Blueprint for Affective Computing

Series in Affective Science

Series Editors
Richard J. Davidson
Paul Ekman
Klaus Scherer

The Nature of Emotion
Fundamental Questions
Edited by Paul Ekman and Richard J. Davidson

Boo!
Culture, Experience, and the Startle Reflex
Ronald Simons

Emotions in Psychopathology
Theory and Research
Edited by William F. Flack Jr. and James D.
Laird

What the Face Reveals
Basic and Applied Studies of Spontaneous
Expression Using the FacialAction Coding
System (FACS)
Edited by Paul Ekman and Erika Rosenberg

Shame
Interpersonal Behavior, Psychopathology, and
Culture
Edited by Paul Gilbert and Bernice Andrews

Affective Neuroscience
The Foundations of Human and Animal
Emotions
Jaak Panksepp

Extreme Fear, Shyness, and Social Phobia
Origins, Biological Mechanisms, and Clinical
Outcomes
Edited by LouisA. Schmidt and Jay Schulkin

Cognitive Neuroscience of Emotion
Edited by Richard D. Lane and Lynn Nadel

The Neuropsychology of Emotion
Edited by Joan C. Borod

Anxiety, Depression, and Emotion
Edited by Richard J.Davidson

Persons, Situations, and Emotions
An Ecological Approach
Edited by Hermann Brandstatter and Andrzej
Eliasz

Emotion, Social Relationships, and Health
Edited by Carol D. Ryff and Burton Singer

Appraisal Processes in *Emotion*
Theory, Methods, Research
Edited by Klaus R. Scherer, Angela Schorr, and
Tom Johnstone

Music and Emotion
Theory and Research
Edited by Patrik N. Juslin and John A. Sloboda

Nonverbal Behavior in Clinical Settings
Edited by Pierre Philippot, Robert S. Feldman,
and Erik J. Coats

Memory and Emotion
Edited by Daniel Rcisbcrg and Paula Hertel

Psychology of Gratitude
Edited by Robert A. Emmons and
Michael E. McCullough

Thinking about Feeling
Contemporary Philosophers on Emotions
Edited by Robert C. Solomon

Bodily Sensibility
Intelligent Action
Jay Schulkin

Who Needs Emotions?
The Brain Meets the Robot
Edited by Jean-Marc Fcllous and
Michael A. Arbib

What the Face Reveals
Basic and Applied Studies of Spontaneous
Expression Using the Facial Action Coding
System (FACS), Second Edition
Edited by Paul Ekman and Erika L. Rosenberg

The Development of Social Engagement
Neurobiological Perspectives
Edited by Peter J.Marshall and Nathan A. Fox

Handbook of Emotion Elicitation and Assessment
Edited by James A. Coan and John J. B. Allen

Emotion and Memory in Development
Biological, Cognitive, and Social Considerations
Edited by Jodi A. Quas and Robyn Fivush

Emotion explained
Edited by Edmund T. Rolls

New handbook of non-verbal behaviour research
Edited by Jinni Harrigan, Robert Rosenthal
and Klaus Scherer

Blueprint for Affective Computing
A sourcebook

Edited by

Klaus R. Scherer

Tanja Bänziger

Etienne B. Roesch

OXFORD

UNIVERSITY PRESS

Great Clarendon Street, Oxford OX2 6DP

Oxford University Press is a department of the University of Oxford.
It furthers the University's objective of excellence in research, scholarship,
and education by publishing worldwide in

Oxford New York

Auckland Cape Town Dar es Salaam Hong Kong Karachi
Kuala Lumpur Madrid Melbourne Mexico City Nairobi
New Delhi Shanghai Taipei Toronto

With offices in

Argentina Austria Brazil Chile Czech Republic France Greece
Guatemala Hungary Italy Japan Poland Portugal Singapore
South Korea Switzerland Thailand Turkey Ukraine Vietnam

Oxford is a registered trade mark of Oxford University Press
in the UK and in certain other countries

Published in the United States
by Oxford University Press Inc., New York

British Library Cataloguing in Publication Data
Data available

Library of Congress Cataloging in Publication Data
Data available

Typeset in Minion by Glyph International, Bangalore, India
Printed in Great Britain
on acid-free paper by
the MPG Books Group, Bodmin and King's Lynn

ISBN 978–0–19–956670–9

10 9 8 7 6 5 4 3 2 1

Whilst every effort has been made to ensure that the contents of this book are as complete, accurate and
up-to-date as possible at the date of writing, Oxford University Press is not able to give any guarantee or
assurance that such is the case. Readers are urged to take appropriately qualified medical advice in all cases.
The information in this book is intended to be useful to the general reader, but should not be used as a means
of self-diagnosis or for the prescription of medication.

Preface and overview

Affective computing is a growing concern both in industry and science. Industry hopes to render technologies such as robotic systems, avatars in service-related human computer interaction, e-learning, game characters, or companion devices more marketable by endowing the 'soulless' robots or agents (which one might reasonably gloss as 'lacking affect') with the ability to recognize and adjust to the users' feelings as well as to send appropriate emotional signals. Scientists are interested in computational models to test theories about human emotions or to perfect detection algorithms for the expression of human affect states and to develop simulation techniques for behaviour of autonomous social agents that is considered as intelligible and appropriate by human interaction partners. Given the commercial and scientific stakes, it is not surprising that many laboratories all over the world are working on different aspects of emotion-oriented systems and affective computing. The numbers of publications—conferences, journals, and books—mapping out the area and the number of members of interest groups and associations are growing at an ever-increasing pace.

A major boost to rapid progress in the area is the increasing realization in many groups of researchers and programmers working in this area that computationally implemented, artificial emotions for applied settings can only be successful if they come close to natural emotional states and are perceived as credible, and thus acceptable, by users. In order to achieve a high degree of authenticity, the work on affective computing and emotion-oriented technologies must be informed by the current state of the art of the affective sciences, all the different disciplines that contribute to the study of natural affect and emotion—including philosophy and other branches of the humanities, psychology, economics, social science, and affective neuroscience (Davidson, Scherer, and Goldsmith 2003; Lewis, Haviland-Jones, and Feldman-Barrett 2008; Sander and Scherer 2009). This constitutes a major challenge, given the multiple contributions to our knowledge about the nature of human emotions and the lack of consensus among the respective scientists about purposes and central aspects of the emotion mechanism (due also to the dearth of pertinent research evidence brought about by the neglect of emotionality during the heydays of cognitivism and the early enthusiasm for artificial intelligence). Given this situation, the only reasonable way forward seems to be the integration of computer science and engineering into the affective sciences.

This volume is intended as a path breaker for such an intensive future collaboration. It is to serve as an introduction and a source book for all those interested in computational models of emotion and affective computing technology based on the state of the art in current scientific investigation of affect in emotion psychology and affective neuroscience. Its aim is to present systematic theoretical conceptualizations of the processes underlying emotional reactions and their implications for various fields in applied affective computing and the design and deployment of emotion-oriented systems. The focus of the core contributions is an accessible description of the structures, functions, and mechanisms underlying emotional reactions—including processes involved in the elicitation of emotional responses, as well as expressive and physiological responses generated during emotional responses, and interpersonal perception of emotional responses.

The volume is also intended to provide an overview of some of the leading work in affective computing and emotion-oriented systems, providing integration of different approaches and quick access to some of the central contributions in this rapidly growing field. As such it can also serve as an introduction to this fascinating field for affective scientists and all those interested in the possibilities and open challenges of computationally modelling one of the most complex aspects of the human mind and behaviour.

The volume is also expected to facilitate the dialogue between conceptualizations and propositions grounded in emotion psychology, in affective neuroscience, and in several areas of affective computing. Its overarching goal is to outline how the perspectives of these different disciplines can inform each other and how this cross-fertilization can give rise to new perspectives and questions in the research fields considered here.

The book is organized in seven sections, the first three devoted to an overview of pertinent concepts, theories, and research findings and the remainder to specific research illustrations and case studies, followed by a brief conclusion. The first section, *Theoretical approaches to the study of emotion in humans and machines*, lays the groundwork for a 'blueprint' to be used as a guiding principle in affective computing research. The first chapter comparatively evaluates the major psychological models and theories and discusses their respective utility to inform computational modelling of emotion. The second chapter consists of an integrative overview of a range of proposed computational models of emotion that can currently be found in the literature, including a systematic comparison of their design features.

The second section, *The emotion process: perspectives from psychology and the neurosciences*, prepares the ground for this volume, presenting the state of the art in current scientific investigation of affect in emotion psychology and affective neuroscience. This section particularly emphasizes the need to relate theoretical propositions as well as empirical data gathered in psychological and in neuropsychological studies to operating computational models used in affective computing. The first chapter in this section presents one of the most comprehensive psychological models of emotion, the component process model. This model also serves to structure the remaining chapters in this section, which review the major components in the architecture of emotion—brain systems (e.g. processes involved in the elicitation of emotional reactions and the organization of the response systems), peripheral physiological response systems (e.g. the heart, vasculature, lung, and sweat glands and their innervation by the autonomic nervous system), and the motor expression system (in particular, facial and vocal expression). The final chapter in the section reviews the role of emotion in social relationships and interpersonal communication. Each chapter in this section includes illustrations of how theories and/or empirical knowledge might be usefully applied to systems engineering. Such propositions might include suggestions from the different disciplines to test specific predictions made in the respective fields using computational models (or complete systems such as expressive embodied agents), as well as suggestions aimed at improving operating models in affective computing (i.e. enhancing the 'affective competence' of autonomous artefacts on the basis of available models and/or data).

The third section, *Emotional expression: ground truth and agent evaluation*, addresses a major conceptual and methodological issue in the area of affective computing—corpora and databases covering an extensive gamut of emotional expressions produced by real human beings in the course of everyday life, media recordings, or acted portrayals. The first chapter in this section justifies the central role of corpora and databases in affective computing, both as models for computational approaches and as a testing ground for the success of artificial emotion expressions, and discusses the advantages and disadvantages of different choices. The second chapter deals specifically with the widely used method of constructing systematic corpora of actor-portrayed emotions for experimental research and the role of strategic emotion presentation in everyday life.

The fourth section, *Approaches to the computational modelling of emotion*, provides an introductory overview of different applications of affective computing by providing two examples for different architectures of computational models of emotion, either in the form of an embodied agent designed for interacting with humans or in the form of a neural network model testing assumptions about fundamental emotion processes. The first chapter illustrates a particular type of rule-based computational model of emotion, informed by both dimensional and appraisal concepts, discussing construction principles and validation procedures. The second chapter provides an illustration of how another type of model, neural networks, can be profitably used to test major emotion mechanisms.

The fifth section, *Approaches to the implementation of emotionally competent agents*, illustrates the concrete operationalization of the theoretical proposals directed at the development of a specific type of agent or model in various types of media and industrial applications, presenting concrete examples for specific implementations of some of the affective competences to be integrated in future artificial agents, such as synthetic production of facial expressions and body movements, emotional speech synthesis, and automatic recognition of human emotions through expression. The four case studies review current approaches to use facial, vocal, and bodily expressions for the perception of emotion by artificial agents or to produce effective emotional signals through simulation and synthesis and summarize the results of empirical research efforts.

The sixth section, *Approaches to developing expression corpora and databases*, provides concrete examples for two methods currently used in the construction of databases and corpora that correspond to the requirements discussed in Section 3. In the first chapter, a new multimodal corpus of systematically designed dynamic actor portrayals for emotional expression research is presented, with a validation study providing ground truth for a shared code in emotion communication. The second chapter describes different emotion induction methods likely to generate emotional expressions that can guide affective computing implementations.

A brief concluding section attempts to organize a coherent picture of some of the views and data presented in earlier chapters, regarding opportunities to further enhance the cross-fertilization across disciplines with respect to the study of emotions in humans and in machines. It outlines currently identified application scenarios and speculates about future developments.

The editors acknowledge the important role of the European Network of Excellence 'Human–Machine Interaction Network on Emotion' (HUMAINE, IST-507422) in the conception and realization of this volume. This collaboration of leading researchers and practitioners in affective computing and affective sciences provided a major platform for mutual acquaintance, informing, and exchange, preparing the interdisciplinary collaboration advocated in many of the contributions. The Network of Excellence has led to the creation of the HUMAINE Association (http://emotion-research.net).

Mirroring progress in the affective sciences, affective computing is a fast moving field and many of the contributions in this volume, while still providing useful entry points, will inevitably be overtaken rather quickly by state of the art. This is why the volume contains a list of websites that will provide updates to many of the contributions in this volume and provide links to the most recent literature in the domains covered.

Klaus R. Scherer
Tanja Bänziger
Etienne B. Roesch

Contents

Contributors

Tanja Bänziger
Faculty of Health and Occupational Studies
Gävle University
Gävle
Sweden
and
Swiss Centre for Affective Sciences
University of Geneva
Geneva
Switzerland

Christian Becker-Asano
Advanced Telecommunications Research
Institute International
Intelligent Robotics and Communication
Laboratories
Keihanna Science City
Kyoto
Japan

Tobias Brosch
Swiss Centre for Affective Sciences
University of Geneva
Geneva
Switzerland

Felix Burkhardt
Deutsche Telekom AG Laboratories
Berlin
Germany

Antonio Camurri
Casa Paganini—InfoMus Laboratory
Department of Communication, Computer
and System Sciences
University of Genoa
Genoa
Italy

George Caridakis
Image, Video and Multimedia Systems
Laboratory
National Technical University of Athens
Zographou
Greece

Ginevra Castellano
Department of Computer Science
School of Electronic Engineering and
Computer Science
Queen Mary University of London
London
UK

Roddy Cowie
School of Psychology
Queen's University Belfast
Belfast
UK

Laurence Devillers
Laboratoire d'Informatique pour la
Mécanique et les Sciences de l'Ingénieur
Orsay Cedex
France

Ellen Douglas-Cowie
School of English
Queen's University Belfast
Belfast
UK

Nickolaos Fragopanagos
Department of Mathematics
King's College London
London
UK

Didier Grandjean
Neuroscience of Emotion and Affective
Dynamics (NEAD) lab
Department of Psychology
Swiss Centre for Affective Sciences
University of Geneva
Geneva
Switzerland

Jonathan Gratch
Institute for Creative Technologies
University of Southern California
Marina del Ray, California
USA

Jennifer Hanratty
School of Psychology
Queen's University Belfast
Belfast
UK

Sylwia Hyniewska
CNRS, Telecom ParisTech
Paris
France

Susanne Kaiser
Psychology Department
University of Geneva
Geneva
Switzerland

Kostas Karpouzis
Image, Video and Multimedia Systems
Laboratory
National Technical University of Athens
Zographou
Greece

Stefanos Kollias
Image, Video and Multimedia Systems
Laboratory
National Technical University of Athens
Zographou
Greece

Nienke Korsten
Department of Mathematics
King's College London
London
UK

Sylvia D. Kreibig
Department of Psychology
Swiss Center for Affective Sciences
University of Geneva
Geneva
Switzerland

Sacha Krstulović
Toshiba Research Europe Ltd
Cambridge
UK

Omar Layachi
Laboratoire d'Informatique pour la Mécanique
et les Sciences de l'Ingénieur (LIMSI)
Orsay Cedex
France

Maurizio Mancini
Casa Paganini—InfoMus Laboratory
Department of Communication, Computer
and System Sciences
University of Genoa
Genoa
Italy

Stacey Marsella
Institute for Creative Technologies
University of Southern California
Marina del Ray, California
USA

Jean-Claude Martin
Laboratoire d'Informatique pour la
Mécanique et les Sciences de l'Ingénieur
Orsay Cedex
France

Gary McKeown
School of Psychology
Queen's University Belfast
Belfast
UK

Edelle McMahon
School of Psychology
Queen's University Belfast
Belfast
UK

Margaret McRorie
School of Psychology
Queen's University Belfast
Belfast
UK

Radosław Niewiadomski
CNRS, Telecom ParisTech
Paris
France

Brian Parkinson
Department of Experimental Psychology
University of Oxford
Oxford
UK

Catherine Pelachaud
CNRS, Telecom ParisTech
Paris
France

Paolo Petta
Austrian Research Institute for Artificial
Intelligence
Vienna
Austria

Etienne B. Roesch
Department of Computing
Imperial College
London
UK
and
Centre for Integrative Neuroscience and
Neurodynamics
University of Reading
Reading
UK

David Sander
Laboratory for the Study of Emotion
Elicitation and Expression
Department of Psychology
Swiss Centre for Affective Sciences
University of Geneva
Geneva
Switzerland

Gunnar Schaefer
Audiovisual Communications Laboratory
School of Computer and Communication
Sciences
Ecole Polytechnique Fédérale de Lausanne
Lausanne
Switzerland

Klaus R. Scherer
Swiss Centre for Affective Sciences
University of Geneva
Geneva
Switzerland

Marc Schröder
German Research Centre for Artificial
Intelligence
Language Technology Lab
Saarbrücken
Germany

Ian Sneddon
School of Psychology
Queen's University Belfast
Belfast
UK

John G. Taylor
Department of Mathematics
King's College London
London
UK

Laurence Vidrascu
Laboratoire d'Informatique pour la
Mécanique et les Sciences de l'Ingénieur
(LIMSI)
Orsay Cedex
France

Gualtiero Volpe
Casa Paganini—InfoMus Laboratory
Department of Communication,
Computer and System Sciences
University of Genoa
Genoa
Italy

Ipke Wachsmuth
Artificial Intelligence Group
Faculty of Technology
University of Bielefeld
Bielefeld
Germany

Stéphane With
Psychology Department
University of Geneva
Geneva
Switzerland

Section 1

Theoretical approaches to the study of emotion in humans and machines

Throughout history android automata have fascinated scientists and the general public, an interest that reached an apex in the eighteenth century (Riskin 2007). It is probably no accident that La Mettrie wrote his influential *L'homme machine* [Machine man] in a period when Jacques de Vaucanson had an immense success with an automatic flute player and a defecating mechanical duck. One of the most remarkable androids from that period is probably the lady musician built by Swiss watchmakers Pierre and Henri-Louis Jacquet-Droz (Voskuhl 2007). This android played several pieces on the harmonium, showing all the skills of an emotionally engaged performer, moving her head, eyes, and lips—and even breathing—in synchrony with musical affect (see Figure 0.1.1). The harmonium player, a sensation in the courts and capitals of Spain and France at the time, might well be considered a first rudimentary effort at *affective computing* in the sense of an embodied agent.

The term *affective computing*, coined by Rosalind Picard (1997), has gradually been accepted as the label for 'computing that relates to, arises from, or deliberately influences emotion or other affective phenomena', as deployed in emotional robots or affectively competent autonomous, and possibly conversational, agents, and which informs emotion theory with the genuine contributions of computational operationalizations and models. In principle, this is a modern update of La Mettrie's machine man endowed with advanced emotional competences—being able to recognize human emotions, to convincingly express emotional signals, and possibly even *have* emotions (or at least an underlying architecture that simulates human-like emotion processes). This is a tall order indeed and one that, as outlined in the preface, can only be attacked through massively interdisciplinary approaches.

One can reasonably argue that any attempt in the direction of creating believable emotionally competent agents requires a guideline, or an architectural blueprint, in terms of a comprehensive, conceptually sound, model of emotion. Unfortunately, currently there is little consensus on such a model, the history of theorizing about emotion in several disciplines having been controversial (see the entries 'emotion definitions' and 'emotion theories and concepts' in Sander and Scherer 2009). In consequence, in this first section, an overview of available approaches is provided.

In Chapter 1.1, 'Emotion and emotional competence: conceptual and theoretical issues for modelling agents', Scherer provides a description of some of the elements theoretically needed to construct a virtual agent with the ability to display human-like emotions and to respond

Fig. 1 'The harmonium player', the first emotionally competent automaton produced by Pierre and Henri-Louis Jacquet-Droz (see Voskuhl 2007; image downloaded from http://drnorth.wordpress.com/category/georges-melies/).

appropriately to human emotion. It includes distinctive definitions of affective concepts and a definition of emotional competence in this context. He presents a comparative overview of major psychological models/theories and their relative advantages or disadvantages with respect to the computational modelling of the proposed mechanisms. As different theories cover different aspects of emotion, the chapter discusses how their contributions can be integrated. The chapter concludes with a survey of desirable features for emotion theories that make them ideal blueprints for agent models.

Then, in Chapter 1.2, 'Computational models of emotion', Marsella, Gratch, and Petta demonstrate how computer simulations of emotion models provide a means to question traditional conceptualizations and expose hidden assumptions. This approach also allows the systematic comparison of the temporal dynamics of emotion processes and makes it possible to formulate predictions about the time course of these processes. Marsella and colleagues point out that findings on the functional, often adaptive role that emotions play in human behaviour have motivated artificial intelligence and robotics research to explore whether modelling emotion processes can contribute to making progress in elusive areas such as perception and sociability, leading to more intelligent, flexible, and capable systems. Most importantly, they provide a detailed discussion of the potential roles for computational models of emotion: a methodological tool for emotion theories; a new approach to artificially intelligent systems; and a means to enhance human–computer interaction. In addition to providing a detailed overview of major computational models described in the literature, Marsella and colleagues discuss their relative advantages and disadvantages in current applications. They conclude by identifying future directions for this research and outlining its potential impact on emotion research.

Chapter 1.1

Emotion and emotional competence: conceptual and theoretical issues for modelling agents

Klaus R. Scherer

Summary

After a brief definition of the term affective competence, it is argued that this notion must be squarely based on a viable architectural model of emotion that reflects the evidence established by centuries of conceptualization and empirical research about the nature and function of emotion. There seems to be massive convergence in the literature on the notion that emotions are mechanisms that facilitate an individual's adaptation to constantly and complexly changing environmental contingencies. In order for this mechanism to be successful it must be based on an evaluation or appraisal of these contingencies using criteria that are specific to the unique motivational structure, both dispositional and transient, of that individual and it must activate action tendencies that are appropriate to the respective situational demands and affordances. As environmental contingencies and also transient motivational states can change rapidly and as information processing may constantly alter situational appraisal, emotion must consist of a recursive process of synchronized changes in several components.

Given these design features of emotion mechanism, competence to manage the continuously evolved emotion mechanism, which integrates both psychobiological and sociocultural determinants, needs to be defined in terms of function or adaptation. I suggest that highly emotionally competent individuals are characterized by an optimal functioning of the emotion mechanism with respect to two major domains—emotion production and emotion perception—each of which is constituted by different facets of competence. Emotion production refers to the total pattern of bodily and behavioural changes that characterizes the adaptive function of emotion, allowing the organism to cope with events of major relevance for well-being. These changes are outwardly visible and constitute important social signals for interaction partners, informing them about the individual's reaction and probable behavioural intention. Given this important role of emotion signalling in social intercourse, individuals need to be able to accurately perceive and interpret the emotional state of others. This is what will be referred to as emotion perception competence.

This conceptualization provides a description of the elements theoretically needed to construct a virtual agent with the ability to display human-like emotions and to respond appropriately to human emotion. It is shown that the computational model of emotion used for the architecture of an emotionally intelligent virtual agent must correspond to the design features of emotion and emotional competence in human individuals—in other words, it must be dynamic, recursive, and emergent.

The main contribution of this chapter is a comparative overview of psychological models/ theories and their relative advantages or disadvantages with respect to the computational modelling of the proposed mechanisms. As different theories cover different aspects of emotion, the chapter discusses how their contributions can be integrated. The chapter concludes with a survey of desirable features for emotion theories that would make them ideal blueprints for agent models.

Defining affective, or emotional, competence

While the term *affective computing* is now widely used to refer to computational modelling of emotion and implementations of autonomous agents capable of affective processing, the notion of *affect* remains ill-defined. I have suggested (Scherer 2005b) that this term is used to cover emotions, preferences, attitudes, affective dispositions, and interpersonal stances that differ widely with respect to event focus, intrinsic and transactional appraisal, degree of synchronization, rapidity of change, behavioural impact, intensity, and duration. In consequence, the term affective competence used with respect to autonomous agents that can recognize and express affective states covers a very wide range of phenomena. However, in virtually all cases the term is mainly used to refer to different types of *emotions*. In consequence, given the absence of an appropriate body of literature on other types of affect, I will focus on the more established notion of *emotional competence* (EC). This term is similar to but not synonymous with *emotional intelligence* (EI). Emotional intelligence has been conceived of in parallel to cognitive intelligence (Mayer and Salovey 1993), defined as a bundle of abilities or skills that have a common underlying factor (small *g*). In contrast, emotional competence is based squarely on the nature and function of the emotion mechanism and describes the abilities and skills needed to use the latter to the best advantage of the individual and/or his reference group. In the following paragraphs, the definition of emotional competence is summarized, based on an earlier overview (Scherer 2007).

The central assumption is that differences in the competence to manage the continuously evolved emotion mechanism, which integrates both psychobiological and sociocultural determinants, need to be defined in terms of *function or adaptation*. Thus, highly emotionally competent individuals are characterized by an optimal functioning of the emotion mechanism with respect to two major domains—emotion production and emotion perception—each of which involves different facets of competence. *Emotion production competence* refers to the total pattern of bodily and behavioural changes that characterize the adaptive function of emotion, allowing the organism to cope with events of major relevance for well-being. In many cases the 'raw' emotion generated on the basis of immediate appraisal is modified, either due to reappraisal of the situation, strategic intentions, or social rules. The capacity to achieve such modification in an efficient fashion will be called emotion regulation competence. The outwardly visible manifestations of the regulated emotion constitute important social signals for interaction partners, informing about the individual's reaction and probable behavioural intention. This function requires two skills that will be subsumed under the notion of emotion communication competence. Given the important role of emotion signalling in social intercourse, individuals need to be able to: (1) generate appropriate and convincing cues of their true emotion (or the emotion they want to advertise to observers) and (2) accurately perceive and interpret the emotional state of other individuals.

We can distinguish three components of production competence: (1) producing the most appropriate emotional reaction to different types of events based on adequate appraisal of internal goal states, coping potential, and the probable consequences of events; (2) being able to adaptively regulate one's emotional states, both with respect to internal set points and according to the sociocultural and situational context; (3) efficiently communicating in social interaction through appropriate expression of one's own emotional state. The discussion of these three aspects is based in part on a specific model of emotion, the component process model (CPM) of emotion (see Scherer 2001, 2009a; Chapter 2.1, this volume).

Appraisal competence

In order to produce an appropriate response, the significance of the triggering events must be correctly appraised (Ellsworth and Scherer 2003; Scherer 2001; see also Chapter 2.1, this volume). One can distinguish two facets of appraisal competence: (1) appropriate emotion elicitation and (2) appropriate emotion differentiation. Appropriate emotion elicitation refers to the ability to rapidly detect significant objects and events that require an emotional response. Our relevance detection ability is of paramount importance, especially as it often relies on unconscious processes. It is one thing to react emotionally when it is required, another to react with the appropriate emotion. The criterion for an emotion being appropriate for a given context is difficult to define and relies in large part on circumstantial evidence. One approach is to define appropriateness negatively, by identifying emotional disturbances such as anhedonia, euphoria, dysphoria, depression, panic attacks, and the like. There is widespread social consensus that such enduring emotional response dispositions are signals of ill health and require therapy, indicating that the emotional reactions of the respective individuals are considered as *inappropriate* or pathological by society at large.

Another approach to defining the appropriateness of an emotional reaction is constituted by the notion of *valid appraisal*. Appropriate emotion differentiation requires evaluating the implications of an event in a realistic fashion and correctly estimating one's coping potential. In addition, emotions such as pride, shame, guilt, and anger require an accurate representation of social expectations, norms, and moral standards. One essential prerequisite for accurate appraisal is to evaluate each event on its merits and to avoid being influenced by evaluative biases or stereotypical judgements. Examples for such biases are causal attribution biases (e.g. tendencies toward other-blaming or self-blaming; exaggerated optimism or pessimism) or an over- or underestimation of one's power or coping potential. Scherer and Brosch (2009) have suggested that cultural goal, belief, and value systems may encourage certain types of appraisal bias and may thus provide an explanation for vestiges of culture-specific emotion dispositions.

If appraisal competence is high and pertinent events are evaluated realistically, appropriate response preparation should normally follow automatically. It seems reasonable to assume that the results of the individual evaluation checks drive changes in the other emotion components, in other words, autonomic physiology, motor expression, and action tendencies (see Scherer 2001, 2009a; Chapter 2.1, this volume). Ideally, synchronized response patterning, appropriately shaped by appraisal, should result in the preparation of adaptive action tendencies. However, it is possible that the translation of appraisal results into response patterning and action tendency preparation will malfunction because of 'hardware' problems (e.g. lesions in mediating brain circuits) or biases produced by specific learning histories (e.g. a preponderance of a specific kind of response due to strong reinforcement in the past). Thus, when an individual responds in a seemingly incompetent fashion to emotionally arousing events, it may be necessary to examine the appropriateness of the appraisal mechanism and the way in which appraisal results trigger response patterns separately.

Regulation competence

Virtually all theories of EI or EC assign a central role to emotion regulation ability. One important function of emotion regulation is to correct inappropriate emotional responses that might have been produced by unrealistic appraisals. Often, our social environment will alert us to the fact that an emotional reaction is inappropriate in kind or intensity. Given a certain sluggishness of the response system, especially physiological arousal, emotions cannot be turned on or off like an electric light, and control and management strategies are required. One might think that emotion regulation skills are not needed if one commands exceptional appraisal competence—in that case the emotions triggered by the appraisal results should always be appropriate. However, this is rarely the case. First, fine-tuning is required, as appraisal changes rapidly and abrupt reappraisal as a result of new information requires strong regulation skills. In addition, emotional reactions are subject to strong normative control in most societies. Thus, even though a strong anger reaction to a veiled insult may be an appropriate behaviour preparation in an evolutionary sense, rules of politeness might prohibit such reactions. Many authors have described the existence and operation of display and even feeling rules in different societies (Ekman 1972; Ekman and Friesen 1969; Hochschild 1979; Matsumoto 1990). Although the importance of emotion regulation is often underlined, relatively little is known about the details of the underlying mechanisms (but see the contributions in Philippot and Feldman, 2004). Three components of regulation competence can be distinguished (Scherer 2007).

1 *Monitoring competence,* which consists of: (a) appropriate reflection and integration of all emotion components; (b) balanced conscious and unconscious processing; and (c) accurate proprioceptive feedback of peripheral responses to a central monitoring system and their appropriate interpretation. Basically, the idea is that the processes of cross-modality and temporal integration (of appraisal results and the corresponding response patterns; see Scherer 2004), as well as the interaction between unconscious and conscious processing (see Scherer 2005a), can operate in a more or less optimal manner (see Scherer 2007 for examples).

2 *Automatic unconscious regulation,* involving the automatic allocation of attentional resources, is of major importance. Upon detection of potential relevance, the executive space needs to be largely allocated to the further processing of the respective stimulus or event. Individuals differ in the rapidity of reactions, task switching capacity, and parallel processing ability. There are major differences in cognitive ability, specifically with respect to executive processes, which could account for differential competence in automatic regulation. Indeed, there is some evidence in the literature that the automatic regulation of emotion may depend on available executive processing resources (Baumeister 2002; Derryberry and Reed 2002; Van der Linden 2004).

3 *Controlled conscious regulation.* Almost all of the research conducted on emotional regulation to date deals with conscious monitoring and control attempts. In particular, the pioneering work of Gross and his associates (Gross and John 2003; John and Gross 2004) has demonstrated the effects of reaction suppression and cognitive reappraisal. Reaction suppression refers to the attempt to reduce emotional intensity by controlling or suppressing physiological reactivity and overt motor expression, with the effect presumably being due to the diminution of proprioceptive feedback. This explanation is consistent with the claim that subjective feeling is an integration of the complete representation of all component changes, including proprioceptive feedback from the periphery (Scherer, 2004; Chapter 2.1, this volume). If less autonomic arousal and motor expression activity is integrated into the total reflection of component changes, subjective feeling will change qualitatively and quantitatively (in terms of intensity).

The effect of reappraisal was early posited and empirically demonstrated by Lazarus and his collaborators (Lazarus 1968). If the results of appraisal determine the nature of the ensuing emotion, a reappraisal of a central criterion will obviously change the nature of the emotion and consequently of the subjective feeling. Modern componential theories, and particularly the CPM, conceptualize appraisal as a recursive process. In consequence, rather than focusing on single acts of reappraisal, these theorists envisage a constant effort to refine appraisal results and bring them into line with reality. This is achieved by continuous processing of incoming information and continuous search for the most appropriate schemata or criteria for the comparison of currently experienced events and their features to internally stored experiences. The result is a constant change of the qualitative nature and intensity of the resulting emotion (and its subjective experience), something that the notion of emotional states in the sense of a few basic emotions hardly does justice to.

Communication competence

Emotions are often socially shared by expressing them or talking about them (Rimé 2009). We can distinguish two major subcompetences, related to: (1) the *sending or encoding* of information about one's emotional state via appropriate verbal and/or non-verbal expression for optimal impact on a receiver (e.g. an interaction partner) and (2) the ability to *receive or decode* the verbal and/or non-verbal expressions of others in the sense of correctly interpreting these signals and being able to correctly infer the underlying emotional state. The second subcompetence comprises the 'emotion perception competence' component of emotional competence.

Sending (encoding) communication competence

Emotional expression, as an integral part of emotion production, informs interaction partners about the way in which an individual has appraised an action or event, the consequent reaction, and, most importantly, the probability of different behavioural consequences (Scherer 1984, 2001). Obviously, then, it is part of EC to produce emotional expressions that are optimally suited to that purpose. At this point production competence and regulation competence converge. Thus, in many cases regulation competence requires that the automatically produced expressions, e.g. as effects of the ongoing physiological changes, be modified. Thus, it is suboptimal to send inappropriate or ambiguous signals about reactions and action tendencies, as this will encourage misunderstanding and seriously complicate interaction processes. If one produces signs toward a partner that he or she can interpret as an anger reaction even though one is worried about the future of the relationship, one is likely to produce unwanted effects of spiralling anger escalation. In some sense, emotion expression always has a strategic aspect that can be more or less pronounced. Scherer and his collaborators have distinguished *push effects*, which represent the automatic motor consequences of the internal processes, from *pull effects*, which reflect cultural templates of socially desirable or strategically useful expressions (see Chapter 3.2, this volume; Scherer 1985).

The appropriate control of emotional expression has been intensively discussed in the literature. Ekman and Friesen (1969) coined the term 'display rules' to refer to cultural norms that govern the licence to express different emotions in social situations (see also Ekman 1972, 2003c; Matsumoto 1990). Clearly, this is a competence that needs to be acquired in the socialization process via which a child becomes a well-functioning member of a particular society. Issues concerning both the understanding and the execution of expression control have consequently been an important part of the literature on the socialization of affect (Ceschi and Scherer 2003; Saarni 1979).

But expression control goes much beyond suppression or modification. Clearly, one needs to add *fabrication*, in other words, showing an emotion one does not feel at all. The strategic use of emotional expression is a central element of emotional skills. A nice example is provided by what may be one of the first formal statements on EC in the history of philosophy and psychology: In his *Nicomachean ethics*, Aristotle (1941) exhorts us to react to an insult with the appropriate amount of anger, at the appropriate time, directed at the appropriate person, in order to avoid being seen as a social fool. The secret is the measured response, avoiding overreacting (to avoid being seen as hysterical or stressed out) or underreacting (being seen as a 'social fool').

The anthropologist Erving Goffman has brilliantly expanded on this important idea by showing the powerful human tendency for positive self-presentation (Goffman 1959). Importantly, emotional expression, even if strategically regulated or manipulated, needs to be credible and convey the impression of being authentic. One of the essential skills in this respect is to produce congruent expression in different modalities, something that requires important skills, given the difficulty of monitoring and manipulating many different cues at the same time In consequence, one would assume that *sending or encoding communication competence*, as an important part of EC, involves being able to produce a skilful blend of push effects, to appear authentic, and pull effects, to conform to norms and pursue one's interactional aims.

Receiving (decoding) communication competence (perception or recognition competence)

In addition to efficient signal production, communication competence requires accurate signal perception and recognition or interpretation (receiving ability). This implies a high ability to recognize emotional states of others in different modalities such as the face, voice, or body, as well as in verbal content, even though the pertinent cues may be controlled or concealed. For example, accurate emotion recognition is important in negotiations to understand when someone gets edgy or irritated to the point that negotiations may break off.

Clearly, individuals differ greatly in this capacity. Not surprisingly, the issue of 'social intelligence', which includes emotion recognition competence, has been early appreciated by the pioneers of intelligence testing, and attempts were made to produce valid tests of these abilities (O'Sullivan and Guilford 1975; Ruisel 1992). Later, the field of non-verbal communication produced a large amount of work on non-verbal sensitivity, which also concerns emotion recognition ability (Hall and Bernieri 2001). It is surprising that current efforts to develop tests of EI either completely ignore this important competence (the personality trait/adjustment approach) or deal with it exclusively from the point of view of socially convergent interpretation (see Scherer 2007). Our group has recently validated a new multimodal performance test of non-verbal recognition ability (MERT; see Bänziger *et al.* 2009).

Emotional competence in virtual agents

Which of these aspects of EC are important for an emotionally competent virtual agent and how can these be implemented? Clearly, this depends on what kind of virtual agent one intends to build. Much of the current effort in affective computing seems to be directed at the development of what I will call a 'service robot', be it in the form of a virtual agent on the screen or a real, physical robot. The EC of such service robots required by the respective applications seems to be limited to the component of EC called *communication competence* above. One widely desired competence is related to the receiving or decoding ability. The robot has to be able to correctly recognize the emotion of the human it is supposed to serve and to adapt its service in consequence, e.g. adopting a soothing attitude upon detecting sadness. Increasingly, sending or encoding competence is equally required. The robot should show the context-appropriate emotion in delivering a specific message, e.g. regret upon having to deny a request, or during a specific service activity, e.g. enjoyment in being able to help. The conceptualization and implementation of such skills are being pursued in many laboratories all over the world, with massive support from industry, as it is hoped that such communication competence will greatly augment the commercial viability of such robots. Obviously, neither the production nor the regulation competence is required as the robot is not supposed to have any emotion. The decoding or receiving competence is limited to successful pattern recognition based on the analysis of spoken utterances or facial or vocal expression configurations. The encoding or sending competence is limited to the operation of pull effects as described above, as the robot has no underlying emotion processes that push out expression. And even these pull effects seem to be limited to the realization of socioculturally desirable or prescribed expression templates, as the robot is unlikely to have his/her own strategic aims that require specific expressions (except possibly those built in by the manufacturer).

While the implementation of such low-level abilities seems rather straightforward, it is fraught with difficulties. In terms of receiving or recognition ability, most current approaches use automatic learning algorithms to acquire prototypical emotion expression patterns (based on the input of stimuli for which the 'ground truth' is provided) in order to detect similar patterns in testing stimuli and classify the underlying emotion accordingly. These approaches consist of *holistic matching* methods as they seem to be based on a match between a particular emotion, conceived of as an invariant unity, and the associated prototypical expression pattern, which is also conceived of as an invariant unity. While such methods enjoy some success in laboratory settings with constrained stimulus material, they do not seem to fare particularly well in more realistic settings. This is not very surprising as there is mounting evidence that neither emotions nor their expressions are invariant unities and that, in consequence, there are no unambiguous prototypical expressions, even for so-called basic emotions, let alone the myriad of so-called complex or of mixed emotions (see Mortillaro *et al.* in preparation; Scherer 1992, 2001; Scherer and Ellgring 2007*a*). To give a single, but powerful example—one would expect that infants show clear prototypical patterns of very basic emotions like surprise; however, a wealth of empirical evidence shows that this is not the case (Scherer *et al.* 2004*b*). Thus, if there are no prototypical emotion expressions, there are no ground truths that could be learned by automatic algorithms (quite apart from the problems of the choice of a representative corpus). The exception might be expression patterns from the extreme end of the pull effect continuum—emoticons. But even actor portrayals of emotion, which can also be considered to be driven mostly by pull effects (Bänziger and Scherer, submitted), are extremely variable and only rarely show the predicted prototypes, for example, in terms of complete facial action unit configurations (Scherer and Ellgring 2007*a*).

It may well be that holistic matching methods lead us into a blind alley. They are unlikely to produce recognition results in realistic contexts that can be reliably used as a guide to behaviour. One could go even further and claim that there is no ground truth in emotion expression, given the variability and the rapid changeability of emotion processes as well as the tremendous amount of individual differences.

What is the alternative? Clearly, the most appropriate approach would be to teach service robots the same perception mechanism that is used by humans. Humans do not use holistic matching but integrative analytic inference. Specifically, I have suggested that human emotion perception can be best described by the Brunswikian lens model (adapted from Bänziger and Scherer, submitted; see also Scherer 2003). The sender expresses (consciously or unconsciously) underlying emotional states by a vector of distal (objectively measurable) cues in facial, vocal, or bodily behaviour. These cues are transmitted via the appropriate communication channels to a receiver. They may be distorted or weakened in the transmission process. The sensorium and brain association areas of the receiver will represent these cues in a proximal fashion, i.e. as subjective impressions, which may be more or less faithful representations of the distal quality of the cues (due to perception, attention, or short-term memory processes). The receiver then infers or attributes an emotional state to the sender on the basis of stored probabilistic relationships. Both encoding and decoding mechanisms are different for push and pull effects.

How can this model help in our quest to improve decoding competence? One important issue is that the model does not assume correct recognition of the true underlying state. This would require that the distal cues completely map the state, that the transmission is flawless, that the proximal cues are equivalent to the distal ones, and that the inference rules exactly mirror the encoding rules. It is unlikely that this happens very frequently. In addition, emotion is a process, not a state and, in consequence, states, and corresponding emotions, change extremely rapidly. Therefore we might best operationally define receiving competence as the ability to infer and attribute emotion processes in others as well or better than the upper quartile of the population (using a quartile is arbitrary of course; it could also be any top percentile of the distribution). What is essential is the definition of a criterion in terms of reaching a convergent attribution as made by a group with known competence in emotion inference from expressive cues, rather than in terms of recognizing the 'true' emotion of the sender (which the latter may also be partially unaware of; see Scherer 2005a).

One might well be able to teach the requisite skills to both humans and virtual agents *if* we had the appropriate empirical data. We can use structural statistical models to represent the process described by the Brunswikian model and estimate its *ecological validity* and the patterns of *cue utilization* by skilled receivers. Such data do not currently exist and unfortunately there is very little research activity in this domain. In addition, the inference and attribution process needs to be broken down further as it is likely that in many cases emotions are indirectly inferred from expressive features that are driven by appraisal and action tendencies. One can hypothesize that receivers first infer these direct causes of the expression and make an emotion attribution on this basis (Scherer 1992, 2003).

What about sending or encoding communication competence? As mentioned above, in the case of service robots, this should be entirely driven by pull effects. If there are no socially desirable or prescribed (or strategic interest) target expressions, no emotional expression should be shown (except possibly noncommittal baseline friendliness). If there are putative sociocultural templates, they should be expressed in a fashion that is as authentic as possible. Again, in order to teach these skills to humans and our service robots we would need empirical data (obtained across cultures and subcultures) concerning the putative templates for different situations and contexts. Obviously, it would have to be certain that the distal cues used in the template are indeed interpreted in the desired way by skilled receivers (using structural modelling based on a Brunswikian approach; see Bänziger and Scherer, submitted). Again, pertinent research hardly exists although the methodology required does not represent any major difficulties.

Differential utility of emotion theories for dynamic modelling

Let us now turn towards more lofty aims—the implementation of autonomous virtual agents that are actually capable of having emotions, albeit only virtual or artificial ones. Clearly, if these agents are to be emotionally competent, the complete list of competencies outlined above would be required. These skills would have to be implemented as part of a complete emotional architecture of the agent. In consequence, it is essential to decide on the definition of emotion one wants to adopt (as there are unfortunately many different ways of defining an emotion; Scherer 2005a), specifying its nature and function, and choosing a theory of emotion that allows computer implementation. In the following section we will examine the different contenders in terms of their utility for the purpose at hand.

Psychological theories of emotion differ with respect to their assumptions on how the emotion components—cognitive processes, peripheral physiological responses, motivational changes,

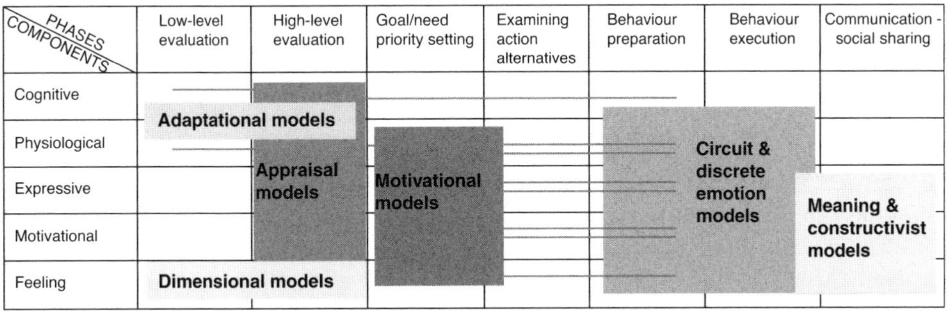

COMPONENTS \ PHASES	Low-level evaluation	High-level evaluation	Goal/need priority setting	Examining action alternatives	Behaviour preparation	Behaviour execution	Communication - social sharing
Cognitive		**Adaptational models**					
Physiological		**Appraisal models**	**Motivational models**		**Circuit & discrete emotion models**		
Expressive							**Meaning & constructivist models**
Motivational							
Feeling	**Dimensional models**						

Fig. 1.1.1 Mapping competing emotion theories in a space defined by phases of the emotion process and type of emotion component. The horizontal lines projecting from the solid areas indicate that a particular model includes in its theorizing at least some of the components/phases crossed by the lines. (Reproduced from Scherer and Peper 2001) (see plate 1).

motor expression, and subjective feeling—are integrated and, particularly, how qualitatively different emotional states are to be differentiated with respect to their patterning. They also differ in their focus on specific stages of the process. Therefore, psychological models of emotion are difficult to assess in terms of their merits for research on, and development of, emotionally competent agents. This certainly makes it difficult for computational modellers to decide which model is the most appropriate for a particular research question or a particular application.

We will now review the major 'families' of emotion theories that are proposed in the literature (for further details, see Moors 2009; Scherer 2000a, 2009c) and that can be considered as competitors for the modeller's choice. The purpose is to unravel some of the different strands pursued by different theorists and to place the different models on a map that can serve for navigation. One can use a two-dimensional coordinate system to plot different psychological theories of emotion (see Scherer and Peper 2001), as illustrated in Figure 1.1.1. One dimension consists of the different components of the emotion, as described above: cognitive processes, peripheral physiological responses, motivational changes, motor expression, and subjective feeling. The second dimension consists of different phases of the emotion process and its consequences: low-level evaluation, high-level evaluation, goal/need priority setting, examining action alternatives, behaviour preparation, behaviour execution, and communication/sharing. Each of the different families of theories described below is marked by a box situated in the region that represents the major preoccupation of each theory with respect to phases and components. Lines emanating horizontally from some theories indicate that the theory also treats other phases in connection with its focus. In what follows, a brief synthesis of the major families of theories is provided (following Scherer and Peper 2001).

Adaptation theories

Under this heading, one can group theorists who emphasize that the emotion system has an important adaptive function, and is primed by evolution to detect stimuli that are vitally significant for the organism's well-being. Öhman (1987) suggests that organisms are evolutionarily 'prepared' for the evaluation of certain contingencies, allowing the detection of threat stimuli in a pre-attentive mode and preparing appropriate physiological orienting or defence reactions. LeDoux (1996) also highlights pre-attentive emotion elicitation and postulates direct projections within the brain from the sensorium and thalamus to the amygdala, which in turn trigger rudimentary viscero-motor and behavioural responses. Both theorists acknowledge that there is a second phase, characterized by higher-level attention-driven evaluation. Because of the emphasis on biologically prepared, pre-attentive processes, both theorists focus on fear-inducing stimuli, such as electric shocks, spiders, or snakes, and the resulting emotion of fear, and were able to confirm their hypotheses in several empirical studies.

Dimensional theories

Emotions can be easily differentiated by their position on a pleasantness–unpleasantness (or valence) and an arousal (or activation) dimension (varying on a continuum from active to passive). This allows one to distinguish between negative and positive emotions of different degrees of intensity and arousal. Dimensional theories have been very popular because of the economical fashion in which they capture valence and arousal differences between emotions. Like Wundt's (1905) pioneering work (who, in addition to pleasantness–unpleasantness and rest–activation, suggested a third dimension, relaxation–attention), most dimensional models focus on the 'subjective feeling' component of emotion. In consequence, much of the research in this tradition uses verbal labels (Davitz 1969; Russell 1980, 1983), in ways that are quite comparable to the earlier three-dimensional model of verbal meaning (Osgood *et al.* 1957). A large number of factor-analytic studies have supported the fact that verbal labels can be very reliably mapped into a valence by arousal space (Barrett and Russell 2009).

Appraisal theories

Appraisal theories posit that most (but not all) emotions are elicited by a cognitive (but not necessarily conscious or controlled) evaluation of antecedent situations and events (see Ellsworth and Scherer 2003; Scherer 1999a; Scherer *et al.* 2001 for overviews) and that the patterning of the reactions in the different response domains is driven by the results of this evaluation process. Arnold (1960) and Lazarus (1968) pioneered the explicit assumption that subjective appraisal, specifically the evaluation of the significance of an event for the organism and its ability to cope with the event, determines the nature of the respective emotion. Appraisal theorists following this tradition have refined the conceptualization of appraisal (see Ellsworth and Scherer 2003; Roseman and Smith 2001; Scherer 1999a). Thus, at one extreme, Lazarus (1991) has postulated a theme-based appraisal reminiscent of discrete emotion theories. The component process model proposed by Scherer (1984, 2001, 2009c), which assumes that there are as many different emotional states as there are differential patterns of appraisal results, is located at the other extreme of appraisal approaches. Intermediate positions are represented by appraisal theorists such as Ellsworth (1991; Smith and Ellsworth 1985), Smith (1989; Smith and Kirby 2001), Roseman (1984; Roseman *et al.* 1994), Frijda (1986, 2007), and Weiner (1985). These theorists take a more eclectic view of the issue concerning the number and the 'basicness' of emotions. However, they all propose that a specific set of cognitive appraisal or evaluation dimensions or criteria allows us to predict which type of emotion will be experienced by an individual on the basis of the results of the appraisal process.

Contrary to other models, appraisal theories render the link between elicitation of emotion and response patterning more explicit. While dimensional emotion theorists doubt the existence of differential emotion patterning (see Barrett 2006) or reduce response specificity to neurophysiological circuits or programs (as in the discrete emotion and circuit models; see Panksepp 1998a), componential appraisal theorists make detailed predictions as to specific physiological, expressive, and motivational changes expected to be driven by appraisal results (Smith 1989; Smith and Scott 1997; Scherer 1984, 1986, 2001, 2009c). This is justified by the assumption that the evaluation or appraisal of an event will lead to specific requirements for further information processing, or to specific response or action tendencies, which are in turn determined by the motivational tendency suggested as an adaptive response by the appraisal outcome. In consequence, appraisal theories include all components and phases of the emotion process shown in Figure 1.1.1, suggesting a central determining role for the results of the evaluation on lower and higher cognitive levels. As will be argued below, this aspect makes appraisal theories ideal candidates for computational modelling.

Over the last 20 years numerous empirical studies based on appraisal theories have been conducted and substantial experimental evidence for many of the predictions has been published. For an overview, the reader is referred to reviews in a volume on appraisal theories (Scherer, Schorr, and Johnstone 2001, in particular, chapters by Johnstone, van Reekum, and Scherer; Kaiser and Wehrle; Pecchinenda, Roseman, and Smith; Smith and Kirby; Scherer). In addition to using self-report, much of the work has made extensive use of objectively measured indicators of appraisal processes such as physiological parameters and expressive behaviour. Thus, several studies have demonstrated the efferent effects of appraisal checks on somatovisceral changes and motor expression as markers of appraisal results (Aue and Scherer 2008; Aue *et al.* 2007; Banse and Scherer 1996; Johnstone *et al.* 2005; Johnstone *et al.* 2007; Scherer and Ellgring, 2007*a*; Van Reekum *et al.* 2004) and evidence for the sequential processing of appraisal check predicted by the CPM (Aue *et al.* 2007; Lanctôt and Hess 2007; Delplanque *et al.* 2009; Flykt *et al.* 2009; Grandjean and Scherer 2008). Preliminary evidence on the synchronization predicted for felt emotional experiences has also been reported (Dan Glauser and Scherer 2008).

Motivational theories

The close relationship between emotional and motivational phenomena is often neglected (Lazarus *et al.* 1982). Some theorists, however, base their models centrally on this relationship. One of the oldest theories in this group is that of Plutchik (1980), who has argued that the major types of emotions can be derived from evolutionary continuous motivational primitives. Thus love is seen as a correlate of parental care, fear as a signal of danger inducing a flight response, and anger as an antagonistic emotion that prepares the organism to fight. Many other emotion theories postulate similar motivational underpinnings (see also Frijda 1986). But Plutchik's theory is a special case in that it bases emotion classification directly on fundamental kinds of psychobiological motivation. Another motivation-based account has been provided by Buck (1985), who views emotions as 'read-outs' of motivational tendencies. There has been relatively little experimental work in this tradition.

Circuit theories

Psychological theories of emotion have continually been influenced by evolving neuroscientific knowledge of pathways or circuits in the brain. Such approaches attempt to use evidence from functional neuroanatomy in order to understand emotion elicitation and differentiation in a comparative perspective. Emotion networks had already been described by the pioneers of affective neuroscience. Prominent advocates of this tradition have been Gray (1990) and Panksepp (1998*a*). These models are all based on the assumption that the differentiation and the number of fundamental emotions are determined by genetically coded neural circuits. They have stimulated a considerable amount of neuropsychological and psychophysiological research with human subjects.

Discrete (or basic) emotion theories

The most popular theoretical accounts of emotion are based on Darwin's (1872/1998) influential book *The expression of emotion in man and the animals*. These theories claim the existence of a limited number of basic or fundamental emotions such as anger, fear, joy, sadness, and disgust. These models can be located close to the end of the emotion process shown in Figure 1.1.1, the differentiation being mostly explained by patterning of effector mechanisms in behaviour preparation or execution (similar to dimensional and circuit models). Following Darwin, theorists in this tradition suggest that, during the course of evolution, a limited number, generally between 7 and 14, of basic or fundamental emotions have evolved. Each of these basic emotions has its own eliciting conditions and its own physiological, expressive, and behavioural reaction patterns.

Discrete emotion theory was pioneered by Tomkins (1962) who argued that a number of basic or fundamental emotions could be conceived of as phylogenetically stable neuromotor programs. These programs automatically trigger a pattern of reactions ranging from peripheral physiological responses to muscular innervation, particularly in the face. This tradition has been most strongly developed by Ekman and Izard, who extended Tomkins' theory. They described the discrete patterning of universal, prototypical facial expressions for a number of basic emotions (Ekman 1972, 1992, 2003c; Ekman and Rosenberg 2005; Izard 1977, 1992; Levenson et al. 1992). A patterning of autonomic–endocrine reactions has also been suggested (Levenson et al. 1990).

Lexical theories

The richness of emotion terms in most languages has given rise to a number of psychological and philosophical models of emotion. One of the basic assumptions of these approaches seems to be that semantic structure will point the theoretician to the underlying organization and determinants of the emotion domain. Thus, Oatley and Johnson-Laird (1996) focus on goal structures implied by major emotion terms. Ortony et al. (1988) provide a theoretical analysis of the semantic implicational structure underlying major emotion words. Shaver et al. (1987) use cluster analysis to show the hierarchical meaning structure of the emotion lexicon. Only a small number of experimental studies have examined these theories.

Social constructivist theories

An approach to defining emotion that is favoured by sociologists and anthropologists suggests that the meaning of emotion is mostly constituted by socioculturally determined behaviour and value patterns (Averill 1980; Shweder 1993). Advocates of this approach consider the psychobiological reaction components of emotion as secondary to the meaning of the emotion in a specific sociocultural context. Often, theorists in this tradition also consider the emotion labels available in a language as indicative of the emotional meaning structures in the respective culture (Lutz and White 1986). Both the lexical and the constructivist theories focus on the final phase of an emotion process: the communication or the sharing of the emotional experience with the social environment. This places heavy, if not exclusive, emphasis on the subjective feeling component. Much of the evidence is based on field work.

Overlap

As is easily seen from the preceding discussion, there is quite a bit of overlap between these traditions. Adaptation and motivation theories are quite compatible with appraisal theories. Similarly, circuit and discrete (basic) emotion theories share many assumptions. These two groups differ mostly with respect to the focus on different phases in the emotion process. Whereas circuit and discrete (basic) emotion theories focus on the response end, assuming specific patterning (elicited by typical situations), appraisal theories (and adaptation and motivation theories) focus on the elicitation and evaluation phase at the beginning of the process, assuming that responses are driven directly by the results. Lexical, dimensional, and constructivist theories focus on a still later stage, that of categorization and labelling in the service of communication. Based on this comparative evaluation, Scherer (2009c) has proposed that three large families of theories be distinguished:

◆ appraisal theories in the widest sense, based on the writings of many philosophers and psychologists, and comprising theories focusing on adaptation and motivation;

◆ basic (or discrete) emotion theories, based on Darwin, including circuit theories;

◆ constructivist theories, loosely based on James (1890/1898) and Schachter and Singer (1962) on the one hand and cultural relativism on the other, comprising dimensional, social constructivist, and lexical theories.

Choosing a theory as the basis for computational modelling of emotion

The preceding review of the competing models suggests that there is reasonable convergence on the view that emotion is considered by most theorists as a *bounded episode* in the life of an organism that is characterized as an *emergent pattern* of *component synchronization* preparing adaptive *action tendencies* to relevant events as defined by their *behavioural meaning* and seeking *control precedence* over behaviour (see also Frijda and Scherer 2009).

Each of the theoretical models described above captures and explains important facets of the emotion phenomenon thus defined. As illustrated by the structural decomposition in Figure 1.1.2, it is essential to determine exactly which of the many aspects of the emotion process are highlighted by the various theories, and to what extent they can be mapped on to each other. As shown above, many of the models can be integrated, if one assumes that different models

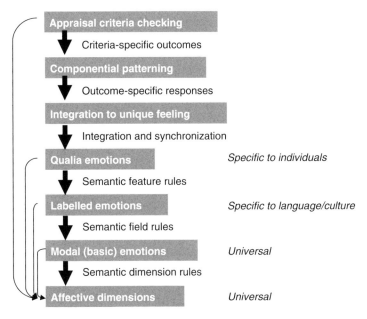

Fig. 1.1.2 The hierarchy of levels of description for emotion processes and their mapping into lower-dimensional space (See plate 2).

describe different components and phases of the emotion phenomenon (see also Scherer 2000*a*). For example, one can argue that the valence and arousal dimensions represent a higher-order factor space into which the so-called discrete or basic emotions can be plotted. Similarly, the basic emotion 'families' (see Ekman 1992) can be seen as higher-order factors with respect to the highly variable outcomes of appraisal processes. Scherer has proposed the concept of *modal emotions* (1984, 1994*b*) to account for the existence of a limited number of such 'families', referring to frequently occurring patterns of appraisal of events that are universally encountered by individuals, such as sadness in the case of loss, or anger in the case of blocked goals. These common elements account for the fact that languages group these states together, using a single label. One may need to go to an even lower level to identify individual emotion family members that share common appraisal profiles (characterized by brief expressions, such as 'righteous anger'). The lowest level might consist of the continuous adaptive changes that—according to component-process theory—are produced by single appraisals. Examples are the startle as well as defence and orienting responses (which may be a part of a higher-order emotion such as surprise or fear). Figure 1.1.2 shows these different levels as well as the mechanisms that seem to underlie the grouping of lower-order units on a higher level. The figure also shows predictions as to which mechanisms are likely to be specific to individuals, to language or culture, or universally shared.

It seems reasonable to start with the most comprehensive and most detailed theoretical approach, and examine how this high-dimensional set of information can be mapped into a lower-dimensional space. It can be argued that the componential appraisal approaches, briefly reviewed above, represent the most comprehensive and detailed attempt to model emotion. This is due to the fact that most of them provide a detailed account of the elicitation mechanisms that produce differentiated emotions (i.e. appraisal criteria checking), predict concrete response patterns based on these appraisal profiles, and consider the construction of subjective feeling as based on these processes. In contrast, most other theories focus on higher levels of aggregation.

What are the elements that would be needed to construct a virtual agent with the ability to respond with something approaching human emotion? If one knows exactly what level of resolution one needs in an emotionally competent agent it is clearly appropriate to choose the model that provides the most economical solution. It is rarely useful to gather a lot of information that is never used thereafter. It is much easier to represent emotion in a two-dimensional space representing pleasantness and arousal, or to use one of a finite number of basic emotions, than to use detailed information on appraisal and response patterning. However, in choosing such an economical model, developers of affective agents need to be aware of their needs, given the design specification of the agents to be built. In what follows, a non-exhaustive and non-systematic list of the requirements for constructing a process model of human emotions is reviewed, and the usefulness of the major theoretical models to fulfil the respective requirements is evaluated.

- *Number of components.* As shown above, despite the consensus that emotions have several components, which interact with one other, many theories emphasize particular components and neglect others (see Figure 1.1.2). If computational modelling or agent implementation requires the participation and interaction of several components, care should be taken to choose a guiding emotion model that provides specifications for this essential feature.

- *Relevant events.* Generally, events or situations are seen as elicitors of emotion episodes. Appraisal theorists assume that it is not the event itself, but the appraisal by the individual, that is decisive and that may change over time, in the course of reappraisal. Constructivist theories do not clearly specify how events affect continuous core affect. According to Russell (2003) individuals may attribute a certain core affect to an event.

◆ *Behavioural meaning.* Appraisal theorists assume that the transactional evaluation of the event constitutes the behavioural meaning for the individual, insisting on the fact that it is only through the specific behavioural meaning of an event for an individual that the action preparation following the appraisal process can have adaptive value. This is not a meaningful feature for basic or constructivist theories. The former take the type of event as the discriminating factor; the latter see categorization and conceptualization of core affect as independent from event evaluation. In consequence, it would seem difficult to model the assumptions of basic or constructivist theories into an agent model as the former would require that specific affect programs for a large number of events would need to be built into the model (which would make the model circular and trivial) and the latter implies that the behavioural meaning of an event can only be understood in an ideographic fashion, which would require the modelling of all possible individual differences and situational effects.

◆ *Adaptive responses.* Most emotion theories assume some degree of functionality of emotion (Nesse 2009). For basic emotion theories, the affect program is pre-programmed to deal with the eliciting event. In contrast, appraisal theories define the adaptive functions in terms of the efferent results of individual appraisal checks that add up cumulatively to prepare appropriate action tendencies (Ellsworth and Scherer 2003; Scherer 2001). Constructivist theories generally endorse the adaptive value of emotion but there is no justification for this claim in terms of the postulated architecture and the criteria for functionality are not defined (see Barrett 2006). However, the modelling of adaptive function seems essential for the attempt to create an emotion architecture for an autonomous virtual agent as adaptation to a specific environment and current goal states is of central importance.

◆ *Component synchronization.* While the componential architecture of emotions is generally admitted, only some appraisal theories, in particular the CPM (Scherer 2004, 2005*a*, *b*; see Chapter 2.1, this volume), strongly insist on a process of synchronization and desynchronization of components within the bounded episode, to the point of making the degree of coherence a central criterion for the existence of an emotion (Scherer 2005*b*; Dan Glauser and Scherer 2008). The synchronization assumption can be considered a major advantage for computational implementation as it allows the building of some degree of coherence between different response modalities into the model, which should add to stability.

◆ *Process modelling and dynamic change.* Despite the general acceptance of the notion that emotion is a dynamic process, most emotion theories deal with discrete, unchanging emotional states and do not specify mechanisms that allow analysing or modelling dynamic change over time. While it is simpler and more economical to restrict modelling to highly circumscribed discrete states, a realistic computational model of emotion requires true process modelling of dynamic change over time with varying inputs. Only componential appraisal theories provide the tools for such an endeavour. While modern constructivist theories (Russell 2003) also propose continuously varying core affect, this is restricted to valence by arousal and no determining input factors are specified.

◆ *Emergent properties.* This refers to unexpected features of the process that may occur and influence the overall process at different levels. The emotion process is intrinsically dynamic and probably nonlinear, and the linear perspective often taken by theorists and modellers may be insufficient to describe its complexity (Scherer 2000*b*, 2009*b*; Sander *et al.* 2005). For instance, eliciting events (input) are not limited to prototypical categories or predetermined locations in a valence × arousal space, and the system should not be equated to simple lookup functions with predetermined databases. Similarly, on the output side, care should be taken to model response patterning in detail, instead of postulating a small number of prototypical affect programs with a single output. The basic emotion model is deterministic on a macro level—a given stimulus or event will determine the occurrence of one of the basic emotions (through a process of largely automatic appraisal). In contrast, appraisal theories are deterministic on a micro level—specific appraisal results or combinations thereof are expected to determine, in a more molecular fashion, specific action tendencies and the corresponding physiological and motor responses. Thus, appraisal theorists espouse *emergentism* assuming that the combination of appraisal elements in a recursive process is unfolding over time and that the ensuing reactions will form emergent emotions that are more than the sum of their constituents and more than instantiations of rigid categories, namely, unique emotional experiences in the form of qualia (see Scherer 2004, 2009*a*).

◆ *Bounded episode*. Consistent with popular assumptions, both basic and appraisal theories consider emotions as bounded episodes in time, having a clear onset and a somewhat fuzzy offset. In contrast, constructivist theories assume that the stream of continuously varying core affect is segmented only by mental categorization and conceptualization. The latter are seen to depend entirely on the individual's construction and will thus vary widely over individuals, which makes it impossible to build a nomothetic model that can be applied, in a lawful manner, to different individuals.

◆ *Number and type of emotions*. On one extreme, we find the notion of a limited number of evolutionarily continuous adaptive emotion systems (held by many basic emotion theorists) and, on the other, that of fuzzy, unpredictable state changes that achieve coherence only by their place in a valence/arousal space and by conceptual classification, espoused by some constructivists. In this debate, appraisal theorists are somewhere in the middle—they neither accept the idea of a limited repertoire of basic, homogeneous emotions with highly prototypical characteristics nor that of emotions being individually labelled points in two-dimensional affect space. Rather, while assuming that there are widely varying types of emotions, they postulate the existence of modal emotion families (Scherer 1994) with frequently occurring appraisal profiles that have adaptive functions in dealing with quintessential contingencies in animal and human life. The insistence of constructivist theorists on individual and situational differences and the absence of predictions do not predestine these theories as guides for model building. Basic emotion theories have the disadvantage that they describe only a few emotions in detail, some of which may not be too useful for modelling in agents (e.g. disgust). In contrast, appraisal theorists allow much more flexibility, including predictions for emotional states that have no standard linguistic labels but can be distinguished on the basis of appraisal-driven response patterns. This may permit the modelling of emotions that are quite specific to agents in a specific environment.

◆ *Variations of intensity and duration*. Regrettably, there has been little interest in the study of emotion intensity and duration (but see Edwards 1998; Frijda *et al.* 1991; Sonnemans and Frijda 1994). In general, emotion researchers working with experimental subjects have recorded self-reported intensity, and sometimes duration, but have rarely used this information in their theorizing. However, in animating an affective agent, the issue of intensity and duration of emotional expressions is crucial. In consequence, care should be taken to choose a guiding model that makes predictions concerning differences in intensity or duration of emotion processes. The guiding theory should at least take account of major differences between members of emotion families such as hot versus cold anger; anxiety versus fear, sadness versus despair, happiness versus elation, etc. (see Banse and Scherer 1996). Currently, all models of emotion are under-specified in this respect, although some, like appraisal models, are more suited to deal with such variations because of their more fine-grained structures.

◆ *Qualia differences.* Specifications of discrimination ability vary for models and agents. In some cases, only the most rudimentary distinctions need to be made, for example, absence or presence of a particular emotion (anger in a client's voice, or the presence of general negative arousal). In others, much finer discrimination is required. Clearly, the choice of model is based on this fundamental requirement. One of the issues of concern should be the capacity of the model to evolve. In many cases, one tends to start with a simple undifferentiated model but quickly sees the need for further development and differentiation. As shown above, a forward mapping from complex, high-information, lower-order models to simpler, low-dimensional, higher-order models is always possible, while the reverse is not true. Thus starting with a simple model allowing little differentiation may impede further development.

◆ *Response patterning.* Virtual agents are becoming increasingly sophisticated, and it is predictable that ever more emphasis will be placed on affective agents that have a highly differentiated repertoire of response patterns in several modalities. Currently, much effort is being made to improve facial and to some extent vocal expression. Interest is also developing in more natural animation of gestures and body movements. It is to be expected that interest in modelling brain and peripheral physiological responses will increase in the future. In consequence, the choice of guiding models should be informed by the capacity of different models to predict complex dynamic processes in response patterning. It would seem to be in the interest of flexibility and realism that this should occur in a molecular and emergent fashion rather than in a holistic and deterministic one.

◆ *Moving back and forth between levels.* As shown above, different emotion theories focus on different levels, dealing with phenomena of lower or higher order. As we have suggested, mapping between theories is possible in one direction, but once information about a lower level is lost, it cannot be retrieved. In consequence, it is important to determine to what extent computational modelling or implementation of virtual agents requires moving back and forth between levels, or whether it is sufficient to remain on a single level of analysis and synthesis. The emotion models presented here vary with respect to affording this possibility.

Conclusion

Stepping back to match these requirements against the many different emotion theories described above, it is easy to see that some theories are better suited to address certain of these requirements than others. Basic emotion theories have been (and still are to some extent) the models of choice in computer sciences and engineering. However, as shown above, if one accepts the central features of emotion outlined above, they do not fare so well both from a point of mapping theory to underlying processes and with respect to the specification of mechanisms that allow the modelling of the essentially emergent nature of dynamic emotion processes. In addition, the notion of fairly rigid affect programs for a small number of basic emotions seriously limits the construction of open, emergent architectures. If the aim is to compute emotion, in terms of a multicomponential process over time, rather than constructively assigned labels of emotion, likely to vary greatly from one individual to another in a rather unpredictable way, constructivist theories need to be discarded (especially as the determining factors are underspecified and precise predictions of mechanisms are absent).

The review of theories above suggests that appraisal theories of emotion constitute the most comprehensive way to represent the complexity of the emotion process, spanning the whole gamut from low-level appraisals of the eliciting event to high-level influence over behaviour. In addition, they present specific hypotheses for the underlying mechanisms that have received consistent support in experimental research. They may thus be the theories of choice for designing adaptive and evolving systems in complex environments as well as for experimental exploration of the emotion mechanism in virtual reality. First attempts to construct partial models based on appraisal theory have yielded promising results (Gratch and Marsella 2004*a,b*; Marsella and Gratch 2009; Scherer 1993; Wehrle and Scherer 2001).

To assure a sufficient degree of ecological validity and flexibility, it is essential to base computational models on the most recent insights concerning the architecture of the emotion process and the essential role of dynamic change. In consequence, modellers should define clearly the aims of their simulations against the requirements described above before choosing a specific emotion theory to guide their work.

Chapter 1.2

Computational models of emotion

Stacy Marsella, Jonathan Gratch, and Paolo Petta

Summary

Recent years have seen a significant expansion in research on computational models of human emotional processes, driven both by their potential for basic research on emotion and cognition as well as their promise for an ever-increasing range of applications. This has led to a truly interdisciplinary, mutually beneficial partnership between emotion research in psychology and in computational science, of which this volume is an exemplar. To understand this partnership and its potential for transforming existing practices in emotion research across disciplines and for disclosing important novel areas of research, we explore in this chapter the history of work in computational models of emotion including the various uses to which they have been put, the theoretical traditions that have shaped their development, and how these uses and traditions are reflected in their underlying architectures.

For an outsider to the field, the last 15 years have seen the development of a seemingly bewildering array of competing and complementary computational models. Figure 1.2.1 lists a 'family tree' of a few of the significant models and the theoretical traditions from which they stem. Although there has been a proliferation of work, the field is far from mature: the goals that a model is designed to achieve are not always clearly articulated; research is rarely incremental, more often returning to motivating theories rather than extending prior computational approaches; and rarely are models contrasted with each other in terms of their ability to achieve their set goals. Contributing to potential confusion is the reality that computational models are complex systems embodying a number of, sometimes unarticulated, design decisions and assumptions inherited from the psychological and computational traditions from which they emerged, a circumstance made worse by the lack of a commonly accepted lexicon even for designating these distinctions.

In this chapter, we lay out the work on computational models of emotion in an attempt to reveal the common uses to which they may be put and the underlying techniques and assumptions from which the models are built. Our aim is to present conceptual distinctions and common terminology that can aid in discussion and comparison of competing models. Our hope is that this will not only facilitate an understanding of the field for outside researchers but work towards a lexicon that can help foster the maturity of the field towards more incremental research.

In characterizing different computational models of emotion, we begin by describing interdisciplinary uses to which computational models may be put, including their uses in improving human–computer interaction, in enhancing general models of intelligence, and as methodological tools for furthering our understanding of human behaviour. We next discuss how models have been built, including the underlying theoretical traditions that have shaped their development. These differing theoretical perspectives often conceptualize emotion in quite different ways, emphasizing different scenarios and proposed functions, different component processes, and different linkages between these components. It should then come as no surprise that such

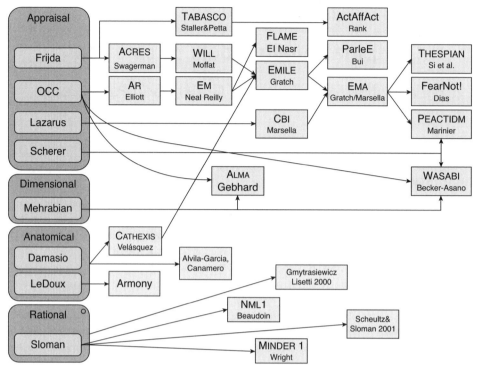

Fig. 1.2.1 A history of computational models of emotion.

differences are also reflected in the underlying design of the computational models. We next narrow our focus to cognitive appraisal theory, undeniably one of the most influential theoretical perspectives within computational research. To help organize and dissect research on computational appraisal models, we introduce a generic appraisal architecture, a *component model view of appraisal models*, that conceptualizes emotion as a set of component models and relations between these components. We discuss how different computational systems address some, but typically not all, of these component models and describe differing processing choices that system developers have used in realizing their component model variants. Finally, we illustrate how this component model view can help guide work in evaluating and contrasting alternative computational models of emotion.

The uses of computational models: an interdisciplinary partnership

New tools often transform science, opening up new approaches to research, allowing previously unaddressed questions to be explored, as well as revealing new questions. To appreciate the transformative role that computational models of emotion can have on research, we consider three aspects in this section: the impact on emotion research in psychology; the impact on artificial intelligence (AI); and, finally, the impact on work in human–computer interaction.

Impact on psychological research on emotion

Work in computational models of emotion impacts research in human emotion by transforming how theories are formulated and evaluated. One way this occurs is through a process of concretizing concepts in the theory. Psychological theories of emotion have typically been cast at an abstract level and through informal (natural language) descriptions. Concepts in the theory are usually not defined formally, and how processes work may not be laid out in systematic detail. The formulation of a computational model enforces more detail. The structures and processes of the theory must be explicitly and formally defined in order to implement them in a computational model, thus making a computer model a particularly concrete realization of the theory. The process of realizing the model can reveal implicit assumptions and hidden complexities, thereby forcing them to be addressed explicitly in some documented fashion. For example, appraisal theories often argue that a key variable in appraisal is an attribution of blameworthiness for an event deemed motivationally incongruent (e.g. Lazarus 1991). But the process by which a person makes such an attribution and therefore whether a particular situation would be deemed blameworthy, and the related required resources and capacities are typically not carefully laid out. And yet this attribution process may in itself be quite involved (e.g. Shaver 1985; Weiner 1995).

As computational modelling exposes hidden assumptions in the theory, addressing those assumptions can extend the scope of the theorizing. Seen in this way, computational models become not only a way to concretize theories, but also a framework for theory construction. In so doing, computational modelling also extends the language of emotion theorizing by incorporating concepts, processes, and metaphors drawn from computation, much as concepts such as *information processing* and *symbol systems* have impacted psychology in general. For example, several computational models have recast the appraisal theory in terms of concepts drawn from AI, including knowledge representation (e.g. Gratch and Marsella 2004*a*), planning (e.g. Gratch 2000; Dias and Paiva 2005), neural networks (Sander *et al.* 2005), and decision making (Lisetti and Gmytrasiewicz 2002; Ito *et al.* 2008). Incorporation of the models into larger simulations can also expose hidden questions behind traditional conceptualizations and extend the scope of theorizing. For example, several computational models of emotion have been incorporated into larger simulation systems that seek to model emotion's role in human mental processes and behaviour (Marsella and Gratch 2001; Dias and Paiva 2005; Becker-Asano 2008; Rank 2009). This has led researchers to address fundamental architectural questions about the relation of appraisal processes to other cognitive processes, perception, and behaviour (Marsella and Gratch 2009; Rank 2009). Of course, a central challenge here is to ensure that increases in the scope of the theorizing do not endanger the parsimony often critical to a model's explanatory power.

Coupled to this transformation of the theory formation process through modelling and simulation runs of the model, the computational realization of a theory can also increase the capacity to draw predictions from theory. In particular, computational models provide a new empirical framework for studying emotion processes that goes beyond what is feasible in more traditional laboratory settings. Computer simulations of the model *behave*: they provide a means to explore systematically the temporal dynamics of emotion processes and form predictions about the time course of those processes. Manipulations of experimental conditions may be explored more extensively first with a computational model, such as ablating certain functionalities or testing responses under adverse conditions that may be costly, risky, or raise ethical concerns *in vivo* (e.g. Armony *et al.* 1997). Simulations can reveal unexpected model properties that suggest further exploration. Additionally, models of emotion and affective expression have been incorporated into virtual humans, software artefacts that look and act like humans, capable of perception and action in a virtual world that they can cohabit with people. These systems essentially allow for the study of emotion in a virtual ecology, a form of synthetic *in vivo* experimentation.

Finally, the computational modelling of emotion and emotional expression has led to new ways to create stimuli for human subject experimentation. Virtual humans are in some ways the experimenter's ultimate confederate. A virtual human can be manipulated systematically to elicit behaviour from human subjects. For example, virtual humans have been used to show that subtle changes in physical appearance or behaviour can profoundly impact social interaction, including changes to people's willingness to cooperate (Krumhuber *et al.* 2007), the fluidity of their conversation (Gratch *et al.* 2007), learning outcomes (Baylor and Kim 2008) and even their level of social aggression (McCall *et al.* 2009).

Impact on artificial intelligence and robotics

Modern research in the psychology, cognitive science, and neuroscience of emotion has led to a revolution in our thinking about the relation of emotion to cognition and social behaviour and, as a consequence, is also transforming the science of computation. Findings on the functional, often adaptive role that emotions play in human behaviour have motivated AI and robotics research to explore whether computer analogues of human emotion can lead to more intelligent, flexible, and capable systems. Early work by Simon (1967) argued that emotions serve the crucial function of interrupting normal cognition when unattended goals require servicing. Viewing emotion as serving this critical interrupt capacity provides a means for an organism to balance competing goals as well as incorporate reactive behaviours into more deliberative processing. A range of studies point to emotions as the means by which the individual establishes values for alternative decisions and decision outcomes. Busemeyer *et al.* (2007) argue that emotional state influences the subjective utility of alternative choice. Studies performed by Damásio and colleagues suggest that damage to the ventromedial prefrontal cortex prevents emotional signals from guiding decision making in an advantageous direction (Bechara *et al.* 1999).

Other authors have emphasized how social emotions such as anger and guilt may reflect a mechanism that improves group utility by minimizing social conflicts, and thereby explains people's 'irrational' choices to cooperate in social games such as prisoner's dilemma (Frank 1988). Similarly, 'emotional biases' such as wishful thinking may reflect a rational mechanism that more accurately accounts for certain social costs, such as the cost of betrayal when a parent defends a child despite strong evidence of their guilt in a crime (Mele 2001).

Collectively, these findings suggest that emotional influences have important social and cognitive functions that would be required by *any* intelligent system. This view is not new to artificial intelligence (Simon 1967; Sloman and Croucher 1981; Minsky 1986) but was in large measure ignored in AI research of the late twentieth century which largely treated emotion as antithetical to rationality and intelligence. However, in the spirit of Hume's famous dictum: 'reason is, and ought only to be the slave of the passions…' (Hume 2000, 2.3.3.4), the question of emotion has again come to the fore in AI as models have begun to catch up with theoretical findings. This has been spurred, in part, by an explosion of interest in integrated computational models that incorporate a variety of cognitive functions (Bates *et al.* 1991; Anderson 1993; Rickel *et al.* 2002). Indeed, until the rise of broad integrative models of cognition, the problems emotion was purported to solve, for example, juggling multiple goals, were largely hypothetical. More recent cognitive systems embody a variety of mental functions and face very real challenges how to allocate resources. A recurring theme in emotion research in AI is the role of emotion in addressing such control choices by directing cognitive resources towards problems of adaptive significance for the organism (Scheutz and Sloman 2001; Staller and Petta 2001; Blanchard and Cañamero 2006; Scheutz and Schermerhorn 2009).

Impact on human–computer interaction

Finally, research has revealed the powerful role that emotion and emotion expression play in shaping human social interaction, and this in turn has suggested that computer interaction can exploit (and indeed must address) this function. Emotional displays convey considerable information about the mental state of an individual. Although there is a lively debate about whether these displays reflect true emotion or are simply communicative conventions (Manstead *et al.* 1999), pragmatically there is truth in both perspectives. From emotional displays, observers can form interpretations of a person's beliefs (e.g. frowning at an assertion may indicate disagreement), desires (e.g. joy gives information that a person values an outcome), and intentions/action tendencies (e.g. fear suggests flight). They may also provide information about the underlying dimensions along which people appraise the emotional significance of events: valence; intensity; certainty; expectedness; blameworthiness; etc. (Smith and Scott 1997). With such a powerful signal, it is not surprising that emotions can be a means of social control (Fridlund 1997; Campos *et al.* 2003; de Waal 2003). Emotional displays seem to function to elicit particular social responses from other individuals ('social imperatives', Frijda 1987) and arguably, such responses can be difficult to suppress. The responding individual may not even be consciously aware of the manipulation. For example, anger seems to be a mechanism for coercing actions in others and enforcing social norms, displays of guilt can elicit reconciliation after some transgression, distress can be seen as a way of recruiting social support, and displays of joy or pity are a way of signalling such support to others. Other emotion displays seem to exert control indirectly, by inducing emotional states in others and thereby influencing an observer's behaviour. Specific examples of this are *emotional contagion*, which can lead individuals to 'catch' the emotions of those around them (Hatfield *et al.* 1994) and the *Pygmalion effect* (also known as 'self-fulfilling prophecy') whereby our positive or negative expectations about an individual, even if expressed non-verbally, can influence them to meet these expectations (Blanck 1993). Given this wide array of functions in social interactions, many have argued that emotions evolved because they provide an adaptive advantage to social organisms (Darwin 1872/1998; de Waal 2003).

To the extent that these functions can be realized in artificial systems, they could play a powerful role in facilitating interactions between computer systems and human users. This has inspired several trends in human–computer interaction. For example, Conati uses a Bayesian network-based appraisal model to deduce a student's emotional state based on their actions (Conati 2002) and several systems have attempted to recognize the behavioural manifestations of a user's emotion including facial expressions (Lisetti and Schiano 2000; Fasel *et al.* 2002; Haag *et al.* 2004), physiological indicators (Picard 1997; Haag *et al.* 2004), and vocal expression (Lee and Narayanan 2003).

A related trend in human–computer interaction (HCI) work is the use of emotions and emotional displays in virtual characters that interact with the user. As animated films (Thomas and Johnston 1995) so poignantly demonstrate, emotional displays in an artificially generated character can have the general effect of making it seem human or lifelike, and thereby cue the user to respond to, and interact with, the character as if it were another person. A growing body of research substantiates this view. In the presence of a lifelike agent, people are more polite, tend to make socially desirable choices, and are more nervous (Kramer *et al.* 2003); they can exhibit greater trust of the agent's recommendations (Cowell and Stanney 2003) and they can feel more empathy (Paiva *et al.* 2004). In that people utilize these behaviours in their everyday interpersonal interactions, modelling the function of these behaviours is essential for any application that hopes to faithfully mimic face-to-face human interaction. More importantly, however, the ability of emotional behaviours to influence a person's emotional and motivational state could potentially, if exploited effectively, guide a user towards more effective interactions. For example, education researchers have argued that non-verbal displays can have a significant impact on student intrinsic motivation (Lepper 1988).

A number of applications have attempted to exploit this interpersonal function of emotional expression. Klesen (2005) models the communicative function of emotion, using stylized animations of body language and facial expression to convey a character's emotions and intentions with the goal of helping students understand and reflect on the role these constructs play in improvisational theater. Nakanishi *et al.* (2005) and Cowell and Stanney (2003) each evaluated how certain non-verbal behaviours could communicate a character's trustworthiness for training and marketing applications, respectively. Several applications have also tried to manipulate a student's motivations through the emotional behaviours of a virtual character. Lester utilized praising and sympathetic emotional displays to provide feedback and increase student motivation in a tutoring application (Lester *et al.* 2000). Researchers have also looked at emotion and emotional expression in characters as a means to engender empathy and bonding between between learners and virtual characters (Marsella *et al.* 2003; Paiva *et al.* 2005); Biswas and colleagues (Biswas *et al.* 2005) also use human-like traits to promote empathy and intrinsic motivation in a learning-by-teaching system.

In summary, computational models of emotion serve differing roles in research and applications. Further, the evaluation of these models is in large measure dependent on those roles. In the case of the psychological research that uses computational models, the emphasis will largely be on fidelity with respect to human emotion processes. In the case of work in AI and robotics, evaluation often emphasizes how the modelling of emotion impacts reasoning processes or leads in some way to improved performances such as an agent or robot that achieves a better fit with its environment. In HCI work, the key evaluation is whether the model improves human–computer interaction such as by making it more effective, efficient, or pleasant.

Overall, the various roles for computational models of emotion have led to a number of impressive models being proposed and developed. To put this body of work into perspective, it is critical for the field to support a deeper understanding of the relationship between these models. To assist in that endeavour, we now turn to presenting some common terms and distinctions that can aid in the comparison of competing models.

A component perspective on the design of computational models

Each of the computational models listed in Figure 1.2.1 is a very different entity, with incompatible inputs and outputs, different behaviours, embodying irreconcilable processing assumptions and directed towards quite different scientific objectives. What we argue here, however, is that much of this variability is illusory. These models are complex systems that integrate a number of component 'submodels'. Sometimes these components are not clearly delineated, but, if one disassembles models along the proper joints, then a great many apparent differences collapse into a small number of design choices. To facilitate this decomposition, this section describes the component processes underlying emotion, with a particular emphasis on components posited in connection with appraisal theory. These components are not new—indeed, they are central theoretical constructs in many theories of emotion—but some of the terminology is new as we strive to simplify terms and de-conflict them with other terminology more commonly used in computer science. We begin by describing the various theoretical traditions that have influenced computational research and the components these theories propose.

A challenge in developing a coherent framework for describing computational models of emotion is that the term 'emotion' itself is fraught with ambiguities and contrasting definitions. Emotions are a central aspect of everyday life and people have strong intuitions about them. As a consequence, the terms used in emotion research (appraisal, emotion, mood, affect, feeling) have commonsense interpretations that can differ considerably from their technical definition within the context of a particular emotion theory or computational model (Russell 2003). This ambiguity is confounded by the fact that there are fundamental disputes within psychological and neuroscience research on emotion over the meaning and centrality of these core concepts. Theories differ as to which components are intrinsic to an emotion (e.g. cognitions, somatic processes, behavioural tendencies and responses), the relationships between components (e.g. do cognitions precede or follow somatic processes), and representational distinctions (e.g. is anger a linguistic fiction or a natural kind)—see Chapter 1.1, this volume, for an overview of different theoretical perspectives on emotion.

Understanding these alternative theoretical perspectives on emotion is essential for anyone who aspires to develop computational models, but this does not imply that a modeller must be strictly bound by any specific theoretical tradition. Certainly, modellers should strive for a consistent and well-founded semantics for their underlying emotional constructs and picking and integrating fundamentally irreconcilable theoretical perspectives into a single system can be problematic at best. If the goal of the computational model is to faithfully model human emotional processes or, more ambitiously, to contribute to theoretical discourse on emotion, such inconsistencies can be fatal. However, some 'fundamentally irreconcilable' differences are illusory and evaporate when seen from a new perspective. For example, disputes as to whether emotion precedes or follows cognition dissipate if one adopts a dynamic systems perspective (i.e. a circle has no beginning). Nonetheless, theoretical models provide important insights in deriving a coherent computational model of emotion and deviations from specific theoretical constraints, ideally, will be motivated by concrete challenges in realizing a theory within a specific representational system or in applying the resulting model to concrete applications. Here we review some of the theoretical perspectives that have most influenced computational modelling research.

Appraisal theory

Appraisal theory, discussed in detail in Chapter 1.1, is currently a predominant force among psychological perspectives on emotion and arguably the most fruitful source for those interested in the design of symbolic AI systems, as it emphasizes and explains the connection between emotion and cognition. Indeed, the large majority of computational models of emotion stem from this tradition. In appraisal theory, emotion is argued to arise from patterns of individual judgement concerning the relationship between events and an individual's beliefs, desires, and intentions, sometimes referred to as the *person–environment relationship* (Lazarus 1991). These judgements, formalized through reference to devices such as *situational meaning structures* or *appraisal variables* (Frijda 1987), characterize aspects of the personal significance of events. Patterns of appraisal are associated with specific physiological and behavioural reactions. In several versions of appraisal theory, appraisals also trigger cognitive responses, often referred to as *coping strategies*—e.g. planning, procrastination, or resignation—feeding back into a continual cycle of appraisal and reappraisal (Lazarus 1991, p. 127).

In terms of underlying components of emotion, appraisal theory foregrounds appraisal as a central process. Appraisal theorists typically view appraisal as the cause of emotion, or at least of the physiological, behavioural, and cognitive changes associated with emotion. Some appraisal theorists emphasize 'emotion' as a discrete component within their theories, whereas others treat the term emotion more broadly to refer to some configuration of appraisals, bodily responses, and subjective experience (see Ellsworth and Scherer 2003 for a discussion). Much of the work has focused on the structural relationship between appraisal variables and specific emotion labels—e.g. which pattern of appraisal variables would elicit hope (see Ortony *et al.* 1988)—or the structural relationship between appraisal variables and specific behavioural and cognitive responses—e.g. which pattern of appraisal variables would elicit certain facial expressions (Smith and Scott 1997; Scherer and Ellgring 2007*a*) or coping tendencies (Lazarus 1991). Indeed, although appraisal theorists allow that the same situation may elicit multiple appraisals, theorists are relatively silent on how these individual appraisals would combine into an overall emotional state or if this state is best represented by discrete motor programs or more dimensional representations. More recent work has begun to examine the processing constraints underlying appraisal—to what extent is it parallel or sequential (Scherer 2001; Moors *et al.* 2005) and does it occur at multiple levels (Smith and Kirby 2000; Scherer 2001)—and creating a better understanding of the cognitive, situational, and dispositional factors that influence appraisal judgements (Kuppens and Van Mechelen 2007; Smith and Kirby 2009).

Models derived from appraisal theories of emotion, not surprisingly, emphasize appraisal as the central process to be modelled. Computational appraisal models often encode elaborate mechanisms for deriving appraisal variables such as decision-theoretic plans (Gratch and Marsella 2004*a*; Marsella and Gratch 2009), reactive plans (Staller and Petta 2001; Rank and Petta 2005; Neal Reilly 2006), Markov-decision processes (El Nasr *et al.* 2000; Si *et al.* 2008), or detailed cognitive models (Marinier *et al.* 2009). Emotion itself is often less elaborately modelled. It is sometimes treated simply as a label (sometimes with an intensity) to which behaviour can be attached (Elliott 1992). Appraisal is typically modelled as the cause of emotion with the specific emotion label being derived via *if–then rules* on a set of appraisal variables. Some approaches make a distinction between a specific emotion instance (allowing multiple instances to be derived from the same event) and a more generalized 'affective state' or 'mood' (see discussion of *core affect* below) that summarizes the effect of recent emotion elicitations (Neal Reilly 1996; Gratch and Marsella 2004*a*; Gebhard 2005). Some more recent models attempt to model the impact of momentary emotion and mood on the appraisal process (Gratch and Marsella 2004*a*; Gebhard 2005; Paiva *et al.* 2005; Marsella and Gratch 2009).

Computational appraisal models have been applied to a variety of uses including contributions to psychology, AI, and HCI. For example, Marsella and Gratch have used EMA to generate specific predictions about how human subjects will appraise and cope with emotional situations and argue that empirical tests of these predictions have implications for psychological appraisal theory (Gratch *et al.* 2009b; Marsella *et al.* 2009). Several authors have argued that appraisal processes would be required by any intelligent agent that must operate in real-time, ill-structured, multi-agent environments (e.g. Staller and Petta 2001). The bulk of application of these techniques, however, has been for HCI applications, primarily for the creation of real-time interactive characters that exhibit emotions in order to make these characters more compelling (e.g. Neal Reilly 1996), more realistic (e.g. Traum *et al.* 2003; Mao and Gratch 2006), more able to understand human motivational state (e.g. Conati and MacLaren 2004) or more able to induce desirable social effects in human users (e.g. Paiva *et al.* 2005).

Dimensional theories

Dimensional theories of emotion argue that emotion and other affective phenomena should be conceptualized, not as discrete entities but as points in a continuous (typically two- or three-) dimensional space (Mehrabian and Russell 1974; Watson and Tellegen 1985; Russell 2003; Barrett 2006). Indeed, many dimensional theories argue that discrete emotion categories (e.g. hope, fear, and anger) are folk–psychological concepts that have unduly influenced scientific discourse on emotion and have no 'reality' in that there are no specific brain regions or circuits that correspond to specific emotion categories (Barrett 2006). Not surprisingly, dimensional theories de-emphasize the term emotion or relegate it to a cognitive label attributed, retrospectively, to some perceived body state. Rather they emphasize concepts such as mood, affect, or, more recently, *core affect* (Russell 2003). We adopt this later term in subsequent discussion. A person is said to be in exactly one affective state at any moment (Russell 2003, p. 154) and the space of possible core affective states is characterized in terms of broad, continuous dimensions. Many computational dimensional models build on the three-dimensional 'PAD' model of Mehrabian and Russell (1974) where these dimensions correspond to *pleasure* (a measure of valence), *arousal* (indicating the level of affective activation), and *dominance* (a measure of power or control).

It is worth noting that there is a relationship between the dimensions of core affect and appraisal dimensions—the pleasure dimension roughly maps on to appraisal dimensions that characterize the valence of an appraisal-eliciting event (e.g. intrinsic pleasantness or goal congruence), dominance roughly maps on to the appraisal dimension of coping potential, and arousal is a measure of intensity. However, they have quite different meanings: appraisal is a relational construct characterizing the relationship between some specific object/event and the individual's beliefs, desires, and intentions and several appraisals may be simultaneously active; core affect is a non-relational construct summarizing a unique overall state of the individual.

Dimensional theories emphasize different components of emotion than appraisal theories and link these components quite differently. Dimensional theories foreground the structural and temporal dynamics of core affect and often do not address affect's antecedents in detail. Most significantly, dimensional theorists question the tight causal linkage between appraisal and emotion that is central to appraisal accounts. Dimensional theorists conceive of core affect as a 'non-intentional' state, meaning the affect is not about some object (as in 'I am angry at *him*'). In such theories, many factors may contribute to a change in core affect including symbolic intentional judgements (e.g. appraisal) but also subsymbolic factors such as hormones and drugs (Schachter and Singer 1962), but, most importantly, the link between any preceding intentional meaning and emotion is broken (as it is not represented within core affect) and must be recovered after the fact, sometimes incorrectly (Clore *et al.* 1994; Clore and Palmer 2009). For example, Russell argues for the following sequence of emotional components: some external event occurs (e.g. a bear walks out of the forest), it is perceived in terms of its affective quality; this perception results in a dramatic change in core affect; this change is attributed to some 'object' (e.g. the bear); and only then is the object cognitively appraised in terms of its goal relevance, causal antecedents, and future prospects (see also Zajonc 1980).

Models influenced by dimensional theories, not surprisingly, emphasize processes associated with core affect and other components (e.g. appraisal) tend to be less elaborately developed. Core affect is typically represented as a continuous time-varying process that is represented at a given period of time by a point in three-dimensional space that is 'pushed around' by eliciting events. Computational dimensional models often have detailed mechanisms for how this point changes over time—e.g. decays to some resting state—and incorporating the impact of dispositional tendencies such as personality or temperament (Gebhard 2005).

Computational dimensional models are most often used for animated character behaviour generation, perhaps because it translates emotion into a small number of continuous dimensions that can be readily mapped to continuous features of behaviour such as the spatial extent of a gesture. For example, PAD models describe all behaviour in terms of only three dimensions, whereas modellers using appraisal models must either associate behaviours with a larger number of appraisal dimensions (see Smith and Scott 1997; Scherer and Ellgring 2007a) or map appraisals into a small number of discrete, though perhaps intensity-varying, expressions (Elliott 1992). For a similar reason, dimensional models are also frequently used as a good representational framework for systems that attempt to recognize human emotional behaviour and there is some evidence that they may better discriminate user affective states than approaches that rely on discrete labels (Barrett 2006).

The relationship between core affect and cognition is generally less explored in dimensional approaches. Typically the connection between emotion-eliciting events and current core-affective state is not maintained, consistent with Russell's view of emotion as a non-intentional state (e.g. Becker-Asano and Wachsmuth 2008; see Chapter 4.1, this volume). Interestingly, we are not aware of any computational models that follow the suggestion from Zajonc and Russell that appraisal is a *post hoc* explanation of core affect. Rather, many computational models of emotion that incorporate core affect have viewed appraisal as the mechanism that initiates changes to core affect. For example, Gebhard's (2005) ALMA model includes Ortony *et al.*(1988) inspired appraisal rules (OCC) and WASABI (Becker-Asano and Wachsmuth 2008; see Chapter 4.1, this volume) incorporates appraisal processes inspired by Scherer's sequential-checking theory into a PAD-based model of core affect. Some computational models explore how core affect can influence cognitive processes. For example, HOTCO 2 (Thagard 2003) allows explanations to be biased by dimensional affect (in this case, a one-dimensional model encoding valence) but this is more naturally seen as the consequence of emotion on cognition (e.g. the modelling of an emotion-focused coping strategy in the sense of Lazarus 1991).

Other approaches

+ *Anatomic theories* stem from an attempt to reconstruct the neural links and processes that underlie organisms' emotional reactions (Le Doux 1996; Panksepp 1998*a*; Öhman and Wiens 2004). Unlike appraisal theories, such models tend to emphasize subsymbolic processes. Unlike dimensional theories, anatomic approaches tend to view emotions as different, discrete neural circuits and emphasize processes or systems associated with these circuits. Thus, anatomically inspired models tend to foreground certain process assumptions and tend to be less comprehensive than either appraisal or dimensional theories, with researchers focusing on a specific emotion such as fear. For example, LeDoux emphasizes a 'high-road' versus 'low-road' distinction in the fear circuit with the latter reflecting automatic/reflexive responses to situations, whereas the former is mediated by cognition and deliberation. Computational models inspired by the anatomic tradition often focus on low-level perceptual-motor tasks and encode a two-process view of emotion that argues for a fast, automatic, undifferentiated emotional response and a slower, more differentiated response that relies on higher-level reasoning processes (e.g. Armony *et al.* 1997).

+ *Rational approaches* start from the question of what adaptive function does emotion serve and then attempt to abstract this function away from its 'implementation details' in humans and incorporate these functions into a (typically normative) model of intelligence (Simon 1967; Sloman and Croucher 1981; Frank 1988; Scheutz and Sloman 2001; Anderson and Lebiere 2003; Doyle 2006). Researchers in this tradition typically reside in the field of artificial intelligence and view emotion as a window through which one can gain insight into adaptive behaviour, albeit it a very different window than that which has motivated much of AI research. Within this tradition, cognition is conceived as a collection of symbolic processes that serve specific cognitive functions and are subject to certain architectural constraints on how they interoperate. Emotion, within this view, is simply another, albeit often overlooked, set of processes and constraints that have adaptive value. Models of this sort are most naturally directed towards the goal of improving theories of machine intelligence.

+ *Communicative theories of emotion* argue that emotion processes function as a communicative system: both as a mechanism for informing other individuals of one's mental state—and thereby facilitate social coordination—and as a mechanism for requesting/demanding changes in the behaviour of others—as in threat displays (Keltner and Haidt 1999; Parkinson 2009). Communicative theories emphasize the social-communicative function of displays and sometimes argue for a disassociation between internal emotional processes and emotion displays that need not be selected on the basis of an internal emotional state (e.g. see Fridlund 1997; Gratch 2008). Computational models inspired by communicative theories often embrace this disassociation and dispense with the need for an internal emotional model and focus on machinery that decides when an emotional display will have a desirable effect on a human user. For example, in the Cosmo tutoring system (Lester, Towns *et al.* 2000), the agent's pedagogical goals drive the selection and sequencing of emotive behaviours. In Cosmo, a congratulatory act triggers a motivational goal to express admiration that is conveyed with applause. Not surprisingly, computational models based on communicative theories are most often directed towards the goal of achieving social influence.

Dissecting computational appraisal theory

Appraisal theory, by far, dominates the work on computational models of emotion so here we spend some time laying out some terminology that is specific to this class of models (although some of this terminology could apply to other approaches). As we discussed earlier, our aim is to promote incremental research on computational models of emotion by presenting a compositional view of model building, emphasizing that an emotional model is often assembled from individual 'submodels' and these smaller components are often shared and can be mixed, matched, or excluded from any given implementation. More importantly, these components can be seen as embodying certain content and process assumptions that can be potentially assessed and subsequently abandoned or improved as a result of these assessments. In presenting this, we attempt to build as much as possible on terminology already introduced within the emotion literature.

Figure 1.2.2 presents an idealized computational appraisal architecture consisting of a set of linked component models. This figure presents what we see as natural joints at which to decompose appraisal systems into coherent and often shared modules, though any given system may fail to implement some of these components or allow different information paths between components. In this architecture, information flows in a cycle as argued by several appraisal theorists (Lazarus 1991; Scherer 2001; Parkinson 2009): some representation of the person–environment relationship is appraised; this leads to an affective response of some intensity; the response triggers behavioural and cognitive consequences; these consequences alter the person–environment;

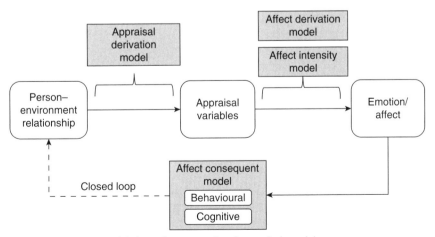

Fig. 1.2.2 A component model view of computational appraisal models.

this change is appraised; and so on. Each of these stages can be represented by a model that represents or transforms state information relevant to emotion-processing. Here we introduce terminology associated with each of these.

Person–environment relationship

Lazarus (1991) introduced this term to refer to some representation of the agent's relationship with its environment. This representation should allow an agent, in principle, to derive the relationship between external events (real or hypothetical) and the beliefs, desires, and intentions of the agent or other significant entities in the (real or hypothetical) social environment. This representation need not represent these relationships explicitly but must support their derivation. Examples of this include the decision-theoretical planning representations in EMA (Gratch and Marsella 2004), which combine decision-theoretic planning representation with belief–desire–intention formalisms, or the partially observable Markov-decision representations in THESPIAN (Si et al. 2008)

Appraisal-derivation model

An appraisal-derivation model transforms some representation of the person–environment relationship into a set of appraisal variables.[1] For example, if an agent's goal is potentially thwarted by some external action, an appraisal-derivation model should be able to automatically derive appraisals that this circumstance is undesirable, assess its likelihood, and calculate the agent's ability to cope, i.e. by identifying alternative ways to achieve this goal. Several computational appraisal models don't provide an appraisal-derivation model or else treat its specification as something that is outside of the system. For example, ALMA (Gebhard 2005) allows domain developers to author the relational model by specifying how certain states or actions should be appraised (e.g. if Sven attacks Valerie, she should appraise this as undesirable). Other researchers treat the appraisal-derivation as a central contribution of their approach. For example, EMA provides a series of domain-independent inference rules that derive appraisal variables from syntactic features of the person-environment relationship (e.g. if the effect of an action threatens a plan to achieve a desired state, this is undesirable). Models also differ in the processing constraints that this model should satisfy. For example, models influenced by Scherer's sequential checking theory incorporate assumptions about the order in which specific appraisal variables should be derived (Marinier 2008). Appraisal-derivation models are often triggered by some eliciting event, though this is not always the case (e.g. EMA simultaneously appraises every goal in an agent's working memory and updates these appraisals continuously as new information about these goals is obtained).

Appraisal variables

Appraisal variables correspond to the set of specific judgements that the agent can use to produce different emotional responses and are generated as a result of an appraisal-derivation model. Different computational appraisal models adopt different sets of appraisal variables, depending on their favourite appraisal theorist. For example, many approaches utilize the set of variables proposed by Ortony et al. (1988) including AR (Elliott 1992), EM (Neal Reilly 1996), FLAME

---

[1] Smith and Kirby (2009) propose the term *relational model* to refer to this mapping, building on Lazarus's idea that appraisal is a relational construct relating the person and the environment. They introduced the term to draw attention to the fact that many appraisal theories emphasize the mapping from appraisal variable to emotion but neglect the situational and dispositional antecedents of appraisal. As 'relation' and 'relational' often have a very different meaning within computer science, we prefer a different term.

(El Nasr *et al.* 2000), and ALMA (Gebhard 2005). Others favour the variables proposed by Scherer (2001) including WASABI (Becker-Asano and Wachsmuth 2008; see Chapter 4.1, this volume) and PEACTIDM (Marinier *et al.* 2009).

Affect-derivation model

An affect-derivation model maps between appraisal variables and an affective state, and specifies how an individual will react emotionally once a pattern of appraisals has been determined.[2] As noted in the discussion of different theoretical perspectives above, there is some diversity in how models define 'emotion' and here we consider any mapping from appraisal variables to affective state, where this state could be either a discrete emotion label, a set of discrete emotions, core affect, or even some combination of these factors. For example, Elliott's AR (Elliott 1992) maps appraisal variables into discrete emotion labels, Becker-Asano's WASABI (Becker-Asano and Wachsmuth 2008) maps appraisals into a dimensional (e.g. PAD) representation of emotion, and Gebhard's ALMA (Gebhard 2005) does both simultaneously. Many computational systems adopt the affect-derivation model proposed by Ortony, *et al.* (1988) whereby 22 emotion labels are defined as conjunctions of appraisal variables—this will be henceforth referred to as the OCC model. Others have implemented models based on the work of Lazarus (e.g. Gratch and Marsella's EMA) and Scherer (e.g. Becker-Asano's WASABI and Marinier's PEACTIDM). Much of the empirical work in psychological appraisal theory has focused on identifying the affect-derivation model that best conforms to human behaviour but the results of these studies are far from definitive and can be interpreted to support multiple proposed models.

Affect-intensity model

An affect-intensity model specifies the strength of the emotional response resulting from a specific appraisal. There is a close association between the affect-derivation model and intensity model (the intensity computation is often implemented as part of the affect-derivation model). However it is useful to conceptualize these separately as they can be independently varied— indeed, computational systems with the same affect-derivation model often have quite different intensity equations (Gratch *et al.* 2009). Intensity models usually utilize a subset of appraisal variables (e.g. most intensity equations involve some notion of desirability and likelihood); how- ever, they may involve several variables unrelated to appraisal (e.g. Elliott and Siegle 1993). Although less studied than appraisal-derivation models, some research has investigated which intensity model best conforms to human behaviour (Mellers *et al.* 1997; Gratch *et al.* 2009; Reisenzein 2009).

Emotion/affect

Affect is a representation of the agent's current emotional state. This could be a discrete emotion label, a set of discrete emotions, core affect (i.e. a continuous dimensional space), or even some combination of these factors. An important consideration in representing affect, particularly for systems that model the consequences of emotions, is whether this data structure preserves the link between appraisal factors and emotional state. As noted above in the discussion of appraisal and dimensional theories, emotions are often viewed as being about something (e.g. I am angry

---

[2] Smith and Kirby (2009) use the term *structural model* to refer to this mapping, drawing analogy to structural equation modelling, the statistical technique for estimating the causal relationships between variables that appraisal theorists often use to derive these mappings (see Kline 2005). As the term 'struc- tural model' is often used to contrast with 'process models' (a distinction we ourselves use later), we prefer the different term.

at Valerie). Agents that model affect as some aggregate dimensional space must either preserve the connection between affect and domain objects that initiated changes to the dimensional space, or they must provide some attribution process that *post hoc* recovers a (possibly incorrect) domain object to apply the emotional response to. For example, EM (Neal Reilly 1996) has a dimensional representation of core affect (valence and arousal) but also maintains a hierarchical data structure that preserves the linkages through each step of the appraisal process to the multiple instances of discrete emotion that underlie its dimensional calculus. In contrast, WASABI (Becker-Asano and Wachsmuth 2008) breaks this link. Some models propose some hybrid. For example, EMA maintains discrete appraisal frames that represent specific discrete emotion instances but then allow a general dimensional 'mood' to moderate which discrete emotion raises to the level of awareness.

Affect-consequent model

An affect-consequent model maps affect (or its antecedents) into some behavioural or cognitive change. Consequent models can be usefully described in terms of two dimensions, one distinguishing if the consequence is inner or outer directed (cognitive versus behavioural) and the other describing whether or not the consequence feeds into a cycle (i.e. is closed-loop).

Emotion can be directed outward into the environment or inward, shaping a person's thoughts. Reflecting this, behaviour consequent models summarize how affect alters an agent's observable physical behaviour and cognitive consequent models determine how affect alters the nature or content of cognitive processes. Most embodied computational systems model the mapping between affect and physical display, such as facial expressions. For example, WASABI maps regions of core affect into one of seven possible facial expressions (Becker-Asano 2008, p. 85) and ParlE (Bui 2004) maps from an emotion state vector (the intensity of six discrete emotion labels) to a facial muscle contraction vector (specifying the motion of 19 facial action units). Emotions can also trigger physical actions. For example, in a process called problem-focused coping, EMA (Gratch and Marsella 2004*a*; Marsella and Gratch 2009) attempts to mitigate negative emotions by changing features in the environment that led to the initial undesirable appraisal. In contrast, cognitive consequent models change some aspect of cognition as a result of affective state. This can involve changes in how cognition processes information; for example, Gmytrasiewicz and Lisetti (2000) propose a model that changes the depth of forward projection as a function of emotional state in order to model some of the claimed effects of emotion on human decision-making. Cognitive consequent models can also change the content of cognitive processes; for example, EMA implements a set of emotion-focused coping strategies, such as wishful thinking, distancing, and resignation, that alter an agent's beliefs, desires, and intentions, respectively.

We can further distinguish consequences by whether or not they form a cycle by altering the circumstances that triggered the original affective response. For example, a robot that merely expresses fear when its battery is expiring does not address the underlying causes of the fear, whereas one that translates this fear into an action tendency (e.g. seek power) is attempting to address the underlying cause. In this sense, both behavioural and cognitive consequences can be classified as *closed-loop* if they directly act on the emotion eliciting circumstances or *open-loop* if they do not.

♦ Open-loop models are best seen as making an indirect or mediated impact on the agent's emotional state. For example, open-looped behavioural consequences such as emotional displays make sense in multi-agent setting where the display is presumed to recruit resources from other agents. For example, building a robot that expresses fear makes sense if there is a human around that can recognize this display and plug it in. Gmytrasiewicz and Lisetti's (2000) work on changing the depth of decision-making can similarly be seen as having an indirect on emotion: by altering the nature of processing to one best suited to a certain emotional state, the cognitive architecture is presumably in a better position to solve problems that tend to arise when in that state.

- Closed-loop models attempt to realize a direct impact to regulate emotion and suggest ways to enhance the autonomy of intelligent agents. Closed-loop models require reasoning about the cognitive and environmental antecedents of an emotion so that these factors can ultimately be altered. For example, EMA implements problem-focused coping as a closed-loop behavioural strategy that selects actions that address threats to goal achievement, and implements emotion-focused coping as a closed-loop cognitive strategy that alters mental state (e.g. abandons a goal) in response to similar threats. Closed-loop models naturally implement a view of emotion as a continuous cycle of appraisal, response, and re-appraisal. In EMA, an agent might perceive another agent's actions to be a threat to its goals, resulting in anger, which triggers a coping strategy that results in the goal being abandoned, which in turn lowers the agent's appraised sense of control, resulting in sadness (see Marsella and Gratch 2009).

The component model in Figure 1.2.2 is, of course, only one of many possible ways to dissect and link emotion components but we have found it pragmatically useful in our own understanding of different computation approaches, as we illustrate below. Additionally, many of the components we identify have previously been highlighted as important distinctions with the literature on emotion research. For example, Smith and Kirby (2009) highlight appraisal-derivation as an important but understudied aspect of appraisal theory. In their work they propose the term *relational model* to refer to this component, building on Lazarus's idea that appraisal is a relational construct relating the person and the environment. As 'relation' and 'relational' often has a very different meaning within computer science, we prefer a different term, 'appraisal-derivation model'. Appraisal-derivation models are frequently identified within the appraisal theory under the term *structural model*, drawing analogy to structural equation modelling (Kline 2005), the statistical technique for estimating the causal relationships between variables that appraisal theorists often use to derive these mappings. As the term 'structural model' is not emotion-specific, and is often used to contrast with 'process models' (a distinction we ourselves use later), we prefer the term appraisal-derivation model. The idea of closed-loop models has been proposed by a variety of appraisal theorists. Most recently, Brian Parkinson (2009) has used the term *transactional model* to highlight the incremental unfolding nature of emotional reactions, although we prefer the term closed-loop, again drawing on computer metaphors.

Processing assumptions

Computational appraisal models can vary, not only by which subcomponents they choose to implement, but how these individual components are realized and interact. Some computational systems make strong commitments to *how* information is processed (e.g. in parallel or sequential?). Others make strong commitments concerning *what* information is processed (e.g. states, goals, plans). Here we introduce terminology that characterizes these different processing choices.

Process specificity

Computational models vary considerably in term of the claims they make about how information is processed. At the most abstract level, a *structural model* specifies a mapping between inputs and outputs but makes no commitment to how this mapping is realized—the term structural comes from structural equation modelling (Kline 2005), a statistical method whereby the relationship between input and output can be inferred. In contrast, a process model posits specific constraints on how inputs are transformed into outputs. For example, Ortony, Clore, and Collins present a structural affect-derivation model that maps from appraisal values to an emotion label, whereas

Scherer's sequential checking theory is a process appraisal-derivation model that not only specifies the structure of appraisal but proposes a set of temporal processing constraints on how appraisal variables should be derived (e.g. goal relevance should be derived before normative significance). The distinction between structural and process is not clear-cut and is best seen as a continuum. Psychological process theories only specify processes to some level of detail and different theories vary considerably in terms of their specificity. In contrast, a computational model must be specified in sufficient detail for it to be realized as working software; however many of these process details are pragmatic and do not correspond to strong theoretical claims about how such processes should be realized. For example, Elliott's affective reasoner implements affect-derivation via a set of *ad hoc* rules, but this should not be seen as a claim that appraisal should be implemented in this manner, but rather as a short cut necessary to create a working system.

Processing constraints can be embedded within an individual appraisal component or can emerge from the interactions of individual components. For example, Scherer's sequential checking theory posits temporal ordering constraints with its model of appraisal derivation. In contrast, Gratch and Marsella's EMA model posits that emotion arises from a continuous cycle of appraisal, coping, and reappraisal and that such temporal properties arise from the incremental evolution of the person–environment relationship (for an in-depth discussion of this point see Marsella and Gratch 2009).

Processing constraints can be asserted for a variety of reasons. In psychology, process models are typically used to assert theoretical claims about the nature of human mental processes, such as whether appraisal is a sequential or parallel process. Within computational systems, the story is more complex. For computational systems that model human psychological processes, the aim is the same: faithfully reflect these theoretical claims into computational algorithms. For example, Marinier (2008) translates Scherer's processing assumptions into architectural constraints on how information is processed in his PEACTIDM model. However, processing constraints can be introduced for a variety of other reasons having nothing to do with fidelity to human psychological findings. These include, for example, formalizing abstract mappings into precise language (Meyer 2006; Lorini and Castelfranchi 2007), proving that a mapping is computable, illustrating efficient or robust algorithms to achieve a mapping, etc.

Representational specificity

Regardless of how component models process information, computational systems vary considerably in the level-of-detail of the information they process. Some model emotional processes as abstract black boxes (exploring, for example, the implications of different relationships between components), whereas others get down the nitty-gritty of realizing these processes in the context of concrete application domains. This variance is perhaps easiest to see when it comes to appraisal derivation. For example, all appraisal models decompose the appraisal process into a set of individual appraisal checks. However, some models stop at this level, treating each check as a representational primitive (e.g. Sander *et al.* 2005), whereas others further decompose appraisal checks into the representational details (e.g. domain propositions, actions, and the causal relationships between them) that are necessary for an agent to appraise its relationship to the environment (e.g. Neal Reilly 1996; El Nasr *et al.* 2000; Gratch and Marsella 2004a; Dias and Paiva 2005; Mao and Gratch 2006; Becker-Asano 2008; Si *et al.* 2008).

Process specificity can vary independently from representational specificity. For example, Sander and colleagues (2005) provide a detailed neural network model of how appraisals are derived from the person–environment relationship, but the person–environment relationship itself is only abstractly represented. Process and representational specificity also vary across component models within the same system. For example, WASABI (Becker-Asano 2008) incorporates detailed representational and process commitments for its model of affect-derivation but uses less detail for its model of appraisal derivation. Such differences often result from the fact that, while specific systems are directed at addressing a subset of the components involved in emotion processes, the authors often require a complete working system to assess the impact of their proposed contribution and these other components may be rudimentary or *ad hoc*.

Domain specific versus domain independent

In addition to their processing constraints and representational specificity, algorithms can be characterized by the generality of their implementation. A domain-independent algorithm enforces a strict separation between details of a specific domain, typically encoded as a *domain theory*, and the remaining code, which is written in such a way that it can be used without modification. For example, planning algorithms operate on a domain theory consisting of a set of states and actions that describe a domain and provide general algorithms that operate syntactically on those representations to generate plans. Computational appraisal models differ in terms of how domain-specific knowledge is encoded and which components require domain-specific input. Most systems incorporate domain-independent affect-derivation models (Neal Reilly 1996; Bui 2004; Gratch and Marsella 2004; Gebhard 2005; Becker-Asano 2008; Marinier 2008). Fewer systems provide domain-independent algorithms for appraisal-derivation (e.g. Neal Reilly 1996; El Nasr *et al.* 2000; Gratch and Marsella 2004; Si *et al.* 2008).

Example of applications of this framework

Viewing a computational model of emotion as a model of models allows more meaningful comparisons between systems. Systems that appear quite different on the surface can be seen as adopting similar choices along some dimensions and differing in others. Adopting a component model framework can help highlight these similarities and differences, and facilitate empirical comparisons that assess the capabilities or validity of alternative algorithms for realizing component models.

Table 1.2.1 illustrates how the component model framework can highlight conceptual similarities and differences between emotion models. This table characterizes three quite different systems. EMA is the authors' own work on developing a general computational model of appraisal and coping motivated by the appraisal theory of Richard Lazarus (Lazarus 1991) and has been applied to driving the behaviour of embodied conversational agents (Swartout *et al.* 2006); FLAME is an OCC-inspired appraisal model that drives the behaviour of characters in interactive narrative environments (El Nasr *et al.* 2000); and ALMA is intended as a general programming tool to allow application developers to more easily construct computational models of emotion for a variety of applications (Gebhard 2005). Some observations that can be made from this table include the following.

- EMA and FLAME both focus on appraisal derivation. They provide domain-independent techniques for representing the person–environment relationship and derive appraisal variables via domain-independent inference rules, although the approaches adopt somewhat different representational and inferential choices. In contrast, ALMA does not address appraisal derivation.

- All systems in Table 1.2.1 use rules to derive affect from a set of appraisal variables. ALMA and FLAME both adopt OCC-style appraisal variables and affect-derivation models, whereas EMA uses a model inspired by Lazarus.

- Each system adopts a different choice for how the intensity of an emotion is calculated.

Table 1.2.1 A component model view of three different systems

	EMA	ALMA	FLAME
Person–enviroment relationship	Domain-independent decision-theoretic plans + BDI	Outside the scope of model	Domain-independent Markov-decision process
Appraisal-derivation	Inference over decision-theoretic plans	User-defined	Fuzzy rules over Markov-decision graph
Appraisal-variables	Lazarus-Inspired, desirability, likehood, expectedness, causal attribution, controllability, changeability	OCC-inspired Good/bad, likely/unlikely event Good/bad act of self/other Nice vs. nasty thing	OCC-inspired Desirabilit Expectation (dis)approval
Affect-derivaton	Lazarus-based structural model that generates discrete emotion and mood state	OCC-based structural model that gives 'Impulsed' into core affect	OCC-based structural model producing discrete emotion lables
Affect-intensity	Expected utility model, Threshold model, Additive mood derivation	User defined	Additive model
Affect	Set of appraisal frames, mood (discrete-emotion vector) with decay	PAD space representing both current mood and emotion	Emotion and positive vs. negative mood state
Behavioural-consequences	Most-intense emotion alters behavior display and action selection. Actions are close-loop via domain-independent rules	Open looped. Mood and emotion alter behaviour display and action selection	Domain-specific fuzzy expression and action rules
Cognitive consequences	Closed-loop via domain-independent emotion-focused coping that changes BDI	Open-looped. Emotion amplifies/dampens intensity of elicited emotions	Closed-loop changes to domain model via reinforcement learning

- All systems incorporate some notion of core affect, though they adopt different representations. EMA has a mood state that summarizes the intensity of all active emotional appraisals and this mood biases the selection of a single emotional appraisal that can impact behaviour. ALMA represents both a current emotion and a more general mood in a three-dimensional (PAD) space (either of which can impact behaviour). FLAME has a one-dimensional (positive vs. negative) mood state that can influence behaviour.

- EMA and FLAME propose closed-loop consequence models that allow emotion to feed back into changes in the mental representation of a situation, although they adopt quite different algorithmic choices for how to realize this function.

Besides allowing such conceptual comparisons, the key benefit of decomposing systems into component models is that it allows individual design decisions to be empirically assessed independent of other aspects of the system. For example, in Table 1.2.1, FLAME and EMA adopt different models for deriving the intensity of an emotional response: both systems calculate intensity as a function of the utility and probability of goal attainment but FLAME adds these variables

Table 1.2.2 Comparing the fit of different affect intensity models

	Hope	Joy	Fear	Sadness
Expectation-Change model	PEACTIDM	ParleE, EM PEACTIDM	PEACTIDM	ParleE, EM PEACTIDM
Expected utility	EMA, ParleE, FearNot! EM BTDE		EMA, ParleE, FearNot! EM BTDE	
Threshold model		EMA, FearNot! BTDE		EMA, FearNot!
Additive model	Cathexis, FLAME	Cathexis, FLAME	Cathexis, FLAME	Cathexis, FLAME
Hybrid model	Price et al, 1985	Price et al, 1985	Price et al, 1985	Price et al, 1985

whereas EMA multiples them for prospective emotions (e.g. hope and fear) and uses a threshold model for retrospective emotions (e.g. joy and sadness). An advantage of the component model view is these alternative choices can be directly compared and evaluated, independently of the other choices adopted in the systems from which they stem.

Gratch and Marsella recently applied this component-model perspective to an empirical comparison of different affect-derivation models (Gratch *et al.* 2009). Besides the two approaches proposed by EMA and FLAME, researchers have proposed a wide range of techniques to calculate the intensity of an affective response. In their study, Gratch and Marsella analysed several competing approaches for calculating the intensity of a specific emotional response to a situation and classified these approaches into a small number of general approaches (this includes approaches used in a variety of systems including: Price *et al.* 1985; Neal Reilly 1996; Velásquez 1998; El Nasr *et al.* 2000; Bui 2004; Dias and Paiva 2005; Marinier *et al.* 2009; Reisenzein 2009). They then devised a study to empirically test these competing appraisal intensity models, assessing their consistency with the behaviour of a large number of human subjects in naturalistic emotion-eliciting situations. In the study they had subjects play a board game (Battleship™ by Milton Bradley™) and assessed subjects' self-reported emotional reactions as the game unfolded and as a consequence of if they were winning or losing (which was manipulated experimentally).

Table 1.2.2 summarizes the results of this study that compared the behaviour of EMA to several other systems proposed in the literature. These include ParleE (Bui 2004), a system that uses appraisal models to drive facial animation; BTDE (Reisenzein 2009), an appraisal theory that attempts to reduce appraisal-derivation, affect-derivation, and affect-intensity to operations over beliefs and desires; FLAME, described above; Cathexis, an anatomical approach that views emotions as arising from drives; FearNot! (Dias and Paiva 2005), an appraisal model based on EMA; EM (Neal Reilly 1996) an OCC-inspired model that drives the behaviour of interactive game characters; and a model proposed by Price and colleagues (Price, Barrell *et al.* 1985) that inspired the design of FLAME. Although these models vary in many ways, when it comes to affect-intensity, they can be described in terms of four basic methods have been proposed in the literature for deriving the intensity of an emotional response.

As noted in the table, different systems used different intensity models depending on the emotion type. The intensity models, listed in the first column, include expected utility (i.e. the intensity of emotional response is proportional to the utility of a goal times its probability of attainment), expectation-change (i.e. the intensity is proportional to the change in probability caused by some event), and additive (i.e. the intensity is proportional to the sum of probability and utility). The cells in the table indicate the intensity model that a particular system applies to calculate the intensity of a given emotion. The table also summarizes the results of how well these different models explain the data elicited from the study. A slash through the box indicates the model cannot explain the results of the experiment. This analysis lends support for the expected utility model for all emotions, with a particularly strong fit for the prospective emotions (i.e. hope and fear), though it allows that some modified version of a threshold model might explain the results of retrospective motions like joy and sadness. If the goal of an emotion model is to realistically model human emotional responses, expected utility is probably a good choice for that appraisal intensity component model.

Of course, the behaviour of a specific component is not necessarily independent of other design choices so such a strong independence assumption should be treated as a first approximation for assessing how alternative design choices will function in a specific system. However, unless there is a compelling reason to believe choices are correlated, such an analysis should be encouraged. Indeed, a key advantage of the compositional approach is that it forces researchers to explicitly articulate what these dependencies might be, should they wish to argue for a component that is repudiated by an empirical test that adopts a strong assumption of independence.

Dividing computational emotion models into components enables a range of such empirical studies that can assess the impact of these design choices on the possible uses of emotion models that were outlined at the start of this chapter—i.e. their impact on psychological theories of emotion; their impact on artificial intelligence and robotics; and their impact on human–computer interaction. Here we touched on some studies that more naturally apply to the first goal and several examples of this now exist including evaluations of the psychological validity of cognitive consequent models (Marsella *et al.* 2009) and appraisal-derivation models (e.g. Mao and Gratch 2006; Tomai and Forbus 2007). However, the same approach can be equally applied to these other overall objectives. For example, de Melo and colleagues present evidence that the appraised expression of emotion can influence human–computer interaction in the context of social games such as iterated prisoner's dilemma (de Melo *et al.* 2009) and it would be interesting to consider how different appraisal-derivation and intensity models might impact the power of this effect. Other researchers have explored how emotions might improve the decision-making capabilities of general models of intelligence (Scheutz and Sloman 2001; Ito *et al.* 2008) and a component model analysis can give greater insight into which aspects of these models contribute to enhanced performance.

Conclusion

In this chapter, we provided an overview of research into computational models of emotion that details the common uses of the models and the underlying techniques and assumptions from which the models are built. Our goals were twofold. For researchers outside the field of computational models on emotion, we want to facilitate an understanding of the field. For research in the field, our goal is to provide a framework that can help foster incremental research, with researchers relying on careful comparisons, evaluations, and leveraging to build on prior work, as a key to forward progress.

To achieve those goals, we presented several conceptual distinctions that can aid in evaluation of competing models. We identified several roles for models, in psychological research, in human–computer interaction, and in AI. Evaluation, of course, must be sensitive to these roles. If, for example, the model is being used as a methodological tool for research in human emotions or in human–computer interaction research as a means to infer user emotional state, then fidelity of the model with respect to human behaviour will be critical. If the model is to be used to create virtual characters that facilitate engagement with, or influence of, humans then fidelity may be less important, even undesirable, while effectiveness in the application becomes more important.

Our assumption is that, regardless of the specific details of the evaluation, research progress in computational models of emotion critically hinges not only on evaluations of specific models but also on the comparison across models. Due to the complexity of some of these models, and their emphasis on different aspects of the overall emotion process, it may not be reasonable or desirable to undertake comparison and evaluation *in toto*. Rather component-by-component analyses, based on a common lexicon, will be both more revealing and often easier. Our hope is that the application of the component analyses exemplified above may serve as a means to facilitate this component-by-component evaluation and lead to additional work in this direction.

Section 2

The emotion process: Perspectives from psychology and the neurosciences

The purpose of the affective computing approach is to create emotionally competent agents that are modelled after or are at least compatible with human emotion processes and individual emotional competence. Consequently, knowledge about the mechanisms underlying the human emotion system is an essential asset for researchers in this area if they want to get as close as possible to the target. This section provides a number of state-of-the-art overviews of the current conceptual framework and the empirical findings concerning major components of emotion, ranging from brain activation to interpersonal processes. In addition to surveying the respective fields of fundamental research on emotion, the authors also make an attempt to demonstrate ways in which insights gained in the respective domains can be profitably applied to affective computing approaches. This includes suggestions to test specific predictions made in the respective fields using computational models (or expressive embodied agents), as well as suggestions aiming at improving operating models in affective computing (i.e. enhancing the 'affective competence' of the computers on the basis of models and/or data available in the respective fields).

In Chapter 2.1, 'The component process model: architecture for a comprehensive computational model of emergent emotion', Scherer provides a general theoretical framework in the form of an appraisal-based componential emotion model. As shown in the overview of different emotion models in Section 1, this family of models has the great advantage of being maximally compatible with other models, as it also allows for evolutionarily continuous 'basic' emotions (here called 'modal' emotions), similar to discrete emotion theories, but postulates a mechanism that accounts for a virtually unlimited number of more complex or blended emotions. At the same time, the highly differentiated predictions of the component process model, which suggests that appraisal at different levels of cognitive processing drives peripheral systems and prepares action tendencies, can also be mapped into a higher-order dimensional space, compatible with classic dimensional theories. By theoretically linking the different components and levels of processing in emotion, the component process model also provides a systematic framework for the following contributions that address individual components and their functioning.

Starting from the appraisal framework, in Chapter 2.2, 'The emotional brain meets affective computing', Grandjean and Sander discuss how advances in cognitive neuroscience allow a better understanding of both the domain and the mode of processing of emotional mechanisms.

First, the authors discuss why the cognitive neuroscience approach is relevant to the issue of implementing affectively competent agents, arguing that a computational analysis of emotional processes, together with the identification of the neural mechanisms subserving these processes, can serve to constrain and inform psychological models of emotion. Then, they focus on four major issues that exemplify the important benefits of a close collaboration between affective computing and neuroscience research and on the potential of using computational approaches to help understand the brain processes generating and regulating emotion: (1) the issue of modularity and domain specificity of the assumed processing model; (2) the central role of the interaction between different levels of processing, demonstrating that the onset of an emotional reaction can occur extremely rapidly, especially if schematic processing based on subcortical brain structures is involved; (3) the temporal dynamics of appraisals that drive emotion processes; and (4) the synchronization between different brain areas in emotion processing, including a review of the dynamic and functional neuronal coupling of distant brain regions involved in emotion elicitation. Throughout the chapter the authors present the results of numerous empirical studies that investigated the neural underpinnings of the processing of several of the major appraisal criteria or checks and the unfolding of appraisal processes (demonstrated through different methods, including behavioural, psychophysiological, and central, brain activity measures). Finally, the contribution discusses how a better understanding of the appraising brain (i.e. neural networks subserving appraisal mechanisms) can guide, and benefit from, computational studies in virtual humans.

In Chapter 2.3, 'The face and voice of emotions: the expression of emotions', Bänziger, With, and Kaiser address the motor expression component and outline how psychological models and empirical research on facial and vocal emotional expressions can both inform and benefit from applications in affective computing. The authors briefly review psychological research in the domain of both production (encoding) and perception (decoding) of facial and vocal emotional expressions, including descriptions of the various determinants theoretically involved in the generation of emotional expressions (e.g. physiological determinants and sociocultural determinants) and descriptions of potential mechanisms involved in the perception (perceptual processing and recognition) of facial and vocal emotional expressions. The chapter compares predictions issuing from an evolutionary–functionalist perspective and from a cognitive approach to emotional reactions and addresses issues related to emotional regulation (automatic and strategic control of expressions) and non-verbal sensitivity to emotional expressions. Finally, the relevance for affective computing (e.g. for the generation of emotional expressions in embodied conversational agents (ECAs), or for the automatic recognition of emotional expressions) of the models and empirical results outlined in this chapter is systematically examined.

In Chapter 2.4, 'Psychophysiological response patterning in emotion: implications for affective computing', Kreibig, Schaefer, and Brosch first introduce concepts and theories of affective psychophysiology relevant for the affective computing domain, including models that delineate how emotions influence physiological reactivity, what constitutes a physiological emotion response, and how the specificity of the emotion–physiology relation may be characterized. They next turn to the question of how to select physiological measures for assessing emotion. Basing their discussion on the structure of the autonomic nervous system, Kreibig and colleagues discuss cardiovascular, respiratory, and electrodermal measures and related measurement devices. In a final section, they consider practical issues of affective computing using physiological sensing. In particular, they argue for a distinction between emotion detection and emotion identification and survey empirical research on this topic. Aspects of the measurement context (e.g. situational and user characteristics), data analysis (e.g. training of classifiers), and technical and ethical constraints are discussed. The chapter concludes with a set of golden rules of physiological measurement for affective computing. A comprehensive appendix provides an overview of physiological measures that can also figure as a guide for selecting the appropriate set of physiological measures for a specific application of affective computing.

In the final contribution in this section, Chapter 2.5, 'Emotions in interpersonal interactions', Parkinson argues that emotions affect and are affected by other people. For example, I may get angry with you for telling someone else something that I wanted kept secret. Another friend may then reassure me that the betrayal was not done out of malice, thus alleviating my irritation. In turn, you may be upset by my anger, feel guilty, and be moved to apologize. More generally, emotions may be viewed as ways of modifying other people's behaviour with respect to shared situations or events. In other words, the point of anger in many circumstances may be precisely to draw attention to a frustrating event and get other people to do something about it.

The component process model: Architecture for a comprehensive computational model of emergent emotion

Klaus R. Scherer

Summary

The component process model of emotion (CPM) postulates that the organism's coordinated subsystem changes that constitute the unfolding emotion process are driven by subjective appraisal. An event happens and we will instantly examine its relevance by drawing from memory and motivation and attend to it immediately if it is considered relevant. In addition, we will assess the implications of the event, its consequences for our well-being, our ability to cope with the event, as well as its normative significance. These appraisal processes, based on criteria determined by values and transient motivational state, draw on resources such as reasoning and self-concept matching. Much of this process occurs unconsciously on different levels of emotion processing that work together seamlessly through parallel processing. The recursive appraisal process changes constantly and so does the nature of the emotion generated by it. Each step in the appraisal process, once the result of the evaluation is relatively stable, will produce a response, inducing a change in the state of the autonomous and motor systems. This physiological response does not trigger a concrete action; rather it prepares plausible types of appropriate behaviour. The component process model postulates that feeling is the reflection of all changes occurring in the different emotion components in the course of a given episode. Both the cognitive appraisal of the event and the response pattern (physiological symptoms, motor expression, and action tendencies) will be centrally reflected (through proprioceptive feedback processes), often in an unconscious fashion. This type of monitoring of all ongoing processes produces automatic regulation processes, including the allocation of resources such as attention. Some of the responses may eventually become conscious and allow more controlled and effortful regulation processes, such as trying to reduce the degree of arousal through various coping strategies. Finally, the conscious emotional experience can be verbalized and communicated, requiring again a variety of regulation and control processes (such as not speaking of or even not expressing certain feelings because of normative social display rules).

The chapter shows how this model is ideally suited to computational modelling and provides an appropriate architecture for an emotionally competent autonomous agent. Each element of the model will be examined with respect to the translation from the human to the agent model and the difficulties that may arise in the computational implementation of the appraisal process. An extensive discussion will be devoted to the notions of 'motivation' and 'action preparation' as well as the potentially mediating role of functional equivalents of physiological system changes. Finally, the important role of categorization and labelling of emotional experiences for social communication will be broached, giving special emphasis to the nature and function of expressive signals in this respect. Again, the considerations will be mapped on the domain of agents and robots, evaluating the possibilities of modelling these features as part of a component process architecture.

Chapter 1.1 suggested differentiating between *service robots* and *autonomous agents*, arguing that the emotional competences to be expected would differ greatly between the two types. This chapter will focus on emotions in autonomous agents, in other words, agents that not only decipher emotional expressions and produce strategic emotion expressions but that rather *have* and possibly *experience* emotions. What does this entail? Given the definition of emotion suggested in Chapter 1.1, it would seem that the central requirement for an autonomous agent capable of having and experiencing emotions is that the agent has *its own needs, concerns, goals, and values* rather than being at the beck and call of a human master. Obviously, this is rather tricky, especially if the agent can act in such a way as to affect human life, as it would mean that our creature is no longer under our control, raising a host of practical and ethical difficulties. For the purposes of this chapter, this complex issue will be left aside as its treatment would require an extensive survey of the literature as well as an in-depth discussion of the philosophical and ethical issues involved. It will be assumed that we can create an autonomous agent capable of emotion by developing a computational model of emotion that allows the simulation of major aspects of human emotions. As argued in detail in Chapter 1.1, one can show that appraisal theories of emotion provide the most promising blueprints for such a computational model.

An important feature of such a model is that it should not include overt instrumental behaviour. In line with the dominant functional or adaptational approach pioneered by Darwin (1872/1998), emotion is seen as a reaction to significant events that prepares action readiness and different types of alternative, possibly conflicting, action tendencies but is not a sufficient cause for their execution. The assumption is that, even though highly emotional behaviours such as angry aggression or flight are *prepared* by emotions, their *execution* is multiply determined, with emotion being only one, albeit potentially important, factor. The prediction of actual behaviour by a general computational model seems rather difficult to achieve, given the multitude of determining factors, contextual mediators, and individual differences that would have to taken into account.

In what follows, the component process model of emotion (CPM) is presented and evaluated with respect to its utility as a blueprint for an emergent computational model of emotion. As the CPM has been described in detail in various publications (Sander *et al.* 2005; Scherer 1984, 2001, 2009*a*), only a brief overview will be provided in the current context, drawing on the earlier treatments. The emphasis is placed on the discussion of computational issues raised by some of the features of the model with an emphasis on *normative* issues, i.e. what the model, respectively the agent, should be able to do, neglecting the practical issues of how that might be done with the modelling tools that are currently available. For this reason, no attempt is made to review the literature with respect to earlier attempts at computational modelling of emotion (see the overview in Chapter 1.2).

A closer look at the component process model

Emotions have developed in the course of evolution to replace rigid instincts or stimulus–response chains by a mechanism that allows flexible adaptation to environmental contingencies by decoupling stimulus and response, creating a latency time for response optimization

Table 2.1.1 Relationships between organismic subsystems and the functions and components of emotion. Abbreviations: CNS-Central Nervous System; NES-Neuroendocrine System; ANS-Autonomic Nervous System; SNS-Somatic Nervous System. (reproduced from Scherer 2001)

Emotion function	Organismic subsystem and major substrata	Emotion component
Evaluation of objects and events	Information processing (CNS)	Cognitive component
System regulation	Support (CNS, NES, ANS)	Neurophysiological component
Preparation and direction of action	Executive (CNS)	Motivational component
Communication of reaction and behavioural intention	Action (SNS)	Motor expression component
Monitoring of internal state and organism–environment interaction	Monitor (CNS)	Subjective feeling component

(Scherer 1984). The price for this flexibility has been complexity involving recursive multisystem multilevel processing. Emotion as a theoretical construct in the component process model (CPM) consists of five organismic subsystems that correspond to five distinctive functions (see Table 2.1.1 for a list of the systems that subserve these functions, and the relevant emotion components):

1 evaluation of objects and events;

2 regulation of internal subsystems;

3 preparation for action;

4 signalling of behavioural intention;

5 monitoring of internal state and external environment.

In the CPM framework, emotion is defined as 'an episode of interrelated, synchronized changes in the states of all or most of the five organismic subsystems'. It is a response to the evaluation of an external or internal stimulus event relevant to major concerns of the organism. Therefore the term 'emotion' is reserved for those periods of time during which several organismic subsystems are *coupled* or *synchronized* to produce an adaptive reaction to a crucial event.

Figure 2.1.1 shows the basic architecture of the CPM, including the dynamic, recursive emotion processes following an event that is highly pertinent to the needs, goals, and values of an individual. As shown in the flow diagram, the model suggests that the event and its consequences are appraised with a set of criteria on multiple levels of processing. The result of the appraisal will generally have a motivational effect, often changing or modifying the motivational state that existed before the occurrence of the event. Based on the appraisal results and the concomitant motivational changes, efferent effects will occur in the autonomic nervous system (in the form of somatovisceral changes) and in the somatic nervous system (in the form of motor expression in face, voice, and body). All of these components, appraisal results, action tendencies, somatovisceral changes, and motor expressions, are centrally represented and constantly fused in a multimodal integration area (with continuous updating as events and appraisals change). Parts of this central integrated representation may then become conscious and subject to assignment to fuzzy emotion categories as well as being labelled with emotion words, expressions, or metaphors. As shown in Figure 2.1.1, these individual components can be grouped into three functionally defined *modules*—appraisal, response patterning, and integration/categorization. The following discussion will be organized around these three modules which represent the fundamental elements of the model's architecture.

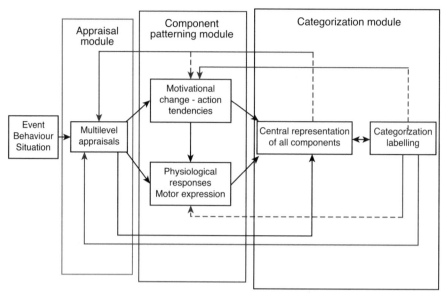

Fig. 2.1.1 General architecture of the component process model of emotion.

The appraisal module

This module is the most basic and most important element in the overall architecture. The results of the information processing carried out in this module will determine whether an emotion episode will be elicited and what its emergent characteristics will be. In other words, the appraisal results will drive the response patterning and constitute a major component of the integrated representation that characterizes the subjective experience of the emotion episode.

There are four major appraisal objectives that an organism needs to reach to adaptively react to a salient event: (1) How relevant is this event for me? Does it directly affect me or my social reference group? (relevance); (2) What are the implications or consequences of this event and how do they affect my well-being and my immediate or long-term goals? (implications); (3) How well can I cope with or adjust to these consequences? (coping potential); (4) What is the significance of this event for my self-concept and for social norms and values? (normative significance). These appraisal goals are pursued by the sequential, cumulative, and recursive evaluation of the event on a number of *appraisal criteria* with the results reflecting the organism's subjective assessment of consequences and implications on a background of personal needs, goals, and values. These criteria (which are, despite somewhat diverging terminology, widely shared among appraisal theorists; Ellsworth and Scherer 2003; Scherer 1999a) are called stimulus evaluation checks (SECs) in the CPM. It should be noted that the outcomes of the SECs are highly subjective, based on the individual's inference, which may not adequately represent the objective characteristics of an event (see Perrez and Reicherts 1995). Thus, individual differences (see van Reekum and Scherer 1997), transitory motivational states or moods (Scherer 2005b), cultural values, group pressures, or other context factors can strongly bias the appraisal outcomes (see Scherer and Brosch 2009; van Reekum and Scherer 1997). In the following, the SECs are described in the context of modelling an autonomous agent, raising some of the issues to be reckoned with in attempting to create a computational model of the CPM and discussing potential implementations. In particular the major appraisal objectives, as defined by the need to prepare adaptive reactions, are successively described.

Appraisal objective 1: How relevant is a given event for the agent? Does it directly affect the agent (or other members of its group)?

Living organisms constantly scan their external and internal environment for the occurrence of salient events requiring attention, further information processing, and possibly adaptive reaction. They also scan their environment for expected events that fail to occur. Presumably, autonomous agents acting freely in a complex environment will need to do exactly the same in order to devote sufficient processing capacity to objects or events that may have important consequences. Three checks are involved:

A check for novelty

Any novel stimulus requires attention and demands further processing as it may represent potential danger or unexpected gains. Three different features of novelty can be distinguished.

1 How sudden or abrupt is the onset of a stimulus event? In nature, abrupt onset is often coupled with a steep rise in the intensity of stimulation, which produces an automatic orientation response in most animals. In consequence, a suddenness detector for the agent could be easily designed by monitoring the rate of intensity changes of perceptible stimuli and focusing attention on steep onsets (and possibly on continuously high intensity levels).

2 How familiar is the object or event? This is important as events one has never encountered before may hold bad (or good) surprises and deserve more detailed examination. In animals and humans, familiarity is checked by using schema matching procedures. In an agent this could be realized in a similar fashion by building up repertoires of static object or dynamic stimulus event schemata in a continuous learning process and matching all current stimulus events against the stored templates. As will become clear throughout this discussion, the agent's ability for learning and memory is an element of central importance in the required architecture.

3 How predictable is the event, based on past observations of regularities and probabilities of particular events? This goes beyond simple matching on the schematic level of processing as probabilities need to be calculated on the basis of past experience and a general knowledge of the word in terms of frequency and likelihood of occurrence. This may not be possible to achieve in an agent, as it requires capacity for several levels of processing, including a conceptual or representational one, extensive knowledge of world facts, a capacity for inference and combination, and massive computational power.

A check for intrinsic pleasantness

Most living organisms evaluate, on a very low level of processing (sensorimotor or automatic–schematic), whether a certain type of stimulus event is likely to result in pleasure or pain (in the widest sense). Such stimuli are automatically relevant. Checking occurs with the help of genetically fixed schemata or overlearned associations. This check is called *intrinsic* because the evaluation is produced by the pre-existing pleasantness or unpleasantness of the stimulus, and is thus independent of the momentary preferences or goal states of the organism. An outcome registering pleasantness encourages approach, whereas unpleasantness leads to withdrawal or avoidance (e.g. a defence response). How could an agent, just off the production line, be made to like sweet and detest bitter tastes, just like newborn babies do? Apart from the issue of the subjective experience of pleasure (which will be discussed later) this could be operationalized by programming into the agent a tendency to approach certain classes of stimuli with certain qualities and avoid others. The automatic detection of the presence of these types of stimuli would serve as intrinsic (un)pleasantness check and provoke the respective appetitive behaviour.

A check for relevance to goals and needs

How pertinent or important is a specific type of event likely to be for one's goals and needs? Relevance varies continuously from low to high, depending on the number of needs or goals that are potentially affected by the event and/or their relative status in the hierarchy of priorities. For example, an event is much more relevant if it threatens one's livelihood, or even one's survival, than if it just endangers one's ability to eat a meal. This is the most complex aspect of relevance detection, as it often implies inference and prediction through checking (and weighing) potential consequences of an event against a large array of expectations generated by different types of motivation (Austin and Vancouver 1996; Moskowitz and Grant 2009).

The existence of needs and values in an agent are, of course, the central prerequisites of a computational agent model. Without needs or goals, no real emotion. The agent equivalents of fundamental needs such as food and shelter are probably fairly easy to implement through energy needs and preferred environmental conditions. But one might even implement need for affiliation through set points (Sollwerte) for number and intensity of contacts with conspecifics (although pair bonding might be difficult to achieve) and need for achievement through set points for rate and number of goal fulfilment feedbacks. The specific characteristic of needs is that they are constantly active and require a certain rate of satisfaction. In contrast, goals are more specific, variable, and time-bound. They can be autogenerated (although it is not quite clear what the mechanism would be in agents) or acquired from outside. Most importantly, the agent must have the capacity to represent a complex hierarchical goal structure with respect to a sequence of plans and subgoals that will finally allow goal attainment (Austin and Vancouver 1996; Moskowitz and Grant 2009). The issue of goal setting and goal representation in agents is, of course, widely debated in the respective literature (Braubach *et al.* 2005: Maes 1991; Ziemke 1998) and will not be pursued here. Suffice it to say that the agent, in order to check the relevance of events for goal attainment, must be capable of determining the extent to which certain events and their consequences will impact its goal path.

The essential task of this check is rapidly to determine the potential goal relevance of an event in order to allocate attention and invest further processing capacity. In humans, this pre-attentive processing is well demonstrated for evolutionarily significant stimuli such as snakes, spiders, faces, and babies (Brosch *et al.* 2008; Öhman *et al.* 2001; Öhman and Mineka 2001), with a central processing role for the amygdala (Vuilleumier 2005). An agent could be similarly equipped with recognition templates for fundamentally significant objects or scenes in its environment, such as conspecifics or predators (presuming that agent worlds are structured along the lines of evolution on earth). The more difficult case concerns events or objects that are not 'prepared' and require inference as to their potential goal relevance, especially in cases in which goal associations have not been established by prior learning. In these cases more explicit object/event recognition and computation with respect to possible implications in the context of current goal pursuits need to be performed.

Appraisal objective 2. What are the implications or consequences of the event, and how do these affect the agents' survival, 'well-being', and immediate or long-term goals?

The potential consequences of an event are difficult to predict. To make a reasonable estimation of implications, consequences, and future developments, one usually needs to find out more about the event and its causation. The following five checks appear to be minimally necessary, for animals, humans, and autonomous agents.

A check for cause

The most important information concerns the cause of the event, in particular, agency and intentionality. In other words, who did it and why? Obviously, the evaluation of the likely development of the situation—in particular the probability of certain outcomes and one's ability to deal with them—will greatly depend on the attribution of agency and intention. For example, if I find my car, parked in the underground garage of my apartment house, on two flat tyres as I am rushing to go to an important appointment, there are many reasons to engage in causal attribution as to agency and intentionality. The attribution processes are quite complex and social psychologists have identified several informational cues or dimensions such as locus of causality (e.g. internal–external, self–other), stability of effect (e.g. stable ability or task difficulty versus sporadic effort or luck), consistency with past behaviour, distinctiveness of effect in the given context, and regularity (see Kelley 1972; Weiner 1985). Humans are experts in causal attribution. However, it will require extensive information search and storage and sophisticated computational routines for agents to perform satisfactorily.

A check for probable outcomes

The individual needs to assess the likelihood with which certain consequences are to be expected. In the example above, the unfortunate car owner must assess the chances that all four tyres might be flat some other day. This check is of particular importance in the case of *signal events*—for example, a verbal threat—where both the probability of the signalled event occurring and its consequences are difficult to establish. As this appraisal depends largely on associations with elements in knowledge storage (including cultural lore and fiction), it may be quite challenging to equip and train agents for this type of extrapolation.

A check of failure to meet expectations

The situation created by the event can be consistent with or vary from the individual's expectation concerning that point in time or position in the sequence of events leading up to a goal. If the car owner had a suspicion that the deviant son of a contentious neighbour might plan a sabotage, the discovery of the flat tyres would not be completely unexpected. This check requires agents to produce constantly updated expectation templates of progress in goal pursuit, depending on past efforts and changes in the state of the world.

A check of conduciveness to goals and needs

The more an action (caused by oneself or somebody else) or an event contributes to goal attainment, directly or indirectly, the higher is its goal/need conduciveness. Conversely, the more an action or event blocks a goal-directed behaviour sequence—putting goal or need satisfaction out of reach, delaying their attainment, or requiring additional effort—the higher their obstructiveness. Typically, conduciveness leads to positive emotions and obstructiveness to negative emotions, quite independently of prior expectations or the intrinsic pleasantness of the stimuli concerned. Obviously, this is a decisive check for agents to master as adaptive behaviour in order to cope with the event directly flows from the result of this check. In particular, if the event is considered to be goal obstructive, the goal pursuit routine needs to be changed—either serious efforts to overcome the obstruction need to be made or another goal implementation plan needs to be developed and pursued. In some cases, the goal may need to be abandoned altogether and substituted by a new and different goal; possibly a different kind of response threshold is needed.

A check for urgency

When high priority goals/needs are endangered, an adaptive response to an event is urgent—the organism must resort to fight or flight. When a delayed response will likely make the situation worse, an urgent response becomes necessary. Urgency depends not only on the significance of an event for an organism's goals/needs, but also on the timeliness of response. Its effect is an immediate increase in action readiness and sympathetic response of the autonomic nervous system (ANS). This check requires that the agent has a powerful capacity for time course and contingency evaluation, allowing it to predict the evolution of events and the potential effects of its own interventions. It may not be sufficient to speed up response time as a function of goal importance.

Appraisal objective 3. How well can the agent cope with or adjust to the consequences of the event?

Organisms are not reduced to passively enduring the effects of events that happen to them. By appropriate action, including the solicitation of help from others, they can prevent the occurrence of negative events or modify their consequences. Thus, the adaptive nature of emotion requires an assessment of one's coping potential. This potential includes (1) the amount of control and power one has to modify the event and its consequences and (2) the capacity to successfully adjust to outcomes that cannot be controlled. In the case of the flat tyres, this might involve calling the police, parking the car in another garage, or quietly resigning yourself to calling for road service each time it happens.

Note the three aspects of coping potential that need to be appraised.

1 *Control*: the extent to which an event or its outcomes can be influenced or controlled by natural agents (i.e. people or animals). If the tyres go flat because of a change in atmospheric pressure, no control is possible, whereas a human tyre deflater could be potentially stopped, depending on one's power. An agent's ability to infer control depends on its capacity to correctly attribute causality, and to infer no or low controllability in the case of environmental causes or of chance (see Weiner 1985).

2 *Power*: one's ability to change contingencies and outcomes according to one's interests. The sources of power can be manifold—physical strength, money, knowledge, or social attractiveness, among others (see French and Raven 1959). As the dimensions of control and power can vary independently from each other it is important to make a clear distinction (which is unfortunately not always the case in the literature, where 'controllability' often seems to imply both aspects). Power computation will present a difficult task for the agent, as this is a transactional concept, especially in the case of dealing with events. Power is differentially defined as the excess of one's own power as compared to that of a potential opponent or the resistance of objects or circumstances. In addition, the different sources of power—strength, money, knowledge, social relations, which can be variously combined—make the assessment extremely complex, as there may not be any common metric.

3 *Potential for adjustment*: one's ability to deal with and accommodate the effects of an event. For example, one might be able to live with being occasionally unable to use one's car if there is a convenient bus stop at a close distance. This is more difficult if the car is one's only reasonable possibility for going to work. In an agent, this check would seem to require the existence of thresholds of acceptability for certain conditions.

The coping potential check represents a feature of critical importance in the agent's appraisal computation as its result will greatly determine the adaptive action to be prepared. In consequence, a constantly updated estimate of the relative power in a situation is required.

Appraisal objective 4. What is the significance of this event with respect to self-concept and to social norms and values?

In species that live in social environments, such as man, the individual needs to evaluate how the majority of the other group members will, in the context of social norms and moral standards, interpret, and possibly sanction, an action. If certain consequences have been caused by the individual's own behaviour, he or she also needs to determine its compatibility with one's self-concept and the consequences for his or her self-esteem. Two subchecks are involved here.

1 A check with external standards: evaluating to what extent an action is compatible with the perceived norms or demands of one's reference group in terms of both desirable and obligatory conduct. For example, tyre deflating might elicit less moral indignation if this type of behaviour is an established and valued custom in an adolescent gang.

2 A check with internal standards: evaluating the extent to which an action falls short of or exceeds internal standards such as one's personal self-ideal (desirable attributes) or internalized moral code (obligatory conduct).

With this pair of checks we may have reached the limit of what is possible to implement in a computational model for an autonomous agent. While one might imagine that a set of behaviour rules corresponding to social norms might be implemented in a group of agents that possess a sense of belongingness, it is difficult to see what equivalent could be found for values such as individualism, justice, liberty, or altruism without the existence of a cultural value structure such as that acquired by many years of learning and socialization (Schwartz and Bilsky 1987). Similarly, it is difficult to see how an agent could develop a self-concept and self-esteem, as this requires a cultural value structure as a backdrop as well as the evaluative feedback of others in the social reference group on one's behaviours.

Concluding remarks on the appraisal module

This concludes the description of the appraisal criteria or SECs as they are defined in the CPM (for further details and references, see Sander *et al.* 2005; Scherer 2001, 2009*a*). The verbal description of these criteria or checks to be processed in the appraisal process seems to require a complex cognitive calculus. However, it can be plausibly claimed that all of the criteria can be processed in parallel at three hierarchically organized levels of different complexity.

1 The sensorimotor level, in which the checking mechanisms are mostly genetically determined and the criteria consist of appropriate templates for pattern matching and similar mechanisms (cf. the notion of 'biological preparedness'; Öhman and Mineka 2001).

2 The schematic level, based on social learning processes, occurring in a fairly automatic, unconscious fashion. This level may in fact consist of two different layers: (a) using well-formed prepotent schemata (based on repeated earlier experiences) on the lower level and (b) facilitated configurations for the spread of associations on a higher level. Both levels share a high degree of automaticity and the potential for unconscious processing.

3 The representational (or conceptual level), relying primarily on cortical association areas and requiring consciousness, involving propositional knowledge, and underlying cultural meaning systems. The different levels continuously interact and can thus produce top-down and bottom-up effects (see Leventhal and Scherer 1987; Power and Dalgleish 1997; van Reekum and Scherer 1997).

Given the postulated multilevel parallel architecture, the model can easily account for both the rapid onset and the rapid change of emotional reactions, as each level of information processing will, depending on the context, allow for automaticity, rapidity, computational power, or the need for consciousness.

This appraisal mechanism requires interaction between many cognitive functions and their underlying neural circuits to compare the features of stimulus events to stored schemata, representations in memory and self-concept, and expectations and motivational urges of high priority. In addition, this process controls attention deployment and relies heavily on implicit or explicit computation of probabilities of consequences, coping potential, and action alternatives. Figure 2.1.2 illustrates the postulated sequence, the cognitive and motivational inputs, and the effects on response systems (to be illustrated below). The architecture assumes bidirectional influences between appraisal and various cognitive functions. For example, minimal attention needs to be given for appraisal to start, but a relevance outcome will immediately deploy further attention to the stimulus. Stimulus features are compared with schemata in memory but strongly relevant stimulus features will, following appropriate appraisal, be stored as emotional schemata in memory. Event consequences are compared with current motivational states, but particular appraisal outcomes will change motivation and produce adaptive action tendencies. These bidirectional effects between appraisal and other cognitive functions are illustrated by the arrows in the upper part of Figure 2.1.2.

As suggested in Figure 2.1.2, the CPM is based on the claim that the SECs described above are processed in sequence, following a fixed order, consisting of four stages in the appraisal process that correspond to the appraisal objectives already described (Grandjean and Scherer 2008; Scherer 1984, 1999b, 2001). This sequence assumption is justified in terms of systems economy

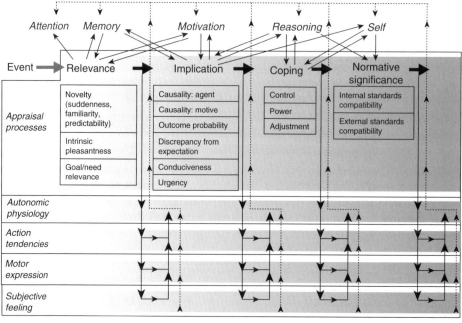

Time

Fig. 2.1.2 Comprehensive illustration of the component process model of emotion (reproduced from Sander *et al.* 2005).

and logical dependencies—the results of the earlier SECs need to be processed before later SECs can operate successfully, that is, yield a conclusive result. Expensive information processing should occur for only those stimuli that are considered relevant for the organism. In consequence, relevance detection is considered to be a first selective filter that a stimulus or event needs to pass to merit further processing. Extensive further processing and preparation of behavioural reactions are indicated only if the event concerns a goal or need of major importance or when a salient discrepancy with an expected state is detected, suggesting that the implications for the organism are assessed next in the sequence. Further, the causes and implications of the event need to be established before the organism's coping potential can be conclusively determined, as the latter is always evaluated for a specific demand.

How can this sequence assumption be reconciled with the existence of massively parallel processing of information in the central nervous system (CNS)? This is in fact a central question for the computational modelling of an agent consisting of multiply layered networks. In the case of humans, the CPM postulates that the recursive checking process repeats the sequence continuously, constantly updating the appraisal results that change rapidly with changing events and evolving evaluation until the monitoring subsystem signals termination of or adjustment to the stimulation that originally elicited the appraisal episode. The level of processing can be expected to move up to higher levels in the course of the sequence, given both the nature of the computation and the likelihood that lower levels have been unable to settle the issue. All SECs are expected to be processed simultaneously, starting with relevance detection. However, the essential criterion for the sequence assumption is *the time at which a particular check achieves preliminary closure*, that is, yields a reasonably definitive result, one that warrants efferent commands to response modalities, as shown by the descending arrows in Figure 2.1.2. The sequence theory postulates that, for the reasons outlined earlier, the result of a prior processing step (or check) must be in before the consecutive step (or check) can produce a conclusive result with efferent consequences. It is indeed feasible to assume that the results of parallel processes for different evaluation criteria will be available at different times, given differential depth of processing.

Figure 2.1.2 also illustrates the requirements that the appraisal module poses for computational modelling in an autonomous agent. As mentioned above, the agent must have multiple needs and goals, as well as normative rules, that can serve as criteria for the checking process and that can change as a function of context and outcomes. At any one time the agent must be capable of determining whether a situation, an event, or a behaviour (of another agent or his/her own) fulfils or thwarts needs, matches or mismatches goal path expectations, furthers or blocks goal attainment, is compatible or incompatible with normative rules.

The central mechanism involved in much of this information processing is valence computing. Given the type of criterion checked, a different type of valence is involved. As shown in Table 2.1.2, the major classes of SECs suggest that there are four types of valence criteria: valence as pleasure (intrinsic pleasantness); as satisfaction (goal/need conduciveness); as self-worthiness (compatibility with self-standards); or as moral worthiness (compatibility with norms/moral standards). One might debate the issue of whether an autonomous agent should be enjoying intrinsic pleasures or indulging in self-esteem as these may not seem necessary to get tasks done or to survive in a complex environment. On the other hand, evolution clearly has produced these criteria in humans and, if one wants to produce a computational model that can generate all or at least most of the human emotion classes, it would seem that the agent must be able to compute these different types of valence as based on the target criteria. The computation of these valences is likely to pose serious problems for modellers. While the sheer fact of the attainment of pleasure or satisfaction can probably implemented relatively easily by a comparison of actual state with target state, the likelihood of future goal attainment is probably extremely difficult to compute as

Table 2.1.2 Varieties of valence and dimensions of the affective space

Evaluation checks	Evaluation outcomes	Type of valence/feeling dimensions
Novelty	Newness–habituation	Unpredictability
Intrinsic pleasantness/beauty	Pleasure–displeasure	Valence as pleasure
Goal/need relevance	Satisfaction–frustration	Valence as satisfaction
Coping potential	Power–weakness	Control/dominance
Compatibility self-concept/standards	Achievement–failure	Valence as self-worthiness
Compatibility social norms/values	Virtue–wickedness	Valence as moral worthiness

it involves a determination of the various implications and consequences of events as well as their probability (or even an adjustment of the goal structure). As suggested above, the computation of self- and moral worthiness may prove to be exceedingly difficult as the respective criteria are internalized in humans over a long period of learning and experiences, especially as based on evaluative feedback from others.

The response patterning module

As shown in Figure 2.1.2, the fundamental assumption of the CPM is that the appraisal results drive the response patterning in all other emotion components by triggering efferent outputs designed to produce adaptive reactions that are in line with the current appraisal results (often mediated by motivational changes). In other words, the result of each consecutive check is expected to affect the state of all other subsystems, differentially and cumulatively. Here is an example (from Scherer 2001, p. 107).

> The detection of a novel, unexpected stimulus by the novelty check will produce:
> 1 an orientation response in the support system (e.g. heart rate decrease, skin conductance increase);
> 2 postural changes in the motivation (or action tendency) system (focusing the sensory reception areas toward the novel stimulus);
> 3 changes in goal priority assignment in the executive subsystem (attempting to deal with a potential emergency); and
> 4 alertness and attention changes in the monitor subsystem.
>
> When, milliseconds later, the next check, the intrinsic pleasantness check, reaches sufficient closure to determine that the novel stimulus is unpleasant, the efferent effects of this result will again affect the state of all other subsystems and thus modify the changes that have already been produced by the novelty check. For example, an unpleasant evaluation might produce the following changes:
> 1 a defence response in the support system (e.g. heart rate increase);
> 2 an avoidance tendency in the executive subsystem;
> 3 motor behaviour to turn the body away from the unpleasant stimulation (thus reducing intake of stimulation in the action system); and
> 4 a negative subjective feeling in the monitor system.
>
> Similarly, all of the following checks will change the states of all other subsystems and will thus further modify the preceding changes.

Thus, the differentiation of emotion is the result of the net effect of all subsystem changes brought about by the outcome of the SEC sequence. These subsystem changes are theoretically predicted on the basis of componential patterning. As shown in Figure 2.1.2, the result of each consecutive check is expected to differentially and cumulatively affect the state of all other subsystems.

Table 2.1.3 shows, for each of the SECs discussed above (column 1), the effect of the check results with respect to functions and component patterning. As shown in Table 2.1.1, in socially living species, adaptive responses are required not only for the internal regulation of the organism and motor action for instrumental purposes (organismic functions), but also for interaction and communication with conspecifics (social functions). Functions (column 2) are described in terms of fairly broad synthetic labels for both organismic functions (mostly concerned with the preparation of the organism for adaptive action) and social functions (mostly signalling the sender's reaction and type of action intention to the social environment). Specific motivational and behavioural tendencies are expected to be activated in the motivation component in order to serve the specific requirements for the adaptive response demanded by a particular SEC result. The CPM makes specific predictions about the effects of the results of certain appraisal checks on the autonomic and somatic nervous systems, indicating which somatovisceral changes and which motor expression features are expected. Column 3 shows the corresponding CPM predictions for the efferent subsystems, especially the ANS (action preparation) and the motor system (expressions in body, face, and voice), based on both the general functions of the emotion components and the specific functions of each SEC.

The preceding description entails a very complex dynamic architecture, involving many different systems in varying states of synchronization. One might ask whether this degree of detail and complexity is really necessary, given that it seems easily possible to select potentially adaptive actions out of a list of pre-scripted command sequences. There are two answers to this. One, if one wants to computationally model the human emotion system as a guide to understanding and the design of appropriate experimental tests, it is clearly necessary to model the proposed mechanisms in as much detail as possible. Two, even if we were content with a functional copy of the human emotion system that does not faithfully replicate all aspects of the human architecture, any simplification would be at the cost of flexibility in the emotional reactions of an agent. It is precisely through the fine-tuning of the response patterns through constant modification driven by the changing results of appraisal results that the organism can adapt in an extremely rapid and precise fashion to dynamically changing and often ambiguous events. A library of prepared action sequences from which a fitting response is to be selected resembles the early instinct theories of human behaviour (McDougall 1923). But it is precisely the rigidity of such subroutine selection mechanisms that has led to the evolution of the emotion mechanism. Thus, in order to model appropriate responses, including complex mixtures and gradations, one needs to model an architecture like the one illustrated in Figure 2.1.2 and Table 2.1.3. A similar point can be made for social signalling in the form of expressions. If standard expression programs had to chosen out of a library (in the form suggested by the neuromotor affect programs postulated by basic emotion theorists; see Chapter 1.1, this volume), the information value to the receiver would be limited to standard classes of messages that would be unable to provide the kind of personalized and contextualized detail that human emotion expression entails (Bänziger *et al.* 2009; Scherer and Ellgring 2007*a*). Thus, a model that drives variable expressive features in a flexible, sequential, and cumulative fashion on the basis of appraisal results will produce much more fine-grained and appropriate information about the agent's state and the resulting action probabilities.

The integration/categorization module and the notion of 'feeling'

The CPM assigns a special status to the subjective feeling component in the emotion process, as it monitors and regulates the component process and enables the individual to communicate its emotional experience to others. If subjective experience is to serve a monitoring function, it needs

Table 2.1.3 Synthetic recapitulation of central elements of the component process model (CPM) of emotion (reproduced from Scherer 2009a)

Stimulus evaluation checks (SECs)	Organismic/social functions	Component patterning
Relevance (A stimulus event is considered as requiring attention deployment, further information processing, and potential action)		
Novelty (abrupt onset, familiarity, predictability)	*Novel and goal relevant:* Orienting, focusing/alerting	Orienting response; EEG alpha changes, modulation of the P3a in ERPs; heart rate deceleration, vasomotor contraction, increased skin conductance responses, pupillary dilatation, local muscle tonus changes; brows and lids up, frown, jaw drop, gaze directed; interruption of speech and action, raising head (possibly also preparatory changes for subsequent effort investment given relevance appraisal at this stage, in particular, increased cardiac contractility as indicated by, e.g. decreased pre-ejection period).
Goal relevance (Does the event have consequences for my needs or goals?)		
Intrinsic pleasantness (Is the event intrinsically pleasant or unpleasant, independently of my current motivational state?)	*Pleasant:* incorporation/recommending	Sensitization; inhalation, heart rate deceleration, salivation, pupillary dilatation; lids up, open mouth and nostrils, lips part and corners pulled upwards, gaze directed; faucal and pharyngeal expansion, vocal tract shortened and relaxation of tract walls ('wide voice'—increase in low frequency energy, F1 falling, slightly broader F1 bandwidth); centripetal hand and arm movements, expanding posture, approach locomotion.
	Unpleasant: rejection/warning	Defence response, heart rate acceleration, increase in skin conductance level, decrease in salivation, pupillary constriction; slight muscle tonus increase; brow lowering, lid tightening, eye closing, nose wrinkling, upper lip raising, lip corner depression, chin raise, lip press, nostril compression, tongue thrust, gaze aversion; faucal and pharyngeal constriction, vocal tract shortened and tensing of tract walls ('narrow voice'—more high frequency energy, F1 rising, F2 and F3 falling, narrow F1 bandwidth, laryngopharyngeal nasality, resonances raised); centrifugal hand and arm movements, hands covering orifices, shrinking posture, avoidance locomotion.
Implications (Following attention deployment, the pertinent characteristics of the stimulus event and its implications or consequences for the organism are determined)		
Outcome probability (How likely is it that the consequences will occur?)	*Conducive:* relaxation/stability	Trophotropic shift, rest and recovery; decrease in respiration rate, slight heart rate decrease, bronchial constriction, increase in gastrointestinal motility, relaxation of sphincters; decrease in general muscle tone; relaxation of facial muscle tone; overall relaxation of vocal apparatus ('relaxed voice'-F0 at lower end of range, low-to-moderate amplitude, balanced resonance with slight decrease in high-frequency energy; comfort and rest positions; plus elements from pleasantness response (however, if a conduciveness appraisal is accompanied by plans for further action, an ergotropic shift is to be expected).
Discrepancy from expectation (How different is the situation from what I expected it to be?)		

Conduciveness (Is the event conducive or obstructive to reaching my goals?) *Urgency* (How urgently do I need to react?)	*Obstructive:* activation/reactivity	Ergotropic shift, preparation for action; corticosteroid and catecholamine, particularly adrenaline secretion; deeper and faster respiration, increase in heart rate and heart stroke volume, vasoconstriction in skin, gastrointestinal tract, and sexual organs, vasodilatation in heart and striped musculature, increase of glucose and free fatty acids in blood, decreased gastro-intestinal motility, sphincter contraction, bronchial dilatation, contraction of m. arrectores pilorum, decrease of glandular secretion, increase in skin conductance level, pupillary dilatation strongly increased muscular tonus; frown, lids tighten, lips tighten, chin raising; gaze directed; overall tensing of vocal apparatus ('tense voice'—F0 and amplitude increase, jitter and shimmer, increase in high frequency energy, narrow F1 bandwidth, pronounced formant frequency differences); strong tonus, task-dependent instrumental actions; plus elements of unpleasantness response.

Coping potential (Once nature of event and consequences are known sufficiently well, organism checks its ability to cope with the consequences to be expected)

Agent and intention (Who was responsible and what was the reason?) *Control* (Can the event or its consequences be controlled by human agents?)	*No or low control:* readjustment/withdrawal	Trophotropic dominance; decrease in respiration rate and depth, heart rate decrease, increase in glandular secretion, particularly tear glands, bronchial constriction; hypotonus of the musculature; lip corner depression, lips parting, jaw dropping, lids drooping, inner brow raise and brow lowered, gaze aversion; hypotonus of vocal apparatus ('lax voice'—low F0 and restricted F0 range, low amplitude, weak pulses, very low high-frequency energy, spectral noise, formant frequencies tending toward neutral setting, broad F1 bandwidth); few and slowed movements, slumped posture.
Power (Do I have sufficient power to exert control if possible?) *Adjustment* (If control is impossible, how well can I adjust to the consequences?)	*High control/high power:* assertion/dominance	Shift toward ergotropic–trophotropic balance; increase in depth of respiration, slight heart rate decrease, increase in systolic and diastolic blood pressure, changes in regional blood flow, increased flow to head, chest, and hands (reddening, increased skin temperature in upper torso), pupillary constriction; balanced muscle tone, tension increase in head and neck; eyebrows contracted, eyes widened, lids tightened, eyes narrowed, lips tight and parted, bared teeth or lips tight, pressed together, nostril dilation; stare; chest register phonation ('full voice'—low F0, high amplitude, strong energy in entire frequency range); agonistic hand/arm movements, erect posture, body lean forward, approach locomotion.

(continued)

Table 2.1.3 (continued) Synthetic recapitulation of central elements of the component process model (CPM) of emotion (reproduced from Scherer 2009a)

Stimulus evaluation checks (SECs)	Organismic/social functions	Component patterning
	Control possible/low power: protection/submission	Extreme ergotropic dominance; faster and more irregular respiration, strong increase in heart rate and heart stroke volume, increase in systolic and decrease in diastolic blood pressure, increase in pulse volume amplitude, vasoconstriction in skin (pallor, decreased skin temperature), gastrointestinal tract, and sexual organs, increase in blood flow to striped musculature, decreased gastrointestinal motility, sphincter contraction, tracheo-bronchial relaxation, contraction of m. arrectores pilorum, decrease of glandular secretion, secretion of sweat (increase in skin conductance level), pupillary dilatation; muscular hypertonus, particularly in locomotor areas, trembling; brow and lid raising, mouth stretch and corner retraction, switching between gaze direction and aversion; head register phonation ('thin voice'—raised F0, widely spaced harmonics with relatively low energy); protective hand/arm movements, fast locomotion or freezing

Normative significance (Overall assessment of the event with respect to compatibility with self-concept, values, social-norms, and moral rules

Compatibility with internal and external standards (Does the event or my behaviour correspond (a) to my self-concept or my values (is it just given my entitlement); (b) to social norms, values, beliefs about justice, or moral principles	*Requirements met or surpassed:* relaxation, bolstering self esteem, norm confirmation	Ergotropic shift plus elements of pleasantness and high power response.
	Incompatible: activation, self-consciousness, highlighting norms	Ergotropic shift plus elements of unpleasantness and low power response (peripheral blood flow to face, blushing; body movements: active avoidance of communicative contact).

to integrate and centrally represent all information about the continuous patterns of change and their coherence in all other components. Thus, feeling is an extraordinarily complex conglomerate of information from different systems.

The notion of subjective experience or feeling invariably invokes the notion of *consciousness*—a delicate issue to address, given the vast number of publications devoted to the issue showing serious disagreement on the nature and function of consciousness, and the special nature of artificial autonomous agent models. Scherer (2004) has proposed that feelings integrate the central representations of appraisal-driven response in emotion. These feelings are conscious, but not exclusively so (see Scherer 2005*b*). The integration of the different components yields extremely complex and constantly changing conglomerates of qualitatively different states—called qualia, which are then categorized and labelled with a word or expression. Below is a brief explanation of how this process works (see Scherer 2004, 2009*a*).

Component integration

The process is conceptualized as shown in Figure 2.1.3, using a Venn diagram in which a set of overlapping circles represents the different aspects of feeling. The first circle (A) represents the reflection or representation of changes in all synchronized components in some kind of central monitoring structure in the CNS, which receives massive projections from both cortical and subcortical CNS structures (including feedback from the periphery). The second circle (B), only partially overlapping with the first, represents the part of the integrated central representation that becomes conscious. This circle corresponds most directly to what are generally called 'feelings'. It feeds the process of controlled regulation, much of which is determined by self-representation and socio-normative constraints. It is the degree of synchronization of the components that generates conscious awareness (Scherer 2005*a*). This synchronization may in turn be determined by the relevance of the event as appraised by the organism.

Note that circle (C) overlaps only partially with the circle representing conscious experience (B), as verbal self-report can only relate part of what is consciously experienced due to selective

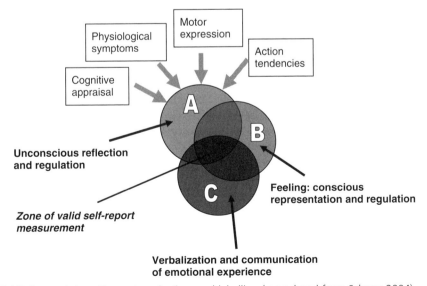

Fig. 2.1.3 System integration, categorization, and labelling (reproduced from Scherer 2004).

reporting, incomplete memories of the eliciting event and the reaction, and the constraints of the language categories available (see below).

The account given above depends largely on the processes of synchronization and integration within and between components. Integration *within components* is required because different structures and processes interact in an extremely complex fashion during emotion. For example, information integration is required within the cognitive component, given the parallel and sequential processing with respect to different evaluation criteria on different levels.

How can we conceive of the mechanism that integrates appraisal results? Appraisal theorists have generally used profile matching or regression analysis (see review in Scherer 1999*a*) to model the integration of appraisal results, but without treating the issue in much detail. Scherer (2004) suggested using Anderson's (1989) integration functions, expected to be strongly determined by the current goals of the organism, to understand the transformation of appraisal results based on individual criteria into a coherent response. For example, van Reekum *et al.* (2004) show that levels of coping potential have a very different effect upon psychophysiological responses as a function of goal conduciveness. This is because coping ability is of less relevance when things are going according to plan. One could predict that the importance of one of the criteria depends on the level of another. Further work in this area will require a high degree of theoretical specification and research sophistication, including a specification of the transfer functions involved (see Kappas 2001). Most likely, linear functions, as specified in the rules proposed by Anderson (1989), will not correctly represent the respective functions in many cases. While up until now the classic linear functions (e.g. regression) have dominated our analysis and modelling methods, Scherer (2000, 2009*b*) has argued that we may need to adopt *nonlinear dynamic system* analysis as a more appropriate framework for emotion modelling.

As shown in Figure 2.1.3, the feedback information from different response components (such as vocal and facial expression or psychophysiological symptoms) must be integrated to yield a coherent representation of feeling. In other words, information must be integrated *across components*. The CPM suggests it is the very process of synchronization between components that elicits and organizes this process of multicomponent integration, largely outside of awareness.

Our knowledge about the integration of proprioceptive cues in the different response components of the emotion process is extremely limited at the present time. This is partly due to a lack of attention to the issue as most emotion researchers specialize in only one specific response component. A great deal of basic research will be required to obtain a better understanding of the underlying feedback and integration mechanisms. It would be useful if such research were guided by explicit hypotheses. Neuropsychological findings about the projection and organization of proprioceptive feedback in different domains could provide extremely useful information in this respect (see Craig 2002; Wiens 2005).

So far, only the *quality* of the subjective experience or feeling and the integration required has been discussed. There is also proprioceptive information, such as feedback, from various parts of the body about the respective *amplitude or intensity* of the changes in different components. This information must, of course, also be integrated toward a common response path. The duration and intensity of feelings has rarely been studied to date (but see Edwards 1998; Ortony *et al.* 1988; Sonnemans and Frijda 1994; Verduyn *et al.* 2009), and little is known about the process of integration. The various integration rules proposed by Anderson (1989) are directly applicable here; amplitudes can be averaged or multiplied, or specific configurational rules may apply.

In summary, when trying to understand integration at different points in the emotion episode and the rules that underlie this process, the key issue is the relative weight given to the different components: appraisal; physiological responses; motor expression; motivation; and action tendencies.

Integration rules are likely to involve differential weighting of various response components, probably using nonlinear functions. Here is an example of configurational weighting: If a person is involved in a negotiation requiring impression management and strategic action, the process of integrating different proprioceptive cues might disproportionately weight the expression component (e.g. facial and vocal behaviours). If he or she is alone, and has to decide on a cause of action, the cognitive appraisal of the event in the light of current goals and values might be more strongly weighted. Thus, as suggested by Anderson (1989), the integration function, particularly the weighting of different components, may to a very large extent be determined by context and goals. In addition, feeling rules (Hochschild 1979) may exert strong, normative effects on the weighting of different proprioceptive cues. Feeling can be proactive, in the sense of defining states to be achieved. It can elicit processes of cognitive reevaluation and of physiological and expressive regulation. It does more than just reactively reflect or monitor changes in the different components.

Emotion processes also need to be integrated *over time*. The term 'emotional state' suggests a static, unitary phenomenon rather than a flow of continuously changing component states. Although we can focus on momentary changes of feeling, we tend to become aware of our feelings in experiential chunks that provide unity to a particular feeling. Temporal integration, in the sense of 'chunking' of experiences, may be determined by the period during which a certain kind of component synchronization takes place. Presumably, the same experiential chunks are available as the basis for verbalization. Additional temporal integration may be required as a result of the packaging by narrative or other pragmatic units in speech (see also Kahneman 2000 for issues of temporal feeling integration).

To summarize, the emotion process is considered as a continuously fluctuating pattern of change in several organismic subsystems that become integrated into coherence clusters and thus yield an extraordinarily large number of different emotional qualities, virtually as many as there are different integrations of appraisal results and consequent response patterns (Scherer 1984, 2001). In line with a philosophical tradition, it is suggested to call these conglomerates 'qualia' (see Scherer 2009*a* for a more detailed discussion of this notion).

Qualia are phenomena that are directly tied to subjective conscious experience. Does it make sense to try to computationally model qualia and would it be possible to do so for autonomous agents? This complex issue is hotly debated at the moment, particularly in computational neuro-science (see review in Cleeremans 2008) and it would go way beyond the focus of this chapter to address it. Suffice it to say that, if an equivalent of qualia representation could be modelled, it would certainly be of great interest for the development of a complete computational model of emotion and of the CPM in particular.

Categorization and labelling of qualia

As outlined above, the CPM predicts that the emotion process, considered as a continuously fluctuating pattern of change in several organismic subsystems, will yield a very large number of different emotional qualities, in fact, as many as there are different integrations of appraisal result profiles and consequent response patterns. However, there are some major patterns of adaptation in the life of organisms that reflect frequently recurring patterns of appraisal and adaptation. Scherer (1994*b*) has suggested using the term *modal emotions* for the states resulting from these outcomes that are due to general conditions of life, constraints of social organization, and similarity of innate equipment.

Table 2.1.4 illustrates the predicted profiles of the antecedent SEC result patterns for four major modal emotions. For each of the SECs, a graded scale of typical result alternatives is assumed. Both the polarity and the grading are used for the predictions. The term 'open' indicates that

Table 2.1.4 Predictions of prototypical appraisal profiles for four modal emotions (reproduced from Scherer 2004)

Stimulus evaluation checks	Joy/happiness	Anger/rage	Fear/panic	Sadness
Novelty	High	High	High	Low
Intrinsic pleasantness	High	Open	Low	Open
Goal significance				
Outcome probability/certainty	High	Very high	High	Very high
Conduciveness/consistency	Conducive	Obstructive	Obstructive	Obstructive
Urgency	Low	High	Very high	Low
Coping potential				
Agency/responsibility	Self/other	Other	Other/nature	Open
Control	High	High	Open	Very low
Power	High	High	Very low	Very low
Adjustement	High	High	Low	Medium
Compatibility with standards/ value relevance/legitimacy	High	Low	Open	Open

many different results of a particular check are compatible with the occurrence of the modal emotion in question. Alternatively, it may mean that the check is irrelevant for that emotion. The fairly high frequency of 'open' entries can be interpreted as the basis for the whole range of variants within a modal emotion 'family'.

Emotions that are closely related in terms of the situation that triggers them may be quite different qualitatively because of grading (or intensity) differences in the SEC results. Consider, for example, the distinction between 'hot anger' and subdued or 'cold' anger, or between worry and fear. The failure to distinguish between such related states may be the reason for the difficulty of replicating results in research on emotional responses. Different investigators may have used similar-sounding labels for emotional states that were in fact qualitatively different (see Banse and Scherer 1996). Combining the predictions for SEC profiles and response patterning, we can determine vocal and facial expression as well as ANS response patterns for these modal emotions (see Scherer 1986, 2001, 2009a for further details).

Thus, one can assume that a sizeable number of qualia representing integrated appraisal configurations and action tendencies (probably including the accompanying somatovisceral response patterns as part of the integrated package) will occur relatively frequently as they are of central importance to the individual's well-being. In consequence, the underlying modal emotions will serve as the basis for categorization of qualia clusters into discrete categories that are generally labelled with a single word or a brief expression in most languages of the world. The availability of such linguistic labels imposes a large degree of separateness and discreteness on particular types of experiences.

Does the modelling of categorization and labelling in an agent require the presence of an integrated representation in the form of qualia? This may not necessarily be the case. For example, Scherer (1993) has developed an 'expert system' that asks users for different appraisals that they may have used in reaction to a certain event and then postdicts, relatively successfully, a specific emotion label that describes the user's emotional experience. More recently, Scherer (2005b) has proposed a new approach to conceive of the semantics of emotion terms in the form of semantic feature profiles of folk concepts of emotions in natural languages. Concretely, emotion terms are rated by native speakers of different natural languages on terms or features representing all components of emotion, representing a *semantic grid*. Participants in a GRID study imagine a person whose emotional experience at a particular point in time is consensually described by observers with a specific term, e.g. 'irritated'. Then they are asked to evaluate the typical eliciting and response characteristics that would warrant the description of the person's emotional state with this label. This includes items on the eliciting event, the type of appraisal the person is likely to have made of the event and its consequences, the response patterns in the different components, the behavioural impact (action tendencies) generated, as well as the intensity and duration of the associated experience and control attempts. Using this procedure, Fontaine *et al.* (2007) studied 24 common emotion terms with 144 features in three languages. Apart from demonstrating the feasibility of the approach, they showed that four dimensions (valence, power, arousal, unexpectedness) rather than two (arousal, valence) are required to map the 24 emotions into a lower dimensional affective space in a satisfactory fashion. This research approach, which is currently being expanded to all major languages of the world, thus generated semantic profiles for major emotion terms. Figure 2.1.4 shows an example for two major emotion terms in the English language (pleasure, fear) using the semantic GRID based on a design feature approach.

Provided that there is reasonable agreement between raters (in the sense of interrater reliability) consensually defining the semantic field, grid profiles for different emotion terms allows the determination of the precise meaning of an emotion term in the respective language. In addition to allowing the examination of subtle differences in the meanings of different emotion terms and providing similarity-of-profile data that can be used to statistically determine the relationships between members of emotion families and the overall structure of the semantic space for emotions, such data for different languages inform us about potential cultural and linguistic differences in emotion encoding.

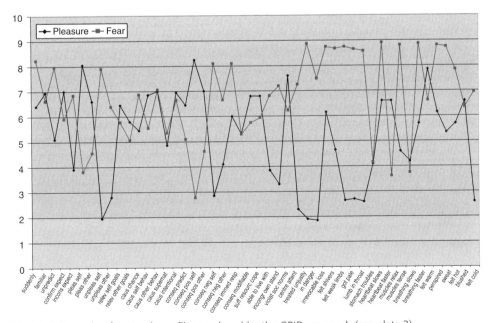

Fig. 2.1.4 Example of semantic profiles produced by the GRID approach (see plate 3).

The success of the two approaches described above shows that one does not need qualia to describe the emotion categories and labels. Language users are apparently able to recover elements from each emotion component that are typical for certain categories and identify these as being important prerequisites for the use of emotion labels. In consequence, the data gathered in the GRID project can be used by agent models to determine the most appropriate category and label to be used to communicate the current emotional state as based on the emergent patterns described by the CPM model. It would be sufficient to establish vectors for the current state in the different parameters used for the process modelling and compare those with the semantic profiles of different emotion terms in a given language. One can reasonably expect that the recognizability of the respective state by human interaction partners is likely to be much better than what can be obtained by coarser approaches (e.g. the OCR model; Ortony *et al.* 1988) that represent only one or two components with very few categories.

Modelling the CPM

In this presentation of the CPM, only the theoretical framework underlying the model has been outlined; empirical research findings have not been discussed. However, there is now much empirical evidence on the predictions of the model, as described in a recent review chapter (Scherer 2009a). On both theoretical and empirical grounds, it can thus be argued that the CPM is an ideal candidate for computational modelling. The elicitation of emotions is not explained by prototypical categories of events, limiting modelling to a lookup of predefined contingencies (as in the module or basic emotion models) or to a limited set of mechanisms, such as conditioning (as in the fear conditioning models). Rather, a set of concrete predictions for an appraisal of low-level features such as novelty, relevance, goal conduciveness, and coping ability are proposed. All of these seem to lend themselves to implementation in computational models where novelty or relevance are standard features in automatic detection and analysis based on system characteristics and state. In addition, the CPM provides detailed hypotheses as to the response patterning that is to be expected on the basis of specific appraisal results. Once these hypotheses are empirically confirmed (as mentioned above, there is already a considerable amount of evidence), the appraisal–response links can be directly implemented to model the visible and audible expression of autonomous agents (and, if desired, a simulation of brain processes or peripheral autonomic responses).

The advantage of synthesizing or animating facial and vocal agent expression with profiles of appraisal results rather than prototypical basic emotion categories (or valence × arousal positions) is greater naturalness and authenticity. In addition, a large variety of subtle emotions can be modelled rather than being restricted to a few stereotypical basic emotions. This is due to the much larger variability of these expressions in comparison with prototypical schemata. Also, in contrast to all other models, the CPM is the only truly dynamical model predicting sequential cumulative changes of appraisal criteria over single appraisal passes and constant change and adaptation due to recursive processing in multiple passes. Again, modelling these dynamic changes should greatly enhance the naturalness and realism of agent reactions and expression. The CPM is the only model to clearly separate subjective feeling state from the underlying process of response patterning based on appraisal results. This allows concentration on event evaluation and appropriate response patterning in interactive applications that do not require higher-order representation. Yet, potentially it also allows modelling of conscious feeling which is particularly important for models that intend to integrate emotion regulation. Conscious feeling may serve important monitoring and directing functions in this respect (see Scherer 2005a). Finally, the structure of the CPM allows seamless integration with other cognitive science models

MODELLING THE CPM | 69

that concern centrally important structures and mechanisms linked to learning and behaviour execution, such as short and long-term memory, executive space constraints, or levels of processing. Figure 2.1.5 (reproduced from Scherer 2001) shows an initial blueprint for such an integrated model (loosely based on Cowan 1988).

A number of computational procedures from simple pattern matching to logical inference, based on schemata and representations that are activated in long-term memory, process sensory input that is coded into brief sensory storage (in the form of sensory registers). This occurs on different levels as suggested by Leventhal and Scherer (1987) and LeDoux's (1996) multiple path model. On a first pass, pertinent schemata are recruited in a largely automatic fashion to determine whether a satisfactory match (including an adaptational response) can be selected, followed by controlled processing based on propositional content activated in long-term memory, giving rise to more elaborate evaluation and inference processes (as shown in the lower part of Figure 2.1.5). As a result, a network of representational units that corresponds to the appraised characteristics and significance of the event will be activated. The activation state of this representational network is constantly updated as the appraisal process unfolds (assuming a single node for each of the checks (see enlarged representation in Figure 2.1.5). Given constant updating, each node will always correspond to the best available estimate of the respective aspect of the stimulus event that is currently processed. The representational network as a whole represents the overall significance of the event for the individual. Even though, as expected under conditions of parallel processing, all checks are performed continuously and simultaneously, the content of the respective node will not necessarily impact on response patterning (see below).

As outlined above, the SEC results provide the four essential types of information required for action preparation: relevance, implication, coping, and normative significance. The contents of the representational units corresponding to individual SECs are continuously integrated with respect to these classes of information. This is illustrated by the connections between the SEC units and the boxes representing these information types (in Figure 2.1.5). The specific integration for each of the information types will vary continuously as a function of information

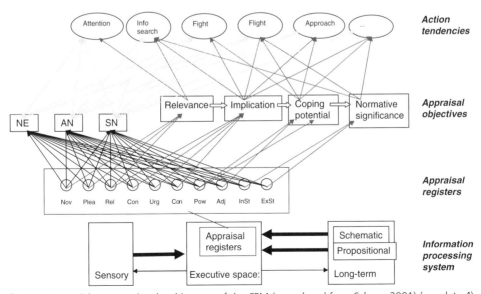

Fig. 2.1.5 Potential computational architecture of the CPM (reproduced from Scherer 2001) (see plate 4).

updating in the network. The different checks are integrated through weighting functions, which may vary depending on the nature of the context (see Wehrle and Scherer 2001).

To graphically represent the connections and activation patterns in the model, a neural network architecture (see Sander *et al.* 2005) has been adopted in Figure 2.1.5. It is predicted that the profile of integrated information in the four major classes will activate potential response mechanisms. To illustrate this, some action tendencies (as part of the executive subsystem) are shown in Figure 2.1.5. Depending on the profile of appraisal results, different action tendencies will be more or less strongly activated and will, in turn, activate the different parts of the support subsystem, the neuroendocrine system (NES), the autonomic nervous system (ANS), and the somatic nervous system (SNS). However, the current version of the model, as shown in Figure 2.1.2 and represented in Figure 2.1.5 by the connections between check units on the one hand and NES, ANS, and SNS on the other, assumes that there are direct connections of the SEC units with these response modalities, independently of action tendencies. However, as mentioned above, it is assumed that such efferent effects will only occur if a minimal degree of closure (or definitiveness) of the evaluation of a specific check has been achieved (to avoid constant vacillation of the organism). It is expected that there will be sequential ordering of the moments of closure. The mechanism for achieving closure that justifies efferent effects at a particular point could consist of markers of confidence or certainty for the contents of the representational units, combined with the temporal persistence of the same informational content in the node (suggesting that there has been no recent updating and that the information is stable and reliable).

Conclusion

Clearly, a more formal attempt to computationally model emergent emotion processes, using leading edge tools, including constraints imposed by what is known by the neural architecture, and modelling the dynamic flow of recursive effects, would be of major importance for the further development of theorizing and research in emotion. It would also greatly enhance the development of the CPM. It is to be hoped that the existence of a dynamic theoretical model like the CPM will encourage concrete modelling efforts in this area. Obviously, one would need to begin by modelling the emotions of a very simple creature, an *organismus simplicissimus* (see Scherer 1984), rather than attempting to start with full-blown human emotions. Given the ever-accelerating increase in both the sophistication of research methods and the resulting understanding of the neural architecture and the dynamic processing underlying our cognitive and affective performances and experiences, the time may be ripe to venture into more complex levels of neural network modelling, including dynamical systems approaches. Currently, the funding policies in the affective computing domain seem to privilege more immediately applicable and much simpler computational models for agent emotion production and recognition over the building of more realistic process models to understand complex recursive mechanisms. But one can paraphrase the old adage that nothing is more practical than a good theory and predict that a good computational model of fundamental emotion processes, being able to account for their emergent properties, might well move the practical applicability of computational agent models to an appreciably higher level.

The emotional brain meets affective computing

Didier Grandjean and David Sander

Summary

What can one learn from the emotional brain in order to synthesize an affectively competent agent? Ideally, one can learn about the explicit biological constraints when formally constructing a computational model of emotion and can then use such a model in order to test functional architectures of psychological mechanisms (e.g. Fellous and Arbib 2005; Korsten *et al.*, in press). In particular, using a cognitive neuroscience perspective, some authors (e.g. Adolphs 2003; Kosslyn and Koenig 1995; Sander and Koenig 2002; Sander *et al.* 2005; Thagard and Aubie 2008) have highlighted the importance of investigating human emotion in the brain at the systems level in order to synthesize computational models that can be implemented in non-human agents. After a brief introduction to such a cognitive neuroscience perspective, this chapter will address four of the most critical elements that the emotional brain can bring to an affectively competent agent.

The first element concerns the specialized *domain of emotional processing* implemented in dedicated neural networks. Without endorsing a so-called modular perspective, a critical question in order to formalize a model is indeed to identify the specific quality of inputs that are processed by a given neural network in order to elicit further processing. Addressing this issue, and with the aim of demonstrating the rationale of the approach, we will focus on the specialized domain of processing of the region that is believed to be the central piece of the emotional brain (e.g. LeDoux and Schiller 2009): the amygdala.

The second element concerns the *level of processing* at which each specialized neural network can operate. Indeed, several theories of emotion have considered that specific emotional processes may take place at various levels of processing (e.g. Robinson 2009). Keeping our focus on the amygdala for the sake of comprehensiveness, we will consider two key questions with respect to the levels of processing, namely, the types of primitives that are processed by the amygdala and whether the amygdala computes information in an automatic way.

The third element concerns the *temporal dynamic* of the specialized neural networks that operate at several levels of processing. Indeed, a critical question in developing an affectively competent agent is whether some computational units function in parallel, and whether others follow one after the other (as a cascade or a sequence). Addressing this issue, we will concentrate on recent evidence demonstrating the possibility of unpacking appraisal processes over time using electroencephalographic measures.

The fourth element concerns the functional connectivity between different brain regions processing different kinds of information and/or processing the same information but at different levels of processing. In this framework we will develop the notion of neuronal *synchronization or coherence* between different components of emotional processing, such as peripheral and central ones. The synchronization refers to different phenomena: (1) a dynamic neuronal phenomenon operating at several levels of processing or (2) a mechanism allowing organisms to build up a representation of integrated outputs from different information processes subserved by different close or distant brain regions. Indeed, after having functionally dissected the different emotion components and processes, a major question is how a coherent emotion can emerge in an affectively competent agent. Addressing this issue, we will present a theoretical framework distinguishing between local and long distance brain synchronization, and discuss recent data highlighting the importance of phase oscillation between the amygdala and the orbitofrontal cortex, two regions well known for their involvement in emotional processing.

On the relevance of the cognitive neuroscience approach in order to synthesize an affectively competent agent

Affective computing can be defined as the type of computing that relates to, arises from, or deliberately influences emotion and other affective phenomena (Picard 2009). In that respect, a close consideration of affective computing can be viewed as being the basis of the implementation of emotion as adaptive mechanisms in autonomous agents (e.g. Cañamero 2009), not only in robotics but also for software agents such as embodied conversational agents (e.g. Pelachaud 2009; Chapter 5.5, this volume). Affective computing is at the basis of the synthesis of affectively competent agents, but what is at the basis of affective computing? Arguably, the basis of affective computing resides in the establishment of computational models of emotion. Such computational models can take various forms (Petta and Gratch 2009), but a particular type of computational model that is most suited for scientific investigations consists of models that are constrained by both psychological and biological plausibility (Korsten *et al.*, in press; Sander and Koenig 2002). In that context, the perspective according to which computational models of emotion should be based on both psychological (Gratch and Marsella 2005) and neuroscientific (e.g. Armony *et al.* 1995, 1997; see Taylor and Korsten 2009) constraints has a strong potential, and corresponds largely to what is more generally known as the cognitive neuroscience approach.

Since its emergence in the 1980s, the cognitive neuroscience approach was first applied to founding domains of cognitive science such as perception, action, attention, memory, and language (see Posner and DiGirolamo 2000). More recently, Davidson and Sutton (1995) pointed to an emerging discipline: affective neuroscience. They argued that studies on emotion require a careful dissection of emotional processes into elementary mental operations, consistent with the cognitive neuroscience approach. Distinguishing affective neuroscience (see also Panksepp 1991) from the cognitive neuroscience of emotion is not discussed here because both disciplines share the fundamental goal of analysing emotional mechanisms in terms of their subcomponents and of understanding how these subcomponents interact in a psychologically and biologically plausible way (see Kosslyn and Koenig 1995). Influential models of emotion have used brain-based evidence at the systems level in order to propose a parsing of emotion into distinct subcomponents.

A first category of such models corresponds to those that do not particularly aim at being formulated in affective computing terms. Therefore, although these models can be extremely useful for the creation of an affectively competent agent, important developments remain to be made in order to use these models in affective computing. For example, with a particular emphasis on clinical and cognitive neuropsychology, Damasio (1998) distinguished between neural systems involved in emotion versus neural systems involved in feeling. In this model, a critical function is given to somatic signals and their integration with other brain signals elicited by external events (see also Thagard and Aubie 2008). In contrast, with a particular emphasis on behavioural neuroscience, Panksepp (1998*a*) proposed four primitive systems described as the emotional operating systems in the brain (seeking, fear, rage, and panic systems) combined with special purpose socioemotional systems (for sexual lust, maternal care, and rough-housing play). With a different emphasis on psychopathology and personality factors, Gray (1994) distinguished three types of behaviour (fight, active avoidance, and behavioural inhibition), each mediated by different neural systems and related to different emotional states. These systems are the behavioural approach system, the fight/flight/freezing system, and the behavioural inhibition system (Gray and McNaughton 2000). Any experienced emotional state may correspond to a blend of activity within all these three systems. Finally, with an emphasis on individual affective styles and psychopathologies, Davidson distinguished between processes involved in the perception and the production of emotionally significant signals, and in addition proposed differential systems underlying approach-related emotions and withdrawal-related emotions, respectively (e.g. Davidson 1995).

A second category of cognitive neuroscience models of emotion corresponds to those that already aim at being formulated in computational terms. Within this category, one can at least distinguish between connectionist (or neural network) models on the one hand (see Levine 2007; Korsten *et al.* 2006), and models that are based on a computational analysis on the other (which can also be connectionist models, but not necessarily; see Sander and Koenig 2002). With respect to connectionist models of emotional processing that adopt a cognitive neuroscience perspective, the most classical example is the work of Armony and colleagues. In a pioneering work, they proposed a computational connectionist model of fear conditioning that was constrained by what was then known about the neuroanatomy and neurophysiology of fear learning, in particular by modelling both cortical and subcortical pathways to the amygdala (Armony *et al.* 1995, 1997). This model was very strongly inspired by the functional neuroanatomy of fear learning, and it is therefore unclear how this model could be extended to other emotions. Connectionist models have also been used to investigate the links between emotion an other systems. For instance, Taylor and colleagues have proposed a neural network model that also integrates some aspect of emotional processing in order to investigate the links between emotion and attention (see, for example, Taylor and Fragopanagos 2005). The authors could show that this model was able to replicate several results obtained in the literature and be useful to propose new hypotheses. For more details on connectionist models of emotion, see Chapter 4.2, this volume.

With respect to models that are based on a computational analysis, most of them are—implicitly or explicitly—inspired by David Marr's notion of 'levels of analysis'. Cognitive neuroscience defines computational analysis as a logical exercise aimed at determining what processing subsystems are necessary to produce a specific behaviour given a specific input (Kosslyn and Koenig 1995). Computational analyses that are both biologically and psychologically constrained gave rise to a rich literature on perception—vision in particular—as well as memory, attention, and action. Marr's approach to computational analysis was also used to propose functional architectures of emotion consisting of interacting specialized subsystems (see Sander and Koenig 2002; Moors 2009). An advantage of computational analysis of emotion is that it invites affective scientists to develop functional architectures that are sufficiently explicit to be tested using computational, neuroscientific, and psychological methods. For instance, a computational analysis of emotion led Sander and Koenig (2002) to specify the model proposed by Kosslyn and Koenig (1995) as constituted of the following subsystems: (1) a somatosensory buffer that represents, as a somatic map, the actual state of one's body; (2) a somatotopic mapping subsystem that specifies the body localization where an internal state change has occurred on the basis of the information provided by the somatosensory buffer; (3) an internal-state preprocessing subsystem that extracts distinctive information about one's internal state; (4) an internal-state pattern activation subsystem that stores in long-term memory representations of previous internal-state patterns; (5) a stimulus–response connection subsystem that implements 'processing reflexes'; (6) an associative memory subsystem that stores amodal representations, and that may be involved in overlearnt appraisals of emotion-eliciting events; (7) an emotion-instructions generation subsystem, that generates an initial specification of the brain/body profile that is appropriate when facing an emotional situation on the basis of information provided by associative memory and appraisal processes; and (8) emotion-execution subsystems that activate 'effector' subsystems in order to modulate the internal state and more generally the emotional expression.

Although existing models at the systems level have often considered critical emotional components—action tendencies, expression, feeling, and peripheral physiology—no model, to our knowledge, has focused on the appraisal component using a cognitive neuroscience approach. In fact, some influential models have already used psychological constraints derived from appraisal theories of emotion in order to produce explicit expert systems (e.g. Scherer 1993) or computational models of emotion (see Frijda and Swagerman1987; Gratch and Marsella 2005; Chapter 1.2, this volume). The next step in the framework of cognitive neuroscience would now be to consider brain-related constraints. In particular, it is critical to understand how neural networks subserve appraisal processes and how they drive the other emotional components. In order to achieve this goal, at least four fundamental aspects of the appraising brain have to be characterized: (1) the extent to which specific appraisals constitute the processing domain of specialized neural networks; (2) the extent to which dissociable neural networks are involved at different levels of processing; (3) the temporal dynamics of the neural networks subserving the appraisals; and (4) the *synchronization* of the specialized neural networks that dynamically operate at several levels of processing. Each of these aspects is addressed below, with the aim of providing evidence for the usefulness of the approach rather than of being comprehensive. As a case study, we have chosen to discuss here advances in the cognitive neuroscience of the amygdala's function. We have chosen the amygdala because this region has received more interest from cognitive neuroscientists than any other region of the emotional brain (see Whalen and Phelps 2009). We have also chosen the amygdala specifically because it has been suggested that it is critically involved in relevance detection (e.g. Sander *et al.* 2003), which is arguably the most important appraisal mechanism (i.e. appraised relevance is often considered as a condition *sine qua non* of emotion elicitation).

Domain specialization

In order to set apart the neural networks involved in specialized domains of appraisal processes, the rationale of the cognitive neuroscience approach consists in constraining the functional organization of the appraisal mechanisms by reviewing converging evidence from the relevant literature and by designing new experiments, in particular, brain imaging experiments on the normal human brain and behavioural experiments testing brain-damaged patients. In this respect, connectionist models (see Taylor and Korsten 2009), and artificial neural network simulations of appraisal processes in particular, may lead to significant theoretical advances. But, in order to be able to simulate appraisal mechanisms with neural networks, it is critical to identify the functional neural architecture that subserves these mechanisms. As discussed above, we have chosen to discuss here advances in the cognitive neuroscience of the amygdala's function.

The amygdala is currently recognized by cognitive neuroscientists as a masterpiece of the emotional brain and has already been used to inspire biologically plausible computational models of emotion (e.g. Armony *et al.* 1995, 1997). Located in the temporal lobe, this structure is thought to play a critical role not only in emotion elicitation, emotional responses, and emotion regulation, but also in allowing prioritized or enhanced neural processing in various systems involved in perception, learning, memory, attention, vigilance, judgement, and decision making. It is, therefore, critical to understand the nature of the computations performed by the amygdala and how it interacts with other neural networks. However, the anatomical unity of the amygdala and the issue of whether it functions as a system remain matters of debate (e.g. Davis and Whalen 2001) with some scholars even arguing that the amygdala does not exist as a unitary structure (Swanson and Petrovich 1998), while others reject this claim (e.g. Barton *et al.* 2003), sometimes suggesting that the unity of the amygdala also includes a so-called 'extended amygdala' containing, for instance, the substantia innominata (see Aggleton 2000; Davis and Whalen 2001). The debate concerning the unity of the amygdala originates mainly from the variety of amygdaloid nuclei and nuclear divisions that compose the amygdala (see Aggleton 2000), the variety of neuron subtypes in each nucleus, and also the confusion concerning the function of the amygdala. Current debates concerning the computational profile of the amygdala concern both the domain and the level of processing of the amygdala. In this section, we will briefly discuss the amygdala's domain of processing, and in the next section its level of processing.

Historically, from the 1930s until the end of the twentieth century, the emotional role of the amygdala was typically associated with one emotion—fear. This association was mainly based on clear evidence from animal research, brain imaging, and patient studies that the amygdala is important for fear learning and, more generally, for the processing of threat-related information (see Phelps and LeDoux 2005). These results ultimately led to the view that the amygdala is central to a 'defence system', 'fear system', or even a so-called 'fear module' (Öhman and Mineka 2001), the latter term implying that the domain of specificity of the amygdala is dedicated to fear-related computations. However, as argued by LeDoux (2008), a critical issue is to understand whether the importance of the amygdala in fear reflects the importance of fear to the amygdala or whether fear is just the function that has been studied the most.

In fact, although the role of the amygdala in fear is unchallenged, it is now clear that the processing domain of the amygdala is not restricted to fear-related information. A large body of evidence—which is too broad to be reviewed here—indicates that the amygdala is involved in the processing not only of information related to negative emotions other than fear, but also of positive information such as humour-related stimuli, happy faces, pleasant pictures, movies, odours, and tastes (see Sergerie *et al.* 2008 for review) and reward learning (see Baxter and Murray 2002). How can the amygdala be considered central to both a 'fear module' (Öhman and Mineka 2001) and a 'reward system' (Baxter and Murray 2002)? As amygdala activity increases with the intensity of both negative and positive events, it was suggested that this structure is sensitive to the intensity or arousal of the emotion-eliciting stimulus, independently of its valence (see Hamann 2003). However, it has been shown that: the amygdala is involved in the processing of stimuli that are low on arousal, such as sadness-related information (see Fine and Blair 2000); equally intense stimuli differentially activate the amygdala (e.g. Whalen *et al.* 2001); arousal ratings in a patient with an amygdala lesion are impaired for negative, but not positive emotions (e.g. Adolphs *et al.* 1999); and neither valence nor intensity *per se* is coded in the amygdala (Winston *et al.* 2005). Moreover, operationalizing the concept of relevance with the notion of 'impact', a recent brain imaging experiment showed increased amygdala activation to images with high impact when compared to neutral images or to low impact images that were matched for arousal ratings (Ewbank *et al.* 2009). Taken together, these results contradict the view that the amygdala codes stimulus intensity or elicited arousal irrespective of valence.

As an alternative, arguing for a unitary function of the human amygdala, Sander *et al.* (2003) proposed that the basic function of the amygdala is to detect events that are subjectively appraised as relevant given the current individual's goals, needs, values, and concerns. This proposal accounts for both inter- and intraindividual differences in amygdala sensitivity and emotional mechanisms. For instance, Phan *et al.* (2003) reported amygdala responses only when subjective ratings were incorporated in the analysis of brain activation as regressors. Another line of research highlighting the importance of taking into account interindividual differences in amygdala sensitivity concerns the fact that amygdala response varies as a function of personality or affective traits. For instance, one can argue that the reason why happy faces particularly activate the amygdala in participants who rate high on extraversion (Canli *et al.* 2002) is because such stimuli are particularly relevant for them. It is also important to consider intraindividual differences in terms of needs and goals. For instance, LaBar *et al.* (2001) showed that the amygdala was more activated by the visual presentation of food-related stimuli when participants were hungry than when they were satiated. Another dimension that may contribute in appraising a stimulus as relevant concerns its novelty or ambiguity, which is consistent with Whalen's proposal that the amygdala — in particular its more dorsal part—may be especially involved in increasing vigilance based on perceived stimulus ambiguity (see Davis and Whalen 2001). The fact that the amygdala is also sensitive to task-related goals and task performance (e.g Schaefer *et al.* 2006; Wright and Liu 2006) also speaks in favour of a role of the amygdala in the processing of goal/need relevance. Other pieces of evidence have shown that human amygdala is also involved in emotional auditory processing (Grandjean *et al.* 2005; Sander *et al.* 2005; Fecteau *et al.* 2007), showing that the involvement of this structure in emotional processing is at least partly independent of the stimulus modality presentation. Importantly, these proposals are consistent with a preferential processing and learning for fear-related stimuli in many contexts, as such stimuli are usually more relevant than stimuli used in the other experimental conditions. Anatomically, the amygdala seems to be particularly well located to serve this function, as it receives information from the thalamus and all sensory cortices, and the amygdalofugal projections to the cortex are massive (see also Aggleton 2000).

To conclude this section, it appears that the amygdala's domain of processing includes, but is not limited to, fear-related information as well as other negative arousing stimuli. Amygdala responses to positive as well as low arousing stimuli that have a particular impact on the individual suggest instead that, as a structure, the amygdala's domain of processing consists of events that are subjectively appraised as relevant given the current individual's goals, needs, values, and concerns. In this section, we have focused on the amygdala as a case study, but current perspectives in cognitive neuroscience may allow a similar analysis of other critical brain regions in order to design artificial affectively competent agents. For instance, including functional specificities of the insula, the striatum, the somatosensory cortices, the orbitofrontal cortex, the ventromedial prefrontal cortex, the dorsolateral prefrontal cortex, or the superior temporal sulcus will certainly be very useful in the design of biologically plausible computational models of emotion.

Levels of processing

In order to set apart the neural networks involved in the various levels of processing, the rationale of the cognitive neuroscience approach is similar to that used for the domains of processing, but with a particular emphasis on two research strategies. First, one can consider that some events might elicit emotions because of their basic sensory properties (e.g. patterns of movements for snakes or spiders, spatial frequencies for faces, or harmonics for musical stimuli). In this context, a critical research question is to determine the primitives that are processed by a given neural network. Second, one can consider that some events might be differentially processed at separate levels as a function of current goal–need demands or task requirements (e.g. explicit/implicit processing, conscious/unconscious processing, degree of intentionality, type of attention). In this context, a critical research question is to determine whether a given processing unit is operating at an automatic level.

Appraisal theories of emotion have proposed that the appraisal process might take place at three different levels (see Chapter 2.1, this volume), but to our knowledge the specific levels of processing suggested by appraisal theories have never been the focus of cognitive neuroscience research. However, keeping with our example concerning the amygdala, the levels of processing of the amygdala can be investigated at least from the two approaches mentioned above: (1) what are the primitives that are processed by the amygdala?; (2) does the amygdala compute information in an automatic way?

Concerning the issue of the primitives that are processed by the amygdala, several results indicate that simple perceptual cues have the power to elicit an amygdala response. This is particularly clear in fear conditioning paradigms in human or other animals during which a simple auditory tone or visual cue can elicit a response in the amygdala, if it has been paired with an emotional stimulus before (see Phelps and LeDoux 2005). Importantly, there is evidence that the amygdala is also sensitive to unconditioned low-level perceptual information such as low spatial frequencies in fearful faces (Vuilleumier *et al.* 2003), the sclera of fearful eyes (Whalen *et al.* 2004), or rising sound intensity (Bach *et al.* 2008). Such results speak in favour of the fact that a rapid processing of coarse emotion-eliciting information takes place in the human amygdala. This is consistent with anatomical and functional evidence suggesting the existence of a dual route architecture to the amygdala. Indeed, experiments of auditory fear conditioning in rats have shown the existence of a direct subcortical pathway from the auditory thalamus to the amygdala in addition to the more indirect cortical pathway (see Phelps and LeDoux 2005). Although uncontroversial anatomical evidence is lacking in humans, functional evidence suggests that a colliculo-pulvinar-amygdala subcortical pathway is involved in coarse and fast processing of visual stimuli in humans (e.g. Vuilleumier *et al.* 2003: see Vuilleumier 2005). A recent model has raised the question of whether such a pathway might be better conceptualized in the context of a two-stage architecture—rather than a dual route—according to which coarse and fast processing first occurs in magnocellular pathways, being then complemented by slower parvocellular visual pathways (Vuilleumier 2005). The existence of a low road in humans—or of a first processing stage—is also consistent with the view that the amygdala processes emotion-eliciting information at an automatic level. Indeed, strong evidence from experiments in blind-sight and neglect patients, as well as from studies using incidental, masking, or non-endogenous attention paradigms in normal individuals, suggests that the amygdala is able to process emotion-eliciting information implicitly, unconsciously, and independently of voluntary attention (see Vuilleumier 2005). It is noteworthy that the amygdala seems also able to process positive—therefore not only negative—stimuli in an unconscious way (e.g. Childress *et al.* 2008). The extent to which such automatic processes take place in a systematic and context-independent way is still a question for further research, as there is evidence that amygdala responses may vary as a function of the attentional constraints of the task at hand (see Pessoa 2008; Vuilleumier 2005). The fact that task-set and top-down context-dependent processing can also modulate processing in the amygdala (see Pessoa 2008; Vuilleumier 2005) makes it flexible, which is consistent with its suggested role of appraising relevant stimuli.

An analogy with the attention-constraints based hypothesis proposed by Smith *et al.* (2001) to account for semantic activation seems useful in order to characterize the amygdala's level of processing. According to these authors, semantic activation can be considered the default setting of the visual word recognition system. By analogy, it can be suggested here that evaluating emotion-eliciting stimuli reflects the default setting of the human amygdala, rather than an automatic process *per se* (in the strong sense of automaticity, implying total independency from capacity demands).

With this suggestion, we mean that, under typical cognitive conditions, processing in the amygdala may be unconscious, uncontrolled, independent of voluntary attention, efficient, and fast (see Moors and De Houwer 2006) but that automaticity is not a necessary condition, in the sense that non-typical conditions (e.g. a highly demanding concurrent task) might not allow the default setting of the amygdala to be expressed (see also Vuilleumier 2009).

In conclusion, we can consider the visual system as an analogy for the theoretical proposal of multiple levels of processing in the emotional system. While the visual system has been classically thought to be fully hierarchical, it is increasingly conceptualized as a mechanism of sequential and simultaneous parallel processing in three visual channels. Indeed, the visual brain, mainly from anatomical considerations, was classically described as consisting of many parallel specialized subsystems (see Felleman and Van Essen 1991) being activated serially by feedforward connections. Because each visual area shows more or less specific receptive field tuning properties, it has been stated that each subsystem mainly processes a specific feature (i.e. colour, motion, texture, or location) of the scene presented on the visual field (see e.g. Palmer 1999). With the development of physiological recording methods, the differences in the timing of activation between lower order areas (e.g. V1) and higher order areas (e.g. V5) have been a topic of great interest in the neuroscience of vision for more than a decade (see Bullier and Nowak 1995). The notion that multiple levels of visual processing of the same stimulus event can take place in parallel was found when considering in detail both the timing of visual processing and the functional differentiation of magnocellular (M), parvocellular (P), and koniocellular (K) pathways in vision (see Patel and Sathian 2000; Cheng *et al.* 2004). In addition to the functional specificities of these visual pathways, a major difference between P and M pathways is the latency difference. For example, as discussed by Bullier and Nowak (1995), it appears that latencies in V1 and V2 overlap extensively and even that many neurons in V2 can be active earlier than some V1 neurons. This result is crucial because it shows that a given M neuron in V2 can drive many P neurons in V1, thereby calling into question the hierarchical model by separating merely simultaneous activity of neurons from areas of different 'levels'. In this context, an alternative to the classical view is to consider that the activation of a conscious visual representation, when one is identifying an attended object, is the result of the interaction between feedback connections from M neurons and feedforward connections from P neurons that fire later within the ventral stream. If enough attention is allocated to the object on the retina, then the result of preprocessing of the M pathway is sent via feedback connections to areas V4, V2, and V1 and, because of the asynchrony of the three pathways, meets the slower feedforward information provided by the P and K pathways (see Bullier 2004; Ullman 1995). Without pushing the analogy between the visual and emotional systems too far, one notices striking similarities between the current perspective on the visual brain and our proposals concerning the emotional brain for multilevel parallel and sequential processing: The stimuli are processed at the three levels in parallel, each sequentially, with some levels being faster than others, thus preactivating representations for further processing by the complementary remaining levels.

To conclude, although the cognitive neuroscience of emotion in general, and of appraisal processes in particular, is not as advanced as the cognitive neuroscience of vision, several lines of research clearly indicate that a given stimulus input can be processed at several levels in the human brain before emotional responses are produced.

Temporal dynamics

The temporal dynamics of emotional processes is a crucial question when someone wants to build up an artificial system able to process emotional information and when modelling the impact of such emotional information processing on the behaviour of an artificial agent.

One of the central features of the Component Process Model (CPM) since its original formulation is the prediction that the processing of major appraisal criteria or stimulus evaluation checks (SECs), while proceeding in a parallel fashion, yields outcomes or results in a fixed sequential order: novelty → intrinsic pleasantness → task–goal relevance → goal conduciveness → coping potential → compatibility with internal and external norms or standards. The essential criterion for the sequence is the point in time at which a particular check achieves preliminary closure, i.e. yields a reasonably definitive result, one that warrants efferent commands to response modalities. What are the arguments that justify this sequence assumption? Relevance detection is considered to be a first selective filter that a stimulus or event needs to pass to merit further processing. It is assumed that only objects or events that surpass a certain threshold on novelty, or intrinsic pleasantness/unpleasantness, or goal/need relevance will pass this filter. Attention will be focused on the event and further processing will ensue. The next step is to assess the causes and implications of the event for the organism. These need to be established before the organism's coping potential can be determined since the latter is always evaluated with respect to a specific demand. Finally, the normative significance of the event, i.e. its consequences for the self and its normative/moral status, is evaluated. The general assumption is that—for logical and economical reasons—the results of the earlier SECs need to be processed before later SECs can operate successfully, i.e. yield a conclusive result. It can also be argued that the microgenetic unfolding of the emotion-antecedent appraisal processes parallels both phylogenetic and ontogenetic development in the differentiation of emotional states (see Scherer 1999b, 2001 for further details on the sequence prediction).

The assumption of sequential processing of the SECs, and the notion of a fixed order of the SECs in particular, has often been challenged (e.g. Ellsworth 1991; Lazarus 1999). It is claimed that the onset of an emotional reaction can occur extremely rapidly, in a single step, especially if schematic processing is involved (Smith and Lazarus 1990). However, the apparent speed of an emotional reaction to an event does not rule out a sequential model, if one assumes that at least some of the checks can be performed extremely rapidly (particularly when subcortical brain structures are involved). As a consequence, this work set out to empirically test the sequence prediction for some of the early appraisal criteria or SECs, and to perform the first mental chronography of appraisals to determine the plausibility of the assumption that sequential checking can occur very early on after stimulus onset and at an extremely rapid rate.

Given the need for high temporal resolution measurement of brain activity required by these aims, we chose to use state-of-the-art electroencephalography (EEG) and event-related potential (ERP) methods in an appropriate experimental design. Two studies were designed using EEG–ERP methods to measure the brain electrical reactions to the visual presentation of affect-inducing stimuli (Grandjean and Scherer, 2008). These methods provide an excellent temporal resolution and thus allow us to test the fixed sequence hypothesis and to obtain precise estimates of the timing of the sequential phases of the appraisal process.

The first experiment tested the sequence hypothesis by experimentally manipulating three different appraisal criteria: novelty; intrinsic pleasantness; and goal relevance (or, specifically, task relevance). On the basis of the CPM, early effects on electrical signal patterns in the brain, specific to the manipulated criteria, were predicted to occur in the following order: (1st) novelty; (2nd) intrinsic pleasantness; and (3rd) goal/task relevance. The second experiment consisted of a full factorial design in which the intrinsic pleasantness and goal conduciveness/obstructiveness appraisals were manipulated. The following order of occurrence of the traces for the respective brain activity was predicted: (1st) intrinsic pleasantness; (2nd) goal conduciveness. The following dependent variables, based on three major analysis techniques for EEG, were used to test these predictions: (1) the timing of ERP topographical maps specifically related to the different manipulated checks; (2) the timing of the amplitude modifications of the global field power related to the manipulated appraisal checks; and (3) the timing of the appearance of differences in amount of energy in the different frequency bands related to the different manipulated checks, see below.

Given the three central issues outlined above, we expected: (1) to obtain evidence for different patterns of brain activities involved in the processing of intrinsic pleasantness and goal conduciveness; (2) to use the results of mental chronography to obtain some indirect evidence on the level of processing (related to automaticity and brain structures involved); and (3) to confirm the theoretical predictions about the sequence of the results of specific checks.

The CPM also assumes that the processing of different appraisal criteria occurs in a simultaneous, parallel fashion on several levels of automaticity, representation, schematicity, rule application—and consciousness (see the useful categorization of multimode distinctions proposed by Moors and De Houwer 2005). This arrangement does not mean that all events are processed in parallel on all levels of processing. Rather, the assumption is that the recursive loop of processing stops when a conclusive result (establishing the behavioural meaning of the consequences with a sufficient degree of certainty and allowing adaptive decisions or actions) has been achieved. The lower levels are assumed to provide leaner processing and to be much faster. Thus, once a conclusive result is achieved, processing may stop without producing any results on higher levels. In other words, higher, more costly—and more conscious—levels are only recruited in cases in which lower-level processing does not achieve conclusive results.

This type of parallel processing does not contradict the assumption of sequential unfolding: novelty → intrinsic pleasantness → goal/task relevance → goal conduciveness → coping potential → compatibility with internal and external norms or standards. The reason is that the essential criterion for the sequence is the point at which a particular check achieves preliminary closure, i.e. yields a reasonably definitive result, one that warrants efferent commands to response modalities. The general assumption is that—for logical and economical reasons—the results of the earlier SECs need to be processed before later SECs can operate successfully, i.e. yield a conclusive result. It can also be argued that the microgenetic unfolding of the emotion–antecedent appraisal processes parallels both phylogenetic and ontogenetic development in the differentiation of emotional states (see Scherer 1999b, 2001 for further details on the sequence prediction). The implication of this assumption is that earlier appraisals are more 'primitive' in level of processing, as well as more unconscious, even if it possible that some processes reach the level of consciousness and then become accessible for an explicit representation and a possible verbal report. For example, a novel object can be processed at an unconscious level before the organism is able to have an explicit representation of this novel object. Evidence for these hypotheses and first indications of the mental chronometry involved comes from a study by Grandjean and Scherer (2008), see also above. In this series of empirical studies, novelty, goal relevance, intrinsic pleasantness, and goal conduciveness SECs were systematically manipulated to test the sequence hypothesis. In two visual experiments (using international affective picture system (IAPS) pictures; Lang et al. 2005) with EEG recordings, characterized by a high temporal resolution, we tested the sequential hypothesis through several types of signal analyses. For example, topographical analyses of the event-related potentials (ERPs) revealed a specific electrical map related to novelty (~90 ms after the onset of the stimulus) preceding another topographical map related to task–goal relevance, indicating that the occurrence of the novel map precedes the task–goal relevance map by about 50 ms (see Grandjean and Scherer 2008 for further details).

To investigate the effects of manipulated appraisals not revealed by the topographical analyses, further analyses were performed on the global field power (GFP) of the ERPs, mainly representing the intensity of signal changes without corresponding modifications of the topography of the electrical fields. These GFP analyses revealed early effects related to novelty and later effects related to the intrinsic pleasantness factor. For the second experiment in which intrinsic pleasant-ness and goal conduciveness were manipulated, the results confirmed that neuronal processing of intrinsic pleasantness precedes the effects related to goal conduciveness checks (see Grandjean and Scherer 2008). The frequency analyses revealed late effects in the gamma band (not present in the analyses of unfiltered ERPs), indicating an effect of goal conduciveness on the so-called induced gamma (Tallon–Baudry *et al.* 1996) at about 600 ms after the onset of the stimuli, sug-gesting that a high level of cognitive processing is involved in this type of appraisal. The results of these two experiments (Grandjean and Scherer 2008) support the CPM predictions and suggest that novelty and intrinsic pleasantness may be appraised early, on an unconscious, automatic, and possibly schematic level, whereas goal conduciveness tends to be evaluated later in the sequence, on a conscious, controlled, and possibly propositional level.

Synchronization

Also of interest in the analogy between the visual system and our theory of the emotional system is that the classical model in vision has difficulties explaining the so-called binding problem. Indeed, to obtain the unified conscious experience that is characteristic of scene perception and to identify objects presented at the same time, it is necessary to bind all the processed features that belong to the same object together. The hypothesis of a single convergence centre that would allow this binding has failed (see Singer 1999*a*). Results from intracortical recording in animals and EEG in humans (see Tallon–Baudry and Bertrand 1999) indicate that the synchronization of oscillatory responses could reflect a binding mechanism rather than a single area. It is important to highlight this point because the search for a single integration structure (such as the 'glande pinéale' of Descartes; Descartes 1649) for conscious perception of emotion might fail, as it failed for vision, and is consistent with the notion of component synchronization as an underlying mechanism for conscious feelings.

Several lines of research on brain-damaged patients or normal participants clearly indicate that both the prefrontal cortex (PFC)—in particular the orbitofrontal cortex (OFC) and the ventrome-dial prefrontal cortex (VMPFC)—and the amygdala are critically involved in emotional process-ing, but the specific levels of processing and types of computations that are performed in these regions are not clearly understood (Davidson and Irwin 1999; Koenigs *et al.* 2007; Rolls 1999; Sander *et al.* 2003). In particular, the important anatomical connectivity between these two regions of the PFC and several nuclei of the amygdala suggests a functional interaction between represen-tations computed in the OFC, VMPFC, and amygdala rather than a functional dissociation between regions of the PFC and the amygdala. For example, Davidson and collaborators (2000) proposed that the mechanism underlying suppression of negative emotion is via an inhibitory connection from regions of the PFC, probably the OFC, to the amygdala. Bilateral anatomical connections between the medial part of the orbitofrontal regions and the amygdala have been recently confirmed in monkey brains (Ghashghaei *et al.* 2007). The functional meanings of these interacting distributed neuronal networks between the amygdala and medial OFC are still not clear. Based on these recent findings of strong anatomical connections between the two regions, we suggest that the latter might form a functional unit involved in the computation of behavioural strategies or action tendencies elicited by emotional perception. Several pieces of evidence indicate that the neuronal synchronization of electric activity between two or more neuronal assemblies is necessary to allow the communication between distant or local neural networks. In particular, Fries (2005) has proposed the communication through coherence (CTC) model, which implies that phase coherence underlies neuronal communication: neuronal assemblies have to be in syn-chronization to exchange information. Based on this model we predict that the amygdala and the

OFC have to be in synchronization to be able to exchange information. Previous findings suggest that neuronal synchronization may indeed be necessary to process emotional information. For example, Luo *et al.* (2007) reported synchronization between the thalamus/hypothalamus and the amygdala in response to facial threat. Distant synchronization between hippocampus and amygdala has also been shown during various stages of fear memory (Narayanan *et al.* 2007). Recently, neuronal synchronizations have been demonstrated between the ventral striatum and the amygdala in the gamma band in rats suggesting the existence of another kind of functional unit involved in emotional processing, especially in reward learning (Popescu *et al.* 2009).

The results of these studies can be interpreted as evidence that different neuronal assemblies, representing different levels of processing in the brain, work in conjunction to assess input of high significance for an individual. This suggestion is reminiscent of the assumption of massive parallel processing in neural network models and is consistent with a recent proposal of a neural network model of emotional consciousness in which emotional coherence, through interactions among multiple brain areas, needs to be achieved for emotional consciousness to emerge (Thagard and Aubie 2008). These synchronizations could occur at different levels including local and distant neuronal synchronies. We suggest that local synchronies, in a specific neuronal network, are necessary to achieve preliminary closure and send information to another neuronal network. For example, to process information relative to the state of the body during an emotional episode, the synchronization of neuronal assemblies inside the insula would be necessary. When a stable representation emerges from this neuronal network, the information might be sent to another part of the brain, to prefrontal brain areas for example (inducing a specific body representation in working memory). In this example, local synchronization would be necessary to build a stable representation, and distant neuronal synchronization would be necessary to exchange this information with another functional unit, here the body consciousness state in working memory. The local synchronies should occur at high frequencies while the distant synchronies would be expected at lower frequencies (Fries 2005).

These empirical findings of neuronal synchronization in the human brain in response to emotional stimuli highlight the importance of the functional coupling between different distant and local neuronal assemblies, and suggest continuous cross-talk between different brain regions during the processing of emotional stimuli. Beyond the specialization and the modular model, the connectivity of different neuronal populations involved in a given decoding (or encoding) would be subserved by neuronal synchronization allowing the different neuronal subpopulations to exchange information and then to build up an integrated representation; this kind of phenomenon should be taken into account while designing artificial systems able of processing or expressing emotions.

Conclusion and perspectives

In this chapter, we have used the cognitive neuroscience approach in order to discuss how one can learn from the emotional brain in order to synthesize an affectively competent agent. The rationale that has structured our approach is as follows: (1) affectively competent artificial agents are agents that perform affective computing; (2) affective computing is always performed on the basis of computational models; (3) computational models are designed on the basis of several constraints, including biological and psychological plausibility; and (4) the aim of cognitive neuroscience is to create explicit models that are testable both in terms of their psychological validity and their neuro-architecture.

We have discussed four aspects for which investigation may follow this rationale, namely: (1) domain specialization; (2) levels of processing; (3) temporal dynamics; and (4) synchronization.

Most of these aspects have been illustrated using the appraisal perspective on emotion, and with a particular interest in the amygdala. We have chosen the amygdala for two reasons. First, the amygdala is the region in the emotional brain that has received the most attention from cognitive neuroscientists. Second, it has been suggested that the amygdala is critically involved in relevance detection, which is arguably the most important appraisal mechanism because relevance is often considered as a condition *sine qua non* of emotion elicitation. Concerning the amygdala, one can hope that future computational models could continue the work started by Armony and colleagues (Armony *et al.* 1995, 1997) and test the alternative hypotheses concerning its function in affectively competent artificial agents. Indeed, in order to accommodate the apparently multifaceted aspects of amygdala functions, at least two alternative hypotheses are possible. One kind of explanation might be that the amygdala can implement as many processes as those directly suggested by the variety of experimental results. According to this view, some subregions within the amygdala might still be considered to implement a specific fear module, whereas other parts might subserve distinct processes, such as intensity coding. Alternatively, another kind of explanation is that an extensive analysis of the different types of stimuli and tasks associated with amygdala involvement may point to a common computational profile. Along this line, a conceptual analysis of the domain and level of processing of the amygdala suggests that the function of the amygdala is best characterized as a default detector of stimuli appraised as relevant given the current individual's goals, needs, values, and concerns. Unfortunately, it is still not possible to draw straightforward conclusions about the functional specialization of the amygdala subnuclei, neither from lesion nor from brain imaging studies in humans. This is why computational models might be particularly relevant at the present time. Therefore, advances in neural network modelling, together with methodological advances in spatial and temporal imaging of the human amygdala, will certainly be extremely precious in order to provide an integrative framework capable of incorporating the current variety of experimental results on amygdala sensitivity to relevant stimuli, including those concerning the precise neuronal circuitry involved in fear learning (see Phelps and LeDoux 2005) and reward processing (see Baxter and Murray 2002). Identifying the neural pathways and temporal dynamics that modulate the human amygdala (e.g. dual route or two-stage architecture), the internuclei connections within the amygdala, and how it interacts with other neural networks of specific cognitive systems remains a conceptual and methodological challenge in understanding how the amygdala is able to play such a central and integrative role in emotional processing.

We feel that the amygdala is an excellent example with which to illustrate the two major options that one can choose from in order to model an affectively competent agent. The first option is to design each basic emotion as independent from any other basic emotion by using a modular approach to emotion (e.g. Öhman and Mineka 2001). The second option is to design common mechanisms and components for all emotions, and then consider unitary emotions as specific profiles of activations of the overall system (e.g. Sander *et al.* 2005; Chapter 2.1, this volume). With this respect, depending on the option chosen, the functional architecture of the amygdala may be used as a basis to model either fear or relevance detection. We have argued in this chapter that the second option is more promising, although certainly more complex. A useful way to describe the basic emotion model is to use the metaphor of basic tastes. Indeed, similar to the fact that the dominant model in taste science is the basic tastes model (see Erickson 2008), the dominant model of emotion during the last century, and probably still the most influential in current emotion research, is the basic emotions model (see Ekman 1992, 1999; Izard 2007). Theorists differ on the number and nature of basic emotions that they propose, but the six following ones are often included: anger; joy; sadness; fear; surprise; and disgust (see Ortony and Turner 1990). These basic emotions, which are also sometimes called primary or fundamental emotions (see Ortony and Turner 1990), are often conceptualized as affect programs that are triggered by specific eliciting conditions to produce emotion-specific response patterns such as prototypical facial expressions, physiological reactions, and action tendencies, and for which specific neural systems exist in the brain (for discussion, see Grandjean *et al.* 2008; Ortony and Turner 1990). Basic emotions are typically being characterized in this tradition as innate, easy, categorical, and immediate (see Russell 2003; Russell *et al.* 2003). It is striking that a very influential representative of the basic emotions model made the explicit analogy between basic emotions and basic tastes as an argument for the existence of basic emotions (Izard 2007). Indeed, Izard (2007) argued that 'It is possible to argue by analogy that the capacity to discriminate among basic-emotion feeling states, like discriminating among basic tastes, is innate and invariant across the lifespan' and, importantly, that 'the data relating to the underlying neural and behavioural processes suggest that the emergence of discriminable basic emotion feelings is analogous to that for basic tastes (...)'. Interestingly, the notion of 'basic tastes' is highly debated, with scholars in the field suggesting that this notion corresponds to a postulate that has never been scientifically validated (see Erickson 2008). If this were to be the case, Izard's (2007) analogy would be misleading for anyone who would aim at designing an affectively competent agent using the basic emotion approach.

The face and voice of emotions: The expression of emotions

Tanja Bänziger, Stéphane With, and Susanne Kaiser

Summary

Expressions of emotions or affects are omnipresent in our daily lives, but still constitute complex and difficult objects for research. Views on emotional expressions will vary widely depending on the researchers' perspectives and the more or less explicit models/theories they have adopted in their work.

Facial and vocal expressions are often conceptualized as the outward (observable) manifestations of more abstract and more 'hypothetical' emotions (or affects), which themselves cannot be measured, quantified, or objectively observed. This view is also reflected in research on human–machine interactions, for example, in cases where the interest is set on the facial or vocal expressions of the human user in order to assess his or her dis/satisfaction with or—more generally—his or her attitude(s) towards the system he or she is using. However, only a few theoretical models offer detailed descriptions regarding the potential associations between a number of behavioural displays and underlying emotional reactions. This chapter introduces those models and their respective predictions. It furthermore presents an overview of the empirical data supporting this view and discusses the implications of the models and findings for affective computing.

Researchers interested in non-verbal communication will often put forward a different perspective. Emotional expressions have doubtlessly become available for social communication, more or less independently of the presence of genuine emotional reactions. Genuine outward signs of comfort/contentment or discomfort/distress are present in newborn human beings and are essential for their survival (to get attention, help, and protection from the caregiver). However, already in infants and toddlers, they will quickly acquire more and more communication value and will get gradually controlled and manipulated in order to influence the behaviour of others (in order to obtain, for instance, compassion or help).

In this second perspective, emotional expressions are more or less 'detached' from genuine emotional reactions. They can (but need not) be manipulated (consciously or unconsciously) by the sender depending on his/her goals, the context of production of the expression, and the status or characteristics of the receiver(s). This view is represented in research on human–machine interactions, for example, when the focus is set on specific communication contexts and especially when the goal is to produce an emotionally believable agent (i.e. a computer interface that displays adequate expressions in order to create a specific emotional impression on a human user in a strategic manner).

In humans, the more or less strategic or automatized regulation of emotional displays (in order to display or to suppress expressions given a specific context) opens the issue of the variability of the expressions displayed and their interpretation in different contexts. This chapter reviews some of the available evidence on sender-, receiver-, and context-dependent production of emotional displays. It also considers how different production contexts influence the emotional attributions of receivers and examines the implications of this line of research for affective computing.

Introduction

Behavioural manifestations of emotions are of primary interest for many researchers. *A priori*, they can be observed and investigated with more ease than other components of emotional responses that are less readily accessible to the researcher (such as emotional feelings, physiological reactions or neurological processes). Yet, in many ways, emotional expressions remain mysterious and represent a challenge for emotion research. We still can endorse the following quote by Charles Darwin, first published in 1872.

> It has often struck me as a curious fact that so many shades of expression are instantly recognized without any conscious process of analysis on our part. No one, I believe, can clearly describe a sullen or sly expression; yet many observers are unanimous that these expressions can be recognized in the various races of man. […] So it is with many other expressions, of which I have had practical experience in the trouble requisite in instructing others what points to observe.

[Darwin 1872/1998, p. 355]

This quote hints to a difficulty that often underlies psychological research. Because we—as humans and as researchers—all understand emotions, because we all produce emotional displays in our daily lives, we are tempted to believe that we are natural experts and easily can get the hang of such phenomena. Unfortunately, this is an illusion; emotional expressions are complex, fleeting, and difficult objects to study, and research in this field can be limited by preconceptions or by restrictive and sometimes implicit models. One of our goals in this chapter will be to outline the main conceptions reflected in various research perspectives. Many of the most influential concepts and models have been presented by their authors as being mutually exclusive. However, and especially with respect to their relevance for affective computing, these models are better understood as being complementary. Therefore, the chapter will describe the strengths and the limitations of each model and present an integrated approach applying a *Brunswikian lens* model to emotional expressions. Brunswik's lens model allows a separation between distal indicators on the part of the sender and proximal percepts on the part of the observer (Brunswik 1956; Scherer 1978). Thus, it can be applied to questions of how emotions are expressed (encoding) and how emotional expressions are perceived (decoding). Starting from the description of two major conceptions of emotional expressions, this chapter describes the methodological and theoretical challenges for emotion synthesis and affective user modelling (see also Kaiser and Wehrle 2008).

We propose to distinguish two conceptions of emotional expressions, on a functional level. On the one hand, *emotional expressions* seen as *symptoms* (outward manifestations) of internal emotional states and, on the other hand, *emotional displays* seen as *social signals* (elements of interpersonal communication). This distinction is relatively often outlined in other—more elaborated—theoretical accounts. For example, Scherer (1985; Chapters 1.1 and 3.2, this volume) recurrently stressed this distinction on the level of the underlying determinants of the expressions. In his account, internal determinants (the emotion elicited in an individual) *push* the expression in a given configuration, while external determinants (the social context) may *pull* the expression into another direction. Similarly, Ekman (1973) proposed to distinguish prototypical emotional expressions, reflecting inborn neuromotor programs, from expressions modified by culture-specific display rules. Although this dual function of (and dual influence on) emotional expressions is well accepted and rather well documented, there are also recurrent controversies or debates on the nature of emotional expressions. Are facial/vocal displays accurate indicators of emotions? Are they universal or culture-specific? Do prototypical expressions occur in social interactions outside the laboratory? (See Elfenbein and Ambady 2002; Keltner *et al.* 2003 for a review on facial expressions; see Juslin and Laukka 2003; Scherer 2003 for a review on vocal expressions.) There is no simple answer to those questions because emotional expressions/displays are multifaceted, with universal as well as culture-specific components, reflecting internal emotional feelings as well as adjustments to social demands.

In this contribution, we take for granted that both conceptions—emotional expressions as symptoms of internal states and emotional displays as social signals (with or without correspondence to an internal emotional state)—are equally valid and we structure this chapter by addressing: first, emotional expressions conceived as symptoms of internal emotional states and, second, emotional displays conceived as social signals. However, we also want to emphasize again that the two conceptions should not be seen as conflicting, but rather as complementary. Sometimes emotional displays required in specific social settings will match spontaneous expressions of internal emotional states occurring in those settings and won't require any adjustments. On other occasions, emotional displays will be used consciously or unconsciously (strategically or not) to signal (social) intentions or action readiness. In many cases 'intentions' or 'action tendencies' are not disconnected from emotional reactions. For example, a threat display produced to unsettle an opponent by signalling an intention to strike will in many cases also reflect a very genuine anger reaction in the sender. Finally, some socially required displays will be totally detached from underlying emotional reactions. This typically happens when requests to produce 'polite' behaviour overrule spontaneous reactions that are regarded as socially inadequate (e.g. a person may be socially required to look happy when actually disappointed after receiving a gift). In this latter case, it will be especially important to acknowledge the influence of (1) internal determinants (emotions) and (2) external social demands on the display, in order to account for the facial or vocal behaviour of the sender.

The present volume addresses emotion research in affective computing, with an emphasis on emotional competence in human–machine interactions. Because the focus is set on *interactions*, it seems likely that most readers will be prone to consider emotional displays as social signals. The emphasis on *emotional competence* further accentuates this assumption, since a 'competent' emotional display is likely to be defined with respect to (sociocultural) display rules (see Chapter 1.1, this volume). Nevertheless, the conception of emotional expressions as symptoms of internal states is at least as prevalent as the social signal conception in affective computing. In this chapter, we will consider how both perspectives can contribute valuable insights on different facets of emotional expressions and will attempt to describe their relevance for affective computing.

The quote by Darwin given at the beginning of this chapter points to a contrast between the ability to automatically and easily attribute affective states to a sender and the difficulty in describing the cues used to make such attributions. It appears reasonable to assume that, whenever emotional attributions can be reliably made, we ought to be able to also uncover the features of the expressions that allow making those inferences. Failure to do so should alert us to the insufficiency of the observations, measures, or descriptions we are using. Furthermore, although there is plenty of data showing that people can indeed accurately identify emotions experienced by others on the basis of their non-verbal displays alone, we should not assume *a priori* that this is always the case (not for all emotions, all social contexts, all persons, etc). Scherer (1978, 2003) proposed distinguishing several steps in the communication process using a *Brunswikian lens framework*. The lens model integrates the study of the production (*encoding*) and of the perception (*decoding*) of emotional expressions. Production and perception are otherwise most often addressed separately by researchers and are also sometimes seen as interchangeable or equivalent.

For example, studies that are essentially centred on production of emotional expressions (e.g. describing facial or vocal features associated with emotions in senders, or questioning the universal/culture specific nature of emotions and emotional expressions) will often rely partly on perception to ensure that emotions are actually communicated in the facial or vocal material under examination. In contrast, the Brunswikian lens view reminds us that an emotion might be reliably attributed to a facial or a vocal display, despite the fact that this emotion might not be present in the sender, and, conversely, that, when receivers cannot reliably attribute emotions to senders, this does not demonstrate that senders do not experience or express emotions.

Obviously *encoding* is taking place on the side of the sender (of an emotional expression) and is more directly related to the conception of expressions as symptoms of internal emotional states, while *decoding* is taking place one the side of the receiver (addressee of an emotional expression) and is more directly related to the conception of expressions as social signals. Nevertheless, we claim that, independently of a main focus on encoding or on decoding processes, on synthesis of emotional expression or on automatic recognition, internal determinants and social determinants act on emotional expressions and both are relevant and important to consider. For example, if we are interested in designing an automatic recognition system in order to detect anger or fear in human users of the system, we should be interested principally in how humans produce (express or display) fear and anger. What expressions are perceived as fearful or angry by most people is not essential for our goal, unless we assume that expression and perception are perfectly matched (i.e. the human perception can be our benchmark but only if we assume that it is accurate). But we should be aware that people can express/display fear and anger as symptoms of internal states and as social signals directed to others (to alert them or warn them). Internal and external determinants act on the expressions/displays the system will have to recognize. In some cases, the two functions will be fulfilled by the same expression, but there could also be cases where this overlap is less present; some specific cues might reflect the internal state (fear or anger response) while other behaviours might be called for in order to fulfil the social signalling function (e.g. a person might try to convey an impression of self-control to others even when reaching considerable levels of panic or exasperation). Hence, although automatic recognition is concerned principally with how humans express emotions (rather than with how they perceive them), the expressions can be influenced by the social requirements of the situation, i.e. by perceptions and attributions real or imaginary receivers might form on the expressions.

Emotional expressions as symptoms of internal states

Facial and vocal expressions are often conceptualized as the outward (observable) manifestations of 'hypothetical' internal states—emotions (or affects)—that themselves cannot be measured, quantified, or objectively observed. Different theoretical conceptions of emotional reactions result in different models to explain the generation of emotional expressions and their relationship to the more global emotional reaction. In the following paragraphs we will briefly outline three models that have been used in the literature and in empirical studies to relate non-verbal expressions to emotions. We will then examine some elements of empirical support to the conception of *expressions as symptoms of emotions* and finally discuss the relevance of this perspective for affective computing and especially for the implementation of emotional competence in human–machine interactions.

Models used to account for emotional expressions

Many models of emotional reactions have been proposed. Some of them were even formulated with a specific intention to allow computational implementation (e.g. Oatley and

Johnson-Laird 1987; Ortony *et al.* 1988). Yet few models extensively address the issue of expressive response patterns. On a theoretical level, the generation of an emotional response is most often described without including elements that would allow a prediction of how this response will be manifested in expressive behaviour. However a few models do formulate such predictions (see also Chapters 1.1 and 3.2).

The most well known predictions for facial expressions have been proposed in the framework of *basic emotion models*. These models—inspired by a Darwinian perspective—state that a specific type of situation or event triggers a specific affect program and produces characteristic expression patterns (Ekman 1972, 1992, 2003c; Izard 1977, 1992). Although Ekman (1999) has acknowledged that affect programs might be executed only partially, the emphasis is clearly set on prototypical situations (or events) that elicit basic emotions and corresponding prototypical expressions. The facial action coding system (FACS, Ekman and Friesen, 1978; Cohn *et al.* 2007) was developed in this tradition and was used to formulate predictions regarding prototypical emotional expressions in the form of combinations of facial action units (Ekman 2003c; Ekman and Rosenberg 2005).

Cognitive appraisal models on the other hand emphasize interindividual variability in the elicitation of emotional reactions. In these models, the focus is set on the evaluation (appraisal) of a situation or an event by an individual and on the reactions—including expressive reactions— elicited when a situation is appraised as relevant for (the goals of) the individual (Chapter 3.2, this volume; Scherer *et al.* 2001). The most detailed predictions regarding the relationship between appraisals and expressive behaviours were formulated by Scherer (1987; see also Scherer and Ellgring 2007a), who relates the *sequential appraisal checks* postulated in his *component process model* (Scherer 2001) to expressive patterns, not only in facial expressions but also in vocal expressions (Scherer 1986).

Predictions of basic emotion models and the predictions formulated by Scherer differ in several aspects. Notably, expressive patterns are related to external triggers (prototypical situations or events) in basic emotion models, whereas, in the perspective of an appraisal model, expressive patterns result from internal appraisal outcomes and cannot be directly related to a type of situation or event. Furthermore, Scherer's component process model makes specific predictions on the dynamic unfolding of the expressive behaviour related to sequential appraisal checks, whereas the notion of expressive prototypes assumes only configurations, without detailed predictions regarding the temporal aspects or the sequential occurrence of expressive patterns for a given emotion. Only a few studies specifically addressed some of the differential predictions formulated by Scherer and by proponents of basic emotion models (Wehrle *et al.* 2000; Scherer and Ellgring 2007a,b) and more work in this area is needed in order to test and refine predictions.

Although Darwin and, more recently, Tomkins (1984) showed a strong interest in emotional vocalizations, it should also be noted that most theoretical and empirical developments in the framework of basic emotion models have focused on facial expressions only. The study of vocal expressions has been relatively neglected and, except for Scherer's predictions and empirical studies (Scherer 1986, 2003; Banse and Scherer 1996), not much research has been driven by theory in this field. A corollary of this lack of theoretical developments has been the difficulty in comparing results of empirical work using widely different definitions of emotional states (Scherer 2003; Scherer *et al.* 2003).

Dimensional models have also been used to account for emotional expressions, although theoretical formulations in this tradition have never included specific predictions on the behavioural displays to be expected for different emotional states. A few studies have showed that similarity ratings for facial expressions (Russell and Bullock 1986) as well as for vocal expressions (Green and Cliff 1975) could be explained by underlying dimensions of arousal and valence.

Russell (1997b) argued that facial expressions reflect *core affect*, a feeling state that, according to his model, is best described by a position in a valence × arousal space. In this perspective, categorical labels (basic emotion descriptors: 'fear', 'anger', 'happiness', etc.) are allocated to expressions on the basis of contextual cues (e.g. aspects of the situation in which the expression is produced or verbal information) and are not primarily derived from the expressions themselves. Furthermore, *arousal models* are sometimes used to describe vocal emotional expressions. *Arousal models* are initially focused on the physiological component of the emotional response (activity of the autonomic nervous system), but can be easily transposed to vocal expressions. Increased emotional arousal is predicted to result in deeper and faster respiration and in increased muscle tension, which in turn are likely to result in increased pitch and more intense vocalizations (Scherer *et al.* 2003). It is, in fact, rather well accepted that vocal expressions reflect emotional arousal. What has been questioned is the capacity of vocal expressions to differentiate other emotional dimensions or categories (Banse and Scherer 1996).

The specific associations between emotions and non-verbal cues (in face or voice) have also been a matter of debate. In the view of *basic emotion* models, phylogenetically evolved, hardwired motor programs are executed to produce specific expressions reflecting specific emotions. But other more flexible associations have been proposed as well. For example, Scherer (1982, 2003) has suggested modelling the relationship between the emotions and expressive cues in a Brunswikian lens perspective. In this view, the relationship between the underlying emotion and the expressive cues is probabilistic and many redundant cues are potentially available for the expression and communication of emotion. In the basic emotion view, the association is deterministic and allows only for little variations (e.g. a motor program might be carried out only partially). In the Brunswikian probabilistic view, several expressive cues are related independently to the emotional reaction; each with a defined probability but none of them is necessarily associated to a given emotion (Juslin and Bänziger 2009). For example, we can speculate that several behaviours are associated with feeling 'sad', e.g. crying but also facial movements. A typical association of facial movements that has been described as a manifestation of 'sadness' is pulling together and raising the inner eyebrows; the resulting oblique shape of the brows is typically used by cartoonists to draw 'sad' faces. There are also vocal features: in the voice 'sadness' is typically manifested in flattened intonation, softer voice, and slower speech. Hence a relatively wide range of redundant cues might all be used as indicators of 'sadness'. But if the association between 'sadness' and any of those cues is a probabilistic one, none of those cues are necessarily and always associated with 'sadness'. 'Sadness' might be manifested sometimes with or without tears, with or without oblique eyebrows, etc. This conception of a probabilistic association between expressive cues and emotions has several implications. In terms of signalling, such a system would not be economical (as several cues convey the same information) but would be very robust. Different configurations of cues could reflect the same emotion. Perfect consistency would not be expected and not be required in order to communicate emotions. It should be noted that this probabilistic view of the association between emotions and expressive cues not only opposes the notion of fixed-action patterns (motor programs) in expressive behaviour but also challenges the need for *gestalts* to recognize emotional expressions.

Empirical findings

In this section we will review some evidence of the existence of reliable indicators of emotions in facial and vocal behaviour. More extensive reviews can be found in other books or meta-analyses (for reviews on vocal expressions see Elfenbein and Ambady 2002; Keltner *et al.* 2003; Ekman and Rosenberg 2005 for reviews on facial expressions; Juslin and Laukka 2003; Scherer 2003; Scherer *et al.* 2003). Overall, researchers have concluded that non-verbal expressions can be accurate indicators of emotions. For example, 'facial expression is not a noisy system but instead provides information about an individual's emotion' (Keltner *et al.* 2003, p. 416). Relations between expressions and other components of emotions have been shown in a variety of studies. In particular, correspondence with expressions has been shown for (self-reported) emotional feeling and for physiological reactions. Relatively more evidence has been collected for facial expressions than for vocal expressions, but evidence exists for both channels (e.g. Johnstone *et al.* 2007).

Much research was driven by the notion that (patterns of) facial and vocal cues ought to be associated with specific emotions. Reviews of the literature show that such associations do exist but that they are less simple than might be expected.

Facial expressions

For facial expressions, the bulk of the evidence was obtained in *perception studies* (relying on *recognition* of expressions). A considerable body of research supports the conclusion that correct identification of a limited number of emotion categories through facial expressions is relatively invariant across cultures. Classic studies by Ekman, Izard, and colleagues (Ekman 1972; Ekman *et al.* 1987; Izard 1971) have demonstrated that prototypical displays of six emotions (surprise, anger, disgust, fear, sadness, and happiness), possibly seven (contempt; Ekman and Friesen 1986; Ekman and Heider 1988) are recognized well above chance level, even across cultures that have had relatively little contact with each other.

It should be noted however that most studies investigating the recognition of facial expressions have used static presentation of intense expressions. The expressions are generally posed by actors who follow strict guidelines on how to produce each specific configuration of cues (Ekman 2007). Moreover, faces are presented in isolation, and pre-selected for maximum discriminability (Barrett *et al.* 2007). Drastic drops or even disappearance of judge's agreement for specific emotion labels have been reported when spontaneously produced facial expressions were used (Motley and Camden 1988; Motley 1993; Yik *et al.* 1998).

There are indications that naturally occurring facial expressions are of weaker intensity, less clear cut, and their interpretation more elusive and ambiguous than posed expressions (Russell 1997*b*). Several *production studies* using well established coding systems—mainly FACS[1]— to specify the configurations of spontaneously produced expressions (including also actor portrayals) report little evidence for the existence of specific prototypical expressions predicted by proponents of Ekman's theory of emotions (Matias and Cohn 1993; Camras *et al.* 2002; Scherer and Ellgring 2007*a*).

In recent years, several further limitations of the study of prototypical expressions have been outlined. A few studies have investigated the combination of facial expression with other non-verbal signals and showed that head orientation (Hess *et al.* 2007), body postures (Aviezer *et al.* 2008), head positions (Krumhuber *et al.* 2007*a*), and gaze orientation (Reginald and Kleck 2005) can all have a modulating impact on the interpretation of facial expressions presented in isolation. Other results suggest that, in social settings, the verbal communication of the circumstances and evaluation of a situation serve to reduce the uncertainty inherent to some facial expressions and constrain their meaning to allow for quick categorization of emotion (Lindquist *et al.* 2006).

---

[1] The Facial Action Coding System or FACS (Ekman and Friesen 1978; Ekman *et al.*2002) is a comprehensive and anatomically based manual coding system designed for the measurement of all visually distinguishable facial activity on the basis 44 action units (AUs) and action descriptors (ADs) as well as several additional categories of head and eyes positions and movements.

Even researchers whose work in the field of facial expressions has relied extensively on judgement studies with static stimuli recognize that studying the natural dynamics of facial expressions could provide information about a sender's mental state that is not available in static displays (Ekman 1982). Indeed, evidence is starting to accumulate concerning the importance of the timing of facial actions on an observer's categorization of subtle expressions (Ambadar *et al.* 2005; Bould and Morris 2008), judgement of genuineness (Krumhuber and Kappas 2005), and judgement of trustworthiness (Krumhuber *et al.* 2007). Moreover, Smith and Scott (1997) have suggested that single components of facial expression might convey meaningful information at a more molecular level than full blown prototypical expressions. In the same line of reasoning, Scherer argues that the temporal sequence in which individual facial displays unfold might reflect a sender's ongoing cognitive processing of emotionally relevant stimuli (Scherer 1992). Even though empirical evidence supporting this view is still scarce (but see Lanctôt and Hess 2007; Aue and Scherer 2008; Delplanque *et al.* 2009), it opens up the possibility that partial expressions that would be seen as meaningless when considered in isolation could, in fact, still be quite informative when preceding and following actions are also taken into consideration.

Despite the current limitations of available results, it appears that there is support for the notion that a number of facial cues might be reliably associated with emotions. However, a majority of studies have used recognition to link facial expressions with emotional attributions rather than with independently identified states in the senders. It is important to observe also that facial expressions are influenced by more than just emotions and probably take different forms in different contexts and that there is relatively little support for simple associations of emotions with prototypical expressions.

Vocal expressions

Vocal expressions have received less attention than facial expressions overall, but a number of studies have aimed at identifying vocal features associated with various emotions. According to a review and meta-analysis of 104 studies performed by Juslin and Laukka (2003), a majority of studies (87%) involving vocal expressions of emotions used actor portrayals. In recent years, more applied studies have tended to include 'naturally occurring' expressions (e.g. Grimm *et al.* 2007; Devillers and Vidrascu 2007a) or experimentally induced expressions (e.g. Batliner *et al.* 2004). Such studies seldom have access to the emotional states experienced by the senders at the time of the recording and therefore most often rely on perception (attributions of expert or lay raters) to identify the emotions underlying the expressions.

The number of emotional states considered in a given study is variable; in most cases four or five categories are included. The categories most frequently considered are 'anger', 'fear', 'happiness', and 'sadness'. But a small number of studies have included more differentiated states (e.g. Banse and Scherer 1996; Burkhardt 2001; Frick 1986; Juslin and Laukka 2001; Katz 1998). Recent studies focusing on expressions recorded in 'natural settings' have been concerned with further emotional states as well. Pragmatically, emotions that are relevant for specific applications are more readily included in such studies (e.g. 'relief' in people contacting a call centre; Devillers and Vidrascu 2007a).

Many studies used acoustic measures to describe or to categorize vocal expressions. Most acoustic parameters are derived from fundamental frequency (F0), amplitude (intensity), or duration of the speech signals. Relatively many studies also include measures derived from spectral analyses (e.g. energy in various bands of the long-term average spectrum). Less frequently used measures include, for example, estimations of formant positions and bandwidths; precision of articulation can be estimated based on the distance between observed formant values for different vowels and the neutral 'schwa' (the closer the observed values are to the neutral reference, the less articulatory effort is involved). Cycle to cycle perturbations of F0 (jitter) or amplitude (shimmer) have been measured. Measures derived from the glottal source signal (estimated with inverse filtering techniques) have also been considered. The latter measures are used less frequently (although they are considered promising in terms of the categorization of emotional states) because they set requirements on the speech data that are not always compatible with the collection of realistic emotional speech.

Table 2.3.1 summarizes the results reported by Juslin and Laukka (2003). Their meta-analysis includes expressions of 'anger', 'fear', 'happiness', 'sadness', and 'tenderness'. The seven most frequently reported acoustic parameters are represented in the upper part of the table. Seven less frequent parameters are shown in the lower part of the table. Juslin and Laukka classified the

Table 2.3.1 Summary of results reviewed by Juslin and Laukka (2003, pp. 792–9). The proportion of studies reporting the result indicated in each cell of the table is shown in brackets

Parameter	Anger	Fear	Happiness	Sadness	Tenderness
Intensity (mean) (high–medium–low)	High (30/32)	High (11/22)	High (20/26)	Low (29/32)	Low (4/4)
Intensity variability (high–medium–low)	High (9/12)	High (7/12)	High (8/13)	Low (8/11)	
F0 (mean) (high–medium–low)	High (33/43)	High (28/39)	High (34/38)	Low (40/45)	Low (4/5)
F0 variability (high–medium–low))	High (27/35)	Low (17/32)	High (33/36)	Low (31/34)	Low (5/5)
F0 contours (rising–falling)	Rising (6/8)	Rising (6/6)	Rising (7/7)	Falling (11/11)	Falling (3/4)
High-frequency energy (high–medium–low)	High (22/22)	High (8/16)	High (13/17)	Low (19/19)	Low (3/3)
Speech rate (fast–medium–slow)	Fast (28/35)	Fast (24/29)	Fast (22/33)	Slow (30/36)	Slow (3/4)
Microstructural regul.[b] (regular–irregular)	Irregular (3/3)	Irregular (2/2)	Regular (2/2)	Irregular (4/4)	Regular (1/1)
Proportion of pauses (large–medium–small)	Small (8/8)	Small (4/9)	Small (3/6)	Large (11/12)	Large (1/1)
Precision articulation (high–medium–low)	High (7/7)	?[a](6)	High (3/5)	Low (6/6)	Low (1/1)
Formant 1 (mean) (high–medium–low)	High (6/6)	Low (3/4)	High (5/6)	Low (5/6)	
Formant 1 (bandwidth) (narrow–wide)	Narrow (4/4)	Wide (2/2)	Narrow (2/3)	Wide (3/3)	
Jitter (high–low)	High (6/7)	?[a](8)	High (5/8)	Low (5/6)	
Glottal waveform[c] (steep–rounded)	Steep (6/6)	Rounded (4/6)	Steep (2/2)	Rounded (4/4)	

[a] Equal numbers of studies reported different levels for this emotion and this vocal description (the number of studies is shown in brackets).
[b] Microstructural irregularities are defined as short-term irregularities of F0, intensity, and/or duration. Irregularities are theoretically associated with negative emotions.
[c] The glottal source is estimated using inverse filtering (Laukkanen, Vilkman, Alku, and Oksanen 1996).

results reported in a relatively large number of studies into three levels (e.g. high, medium, low intensity) or sometimes only two levels (e.g. raising versus falling F0 contours). For each acoustic parameter and each emotion we indicate the level most frequently reported in the studies examined by Juslin and Laukka. In parentheses, the first number is the count of the studies that reported this level, while the second number is the count of the studies that included this measure.

This table shows the relative use of different parameters used to describe different emotion categories in the studies reviewed by Juslin and Laukka (2003). Obviously, other acoustic parameters have been used and other emotions have been studied (for a full account see Juslin and Laukka 2003) but very little cumulative evidence is available for emotional states or parameters that have been less frequently considered. The table also allows us to see the relative consensus across studies. For some emotions and some acoustic features there was complete consensus (e.g. for 'anger', 22 studies out of 22 reported high levels of energy in the high frequency regions), whereas for other emotions and parameters there was much more divergence across results (e.g. for 'fear', 17 studies out of 32 report low F0 variability, while 15 studies reported either medium or high levels of F0 variability).

At this rather abstract level of description, the emotion discrimination achieved by the most frequently used measures (upper part of the table) is quite poor. This has also been reported in other reviews. The most usual acoustic measures, which sometimes yield interesting results in isolated studies, achieve only little emotional discrimination when the results are considered on a broader scale. Reviews often point to the fact that different measures might reflect a single underlying dimension of emotional arousal, with 'anger', 'fear', and 'happiness' being relatively high-aroused states, while sadness and tenderness involve less emotional arousal.

In contrast to this finding, *perception studies* report relatively high accuracy in emotion *recognition* based on vocal expressions. Although vocal communication of emotion appears to be somewhat less accurate than facial communication of emotion (e.g. Chapter 6.1, this volume), the communication works much better than what is suggested by the apparent lack of discrimination on the acoustic level. Several reviews of recognition studies point to consistent differences across emotions (Johnstone and Scherer 2000; Juslin and Laukka 2003; Scherer 2003). 'Sadness' and 'anger' are repeatedly recognized with higher accuracy than 'fear' and 'happiness'. The replication is striking, as different studies use variable definitions of emotions, as well as variable methods to record expressions and to gather ratings. Expressions of 'disgust' have been yielding especially low recognition accuracy in speech-based vocal expressions, but appear to be rather well communicated in *affect bursts* (Chapter 6.1, this volume; Hawk *et al.* 2009).

In view of the relatively good discrimination of emotional states by receivers and the relatively poor discrimination on the acoustic level, several potential explanations can be raised. One of them is that the acoustic measures used in this field are fairly good descriptors of the signals but don't account for perceptual processes (i.e. listeners extract information—for example, micro-events disrupting the speech—that is not captured by the acoustic features used to describe the signals). Another potential explanation might be that the emotional descriptors are too unspecific. A broad category such as 'anger' might include many nuances (irritation, rage, frustration, etc.) which all might result in different vocal expressions but could still be classified by receivers in the overarching 'anger' category. A further possibility is that a given emotion can result in more than one expressive pattern, even when it occurs in a very standard experimental context (i.e. under similar conditions of production and with the same audience). The latter hypothesis would be true if the non-verbal expression and communication of emotion is based on probabilistic associations between cues and emotions instead of the often-assumed prototype/gestalt view.

Other research

Aside from the numerous studies dedicated to the investigation of the association between facial or vocal cues and emotions or recognition of facial and vocal portrayals, a few other lines of research have been pursued.

For facial expressions, some work has focused on the association of expressions with emotional feelings and/or physiology, taking a proprioceptive feedback perspective (Levenson *et al.* 1990). In this perspective, expressions and feelings or physiology are seen as so tightly connected that the elicitation of a prototypical emotional expression might induce a corresponding feeling and/or a distinctive physiological response. This proposition has been supported by experimental work (Strack *et al.* 1988; Levenson *et al.* 1990; Soussignan 2002) and makes a strong case for the association between feelings, physiology, and expressions in the framework of emotional reactions.

Studies on lying and deception as well as some clinical studies furthermore suggest that facial or vocal expressions can be especially good indicators of emotions, when compared to other sources of information. There is, for example, research showing that in some instances a verbal report can be biased or disguised, while the non-verbal expression still provides information regarding the 'genuine' feelings or reactions of the sender. Ekman refers to 'leakage' of emotional cues when involuntary expressions of emotions are present despite a person's efforts to disguise them (Ekman *et al.* 1988; Ekman and Rosenberg 2005).

Other results suggest that, compared with physiological manifestations of emotions (peripheral measures reflecting the activity of the autonomous nervous system), facial expressions are more able to convey the emotional valence of a person's reaction to a given stimulation. The peripheral physiological activity might mostly reflect the presence of emotional arousal, while the facial expression would allow to assess if the reaction is positive/pleasant or negative/unpleasant (Dimberg 1990).

On the other hand, several theoretical postulates have been challenged by empirical results. One example can be found in Camras *et al.* (1996). They reported that prototypical emotional expressions in infants (5–7 months old) are produced in the absence of prototypical elicitors. Camras *et al.* (1996) investigated prototypical expressions of surprise that occurred, for instance, when an infant was reaching a desired object (i.e. not in response to a prototypical elicitor of surprise). They also reported that prototypical elicitors do not consistently result in prototypical expressions in infants (e.g. violation of expectations does not always produce an expression of surprise). Their observations are especially relevant since they were made on babies and it is unlikely that infants would have manipulated their expressions in order to disguise them (an explanation that is sometime invoked to account for similar results in adults). Other authors also report expressions in infants (4 months old) that are not situation-specific (Bennett *et al.* 2002; Scherer *et al.* 2004*b*).

This observation leads back to the issue of the type of emotional information reflected in the face or the voice. It has been argued that *basic emotions* (e.g. 'anger', 'fear', 'happiness'), *dimensions* (e.g. 'valence', 'arousal') and *cognitive appraisals* (e.g. 'relevance' of the elicitor for the sender, 'coping resources' of the sender) might be reflected in facial and in vocal expressions. The results of Camras *et al.* (1996) and Bennett *et al.* (2002) speak against a tight and systematic association between prototypical elicitors and prototypical expressions. This can be accounted for with the argument that the expected basic emotion was not elicited despite the presence of a prototypical elicitor and it raises the importance of the *appraisals* that mediate the response of an individual to a given stimulation. Few studies tried to compare predictions made by different models (e.g. Wehrle *et al.* 2000; Scherer and Ellgring 2007*a*; Laukka 2004). The validity of different models in terms of their capacity to account for a variety of observation is obviously an important issue. Nevertheless, it is probably equally important for applied research to take into account that different models might be simply more or less adapted for different applications.

Expressions as symptoms: relevance for affective computing

In the following paragraphs, we will address the relevance of different notions and findings derived from the study of human facial and vocal expressions for two major domains of affective computing (see also Wehrle and Kaiser 2000): (1) *automatic expression recognition* (identification of emotional reaction of users) and (2) *expression synthesis* (production of emotional expressions in animated intelligent agents). We will consider the validity of using expressions as accurate indicators (symptoms) of emotions in both domains and we will raise a number of specific issues in order to outline their importance for both domains.

Starting with *automatic recognition*, based on the elements outlined previously, we can assume that it is of interest for many applications to gain some insight into the emotional (i.e. also motivational) states of users. There are good reasons to believe that facial and vocal expressions can be seen as valid indicators of emotions and that they provide important informations about people's feelings, preferences, or even behavioural orientations. Non-deceptive emotional expressions could be very good predictors of, for example, satisfaction (or dissatisfaction) with the system or the service that the system provides. Thus the expressions of the human user might be used to get access to his or her feelings (or attitudes) and to predict relevant behavioural outcomes affecting the interaction with the system. We can further postulate that an *affectively competent* system ought to be able to make accurate inference about the emotions of its users by definition (since this capacity is seen as a prerequisite to other forms of emotional abilities; see Chapter 1.1, this volume).

Hence the goal seems valid, but its realization involves a few challenges. We will consider some aspects related to the emotional representations that can be used (*what* is it that an automatic recognition system has to recognize?) and aspects related to the encoding into expressive features (*how* is it expressed, *how* can an automatic classifier extract relevant information?).

What emotion representation is suited for automatic recognition?

Different models have been proposed to account for emotional reactions and their relationship with expressive behaviour. We outlined three types of models (basic emotion models, dimensional models, and appraisal models). Those models propose different representations of emotional states. Hence, depending on the model used, the task of the system would be to extract different information, e.g. it could attempt to discriminate between 'fear' and 'anger' (or other discrete categories), or it could try to assess a degree of emotional 'arousal' (or other emotional dimensions), or to estimate the relevance of a given situation/event as appraised by the user (or any other appraisals, such as the goal-conduciveness/obstructiveness, the appraised fairness/unfairness, etc).

At this date, the most widespread model remains the basic emotion model, i.e. the goal set for *automatic recognition* is most often to discriminate between a limited number of discrete emotional states. However, when considering empirical evidence, some limitations of this model become manifest. For example, the relationship postulated between prototypical situations and basic emotions (and their respective prototypical expressions) has been seriously challenged by the fact that on an empirical level it is often difficult to relate specific emotional expressions with specific emotional elicitors. On an even more general level, attempts to find prototypical patterns in spontaneously produced expressions have met only little success. We also mentioned earlier in this chapter that the categories that are typically used ('anger', 'fear', 'sadness', 'happiness', etc.)

might be too unspecific and might encompass a variety of differentiated states and differentiated expressions. The common features between, for example, 'anxiety' arising when thinking of an anticipated challenging task and a 'panic' response in an acute and immediate life-threatening situation are probably not to be found in their associated facial or vocal displays but rather on a more abstract conceptual level (both situations potentially elicit 'fear' or 'stress' responses as they both involve a form of threat). In complete contradiction with this notion, some authors have formed the hypothesis that discrete categories are not shown in facial or vocal expressions and that people infer them from other knowledge they gather on the context of the production of expressions that are themselves seen as relatively undifferentiated (Russell 1997b).

In summary, there are several models, which differ in their conceptions of emotions themselves and which ultimately question simplistic relationships between expressions and emotions (which appear as hypothetical and fuzzy concepts in the light of competing models). However we want to stress again that, although a simple one-to-one association between emotions and facial or vocal expressions is not supported, there still are indicators of emotional reactions in facial and vocal behaviour and they can be exploited by automatic recognition.

Pragmatically, we argue that, although the issues of the models that best account for emotional behaviours at large are of essential relevance to fundamental research, for specific applications those issues are not always relevant. What matters for specific systems is to make predictions about the relevant emotions (categories or emotional dimensions, or appraisals) that might occur in interaction with the system. It might well be that some systems could already be displaying sufficient emotional competence if they simply manage to accurately assess the presence/absence of whatever emotional reaction in a user, whereas for other applications it might be important to distinguish a mild irritation that could signal a dissatisfied user but with little consequences for the interaction, from a full blown angry response that might result in an interruption of the interaction with the system. However, in such a pragmatic view, it is also essential to consider the feasibility of a given goal (e.g. is it realistic to think that it will be possible to differentiate subtle variations in emotional states, when some models claim that expressions don't carry this kind of information about the states of senders). Unfortunately, this remains to be tested in the context of specific research questions that have not been fully addressed yet.

This is, however, an aspect where automatic recognition research has the opportunity to make significant contributions to fundamental science, for example, by testing more systematically which representations best account for the users' behaviours in a variety of contexts, e.g. comparing how efficiently the same set of facial or vocal cues can be used to extract alternative emotion representations in the same data set. An important prerequisite for this goal, however, would be that research on automatic recognition takes into account alternative models and their propositions regarding emotion representations.

How can expressive cues be used to detect emotions

For automatic recognition it seems important to consider not only *what* might be encoded in the face/voice, but also *how* it might be encoded. Automatic recognition sometimes relies on features and analyses that are empirically selected because they achieved good discrimination in related fields, e.g. for vocal expressions the first emotion classifiers used a technology developed for speech recognition. Nevertheless, there are some specific considerations deriving from fundamental research on emotional expressions that ought to be taken into account.

Specifically, we described in earlier sections that simple associations between emotions and prototypical configurations of cues (especially for the study of facial expressions, which has often been limited to the postulated configurations of basic emotion theories) are supported essentially by recognition studies. There is data showing that receivers reliably use certain expressive features to make emotional attributions. However, there is a lot less evidence for simple associations of emotions and expressions on the production side. Among the aspects that have been questioned we listed the limitations imposed by the methods available to extract and analyse expressive cues. For example, the timing of sequential expressive cues, i.e. the succession in time of expressive features, their relative duration, etc., is seldom considered but the few studies that examined such aspects showed promising results. With the same line of reasoning it might be that emotions are sometimes behaviourally manifested in extremely brief expressive 'events', a notion that has already been partially supported in the recent attention allocated to affect bursts (Scherer 1994*a*; Schröder 2003; Hawk *et al.* 2009) and their capacity to convey emotional meaning.

Research on automatic recognition ought to take those notions into account when attempting to develop methods for the extraction of emotional symptoms in facial or vocal expressions. There could be important contributions to fundamental research in terms of identifying the best indicators of emotional reactions if different approaches to cue utilization would be systematically considered, tested, and compared in automatic recognition research.

If we consider *expression synthesis*, it appears at first sight that it is a very valid goal for affective computing to consider how expressive patterns can convey emotional impressions. There are plenty of results showing that people readily attribute emotions to voices and faces and that they are fairly consistent in their attributions, despite the fact that those attributions can also be biased or manipulated. There are even results showing that very simplified cues (e.g. schematic faces; Öhman *et al.* 2001*b*) lead to emotional attributions and other reactions in the sender (e.g. schematic angry faces attract attention).

Nevertheless, it can be argued that the actual presence of an emotion model in a machine (robot, computer, embodied agent, etc.), reflected in emotional expressions similar to emotional expressions in humans, might be of relatively little relevance for the users who interact with such systems. For an intelligent system and taking a pragmatic stance, the most important aspect is that the users rate the *behaviour* of the system as *adequate* (i.e. adapted to the interaction). We can assume that users will (or will not) attribute emotions to an artificial system depending on their preconceived ideas and expectations about this system, much more than on the capacity of the system to generate patterns of expressive cues matching human expressions. Our speculation is that a user who is pre-inclined to allocate emotions to an artificial system (because they believe that the system ought to have and express emotions) will readily do so, based on minimal and simple cues emitted by the system. Whereas a user who does not expect emotions to be present or expressed by an artificial system will be reluctant to do so and might even judge emotional cues as inadequate if they are emitted by the system.

However many of the issues we have previously raised for automatic recognition can also be transposed to the development of emotional expression synthesis, in particular, the issue of the most functional emotion representation. Eventually, synthesis might become a tool to test predictions formulated by various models in recognition studies. Such tools are currently developed. For example FACSGen (Roesch *et al.*, in press) is a system designed to produce dynamic expressions on an agent face. The agent's expressions are implemented according to the specification of the facial action coding system (FACS; Ekman and Friesen 1978; Ekman *et al.* 2002). With FACSGen, a programmer can specify the onset, apex, and offset duration and intensities of each FACS action unit. This allows the user both to implement copies of naturally occurring dynamic expressions[2] and to test different predictions made by different emotion representation models.

---

2 Using timing parameters and facial configuration patterns identified in spontaneous expressions databases coded with FACS (see With and Kaiser 2009).

This example allows us to see that the other issues we have addressed such as the importance of the timing and sequencing of the cues are automatically taken into account in the framework of expression synthesis. On the other hand, we also mentioned that insufficient attention has been devoted so far to the possibility that redundant and interchangeable cues might express emotions. Most research has been focused on identifying expressive profiles, with a one-to-one understanding of the relationship between emotions and expressions (e.g. a prototypical expression for a basic emotion). However, a conceptually distinct emotion (e.g. sadness) might correspond to a variety of redundant expressive cues (e.g. stretched mouth, tears, frown, subdued, or jittery voice) that might be only partially present in specific occurrences and that might also appear in connection with other emotional states. There is a possibility that probabilistic associations between non-verbal cues and emotions will be more fruitful than strictly deterministic associations, both for generating expressions (synthesis) in humanoid computer systems and for implementing recognition rules (decoding the emotional state of the user). Currently, it seems that this notion is better accepted when it comes to recognition/inference of emotions in humans by machines, than when it comes to synthesis of emotional expressions by machines.

Emotional displays as social signals

Emotional expressions, even if they have evolved as part of emotional responses, have doubtless become available for social communication, more or less independently of the presence of genuine emotional reactions. There is evidence that emotions and emotional expressions are automatically regulated in social interactions and also that they can be strategically manipulated. Some authors have argued that, because of their function as social signals, emotional displays are primarily driven by the effects they have on receivers and have little or no connection with internal ('private') states of the sender. Although there is no doubt that emotional expressions are shaped by their social functions, there are no exhaustive models to account for the numerous factors that can be included in this perspective. In the following paragraphs we will present the dominating directions of research in this field and their most crucial findings. We will again conclude this section with some consideration on the relevance of those conceptions and findings for affective computing (affectively intelligent systems).

Effects on receivers

The reaction of the receiver is a crucial aspect in the perspective of emotional expressions as social signals. Independently of the question of the shaping of the expression by the social context, it is very well known and documented that emotional expressions are perceived by others and affect them in various ways.

Receivers can make many inferences about a sender from looking at their facial expressions or hearing their vocal expressions without any further information being available. Importantly, the voice and the face will allow them to form impressions not only of emotions but also of other characteristics of the senders, such as age, gender, health, attitudes, or personality. Some of these other attributions might be used when attributing emotions to a sender. For instance, the gender of the sender seems to be important when attributing emotions. This might be related to different expectations on emotions that are considered to be socially appropriate for women (e.g. sadness or fear) and emotions that are considered to be socially appropriate for men (e.g. anger) (Wallbott 1988; Widen and Russell 2002).

Furthermore, emotional expressions affect receivers in more implicit ways. Even subliminal perception (outside awareness) of facial expressions produces mimicry (imitation) of the expressions presented (Dimberg et al. 2000). Subliminal exposure to angry faces has been shown to increase skin conductance responses (Esteves *et al.* 1994), suggesting an unconscious orienting response towards the angry/threatening face. Similarly, Grandjean *et al.* (2005) showed that angry voices are processed even when attention is directed away from the angry/threatening voice. Overall, there is good evidence that emotional expressions affect the receivers' own emotional reactions and therefore might reorient attentional resources to the sender.

Expressions as social messages

Some authors who focused on emotional displays in social interaction have proposed that non-verbal expressions have very little to do with emotions altogether and would be better understood as displays signalling social intentions (social messages). According to this view, the face or the voice doesn't show anger or fear, but intentions to strike or to flee (Fridlund 1991). In this perspective we can also include the notion that the face or voice might carry information about the relationship that exists between the sender and the receiver (e.g. the voice or face could signal dominance or submission, compassion, liking, etc.) and the context in which the expression occurs (e.g. an expression that would be considered fearful with a focus on the sender, might be considered as signalling a danger in the environment).

The focus on the receiver and the social message is supported by the notion that in a social situation the 'private' emotional reaction is often not displayed and is replaced instead by a socially appropriate display. Fridlund and collaborators (Fridlund 1991; Fridlund *et al.* 1992) provided some evidence supporting this view. In a series of experimental studies, they showed that the expressions of participants in the laboratory varied more as a function of the presence of others than as a function of emotion inducing material (pictures or films). This view was however questioned by other authors who didn't replicate the larger influence of the audience on the expressions (Hess *et al.* 1995).

Following Fridlund, some authors (e.g. Krämer and Bente 2003) have even argued that emotions are not relevant at all in social interactions. In consequence, emotions would also not be relevant for interactions between humans and artificial agents. There is some truth in this idea, especially when focusing on perception of expressions. For example, an 'angry' face or an 'angry' voice is indeed a potential threat for a receiver. However, there is also very much evidence pointing to the fact that receivers do make emotional attributions when confronted with faces and voices. The 'angry' face might be perceived as a threat but—at the same time—the receiver will also form other attributions, and emotions are very prevalent attributions to faces and voices. Scherer and Grandjean (2008) showed, for example, that, on the level of the perception of emotional faces, social intentions are not the most prevalent attribution made by receivers.

Sociocultural influences on the production of expressions

We have already described in the preceding sections how expressions in infants have been used to argue against a very tight connection between prototypical elicitors and prototypical expressions. However, it should be noted that there is evidence of emotional displays in newborn babies and that those displays can be considered as reflecting emotional reactions (Stroufe 1996; Oster 2005). For example, facial expressions of 'disgust' (negative affect) can be induced with bitter tastes, while 'contentment' (positive affect) expressions can be induced with sweet tastes; newborn babies cry when they appear to experience discomfort or pain (etc.). But those initial reactions are very quickly 'modulated' by the environment, essentially through the impact they have on caregivers. The most well known examples are smiles and cries. Smiles appear to be first produced randomly and to mostly reflect internal states, but infants very soon learn to produce them in response to the solicitations of parents and caregivers. Cries are considered to be initially pure expressions of 'discomfort' (or psychophysiological arousal), but the social environment affects them as well. Recent research has shown, for example, that the cries of newborns already differ depending on the language spoken by their parents (Mampe *et al.* 2009). Furthermore, parents will claim that their very young babies send them messages in the form of differentiated cries. Although there are debates regarding the actual source of these attributions (baby cries are perhaps less differentiated than caregivers believe and caregivers probably use other cues to interpret the cries), the cries have an effect on the caregivers and the caregivers influence the cries in return (Lagasse *et al.* 2005; Soltis 2004). The expressions will become gradually more and more influenced by and addressed to social partners. Older children will sometimes screen the surroundings after an emotion-inducing event (e.g. after hurting themselves) and subsequently choose to cry or show other emotional reactions depending on the 'audience' (parents, strangers, peers) and the reactions of the audience (Zeman *et al.* 1997, 2006).

The same functional view of expressions is also represented in animal studies both in experimental and in ethological settings. The best example might be found in the ethological study of vervet monkey calls. Vervet monkeys in their natural habitats use three different types of alarm calls to indicate the presence of three different types of predators (leopards, eagles, and snakes). While all predators probably evoke a fear response in the animals, they send out differentiated calls to orient the behaviour of the other monkeys. Vervet monkeys who hear the calls initiate distinct escape behaviours: for a leopard-alarm they run to hide in trees; for an eagle-alarm they look up and sometimes hide in bushes; for a snake-alarm they look down and screen the ground (Seyfarth *et al.* 1980).

Cross-cultural comparisons further point to how expressions can be modified by social rules. Several authors have reported observations of culture-specific display rules. One example provided by the studies of Matsumoto and collaborators (Matsumoto 1992; Matsumoto *et al.* 2002) points to differences in display rules between Japanese and American individuals. Matsumoto *et al.* (2002) argued that Americans apply rules that encourage the amplification of emotional expressions, while Japanese rules, on the contrary, prescribe minimization of emotional expressions. Matsumoto *et al.* (2009) further argue that such differences in expressivity regulation can be extended to individuals from 'individualistic' cultures for whom it is appropriate to display more emotions than for individuals from 'collectivistic' cultures.

Altogether, there is indisputable evidence that emotional expressions are used in social communication. But it is important to note also that in the previous examples we have not yet addressed the issues of deception or fabrication of expressions. While the expressions are directed to specific receivers and are influenced by them (e.g. a child cries after falling, but only after seeing her mother wince at the fall), there is still a close correspondence between the reaction of the sender and the emotions displayed. In fact, for many of those 'socialized displays' one could argue that the emotional reaction of the sender itself is transformed by the social context (e.g. the child is 'afraid' after seeing that her mother winced).

Emotion regulation and strategic use of expressions in interactions

Most authors accept that emotional reactions sometimes need to be regulated in order to suppress reactions that are socially undesirable or simply to decrease unpleasant feelings associated with negative emotions or potential undesirable outcomes of negative emotions. There is a vast literature on emotion regulation and much of it is also concerned with emotional expressions. The model proposed by Gross (Gross 1998; Gross and Thompson 2007) in particular sets a relatively strong focus on expressions. Gross opposed two sets of strategies: *antecedent-focused emotion regulation* and *response-focused emotion regulation*. Response-focused regulation targets the emotional reaction itself and includes various strategies such as 'intensifying, diminishing, prolonging, or curtailing ongoing emotional feeling, *expression,* or physiological responding' (Gross 1998). In an experimental study (Gross 1998) showed that—while both types of emotion regulation could be effectively used to modify emotional expressions—*cognitive reappraisal* (a form of antecedent-focused emotion regulation, targeting the evaluation of the emotion-inducing situation in order to prevent the emergence of the emotional response) appeared to effectively decrease emotional feelings, whereas *suppression* (a form of response-focused emotion regulation targeting the already elicited emotional expressions) appeared to increase physiological arousal (sympathetic activation) and did not decrease emotional feelings.

In summary, this perspective assumes that individuals will make strategic—including also automatic—attempts to suppress emotional expressions either directly or via the reappraisal of elicitors. Another research tradition, focusing on *deception*, holds the same perspective but with an even stronger focus on expressions and their deliberate alteration for strategic purposes. Much research was conducted on deception (Lewis and Saarni 1997; Ekman and Rosenberg 2005). Two recurrent finding are of central interest for our discussion. First, attempts to conceal or, on the contrary, to fabricate emotional expressions seem to occur often in everyday life and occur even among small children and in other species. Second, detecting deception is difficult (reliable 'lie-detectors' have not yet been engineered) but should be possible according to Ekman and collaborators. According to those authors, subtle micro-expressions or small deviations in the temporal unfolding of the expressions might indicate that emotional expressions are not authentic (Ekman and Rosenberg 2005).

The elements exposed in the preceding paragraphs all support the notion that facial and vocal expressions are influenced by more than just emotions and that emotional communication is shaped by sociocultural rules. Many of those influences are integrated very early on (starting at birth or even before birth) and their influence on the production of facial and vocal expressions occurs outside the awareness or the conscious control of the senders. Conscious and deliberate manipulations of facial and vocal expressions can obviously also occur and we have little knowledge regarding the differences that might exist between automatic and deliberate regulations. We won't discuss further a nevertheless important issue, namely, the concomitant shaping (or construction) of the emotional reactions themselves (possibly via the constraints imposed by sociocultural influences on emotional expressions). But we point the reader to the fact that there is a substantial literature discussing such issues (e.g. Averill 1980).

Expressions as signals: relevance for affective computing

Different conceptions of the social signalling function in emotional communication are described in the preceding section. We will consider successively a few implications for applications in affective computing and relate them more directly to different conceptions.

The strongest hypothesis is to be found in Fridlund's position stating that facial and vocal expressions are interpreted primarily as social messages (not as expressions of emotions) and that the real or imaginary receiver of an expression shapes the expression. In this view, emotions become (almost) irrelevant for social interactions and might be replaced with a set of social intentions. This would, of course, mean that emotions are also irrelevant categories for socially competent agents. *Expressive synthesis* would aim at implementing facial or vocal features to convey social messages, and *automatic recognition* would attempt to identify the social intentions (instead of the emotions) of users. But, pragmatically, the same research questions would subsist (i.e. what are the relevant social intentions; how are they shown in facial and in vocal displays?). However an important implication of this view is that the focus of interest is displaced from the reaction of the sender to the reaction of the receiver. This would not affect the development of *expressive synthesis* systems as they should anyway be oriented primarily on the response (perception) of human receivers. On the other hand, for *automatic recognition*, this view implies that the expressions of the user are essentially dependent on whom they are addressed to. This obviously raises a number of issues about the way users will interact with computers or robots. We cannot predict with certainty that all users will address social messages to all artificial agents. Automatic recognition might need to take into account the possibility that (human) emotional behaviour directed to a specific agent is specific to this agent. This might be examined, for example, in wizard-of-oz studies simulating different agent behaviours (or more simply by allocating various attributes to artificial agents even if they do not translate directly into the agents' behaviours) in order to test their effect on the expressive behaviour of the users.[3]

If we consider the developmental and the intercultural (or even the interspecies) evidence, it becomes apparent that vocal and facial expressions are differentially shaped depending on the sociocultural background of the sender. A central implication of this observation is that many individual differences shaped by sociocultural factors might emerge. Taking an example, if it is true that Japanese individuals and American individuals have different views on socially adequate emotional displays, as Matsumoto and collaborators have argued, *expressive synthesis* ought to be adjusted for the nationality of the human receiver in order to be rated as adequate by the (Japanese or American) receiver. Likewise *automatic recognition* might need to be informed of the nationality of the user in order to achieve good performance. Obviously, this example could be extended to almost any other individual differences that are likely to affect the production or the perception of emotional expression (e.g. gender, age, personality, and intelligence are potential candidates).[4]

Hence when focusing on communication and on how emotional expressions might be affected by social factors, it becomes quickly apparent that a large variety of influences exist. There appear to be almost countless potential rules as to what 'emotions' (or emotion-related aspects) ought to be expressed by whom and under which circumstances. This is even reinforced if we also take into account the perspective of emotion regulation models. This perspective mainly implies that some facial or vocal displays are desirable and others not, depending on social situations and social roles. Consequently, individuals will automatically or deliberately modify their expressions in order to hide certain expressions and to show other expressions.

In order to implement 'emotional competence' (or social competence) in human–machine interactions, both automatic recognition and expression synthesis would have to take into account complex models of social interactions (see Chapter 2.5, this volume). In the domain of expressive synthesis, emotionally (socially) believable agents would not need to experience genuine emotions, but would need to display socially adequate behaviours. Likewise, automatic recognition systems would not need to identify hypothetical emotions in users but would be confronted with even far more complex issues. The difficulties arising from the large number of rules governing socially appropriate emotional displays are considerable and will require that adequate models of the social constraints acting on emotional expressions are developed.

---

[3] This would be important also in a view centred on emotional reactions only, provided that we take into account potential emotional reactions of the users/senders. Attributes or behaviours of agents might be used to elicit emotional responses in the users, which (in an 'expression as symptoms' view) would translate into expressive behaviours.

[4] This would as well matter in an expression as symptom of emotion view, provided that we assume that the emotional reactions themselves (and not only the facial or vocal expressions) are affected by sociocultural variables and interindividual differences.

Conclusions

Although we structured this chapter by separating emotional and sociocultural determinants of facial and vocal expressions, they do not reflect opposing, but rather complementary perspectives on facial and vocal expressions. Essentially, the separation is conceptual. Facial and vocal expressions are shaped both by emotions and by social factors (see also Parkinson 2005).

We have stressed that social determinants act on expressions in several different ways and that part of their influences is progressively integrated in the course of individual development and will be translated into automatic expressive behaviours. Furthermore, emotions themselves are also subjected to social learning; what people like or dislike, what shames them or makes them feel proud is not free from sociocultural influences. Facial and vocal expressions are always socialized, even when they are not directed at any actual receiver. In addition, cultural rules also prescribe when to show and when to suppress spontaneous emotional displays in given social contexts. As a consequence it will be very rare to find expressions that are totally devoid of sociocultural influences.

On the level of the production of emotional expressions, the difficulty of linking specific emotions (or emotion elicitors) with specific configurations of facial or vocal cues has been used to question the reliability of the association between emotions (or emotion elicitors) and expressions. Ultimately, the usefulness of emotions as concepts to account for facial or vocal behaviours is again challenged by this view. Evidently, if there were no reliable cues reflecting emotional reactions in facial or in vocal behaviour, it would be pointless to try to implement emotions in human–machine interactions. Still, there is enough evidence to ascertain that emotional information is expressed and perceived in facial and in vocal features. The lack of simple associations between expressive patterns and emotional feelings, emotional elicitors, or emotional attributions could be attributed to the existence of more complex associations than are usually considered. For affective computing, this would means that the task at hand is more complex than to match a triggering event with an emotional response and an emotional response with a defined and fixed set of vocal and facial features. A frequent misunderstanding seems to be that, with a few emotion categories (maybe five, or seven, or ten) and simple expressive prototypes for each category, the problem will be solved. Unfortunately, the literature shows that this is a very naïve understanding given the great complexity of emotions, emotional expressions, and emotional communication in social interactions. But this complexity is also what makes emotional expressions interesting and worthwhile to study and to implement in human–machine interactions.

Chapter 2.4

Psychophysiological response patterning in emotion: Implications for affective computing[1]

Sylvia D. Kreibig, Gunnar Schaefer, and Tobias Brosch

Summary

In this chapter, we introduce concepts relevant to emotion measurement in the domain of physiological activity. In the first part, we review theoretical accounts of why and how emotions are believed to influence autonomic nervous system (ANS) activity and what we can learn about emotion from monitoring physiological activity. The notions of indicand (an abstract quality), indicator (a concrete measure of that quality), and the nature of their relation are introduced for conceptualizing the intersecting fields of affective computing and autonomic physiology. In the second part, we turn to the question of which physiological parameters to measure. Based on the structure of the ANS, measures that index activation of the cardiovascular, respiratory, and electrodermal organ systems are introduced and sensor concepts are reviewed. In the third part, we address the question of how to design a particular measurement. Practical issues of the differentiation between emotion detection and emotion identification, characteristics of the measurement context for collecting physiological data, as well as aspects of physiological data analysis are addressed. We also give consideration to possible application contexts afforded by the measurement of emotion via physiological activity as well as ethical considerations in the physiological measurement of emotion. In conclusion, we offer a set of 'golden rules' of physiological measurement for affective computing as a practical guide to researchers and engineers.

Introduction

Research on emotion has long moved on from the fundamental question of *whether* emotion can be measured to the question of *how* emotion can be measured. Psychologists and neuroscientists are proud of their toolboxes for the measurement of emotion, allowing them to assign a set of numbers to this ephemeral phenomenon. In this way, emotion questionnaires map subjective emotional experiences of, for example, anger, fear, happiness, or sadness, on to a scale that may span from 0 to 10 with endpoints labelled *not at all* to *very much*, respectively. Individuals can then rate the quality and intensity of their emotion on this instrument. If adequately quantified, the subjective experience of emotion becomes comparable between different individuals. Similarly, quantification of facial expression is achieved by coding the movement of certain

---

[1] Preparation of this manuscript was supported by the National Center of Competence in Research (NCCR) Affective Sciences, financed by the Swiss National Science Foundation (51NF40-104897) and hosted by the University of Geneva.

muscle regions, measurements of brain activity are used to quantify differences in information processing of emotion, and assessment of physiological measures innervated by the autonomic nervous system (ANS) allows us to characterize different activation states caused by emotion.

Scientific progress is now moving beyond *affective measurements*, where, given an emotion, a certain value is assigned, to *affective computing* or—more precisely in the present context—*affective inference*. This approach takes the opposite position, aiming at drawing conclusions about emotion from some numerical representation, i.e. given a certain value what emotion may be present? To take up the above examples, given a certain kind of facial muscle movement, can we infer that this person is experiencing joy? Given a certain pattern of brain activation, can we infer that this person is experiencing sadness? Or given a certain physiological state activation, e.g. racing heart and fast breathing, can we infer that this person is experiencing fear?

The present chapter discusses theoretical and practical issues of affective computing based on the measurement of physiological responses. To this end, we review theoretical accounts of why and how emotions are believed to influence physiological activity and what we can learn about emotion from measuring this activity. We then turn to the question of what parameters to measure. We conclude with a discussion of practical aspects related to designing the measurement.

Why measure physiological activity to probe emotion?

Common language associates the guts with the basic visceral or emotional part of a person ('gut'; *Merriam-Webster Online Dictionary* 2009). The heart, in particular, is viewed to be linked with the emotional nature as distinguished from the intellectual nature of a person, such as in having a generous disposition or compassion (e.g. a leader with heart), love and affection (e.g. winning her heart), courage and ardour (e.g. never lose heart), and one's innermost feelings (e.g. knowing it in your heart; 'heart', *Merriam-Webster Online Dictionary* 2009). This connection between the viscera and emotion dates back at least as far as Greek philosophy: Plato (400 BC) suggested that, whereas rational faculties were located in the head, the passions were located in the spinal marrow and the heart. Modern research on physiological effects of emotion traces back to William James who formulated a controversial theory of emotion. James (1884, p. 189) proposed that 'the bodily changes follow directly the *perception* of the exciting fact, and that our feeling of the same changes as they occur *is* the emotion'. This thesis, equating the sensation of bodily changes to the experience of emotional feelings, laid the cornerstone for the derived idea that at least some emotions may be related to particular occurrences of physiological activity.

Ever since James (1884) proposed *peripheral perception theory*, scientific debate and investigation have addressed the relation of physiological activity and emotion. Besides the source of emotional feelings, several different functions have been assigned to physiological activity in emotion, including action preparation, body protection, facilitation of information processing, and communication of appraisals and intentions to others (e.g. Frijda 1986; Pecchinenda 2001; Smith 1989; Stemmler 2004).

Just as the colour red can be used to indicate different psychological states under different circumstances (e.g. red roses symbolize love, whereas seeing red symbolizes anger), physiological activation may indicate different psychological events. Does increased heart rate unanimously indicate fear, or does it also occur under anger and joy? Does shallow breathing unanimously indicate fear, or does it also occur under disgust and sadness? This question of the relation between emotion and physiological activity can be formalized into a question of specificity (Stemmler 1984, 1989, 1992*b*). Peripheral physiological emotional response specificity proposes unique physiological profiles across most or all individuals under a certain emotion. Response specificity is a three-valued concept in that *something* (the indicator or physiological measure) is specific *in a certain way* with respect to *something else* (the indicand or emotion construct). In terms of the above example, it can be said that red symbolizes love when it appears in the context of roses.

A sound theoretical conceptualization of (a) the indicand domain and (b) the indicator domain as well as of (c) the nature of relation between the two is thus central for an informed use of physiological measures for probing emotion. We discuss each one of these in more detail in the following.

Indicand domain: The nature of psychological emotion differentiation

To what degree can we expect emotions to be differentiated? Various emotion theories conceptualize emotion in different ways. Still, they all agree on the fact that emotions have certain quantitative (the emotion intensity), qualitative (in the broadest sense positive or negative valence), and temporal aspects (including onset, peak, and decay) that may all contribute to some degree of inter-emotion differentiation. Emotion models typically conceptualize emotions in a componential manner (Mauss and Robinson 2009); we adopt this consensual view and consider emotion as a multicomponent response, involving effects on subjective feelings, facial expressions, action tendencies, and—of interest to the present chapter—physiological activation. A general overview of emotion models is presented in Chapter 1.1, this volume. We here focus on physiological aspects of emotion models, in particular, what kind of predictions they make regarding physiological differentiation in emotion. From this point of view, emotion models can be distinguished with respect to the level of abstraction that they take in specifying the mechanism of physiological response organization in emotion.

- *Constructivist models of emotion* ascribe the qualitative differentiation of emotion to higher cognitive functions. Models in this tradition do not acknowledge physiological differentiation of emotion (Feldman-Barrett 2006; Russell 2003).

- *Discrete emotion theory*, as originally proposed by Tomkins (1962, 1963), Ekman (1972), and Izard (1977), suggests that each of the basic emotions is produced by an innate hardwired neuromotor program with characteristic neurophysiolopigcal, expressive, and subjective components. In particular, discrete emotion theory assigns autonomic response differentiation to emotion-specific behaviours, such as fight in anger and flight in fear, and argues that such behaviours require different autonomic activation to support them. Thus, for anger, it predicts increased blood perfusion of the hands to mobilize for violent quarrels and increased perfusion of the face to display angry arousal. In contrast, for fear, it predicts increased perfusion of the limbs to mobilize for quick running; this redistribution of blood to the extremities might cause a pale face; moreover, increased sweating is predicted to occur that may be functional to escape the grip of a predator. Even if such behaviour is not overtly expressed, a preparatory response is predicted to happen inevitably (Levenson 1988). This preparatory mobilization may be noticed in such situations as a just-avoided car crash where we feel our knees shaking or the inner arousal that occurs in case of an anger-eliciting provocation that we wish to not act out against a superior.

- *Dimensional models of emotion* criticize the tight coupling proposed by discrete emotion models between specific emotions and certain behaviours that in turn are believed to organize ANS activation. They base their argument on the observation that there exists no one-to-one correspondence between emotions and behaviours. For example, stimulating an animal with an electric shock may result in the attack of another animal in the presence of conspecifics (i.e. an anger response) or, if alone, may entail either freezing or, given an escape path, fleeing (i.e. various fear responses). Dimensional emotion models rather view all of these emotion behaviours as being driven by activation of a defence system. In particular, the organization of emotion is assumed to be based on a few underlying dimensions. Bradley and Lang (2000), for example, view emotions as action dispositions, i.e. tendencies of movement toward positive, appetitive things and away from negative, unpleasant ones. Emotions are thus conceptualized according to two motive features of behaviour, affective valence (positive/negative) and intensity of activation, defining a two-dimensional space that is believed to underlie all action. Two motive systems are proposed to exist in the brain—appetitive and aversive/defensive— reflected in the valence dimension in affective expression. Arousal is viewed as representing activation (metabolic and neural) of either the appetitive or aversive system. Assuming that emotion is organized by the brain's motivational systems, physiological and behavioural reactions to affective stimuli should also reflect this organization. A large research corpus relates such changes in heart rate to the valence dimension and changes in skin conductance to the arousal dimension (Hamm *et al.* 2003). The diversity of expressed emotions is believed to have developed from different contextual tactics of approach and withdrawal but being based on the same strategic frame viewed as fundamental to the organization of emotion.

♦ *Appraisal models of emotion* suggest breaking up the emotion process into molecular appraisal processes. According to this view, appraisals produce a nuanced emotional reaction and the outcome of each appraisal—rather than whole emotions—is suggested to cause direct changes in brain, body, and subjective feeling (Ellsworth 1994; Ellsworth and Scherer 2003; Scherer 1984, 2001). Thus, instead of action tendencies as mediator between appraisal outcomes and physiological responding, it is assumed that there exist direct connections of appraisals with response modalities, independently of action tendencies. Ellsworth (1994, p. 228, emphasis in original) described the onset of an emotion as follows:

> At the moment when the organism's attention is aroused by some change in the environment or the stream of consciousness, certain neural circuits in the brain are activated [...], the heart may slow, the head may turn, and the organism *feels different* than it did before the event. Arousal of attention does not necessarily lead to emotion [...] but attention is very often the first step in emotional arousal. No nameable emotion has yet developed, but already there are cognitive, physiological, behavioural, and subjective changes. If the organism senses that the stimulus is attractive or aversive, the feeling and the bodily responses change again. As each succeeding appraisal is made, mind, body, and feeling change again. The sequence may seem to burst forth all at once, or it may unfold over a much longer period of time.

Thus, each appraisal outcome is proposed to have a certain effect on physiological activity; the combination of appraisal effects is believed to form the highly differentiated physiological emotion response.

This brief overview shows that contemporary emotion models propose different degrees of emotion differentiation as well as different pathways (behaviour, action tendencies, appraisal) via which emotion affects physiological responding.

Indicator domain: The nature of physiological emotion differentiation

From the perspective of embodiment, physiological processes form an integral part of all psychological phenomena, from behaving, to thinking, to emoting. Not only ambient temperature, circadian rhythms, body postures, physical tasks, and their associated motor behaviours, but also psychological influences, such as attention, anticipation, mental effort, as well as emotion exert an effect on physiological responding. Non-emotional physical, behavioural, and psycho-logical factors—typically termed *context effects* (Stemmler 2003)—influence physiological activation before, during, and after emotion, producing a complex amalgam of influences on physiological activation. Physiological responses can therefore not be taken as a direct window to affective states; too many factors influence physiological activation at any one time as to allow one specific factor—emotion—to be detected unconditionally. This means that measurement of emotion by assessment of physiological activity necessitates a disentangling of emotion and context effects. The emotion theory and measurement model, based on which measures are interpreted, are central to giving peripheral physiological changes a meaningful indicator function for emotional processes.

A first question that needs to be addressed is *when* to measure or, more precisely, during which time window one can expect to observe emotional effects on physiological responding. Emotions are relatively brief affective phenomena, lasting from subsecond duration to only a few seconds or minutes (Ekman 1984, 1994*a*). It is in that narrow time window when emotion-relevant physiological effects are expected to occur. Once a behavioural reaction has been initiated, the physiological activity is in the service of that behaviour and any physiological differences between emotions will be obscured (Levenson 2003; Stemmler 2004). Before the emotion and after it subsides, physiological activity reflects forces other than emotion.

This leads to a second question of how the onset of emotion might be identified in an ongoing stream of physiological activity. Emotions are typically conceptualized as being elicited by a stimulus event, an occurrence of a stimulus under certain presentation conditions. A stimulus can be of exogenous origin, such as visual, auditory, or haptic, affecting the organism via sensory pathways. A stimulus can also be of endogenous origin, such as thoughts or memories. Event-relatedness is a distinctive feature of emotion in contrast to mood. Monitoring the situational context for cues of stimulus events is an important, albeit insufficient, correlate for identifying the onset of an emotion. Emotion elicitation due to inner processes will be missed and not all stimulus events are emotionally significant for the organism; those that are, typically signal a state change, i.e. the current mode of operation of the organism needs to be adapted to changed environmental demands. Emotion has thus been conceptualized as a discontinuity of activation (Kreibig, Gendolla, and Scherer, 2010), directly affecting physiological functional activation. Similar views have been expressed in the literature, conceptualizing emotion as a behavioural reset or interrupt mechanism (Simon 1967).

Third, it needs to be asked *how* physiological effects of emotion may be expressed. The construct 'emotion' cannot be captured with any single measure (Lang *et al*. 1988; Mandler 1975; Rachman 1978). This assertion is based on the fact that physiological responses are fractionated (Lacey 1967), i.e. show different levels and directions of activation across measures, rather than mere intensity variations of an undifferentiated arousal. Physiological effects of emotion are thus expected to be expressed in a combination of variables and their specific response constellation (see profile analysis; Stemmler 1989, 1992*b*). The idea of pattern formation is inherent in a conceptualization of emotion as a spatial organization of response components (Stemmler 1984).

Many emotion theories have integrated the concept that emotions are marked not only by spatially, but also by temporally organized effects, acknowledging emotion as a dynamic continuous process. Bradley and Lang (2000), for example, propose a cascade of different response events, changing in different ways and at different levels over time. Appraisal theories hold the idea that appraisals occur in a temporal sequence and directly affect each response system, among these the physiological response level, each time a new appraisal outcome is reached (Ellsworth and Scherer 2003; Scherer 1984; see also Chapter 2.1, this volume). Scherer (2000*b*), in particular, conceptualized emotions as episodes of subsystem synchronization, suggesting an organization between response systems and over time. Finally, temporal dynamics operate not only within emotion, as they evolve, but also in the transition between emotions. The initial emotional response may change over time in quality or type as the event is reappraised.

Fourth, we need to address how to conceptualize *what* is being measured, i.e. what part of the measurement reflects emotion. Although emotional factors might dominate physiological activation in a time window of milliseconds to a few seconds (or even minutes), co-occur with a stimulus event, and be marked by spatial and temporal organization, still a myriad of non-emotional physical, behavioural, social, and psychological factors additionally influence physiological activation at that point in time. To disentangle the potential confounding context effects from emotional effects on physiological activation, three major factors have been recognized that influence physiological responding (Stemmler 2004; Stemmler *et al.* 2001).

- *Effects of the non-emotional context* include posture, ambient temperature, ongoing motor activity, or cognitive demands that are not in the service of emotion. This component constrains the physiological effects that the other components may exert.

- *Effects of the emotional context* include organismic, behavioural, and mental demands of enacting the emotion, given the specific momentary situational allowances and constraints on the emotional behavioural response. Any motivational and actual behavioural direction, e.g. attacking or running toward a safe place, fall hereunder. This component represents context-dependent effects of emotion that may be variable across situations.

- *Effects of the emotion proper* reflect specific physiological adaptations with the function to protect the organism through autonomic reflexes and to prepare the organism for consequent behaviour, occurring in a rather short temporal window after the elicitation of an emotion and before actual behaviour has started. This component represents context-independent effects of emotion, which are expected to be stable across situations.

According to this model, emotion–context confounds may operate in two distinct ways: A first component of response organization is independent of the emotion, whereas a second one is intertwined with the emotion. The third component of the model, the emotion signature proper, is expected to allow statistical identification of specific, non-overlapping emotion responses (Stemmler *et al.* 2001).

In a measurement situation, non-emotional context effects can be accounted for by measurement of physiological activation during a non-emotional period[2] (Stemmler *et al.* 2001). Effects of the emotional context can only be separated from effects of the emotion proper by independently varying effects from these two sources (for an empirical investigation differentiating these two components, see Stemmler *et al.* 2007). If effects of the non-emotional context and effects of the emotional context have been identified, and influences are assumed to exert additive effects, calculation of difference scores allows for the identification of effects of the emotion proper.

This decomposition of contextual effects is based on a conceptualization of physiological responses as reflecting effects of stimulus or situational response specificity (SRS). While physiological responses may display such trans-individual generalizability of situation-specific patterns, trans-situational consistency of individum-specific patterns has likewise been found to significantly influence the pattern of physiological responding (Hinz *et al.* 2000; Lacey and Lacey 1958; Marwitz and Stemmler 1998). Individual response specificity (IRS) refers to the

---

[2] This non-emotional episode should be identical to the emotional episode, only with the emotional component removed. For example, when measuring emotional responses within the context of film viewing, the viewing of a non-emotional film would allow measurement of non-emotional contextual effects.

observation that individuals tend to respond with the same pattern of physiological activation, whatever the stress or stimulus. Both SRS and IRS exert independent as well as interactional effects on physiological responding.

It will be an important task for affective computing to incorporate these measurement models, developed in affective psychophysiology, into the measurement situation of affective computing to make affective inference more powerful.

The nature of relations: Projections and possible inferences

Thus far, we have discussed what kind of emotional differentiation may be expected and how emotional effects may be expressed on the physiological level. In this part, we integrate these two aspects, addressing the way in which the psychological domain of emotion may be related to the physiological domain.

When observing a physiological response found previously to vary as a function of emotion, the data are often interpreted as indicating the occurrence of that emotion. For example, the observation of increased skin conductance might be interpreted as indicating that the person is anxious, decreased heart rate as indicating that the person is sad, or a faster breathing rhythm as indicating that the person is happy. We may, however, only make such inferences when a one-to-one mapping between the psychological domain of emotion and the physiological domain of ANS responding has been established (Cacioppo *et al.* 2000*a*). If that is not the case, this form of inference, known as *affirmation of the consequent*, produces an invalid conclusion.

Peripheral physiological activation as a function of emotion can occur in a number of different forms of projections or mappings between the domain of the indicand (here, emotion) and the domain of the indicator (here, physiological activation; Cacioppo and Tassinary 1990*b*; see Figure 2.4.1). Unless empirically tested, one cannot presume any particular form of projection of the many possible.

- In a *one-to-one projection* (injective mapping; Figure 2.4.1(a)), an element in the psychological domain is associated with exactly one element in the physiological domain, and vice versa.

- In a *one-to-many projection* (Figure 2.4.1(b)), an element in the psychological domain is associated with a subset of elements in the physiological domain. One-to-many relations can be reduced to one-to-one relations by replacing the subset of physiological elements associated with the psychological element with a physiological syndrome or response pattern.

- In a *many-to-one projection* (Figure 2.4.1(c)), two or more psychological elements are associated with the same physiological element.

- In a *many-to-many projection* (Figure 2.4.1(d)), two or more psychological elements are associated with the same (or an overlapping) subset of elements in the physiological domain. Many-to-many relations can be reduced to many-to-one relations by viewing elements within the physiological domain as representing singular physiological responses or physiological response syndromes.

- In a *null relation* (Figure 2.4.1(e)), there is no association between an element in the psychological domain and that in the physiological domain.

The definition of physiological elements need not be confined to single response measures, but can also accommodate sets of physiological responses that form an element based on their unfolding over time (temporal information) or across response systems (spatial information). This way, many complex psychophysiological relationships can be reduced to one-to-one or many-to-one relations (Cacioppo *et al.* 2000*a*). Only these two types of projection allow a formal specification of psychological elements as a function of physiological elements. Possible inferences that can be

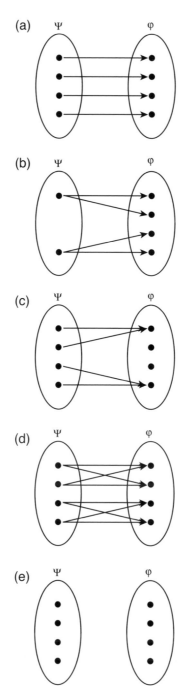

Fig. 2.4.1 Various types of projections between the psychological domain of emotion (Ψ) and the physiological domain of ANS activation (φ). (a) One-to-one; (b) one-to-many; (c) many-to-one; (d) many-to-many; (e) null.

drawn, given a certain type of projection, are the following (for more detail, see Cacioppo and Tassinary 1990*a,b*; Cacioppo *et al.* 2000*a*, 2007*a*).

♦ *Context-dependent inferences about the absence of emotion* are possible when a physiological response has been identified to vary as a function of emotion, i.e. is a *psychophysiological outcome*. The projection is of the form many-to-one, such that many psychological processes, of which one may be emotion, may influence the physiological measure of interest. Moreover, such relations may have a very limited range of validity, i.e. be highly situation-specific. Results stemming from psychophysiological laboratory experiments are typically of this nature, although subsequent investigations may establish generalization of the found relationship, i.e. context-independence and/or a one-to-one projection between the two domains, likely based on further refinements of the measure. The identification of a physiological response profile that differentiates emotional from non-emotional episodes or between types of emotions is sufficient to infer the absence of that psychological phenomenon, but it does not allow us to infer anything about its presence. Measures based on such findings thus cannot figure as indices of emotional processes, as it is simply not known what other factors might have influenced the observed response. Overestimation of the presence of the psychological element is a problem if the probability of the physiological element is greater than the probability of the psychological element in question.

♦ *Context-independent inferences about the absence of emotion* are possible when a physiological response has been identified to vary cross-situationally as a function of emotion, i.e. is a *psychophysiological concomitant or correlate*. The projection is of the form many-to-one and has been shown to generalize to different situations. Typically, results from replication studies of psychophysiological laboratory experiments or ambulatory monitoring studies are used to demonstrate that findings have a larger range of validity. The empirical establishment of a psychophysiological concomitant allows a probability statement about the absence or presence of a particular element in the psychological domain when the specific physiological response is observed. Still, given the nature of a many-to-one projection, the physiological event is not a strong predictor of the psychological phenomenon of interest. Again, base rates of the occurrence of the physiological event across situations must be considered.

♦ *Context-dependent inferences about the occurrence and nature of emotion* are possible when a physiological response has been identified as predicting the occurrence of a psychological event within a given context, i.e. is a *psychophysiological marker*. The projection is of the form one-to-one that has been established in a specific context, i.e. it may be valid only in a limited range of situations. Establishing a physiological measure as a marker allows inferences about the nature of emotional processes as a function of that measure. This presupposes demonstration of the following three properties: (a) presence of the physiological response reliably predicts the psychological construct of interest; (b) presence of the physiological response is insensitive to other psychological phenomena; and (c) the boundary conditions for the validity of this relationship are specified. The *specificity* of a psychophysiological marker characterizes the degree to which the physiological event would occur in the absence of the psychological phenomenon: the higher the specificity, the greater the likelihood of establishing a one-to-one relationship between the physiological event and the emotion construct and the greater the likelihood of establishing a large range of validity of this relationship. The higher the *sensitivity* of a psychophysiological marker, the more information it provides: at low sensitivity, the physiological measure may indicate the presence or absence of the psychological phenomenon, whereas at high sensitivity, it may indicate its temporal course, signalling onset, offset, and amplitude of the psychological event.

◆ *Context-independent inferences about the occurrence and nature of emotion* are possible when a physiological response has been identified to cross-situationally predict the occurrence of a psychological event, i.e. is a *psychophysiological invariant*. The projection is of the form one-to-one and has been shown to generalize to different contexts. Establishing a physiological measure as an invariant provides a strong basis for psychophysiological inference; only in this case is the logical error of affirmation of the consequent not a problem. This presupposes demonstration of the following three properties: (a) the physiological event is present if the psychological phenomenon of interest is present; (b) the psychological phenomenon is present if the physiological event is present; and (c) this relationship holds across different situations.

What to measure?

The ANS is a major output system of the brain. Because functional activation patterns are hypothesized to be at the core of physiological responding in emotion, it is important to know the underlying system's structure well. We therefore first turn to a description of the structure and functioning of the ANS. We then discuss the parameters of those organ systems innervated by the ANS that are most accessible to measurement in the context of affective computing. An appendix provides more detailed information and background on measures of physiological functioning as well as an overview of assessment methods.

Structure and functioning of the ANS

The ANS, shown in Figure 2.4.2, consists of a system of nerves that regulates organ functioning throughout the human body, including the viscera, vasculature, glands, and other tissues, except for striated muscle fibres (Jänig 2003; Langley 1903, 1921). The ANS is divided into the sympathetic (SNS), the parasympathetic (PNS), and the enteric nervous systems, of which only the first two will be further discussed here. This distinction is based on the anatomical structure of the autonomic innervation from the central nervous system to the peripheral target tissues. Every organ is innervated by one or both of the sympathetic and parasympathetic outflows. As shown in Figure 2.4.2, the SNS and PNS innervate the following target tissues.

◆ *Sympathetic nervous system*:
  • heart;
  • smooth musculature of blood vessels, erector pili muscles, pupils, lungs, evacuative organs;
  • sweat, salivary, and digestive glands;
  • adipose tissue, liver cells, pineal gland, and lymphatic tissues;
  • adrenal medulla (endocrine gland) releases adrenaline and noradrenaline into blood, which circulates to reach tissues throughout the body.

◆ *Parasymphetic nervous system*:
  • heart (pacemaker cells and atria);
  • smooth muscles and glands of the airways;
  • intraocular smooth muscles;
  • smooth musculature, exocrine and endocrine glands of the gastrointestinal tract;
  • pelvic organs (lower urinary tract, hindgut, reproductive organs);
  • epithelia and mucosa throughout the body;

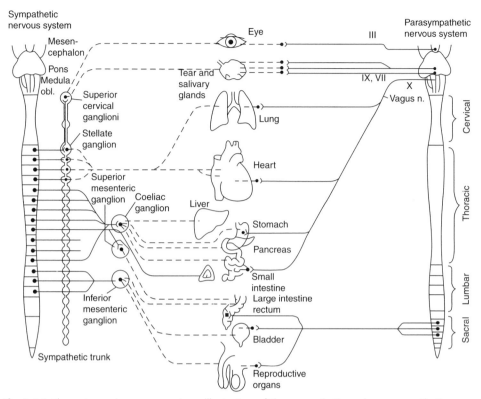

Fig. 2.4.2 The autonomic nervous system; illustration of the sympathetic and parasympathetic branches. The enteric division, not shown separately here, consists of groups of cell bodies and nerve fibres embedded in the walls of the oesophagus, stomach, and intestines. (Redrawn from Jänig and Häbler 1999.)

- exocrine glands of the head;
- some intracranial, uterine, and facial blood vessels not contributing to blood pressure regulation.

Most target tissues respond to only one of the systems. A few respond to both the SNS and PNS, such as the iris and the heart's pacemaker cells and atria. Opposite effects of the SNS and the PNS are—in contrast to common conception—rather rare (Koizumi *et al.* 1983). The systems typically work either synergistically or under separate functional or temporal conditions. A systematic differentiation of autonomic regulatory states has been proposed by Berntson *et al.* (1991). This model differentiates between coupled and uncoupled modes of functioning of the sympathetic and parasympathetic divisions of the ANS. Coupled modes include the traditional view of reciprocal functioning as well as modes of coactivation and coinhibition. In uncoupled mode, the two autonomic divisions function independently. Thus, in order to infer the specific mode of autonomic control, activation measures of dually innervated target organs need to parse sympathetic and parasympathetic activation components.

The ANS regulates body functions to adjust its performance to the varying internal and external demands placed on the organism (Jänig 2003). This allows the organism to act in a coordinated way under various challenging conditions. Autonomic regulation is normally fast, occurring within subsecond time range. Autonomic regulation is moreover highly differentiated.

The brain continuously monitors the environment via the sensory systems and selects the most appropriate available reaction pattern for coping with the perceived situation. Neural programs implemented in the upper brainstem, hypothalamus, and limbic system generate corresponding response patterns to adjust to the new situation. Efferent commands to the peripheral organs are sent through autonomic and endocrine pathways. A precise neural regulation of homeostatic body functions is achieved by an anatomically and physiologically distinct organization of the SNS and PNS that consists of several different, functionally distinct subsystems. Each subsystem is associated with a different type of target tissue. Very little or no cross-talk exists between these different peripheral pathways (Jänig and Häbler 2000; Jänig and McLachlan 1992a,b). This highly differentiated organization supports adaptive responses of the body during different types of behaviour, including emotional responding. Thus, unlike the hypothesis of a sympathico-adrenal 'fright, fight, or flight' response (Cannon 1929, 1939), believed to similarly affect all effector organs in an 'all-or-none' fashion, current physiological models acknowledge highly differentiated effects of the SNS and PNS on target organs (Jänig 2003; cf. Langley 1903, 1921). The simple dichotomy of the PNS promoting energy conservation, resource replenishment, and recovery after stress (i.e. trophotropic functions) and of the SNS mobilizing bodily resources and adapting the body to external challenges (i.e. ergotropic functions; Hess, 1948) has been criticized as being 'far too general to explain the complexities of the central control of autonomic systems' (Jänig and Häbler 1999, p. 17; see also Vingerhoets 1985).

Major organ systems innervated by the ANS are the cardiovascular, respiratory, and eccrine (electrodermal) systems. Measuring changes in their functioning allows conclusions about the activation level of the SNS and PNS. Still, inferences about ANS functioning derived from measurements of one organ system do not have to indicate the same as inferences based on measurements of another organ system (cf. functionally distinct subsystems of the SNS and PNS, above, also known as directional fractionation). Moreover, complex cross-system interaction exists between the cardiovascular, respiratory, and eccrine systems. Heart rate, for example, changes as a function of the respiratory cycle, a phenomenon known as respiratory sinus arrhythmia (RSA; Grossman 1983; see also Engel and Chism 1967). Respiration also affects electrodermal activity (Rittweger et al. 1997). Therefore, conclusions about autonomic activation will be incomplete, if they are based on measurements of only one system without concurrent measurement of other relevant systems.

Physiological measures

The ANS is an extremely dynamic system. Many autonomically innervated organs exhibit rhythmic processes, such as heart beat or breathing cycle, of which recurrent events can be monitored. Observation of such events may be quantified by their rate, as, for example, found in the measure of heart rate (HR, counting the number of beats per minute) or respiration rate (counting the number of breaths per minute). Cyclical events moreover allow for quantification of time intervals, as evidenced in measures of the time between two consecutive heart beats (interbeat interval) or a temporal subdivision of the cardiac cycle into such time intervals as pre-ejection period (the isovolumetric phase, during which pressure is built up in the heart), or left ventricular ejection time (the subsequent phase, during which blood is ejected from the heart). Similarly, for the respiratory system, one can quantify the duration of one full breath (total respiratory cycle duration) or subdivisions of a breath, such as inspiratory, expiratory, and respiratory pause times. Furthermore, the amplitude of characteristic waveforms of the electrocardiogram (ECG, e.g. P-wave or T-wave) or the amplitude of arterial blood pulsation can be quantified. Stroke volume or cardiac output are volumetric measures of heart functioning that indicate the amount of blood ejected from the heart during one heart beat and the amount of blood pumped from the heart during one minute, respectively. For the respiratory system, different quantifications of lung volume include vital and inspiratory capacity, inspiratory and expiratory reserve volume, and tidal volume, of which the latter, i.e. the normal volume of air inhaled after exhalation, is most commonly employed. Moreover, pressure changes occur over the course of a cardiac cycle that are quantified by blood pressure measures of systolic, diastolic, and mean arterial pressure. Likewise, for the respiratory system, blood gas saturation varies over the course of a respiratory cycle, which can be measured by means of carbon dioxide and oxygen partial pressures. Temperature changes also occur in cyclical, though typically slower, fashion (circadian rhythm). Finally, all natural processes show a certain degree of variability. This is also true for the cardiac and respiratory organ systems. Such variability can be quantified by measures of heart rate, blood pressure, and respiratory period variability, as well as tidal volume variability, based on time-or frequency-domain analysis. Spectral variance decomposition further allows for the calculation of transfer functions between two such spectra, which are informative with respect to response coherence (Berger *et al.* 1989; Saul *et al.* 1991). Heart rate variability is known to relate to parasympathetic control of the heart (cf. respiratory sinus arrhythmia; see Allen *et al.* 2007, for a primer on its different metrics). Respiratory variability particularly relates to the occurrence of sighs, which can be further analysed regarding rate and amplitude (cf. Vlemincx *et al.* 2009).

Event occurrence typically causes a change in the cyclical functioning of the cardiovascular and respiratory systems. For example, one can observe an orienting response, characterized by heart rate slowing and breathholding, when an unexpected event occurs (Stekelenburg and van Boxtel 2002). Whereas these cyclical systems evidence inhibition of activity, another organ system, the eccrine system, typically shows increased activation to event occurrence, such as a skin conductance response. Such event-related responses are superimposed onto a relatively constant level of base activation (skin conductance level). Event-related skin conductance responses can be further characterized by such measures as onset latency, rise time, half recovery time, and amplitude. The eccrine system moreover shows spontaneous activity or nonspecific skin conductance responses that are quantified as the number of responses per minute or skin conductance response rate. Table 2.4.1 gives an overview of discussed measures and possible ways to assess them. A detailed description of each organ system and definition and background on the physiological measures is provided in the Appendix.

How to measure?

We have thus far addressed the *why* and *what* of physiological measurements for probing emotion, leaving discussion of practical issues to this final section. How might affective psychophysiology contribute to the aims of affective computing? The cross-fertilization of disciplines addressing converse research questions needs to be considerate. A large number of empirical findings regarding emotional physiological response patterning exists in affective psychophysiology, as summarized, for example, in a recent review by Kreibig (2010), in a meta-analysis by Cacioppo *et al.* (2000c), or in *The handbook of psychophysiology* (Cacioppo *et al.* 2007b). However, the applicability of mere lists of results of emotion-specific responding, as found in psychophysiological studies, to the affective computing context will be limited. Still, with the necessary prudence in questions of generalizability, they might be instructive in certain ways. Similarly, research paradigms developed and used in affective psychophysiology are relevant for the study of emotion detection and identification in affective computing, but cannot be applied one-to-one. It needs to be kept in mind that, although both disciplines address related questions, research strategies take opposite approaches in many ways. Main differences in the measurement approach lie in: (a) the characteristics of the measurement context; (b) the approach to data analysis; and

Table 2.4.1 Overview of measures and assessment methods

Full name (abbreviation)	Measure of	Quantification of
Electrocardiography (ECG)	Voltage changes	HR, IBI, PWA, TWA, HRV, RR (spectral)
Impedance cardiography (ICG)	Impedance changes	HR, IBI, PEP, LVET, SV, CO, RR
Photoplethysmography (PPG)	Volume changes	HR, PA, PTT (in combination with ECG)
Sphygmomanography	Pressure changes	HR, SBP, DBP, MAP, TPR (in combination with ECG)
Temperature (TMP)	Temperature changes	FT
Respiratory inductive plethysmography (RIP)	Volume changes	w
Impedance pneumography (IPG)	Impedance changes	RR, Ttot, Vt, Ti/Ttot, Vt/Ti
Phonospirometry	Sound changes	RR, Ttot, Vt, Ti/Ttot, Vt/Ti
Temperature	Temperature changes	RR
Capnography	Changes in blood gas saturation	pCO_2
Pulse oximetry	Changes in blood gas saturation	SO_2
Electrodermography (EDG)	Conductance changes	SCL, NS-SCR, SRA

Abbreviations. HR, Heart rate; IBI, interbeat interval; PWA, P-wave amplitude; TWA, T-wave amplitude; HRV, heartrate variability; RR, respiration rate; PEP, pre-ejection period; LVET, left ventricular ejection time; SV, stroke volume; CO, cardiac output; PA, pulse amplitude; PTT, pulse transit time; SBP, systolic blood pressure; DBP, diastolic blood pressure; MAP, mean arterial pressure; TPR, total peripheral pressure; FT, finger temperature; Ttot, total respiratory cycle duration; Vt, tidal volume; Ti/Ttot, duty cycle; Vt/Ti, respiratory flow rate; pCO_2, end-tidal carbon dioxide partial pressure; SO_2, blood oxygen saturation; SCL, skin conductance level; NS-SCR, non-specific skin conductance response rate; SRA, skin conductance response amplitude.

(c) certain ethical and technical constraints. We conclude this chapter with a discussion of each of these issues and their implications for affective computing. Before that, we take a look at the current state of research on emotion detection and identification.

Emotion detection and emotion identification

Building a system that is sensitive to a user's emotions requires addressing two problems: first, emotion detection, i.e. the fact *that* an emotion has occurred, and, second, emotion identification or differentiation, i.e. *which* emotion has occurred (compare to the notion of emotion elicitation and emotion differentiation introduced in Chapter 1.1, this volume). Only a system that incorporates both of these aspects is truly sensitive to a user's emotions and may adapt appropriately.

Whereas in psychophysiological studies of the effects of emotion (for an exemplary summary, see Cacioppo *et al.* 2000c) emotion is the independent variable and physiological reactivity is the dependent variable, the converse perspective is taken in affective computing, aiming at a prediction of emotion based on psychophysiological measures. Surprisingly, many investigations conducted under the label of affective computing take the very same approach to study design as in affective psychophysiology, feeding such collected data subsequently to various types of classifiers (e.g. Kim and André 2008; Lisetti and Nasoz 2004; Picard *et al.* 2001). These studies thus only address emotion identification, leaping to the second step of the above-outlined two-step problem, without addressing emotion detection.

Study designs of affective psychophysiology are, however, inherently imperfect for addressing questions of affective computing for two reasons.

* *Frequency.* Statistical procedures typically used in psychophysiology prescribe a balanced experimental design, with equal numbers of experimental units in each of the different (emotional) conditions. Yet in real life, equal probabilities of event occurrence can be assumed neither for emotional and non-emotional events nor for different qualities of emotion. This is not a problem for the type of questions asked in affective psychophysiology. For the purpose of affective computing, however, sample data needs to faithfully model base rates of emotion occurrence, or else, real-life applications will be unsuccessful.

* *Type and intensity.* Psychophysiological paradigms for emotion induction are used as highly controlled and standardized models of emotion, which should be replicable independent of location and experimenter and should assure the very same treatment for each and every participant, to allow comparability between studies and accumulation of results. Consequently, the range of types and intensities of emotions studied in the laboratory may be restricted compared to real-life processes. While only of secondary concern to affective psychophysiology, this aspect should constitute a central concern for affective computing. As for frequency, an appropriate modelling of the types and intensities of emotion occurrence is a mandatory prerequisite for the usefulness and applicability of results of affective computing.

While research on emotion identification or emotion classification has meanwhile become mainstream, a search of the computing and engineering literature through IEEEXplore returned merely five publications that fell under the descriptor of physiological emotion detection, none of which truly address that topic, but rather only emotion identification. A notable exception presents a series of studies by Myrtek *et al.* (Myrtek *et al.* 1988, 2005; Myrtek and Brügner 1996). Myrtek and colleagues implemented an emotion detection monitor based on a portable minicomputer that carried out an online analysis of both heart rate (HR) and physical activity (recorded with motion detectors) during 24 hours of the participants' regular life. The monitor was programmed such that it signalled the user to report their emotion under two types of conditions: (1) every time an increase in HR was detected that was not accompanied by concurrent increases in activity (hypothesized to indicate the occurrence of emotion) and (2) random events not related to HR increases (hypothesized to not be related to emotion, i.e. false alarms). Results were, however, not favourable for the emotion detection performance of this algorithm: such detected 'emotional' situations as contrasted to randomly selected situations did not differ significantly with respect to reported emotion.

This null finding need, however, not be taken to indicate that physiological activation does not co-vary with emotional activation. The algorithm used may have generated a large number of false positives and false negatives. First, it may have falsely detected situations as emotional (i.e. false positives), because HR increases not only occur with emotion, but also with other psychological processes, e.g. mental effort. Second, randomly selected situations may, in fact, have been emotional (i.e. false negatives), even if they did not meet the criterion of increased HR and *no* change in physical activity. Especially in real-life contexts, it is very likely that emotions (and related HR changes) will co-occur with increased physical activity, for example, when a person is venting his or her anger. Thus, the absence of differences of reported emotion between the 'emotional' and 'random' conditions may have been due to incorrect detection of emotional and non-emotional or random situations.

Moreover, the series of studies by Myrtek *et al.* used but one physiological indicator variable. HR, in particular, is a relatively unspecific indicator of ANS activation, as it reflects the joint influence of sympathetic and parasympathetic effects on the heart. Physiological variables that more specifically indicate changes in ANS activation, such as the relative influence of sympathetic or parasympathetic effects, could give better results (Kolodyazhniy *et al.* in preparation; Wilhelm *et al.* 2007).

More promising results may also be expected with multichannel measurements. Wilhelm *et al.* (2006), for example, found that many parameters, including HR, RSA, skin conductance level, and rate of non-specific skin conductance responses, and respiratory timing parameters are strongly and non-specifically affected by both emotion (anxiety in the context of their study) and physical exercise. In contrast, parameters of respiratory volume were selectively responsive to exercise, and certain parameters of irregularity in breathing responded to anxiety only. Still, additional context awareness may be useful for more confident emotion detection. For example, cameras and microphones might be able to provide disambiguating information about a situation that was ambiguous on the basis of physiological data alone.

Furthermore, participants may not always be able to correctly report on their emotional feelings. It could be imagined that a certain activation threshold needs to be passed in order for emotions to enter consciousness (Winkielman and Berridge 2003). Emotions below this threshold would not be accompanied by conscious emotional feelings. If emotions cause proportional changes in physiological activation, then the threshold, above which participants are able to give a correct indication of their emotion, could be identified. This threshold may well be individuum-specific.

Finally, how to appropriately assess emotion with self-report measures is itself still a matter of research. Self-report scales that collect emotion ratings on basic dimensions such as valence and arousal, or excitement and enjoyment as in the studies by Myrtek and colleagues (Myrtek *et al.* 2005, 1988; Myrtek and Brügner 1996), are often used, but may not differentiate sufficiently to capture the full scope of the emotional space. Similarly, basic emotions, of which happiness, anger, anxiety, sadness, surprise, and disgust were assessed by Myrtek *et al.* (2005), may provide emotion labels with which participants cannot identify or that are not appropriate for the emotion experienced in the real-life context. Solutions may be offered by measurement instruments such as the *Geneva Emotion Wheel* (Scherer 2005*b*), which samples a large variety of possible emotional feelings. Another alternative is the assessment of appraisal dimensions (e.g. *Geneva Appraisal Questionnaire*; Scherer 1997; Smith and Ellsworth 1985).

Characteristics of the measurement context

Besides the opposing directions of the research questions of affective psychophysiology and affective computing, several other noteworthy methodological differences exist between the two fields.

Most psychophysiological studies on emotion are conducted in the laboratory. Psychophysiological laboratories range from simple office rooms equipped with a chair, desk, and psychophysiological recording equipment, to cosy living room-like setups, to soundproof Faraday cages. Participant selection criteria often exclude certain populations, such as smokers or people with physical diseases (e.g. cardiovascular problems or asthma) or psychological disorders (e.g. anxiety or depressive disorders) because their physiological responses differ from those of nonsmokers or 'healthy' participants. Participants are moreover often instructed to refrain from caffeine and alcohol consumption for a certain time prior to the experiment. They are furthermore asked to assure a sufficient hydration level and to not have just eaten. This is done to limit possible between-participants differences with respect to ANS arousal (i.e. base activation) and arousability (i.e. reactivity).

Experimental conditions are highly controlled. Participants are usually seated and movement is restricted, both in order to not disturb physiological measures and because of the physically restricting range of sensors and cables of monitoring equipment. The sequence of stimulus presentation or experimental tasks is scripted and controlled by an experimenter. Manipulated events, hypothesized to be of emotional relevance, are time-stamped with an event marker for subsequent data processing.

Typical research results are based on measurements taken after participants were physically inactive for a few minutes. This rest period, during which participants may simply be instructed to sit quietly, view a relaxing film, or perform a minimally activating task, is used for returning participants' physiological activation to a base level (Kreibig *et al.* 2007). Measures of this habituation period are used as an estimate of each individual's base activation. Because individuals differ in their physiological basal activation (i.e. arousal level), knowledge of each individual's base activation allows statistical control and, by this, reduction of one source of between-participants variability (Stemmler 2003). The baseline estimate is used to calculate change scores by subtracting baseline levels from task levels (Llabre *et al.* 1991). It is, however, still a matter of research, when to record the baseline (Fahrenberg *et al.* 1987; Obrist 1981), for how long to record the baseline (Jennings *et al.* 1992; Saab *et al.* 1992), and under what kind of task to record the baseline (Jennings *et al.* 1992; Kreibig *et al.* 2007; Kreibig *et al.* 2005; Piferi *et al.* 2000). Particularly in the context of emotion research, it has been discussed whether such baselines should in fact assess base activation or rather aim at assessing modal activation (Levenson 1988).

Physiological responding found in the 'emotion' condition (i.e. average values based on milliseconds, seconds, or even several minutes) is either contrasted against physiological responding found in the same condition without the emotion component (i.e. same task/stimulus, but without emotional significance) or contrasted against physiological responding in another 'emotion' condition that differs from the first 'emotion' condition in emotional quality but is otherwise exactly the same. Results reported in psychophysiology are typically based on group averages across a number of individuals. These results are statistically significant, i.e. chance occurrence of the observed effect is small. Still, between-participants variability or error variance can be high in physiological data (Stemmler 2003).

Naturally, results strongly depend on the choice and number of variables assessed in a given study. Differential fractionation of physiological response variables implies that some variables may indicate differences between emotions whereas other variables may not. Looking at only a few variables can mean that variables that differentiate between emotions are missed. Because physiological variables serve specific functions in an overall regulation pattern, single variables cannot adequately identify such regulation patterns (Stemmler 1992*a*). Also, for the understanding of mechanisms rather than the enumeration of significant differences of physiological variables between emotions, it is advantageous to assess a well-selected array of such variables (Cacioppo *et al.* 2000*c*; Stemmler, 2004). Because, in most instances, physiological changes are the result of interaction among activation components, it is suggested that variables be sampled that are good estimators of basic activation components (Stemmler 1992*b*) or of the autonomic space (Berntson *et al.* 1991, 1993) and that reflect unique sources of variance (i.e. selecting measures based on non-redundancy).

In contrast to the laboratory, the context of affective computing is diametrically different. Minimal control of environmental stimuli and no selection according to person characteristics is possible. Rather, the user will be in full control over the interaction with the system, changing or interrupting the current action ad libitum. Clearly, the more that is known about physiological activation in non-emotional situations, the better the signal-to-noise ratio for subsequent detection and prediction of emotion (Stemmler 2003). Therefore, it will be of major importance to learn as much as possible about the situation and the person. The context can be monitored by audiovisual means, and a 'person-history' can be established both on the micro- and macro-level. For example, taking physiological measurements as early as possible allows one to estimate person characteristics, such as habitual arousal level. Running averages (mean or mode) could be one approach to estimating base activation. A context to which a user returns allows an even longer history of person-specific data. Such aspects allow implementation of knowledge of IRS (see the section on 'Indicator domain', this chapter).

Comprehensive physiological assessment and flexible data processing should aim at a large array of physiological parameters, including both traditional and more exploratory indices of variability, for example, those based on time and frequency domain analyses (Blechert *et al.* 2006; Friedman and Thayer, 1998; Van Diest *et al.* 2006).

Data analysis

Data analysis in psychophysiology targets mean differences between groups or conditions. This analysis technique is used to average out random noise from the 'true' signal. Inherent in the mean calculation is that none of the individuals, on the basis of whom the mean was calculated, necessarily need to display this average response. Moreover, common test statistics address statistical significance; even differences small in size may be found to be statistically significant with sufficiently large sample size. In contrast, effect sizes give information about the magnitude of effect. In the context of emotion differentiation, Stemmler (2003) argues for the use of multivariate analysis techniques because these consider variables not separately, but rather make use of all information, i.e. effects of single variables as well as of the configuration of variables to each other, which may be captured in a pattern, consisting of elevation, scatter, and shape (Stemmler 1988, 1992*b*). Such multivariate data analysis methods include multivariate analysis of variance (MANOVA) and pattern analysis.

Once again, the computing context takes the complementary perspective: detection and identification of emotion, based on the monitoring of physiological activation of individuals (i.e. a single unit). The computational interface typically constitutes an emotion detection algorithm and/or training of a classifier algorithm for emotion identification (Kolodyazhniy *et al.*, in preparation; Wilhelm *et al.* 2007). Using template matching to identify certain physiological response configurations, as in predictive discriminant function analysis or nonlinear approaches, relies on prior learning. Internal predictability refers to training and testing of a classifier on the same sample. This usually results in overestimation of the performance of the classifier on unknown data. External predictability refers to training and testing of a classifier on two disjunct data sets. The test data set can vary such that either unknown individuals occur or that known individuals occur in response to unknown stimuli or contexts or both (Kolodyazhniy *et al.*, in preparation; Wilhelm *et al.* 2007). Neural network systems that learn to detect and identify emotions based on initial user input are another possibility. This training can be achieved in different ways: (1) users prompt the system upon experience of an emotion and identify the kind of emotion or (2) the system prompts the user to identify their emotion, given detection of an event of interest, e.g. the presence of certain response patterns (template matching), synchronization of physiological variables as expressed in temporal correlation, or surpassing of an intensity of activation threshold.

When using training for emotion identification, verification of emotional responding is very important, as otherwise the trained response patterns will be blurred (Stemmler 2003). Self-report can be used for this (Sinha and Parsons 1996), although response fractionation may impair the verification. That is, if the emotion response system, from which the verification variable is derived (e.g. self-report of emotion), is uncoupled from the response system under investigation (e.g. physiological variables), the selection of cases would risk severe misclassification (cf. Mauss *et al.* 2005). For different reasons, participants might report that they are not feeling the target emotion, even though the target emotion and its physiological manifestations actually exist. An individual could be 'blind' to his or her feelings or might want to suppress any socially visible signs of an emotion (Stemmler 2003). Such cases critically compromise the validity of the training data. Whenever possible, indirect measures, such as facial expressions or gestures, should be used to substantiate self-report data (for a study implementing such a criterion, see Lerner *et al.* 2005).

To evaluate the performance of an emotion detection and identification system, several issues regarding the patterning of emotion need to be addressed.

(a) *Contextual–emotional response decomposition.* Does the system correctly differentiate between the emotion and its context?

(b) *Transsituational emotional response consistency.* Does the system recognize one and the same emotion across different contexts?

(c) *Transindividual emotional response consistency.* Does the system recognize one and the same emotion across different individuals?

(d) *Transtemporal emotional response consistency.* Does the system recognize one and the same emotion across different time points?

(e) *Emotional response gradation.* Does the system recognize one and the same emotion across different intensities?

(f) *Emotional response specificity.* Does the system correctly differentiate between different emotions in the same context?

Issues (b) through (e) also need to be demonstrated in the context of between-emotion differentiation.

Technical and ethical constraints

The application of physiological sensors is straightforward in the laboratory context. Given participant consent, sensor placement can be performed so as to maximize data quality. In the laboratory, where the participant remains relatively immobile, well-established wired solutions are the method of choice. They are well-validated, allow high data rates, and recent systems have become very robust to electromagnetic interference.

The picture changes dramatically when turning to the monitoring context of affective computing. Here, sensor application is one of the greatest challenges. It is desirable to take measurements, such that intrusion is minimal, preferably without actually gluing sensors to the skin or applying belts or clips. Technologies, such as the *Emotion Mouse*, that measures skin conductance over inbuilt sensors (Ark *et al.* 1999) or pressure-sensitive mouse devices that measure the force applied to the mouse (van den Hoogen *et al.* 2008) offer possible solutions for this, although the problem of high susceptibility to motion artefacts resulting from varying pressure of electrodes to the skin needs to be resolved in such contexts. Sensors may also be integrated into the chair, on which the person is seated (Dokhan *et al.* 2007). The use of infrared telethermography for measurement of body surface temperature may prove advantageous in such contexts, as this device is noninvasive (a camera is directed toward the body) and allows monitoring of larger areas of the skin than the limited region under an electrode (Rimm-Kaufman and Kagan 1996). Similarly, thermal imaging techniques may be useful for the measurement of facial expressions (Jarlier, Grandjean *et al.* 2008).

If users were to wear sensors directly on their body, for which wearable sensor technologies are being developed (Anliker *et al.* 2004; Locher *et al.* 2005; Roggen *et al.* 2006), wireless technologies would allow a larger range of free movement than wired solutions. Wireless systems may imply that either the sensors themselves are wireless, conceptualized as a wireless body area sensor network (WBAN), or that sensors are cabled to a portable wireless relay, such as a cellphone or PDA, or to a simple data logger. In ambulatory settings, both WBANs and wireless relays can be of great impact in terms of unobtrusiveness and real-time monitoring.

Lastly, in deciding to take such measurements, it is important to consider what consequences they may have for the human being involved. People have individual rights regarding what information they wish to disclose and what information to keep private. Taking such recordings also involves questions of authorized data usage as well as data security, including anonymity.

Taking physiological measurements of humans also calls for consideration of the possibility of disease transmission, on which Putnam *et al.* (1992) give a useful primer. Moreover, issues related to medical diagnosis arise. Measurement situations of affective computing are neither constructed to allow for medical diagnosis, nor are the instruments used necessarily of the needed precision. Still, certain abnormalities might be so pronounced that they impose the question of whether one has the obligation to inform versus the right to disturb the person. Such questions need to be answered *before* starting measurements.

Conclusion: The seven golden rules of physiological measurement for affective computing

To conclude, we provide guidelines that should be taken into account for the successful measurement of emotion-relevant physiological activation in an affective computing context.

1 *Mind the plurality of influences.* At a given point in time, physiological activation is influenced by effects of the non-emotional context, effects of the emotional context, and effects of the emotion proper ('Indicator domain: The nature of physiological emotion differentiation', this chapter). Thus, physiological responses are not a direct window to emotional state. It is hence important to disentangle emotion effects and context effects using appropriate data and measurement models.

2 *Ensure specificity.* To use a certain physiological measure as an indicator of emotion, it needs to be specific in a certain way with respect to a certain emotion construct. When relating physiology to emotion, properly conceptualize the indicand in the emotion domain (e.g. based on valence and arousal dimensions, basic emotions, or appraisal outcomes; see 'Indicand domain: The nature of psychological emotion differentiation', this chapter), the physiological indicator(s) (see 'Indicator domain: The nature of physiological emotion differentiation', this chapter), and the expected nature of the relation (see 'The nature of relations: Projections and possible inferences', this chapter).

3 *Know what you measure.* Familiarize yourself with the ANS and the respective measurement methods (see 'What to measure?' and the Appendix, this chapter), so that you can make an informed choice of which parameters to assess and which measurement device to use in order to obtain informative data. In the measurement situation, collect information about the specifics of the person (physiological baseline) and the situation (audiovisual recordings), as physiological responses are influenced by both.

4 *Know when to measure.* Emotions are related to relevant internal or external stimuli or events. Emotion-relevant physiological effects occur in a relatively narrow time window around the occurrence of such an event (from milliseconds up to several minutes).

5 *Measure multiple systems.* Due to the interactions between different physiological response systems, conclusions about autonomic activation based on measurements of only one system

will be incomplete. Always try to assess a broad array of physiological variables, selected according to their non-redundancy.

6 *Analyse patterns.* Physiological effects of emotion are expressed in the combination and interrelation of different variables and their specific response profiles. Use analysis methods that tap the interrelation between different measurements, such as multivariate analysis or pattern analysis, taking into account both the spatial and temporal organization of the response pattern. When training a pattern recognition algorithm, use both direct (e.g. explicit self-report) and indirect measures (e.g. implicit facial expressions) to verify emotional experience.

7 *Beware of inferential fallacies.* If you observe a physiological activation that has previously been found to vary as a function of emotion, do not automatically interpret this as indicating the occurrence of an emotion. Take into account the kind of projection between physiological indicator and emotion, then make the appropriate kind of inference about the absence or occurrence of certain emotions (see 'The nature of relations: Projections and possible inferences', this chapter).

Embarking on the journey of affective computing offers exciting possibilities. We wait curiously to see whether emotion-sensitive systems outlined in this chapter will be developed and to what extent they will be able to accurately interact with an emoting user, based on detection and identification of emotion.

Appendix. A guide to physiological measures

This appendix provides background information for selecting specific physiological response variables and deciding how to measure them. This guide is organized according to organ systems, wherein we present physiological response variables according to the kind of physical quality being assessed (e.g. changes in voltage, volume, or impedance). We focus on general measurement principles and point to guideline papers for measurement specifics.

The cardiovascular system

The cardiovascular system consists of the heart and vascular pathways that deliver oxygenated blood to the organs and tissues and return deoxygenated blood to the lungs. The heart is one of the few organs innervated by both the SNS and PNS, resulting in complex patterns of interaction and coactivation (Berntson *et al.* 1991). This is why, especially at the heart, an independent assessment of effects of the SNS and PNS is of high interest to decompose autonomic influences.

The heart produces measurable signals in a number of domains. First, and most prominently, electrical changes occur during the polarization and depolarization associated with the contraction and relaxation of the heart muscle (myocardium). The *electrocardiogram* (ECG) is the measurement of such **voltage changes** in the body over time (for recording guidelines, see Jennings *et al.* 1981). A typical ECG tracing of a normal heartbeat (or cardiac cycle) consists of P wave, QRS complex, and T wave. Each cardiac cycle starts with an impulse from the sinoatrial (SA) node near the top of the atrium. The spreading of electrical activity over the atrium (i.e. atrial depolarization) produces the P wave on the ECG. The QRS complex marks the depolarization of the ventricles, i.e. ventricular contraction. The ST segment is the time when the ventricle is contracting, but no electricity is flowing. The T wave represents the repolarization (or recovery) of the ventricles. A number of time-dependent measures can be derived from the characteristic points on the ECG. For example, the time interval from one R-wave peak to the next quantifies the time of one complete heart cycle, i.e. one heart period or interbeat interval (IBI). The inverse of this measure corresponds to heart rate (HR, in beats per minute). Heart rate reflects effects of both SNS and PNS innervation, which function independently (i.e. reciprocally or unreciprocally): an increase in HR may be caused by increased SNS or decreased PNS stimulation. Heart rate variability (HRV) is a measure that quantifies the variability of heart rate over a certain period of time. The systematic variation of heart rate with the respiration cycle, known as respiratory sinus arrhythmia (RSA), describes the phenomenon that heart period increases during exhalation and decreases during inhalation. Properly quantified, RSA is an index of PNS influence on the heart (Allen *et al.* 2007; Grossman and Kollai 1993; Hirsch and Bishop, 1981; Ritz and Dahme 2006; Task Force of the European Society of Cardiology and the North American Society of Pacing Electrophysiology 1996; see the latter for recording guidelines).

Volume changes resulting from fluctuations in the amount of blood or air in an organ or the whole body are measured in *plethysmography*. *Photoplethysmography* (PPG) obtains a volumetric measure via optical means by emitting infrared light into the skin and measuring **the change in the amount of light** that passes through. PPG can be obtained from transmissive (as at the finger tip) or reflective absorption (as on the forehead). Depending on the blood volume in the skin, more or less light is absorbed. *Pulse photoplethysmographs* are commonly worn on the finger or ear. The measured signal records venous blood volume changes as well as the arterial blood pulsation in the arterioles. PPG allows derivation of pulse amplitude (PA), the difference between peak and valley of the pulse waveform, indexing peripheral vasoconstriction, and, in combination with the R-spike of the ECG, pulse transit time (PTT), the duration of time that the pulse wave takes to travel to the periphery.

Impedance plethysmography (IPG) obtains a volumetric measurement by observing **changes in impedance** as blood or air volume varies by passing a small alternating current through the body. *Impedance cardiography* (ICG) is an application of IPG to assess the mechanical functioning of the heart, providing a number of parameters relevant to flow, volume, and contractility related to myocardial performance (Sherwood *et al.* 1990). ICG measures impedance changes in the thorax caused by changes of fluid content over the cardiac cycle, in particular those related to thoracic blood volume changes. The method applies a high-frequency constant current flow across a set of thoracic electrodes and records the associated voltage across another, inner set of electrodes (Berntson *et al.* 2007). According to Ohm's law, when the current flow is held constant, the measured voltage varies inversely with the resistance of the thoracic current path. The body components with the lowest resistance are blood and plasma, so the measured thoracic impedance is highly sensitive to changes in the cardiac and aortic distribution and flow of blood during the cardiac cycle (Hoetink *et al.*2004). Two types of measures can be derived from the impedance signal: (1) measures of systolic time interval, related to the duration of myocardial contraction, driving blood into the aorta and pulmonary arteries, including pre-ejection period (PEP), the time interval from onset of ventricular contraction to the onset of ventricular ejection, a measure of myocardial contractility that is used to index sympathetic cardiac control; and left ventricular ejection time (LVET), the time interval from opening to closing of the aortic valve; and (2) volumetric measures, including stroke volume (SV; Kubicek *et al.* 1966; Lozano *et al.* 2007), the amount of blood ejected from the heart during one heart beat; and cardiac output (CO), calculated as the product of stroke volume and heart rate, indicating the amount of blood pumped from the heart during one minute (for recording guidelines, see Sherwood *et al.* 1990).

Pressure changes over the cardiac cycle are another vital sign that provides information about autonomic activation. Common parameters derived from a sphygmomanometer are systolic blood pressure (SBP, the pressure when the heart is contracting, indicating maximum arterial pressure), diastolic blood pressure (DBP, the pressure when the heart is in relaxation and filling with blood, indicating minimum arterial pressure), mean arterial pressure (MAP, the average pressure over a cardiac cycle), and pulse pressure (the difference between systolic and diastolic pressure). The *auscultatory method* for blood pressure measurement is based on body sounds. Typically, a cuff with an embedded microphone is placed on the upper arm. Application of external pressure is used to estimate intra-arterial pressure, where so-called Korotkoff sounds are used to indicate different stages in the measurement process relevant for the estimation of different pressure readings. The *oscillometric method* is based on measurements of pressure oscillations in the cuff transmitted from the underlying vessel (Borow and Newburger 1982). High temporal resolution blood pressure measurements can be obtained from small finger cuffs (Brownley *et al.* 2000). A fast-response servo control system responds to finger volume increases with increased cuff pressure as to re-establish original arterial size and blood volume. Fluctuations in cuff pressure thus closely follow intra-arterial pressure.

The combination of ECG, ICG, and blood pressure measurement allows for the assessment of cardiovascular changes. For example, total peripheral resistance (TPR), calculated from blood pressure and cardiac output, provides information about resistance of all peripheral vasculature in the systemic circulation and is related to vasoconstriction.

Changes in surface temperature are another easily accessible measure that also provides information about the constriction or dilatation of the vasculature. Typically, measurements are taken from the finger (finger temperature, FT or skin temperature in contrast to core body temperature). *Thermocouples* (thermoelectric effect) or *thermistors* (temperature-dependent resistors) are often used as temperature sensors.

The respiratory system

The respiratory system consists of the lungs, the airways, the muscles of respiration (i.e. diaphragm, intercostals, rib cage) and their central control, as well as the chest wall. Inspiration is initiated by the contraction of the diaphragm, which forces the abdominal content down and forward, lifts the rib cage, and thus increases thoracic volume. This creates a negative pressure differential in the lungs and air is drawn in. In expiration, the lungs recoil and return to end-expiratory volume. The respiratory system primarily supports gas exchange between the atmosphere and the blood, delivering oxygen to the blood stream and removing carbon dioxide produced by cellular metabolism. It is also implicated in speech production and odour perception (Lorig 2007).

Breathing is a phenomenon that falls under both conscious and unconscious control. We can voluntarily hold our breath, concentrate, and regulate our breathing pattern, for example, in meditation practice, but typically rely on the automatic regulation of the ANS to adjust breathing to bodily demands, be that exercise or sleep (Wallace *et al.* 1971). Drawing attention to respiration, such as instructing participants to 'breathe normally', causes an abnormal type of breathing (i.e. arrhythmic and irregular breathing patterns; Harver and Lorig 2000), and should thus be avoided in measurement contexts.

Variables typically recorded in studies measuring the respiratory system are the following: breathing frequency or respiration rate (RR) is the number of respiratory cycles per minute (cpm). Tidal volume (V_t) is the normal volume of air inhaled after an exhalation, i.e. depth of breathing. The duration of the phases of the breathing cycle are another commonly quantified parameter, including inspiratory time (T_i), expiratory time (T_e),[3] and total time of the respiratory cycle (T_{tot}). The ratio of inspiratory and total breath time (T_i/T_{tot}) indicates the duty cycle, and

---

[3] Parametrizations of T_i and T_e may include or exclude inspiratory and expiratory pauses (P_i and P_e, respectively).

the ratio of inspiratory volume and inspiratory time (V_i/T_i) indexes inspiratory flow rate. End-tidal carbon dioxide partial pressure (end-tidal pCO_2) is the proportion of carbon dioxide at the end of a respiratory cycle, i.e. at the end of expiration. These parameters can be derived from a number of physical expressions of the respiratory cycle, such as changes in thoracic distension, impedance, temperature, sounds, and breathing gas composition.

Changes in thorax circumference are evident as expansions of the chest and/or abdomen. Recording is typically accomplished by applying a belt-like device. This method is relatively non-invasive; however, it always provides external feedback because the belt must be tightened during breathing. Such devices provide estimates of time-dependent parameters, including respiration rate and duration of phases of the respiratory cycle, and relative breathing amplitude, but do not provide volume-dependent parameters of tidal volume or inspiratory flow rate because sensors typically do not respond linearly to volume changes. Recording of both thoracic and abdominal changes is recommended because these two compartments have independent contributions to total respiratory volume (Konno and Mead 1967). Belt sensors typically rely on *strain gauges* (strain-sensitive resistors) or *piezoelectric sensors* to quantify changes in breathing. Similarly, in an *air-pressure pneumograph*, bellows are connected to a band fitted around the abdomen or chest. Changes in pressure occur within the bellows as the chest stretches the bellows and reduces the pressure within it, readily recordable with a pressure transducer. *Respiratory inductive plethysmography* (RIP) consists of two coils that are sewn into elastic bands encircling the rib cage and abdomen and are connected to an oscillator module (Cohn *et al.* 1982; Tobin *et al.* 1983). Changes in thorax circumference alter the self-inductance of the coils and the frequency of their oscillation. Inductive plethysmography allows for reliable measurement of both time- and volume-dependent respiratory responses in combination with appropriate spirometry calibration (cf. the LifeShirt; Wilhelm *et al.* 2003). *Magnetometry* is another technique that makes use of the distension of the chest wall and abdomen (see McCool *et al.* 2002 for a portable version of this device).

Transthoracic impedance changes, related to the volume of air in the thorax over a respiratory cycle, are another way of measuring temporal and volumetric parameters of respiration (Stein and Luparello 1967). Electrodes placed on the thorax apply an alternating current to the chest wall. Impedance increases during inhalation when air is drawn in and the chest expands and decreases during exhalation when air moves out and the chest deflates. This method is often used to measure the heart (cf. impedance cardiography), and algorithms allow extraction of *impedance pneumography* data from impedance cardiography recordings (Ernst *et al.* 1999).

Temperature changes measured near the mouth or nose, related to differences in temperature between inspired and expired air, are yet another way of measuring respiratory activity. This method makes use of the fact that air is warmed in the lungs before being exhaled. Thus, an increase in temperature indicates exhalation. As for cardiovascular surface temperature, thermistors or thermocouples may be used to quantify changes in temperature. Use of these sensors strongly depend on the cooperation of subjects to breathe continuously through either their mouth or nose only.

Changes in blood gas saturation can be estimated from analysis of the chemical composition of the exhaled air, which is close to alveolar and arterial values in healthy people (Gardner 1996). The *capnogram* is a device for the analysis of breath-by-breath variations in the rate of CO_2 production. Measurements can be made by sampling from the nostrils or mouth. Transdermal probes have also been employed to sense CO_2 levels in the capillary beds (transcutaneous pCO_2). Such measurements can be used to index hyperventilation, a physiological state of breathing in excess of metabolic requirements (Gardner 1996), as indicated by reduced levels of pCO_2 (i.e. hypocapnia) due to higher ventilation than the rate of CO_2 production. *Pulse oximetry* can also be used to estimate changes in the saturation of blood haemoglobin with oxygen. Similar to a photoplethysmograph, a pulse oximeter detects the ratio of absorbed light for two different light sources, one of which is specifically absorbed by oxygen-bound haemoglobin.

Sounds related to the respiratory cycle provide yet another means of measuring respiratory activity. A microphone placed near the nares records different sounds for inhalation and exhalation. Clearly, this technique is exposed to artefacts from ambient noise. *Phonospirometry* is a technique that uses a tracheal microphone to analyse sounds related to air flow in the lungs and is described to allow estimates of both time- and volume-dependent respiratory parameters (Que *et al.* 2002). Ritz *et al.* (2002) provide measurement guidelines for mechanical lung functioning.

The eccrine system

The eccrine sweat glands are part of the body's exocrine gland system that regulates the release of fluids through the skin. The eccrine glands have been called the 'skin's sprinkler system' (Hurley 2001, p. 47), as they secrete sweat, a fluid comprising water and various minerals. These glands are widely distributed over the body surface, with highest density on the palms of the hands and the soles of the feet, intermediate density on the head, and lowest density on the arms, legs, and trunk (Andreassi 2006). The eccrine glands are simple, tubular structures with a round secretory portion, located in the dermis, the underlayer of the skin, and a duct that opens as a small pore at the surface of the skin. The eccrine system is solely innervated by the SNS (Critchley 2002; Wallin 1981). The neurotransmitter at the postganglionic synapse mediating eccrine gland activity is acetylcholine (Shields *et al.* 1987; Venables and Christie 1980), not noradrenaline, which is the postganglionic transmitter at all other sympathetic innervations. Because activation of the eccrine system has been found to dissociate from activation of other sympathetic indicators (cf. directional fractionation of response; Lacey 1967), it should not be taken as a general indicator of sympathetic activation, despite its easy accessibility for measurements.

Perspiration occurs not only in the context of thermoregulation, but also in response to psychological stimulation, including emotion, attention, arousal, and mental effort, as well as locomotion (Andreassi 2006; Boucsein 1992; Cacioppo and Tassinary 1990a; Dindo and Fowles 2008; Siddle 1991). When sweat levels change in the eccrine glands, the **skin's electrical characteristics** change as well, a phenomenon referred to as *electrodermal activity* (EDA; Christie 1981). Measurable properties of sweating are changes in skin conductance[4] (SC; based on the passage of an external current across the skin, i.e. exosomatic method) and skin potential (SP; recording of internal current, i.e. endosomatic method). Measurement of skin conductance is typically the method of choice, which is expressed in units of microSiemens (μS).

EDA is composed of tonic and phasic components (Dawson *et al.* 1990; Lim *et al.* 1997). Tonic EDA is a slowly changing base signal, not directly related to a stimulus. Quantified as skin conductance level (SCL), the absolute level of conductance at a given moment in the absence of a measurable phasic response, it indicates basal activity. Superimposed on the tonic level are phasic increases in conductance, i.e. skin conductance responses (SCRs). The phasic EDA component indicates a response to stimulation. It can occur after stimulus presentation, called an event-related SCR (ER-SCR; exogenous activation), or it can occur spontaneously, called nonspecific SCRs (NS-SCRs; endogenous activation). When a stimulus is presented, several parameters of the response, such as SCR size, can be computed. Averaged over multiple repetitions, magnitude is the mean value computed across all stimulus presentations including those without a measurable

---

[4] Skin conductance, in contrast to skin resistance, has become the preferred measure for reasons of measurement model; see Dawson, Schell, and Filion (2007).

response, whereas amplitude is the mean value computed across only those trials where a measurable (nonzero) response occurred. Temporal characteristics of the SCR include onset latency, rise time, and half recovery time. Under conditions of high activation, high SCL, frequent NS-SCRs, large SCR amplitude, short latency, short rise time, and short recovery time tend to co-occur. Because correlations among EDA components are, however, generally less than 0.60 (Lockhart and Lieberman 1979; Schell *et al.* 1988; Venables and Christie 1980), these components are regarded as representing partially independent sources of information (with the exception of high correlation between SCR rise time and recovery time, and a consequent preference for the measure of rise time, because recovery time is not always calculable if subsequent responses occur; Venables and Christie 1980). Measurement guidelines for EDA have been outlined by Fowles *et al.* (1981).

Chapter 2.5

Emotions in interpersonal interactions

Brian Parkinson

Summary

Emotionally competent agents must orient to relations with other people in order to model the operation of emotions in their everyday social context. This chapter maps out the territory they need to negotiate by outlining ways in which emotions function in the interpersonal world. For the purposes of exposition, three different kinds of relation are distinguished, each of which may operate at either an explicit or an implicit level. Roughly speaking, these relations may be strung out into a narrative episode, wherein interpersonal factors may activate emotions (or otherwise influence the process of non-social activation), affect their real-time emergence and regulation, and in turn be affected by emotions. First, I consider how interpersonal factors impact on appraisals, both by providing content for appraisal mechanisms to process and by shaping how these mechanisms operate on emotional content. Although many interpersonal effects on emotion are mediated by appraisal, some varieties of emotion contagion and social appraisal may operate more directly, and depend on bottom-up mutual adjustment rather than top-down coordination. Turning to modulators, emotion expressions and experiences are not only adjusted in response to interpersonal pressures, but also depend on co-regulated patterns of cognition and orientation between interactants. Further, emotions bring consequences, not only for other people's emotions but also for interpretation, action orientation, and attention. These interpersonal effects are important for modellers because they help to constitute the dynamic social environment within which emotions unfold and to which they respond. Finally, I present an integrative relation-alignment approach to interpersonal emotions, arguing that many social emotions (and social instances of non-social emotions) are attuned and oriented in real time to the effects that they exert on others. Emotions operate not only as strategic social influence attempts but also as on-line adjustments to the unfolding affordances of other people's mutual orientations. In short, emotion's interpersonal causes, modulators, and effects fit together into functional modes of dynamic engagement with the interpersonal environment. Modelling such interpersonal processes requires fully embodied agents embedded in and continually sensitive to responsive social environments.

Introduction

Emotions are about things that matter to us, at least for as long as we feel emotional about those things. Some of the things that matter to us most are other people, especially to the extent that what they feel, do, think, or say impacts on our lives. It follows that emotions are often focused on other people in some shape or form. Even ostensibly inner-directed states such as guilt and sadness often relate to interpersonal events rather than purely private calculations about a socially isolated or decontextualized self. And when it comes to anger, affection, hate, gratitude, or jealousy, their characteristic interpersonal orientation forms an inextricable part of the associated appraisals, action tendencies, and facial expressions. Anger, for example, is characteristically directed towards some social or quasi-social object. We do not simply get angry as a free-floating condition; we get angry *with someone* for doing something we take exception to, and even when we are angry with our car or computer, we want to bring its behaviour into line as if it were a responsive agent too. So emotions are often caused by, and directed at, interpersonal states of affairs. Further, their implicit function may be to readjust these states of affairs and the ongoing responsivity of the interpersonal environment in turn will affect their enactment in real time.

Although these observations about the interpersonal context of many emotions are mostly uncontroversial, contemporary theories of emotion and models of emotional agents still often seem most relevant to contexts in which a passive individual is exposed to a non-social stimulus (see Hareli and Rafaeli 2008; Parkinson *et al.* 2005): 'We meet a bear, are frightened and run' (James 1890/1898, p. 190), we lose our job and feel depressed, we win a lottery and it makes us happy (at least in the short term). Although the principles shaping reactions to such prototypically emotional events may be extended to cover future-oriented operations performed on responsive interpersonal objects (e.g. Marsella and Gratch 2009), another way of dealing with the latter emotion instances would be to look for their distinctive principles and processes. In short, an emotionally competent agent may need to follow different kinds of rules and procedures when operating in a dynamic social world.

Social and non-social emotions

Emotions may be divided into categories of various kinds. A commonly applied distinction separates social emotions from other (non-social) emotions. Clear cases of social emotions include embarrassment, shame, jealousy, love, and hate because these emotions characteristically relate to social objects. In other words, the focus of evaluation, desire, or appraisal is something to do with other people or the self's relation to other people. Even if these emotions can occur in private, the thoughts and feelings associated with them concern events that have happened, are happening, or might happen in the social world (see Hareli and Parkinson 2008).

According to some theorists, social emotions emerge later in development and are more cognitively complex than non-social basic emotions (e.g. Lewis 2000). However, some of the emotions that seem to emerge earliest in our lives are directed at interpersonal states of affairs (e.g. attachment-related affect; see Nadel and Muir 1995; Trevarthen 1984). It therefore seems mistaken to conflate the social basis of an emotion with its developmental trajectory (Draghi-Lorenz *et al.* 2001).

Are any emotions truly non-social? According to most evolutionary accounts, the emotion of fear originated as a strategy facilitating escape from predators among our hunter–gatherer ancestors. If this is the primary function of (and *raison d'être* for) fear, then this emotion is not exclusively social, because it can be directed at non-social objects. However, many of the events that frighten us in contemporary society have some social element (status anxiety, social phobia, fear of public speaking, etc.). Furthermore, a case might be made for fear serving as a means of soliciting protection from more powerful others rather than being a direct preparation for the physical demands of escape from dangerous events (see Parkinson *et al.* 2005). Indeed, our earliest experiences of fear (during infancy) probably occur before we are capable of running away from dangerous animals. Why then should natural selection preprogram an integrated response that does not need to be activated until infants have been socially attuned to the specific threatening aspects of current environments and learnt tactics for dealing with them?

Regardless of whether it is possible for emotions to be entirely non-social, everyone agrees that some emotions are necessarily social and that others can sometimes be provoked by social events and bring social consequences. When we get emotional, it is usually but not always about something happening in our social lives that changes the way we operate in the social world (Parkinson 1996). What then are the causes and effects of emotions that operate in interpersonal interactions?

Interpersonal causes

Other people's actions and experiences constitute one of the most common classes of emotion-inducing events (e.g. Scherer *et al.* 1986). In this section, I consider some of the ways in which something that someone else does, thinks, or feels can affect emotions. In particular, I discuss how emotional appraisals may be directed at interpersonal considerations, how interpersonal factors may shape the dynamic course of these appraisals, how other people's emotions might impact on our own emotions, and whether all interpersonal effects on emotion can be fully explained by appraisal approaches.

Appraisal content

For many theorists, a defining feature of emotion is its object-directedness or intentionality (e.g. Ortony *et al.* 1988). Emotions are about events that have happened, are happening, or might happen, or about things in the world (or in our heads) and our relationship to them. From an appraisal perspective (e.g. Frijda 1986; Lazarus 1991), what activates and shapes an emotion is our interpretation and evaluation of these objects or events. In this section, I will discuss the range of interpersonal considerations at which emotional appraisals may be directed (appraisal *content*) before turning in the following section to how the *process* of appraisal may be affected by interpersonal factors even when appraisal content is not itself interpersonal.

The emotions that we experience during interactions with others may relate either to events that are part of the dialogue itself or external events from the past, present, or future. In some cases, we remain focused on an unchanging concern (e.g. a recent traumatic loss or cause for celebration, an impending threat or an anticipated reward) despite changes in incoming information, but more usually our appraisals are continually updated to track unfolding events. For example, we may be anxious about impressing another person and closely monitor her dynamic facial expression to check how her attitude towards us is changing in response to our unfolding social influence attempts. In such circumstances, appraisals and their associated emotions relate to an ongoing stream of information and its implications for current (and continuously adjusting) actions by the self (Lazarus 1991).

In the above example, the central object of emotion is the other person's appraisal, which continually changes as we attempt to influence it. Our own influence attempts may in turn be seen as forms of problem-focused coping (e.g. Lazarus 1991) and their appraised success or failure also has a real-time relation to our developing interpersonal stance. Further, our influence attempts may themselves involve presentation of emotion. For example, we may have learnt to suppress social anxiety in order to create a better impression. Thus, we will also monitor our own emotion expression and check the other person's developing response to that. Under these circumstances, it becomes increasingly difficult to specify where appraisal ends and emotion begins and whether regulation and coping are objects of appraisal, aspects of emotion, or external processes intended to modify emotion. However, at least one thing seems clear: emotions in interpersonal interaction are often focused on social concerns and respond in real-time to the changing nature of these concerns in relation to the self.

The above discussion paves the way for a preliminary classification of possible sources of appraisal information that are operative in interpersonal interactions. First, other people may represent the primary object of appraisal in episodes characterized by love, hate, contempt, and so on. Second, appraisal and emotion may focus on some relatively enduring characteristic of the other person, as occurs in envy or admiration directed at someone else's charm, intelligence, or good looks, or disgust at their personal hygiene. Third, some more temporary behaviour may provoke an emotional response, such as when the other person insults or praises us, or suddenly confesses undying devotion. Fourth, as illustrated above, their responses to our behaviour may become the focus of our appraisals of the success or failure of our own emotional projects or coping efforts. Although this list is by no means exhaustive, it still serves to demonstrate that emotions occurring in interpersonal interactions are often directed at social objects of some kind. Of particular interest is the fact that the precise focus of appraisal (as well as its output) often changes quickly over time and modellers need to be attentive to this rapid dynamic attunement to the interpersonal environment (e.g. Marsella and Gratch 2009).

Appraisal processes

Moving from appraisal content to process, interpersonal factors may influence how social or non-social input is registered or transformed. These processing effects may operate at a number of different levels, ranging from sensorimotor to articulated conceptual effects (e.g. Leventhal and Scherer 1987). In other words, both the dynamic affordances offered by other people's actions and their perceived meaning can impact on the emotion generation process.

One of the clearest examples of how appraisals may be affected by interpersonal processes is provided by the phenomenon of social referencing. Sorce and colleagues (1985) demonstrated that 1-year-old infants approaching a visual cliff were more likely to cross towards their mothers if she was showing a happy face than if she was showing a fear face. These researchers concluded that the caregiver's emotional communication shaped the infant's appraisal of threat, with a smile signalling safety and a fearful expression signalling potential danger.

Some studies have shown that vocal cues may enhance the effectiveness of visual emotion displays during social referencing (Mumme et al. 1996), perhaps because they can be picked up even when infants are not specifically attending to the adult (Campos et al. 2003). In fact, some theorists argue that one of the functions of vocal cues is to draw visual attention to the face of the person whose voice is heard (D'Entremont and Muir 1999).

What exactly is communicated by the adult's expressions in social referencing situations? Because emotions are relational processes (e.g. Frijda 1986; Lazarus 1991), they embody the actor's orientation towards some intentional object (which may be another person). For example, the mother's apparent anxiety in the visual cliff studies carries the meaning that she is concerned about the potential negative consequences of the infant moving further forward. This simultaneously conveys information relating to the other person (that she is concerned about potential negative consequences) and the intentional object (that it is potentially dangerous). Any emotional impact of the other's presented emotions may therefore depend on changes in appraisal of the other person, of the object to which the other is oriented, or both (e.g. the relation between person and object or between person, person, and object).

This possible duality of social appraisal effects raises the issue of whether they genuinely influence the process of appraisal or simply its content. Manstead and Fischer (2001) coined the term social appraisal to cover situations in which the other person's reaction to an object or event provides input to the appraisal of a separate object. For example, in social referencing experiments, the mother's expression of fear signals that the visual cliff should be appraised as dangerous. However, in an ambiguous situation such as this, it may simply be that the toddler separately appraises the visual cliff and the potential reaction of the mother to crossing it. In other words, social referencing may leave the appraisal of an emotional object unchanged but add another appraisal relating to the other person.

Moving to adult–adult interactions, Manstead and Fischer (2001) discuss situations in which people take other people's emotions into account when arriving at their own appraisals of potentially emotional situations. For example, I may be less amused by a risqué comedy film if I sense that my companion disapproves of some of its off-colour humour. One interpretation of such episodes is that my companion's emotion changes my appraisal of the jokes so that I find them less funny. Alternatively, as implied above, any change in emotion may result from appraisals of, and emotions directed towards, my companion rather than the joke. In particular, my concern that he is not enjoying the film may detract from my own enjoyment of the overall situation. Another possibility is that I actively try to regulate my amusement because I recognize that my companion will be displeased by overt hilarity in this context. Although each of this possible processes might be subsumed under a generic concept of social appraisal (e.g. Fischer *et al.* 2003), there are obvious theoretical and operational advantages to maintaining principled distinctions between them.

In sum, a number of possible processes may underlie the social appraisal effects described above (see also Scherer 2001).

- *Interpersonal effects on active concerns.* The other person's emotion may lead to reprioritizing of goals, motives, or concerns (Scherer 2001), thus providing a different relational context for appraisal. For example, our co-viewer's outrage at sensitive comedy material may make us view jokes from a moral rather than humorous perspective.

- *Interpersonal appraisal objects.* The other person's emotion or anticipated future action may be an object of appraisal (Manstead and Fischer 2001; e.g. being upset that someone else is upset, being anxious about how anxious an action is making the other feel).

- *Interpersonal effects on appraisal objects.* The other person's actions or expressions may alter the nature or severity of a separate object of appraisal, e.g. by providing direct assistance in warding off a threat.

- *Interpersonal appraisal information.* The other person's emotion may provide direct information that affects appraisals, e.g. about available social support feeding into the appraisal of coping potential (Saltzman and Holahan 2002).

- *Interpersonal appraisal calibration.* The other person's emotion may be explicitly taken into account when arriving at appraisals (as implied in the original social appraisal model).

- *Interpersonal emotion regulation.* The other person's actions or expressions may provide regulatory resources that change the outputs of an already unfolding emotion (see also below).

None of these principles are beyond the scope of existing implementations of appraisal theory; they simply specify that social factors may affect what is appraised (appraisal content) or provide information that influences how appraisal unfolds (appraisal process). Appraisal processes remain the proximal mediators of emotional reactions but there is increased acknowledgement of the interpersonal context for these processes. As such, the implications for modelling of emotionally competent agents only relate to how social information is processed.

However, some forms of social appraisal may involve a more serious reconsideration of appraisal principles because they seem to obviate the need for either implicit or explicit apprehension of the personal significance of an emotional situation. For example, Parkinson (2001*a*) suggests that, during interactions, actors' continuing adjustments in mutual orientation may lead them to adopt co-constructed relational stances without either party registering the emotional meaning that these stances convey.

For example, I sometimes find myself adopting an angry tone of voice when I am escalating the emphasis of my expression in order to convey even a trivial point under circumstances when there is resistance to information transfer (e.g. when trying to talk to someone who is in the next room, or someone who does not know the background information that would make my point clear). More generally, situated lines of interpersonal action are continually responsive to the adjustments made to them by others. Sometimes they interlock in ways that are readable as emotional even though neither interactant has registered information directly relating to the personal significance of what is happening. Such emotional outcomes are not wholly mediated by individual processes of meaning extraction but rather emerge interactively from the resonances and resistances characterizing ongoing relational dynamics. As yet, proposals for modelling such episodes remain mostly speculative (e.g. Gratch 2008).

Emotion contagion

As described by Hatfield and colleagues (1994), emotion contagion explains the phenomenon of finding yourself in a similar affective state to someone with whom you are interacting, for example, by catching their enthusiasm or feeling enervated after exposure to their depressed or lethargic demeanour. According to these authors, the process underlying such effects depends on automatic mimicry of expressive behaviours. Internal feedback from these copied expressions (or from the neural commands provoking them) in turn leads to corresponding emotional experience because of the operation of self-perception processes. Other theorists (e.g. Neumann and Strack 2000) have placed less emphasis on direct mirroring of another's movements and merely assume that action codes directly activated by perception of another's perceptions can trigger associated affect.

A number of studies have attempted to distinguish the operation of automatic emotion contagion from more controlled or inferential processes (including social appraisal) in both laboratory (e.g. Hsee *et al*. 1992; Neumann and Strack 2000) and field (e.g. Totterdell *et al*. 1998; Parkinson and Simons 2009) settings. Their general conclusion is that interpersonal affect transfer is not entirely mediated by reported appraisals of events. However, no research yet provides direct evidence that emotion contagion based on either expressive mimicry or activation of interpersonally attuned action codes specifically explains these appraisal-independent effects on emotion. One alternative possibility is that people are automatically aware of another's relational stance during an interaction (based on innate relational capacities, e.g. Trevarthen 1984; or early acquired relational habits and skills arising from experiences of primary and secondary intersubjectivity, e.g. Hobson 2002). People are implicitly able to take the other's perspectives without having to copy their exact physical movements (although this may also occur in some circumstances) and this brings emotional effects depending on the level and nature of identification with the other person. Instead of seeing emotion contagion as an explanation for empathy, perhaps basic empathic processes can lead to emotion contagion when the conditions are right (see also Ruys and Stapel 2009).

It seems undeniable that the tone of an interaction is often influenced by subtle indications of affective state, conveyed not only by the face, voice, and body, but also by the rhythm and tempo of the exchange, its enmeshment, and the way different parts relate to each other. However, it is less certain that the emotional aspects of these phenomena are produced purely as a function of direct individual sensory feedback. People read their emotional states not only from observation of their own reactions, but also from the reactions of others who reflect it back to them. We tend to feel happier when smiling mainly because others often smile back and their apparent happiness makes us feel better. In other words, interpersonal rather than intrapsychic feedback may mediate many real-life examples of emotion contagion.

Appraisal-independent effects?

Evidence that interpersonal emotion transfer operates independently of reported appraisals does not rule out mediation by appraisals operating at an unreported or unreportable level (e.g. unconsciously; Moors, 2010). Indeed, seeing contagion as a function of implicit perspective taking and identification is compatible with accounts in terms of automatic self-relevant appraisals. For example, your happiness may make me happy because I automatically see things from your point of view and want you to experience pleasure. Of course, if our relationship were antagonistic or competitive, my automatic perspective-taking might lead to a more negative reaction to your apparent delight.

However, Scherer (2001) proposes a way in which interpersonal effects might bypass appraisal processes including unconscious ones. Even if subcomponents of emotion are normally integrated by the appraisal register, they are also susceptible to influences from other sources (e.g. pharmacological, homeostatic, etc.). In principle, then, the pattern of bodily activity that characterizes emotional function might be assembled from co-occurring bottom-up processes (e.g. dynamic facial mimicry or countermimicry) and their coordination might derive not from central integration but from dynamic concordance of external pressures (including interpersonal pressures; see Parkinson 2001a).

Thus, emotions may emerge as co-regulated modes of engagement with ongoing events whose emotion-relevant features do not need to be extracted by any appraisal mechanism. For example, a child's escalating struggle against physical restraint does not necessarily depend on the detection of novelty, intrinsic unpleasantness, norm incompatibility, and so on, but instead may emerge as part of an already situated line of action. Of course, moment-by-moment postural adjustments and nascent actions need to be sensitive to the physical constraints and affordances of their unfolding ecology, but this does not require detection of abstract features that specify the appropriate emotional response because the structured, dynamic environment shapes behaviour on-line. In short, emotions may emerge as part of a low-level process of adjustment to ecological constraints (including interpersonal constraints) without the intervention of any appraisal- or emotion-specific processing of perceptual inputs. Modelling such processes involves fully embodied agents that adjust to dynamic changes in their relations to other agents.

Interpersonal modulation

According to Scherer (2001), another way in which interpersonal factors might exert appraisal-independent effects depends on regulation of emotions that have already been activated by stimulus evaluation checks. For example, we may register our superior's disapproval of our developing anger and actively attempt either to suppress its symptoms or adjust our interpretation of the anger-provoking incident in order to prevent further aggravation.

At the former, more strategic level, emotions are deployed as moves in interpersonal negotiation and become oriented to real and anticipated social consequences. For example, the presentation of my growing anger at your failure to follow my argument is attuned to my registration of the real-time feedback that your expression of increasing confusion provides me. In certain circumstances, people may deliberately control their emotion presentations as a way of exerting interpersonal influence, but such control is rarely perfect or complete. More commonly, the significance of interpersonal feedback is registered implicitly. In either case, emotions are other-directed, not only in the sense of taking an interpersonal object, but also by virtue of adjusting to the implications of others' responses to emotion presentation.

More generally, a second way in which other people can impact on emotion is by influencing regulatory processes such as problem-focused and emotion-focused coping, or by directly altering the emotional situation that is being appraised. Of course, many of the interpersonal factors that impact on emotion activation as considered above can equally affect emotions that are already activated. For example, someone else's contagious enthusiasm may alleviate our anxiety either directly or by changing our appraisals of the riskiness of what we are doing (e.g. Parkinson and Simons 2009). Other examples of interpersonal emotion modulation *only* apply to emotions that are already underway and detectable to others. It is these latter effects that are the focus of the present section.

Audience effects on expression

In the earlier discussion of social referencing, I described some of the effects of facial expressions on others' behaviour. Sensitivity to these interpersonal consequences also leads people to regulate their facial expressions in accordance with display rules (Ekman 1972; see also Chapter 3.2, this volume). In general, presentation of emotion depends on your relationship with the other person who is present, your current motives, and the culture-defined acceptability of showing the expression in question in this particular situation. For example, 'happy' expressions may be enhanced when in the presence of friends but less so in the presence of strangers (e.g. Wagner and Smith 1991), whereas 'sad' expressions are often strongest when no-one else is present (e.g. Jakobs *et al.* 2001).

An ongoing debate concerns whether regulation of expression should be conceived as a process that is imposed on a separate spontaneous emotional response, or whether it is bound up with the initial activation of the facial expression (see Parkinson 2005). In either case, interpersonal interactions often bring conflicting demands on expression with different audiences (present or implicit) demanding different expressive stances. For example, I may be attuned not only to your delight at winning a prize but also to our other companion's disappointment at only being runner up, while personally believing that the whole contest was a waste of time in the first place. My responses to these various pushes, pulls, and pressures are also shaped by ongoing direct feedback from the expressions of the other interactants, whose own expressions are correspondingly regulated with due attention to my emotion presentation (and feedback about their presentation).

Studies of 'audience effects' on facial expression rarely acknowledge such levels of complexity. However, they clearly reveal that the presence of others can either intensify or dampen expressive responses depending on a variety of contextual factors. Fridlund's (1994) motive-communication theory provides a useful explanation for many of these effects, arguing that facial displays are designed to provide information about social motives to specific addressees under circumstances when communication serves survival or reproduction. However, the theory does not permit specific predictions about exactly when the presence of a particular other will lead to a particular form of display (see Parkinson 2005). Selection from the range of alternative responses to any given interpersonal movement may depend on tighter specification of ongoing non-verbal dynamics within a particular relationship. This represents a challenge to models that depend on unconditional rules based on intrinsic features of facial expressions. In reality, facial conduct derives its significance and functionality from its ongoing sensitivity to the unfolding interpersonal context.

Interpersonal effects on emotion regulation

Regulatory processes not only apply to symptoms or expressions of emotion but also operate on other components including cognitive and subjective aspects (e.g. Gross 2007). Some emotion-regulation attempts are responses to various forms of social pressure and some are implemented using interpersonal resources. For example, I may try to stay calm despite a sense of growing panic because I do not want to make you panic too and talking with you about something else may help to alleviate my fears. You may even be able to take more direct action to reduce the dangers that we both face. Correspondingly, your apparent panic may exacerbate rather than soften my anxiety or may keep you from doing anything constructive about our plight.

In this section, I illustrate some of these interpersonal effects on emotion regulation by reference to research into social support and maladaptive styles of interpersonal interaction (specifically co-rumination). Thus, I will consider examples where others' actions make our emotions less unpleasant and where they make them worse.

Social support is a broad concept covering perception and experience of other people's actual, intended, and potential assistance with emotional problems. Despite the apparent positive effects of feeling that you can call on others for practical and emotional help (see Cohen 2004), studies that have assessed responses to actually receiving support often find negative effects (e.g. Liang *et al.* 2001). With a few exceptions (e.g. Feeney and Collins 2003), people generally seem to be feel worse not better following support experiences. This effect does not seem to be wholly explained by the fact that support is more likely to be received when stress is at higher levels (Gleason *et al.* 2008).

One reason why receiving social support may have negative effects on emotions is that it is often associated with focusing attention on a negative concern. Similarly, Nolen-Hoeksema and colleagues (e.g. Nolen-Hoeksema *et al.* 2008) have consistently argued that ruminating about problems rather than distracting oneself can intensify depressive responses. Rose (2002) identified a relational pattern of co-rumination in which friends tend to chronically work over and discuss each other's problems. In other words, rumination may operate as an interpersonal as well as an individual process. Female friends with a co-ruminative style tend to experience greater anxiety and depression but also greater relational closeness (Rose *et al.* 2007), yielding a pattern of findings that corresponds neatly with those reported for responses to receiving social support. Research findings therefore converge on the conclusion that social interaction at times of trouble can make people feel worse rather than better and that a problem shared is not usually a problem halved.

However, it would be premature to recommend a life of solitary problem-solving as the true path to happiness and emotional well-being. For one thing, Gleason and colleagues (2008) did find exceptions to the negative impact of receiving social support. In particular, on days when both partners reciprocally provided support to each other, distress was reduced and relational closeness increased.

Certain kinds of social support may be effective precisely because they provide practical resources (instrumental support, e.g. providing funds, helping with tasks; House and Kahn 1985). In these cases, assistance from others changes the object of the appraisal guiding emotional response with corresponding consequences for affect. Similarly, talking things over with someone else can clearly alter the way we interpret and evaluate events and bring social appraisal effects as discussed above (informational support; House and Kahn 1985). Indeed, the demonstrated efficacy of cognitive therapy for depression (e.g. Dobson 1989) attests to the fact that receiving informational social support can at least sometimes make people feel better about things.

In principle, many aspects of interpersonal regulation may be captured by models that assume that appraisal input is continuously updated in response to input from other people (e.g. Marsella and Gratch 2009). However, realistic simulation of these processes also requires appreciation of the context dependence of effects of regulatory attempts and the socially interactive nature of the processes that are involved. Further, the interpersonal process depends not only on how emotions are presented by an emotionally competent agent but also on how emotion presentations are interpreted in context by their recipients (see Chapter 1.1, this volume). Others' regulatory responses to our emotions partly depend on what they think we are feeling and what effects they believe our feelings will have on us and on them.

Social consequences of emotion

As indicated above, many of the events that provoke emotion include interpersonal aspects. Interpersonal factors contribute to the causation and regulation of emotion, such as when the other team's gloating makes losing a game more upsetting. Often, as in this example, the thing that we are emotional about (the emotion's intentional object) is an interpersonal object or event too. Our anger may have been encouraged by someone else's expressed outrage but also the anger is directed at something reprehensible that someone else has done in the first place. This other-orientation of social emotions (and social instances of non-social emotions) does not only apply to associated appraisals but also to action tendencies, gestures, and facial expressions. Because other people are likely to respond to the emotional behaviour that we direct at them, it follows that they are often affected by our emotions too.

This section discusses the literature concerning interpersonal effects of emotion, including the use of emotions in negotiation. Many interpersonal consequences of emotion have already been addressed as part of the earlier discussion of contagion and social appraisal processes as causes of emotion. Findings showing that one person's emotion causes a corresponding or conflicting emotion in a second person not only provide evidence for interpersonal causes of emotion but also for its interpersonal effects. However, just as not all interpersonal causes of emotion depend on the emotions of the person bringing the emotional influence, not all interpersonal effects of emotion relate directly to the emotions of the person being influenced. In this section, then, I focus on non-emotional responses to another person's emotions.

Although some of these effects may still depend on interpersonally induced changes in emotion, others operate more directly on cognition, communication, or action. It is also worth distinguishing interpersonal effects that are exerted intentionally as part of the strategic presentation of emotion and those that happen irrespective of the intentions of the agent of emotional influence. For example, an anger expression may induce concessions from the other party regardless of whether it is intended to exert that effect (e.g. Sinaceur and Tiedens 2006; van Kleef et al. 2004), but people may also systematically deliver anger expressions at certain moments in order to get others to back down. The latter strategic functions of emotion are addressed in the final sections of this chapter. For now, I focus on how interpersonal feedback is registered and responded to in these two modes of interaction. Interpersonal effects of emotion presentation over more extended timescales as covered in the literatures on social sharing (e.g. Rimé 2009) and protracted emotion cycles (Hareli and Rafaeli 2008) are beyond the scope of the present chapter.

Responses to the meaning of others' emotions

Research into social referencing discussed above suggests that someone else's apparent emotion can convey information about that person's orientation to something. For example, toddlers recognize that a caregiver's fear expression implies potential danger. The perceived emotion not only carries information about the object of the emotion (e.g. that the cliff may be dangerous) but also about the emotional person's orientation towards that object (that they appraise it as dangerous and are inclined to withdraw or escape from it; see also Steinel et al. 2008). Similarly, a companion's apparent fear while watching a horror movie may lead us to see her as timid (cf. Zillmann *et al.* 1986) or the film as frightening, and close others' feelings of trepidation about impending decisions may lead to inferences not only about the direct dangers of possible courses of action but also about potential harm to the other person's well-being (Parkinson and Simons 2009).

Most of the research into interpersonal effects of emotion has focused on negotiation contexts, partly because of their obvious practical implication (in these settings, the value of information gleaned from others' expressions is likely to be high). Studies have consistently found that participants perceive someone expressing anger as tougher (Knutson 1996), higher in status (Tiedens 2001), and less willing to make concessions (Sinaceur and Tiedens 2006; Van Kleef *et al.* 2006*b*) than someone expressing happiness or no emotion. These perceptions directly affect participants' own behaviour leading them to make greater concessions to angry than non-angry negotiators, especially when they perceive their own power as lower (van Kleef and Côté 2007).

Effects also depend on the perceived object of the negotiator's anger. For example, Steinel and colleagues (2008) found that anger explicitly related to an offer made by the participant yielded more concessions than anger explicitly directed at the participant. The investigators concluded that anger directed at the offer provides specific information about how low an offer the negotiator is likely to accept whereas person-directed anger provides no information that is directly relevant to the offer. Indeed, if the other person is angry with you personally, there is no reason to suppose that this anger will be defused by changes in your behaviour.

The effects of emotions other than anger have also been studied. For example, Van Kleef *et al.* (2006) showed that participants made fewer concessions to negotiators who expressed guilt than to negotiators who expressed disappointment about previous offers. Guilt apparently signalled that the negotiator wished to make amends for previous low offers, whereas disappointment signalled dissatisfaction with previous low offers and reluctance to engage in future concessions. Interestingly, these effects were moderated by levels of trust, with trusting participants more susceptible to the effects of the other's emotions than untrusting participants. The most likely explanation is that untrusting participants suspected negotiators of expressing emotions strategically in order to influence their offers.

The research described in this section shows that people are able to extract information relating to appraisal and action readiness from other people's emotion communications and adjust their own behavior accordingly. One possible explanation for these explicit interpersonal effects is that emotional information was presented in the form of verbal statements in most of these studies. Participants reading another person's statement that they are angry about an offer may be more likely to extract appraisal information than participants who simply catch sight of an angry expression on the other person's face, because the emotional meaning has already been encapsulated explicitly by the linguistic formulation in the former case. Indeed, the fact that the emotion has been expressed verbally means that the agent is aware of the emotion and its connection to the current situation and has made a relatively conscious decision to communicate this information. All of these factors may increase the probability that the recipient factors the other's presented emotion into their judgements and decisions. Correspondingly, from a modelling perspective, it is important to recognize that interpersonal effects of emotion need not depend on explicit categorization of emotion presentations, but may operate on-line at a more implicit level.

Another limitation is that information about the other's emotion is provided at a single moment in time and there is no direct face-to-face contact between negotiators. In many real-world emotional interactions, emotional communication unfolds responsively in real-time between co-present interactants. Under these circumstances, there may be less need to infer implications from others' emotions because they are already attuned to one's own apparent appraisals.

Responses to facial configuration and movement

As outlined in the earlier section on emotion contagion, emotions can bring emotional effects that are not dependent on apprehending implications concerning emotion objects, appraisals, or action tendencies. In the present section, I consider evidence that similar effects operate on other people's cognition and behaviour. For example, the fact that people often become physically agitated in states of panic may induce higher activity levels in others regardless of whether the physical agitation is interpreted as a symptom of panic. Possible mechanisms for such effects depend on the dynamics of the stimulus configuration presented by the other person and may involve low-level mimicry-based processes, or direct modulation of attention and orientation. To illustrate, shouting, crying, stroking, and yawning are all emotion-related responses that can have automatic effects on other people's behaviour regardless of their interpretation as indications of what the other person is feeling.

The present section's main focus falls on interpersonal effects of facial movements associated with emotions (see also earlier section on social referencing) and I shall consider specifically whether such effects are necessarily mediated by the receiver's extraction of emotional meaning. If so, then the effects of exposure to facial representations of emotion are directly analogous to the effects of verbal representations of emotion as described in the previous section. If not, then they constitute a partially independent basis for emotion's interpersonal influence that needs to be modelled according to different principles.

The most extensive literature on social effects of facial expressions probably relates to smiling. In general, smiling faces are viewed more positively by other people than non-smiling faces. Further, the dynamics and configuration of the smile make a difference. For example, Krumhuber and colleagues (2007b) found that videos of smiles digitally manipulated to have a temporal pattern that appeared 'genuine' (i.e. more gradual onset and offset and briefer peak) elicited perceptions of greater trustworthiness and higher levels of cooperation. Krumhuber et al. (2009) also found that targets showing similarly manipulated smiles were more likely to be successful in simulated job interviews.

Turning to configural features, Johnston et al. (2010) found that still photos of 'enjoyment' smiles (including contraction of orbicularis oculi) induced greater levels of cooperation than photos of non-enjoyment smiles. Similarly, Miles (2009) found that participants tended to move their head more towards a looming face showing an enjoyment smile than towards a face showing a non-enjoyment smile or neutral expression. Miles concluded that facial expressions of enjoyment are perceptual stimuli that directly afford approach behaviour.

Research into attentional responses to pictures of facial expressions also suggests that the adult visual system is specifically attuned to certain configurations. For example, Hansen and Hansen (1988) showed that people can more quickly pick out a single angry face from an array of smiling faces than a single smiling face from an array of angry faces. Such effects probably depend on the threat value of angry faces, which makes it beneficial to monitor automatically for their presence. Indeed, participants with higher levels of trait anxiety seem more sensitive to angry faces than low-anxious participants (Bar-Haim et al. 2007). The current consensus is that pre-attentive processing of threatening faces permits their rapid detection (e.g. LoBue 2009).

Most of the above findings may be interpreted in terms of the perceived emotional meaning of presented faces. For example, a fixed smile is interpreted as indicating simulated pleasure rather than a spontaneous reaction to a pleasant event and for this reason participants are more favourably disposed towards targets displaying the latter form of expression than towards those displaying the former. More generally, smiles that are more likely to reflect happiness yield more positive reactions. Correspondingly, faces that may indicate anger and readiness to aggress or fear and detection of danger have threat value precisely because they reflect those emotions, appraisals, and action tendencies. Regardless of whether their detection occurs pre-attentively or after conscious processing, it is the significance of the stimulus as a whole that guides its effects. However, it is also possible that specific features of facial movements induce reactions that do not depend on the overall meaning of the facial configuration.

For example, research into gaze-cued orienting demonstrates that people are acutely sensitive to the direction of other people's visual attention (see Frischen *et al.* 2007). In particular, there is a strong, early acquired, and automatic tendency to direct our gaze towards objects that others are looking at (e.g. Friesen and Kingstone 1998; Hood *et al.* 1998). Further, our perceptions of other people are strongly affected by the direction of their gaze toward or away from us. Eye contact leads to perceptions of approachability and trustworthiness, whereas gaze aversion or withdrawal can signal social rejection. Because emotions regulate attentional attunement (e.g. Oatley 1992), such interpersonal effects may also occur in different emotional situations. For example, gaze directed at a potentially threatening object in fear may draw others' attention to this object whether or not they have interpreted the gaze as an indication of fear. More generally, some of the effects of emotion-related responses may not be mediated by either automatic or controlled categorization of another person's emotion.

However, the context dependence of many of these effects suggests that they are sensitive to the goals or lines of action being pursued by interactants. For example, in a study by Jones and colleagues (2006), gaze direction indicating eye contact only increased preferences for attractive over unattractive faces when the expression was a smile and not when it was neutral. In a related study, Wilkowski *et al.* (2009) found that participants were more influenced by schematic faces indicating gaze direction when they were motivated to increase their sense of social belonging. Clearly, our attunement to social stimuli associated with emotion is moderated by various attentional and motivational factors.

In this section, I have considered some of the ways in which other people's emotions and emotion expressions can influence our attention, cognition, and behaviour (for further examples, see Hareli and Rafaeli 2008; van Kleef 2009). Some of these effects seem to depend on apprehending the emotional meaning of social stimuli (either pre-attentively or consciously). In these cases, responses are guided by knowledge about the implications of different emotions for the nature of the emotional object, appraisal of that object, and action tendencies towards that object. For example, knowing someone is angry suggests that they have something to be angry about, appraise that thing as somehow illegitimate, and are inclined to push it away or otherwise act against it. However, it is also possible that other people's emotions can affect us because of lower-level reactions to their associated response components. Regardless of whether I recognize another's gaze as an angry gaze, I may be inclined to look in the direction it indicates, thus affecting my perception of what is happening and reaction to it. Again, realistic models of agents and social perceivers need to incorporate responses to subcomponents of the emotion syndrome and not just its overall integrative meaning (see also Parkinson 2009).

Emotion as relation alignment

Research reviewed above suggests that people may strategically adjust their behaviour based on their interpretations of others' emotions. In this section, I consider the possibility that people's emotion presentations adjust to take into account their effects on others. Indeed, one of the main purposes of many social emotions may be to exert these interpersonal effects. To take this further, emotions may be a means of influencing others' emotions that in turn are means of influencing our own emotions reciprocally. I may be angry that you are angry, while your anger in turn may be exacerbated by my anger about it, leading to a mutually vicious cycle. Indeed, the aim of each party's simultaneous anger may be to reduce the other's anger. Correspondingly, a more virtuous circle may operate when I begin to show guilt about the thing you are becoming angry about. In both cases, emotions are either strategic moves in a dialogic process or adjustments to mutually adjusting processes in the other.

In previous writings (e.g. Parkinson 2008), I have argued that emotions generally serve to align relations between people and objects (including other people). These relations may be two-part relations between one person and another person or object, or three-part relations involving the respective positions of two (or more) persons towards an object of mutual concern (compatible or incompatible), which may be another person. For example, my anger about your insult not only aligns the relations between me and you and between you, me, and your insult, but also presents my orientation to your behaviour as insulting to others present, thus aligning their relations with you, me, and the insult. Some intrinsically social emotions always take another person as their object and function as moves away, against, or towards that other person. Other emotions are sometimes oriented to non-social objects but also adjust (reciprocally) to others' orientation to that object. Here the focus will fall on social emotions of the first kind and non-social emotions when they are directed at interpersonal objects.

In my view, emotion presentations may be integrated strategic attempts to exert the meaning-based interpersonal effects considered in the previous section. For example, I may become angry because anger draws your attention to what I see as an unfair situation and encourages you to adjust your behaviour in a way that helps me deal with it. My anger communicates an appraisal of the emotional object (e.g. that I am offended by such a low offer in a negotiation; van Kleef *et al.* 2004 above) and carries implications about my own relational position with respect to that object (e.g. that I feel I deserve a better offer). Of course, this need not imply any conscious intention to influence you on my part. Instead, over the course of early interaction with others and socialization, angry relational modes may have become implicitly associated with certain relational dynamics or contextualized unfolding reactions from others.

In addition to the top-down strategic operation of anger as a communication of other-blame or a threat of retaliation, my low-level adjustments to specific aspects of a frustrating situation (e.g. visual attention and physical orientation directed towards an obstacle) may lead others sharing my situation to make corresponding adjustments without necessarily drawing any (implicit or explicit) inference that I am angry. These processes require no integrated anger agenda to shape either party's actions, but a mutual angry relational orientation may still develop towards the object of the emotion.

In my view, emotions first emerge in ontogenesis as lines of action rather than reaction to information (see also Parkinson 2007). In other words, emotions are initially activated in development by relational demands whose specific components do not need to be registered by an appraisal process. The infant's earliest affective presentations of pleasure or discontent mesh with the caregiver's unfolding receptivity and emerge as meaningful emotional states without the need for sequential stimulus checks. Emotions even at this stage are not simply reactions to registered information but also active relational moves that are sensitive to interpersonal and environmental feedback. Later in development, the articulation of emotions as meaningful cultural entities requires an implicit appreciation of their other orientation as well as their dependence on perceived meaning.

Examples of how social emotions are oriented to the actual or anticipated consequences of others include studies of anger and embarrassment. Parkinson (2001*b*) argued that anger has developed as a strategy for regulating others' conduct in face-to-face interactions. Real-time responsiveness to posture, gesture, and facial movement allows people to adjust their own orientation so that full-blown anger is often averted. Initial symptoms of disapproval may be met by conciliatory signs or backtracking movements.

However, this non-verbal negotiation process can break down when the usual modes of interpersonal contact are disrupted. For example, driving situations do not usually permit close proximity between interactants and noise levels prevent easy vocal communication. Thus, when a driver wants another driver to acknowledge or apologize for a transgression, communication needs to be escalated before the message gets across. Before the other driver even notices what is happening, the first driver may be shouting, shaking fists, honking horns, or driving so close that the other driver can no longer ignore the communicated anger. Correspondingly, any signal of acknowledgement or apology from the other driver needs to be highly perceptible if it is to be registered by the offended party. Consistent, with this account, Parkinson (2001b) found that the intensity of anger while driving was independently predicted by ratings of how quickly the target of anger registered the participant's emotion, even after controlling for other-blame appraisals. One implication of this research is that models of emotionally competent agents need to factor in the nature, fidelity, temporal resolution of available communication channels when simulating interpersonal emotion episodes. In particular, interpersonal emotion presentation is likely to be modulated by directness of its transmission to the other party to the exchange, and of the other party's response back to the agent (see Parkinson 2008).

Leary *et al.* (1996) presented comparable data for the emotion of embarrassment. In their study, participants stopped being embarrassed more quickly when they believed that the person who had witnessed their performance had registered that they were embarrassed. Again, the conclusion seems to be that emotions can be oriented to their interpersonal effects and dissipate only when their interpersonal functions have been perceived to be served.

Both these examples may be explained by reference to shared knowledge about the common meanings and implications of emotional states. The emotion serves its social function partly because others recognize its nature and meaning (in terms of emotional objects, appraisals, and action tendencies). However, I argued above that separate aspects of emotional presentations may also exert low-level interpersonal influence so that the emotion serves its social function in a more bottom-up fashion. The following example illustrates this principle by demonstrating that facial and bodily movements can regulate another person's visual attention in real time, and reinforces earlier points about sensitivity to other people's gaze which seems to be present from a very early age.

Reddy (2000) documented 3-month-old infants producing 'coy smiles' as common responses to sustained attentional contact with mothers, experimenters, or themselves reflected in a mirror. This pattern of movement involved turning away the eyes or head while a smile developed. Uninformed observers of the videotape spontaneously labelled this reaction as coy, bashful, or embarrassed (Draghi-Lorenz *et al.* 2005) and, indeed, the observed dynamic pattern of facial expression corresponds closely to the specifications of an adult embarrassment display outlined by Keltner (1995).

There are clearly practical as well as communicative functions to these specific movements. Turning away represents a withdrawal from attentional contact, ceasing exposure to the continuing gaze of the other, which has become uncomfortable (or has increased the degree of arousal beyond a tolerable level). Furthermore, this movement is highly visible to the other person who can easily pick up the signal that attentional contact is no longer desired. Finally, the coupling of this movement with a smile communicates that withdrawal occurs in the context of an affiliative relationship that is not being abandoned during this temporary disruption in communion. Thus, the infant's response to prolonged attentional contact may convey a coherent emotion to the perceiver but may still be driven by more local responsivity to interpersonal pressures and demands.

Emotionally competent interactants?

According to the relation-alignment approach, emotions can be activated as emergent patterns of co-regulated activity or as integrated (though often automatized) means of communicating appraisals or signalling social motives. This two-level, situated, dynamic, and flexible perspective may present difficulties for some computational models that require abstract generative mechanisms for outputting differential emotions. Simple rule-based systems for extracting emotionally relevant cues may sometimes be overly restrictive to capture the operation of functionally organized and interpersonally attuned dynamic emotions. For example, if emotion presentations are attuned to the real-time responsiveness of another agent, then factors relating to mode of contact, mutual positioning, mode of information transmission, and so on need to be properly specified to enable realistic simulation. Models that specify emotional information only in terms of integrated appraisal agendas rarely do full justice to these considerations.

In a realistic emotion model, the agent needs to be more tightly embedded in a continually responsive environment and to be oriented from the outset to the relational positions of other agents (see Gratch 2008). Further, the emotion should be seen as part of the process of active adjustment to other agents and the environment rather than as an indirect side effect of these transactions. In principle, much of this may be achievable by implementing interlocking dynamic feedback systems at several levels and by specifying when and how top-down monitoring and regulation need to kick in or out. The nature of this regulation may be open to modification as a function of learning and socialization.

Alternatively, an extended appraisal model incorporating additional dimensions of relational meaning and conditional context-based rules specifying alternative prerequisites for similar emotions may be sufficient for certain purposes, especially if there is no requirement for real-time responsiveness. At one level, there is no doubt that it is possible to specify emotions in terms of cues that shape their emergence and rules whereby those cues are transformed into meanings. However, it is important to acknowledge that real-world emotions are often attuned to anticipated consequences in addition to unfolding and responsive dynamic feedback and that the extraction of relational meaning does not always represent the sole driving force behind the emotion process, especially when emotions occur in the context of unfolding interpersonal interactions.

One possible way forward suggested by Gratch (2008) is to integrate emotion-production and recognition-systems with existing dialogue systems (e.g. Poggi and Pelachaud 2000). The challenge facing such syntheses concerns the tension between seeing gestures and facial movements as emotion expressions or as communicative signals (cf. Parkinson 2005). However, emotion expressions clearly do communicate information and others' responses to communicated information in turn affect the agent's emotions. The remaining issues then concern possible differences in the interpersonal consequences of strategic communication and more spontaneous emotional expression. Does a smile underwritten by authentic happiness have different interpersonal functions and effects from a simulated smile with similar objective characteristics? Further, are some of the effects of smile-related movements independent of the meaning they convey to the other?

In this chapter, I have argued that emotions are often directed at interpersonal objects, whose appraisal may depend on evaluative responses from other people. Further, the emotion may change in response to other people's activities that either change the emotion's object or provide resources for reacting to it differently. Finally, emotions exert effects on other people either by providing information about the emotional person's relation to the emotion's object or by activating responses more directly. Given that emotions are so intricately embedded in their social context, it might seem surprising that, historically, most psychological research into emotion has focused on individual responses to non-social stimuli. That situation is beginning to change (e.g. Keltner and Haidt 1999; Van Kleef 2009) but theoretical models continue to treat interpersonal variables as extraneous inputs or outputs to an intrapsychic emotion process. The alternative as sketched out here is to consider social emotions (and social examples of non-social emotions) as phenomena worthy of purpose-built relation-alignment explanations. These explanations imply corresponding extensions to models of emotionally competent agents, operating in a dynamic and responsive interpersonal environment, where interactants adjust to each other's responses and communications in addition to their appraised meaning.

Section 3

Emotional expression: Ground truth and agent evaluation

A central methodological issue is common to the majority of the perspectives covered in this volume—the use of corpora containing recorded samples of emotional behaviour, in particular, emotional expression, and of databases containing systematic documentation of data or other material relevant to emotion elicitation and emotional responses. These corpora and databases are generally used to inform the rule systems built into artificial systems, considering the material in some sense as 'ground truth', as well as to evaluate the plausibility and stringency of simulation or analysis outcomes. While there are an enormous number of different databases with relevant material and past findings of relevance for affective computing (too many to be inventoried here), there are two major types of corpora: (1) recordings of naturally occurring or experimentally induced emotional behaviour samples and (2) actor portrayals of emotional behaviour.

In Chapter 3.1, 'The essential role of human databases for learning in and validation of affectively competent agents', Cowie, Douglas-Cowie, Martin, and Devillers, focusing on the first type, assert that much of what is covered in Section 5, in which different approaches to the implementation of affective competent agents are discussed, requires learning by computational models from human example and validation of agent models in terms of human emotion processing and expression. In consequence, properly conceived databases are essential for the design of affectively competent agents and the assessment of their performance. According to the authors, in contemporary technology, the only practical way to engineer many subsystems is by constructing suitable databases and applying learning algorithms to them, not by a human designing in the conventional sense. These learning-based parts of the design process obviously require suitable databases to learn from and there are obvious advantages if the research can exploit permanent databases of carefully assembled and validated recordings, rather than trying to generate the required kind of material for every new study (and perhaps not succeeding completely). The authors provide an in-depth analysis of the problems that need to be addressed at multiple levels: psychological (what should ideally be recorded and how should it ideally be described); practical (suitable recording techniques, reliability of labelling, ease of use); and legal/ethical (consent, ownership and data protection). They also describe emerging ideas in the field in the context of particular databases that reflect the state of the art and are linked to the technology described in the previous chapters.

In Chapter 3.2, 'On the use of actor portrayals in research on emotional expression', Scherer and Bänziger first analyse the central issue concerning corpora of emotional behaviour, in particular, expression—the extent to which the recorded behaviours can be considered 'natural' or 'authentic'. They show the difficulties in defining these terms, as well as the almost insurmountable problems in empirically establishing that specific behaviours, especially in media recordings of emotional behaviour or in experimental induction, are really 'natural' or 'authentic'. The authors suggest using the criteria of 'believable' or 'plausible' instead, arguing that emotional expression is always determined by both internal push factors (e.g. physiological emotion concomitants producing motor expressions) and external pull factors (e.g. modelling the expression in line with strategic intentions or normative constraints). They argue that an attempt to capture and analyse pure push factors, spontaneous unregulated expressions, is unrealistic, given the scarcity of such expressions in social life and the high likelihood that seemingly spontaneous expressions are in fact at least partially subject to manipulation by self-presentation strategies of the sender and/or the constraints of social expectations. The authors suggest that current research in psychology and affective computing should pay more attention to the study of pull effects. For this purpose, they advocate the use of actor portrayals as a highly appropriate methodological choice, an option that has been taken by many researchers in the field.

Chapter 3.1

The essential role of human databases for learning in and validation of affectively competent agents[1]

Roddy Cowie, Ellen Douglas-Cowie,
Jean-Claude Martin, and Laurence Devillers

Summary

Databases are fundamental to affective computing. Directly or indirectly, they provide a large proportion of the information about human affective functioning that is used by affective systems. Information may be drawn from them in many ways—by machine learning, by direct use of extracts, or by a combination of human judgement and machine measurement. They are also the key to comparisons between systems. Numerical measures of performance mean very little unless they are based on the same material, which in practice means using standard databases.

The databases used differ widely in form and scale, depending on the diverse functions that they serve and the modalities involved. There are also different criteria that they may be expected to satisfy, which are not always easily reconciled. For instance, the importance of ecological validity has become increasingly widely accepted, but automatic processing depends on highly artificial lighting and sensor configurations.

Constructing a viable database depends on understanding the different issues that arise in different areas. Databases for speech synthesis need to represent at least all the vowels in the language in all phonetic evironments for each emotional style to be produced. There is less need for structure in databases for synthesis of visible actions, because control is typically based on rules extracted from them by human scientists. In research on the recognition of affect in speech, the consensus is that the material in training databases needs to come from the application context or something very similar to it. In visual recognition of affect, there are multiple levels. General databases can be used to train recognizers concerned with elementary features (such as facial points or action units), but going beyond that to recognize affective significance seems to require application-specific data. Text databases tend to contain very large numbers of items and, with current technology, support only very coarse affective classifications.

The varied nature of the demands means that constructing a genuinely competent agent requires a suite of very different resources. The development of SAL, an agent that carries out a very rudimentary affectively coloured conversation, involved 11 separate databases, some of which were used to generate several smaller, specialized datasets.

---

[1] This work was supported by the European Community's Seventh Framework Programme (FP7/2007-2013) under grant agreements no. 211486 (SEMAINE) and 231287 (SSPNet).

The fact that contemporary technology depends on acquiring and transmitting very large bodies of information appears to be fundamentally inefficient, particularly if each application needs data tailored to its specific characteristics. Several kinds of research may contribute to reducing that inefficiency. These involve both new techniques in machine learning and perception and work by human scientists, guided by databases, on the kinds of abstraction that may be possible. The prospect of progress in these and other areas means that the demand for databases may change. Some databases that were standard a decade ago are still used, but others have been largely relegated to history. That process is likely to continue.

Introduction

Empirical information about human beings always plays a part in designing systems for human use, but the information can take very varied forms. In affective computing, major parts of it take the form of databases. Hence, a good deal of the work that goes into building an affectively competent agent is likely to be spent creating suitable databases.

People who are not familiar with the area may be surprised that databases play an important role in it, and it is useful to provide a preliminary context for them. The premier conference in the area is Affective Computing and Intelligent Interaction (ACII). ACII 2009 was held while this chapter was being written. The proceedings contain 130 full papers and posters. In 55 of those, databases were not only mentioned, but played a substantial role in the work.

The single most prominent use of databases involves applying machine learning procedures to train recognizers, and a sketch of that application is a useful point of reference. The database will contain raw records (assume for the sake of illustration that these are audio recordings, each containing one spoken sentence) and, associated with each record, there are verbal or numerical descriptions, which will be called labels (e.g. a label might describe the speaker's arousal level when he or she utters the relevant sentence). The aim of the learning procedure is to find statistical relationships between the records and the labels. These relationships are typically quite complex. They identify features of the records that appear to be usefully related to the labels (e.g. the pitch contour or the average spectrum), the parameters of the features that are relevant (e.g. the mean of the pitch contour or the slope of the spectrum), rules for weighting and combining these parameters to derive an overall measure of fit between a given stretch of speech and a given label, and a rule for deciding whether the label should or should not be considered to apply. Together, these elements define a function that can be used to assign labels. Its construction ensures that, if it is applied to the material used for training, the labels it generates will agree reasonably well with the labels in the training material. Its practical use lies in the fact that it can be applied to a sentence that has not been labelled and can estimate what the speaker's arousal level was in that case. The function typically does not make much intuitive sense to a human being.

That kind of learning is a central example of the way databases are used, but variation around the centre is enormous. The databases used in ACII varied radically in their forms and functions. They involved many modalities—including audio, visual, audiovisual, text, music, and motion capture—and featured in all sections of the conference: recognition; synthesis; tutoring; robotics; individual differences; information retrieval; and so on.

The databases were very diverse numerically: some were based on a single individual; some on hundreds. That depended partly on function and partly (perhaps less intuitively) on modality. Two reasonably representative papers illustrate the point. One, dealing with affect in text, considered 116 533 entries, and aimed to assign each to one of three categories (Xu *et al.* 2009). In contrast, one dealing with video used a database of 247 clips, and assigned each to one of 8 classes (Afzal and Robinson 2009).

The contents of the databases may also surprise readers who have a traditional background in psychology. What was until recently the archetypal example of a database, the Ekman and Friesen photographs of faces simulating basic emotions, was cited by only two papers, and one of those was concerned with pointing out its limitations. The Cohn–Kanade database—still posed, but to less precise specifications—was used by five. The great majority sought some kind of naturalism. Four papers used databases concerned with clinical material, four with human–machine interactions, and eight with other application scenarios. Eight used extracts from film or TV, five involved text corpora, and three used material from the web.

A realistic discussion of databases needs to recognize not only the centrality and diversity of databases, but also the fact that their use is surrounded by genuinely difficult questions. Some of the questions are couched in abstract terms, some practically, but they have a common implication, which is that it is far from clear what the pattern of databases and database use will be in a mature technology of affectively competent agents. The work that is being done with contemporary databases is among other things a key medium for the attempt to identify a long-term shape for the field.

The most abstract question hinges on the fact that databases are large. They typically include large amounts of data from sensors (cameras, microphones, etc.). The labelling systems associated with these may be very elaborate, detailing not only affective content, but also the signs that convey it, the context, and various other issues.

People in the human sciences would not normally expect to transmit empirical information in such an uneconomical format. Psychologists in particular expect that information about human behaviour, thoughts, and feelings will be captured by expressions, verbal and/or numerical, that are both selective (i.e. they consider a few features of the situations they describe, and ignore the rest as irrelevant) and general (i.e. they describe patterns that hold across a range of situations, not a particular case). That kind of formulation is vastly more economical than a database, which is quite likely to include gigabytes of sensor data. It is clearly important to know whether affective computing needs to rely so heavily on the apparently uneconomical format and, if so, why.

A closely related question is raised by the fact that research teams working on particular applications tend to assume that they need databases tailored to their specific applications. That reflects a consensus that is widespread, though not often stated, that, in practice, the kind of generalization that learning and related procedures can achieve is very limited indeed. If that remains the case, then one of the main limits on the rate at which affective computing develops will be the time and effort needed to generate tailored databases for each application.

A more obviously practical problem is how to accommodate engineers' concern with issues like recording quality, balanced sampling, and 'ground truth'. These are important from an engineering point of view. However, reconciling them with demands for realism is at best very difficult. Some kinds of human behaviour can be obtained to order in a meticulously controlled environment, but it is reasonable to doubt whether displays of spontaneous, natural emotion are among them.

Behind many of these issues is the uncertain relationship between data, mechanical procedures for exploiting it, and human scientific intelligence. It may be that the details of emotional expression are simply not amenable to the kind of selective, general description that the human sciences have traditionally aimed to achieve and that, in effect, every application needs its own database (or system of databases). It may also be that research will find ways of abstracting rules that can be applied in a wide range of situations—either by understanding the key issues, or by improving machine learning, or both. Similarly, technology may or may not find ways to overcome its current dependence on careful control of lighting, sensors, and so on.

The various complexities outlined here have a straightforward implication. Affective computing is eager to acquire databases, but teams who are considering developing them need to be very clear about the particular demands that they aim to meet. The demands vary massively according to modality and function. Conceptually interesting data may go unused because they do not meet the requirements of contemporary technology, but, conversely, if those requirements change, data designed specifically to meet them may also become redundant. The general aim of this chapter is to alert people to the distinctions that they need to understand in order to make informed choices in an area that is fascinating, but far from straightforward.

Major functions, elements, and criteria of adequacy

The point has been made that databases in affective computing are very diverse. They also have multiple kinds of internal component. This section expands those observations into a more systematic overview of the main elements and issues to be considered.

One of the key differences between applications is how directly material from databases is used. Speech synthesis is at one extreme. In the standard approach, unit selection, the speech that systems output consists of segments selected at runtime from a database of recordings and recombined to produce the intended utterance. Recognition follows a different pattern, which has already been outlined. Databases typically provide the input to machine learning procedures, producing rules that the system uses to classify the inputs that it encounters. The synthesis of gestures is somewhat similar, but there is typically more human involvement: scientists identify relevant categories by observation, but the parameters that distinguish instances are derived by machine analysis. Beyond that, the systems to describe both relevant features and affective content tend to be chosen by human beings as a result of working with material in databases: descriptive tools are chosen because they are needed to do justice to the material. Over and above all of these, databases have an essential part to play in testing systems, because they allow the performance of different systems to be compared on the same material.

As might be expected, the databases needed for these different purposes have very varied internal structures. However a few main kinds of element are generally involved. It is useful to recognize at least four broad divisions.

◆ *Raw records*. These are minimally processed records of individual events. They are typically the outputs of video, audio, or physiological sensors, though some applications use force sensors in chairs or steering wheels, motion capture data, records of moves in a game, and so on. It is artificial not to extend the term to the texts, transcripts, etc. that form the basis of verbal corpora.

◆ *Sign labels*. These provide an intermediate level of description, concerned with patterns that can be identified mechanically and with high confidence. They may describe physical patterns (fundamental frequency, distance between the hands, etc.) or actions (asking a question, clapping, etc.). It is debatable whether labels like 'smile of enjoyment' (Ekman and Friesen 1982) that imply an emotional significance belong at the same level of description.

◆ *State labels*. These describe the affective content of episodes in the database. They may use descriptors drawn from everyday language, or from a range of theoretical formulations (e.g. dimensional or appraisal theories). One might expect them to describe the objects of emotion (is the person angry with me or with my opponent?), but very few databases actually do so.

◆ *Context descriptions*. These provide background information about the people and the environments involved. For the people, relevant issues include individual characteristics (gender, personality, etc.) and cultural background. For the environment, they may be physical, task-related (e.g. what stage a task has reached, how successfully it is being accomplished), social (others present, norms in force, etc.), and communicative (form of communication, phase of discourse, etc.).

It has been noted that the area is marked by questions about best practice that are far from being resolved. In fact, there are multiple controversies, associated with different applications and elements.

For raw records, one key issue has already been raised. The devices that will use recordings are much less sophisticated than human perceptual systems. Providing inputs that they can process favours situations that are far from conducive to natural emotion. Less obviously, different psychological models also contrast. Some studies stress discriminability or availability of a clear 'ground truth'. Others stress authenticity or ecological validity. At present, different balances need to be struck for different applications. Images of faces intended for automatic analysis simply must meet very stringent requirements: material that looks perfectly acceptable to the human eye may be quite impossible to process. In contrast, the natural desire to have a clear 'ground truth' can be set aside in some cases, for reasons explained in the discussion of labelling later in this section.

For sign labels, there is relative consensus in some areas, such as the use of the facial action coding system (FACS) to code facial expressions, but in many areas radically different schemes are available. The issue is not simply at the level of choice between individual descriptive systems. Some databases provide complex hierarchies of intermediate descriptions; others provide none. A related issue is whether labels should reflect the way humans categorize the relevant patterns: for instance, should databases use linguistic descriptions of intonation or voice quality to annotate speech? These issues are related to long-running debates about intermediate variables in human perception and action. Psychological knowledge in these areas does not dictate best practice. In fact, building databases that make sophisticated analysis possible is one of the keys to reaching a consensus.

With state labels, the most basic questions hinge on the case for ensuring that the labels are correct, or, at least, that raters agree on the labels. These are variants of standard psychometric criteria, validity and reliability. The issues here are complex.

◆ Emphasizing correctness has far-reaching consequences. Judgements about correctness, raw records, and context are interlinked, because it is difficult to ensure that emotion-related descriptors are correct outside very specific contexts—which may not be the ones that agents are likely to face. Logically, though, correctness is only required if the aim is to build a system that identifies a person's emotions correctly. If the aim is to form the kind of impression that similar signs would evoke in a human observer, then the appropriate goal is to find ways of capturing observers' impressions, whether or not they are correct.

◆ Requiring that raters should agree can be seen as an alternative, but it too is less straightforward than it might seem. People's interpretations of the same signs may differ according to many factors, including mood (Niedenthal et al. 2000), personality (Melfsen and Florin 2002), emotional intelligence (Mayer et al. 1990), gender (Hall and Matsumoto 2004), and culture (Matsumoto 2001), and it is an important feature of some displays that they do evoke divergent impressions (Cowie et al. 2009). That suggests the key target is usually reflecting the range of responses that signals may evoke. A key qualification is that, in some applications, it is critical that the system identifies actual emotions (e.g. in a diagnostic context). It is known that perceived and actual states can be quite divergent (Tcherkassof et al. 2007), and so data that is to be used for that kind of application should not rely on ratings by non-expert observers.

The importance of context is only gradually being registered, and there is very little consensus on suitable ways of describing relevant factors. Above all, a good descriptive system should reveal the relevant similarities and differences between contexts. Obviously, similar emotions are likely to be expressed in different ways in different contexts—on the football field, driving a car, in a courtroom. It would invite disaster to base the design of an agent intended for one of those contexts on databases drawn from the others. The difficulty is that we do not know which features of the context are relevant to transfer. It may be that the only way to construct an agent that can operate effectively in a particular context is to obtain raw records in exactly that context. But, if that is not the case, then we need ways of describing context that indicate which existing databases are likely to be suitable for the development of a new agent. The process of finding good ways to classify context is an intellectual challenge that is as much part of database research as understanding the practical constraints that have to be observed in order to produce a database that will be used; it will shape both the descriptive systems that future databases incorporate, and the body of records that it is seen as necessary to accumulate.

A final point about function is implicit in several others that have been made throughout this section. The databases that the community regards as standard define the phenomena that it is committed to dealing with: the quality of records that it should be able to process; the kinds of state and relationship that systems should be able to recognize; and the kinds of behaviour that it should be possible to synthesize. Hence there is a strong and highly practical sense in which assembling relevant databases amounts to defining the field.

Basic categories of database

It has been noted that two issues have a major bearing on the differences between databases, namely, modality and function. This section uses those distinctions to structure a basic discussion of the contributions that databases make and the various requirements associated with them. It looks first at databases for synthesis, then at databases for analysis. Within each type of function, different modalities are considered in turn.

Databases for speech synthesis

The point has already been made that databases underpinning speech synthesis represent an extreme. As such, they bring out some key issues particularly clearly. Until the 1990s, the dominant model of speech synthesis—synthesis by rule—involved constructing a general model of the vocal tract, and inputting the parameters needed to generate individual utterances. Systems using that approach sounded unacceptably unnatural, and they were succeeded by 'unit selection' systems. These incorporate a database of recorded speech, and create the required utterance by concatenating extracts. Early versions used a database containing every vowel in all possible phonetic environments. Better quality was achieved by including several realizations in the database and using rules (partly or wholly learned) to select the most appropriate for a given context. Schröder (2009; see also Chapter 5.2, this volume) reviews these trends.

The different methods involve very different relationships between agents and databases. In synthesis by rule, a process of abstraction obtains what are expected to be the relevant parameters and discards details that are presumed to be irrelevant. The problem is that the details turn out not to be irrelevant to the human ear. That may be because speech decoding mechanisms are attuned to the biomechanics of speech production, as motor theories of speech have argued for decades and continue to (Moore, 2007). Currently, the standard solution to that problem is to give the agent fragments of relatively raw speech from a database and combine them to produce the utterances it needs.

Generating emotional speech deepens the problem. In synthesis by rule, it can be stipulated that, to signify anger, speech should be made louder, the pitch raised, and the rate increased. In unit selection, the only obvious option is to add a complete database for each new emotion. That can be done when only a few emotion types are needed (Iida and Campbell 2003), but sheer scale makes it difficult to extend it to a substantial emotional range, let alone different levels of emotion.

This area provides a nice illustration of a general point, which is that database requirements are not static—they change, sometimes quite radically, as technology develops. Direct dependence on databases was introduced because standard ways of abstracting from data to rules discarded detail that mattered to humans. That approach in turn faced problems involving database size. Part of the solution may be to find deeper ways of abstracting from data. There has been renewed interest in speech generation based on models of vocal physiology (e.g. Birkholz 2007). It is often argued that a coherent set of physiological changes underpins the surface phenomena of emotional speech (Banse and Scherer, 1996). Hence the new approach may provide a way of synthesizing emotional speech without the direct use of recorded samples that marks the current state of the art, and put a premium on databases that capture patterns of physiology rather than sound. Issues of that general kind return in various guises throughout this chapter.

Databases for the synthesis of visible actions

A naïve onlooker might assume that the issues involved in synthesis would be essentially similar, whatever the modality. In fact, databases for the synthesis of visible actions function very differently from databases for the synthesis of speech and there are also significant differences between different types of visible action.

A great many kinds of visible action are potentially relevant to affective agents. Facial signs of emotion are the most obvious, but head movement, gesture, and body posture are also relevant. If the agent is shown full body, then mode of locomotion is also relevant (Dittrich *et al.* 1996; Gunes *et al.* 2008).

The immediate contrast with speech is that synthesizing visible action is an area where traditional approaches to formulating rules have worked comparatively well. The most striking example is facial expression of emotion. A highly influential scheme due to Ekman and Friesen (1975) describes the state level in terms of basic emotion categories, and the sign level in terms of 'facial actions'. Mapping between them is quite complex, as each basic emotion can be described as a family of expressions. For instance, surprise can be divided into different types such as questioning surprise, astonished surprise, dazed surprise, or full surprise. These are generally assumed to involve different areas of the face. So-called blends of emotions also involve different patterns in different areas of the face. Mappings that reflect these distinctions adequately continue to be developed.

Additional rules are needed to generate actual images from descriptions of facial action units. The range of variation that occurs can be modelled using standard databases (Tsapatsoulis *et al.* 2002), but specialized recordings are needed to model the way emotion affects a speaker's lip movements (Bevaqua and Pelachaud 2004).

A more fundamental gap involves context. Studies suggest that people who express emotion in the course of an activity rarely show the archetypal patterns described by Ekman, with the exception of happiness (Carroll and Russell 1997; Scherer and Ellgring 2007*a*). Fewer units tend to be active simultaneously. Patterning across time and modalities contributes to distinctiveness, but explains only part of it (Scherer and Ellgring, 2007*b*). A central challenge in the area is to develop databases that capture that kind of patterning. An integral part of the challenge is to identify the contextual variables that determine which kind of patterning will occur.

There are also well established ways of using databases to derive appropriate parameters for large amplitude actions (e.g. amplitude of gesture, rate of movement, likelihood of bilaterality, likelihood of repetition). Those parameters are then used to resynthesize a comparable gesture, and the resynthesis is assessed for similarity to the original sample from the database (Buisine *et al.* 2006, Martin *et al.* 2006). If the match is acceptable, the parameters are used to control resynthesis. The database plays no further role.

It is not clear how much that kind of light reliance on databases can achieve. As with speech, movement synthesized by rule is not altogether natural. Some research synthesizes images directly from records of body movements, using databases such as AffectMe (Kleinsmith *et al.* 2006), which includes motion capture data about acted bodily expressions of four basic emotions. If that level of naturalness matters, then the problem of large databases arises in the same way as with speech.

Databases for the recognition of affect in speech

Work on recognizing emotion from speech highlights three linked issues: naturalness; context; and description. They are well illustrated in a series of studies by Batliner and his colleagues.

A landmark study by Batliner *et al.* (2003) considered recognition of emotion in calls to a flight booking service. The objective was to recognize the emotion in the voices of people using the service. The recognizers were constructed in the standard way, by applying machine learning procedures to databases. Databases of three contrasting types were used for training. The first database contained recordings of actors who had been asked to generate archetypal examples of the emotional patterns that would be expected. The second contained recordings of people inter-acting with another person who simulated the behaviour of the system. The third contained recordings of people interacting with the system itself. The team expected that recognizers trained on the first two databases, containing material from actors and simulations, might give better performance, because the training material provided clearer examples of the relevant emotion categories. In fact, that was not the case. Recognizers trained on the idealized material performed poorly on real interactions. The best performance by a considerable margin came from training with the database containing material taken from the application scenario itself.

The usual conclusion is that training material should be naturalistic, not acted (Devillers *et al.* 2005; see also Chapter 5.3, this volume). However, the problem could hinge on context rather than naturalness *per se*, i.e. natural material would be just as inappropriate if it were taken from the wrong context. To illustrate, Ruzanski *et al.* (2005) recorded speech where fear had been induced by appearing before a military tribunal. Presumably the fear was genuine, but the record-ings would not be good training material for recognizing equally genuine fear in, for instance, crowd disturbances. The conclusion that speech research seems to have drawn in practice is that training material needs to be obtained in the same context as the application.

Context is also pivotal in the issue of description. For example, later research by Batliner stud-ied children giving commands to an Aibo robot. One of the main forms of speech was described as 'motherese' (Batliner *et al.* 2006). It is not a category that would be expected to occur either in their call centre study or in Rusanki *et al.*'s tribunal. Similarly, Devillers *et al.* (2005) looked at data from different call centres, financial and medical, and found very different patterns for, e.g. fear for one's life and fear of losing money. Clearly, descriptors should not be independent of the states that occur in the context. However, if every context used its own set of descriptors, research on one context could not inform research on another; and there would be severe difficulties in developing an agent that could operate across multiple contexts.

In the case of speech, there are reasons to doubt whether state level labelling should use every-day categories at all. It has been argued that most of the affective information in natural speech relates to abstract dimensions identified by psychological theory, arousal (or activation) and, to a lesser extent, valence. Raters can use 'trace' procedures to assign those labels, moving a cursor to indicate where the person being rated lies on each dimension at a given time (Cowie *et al.* 2000; Douglas-Cowie *et al.* 2007). Recognizers can match human application of those labels rather well (Wollmer *et al.* 2008).

Associated with those issues is a contrast of aims. In the military tribunal studied by Ruzanski *et al.* (2005), speakers are likely to conceal fear; and the natural task is to detect leakage, which non-expert human hearers might well miss. In conversational exchanges, the goal is more likely to be ensuring that the agent responds in the same way as a human listener would, whether or not the human listener would have been correct. Agents intended for these different goals need state labellings that meet different criteria.

One important kind of material clearly does presuppose a correctness criterion. It involves material from call centres (Devillers *et al.* 2005). Call centres are an interesting source because the material is authentic. However, they also raise distinctive problems. The goal may be, for instance, to detect when a caller is distressed, and should be routed away from an automatic answering service to a human. In that context, there is an obligation, which is ethical as well as technical, to ensure that labelling satisfies stringent criteria. There are also recurring issues about availability: companies rarely release recordings to the research community in general, and so it is very difficult to interpret the work done on a specific database.

These examples raise conceptual issues that are central to the field, and need to be brought out. However, it is also useful to provide some basic technical information.

- By speech standards, the size of database needed to recognize emotional colouring in conversational interaction is quite modest. Wollmer *et al.* (2008) reported good recognition of arousal, and reasonable recognition of valence, with a database containing about 80 minutes of speech from four speakers.

- Balance is an issue as well as size, particularly with naturalistic material. For instance, in 14 hours of recordings studied by Ang *et al.* (2002), the commonest strong emotion was frustration, of which there were 42 clear samples. Statistical learning rules applied to that kind of data simply conclude that they should call everything neutral. The problem can be mitigated, but balanced databases are strongly preferred for machine learning.

- Sign labelling raises particular issues of scale. It is common for work on recognition to derive 5000 features from each segment of the speech waveform. It is typically assumed that most of them will be generated at need rather than stored.

- The stored features are typically those that cannot be extracted automatically. Pitch contour is an obvious example. There are well-known methods of extracting the physical correlate of perceived pitch (which is known as F0). Automatic extraction is prone to errors (such as octave jumps), and so there is a case for including corrected descriptions in a database. Some databases take the same principle a step further, and include standard linguistic descriptions of intonation, such as TOBI, which describe variation in pitch and intensity in terms of categories that are meant to encapsulate what is perceptually significant for humans. In fact, where there is direct evidence, they do not seem particularly relevant to the perception of emotion (Batliner *et al.* 2006). It remains a controversial issue how useful it is for databases to include descriptions based on human impressions of the signal rather than the state of the person.

Most of the issues discussed in this section have implications beyond speech. They take different surface forms, but similar underlying problems arise in other modalities; and finding workable solutions is fundamental to progress.

Databases for the recognition of visible patterns

This heading covers very different subtopics. Recognizing visible signs raises different issues from recognizing states. The category of signs itself is very diverse, from eyebrow raising to body shape. Several other topics could be considered here, but are covered later. They involve databases where information is multimodal and/or resides in the way people carry out a task.

Recognizing visual signs is a comparatively standard engineering problem. Recognition of action units in the face and hand shapes in gesture is not specific to emotion, and so research can use databases that are controlled for lighting, head position, resolution, and so on. For instance, Bartlett *et al.* trained recognizers to classify action units on the Cohn–Kanade DFAT-504 dataset (Kanade *et al.* 2000) and material from Ekman's group (Donato *et al.* 1999), and applied the trained system to recordings of spontaneous facial behaviour. Agreement with human FACS raters was 90.9% for the training data, and 93% for the spontaneous data.

With controlled sources, training requires surprisingly few examples—as low as about 16 instances to train a support vector machine, about twice as many to train a Bayesian recognizer. In practice, larger numbers are preferred: the Bartlett study used 100 subjects from the Cohn–Kanade database and 24 from the Ekman material.

Beyond faces, databases developed for research on sign language (Ding and Martinez 2002) are relevant to problems like recovering hand position and configuration. Emotion-related gestures during dyadic interaction are shown in the EmoTaboo (Zara *et al.* 2007). The SEMAINE SAL database (described later) is concerned with various types of head movement that are relevant to the emotional colouring of interaction (nods, shakes, lowering, etc.).

As with speech, the databases most often used for state recognition show actors simulating a specified emotion in isolation. Evidence is accumulating that there are substantial differences between that kind of posed emotion and emotion in the course of a meaningful interaction (Cowie *et al.* 2009). The appropriate response is not simply to collect authentic visual signs of emotion, because authentic signs are likely to vary substantially in different contexts (during conversation with a friend, in a boardroom, on a football terrace, or during a marathon). It is a clear research priority to assemble material that captures the range of variation, as a preliminary to assembling databases that support training in significant areas of the domain.

Similar issues apply to state description. Categorical descriptions tend to fit acted databases—often basic emotions, sometimes subtler affective states, as in the 'mindreading CD' compiled by Baron-Cohen *et al.* (2004), which includes 'cognitive-epistemic' states such as doubt and confidence. Databases of naturalistic material may use categorical state labels, but the number of categories tends to be large, often multiplied by allowing combinations and/or specifying how well a given label fits. Dimensional labels provide a natural alternative. Since dimensions tend to be chosen by reference to a body of data, judgements about relevant dimensions interact with the task of assembling appropriate recordings.

Verbal databases

Affective use of language has tended to be rather separate from work with non-verbal channels. It involves both recognition of affect in text and generation of text with appropriate affective colouring. Research there hinges on large corpora, such as WordNet (Fellbaum 1999) and SenseNet (Shaikh *et al.* 2007a). They have been used to develop methods of estimating positive or negative sentiment in words, phrases, sentences, and documents, using very varied techniques: keyword spotting; lexical affinity; statistical methods; fuzzy logic; and direct assignment of valence by human raters (Shaikh *et al.* 2007b).

Databases for the recognition of relevant actions and interactions

Intuitively, it seems obvious that emotion is often revealed by the way people carry out a task. Relatively few databases address that problem. Pollick *et al.* (2001) have collected point light displays showing how people in various emotional states knock at a door. The 'spaghetti database' (Douglas-Cowie *et al.* 2007) shows people feeling in a box and finding various unexpected things (cold spaghetti, a spider, a buzzer). McMahon *et al.* (2008) have collected records of the way people drive after the induction of elation or anger.

That kind of material highlights the problem of scale vividly. There seems to be literally no end to the number of activities that could potentially yield information about affect, and collecting databases that document all of them would seem to be an endless task.

That argument points back to general questions. It seems likely that emotion is revealed by the way people do things because of underlying changes that affect all actions—concentration, judgement of risk, energy levels, and so on. Hence, it would seem that the way to tap into that kind of information is not to amass larger and larger databases, but to discover ways of inferring central changes from abstract characteristics of performance. But, although the idea seems logical, it is not clear how to implement it.

Issues that cut across the basic categories

Many key issues in database research are dependent on modality and function, but not all. This section considers issues that cut across those distinctions.

Multimodal databases

The term multimodal is often used loosely to describe material that includes different channels even if they are technically in the same modality, such as face and gesture (Martin *et al.* 2007), and it is used in that way here.

There has recently been a strong trend towards multimodality. It is linked to growing emphasis on naturalistic material, which tends to be intrinsically multimodal. However, there are also sophisticated multimodal databases using acted material, notably GEMEP (Bänziger and Scherer 2007; see also Chapter 6.1, this volume).

Early work on multimodality tended to look for material where all the major modalities were engaged simultaneously. In fact, it seems increasingly likely that different combinations of modalities tend to come into play in different contexts. For instance, gesture is quite sensitive to physical position and culture; and modalities often systematically conflict (e.g. smiling to offset the effect of very negative words). As elsewhere, the idea that modalities combine in different ways raises issues about scale.

The problem of interconnection

It is a feature of emotion that elements are profoundly interconnected. Databases can make interconnections more or less easy to discover.

◆ *Temporal units*. The raw recordings in a database need to be subdivided into functional units (often called 'clips'). Various units have been used as clips—words, phrase-like units, turns, episodes. Shorter clips have the advantage of neatness; longer clips have the advantage of providing context. Different units probably suit different functions. For instance, a relatively brief apex may be the relevant unit when units are being trained to recognize a particular facial configuration, but some kinds of state are difficult to recognize without quite a long prior context. What is important is that the issue is thought through.

- *Grouping.* Registering that certain features go together may be fundamental to understanding affect (e.g. that a grimace goes with a particular word, or direction of gaze indicates the object of emotion). Currently, databases of verbal material do use complex ways of representing relevant relationships, between words, phrases, phases of interaction, and communicative goals. Extending that kind of annotation to non-verbal material is an obvious goal, but not an easy one.

- *Interpersonal issues.* Emotion may be fundamentally social, and it certainly has interpersonal functions. The consequences have still to be absorbed. Clearly, some issues can only be addressed if databases record all the parties to an interaction. That is common practice for meeting databases, but they tend not to be particularly rich affectively (Heylen *et al.* 2006). Simply recording both parties is not necessarily enough. For instance, active exploration of another's emotion is an important competence. Understanding it may depend on access to an agent that will react to exploration rather than a static database.

The SAL paradigm, described below, goes some way to addressing those issues. It provides records of two parties interacting, and a context where interactions with an agent can be generated to support learning online rather than offline from databases.

Databases for evaluation and conceptual development

The principles that have been raised above have far-reaching implications for innovation, both technical and conceptual.

Evaluation is a glaring problem for technical innovation, particularly in the area of recognition. In speech recognition, studies using selected material obtain recognition rates about twice as far above chance as studies using naturalistic material directly (Cowie 2009). When material has effects on that scale, it is impossible to gauge the effect of technical innovation. Hence it is critical to have material that different techniques can be applied to.

The CEICES project (Batliner *et al.* 2006) represents a sustained effort in that direction. However, it highlights problems as well as ideals. The project uses a very particular kind of data, segmented and annotated in a specific way. If performance on that dataset became a recognized benchmark, it would presumably favour particular kinds of technique (as arguably happened when the Ekman database became a standard for face recognition).

There appears to be a need for a range of datasets that are recognized as standard, and that represent the different types that may be important. That is closely related to the conceptual problem of describing context, which has been emphasized repeatedly.

Other conceptual problems need similar resources. To find adequate ways of describing context, there needs to be a range of raw records that spans the important kinds of context and against which alternative ways of describing context can be assessed. The same goes for the problem of finding state level descriptions that apply across contexts rather than having to be constructed *ex nihilo* for every new application.

A case study: the database system for SAL

The discussion so far has considered different types of database in isolation. It does not convey the level of resource that is needed to develop an integrated agent. A useful way to do that is to return to the ACII 2009 conference. The system which won the prize for best demonstration, the 'sensitive artificial listener' (abbreviated to SAL), was designed to achieve an ongoing, affectively coloured interaction with a human user. To do that, it needed to incorporate multiple abilities—recognition, planning, and output—in multiple modalities. Hence, it provides a useful indication of the database support that is needed to implement an agent with even minimal affective competence.

SAL is not so much an application as a testbed that draws together the technical challenges involved in conducting a sustained, affectively coloured conversation with a person. The system's conversation consists of stock phrases chosen for their affective impact, and it provides 'back-channelling' while the user is speaking: both have to be synthesized in an emotionally appropriate way. What it does at any given time is based on non-verbal signs from the user, particularly signs concerned with affect: hence, it needs to register the signs. To maintain interest, it simulates four 'operators' with different affective styles: Spike, who is angry; Obadiah, who is gloomy; Poppy, who is exuberant; and Prudence, who is pragmatic. Each tries to detect the user's mood, and choose responses that steer his/her mood towards its own. That crude scenario creates a dynamic that is interesting enough to engage users for tens of minutes, long enough to expose core issues in affective human–machine interaction.

The system is shallow in the extreme, but developing it required an extensive and diverse set of database resources. Reviewing them provides a concrete sense of what is needed to develop anything approaching a credible agent with current technology.

Pre-existing sources

Well-established databases met some needs, particularly those concerned with extracting comparatively simple signs. Thus, in the visual domain, Feret and BioID were used to train detectors for facial points, and MMI was used to train recognizers for action units. Similarly, in the audio domain, AVIC, the AMI database, TIMIT, and WSJ were used to train word recognizers, AVIC and AMI were also used to train natural language models, AVIC was used to train interest recognizers, and AMI was used to train recognizers for discourse type. On the synthesis side, a standard XML lexicon was used to define relevant behaviours.

Beyond these, a range of resources specific to the project were used. The categories introduced above provide a way of describing them.

Raw records

- *Operator speech recordings*. Four actors, one for each operator personality, made audio recordings of all the stock phrases for each character, plus a phonetically balanced set of sentences (so that new utterances could be synthesized).

- *Role play recordings*. Trained humans simulated each operator responding to users in each affective category. This material guided synthesis of operator behaviour, particularly backchanelling.

- *Wizard of Oz recordings*. Users interacted with a system that replayed the pre-recorded utterances, but used a (hidden) human operator to choose the most appropriate utterance at any given juncture.

- *Transcripts*. Transcripts of the role play recordings provided a basis for developing rules to govern dialogue management.

The core recordings used five high-speed, high resolution cameras, and four high quality microphones. Teleprompters were adapted to give the impression of eye contact but allow cameras to be directly in front of the face.

Sign level annotation

- Operator speech recordings were annotated phonetically for synthesis of new utterances.

- Role play recordings of the operator were annotated to identify head nods and shakes, eyebrow raises and frowns, and other gestures relevant to synthesizing backchannelling.

♦ Extracts from recordings of the user were annotated to train sign-level analysers. They were chosen to provide clear examples of the following key categories:

  • head actions, nodding, shaking;

  • 9 gaze directions, each in varied contexts;

  • 20 specified facial action units in varied contexts.

About 30 instances were selected for each category, balanced across users and moods.

State level annotation

Labelling of the user's affective state was used to train audio and visual recognition of affective states and states' relevant dialogue management. It operated at two levels. In the first, raters traced apparent rise and fall of overall emotional intensity and the four affect dimensions identified by Fontaine *et al.* (2007): valence; potency; activation; and novelty. In the second, raters decided whether an extract contained a clear-cut example of a relevant category. The categories were simple emotions (fear, anger, happiness, sadness, disgust, surprise, and amusement); epistemic/affective states (certain, agreeing, interested, at ease, thoughtful, concentrating); and interaction process analysis discourse categories described by Bales (1950).

Contingencies

Labelled role play recordings were used as a basis for a separate database detailing what informants felt would be appropriate responses to particular statements by users in the role play, taking account of the emotion labels assigned to them. The function of this database was to provide an empirical basis for choosing the agent's response to a particular kind of user utterance.

Producing the specialized databases absorbed a considerable proportion of the project's resources. About 20% were directly allocated to the task. The proportion of effort actually consumed was considerably higher, because consumers were heavily involved in ensuring that the material was suitable.

Synthesis and prognosis

Databases are at the centre of affective computing. Reviewing the various forms that they take helps to clarify why that is, and what the implications are. Several underlying issues seem critical.

In emotion, the norm is for many variables to be changing simultaneously and subtle features of the way they change and interrelate may materially change outcomes. Hence, they need to be captured in a way that allows them to be analysed, or processed, or reused, both separately and together, if necessary over a long period. In practice, that means that both the raw materials, and the results of time-consuming analyses, need to be consolidated into databases. The one-shot experiments classically favoured by experimental psychology are simply not an appropriate medium.

A deeper issue is whether there is something special about the kind of relationship that holds between affective states and the actions that signal them. The human intellect is excellent at seeing past irrelevant detail to simple underlying relationships. But in areas such as recognizing emotion in speech and action hugely complex relationships among multiple types of detail seem to be of the essence. It seems entirely possible that these relationships are intrinsically opaque to the human intellect; and that, as a result, the only practical way to capture them is by applying learning and selection rules to databases.

It may also be that, because of the form of relationships between affective states and the actions that signal them, it is intrinsically difficult to find rules that hold across a very wide range of contexts.

However, there are some kinds of development that it seems likely could make it easier to discover relationships that are not tied to particular sensor configurations or task settings.

- Human beings achieve 'constancy' across sound environments, lighting, camera orientations, etc. Currently, machine perception cannot do the same. However, matching the 'constancies' that humans achieve does not seem an unattainable goal. Progress towards it would reduce the need to build new databases for every configuration of sensors and ambient energy.

- Logically similar, but deeper, is the problem of going beyond surface images of an action to infer levels of control, risk-taking, and so on. If progress were made on that problem, the need for situation-specific databases could be hugely reduced.

Even if these issues were solved, it would remain a major challenge to deal with the way expressions of emotion depend on context. The challenge has two parts. The practical part is collecting and labelling data on the appropriate scale. It seems increasingly clear that the scale required is very large. The conceptual part is understanding what the different contexts are, and finding suitable ways to describe them. Very little has been written on the subject, and what there is barely scratches the surface.

The future shape of research on affectively competent agents depends fundamentally on the progress that is made in these areas. At best, new discoveries may mean that teams building a new system can usually access existing databases, or subsystems developed using those databases. At worst, constructing databases specifically, each new agent will consume a large part of the effort needed to build it, and will depend on quite specialized skills. It is not clear which future is more likely.

On the use of actor portrayals in research on emotional expression

Klaus R. Scherer and Tanja Bänziger

Summary

In this chapter we address the hotly debated issue of the utility of using actor portrayals in research on emotional expression in psychology, neuroscience, and affective computing. We argue that emotions are rare and fleeting events that are difficult to capture in a purely spontaneous fashion, especially as they are likely to be constantly manipulated for the purpose of self-regulation or social constraints. We propose an account of the fundamental mechanism underlying emotional expression and present a theoretical analysis that distinguishes between push (physiologically driven) and pull (social regulation and strategic intention) factors, suggesting that corpora with unobtrusive recordings of real-life expressions, laboratory induction, recording of expressive behaviour from media shows, and explicit actor portrayals all have their place in emotional expression (EE) research and vary continuously on several dimensions rather than representing completely different classes of expressions. We argue that an analysis of pure push factors, spontaneous unregulated expressions, is unrealistic in practice and probably of little interest, given the scarcity of such pure expressions in social life. We suggest that one focus of current research should instead be directed toward the explicit study of pull effects, the use of actor portrayals being a highly appropriate methodological choice for this aim, given the possibility of manipulating and standardizing pull effects. The central role of actor portrayals clearly lies in the empirical and experimental study of the shared code of emotional signalling and the examination of cue utilization in emotion perception and inference.

Introduction

The study of emotional expression (EE) plays a central role in emotion research as visible or audible expressions externalize an internal state and thus become a major aspect of social communication, informing others about the person's reactions to events and intentions to act. Not surprisingly, then, EE research constitutes a sizeable proportion of emotion research in psychology, ethology, neuroscience, and affective computing. A major problem for such research efforts is the fact that strong emotions that are likely to be forcefully expressed are relatively rare, fleeting phenomena that are generally hidden from public view or covered up. The fact that strong, prototypical emotions are relatively rare is suggested by indirect evidence. Thus, when one tries to report a representative instance of certain emotion experiences, for example, intense sadness, one often has to go back in time for several months to find an appropriate example in memory (Scherer and Wallbott 1994, p. 319). Only relatively frequent emotional experiences, such as minor anger episodes, come readily to mind by recalling events from previous days or weeks. In an actuarial study of emotional experiences, asking a quasi-representative sample of the Swiss population to report the most important emotion that they experienced yesterday, only anger or joy were reported by more than 10% of the sample, whereas emotions such as sadness or fear were reported only by about 2–3%, suggesting that such strong emotions occur rather less frequently in daily life (see Scherer *et al.* 2004*a*).

Even EEs that occur relatively frequently in everyday life are often quite unpredictable, which makes them hard to catch for the researcher. EEs are fleeting, evanescent events that come and go rapidly. This means that, if one wants to go beyond impressionistic description and interpretation, EEs need to be recorded audiovisually at sufficiently high quality to allow objective measurement and analysis.

Unfortunately, apart from lack of opportunity, i.e. the difficulty of catching appropriate incidents of EEs in a naturalistic fashion in the field, EEs are also almost impossible to systematically observe or even record for further analysis because of privacy and ethics constraints. Even if it were possible to obtain the informed consent of all concerned, the recording conditions (camera angle, image resolution, sound quality) are often hampered by the available technology or the local setting. Even more important, in general only public settings provide ethically admissible observation and recording options so the likelihood is strong that senders will closely monitor and control their expressive behaviour, conforming to sociocultural display rules (Ekman and Friesen 1971; Matsumoto 1990). This tendency will be even more pronounced in the presence of cameras and microphones, producing the danger that the authentic expression of the respective emotions will be completely suppressed or modified and sometimes replaced by stereotypical expression patterns that are in accordance with cultural expectations for the respective event and setting.

An alternative approach consists of inducing an emotion in the laboratory and observing or recording the corresponding expression. Although psychologists have created an impressive number of induction techniques (Coan and Allen 2007), some of which produce relatively reliable effects, the intensity of the resulting states is generally low, with little outwardly observable expression, for example, in the case of emotion induction through picture viewing, listening to music, or imagination and memory retrieval. Ethical constraints, as well as cost and practicality, often prevent researchers from confronting participants with stimuli or events of sufficiently high importance or relevance that are likely to produce bona fide emotions. Most important, expressions are often generated by action tendencies (Darwin 1872/1998; Frijda and Tscherkassof 1997; Scherer and Ellgring 2007*a*) and, because most experimental inductions and manipulations in the laboratory do not require or allow adaptive action, the potential for the production of EEs is limited. Furthermore, as in the case of observation in natural field settings, artefacts cannot be excluded. Thus, by using social or personal display rules, participants may suppress or modify naturally occurring expressions that they consider inappropriate, or may even simulate emotions that they do not experience to show that they are 'good participants' who give the experimenter what is expected.

Methodological requirements for emotion induction

In sum, neither natural field observation nor experimental induction are particularly conducive to EE research—neither for the study of the mechanisms underlying EE production nor in the way in which they are perceived and interpreted by observers. At the same time, the methodological demands on this research with respect to experimental design and procedures are extensive as the following issues have to be taken into account.

◆ *Individual differences.* The evidence for strong individual differences in emotional reactions is abundant. Different individuals (or the same individual at different times) may react with different emotions to the same situation because differentially salient goals and values that are specific to an individual may lead to different appraisals (Scherer and Brosch 2009). Individuals also have different response or coping styles (including expression, e.g. externalization versus internalization). For this reason, expressions of several different emotions and repeated expressions of each emotion need to be sampled for each individual studied. This sampling needs to occur under highly controlled situational conditions because even minor differences in event appraisal may lead to widely different emotions (Ellsworth and Scherer 2003; Scherer *et al.* 2001).

♦ *Emotion differences.* As mentioned earlier, many EEs are generated by action tendencies and, because each emotion can generate a variety of partially overlapping action tendencies, the study of EE differences between emotions requires the study of widely different emotions. In consequence, studies on EE need to sample as large and as complete a set of emotions as possible.

♦ *Technical requirements.* The need for objective coding and measurement of multimodal EEs requires audiovisual recording and a high level of sophistication to ensure a high recording quality required by the advanced annotation and analysis methods in this domain (see Harrigan *et al.* 2005).

Clearly, these conditions are hard to meet, especially at a reasonable cost in time and money, if one wants to record naturally occurring EEs for many different emotions, in a repeated fashion, for a sizeable number of comparable individuals in everyday life or to induce many different strong emotions in a repeated fashion in the laboratory. The limited suitability of field observation and experimental induction paradigms for the systematic study of EEs and the need for large-scale sampling, repetition, situational control, and sophisticated methodology have led expression researchers to have recourse to actor portrayals of emotion. It is no surprise that the bulk of expression research reported in the literature, particularly for the perception and interpretation of EEs, has used this approach, generating a remarkable body of pertinent and highly replicable findings.

The portrayal paradigm generally consists in asking trained lay persons or professional actors to produce an EE that can be considered a plausible or believable instance of a prototypical expression of a given emotion. In some cases, encoders are only given an emotion label and asked to produce the appropriate expression. More frequently, however, more elaborate encoding instructions are used, for example, providing typical emotion scenarios that the actors are to act out, or a procedure that approaches induction procedures, namely, the Stanislavski or method acting approach that requires the actors to generate a rudimentary feeling state corresponding to the respective emotion by using memory recall or vivid imagination techniques. Providing standard scenarios serves to define the emotion more precisely beyond the semantic meaning of words and is likely lead to more comparable portrayals across actors for a given procedure. In contrast, a Stanislavski procedure, through the implication of personal experiences and images, encourages somewhat more idiosyncratic expressions. Both procedures are likely to increase the authenticity and believability of the portrayals as they discourage the use of stereotypical patterns. In some cases, both approaches are combined for maximal effect (see Chapter 6.1, this volume).

Unfortunately, actor portrayals are often misunderstood. The purpose of using actor portrayals is *not* to study spontaneously occurring emotions or to detect underlying emotions in actors. Actors are asked to produce expression patterns that are plausible and believable replicas of real, spontaneous expressions typical of certain emotions. Participants in judgement studies are asked to judge what emotion is *represented* by the portrayal, not what emotion the actor feels. And the purpose of the research is to identify the prototypical representation of emotions in social communication, not to study the nature of spontaneous emotion expressions in real life.

Clearly, there are differences between the two. For example, differences in timing and dynamic patterning have been shown between 'true' and 'fake' smiles despite the fact that the facial movement is the same (Krumhuber and Kappas 2005; Schmidt *et al.* 2006). But the purpose of using actor portrayals in emotion perception research is to examine the expressive *code* used in social emotion communication.

Studying a code requires that it is understood by the decoder and thus portrayed expressions are generally selected on the basis of their recognizability, something which some critics fail to understand. Thus, Barrett (2006) writes: 'For example, one very influential study (Banse and Scherer 1996) attempted statistical classification of only 16.9% of the vocal samples that were actually recorded. It is difficult to interpret the findings from meta-analyses like the one by Juslin and Laukka (2003) when the utterances being classified are carefully selected to represent only a small subset of those that occur within the lab.' There is a fundamental misunderstanding here. Studying a communication code requires the selection of well-recognized tokens; otherwise, the precondition of socially shared iconic representations is not met. Generally, in portrayal studies, many more repetitions are recorded than stimuli are needed and a selection of the most reliably rated and best recognized stimuli is made to ascertain that a shared iconic representation is captured.

In consequence, the utility of actor portrayals is intrinsically limited to the study of the shared code of EE in emotion communication and care has to be taken to avoid using such material in an inappropriate fashion, Clearly, EE corpora or databases need to be adapted to the specific research aims pursued by the researcher and a careful analysis of the specific needs should made in each case (see Chapter 3.1, this volume; Douglas-Cowie *et al.* 2003*b*). In many cases one may need to resort to different techniques to obtain pertinent samples of EE, using systematic induction, media material, field observation, or other techniques (see Chapter 6.2, this volume; Campbell 2000; and http://www.acii2009.nl/program/show_slot/42). However, care should be taken to avoid using a simple dichotomy between actor portrayals, considered as artificial and inauthentic, and corpora obtained through laboratory induction, from media records, or through surreptitious field recordings, considered as natural or authentic. We believe that it is necessary to examine the underlying conceptualization of the distinction between 'natural and artificial' to evaluate this suggestion. The general assumption seems to be that expressions can be arranged with respect to a simple binary distinction:

- natural, realistic, authentic, genuine, real, believable, sincere, trustworthy versus
- unnatural, unrealistic, counterfeit, artificial, fake, not believable, feigned, unreliable.

We argue that this is an unrealistic claim as expressions tend to vary continuously on several dimensions. Thus, closer inspection of the above enumerations shows that these qualifiers take different objects and have different meanings. The following list provides a small sampling of different pairs of terms and suggests criteria that might be used for deciding which term of the pair should be applied.

Terms	Criteria
Natural versus unnatural	Biological determination
Realistic versus unrealistic	Probability of occurrence
Genuine versus artificial	Original versus. copy
Real versus fake	Original versus copy
Authentic versus counterfeit	Deception intention
Sincere versus feigned	Deception intention
Believable versus not believable	Observer judgement
Trustworthy versus unreliable	Observer judgement

Of course, this is a very hazardous procedure as many of the terms are semantically highly complex. Naturalness seems to refer to something that is biologically given and immutable, whereas something unnatural would go against preordained practice. The quality of being realistic, corresponding to facts rather than abstract ideals, could be glossed as the probability of occurrence of a specific behaviour in a given situation determined by its actuarial frequency and prototypicality. Unrealistic would apply to figments of the imagination. Genuineness seems to depend on whether the object or behaviour in question is the original or a copy, implying the existence of a certain uniqueness. Sincerity or authenticity can only be judged on the basis of a person's intention to deceive about a true underlying state, feigning or faking another. And believability or trustworthiness surely depends entirely on subjective observer judgement rather than on some objective quality of the behaviour. From this analysis, we suggest distinguishing three underlying perspectives for classifying EEs:

1 A *behaviour perspective* that examines the frequency and typicality of a given EE in the context of a specific situation, thus defining its realism or naturalness, as the biologically determined should also be the most frequent. This perspective requires an examination of the biological determination of EE and actuarial investigation of frequency and typicality.

2 A *sender or encoder perspective* that examines the EE from the point of view of the production, taking into account communication intentions in particular. Here, issues such as spontaneous versus voluntary, strategic production, raw versus regulated, controlled expression, and conscious versus unconscious production have a role. The true underlying intention is exceedingly difficult to determine, even by questioning the sender, because the production factors may be unconscious or the sender may want to dissimulate strategic intentions. Most important, both types of factors may be involved in close interaction.

3 A *decoder or observer* perspective that is orthogonal to the preceding factors because observers may form subjective impressions about prototypicality and thus realism, or about sender intention and thus authenticity, or about sincerity versus strategic intention. Genuine observer judgements are perceived believability or plausibility (an evaluation that combines realism and authenticity) and perceived reliability or trustworthiness of the sender (a derived judgement about sender dispositions).

Given these three perspectives, it is possible to analyse more precisely the differential utility of different types of sampling of EE as corpora or databases for research, such as actor portrayal procedures, excerpts from media game or reality shows, laboratory induction, or surreptitious or open recording of spontaneous, real-life EEs. Which of these research paradigms come closest to the natural, authentic, and genuine expressions in spontaneous emotion expressions that are presumably biologically determined, untainted by devious encoder intentions, and thus automatically believable and trustworthy? Cowie, McKeown, and Gibney (2009) show, using examples in which spontaneous emotion is perceived as acted and acted emotions as spontaneous and authentic, that this question has no simple answer. They focus on the third perspective outlined above, concerned with observer judgement, and demonstrate the need to study the nature and distribution of expressive cues in multiple modalities that underlie authenticity judgements of observers. They note that the differences between the various types of sampling needed to be discussed with respect to their relative importance and the research questions and demands on analysis in specific cases. The perspectives we have outlined above can help to examine these issues. Thus, the first, behaviour perspective is obviously central in cases in which there are clear context constraints and in which it thus makes sense to require high frequency and prototypicality of expressions. The third, decoder or observer perspective is most important in research questions that examine the mechanisms underlying emotion perception, the nature of the cues, and the impression formation and inference processes (see also Figure 3.2.1). Both of these

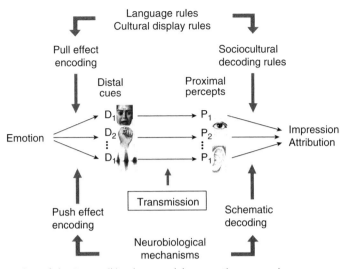

Fig. 3.2.1 Adaptation of the Brunswikian lens model to emotion expression.

perspectives play a major role in the study of the interpersonal communication of emotion. The most difficult is the second, sender or encoder perspective as it requires the observer to identify the 'real state' and communication intentions of the sender which are often unconsciously or purposively hidden from public inspection. This perspective is of central relevance for diagnostic purposes in which the investigator wants to use EE to uncover the sender's innermost feelings and true intentions, for example, in the case of detecting deception (Ekman 2009). The problem is that the distinction between true and faked feeling is a very difficult one. We will devote the bulk of this chapter to addressing some of the underlying theoretical issues for this distinction.

A good starting point, as so often, is Aristotle, who, in remarkable anticipation of the notion of emotional competence or intelligence, pointed out that to qualify as a socially skilled person one needs 'to be angry in the manner, at the things, and for the length of time, that the rule dictates' (see Aristotle 1941, p. 996); in other words, anger expression has to conform to social standards and expectations. This theme was echoed and enlarged by Goffman's (1959) notion of impression management, in which one's emotions are expressed in accordance not only with sociocultural norms, but also with one's strategic intentions. Clearly, it is not enough to closely control EE; rather, the expression has to be appropriate for cultural and contextual expectations. As shown by work on *display rules* (Ekman *et al.* 1969; Matsumoto 1990; Scherer 2000*b*), people need to actively produce the *appropriate* expression. These mechanisms are clearly incompatible with the pure natural, genuine, and authentic view espoused by many researchers.

A dual mechanism in expression generation

So what exactly are the determinants of emotional expression? Scherer and his collaborators (Kappas *et al.* 1991; Scherer 1985, 1986, 1988; Scherer *et al.* 1980; Scherer, and Kappas 1988) have suggested settling the conundrum by differentiating *push and pull effects* in EE. In the case of push effects, internal factors, such as physiological arousal in strong emotions, 'push' motor behaviour into certain directions (such as adaptive actions) but do not necessarily target particular configurations. Thus, the underlying emotion processes are highly variable and volatile; in consequence, the resulting expression is also highly variable and may rapidly change over time.

In contrast, external pull factors are in the service of specific communication intentions or of culturally defined norms or expectations that require the production of relatively unambiguous expressive features in a specific signal structure. The sender needs to produce this pattern to achieve a particular effect. In this case, the expression outcome or target is fixed, or at least constrained, although the processes by which it is brought about can be variable.

Much research on EE has been conducted with an implicit focus on push factors in an attempt to use expression as direct readout of the underlying emotional state of the individual. This research is often frustrating because researchers rarely have access to bona fide emotions in natural social settings, individuals differ strongly in their expressive behaviour, and it is difficult to objectively determine the precise nature of the underlying emotion without using verbal report (which is often biased by defense strategies or conventional response rules). In this chapter, we attempt to redress the balance and to focus on the pull effects in emotion expression and communication.

Figure 3.2.1 shows an adaptation of the Brunswikian lens model that Scherer (1978, 2003) has suggested as a guide to theorizing and research in the area of EE. The model suggests that the expresser encodes an emotion by producing a number of distal cues in bodily posture, gestures, facial movements, and vocal cues. These distal cues are transmitted via the auditory and visual communication channels to a perceiver, where they give rise to proximal percepts, the correspondence to the original distal cues depending on transmission quality and the capacity of the sense organs. In the process of impression formation, the perceiver uses inferential mechanisms to attribute an emotion to the expresser (with variable degrees of accuracy). Unfortunately, this model has rarely been used to describe EE and the mechanisms underlying both the generation of distal cues as a function of the underlying emotion on the one hand and the inference and attribution of emotion on the basis of the proximal percepts on the other (but see Bänziger 2004; Juslin 1998, 2001). In particular, most research has focused on single expression modalities such as facial or vocal cues, making it impossible to study the coherence between the different modalities that may have a major role in constituting the emotion (see Scherer 2009a) and in determining perceiver inference (see below).

The proposed distinction between push and pull effects implies specific hypotheses about the nature of the underlying mechanisms. As shown in Figure 3.2.1, in the case of push factors, one expects the operation of neurobiological mechanisms that generate specific expression patterns as part of the emotion process. Push effects are biologically determined externalizations of naturally occurring internal processes of the organism, particularly information processing and behavioural preparation. Examples for cases in which push effects dominate are reactive animal expressions, infant grunts and cries, affect bursts, or sudden, uncontrolled emotional utterances.

Mechanisms underlying the operation of push and pull factors

What is the underlying mechanism? In his component process model, Scherer (1984, 1992, 2001, 2009a) proposes that efferent effects of sequentially accrued appraisal results cumulatively constitute the unique, context- and individual-specific response pattern for a given emotion episode. The component process model is based on the idea that during evolution, emotion has been optimized to serve the following functions: (a) evaluation of objects and events; (b) system regulation; (c) preparation and direction of action; (d) communication of reaction and behavioural intention; and (e) monitoring of internal state and organism–environment interaction (see Scherer 1984, 2001). In consequence, the model predicts that the results of sequential appraisal checks will generate appropriate response patterns including, particularly, the generation of the expression patterns. Predictions for facial, vocal, and gestural expressions have been elaborated (Johnstone *et al.* 2001; Kaiser and Wehrle 2001; Scherer 1986, 1987, 2001, 2009a) on the basis of several classes of determinants: (1) the effects of the physiological change; (2) the preparation of specific instrumental motor actions; and (3) the production of socio-communicative signals. The first two determinants can be subsumed under the push effects.

As shown in Figure 3.2.1, push effect encoding is determined by neurobiological mechanisms. Of particular importance are three major instrumental functions of the facial organs (lips, nose, ears) and the vocal tract (mouth, pharynx, larynx): (1) passing matter (light, air, liquids, solids) to and from internal organs (e.g. in the service of respiration, metabolism, and glandular secretion); (2) positioning sensory organs for optimal reception of stimulation (e.g. raising eyebrows, flaring nostrils); and (3) acting directly on objects and other organisms (biting, licking, kissing). Table 1 in Scherer (2009a) shows the predictions for facial, vocal, and gestural expressions resulting from individual appraisal checks.

The model suggests that the cumulative results of a sequential series of checks (1, relevance of the event; 2, implications for major needs, goals, and values; 3, ability to deal with these consequences or coping potential; and 4, normative significance of the event) produce a wide variety of complexly patterned emotion episodes. Despite this variability, a number of modal emotions, such as anger, fear, or joy, can be identified (Scherer 1994b). Yet, one can expect relatively strong interindividual differences in the expressive patterns produced by push effects (as the underlying biological processes are dependent on both the idiosyncratic nature of the individual and the specific nature of the situation).

In contrast, the social signalling function is served by pull effects, that is, particular visual or auditory signal configurations that are part of a socially shared communication code. This pull effect encoding is determined by linguistic rules for the encoding of syntactic, semantic, and pragmatic aspects of meaning and socioculturally variable norms, or molds, concerning the signal characteristics required by the shared codes for the communication of internal states and behavioural intentions. Examples for pure pull effects are sound symbolism, symbolic coding systems such as language, conventionalized expression rules, affect emblems, the mimicking of push effects, or constraints due to specific communication channels. Because pull effect encoding is characterized by a high degree of symbolization and conventionalization, one would expect comparatively few and small individual differences.

Just as push and pull effects differ in their underlying production or encoding mechanisms, they also differ in the corresponding perception or decoding mechanisms. As shown in Figure 3.2.1, one would expect animals and humans to have innate or prepared recognition schemata and efficient learning strategies for push effect expressions, whereas pull effects are likely to be decoded on the basis of socially transmitted, and explicitly taught, decoding rules that determine inference and attribution of the transmitted emotional meaning.

Pure push or pull effects are rare, because these two classes of determinants always closely interact (Kappas *et al.* 1991; Scherer 1985, 1988; Scherer and Kappas 1988). This is why Figure 3.2.1 illustrates the simultaneous effects of push and pull production and perception mechanisms in the ongoing process of emotion transmission. Once the emotion process has started, the resulting patterning becomes itself subject to appraisal (see also Frijda 1993) and thus subject to different kinds of regulation. Furthermore, emotion, although originally elicited in a spontaneous fashion, may, in the ongoing process of emoting, become of strategic importance in interaction, as the claims by Aristotle (1941) and Goffman (1959), mentioned earlier, show. Thus, once the emotion process is ongoing, one expects various mixtures of biologically driven (often automatic) and socially learned (sometimes intentional) affect expression, depending on the nature of the situation, the strategic goals of the actor, and his or her cognitive and social development. In consequence, one of the major issues to be dealt with in the study of behaviour control under emotion is the relative mix of push versus pull, or more spontaneous versus more deliberate, aspects of expression control.

One can assume that most real-life EEs have a strong pull effect component because much behaviour in social settings is closely regulated and controlled. Thus, even in the case of the most primitive expressions, the affect bursts (Scherer 1994*a*), one is much more likely to find them in a 'domesticated' version (Wundt 1900) in the form of affect emblems or interjections. Yet, many researchers in the domain of EE research pursue a quest to study the natural, true, authentic expression of the observed individual's innermost feelings, in other words, pure push effects. Apart from the problem that such cases are likely to be rare, they are unlikely to happen in the presence of research teams with the capacity for high-quality multimodal recordings of such instances. Much of the EE research has a focus on expressions that have a strong pull component, including signals that the individual wants his social environment to notice and interpret correctly. We believe that it is essential to systematically investigate the distal cues that are produced by senders in such cases and to examine how these cues are "utilized", in the Brunswikian sense, by decoders or receivers who try to make sense of the proximal cues they perceive. Given the difficulty of studying pure push effects in EE, and given the pervasiveness of cases with mixed origin, often with considerable pull effects, this investigation seems to be an important and realistic aim.

Furthermore, the existence of pull mechanisms implies that specific expressions are socially appropriate for specific senders in specific social situations and that observers (receivers of the displays) will interpret the expressions according to the context of their production. Many examples can be used to illustrate this point, for instance, the reaction of the 'winner' and the 'loser' in the final of a beauty pageant. These contests almost always include a finale in which two candidates are singled out and where the tension and anticipation rises while everyone awaits the nomination of the winner. Rules for appropriate emotional displays and rules for the interpretation of the behaviour of the contestants are well established. The loser is probably disappointed but does not display this emotion, instead showing happiness (for the sake of the winner) and good humour. The winner is mostly happy, but the display must also include tears, tremors, and signs of surprise or disbelief. Viewers are aware of this scenario; both contestants hope to win, yet both act as if they expected the other one to win (this rule seems to apply to other/competitions as well, but not to all types). Viewers would probably be shocked if the expected scenario were not fulfilled. However, someone foreign to the rules of this specific situation might not understand the scenario and might interpret the reactions in a different way. Likewise, in most social situations there are well-established rules that orient the interpretation of the non-verbal displays presented by specific social actors. Although the context is inseparable from the non-verbal displays in everyday experience, the ensuing confounding of context and non-verbal displays constitutes a problem for the advancement of research into EEs. When a non-verbal display (EE) is embedded in other contextual cues that provide information about the probable emotion(s) of the sender (e.g. in the example of beauty pageant it would be impossible to witness the ongoing non-verbal reactions of the contestants without getting information about the underlying scenario at the same time), it becomes impossible to assess the specific contribution of the non-verbal displays to the formation of an impression in the viewers. To find out if and how the non-verbal displays contribute to the interpretation of the emotions experienced by the senders, one would need to isolate the non-verbal displays and to present them in different contexts or to present different non-verbal displays in the same context.

If we analyse media recordings of EEs from a push–pull perspective, one may conclude that many takes do not seem highly natural or realistic (except in their own contexts, e.g. TV game shows) and are unlikely to be devoid of strategic intentions (given the evaluation apprehension in the recording situation). Similarly, laboratory-induced EEs, if one could produce them in a reliable fashion, would suffer from some of the same shortcomings: the expressions might be specific to the experimental context and demand characteristics are likely to play a major role.

Although media conditions may increase the chances that strategic impression intentions will have a role, the same is true in real life, as our review of the Goffmanian approach, highlighting the 'presentation of emotion in everyday life', has shown (see also the writings of ancient rhetoric teachers such as Aristotle, Cicero, or Quintilian). Thus, the difference to explicit portrayals by actors may be much less important than is generally held. As argued above, all expressions of emotion vary continuously on the dimensions outlined above and we can expect gradients rather than categorical distinctions. Obviously, it is highly instructive to obtain corpora with media recordings, chance unobtrusive recordings from 'real life', as well as to induce a variety of emotional states in the laboratory and observe the expressions. In every single case, there will be an interaction of push and pull effects and it would be of great benefit to pull these apart. What we want to warn against is to treat the difference to explicit actor portrayals as a fundamental categorical distinction that opposes the natural to the artificial.

Using actor portrayals in systematic research on pull factors

Rather, we argue that the use of actor portrayals of EEs provides a royal road to examine the questions outlined above in a principled fashion. In the last quarter of the eighteenth century, the French philosopher and encyclopedist Diderot wrote an essay on the 'actor's paradox' ('Le paradoxe du comédien') in which he debated the question of whether and how actors can produce authentic, believable emotions on the stage without simultaneously experiencing these emotions. The issue of the 'player's passion' has been passionately debated ever since by both actors and scholars alike (see Roach 1993) and it is of central relevance to contemporary emotion research. Recently, this debate has acquired new timeliness, given the growing dissension about the 'right' way to study EEs in voice, face, and body (Douglas-Cowie et al. 2003b). The use of actor portrayals has a long history in the study of emotion research because of the inherent limitations of studying naturally occurring EEs.

We have attempted to show that neither sampled media nor real-life EEs are devoid of strategic intentions leading to simulation, fabrication, control, and so forth. Furthermore, in many of these cases, the nature and strength of these intentions are unknown or extremely difficult to determine reliably. Thus, it may be overly optimistic to expect to obtain natural, authentic, spontaneous, sincere, and believable EEs through media sampling or laboratory induction. Furthermore, as long as one does not have an exact inventory of all the components of an emotional episode, including the person's conscious feeling state and label, one has no clue as to the authentic, natural emotion that is expressed, and it is dubious if such a state exists at all because, in all emotion episodes, control and regulation enter from the start.

How do actor portrayals fare in comparison? One central point is that the use of actor portrayals in research is not an attempt to study natural, authentic, spontaneous, sincere, and believable EEs. It is clear from the outset that the actor will intentionally produce an EE that may be completely unrelated to his or her current emotional state. The major advantage of actor portrayals, in contrast to media sampling or laboratory induction paradigms, is that the strategic intentions of the actor are known and can be standardized. The actor is told to produce a believable or plausible expression that will be recognized by observers and that must be prototypical and consequently natural and realistic. This, we hold, will make it possible to study the pull effects of EE and communication in the sense described earlier, because the actor's expressions are likely to come close to the templates that would be, consciously or unconsciously, used in producing expressions that are 'pulled' into the direction of a specific strategic or culturally imposed target.

However, we assert that, to achieve satisfactory results, asking students or members of one's laboratory to 'do' certain emotions is not sufficient. From Diderot on, the consensus has been that it is an art to produce believable emotions on the stage and that only the best professionals succeed in this enterprise. On the basis of theory and our own experience (Banse and Scherer 1996; Gosselin *et al.* 1995), we suggest that professional actors should be used, who are coached by a professional director and who use Stanislavski (1980) or method acting techniques that involve role taking, personal memories, and empathy, because this technique is likely to increase the believability of the portrayals. The concept is not to simply ask an actor to produce an expression, but to ask an actor to produce an authentic emotion that will automatically carry an expressive component.

Much EE work has always emphasized, and rightly so, pull effects and, in particular, cue utilization by observers. For this purpose, it is essential to create a sufficient number of conditions, repetitions, and controls, as well as a high degree of standardization. In consequence, we strongly reassert the utility of actor portrayals (see also Bänziger and Scherer 2007) in studying EE and we present a new corpus constructed according to the theoretical and methodological desiderata outlined earlier and based on our past experience with similar attempts (Chapter 6.1, this volume).

Conclusions

Our intention in this chapter was to deliver three central messages. First, on a theoretical level, we wanted to clarify what the aim of EE research is. Should it really be the analysis of the spontaneous, sincere, unregulated expression of ongoing emotion processes in naturalistic settings? We argue (1) that current research procedures are incapable of obtaining access to such expression instances and (2) that these are a rare species indeed. Instances of pure push expressions occur very infrequently in adult members of modern society in which expressions are almost always determined by an interaction or combination of push and pull effects. We have suggested that it may be very useful to engage in a systematic examination of pull effects, including the iconic representations of specific emotions by patterns of expressive features, which probably account for a sizeable portion of EEs encountered in everyday life. We hold that, for this purpose, actor portrayals provide a royal road.

It is obvious that actor portrayals cannot be treated as expressions of spontaneously occurring emotions. Actors pose an expression and, although they may not be devoid of emotion when they use Stanislavski techniques to conjure up appropriate memories or images, the purpose of posing is clear—to provide a plausible and believable impression of the emotion in observers. And the purpose of the research is obviously not to examine the nature of spontaneous emotion expressions or their underlying production mechanisms with the help of actor portrayals (although they can help to develop hypotheses; see Scherer and Ellgring 2007a, b). The aim is to examine a shared code of emotional signalling in social communication and to determine the way in which different types of facial, vocal, and bodily cues are used in signalling and in interpreting these signals. In this sense, systematic corpora of well designed actor portrayals can play a major role in examining the neurological and psychological processes that occur when we encounter certain patterns of multimodal emotion expressions. It seems to us that such corpora can also be of immense value for affective computing research and implementation, feeding the learning process described by Cowie *et al.* (Chapter 3.1., this volume) and serving as appropriate criteria to evaluate automatic detection algorithms and synthetic expressions of emotional competent autonomous agents. It is to be hoped that the fruitless debate about what is natural and spontaneous in emotional expression and the rigid rejection of certain research paradigms, many of which have, like actor portrayals, shown their utility in EE research, can be rapidly overcome. Given our evanescent object of study, we need to use every possible angle of approach that is feasible.

Section 4

Approaches to the computational modelling of emotion

In this section two types of computational models are illustrated, serving different purposes: a rule-based agent model with a sophisticated approach to emotion computation that can serve as the basis for interactive autonomous agents and a neural network model oriented toward simulating and testing essential mechanisms involved in the emotion processing of many organisms—attention deployment.

Taking the overview of computational agent models in Section 1 (see Chapter 1.2) as a framework, in Chapter 4.1, 'WASABI as a case study of how misattribution of emotion can be modelled computationally', Becker-Asano and Wachsmuth present a computational architecture for emotionally believable agents that are supposed to interact autonomously and socially with humans. In contrast to most other approaches to modelling emotions, the idea of an emotion dynamics in three-dimensional affect space is central to the WASABI architecture, which naturally sustains mood congruency of emotions. The authors adopt the distinction between primary, genetically earlier types of emotions and secondary, cognitively elaborated emotions, which are both seen as influencing the agent's bodily emotion dynamics. Dynamics in three-dimensional affect space are interpreted as representing aspects of an agent's 'subjective feeling' that are partly cognition-independent.

In Chapter 4.2, 'Emotions in artificial neural networks', Roesch, Korsten, Fragopanagos, and Taylor link artificial neural network (ANN) modelling to theories of emotion and explore how modellers addressed a selection of phenomena in psychology and cognitive neuroscience, namely, emotional learning, attention, the subjective feeling of emotion, and decision making. In doing so, they attempt to answer two questions. What have we learned from computational neuroscience about the neural correlates of emotion? And, what can neural network simulation contribute to the scientific study of emotion? For each phenomenon, after reviewing the most influential theories, they describe a selection of computational models that have been used to put to the test the theories and formulate new hypotheses. They conclude by pointing out possible avenues for bridging the gaps between experimentalists and modellers.

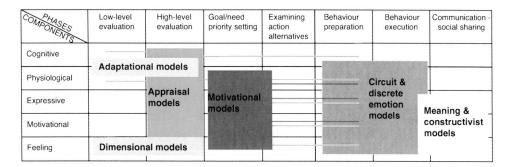

Plate 1 Mapping competing emotion theories in a space defined by phases of the emotion process and type of emotion component. The horizontal lines projecting from the solid areas indicate that a particular model includes in its theorizing at least some of the components/phases crossed by the lines. (Reproduced from Scherer and Peper 2001) (see Fig. 1.1.1).

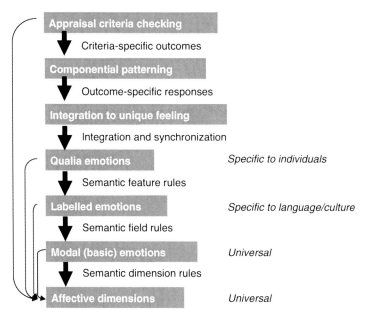

Plate 2 The hierarchy of levels of description for emotion processes and their mapping into lower-dimensional space (see Fig. 1.1.2)

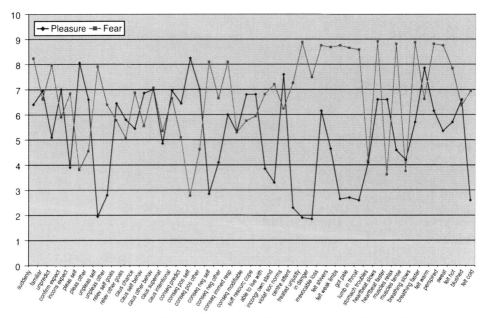

Plate 3 Example of semantic profiles produced by the GRID approach (see Fig. 2.1.4).

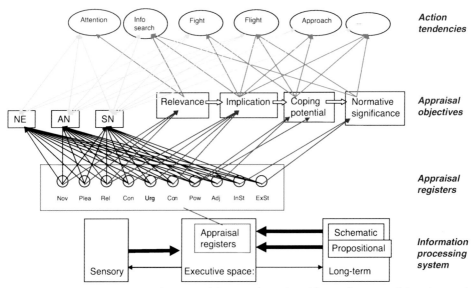

Plate 4 Potential computational architecture of the CPM (reproduced from Scherer 2001) (see Fig. 2.1.5).

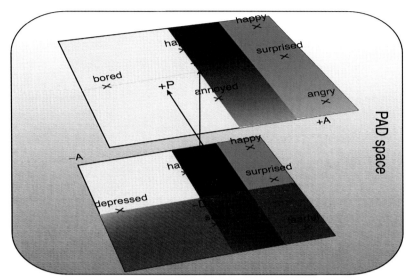

Plate 5 The (P)leasure–(A)rousal–(D)ominance (PAD) space with nine primary emotions (indicated by the labelled red crosses) and three secondary emotions—'hope' (green), 'relief' (blue), and 'fears-confirmed' (red)–assigned to the high and low dominance planes (see Fig. 4.1.3).

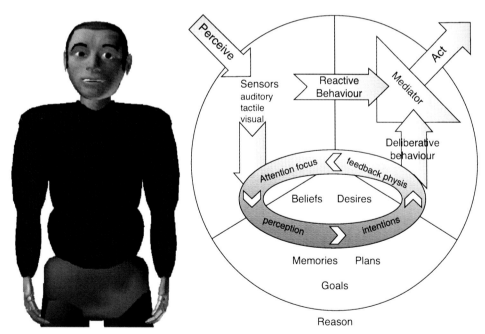

Plate 6 The virtual human 'Max', left, and an outline of its architectural framework, right. (Reproduced from Leßmann, Kopp, and Wachsmuth 2006) (see Fig. 4.1.4).

Plate 7 Screen shot of Max playing Skip-Bo against a human opponent in the virtual reality installation of the Artificial Intelligence Group at Bielefeld University, Germany. The red areas in front of the human's hand cards are her stock piles, which are visible to Max and enable him to generate expectations about which cards she might play next. Accordingly, in the moment depicted here Max expresses his fear of her playing the '8' on top of the '7' on one of the three shared target piles to the right of the virtual table (see Fig. 4.1.6).

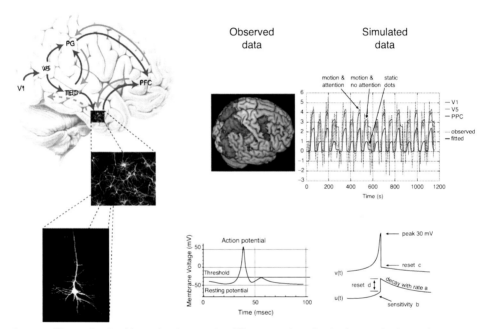

Plate 8 Different levels of investigation require different tools. Left: The human brain can be seen as a network of brain areas, each of which can be seen as a network of neurons. The brain contains approximately 10^{11} neurons. Right: Simulating a particular level of investigation requires a particular tool (e.g. fMRI on top, single cell recording at the bottom) and produces different results (e.g. simulated blood oxygenation level dependent signal on top, a single spike at the bottom) (see Fig. 4.2.1).

(a)

(b)

Plate 9 (a) A measure of quantity of motion using silhouette motion images (the shadow along the pianist's body) and (b) the tracking of the head. (From Castellano *et al.* 2008*b*) (see Fig. 5.4.2).

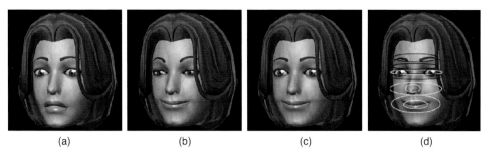

(a)　　　　　(b)　　　　　(c)　　　　　(d)

Plate 10 Disappointment masked by happiness. From left to right: (a) disappointment; (b) happiness; (c) disappointment masked by happiness; (d) disappointment masked by happiness with significant areas marked (see Fig. 5.5.3).

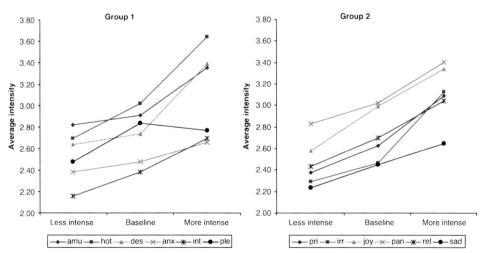

Plate 11 Intensity ratings for different emotions and types of regulation in two groups of actors portraying different emotions. amu, amusement; hot, hot anger; des, despair; anx, anxiety; int, interest; ple, pleasure; pri, pride; irr, irritation; joy, joy; pan, panic fear; rel, relief; sad, sadness (see Fig. 6.1.6).

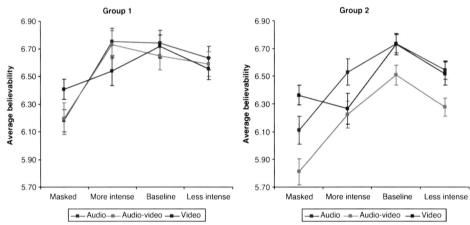

Plate 12 Believability ratings for different emotions and types of regulation in two groups of actors portraying different emotions (see Fig 6.1.7).

WASABI as a case study of how misattribution of emotion can be modelled computationally

Christian Becker-Asano and Ipke Wachsmuth

Summary

Cognitive scientists, psychologists, neurobiologists, and computer scientists achieved significant progress in understanding and modelling the fuzzy concept 'emotion' and more general 'affect'. Accordingly, a variety of computational realizations (discussed in Chapter 1.2, this volume) stem from a number of different psychological theories and philosophical conceptions. As correctly classified in Chapter 1.2, the computational realization we propose, labelled WASABI ([W]ASABI [A]ffect [S]imulation for [A]gents with [B]elievable [I]nteractivity), performs a mapping of appraisal outcome into a three-dimensional space of pleasure, arousal, and dominance, or PAD space in short, and it thereby 'breaks the link' between the internal representation of affect and its external domain object. Accordingly, we will present and discuss here, how the phenomenon of post hoc misattribution, i.e. a mismatch between an emotion's objective and its subjective cause, can be modelled and explained by the WASABI architecture.

The central idea of this architecture is to combine two dimensions, namely, emotional valence and valence of mood, such that their mutual influence generates a continuously changing, self-rebalancing internal state, which can be interpreted as constituting a very basic, non-relational, short-term memory of affect. Whenever some external or internal event (the latter, for example, resulting from cognitive reasoning processes) is appraised as having an emotional effect, this effect is translated into an impulse of emotional valence, which then disturbs the internal emotion dynamics. At the same time internal cognitive reasoning further analyses the event to determine if it is a candidate for elicitation of an emotion. In the current state of the architecture this reasoning is limited to the generation and checking of expectations within the context of a well-defined interaction scenario serving as proof of concept. The emotions are represented in PAD space such that a particular emotion can only be elicited (or in more philosophical terms 'become aware to the agent') if the agent's current internal feeling state represented in PAD space allows for it.

Although this architecture is already considerably complex, we admit that this is only our first attempt to grapple with the complex dynamic interplay of cognitive and bodily processes from which emotions are assumed to arise. Accordingly, we hope that the WASABI architecture, on the one hand, provides fruitful impulses to the interdisciplinary endeavour of understanding human emotionality and, on the other hand, can serve as one example of a blueprint for how to increase a conversational agent's affective competency.

Introduction to WASABI's core ideas

As pointed out in Chapter 1.2, this volume, a variety of computational models of emotions stem from different psychological and philosophical theories. When we started developing our own computational model of affect, which was later entitled WASABI, it was tempting to follow the ideas and conceptions of the by then famous structural model of emotions (Ortony *et al.* 1988), or OCC model in short, as many other computer scientists had done before. The limitations and problems of this model, however, had already become apparent (Bartneck 2002) so that we decided to first concentrate on modelling the temporal dynamics of emotions instead (Becker *et al.* 2004). We furthermore limited ourselves to only simulate the temporal unfolding of an emotion's intensity, postponing the question of how to realize cognitive appraisal. We also did not follow the 'basic emotions' idea (Ekman 1999), but instead combined simple hedonic valence with a very basic conception of positive versus negative mood. These two dimensions were arranged to form an orthogonal space, which is labelled 'emotion dynamics' and can be found in the lower left corner of Figure 4.1.1. Within this space the mutual interaction between hedonic valence (represented on the *x*-axis) and mood (represented on the *y*-axis) is simulated such that a so-called emotion dynamics continuously unfolds over time.

Eventually we added a third, orthogonal dimension to this space to account for those cases when nothing emotionally relevant happens over a certain period of time. This *z*-axis is labelled 'boredom' to indicate that any value along this axis represents an agent's level of boredom (see Figure 4.1.2).

The temporal unfolding and mutual interaction of emotion and mood is realized as follows.

1 The *x*-value is interpreted as a gradient, in relation to which the *y*-value increases or decreases. The more positive the value on the *x*-axis, the faster the *y*-value increases; the more negative the *x*-value, the faster the *y*-value decreases. Speaking in the language of affective sciences, this models a fortifying and alleviating effect that emotions are assumed to have on moods, which is graphically indicated by the white up and down arrows in Figure 4.1.2.

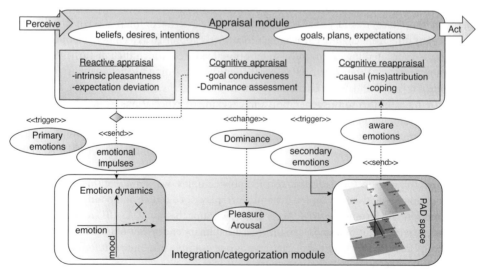

Fig. 4.1.1 A general overview of the WASABI architecture with its 'appraisal module' on top and the internal 'integration/categorization module' at the bottom.

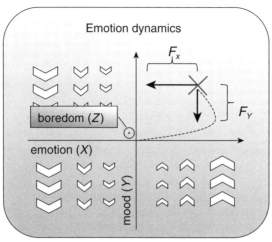

Fig. 4.1.2 Details of the emotion dynamics part inside the integration/categorization module of the WASABI architecture.

2 Any nonzero value on either of the two axes is constantly pulled back to zero by applying two simulated forces F_x and F_y, which are exerted by two independently simulated spring-mass systems virtually attached to the reference point; see Figure 4.1.2. In terms of modelling affect, the simulation parameters are normally chosen such that in case of equal displacements for x and y the reset force F_x is greater than the reset force F_y, because emotions are commonly considered to last less long than moods.

With this basic setup in place (described in more detail in Becker *et al.* 2007), a single emotional impulse of hedonic valence (see Figure 4.1.1) is sufficient to start the emotion dynamics. The impulse causes an instantaneous displacement of the reference point and an agent's internal emotional state will change dynamically over time (as indicated by the dashed line connecting the coordinate system's origin with the point of reference in Figure 4.1.2) until it reaches the point of origin again, if no further impulses have arrived in the meantime. When, for a longer period of time, no emotional impulses disturb the emotion dynamics, the z-value changes linearly to simulate an agent's increasing level of boredom.

Next, the three values x (emotion), y (mood), and z (boredom) need to be integrated in order to allow them to be mapped on named emotions, which are finally transmitted back to the appraisal module (see Figure 4.1.1). At this point, we decided to map into pleasure–arousal–dominance space, PAD space in short (Mehrabian 1995), as described by the following equations.

$$PAD(x_t, y_t, z_t) = (p(x_t, y_t), a(x_t, z_t), d(t)), \text{with}$$

$$p(x_t, y_t) = \frac{1}{2} \times (x_t + y_t) \text{ and } a(x_t, z_t) = |x_t| + z_t, (\text{with } z_t \leq 0) \tag{4.1.1}$$

All variables in eqn (4.1.1) are indexed with t, because the emotion is updated 25 times per second to achieve a seemingly continuous simulation of the internal feeling state. In PAD space primary emotions are located as indicated by the crosses in Figure 4.1.3 and secondary emotions occupy areas on the levels of high and low dominance. The smaller the distance between an agent's emotional state, as represented by the continuously updated PAD triple $PAD(x_t, y_t, z_t)$ (see eqn 4.1.1), and any of the primary emotions, the more likely it is that the agent becomes aware of this emotion with an intensity that is inversely proportional to this distance. If the agent's emotional

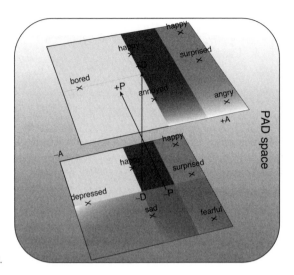

Fig. 4.1.3 The (P)leasure–(A)rousal–(D)ominance (PAD) space with nine primary emotions (indicated by the labelled red crosses) and three secondary emotions—'hope' (green), 'relief' (blue), and 'fears-confirmed' (red)– assigned to the high and low dominance planes (see plate 5).

state enters a region representing a secondary emotion, which was triggered just before, then the agent becomes aware of this secondary emotion with an intensity derived from its intensity distribution in PAD space (see Becker-Asano and Wachsmuth 2010 for details).

The motivation for this quite complex interplay between cognitive reasoning and emotion dynamics will be clarified in the light of the interdisciplinary background and it will be contrasted with related work in affective computing. Basically, we can explain our motivation in relation to Marsella *et al.*'s conceptions (see Chapter 1.2, this volume). The dynamic simulation explained so far makes detailed representational and process commitments for affect-derivation, but leaves open how an agent's relationship with the external world influences its appraisal of events, other agents, or objects within that world. An emotional impulse can be derived from any kind of cognitive appraisal process, but it might also be a byproduct of hard-wired, reactive perception–action patterns. From an engineering point of view, this flexibility allows for the core emotion dynamics to be combined easily with different computational architectures as long as they feed the emotion dynamics with emotional impulses, trigger primary and secondary emotions whenever appropriate, and make reasonable use of the set of aware emotions they receive in return. From a psychological point of view, we naturally assure mood-congruency of emotions because, for example, only in the case of bad mood do negative emotional impulses have the immediate effect of eliciting anger in the WASABI architecture. When the agent is in a good mood, in contrast, negative impulses will only dampen the good mood first, before it might get negative enough to allow for the elicitation of negative emotions. Furthermore, by decoupling the domain object from the subjective emotional response, post hoc reasoning about what might have been causing an agent's current emotional state can reasonably be performed. As a result, the subjective cause might not match the objective cause and, thus, an agent driven by the WASABI architecture is susceptible to misattribution.

Interdisciplinary background

Our approach to modelling affective competency for our virtual human 'Max' is derived from and relates to a multitude of different ideas, conceptions, and theories of psychologists, cognitive scientists, philosophers, and neurobiologists. WASABI's core of simulating an emotion dynamics in three-dimensional affect space can be traced back to the ideas of the psychologist and philosopher Wilhelm Wundt (1922/1863), who claimed that any emotion can be characterized as a continuous progression in such a three-dimensional affect space. By now the validity of dimensional theories of affect is widely accepted and the interested reader might kindly be referred to (Becker-Asano 2008) for an introduction to the history of this class of theories.

In the following, however, we will concentrate on explaining how our architecture relates to Scherer's component process model (CPM; see Chapter 2.1, this volume), from which it derives a number of ideas. Afterwards, the neurobiological background of the WASABI architecture will be outlined in order to explain the rationale for distinguishing two classes of emotions, namely, primary and secondary emotions.

WASABI in relation to the CPM

Scherer distinguishes the following five functions for the theoretical construct of emotions in the context of the CPM (see Chapter 2.1, this volume):

1 evaluation of objects and events;

2 regulation of internal subsystems;

3 preparation for action;

4 signalling of behavioural intention;

5 monitoring of internal state and external environment.

Although the WASABI architecture is not directly derived from Scherer's CPM, we follow the above distinction and believe that we can account for a subset of these functions as follows (see Figure 4.1.1).

- *Evaluation of objects and events.* Appraisal processes that enable our agent to evaluate external objects and events are realized in a software module, which is based on the belief–desire–intention (BDI) approach to modelling rational reasoning (Rao and Georgeff 1991). In this module goals and plans are explicitly represented, expectations are generated, and current events are evaluated against previous expectations. This cognition module, which contains the agent's *Appraisal module*, will be explained in the section 'Technical realization and example of an interaction', this chapter, in the context of the general explanation of our virtual agent Max.

- *Regulation of internal subsystems.* According to Scherer (2001) this function is served by the 'peripheral efference component' and in Scherer (1984) 'the physiological component of activation and arousal' is made responsible for this function. Therefore, we assume that our simulation of emotion dynamics, which is driven by external and internal forces and continuously updates an agent's arousal level, can—at least in some respects—fulfil this function.

- *Preparation for action.* This function is realized in the WASABI architecture by letting our agent's breathing and eye blinking frequency be modulated by the simulated arousal, which might be interpreted as 'preparing for action' by an outside observer. We have to admit, however, that we do not explicitly model 'behaviour tendencies', which are postulated by Scherer (1984) as being part of this function.

- *Signalling of behavioural intention.* Our agent's facial expressions are directly driven by the primary emotions of the WASABI architecture such that the 'motor component' is realized in a quite straightforward manner. Furthermore, in the case of secondary emotions such as hope or relief, the agent's cognition generates appropriate verbal expressions that are seamlessly combined with non-verbal expressions driven by primary emotions.

◆ *Monitoring of internal state and external environment.* Although the WASABI architecture simulates a continuously changing internal state through the implementation of an emotion dynamics, we do not explicitly model a monitoring process that, according to Scherer (Chapter 2.1, this volume), is necessary to achieve subjective feeling states. We believe, however, that our architecture is a promising candidate for extensions toward the simulation of such subjective aspects of emotions.

In addition to these functional similarities the WASABI architecture as it is outlined in Figure 4.1.1 can conceptually be divided into two modules that are comparable to two of the three CPM modules presented by Scherer in Figure 2.1.1, p.50, this volume.

Scherer's *appraisal module* consists of one submodule labelled 'multilevel appraisal', which is responsible for very sophisticated and detailed 'sequential evaluation checks'. In contrast, the computationally realized *appraisal module* of the WASABI architecture permits a much less sophisticated appraisal than that proposed by the CPM. Nevertheless, we believe that we can account for some of the proposed evaluation checks as will be detailed in the section, 'The virtual human Max', where our agent's cognitive reasoning abilities are described.

Although the *component patterning module* is omitted in our architecture, the changes within the emotion dynamics part of the *integration/categorization module* (see Figure 4.1.1) can be understood as simulating physiological responses, which are part of Scherer's module. In addition, motor expression of emotions is achieved within the *integration/categorization module* of the WASABI architecture as well, after emotion, mood, and boredom have been mapped into PAD space as described above.

By representing emotions in PAD space we also account for 'categorization/labelling', which is part of Scherer's third *categorization module* (see Figure 2.1.1, Chapter 2.1, this volume). We lack, however, a *central representation of all components*, unless one argues that this representation is achieved by the dynamically changing, emotion-related belief-structures within the BDI-based *appraisal module*.

Primary and secondary emotions

A major difference between the WASABI architecture and the CPM consists of the distinction of two classes of emotions in WASABI—primary and secondary emotions. These two classes are derived from neurobiological research findings of Damásio (1994).

Primary emotions are supposed to be innate and they are understood as prototypical emotion types that can already be ascribed to 1-year-old-children (Damásio 2003). Secondary emotions are assumed to arise from higher cognitive processes and to be acquired during ontogenesis through learning processes in a social context. Damásio (1994) uses the adjective 'secondary' to refer to 'adult' emotions, which 'utilize the machinery of primary emotions' by influencing the acquisition of 'dispositional representations', which are necessary for the elicitation of secondary emotions. These acquired dispositional representations, however, are believed to be different from the 'innate dispositional representations' underlying primary emotions.

In the WASABI architecture this representational difference is reflected in the following two ways.

1 The PAD space representation of secondary emotions is much less precise than that of primary emotions (see Figure 4.1.3), because the former require much more elaborate cognitive reasoning than the latter.

2 Appraisal processes do not necessarily need to trigger primary emotions, before they can be elicited in PAD space. For secondary emotions to be elicited, however, this triggering in PAD space is a necessary precondition, as will be explained in the section 'Misattribution of an emotion's cause'.

We follow Damásio's distinction, because it allows us to start with a set of more 'primitive' primary emotions that can already be elicited by fast, hard-wired perception–action patterns without the need for complex deliberation. This is, of course, mostly a rather technical motivation, but doing so might eventually allow us to investigate developmental aspects of emotions. In fact, the results of an empirical study confirmed the hypothesis that an agent simulating secondary emotions in addition to primary ones is judged older than one that only simulates primary emotions (Becker-Asano and Wachsmuth 2010).

The virtual human Max

The virtual human Max (see Figure 4.1.4, left) developed at Bielefeld University's Artificial Intelligence Laboratory has been employed in a number of scenarios in which Max's conversational capabilities have been steadily extended. In a museum application, Max conducts multimodal small talk conversations with visitors to a public computer museum. In this setting, the emotion dynamics lead to a greater variety of often unpredictable, yet coherent emotion-coloured responses, which add to the impression that the agent has a unique personality. Furthermore, the WASABI architecture has also been applied to a gaming scenario, in which secondary emotions were simulated in addition to primary ones.

In the following we give a brief overview of our agent's cognitive architecture, before we explain in detail how different levels of appraisal are realized inside it.

The architectural framework of Max

Max has been developed to study how the natural conversational behaviour of humans can be modelled for face-to-face encounters in virtual veality. Max's cognitive architecture (see Figure 4.1.4, right) realizes and tightly integrates the faculties of perception, action, and cognition required to engage in such interactions (Leßmann *et al.* 2006). Although in general it employs the

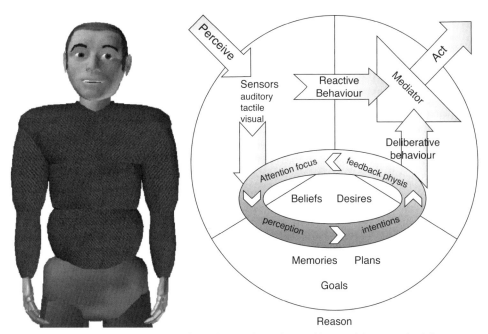

Fig. 4.1.4 The virtual human 'Max', left, and an outline of its architectural framework, right. (Reproduced from Leßmann, Kopp, and Wachsmuth 2006) (see plate 6).

classical perceive–reason–act triad, all processes of perception, reasoning, and action run concurrently within the architecture.

Reflexes and immediate responses to events are realized by a reactive connection between perception and action. Such fast-running stimulus–response loops enable Max to also react to internal events and his reactive behaviours include gaze tracking as well as focusing on the current interaction partner in response to prompting signals. In addition, continuous secondary behaviours reside in this layer, which can be triggered or modulated by deliberative processes and by the emotional state of the agent. These behaviours let Max appear more lifelike and they include eye blink, breathing, and sway.

Perceptions are also fed into deliberative processes that are responsible for interaction management by interpreting input, deciding which actions to take next, and composing behaviours to realize them. This reasoning is implemented following the BDI approach to modelling rational behaviour and makes use of an extensible set of self-contained planners. The architecture further comprises a cognitive, inner loop that feeds internal feedback information upon possible actions to take back to deliberation.

Three different levels of appraisal

By exploiting the functionality of the architectural framework described above, three levels of appraisal are computationally realized for Max within the *Appraisal module* (see Figure 4.1.5). *Reactive* as well as *cognitive appraisal* submodules serve as input for the *integration/categorization module*, whereas the *cognitive reappraisal* submodule evaluates the resulting set of aware emotions in the light of cognitively represented situational context information.

1 *Reactive appraisal.* This submodule realizes aspects of the first appraisal objective postulated by Scherer's CPM (see Chapter 2.1, this volume). Max uses a look up table to assess an event's intrinsic pleasantness and checks if the event complies with his expectations. The intrinsic pleasantness directly translates into an emotional impulse to be sent to the emotion dynamics. Only if the event is unexpected is the primary emotion 'surprise' triggered in PAD space (see Figure 4.1.1), so that Max is not surprised by events he could expect to happen. A similar assessment lets the *Appraisal module* trigger the primary emotion 'fear', when Max expects some negative event to happen in the near future.[1]

2 *Cognitive appraisal.* Central to this submodule is the evaluation of an event's goal conduciveness (or its obstructiveness, respectively). As described in the context of Scherer's CPM (see Chapter 2.1, this volume), an intrinsically pleasant event (e.g. the delicious cake offered by a friend) can nevertheless be negative, if it hinders an individual from achieving a higher-level goal (e.g. sticking to a diet). With respect to secondary emotions, deliberative reasoning about goal-conduciveness of possible future events takes place in this module as well. This prospect-based deliberation might give rise to emotions such as 'hope' or 'fear' ('hope' being considered a secondary emotion) and, after an undesired expected event is confirmed or disconfirmed, the secondary emotions 'relief' or 'fears-confirmed', respectively, are triggered in PAD space.

These appraisal processes are both part of the second appraisal objective in Scherer's CPM. Another appraisal target of this submodule—changing the agent's 'dominance'—is considered to

---

[1] 'Fear' is a very special primary emotion within the WASABI architecture, because it is the only prospect-based emotion that does not belong to the class of secondary emotions. Accordingly, a strict distinction between primary and secondary emotions is sometimes problematic and we hope our architecture can serve as a basis for further discussion.

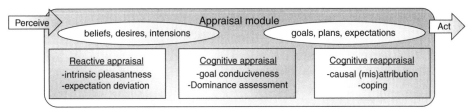

Fig. 4.1.5 The 'Appraisal module' of the WASABI architecture with its subcomponents 'Reactive appraisal', 'Cognitive appraisal', and 'Cognitive reappraisal'.

be part of appraisal objective three in the CPM. We use an agent's 'dominance' in a similar way to Scherer's conception of 'power' and 'control', in that it reflects our agent's level of control over the situation as well as his social status. For example, whenever it is Max's turn in a game, the *appraisal module* changes his level of dominance to maximum and vice versa.

These appraisal mechanisms generate all necessary input for the *integration/categorization module* (see Figure 4.1.1). Emotional impulses are derived from reactive and cognitive appraisal, primary emotions are triggered by reactive appraisal, and, finally, secondary emotions are triggered and the agent's level of dominance is changed as a product of cognitive appraisal.

As a result, the *integration/categorization module* eventually sends back to the *appraisal module* a set of aware emotions with their respective intensities. These primary and secondary emotions are then reappraised in the *cognitive reappraisal* submodule (see Figure 4.1.5). One target of this reappraisal is the assessment of coping potential (see Scherer's third appraisal objective of the CPM; Chapter 2.1, this volume). We have to admit, however, that our implementation of coping behaviour so far is rather simple. In the museum guide scenario Max leaves the scene whenever he gets very angry and only comes back after he has calmed down again. This 'calming down' results from WASABI's internal emotion dynamics, which drift back to zero automatically in the absence of emotional impulses. We believe that the WASABI architecture is well suited for more elaborate realizations of coping-related reasoning, as, for example, implemented by Marsella and Gratch (2006) for their EMA model (see Chapter 1.2, this volume).

Due to the cognition-independent emotion dynamics simulation the cause of any of the aware emotions arriving in the *cognitive reappraisal* submodule needs to be re-established. For secondary emotions the cognitive architecture keeps track of the emotion's cause by memorizing it explicitly. Thus, Max can tell, for example, what he is relieved *about*, or *why* he sees his fears confirmed. The causal reasons for experiencing primary emotions such as anger or happiness, however, cannot be memorized during the *reactive* or *cognitive appraisal* steps, because they might result from an accumulation of equally signed emotional impulses which might have originated from purely reactive appraisal alone. Accordingly, the WASABI architecture allows for misattribution of an emotion's cause to happen. The processes leading to this effect are detailed along the lines of an example of an interaction in the next section.

A case study of causal misattribution in WASABI

The dynamic interplay of the agent's appraisal and his emotion dynamics is best demonstrated using as an example an interaction between Max and a human opponent in the card game Skip-Bo. We decided to use a playful interaction scenario assuming that humans will more openly show their feelings and, thus, also more easily accept a virtual agent's direct way of expressing its emotions. In addition, a game provides well-defined boundaries to the set of plausible actions and its rules allow for the computational generation of meaningful expectations for the agent.

Fig. 4.1.6 Screen shot of Max playing Skip-Bo against a human opponent in the virtual reality installation of the Artificial Intelligence Group at Bielefeld University, Germany. The red areas in front of the human's hand cards are her stock piles, which are visible to Max and enable him to generate expectations about which cards she might play next. Accordingly, in the moment depicted here Max expresses his fear of her playing the '8' on top of the '7' on one of the three shared target piles to the right of the virtual table (see plate 7).

The commercial card game Skip-Bo was adapted for our three-dimensional cave-like virtual reality environment such that humans can play it against Max (see Figure 4.1.6). A set of carefully crafted plans allows Max to follow the rules of the game based on simple heuristics and all human opponents agreed that it is fun to play against him, although he is not a particularly strong player.

The WASABI architecture was employed to let Max react emotionally throughout the game and it led to believable interactivity as will be outlined next.

Technical realization and example of an interaction

The virtual human Max is based on a multi-agent system that encapsulates his cognitive abilities inside specialized software agents (see Figure 4.1.7). These software agents communicate with each other by passing messages.

The *integration/categorization module* is implemented as a so-called 'emotion-agent', which acts in concert with a number of other agents. In the Skip-Bo scenario the emotion-agent receives emotional impulses from the BDI-agent, which is continuously being updated with the set of aware emotions. The reasoning processes within the BDI-agent also derive the actual state of dominance from the context of the card game, such that Max feels dominant whenever it is his turn and non-dominant, i.e. submissive, otherwise. Thus, whenever the human opponent fails to follow the rules of the game, Max takes the turn to correct her and accordingly feels dominant until giving the turn back to the human. Concurrently, the BDI-agent keeps the visualization-agent updated about the actual primary emotions and PAD values.

Figure 4.1.8 illustrates an example of an information flow within the WASABI architecture. In this sequence diagram the three agents, BDI-agent, emotion-agent, and visualization-agent ('Vis.-Agent'), are represented as boxes at the top. In the top-left box, labelled BDI-agent, three plans —generate-expectation ('gen. exp.'), check expectations ('check exp.'), and react-to-secondary-emotion ('react sec.')—are rendered as three white rectangles to show their activity below. The same rectangles are used to depict the PAD space as well as the emotions *fearful* and *fears-confirmed*

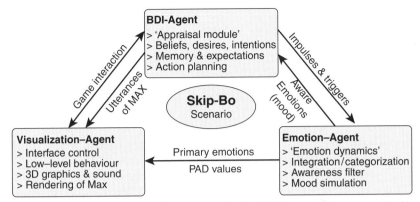

Fig. 4.1.7 The three most important software agents in the Skip-Bo scenario are presented together with their interconnection realized by means of message passing. The *appraisal module* is part of the BDI-Agent, the *integration/categorization module* resides inside the Emotion-Agent, and the Visualization-Agent renders the three-dimensional graphics including the game and the Max agent. A user's interaction with the game is also handled by the Visualization-Agent and then forwarded to the BDI-Agent.

('Fears-Conf.'), which all reside in the emotion-agent. The internals of the visualization-agent are not detailed here. In this example it only receives messages from the other agents, although in reality it also distributes information about the human player's interaction with the game by sending messages to the BDI-agent (see Figure 4.1.7).

We will now explain the sequence of message communication between these agents for which the time-line runs from top to bottom in Figure 4.1.8. At first, the generate-expectation plan is called, e.g. after Max ends his turn by playing one last card on one of his stock piles in front of him (see Figure 4.1.6). This plan, first, results in a negative impulse ('send impulse neg.') which is sent by the *reactive appraisal* sub-module to the emotion dynamics of the emotion-agent thereby indirectly changing Max's emotional state in PAD space (see the section 'Introduction to WASABI's core ideas'). Subsequently, while following the same plan, the primary emotion *fearful* is triggered

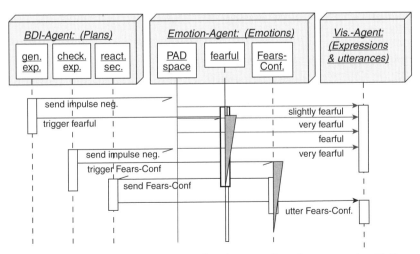

Fig. 4.1.8 Sequence diagram of an information flow between the software agents with the time-line from top to bottom.

('trigger fearful') by the same *reactive appraisal* submodule of the BDI-agent, because Max expects the human player to play an important card that would hinder him from fulfilling his goal of winning the game.

In the emotion-agent, however, the negative emotional impulse pushed the reference point in PAD space already close enough to the (not yet triggered) emotion *fearful* to let Max experience fear with low intensity. This is possible, because we decided to set *fearful* to a slightly positive base intensity of 0.25 (see Becker-Asano and Wachsmuth 2010 for details). In Figure 4.1.8 this base intensity is indicated by a small double line along the dashed, vertical lifeline of *fearful*. Accordingly, *slightly fearful* is sent to the visualization-agent even before the BDI-agent triggers the emotion *fearful*. Because the intensity of *fearful* in the emotion-agent abruptly changes with the incoming *trigger fearful* message, Max's emotional state changes from *slightly fearful* to *very fearful*. This sudden change in intensity is reproduced in Figure 4.1.8 by the two grey triangles drawn along each emotion's lifelines. Accordingly, in that moment Max shows a clear expression of fear in his face (see Figure 4.1.6).

The intensity of *fearful* decreases within the next 10 seconds and the reference point changes its location in PAD space due to the implemented emotion dynamics. Thus, *very fearful* automatically changes to *fearful* (see right side of Figure 4.1.8) in the absence of any further impulse or trigger messages.

Next, the *cognitive appraisal* module of the BDI-agent uses the 'check expectations' plan to check if a human player's action matches any of the previously generated expectations. In this example, the BDI-agent first sends a negative impulse to the emotion-agent, because it is assumed here that such a previous expectation exists. The reference point's location in PAD space is thereby changed such that Max gets *very fearful* again. This sequence of different emotion intensities (*slightly fearful*, *very fearful*, *fearful*, *very fearful*) can happen in the case of every primary or secondary emotion, although it is exemplified here only for *fearful*. It results from the dynamic interplay of the *appraisal module* and the *integration/categorization* module.

The 'check expectations' plan, then, triggers the secondary emotion *fears-confirmed* ('trigger Fears-Conf.') in the emotion-agent, thereby maximizing its base intensity. Together with the negatively valenced mood, *fears-confirmed* reaches the agent's level of awareness and is sent back to the BDI-agent ('send Fears-Conf.'). In effect, the plan react-to-secondary-emotion is executed within the *cognitive reappraisal* submodule to process the incoming message. This results in an 'utter Fears-Conf.' message, which is sent to the visualization-agent letting Max produce an appropriate utterance.

Misattribution of an emotion's cause

A human opponent would possibly explain Max's behaviour like this:

> After Max ended his turn with playing a hand card to one of his stock piles, he seemed to realize within one or two seconds that I could now directly play one of my four stock pile cards. I could derive this from his fearful facial expression and the fact that he seemed to inhale sharply producing the characteristic sound of someone being afraid. When I then actually played that stock card, Max admitted that he had been afraid of that before.

In the *appraisal module* of Max's cognitive architecture, however, the event that caused the fear is disconnected from the finally elicited emotion itself. Thus, if Max were asked why he shows fear, he would have to recapitulate which events of the recent past could have caused his fear. In principle, a number of events could have influenced Max's emotion dynamics negatively rather directly through *reactive appraisal* alone leaving no trace in the form of cognitive representations. For example, if we additionally simulated an artificial hunger level for Max, his slowly getting hungry could result in small negative impulses, which are sent repeatedly to the emotion-agent and could slowly worsen Max's mood. Assuming this process to be realized in parallel to the BDI-based reasoning module, Max would be unable to consider his being hungry as one factor causing his experience of fear (or any other negative emotion).

Even without modelling additional influences outside of Max's cognitive awareness misattributions could happen in situations in which a high number of events quickly succeed each other. For example, if Max cognitively perceived a new person entering the scene directly after realizing that the human opponent is likely to play a fear-inducing card (see example above), he might later misattribute this new person's appearance to be causing his fear. In fact, this can happen even if the new person's appearance itself had no emotional impact at all. Accordingly, Max being asked about why he shows fear in the above example could then be prone to the following misattribution, 'I think I fear that person next to you who just entered the room.'

Before we further discuss the pros and cons of our architecture, we will contrast it next with related work in the field of affective computing.

Related work

El Nasr *et al.* (2000) present FLAME as a formalization of the dynamics of 14 emotions based on fuzzy logic rules. It includes a mood value, which is continuously calculated as the average of all emotion intensities to provide a solution to the problem of conflicting emotions being activated at the same time. Our conception of emotion dynamics in the WASABI architecture is quite similar to their realization of mutual influence of emotion and mood.

Marsella and Gratch (2006) focus with their EMA model of emotions on the dynamics of emotional appraisal. They also argue for a mood value as an addend in the calculation of otherwise equally activated emotional states following the general idea of mood-congruent emotions. Their framework for modelling emotions is certainly much better suited to explain the cognitive underpinnings of emotions than the WASABI architecture can possibly be. Furthermore, it has successfully been evaluated as modelling human emotion dynamics quite accurately (see Chapter 1.2, this volume). The strength of the WASABI architecture, however, seems to be the relative simplicity with which convincing emotion dynamics (at least of primary emotions) can be achieved. With EMA's rational reasoning approach it also seems much more difficult to explain misattribution of an emotion's cause, because of the direct linking of a domain object and its emotional effect.

Central to the architecture proposed by Marinier and Laird (2007) is the idea of 'appraisal frames', which are based on the EMA model and 11 of Scherer's 16 appraisal dimensions (see Chapter 2.1, this volume) and are modelled for integration in the Soar cognitive architecture (Laird *et al.* 1987). They distinguish an 'active appraisal frame', which is the result of a momentary appraisal of a given event, from a 'perceived appraisal frame', which results from the combination of the actual mood and emotion frames. Thereby, they take Damásio's distinction between emotion and feeling into account—similarly to the conception underlying the WASABI architecture. It has to be noted, however, that Damásio defines a feeling as 'the perception of a certain state of the body along with the perception of a certain mode of thinking and of thoughts with certain themes' (Damásio 2003, p. 86). This definition seems to be even more difficult to operationalize than Scherer's assumption that 'feelings integrate the central representations of appraisal-driven response in emotion' (Chapter 2.1, this volume). Although it remains a challenging question, if we can ever reasonably ascribe feelings to autonomous agents, we believe that following a component approach to modelling affect is most promising and in that respect Damásio and Scherer seem to agree.

Aiming at the development of believable conversational agents Pelachaud and Bilvi (2003) are continuously improving their 'Greta' agent, which is capable of producing bodily as well as facial gestures that are consistent with the situational context. This consistency is guaranteed by BDI-based modelling of Greta's 'mind' (Rosis *et al.* 2003) resulting in an architecture that allows for the inclusion of an emotion model. The latter builds upon a 'dynamic belief network' to account for the inherent dynamics of emotional processes, which is also central to our work as outlined above. Recently, Ochs *et al.* (2006) presented another BDI-based approach to implement OCC-based appraisal for Greta.

The layered model of affect, ALMA, uses PAD space to derive an agent's mood from emotions that are themselves the result of OCC-based appraisal (Gebhard 2005). ALMA is rooted in a purely cognitive approach to modelling affect, which was only later extended by a representation of all 22 OCC emotions (plus 'liking' and 'disliking') in PAD space. Accordingly, in evaluating ALMA, Gebhard and Kipp (2006) heavily rely on third person rational judgement of the believability of emotion and mood labels, which ALMA generates for two interacting conversational agents. For WASABI, in contrast, the emotional effect of Max's affective behaviour in direct playful face-to-face interaction has been evaluated to be beneficial (Becker *et al.* 2005). In Chapter 5.2, this volume, Schröder and colleagues introduce an approach to emotional speech synthesis that is also based on PAD space (see also Schröder 2004).

Conclusions and discussion

In contrast to most existing computational affect simulation models, the WASABI architecture focuses on capturing the temporal dynamics of emotions and mood and makes only very few commitments regarding how cognitive appraisal is to be realized. Furthermore, the WASABI architecture breaks the link between an emotion-eliciting domain object and the resulting emotion itself and we outlined how this can be exploited to realize misattribution of an emotion's cause.

We admit, however, that the conceptual decisions taken in designing the WASABI architecture are not without questionable consequences. A major challenge is the question of how WASABI can account for the occurrence of mixed emotions. For example, imagine yourself queuing up to take a ride in a roller coaster, which is likely to produce an adrenaline rush. In such a moment the happiness of expecting a pleasurable ride appears to be mixed with the fear of possible negative consequences of the same event in case of an accident. Although both emotions, happy and fearful, might be triggered by the *reactive appraisal* submodule (see Figure 4.1.1), the distance between these two emotions in PAD space makes it impossible for Max to be aware of them simultaneously. In fact, the assured mood-congruency of emotions prevents in this case the simultaneous elicitation of positively valenced happiness and negatively valenced fear. It can be argued, however, that in humans these two emotions are also not experienced simultaneously, but in quick succession one after the other depending on a human's focus of cognitive attention.

Another challenge to be addressed in future research is how we can model and test the emotion-related effects on an agent's personality. So far, we have heuristically determined reasonable values for the parameters of the emotion dynamics simulation. We believe, however, that by changing these parameters we can systematically change an observer's judgement of the agent's personality. Although the 'Big Five' personality schema with its proposed relation to PAD space (Mehrabian 1996) is commonly used to realize an agent's personality (Gebhard 2005), we believe that our conception of an emotion dynamics is already powerful enough to allow for the creation of different personalities within WASABI-driven agents.

Finally, how to realize cognitive reappraisal is still an open topic for the WASABI architecture. The BDI-based architectures discussed in the section, 'Related work', are much better suited to explain the *why* of an emotion, because their emotion elicitation is explicitly based on rational reasoning processes. Thus, we believe that combining WASABI's core ideas (see the section 'Introduction to WASABI's core ideas') with these more cognitively motivated affect simulation architectures would yield interesting results and in doing so we might also achieve a more complete picture of a human's emotional life.

In summary, we hope that the WASABI architecture contributes to the diverse theories and ideas within the emotion research community and also provides a valuable technical contribution to the question of how to endow embodied agents with affective competency.

Chapter 4.2

Emotion in artificial neural networks

Etienne B. Roesch, Nienke Korsten, Nickolaos Fragopanagos, and John G. Taylor

Summary

What have we learned from computational neuroscience about the neural correlates of emotions? What can neural network simulation contribute to the scientific study of emotion? With a view to answering these two questions, we review the recent progress in the field of biologically plausible neural simulation in understanding the neural processes that give rise to emotional phenomena.

Emotion is amongst those topics that elicit much ado, even in groups of well-intentioned academics. Part of the discord is due to different perspectives that emphasize certain aspects of emotions over others. We argue that addressing a topic as complex and multifaceted as emotion requires engaging in an iterative dialogue between theoretical, computational, and empirical work. From this standpoint, approaches that ground computational neuroscience in empirical work are capable of generating novel and innovative hypotheses about the brain. However, in addition to being constrained by empirical results, computational models should also be evaluated within similar experimental paradigms if their predictions are to be truly insightful.

In this chapter, after a brief overview of some of the techniques used to simulate different scales of interaction in the brain, we review a number of affective phenomena and focus on the interactions between the underlying processes, as perceived through the lens of computational neuroscience.

◆ Emotional learning relates to the ability of the organism to associate signals from the external (or internal) world with a corresponding affective value, and to use this knowledge to develop strategies for future encounters. Neuroscientists investigated this area of research by focusing on both reward and punishment conditioning procedures. Computational models emphasized the role of particular brain areas in generating and sustaining the neurodynamics responsible for the predictions of sensory input, and the general sensitivity of the learning system to information related to adaptive timing.

◆ Attention plays a major role in the general functioning of the organism by providing the ability to process selected stimuli from the environment. Not only does it allow the filtering of incoming information, but it also provides support for the coordination of the many stages involved in its processing, by resolving competition for resources and preventing interference. The 'emotion system' biases this compound of processes by quickly evaluating incoming information and influencing each stage of the subsequent processing.

◆ The subjective feeling, and its embodiment, refers to the felt part of emotion. It is the end-result of a series of evaluating processes that involve interactions between a widespread network of brain areas and different aspects of the body. Computational neuroscience investigated the integration of all this information, which grounds the organism in the occurring event and supports many other processes (e.g. general inference).

◆ Decision-making and value systems involve emotions at many levels. In recent years, neuroscientists even demonstrated that emotion was at the core of decision-making, in contrast to the traditional opposition reason–passion. Computational modellers investigate this affective phenomenon by focusing on the incremental dynamics in emotional circuits that influence decisional processes.

The covert agenda of our enterprise is to initiate the healthy dialogue required to cross disciplinary boundaries and bridge some of the conceptual gaps that exist between experimentalists and modellers. With the hope that this chapter will arouse curiosity, we invite the reader to follow the threads of publications we reviewed with a fresh and open mind.

Introduction

This chapter is concerned with the use of artificial neural networks to study emotions as experienced by humans. Artificial neural networks (ANN) are computer programs based on the approximation of the workings of several components of the brain, including neurons, neurotransmitters, and networks of brain structures. We refer to a particular category of neural networks, namely, *biologically plausible* neural simulations, which aim at representing and studying the processes actually occurring in the brain.

We focus on neural simulations whose explicit goal is to investigate the mechanisms in the brain that give rise to emotion and emotional processing (Levine 2007). We review selected models that allow for the investigation of a wide range of affective phenomena, spanning learning through conditioning, decision making, attentional and memory biases, as well as the 'felt' part of emotion, the subjective feeling. From this exercise, we attempt to answer the following questions. What have we learned from computational neuroscience about the neural correlates of emotions? What can neural network simulation contribute to the scientific study of emotion?

More specifically, we are interested in what computational neuroscience has to say about what emotions do, and what can be learned about human emotions. In this particular context, emotions are sometimes seen as interruption signals (Simon 1967; Sloman and Croucher 1981; Sloman 2002) or as a system that allows for a fast reaction to potentially important events in the environment (Armony *et al.* 1997). It has also been described as an evaluative system that taints perception (Fellous *et al.* 2003) or as one of the core systems underlying broader concepts like motivation, personality, or volition (Tomkins and Messick 1963; Levine and Leven 1992; Moffat and Frijda 1995). Although proposed in the particular context of computational science, all of these descriptions originated from the study of emotions in humans, and are largely based on emotion theories proposed by researchers in psychology and neuroscience.

Emotion and emotional processes

There has been much argument about what emotions are, and we will not address this topic here, as it is described at great length elsewhere (e.g. see Chapter 1.1, this volume). Emotion is generally described as a multifactorial psychological concept that refers to five functions, encompassing all aspects that situate an organism in its environment. It includes the evaluation of (1) what is happening in the environment, (2) the monitoring and (3) the regulation of the organism's internal systems, (4) the preparation for action, and (5) the communication with conspecifics (Fontaine *et al.* 2007). From this description several trails of research arise. In the field of neuroscience, a growing body of results offers insights into the parts of the neural correlates of emotions involved in each of these functions (see Chapter 2.2, this volume). Of particular importance is the evaluative function of emotion, which allows the organism to appraise an occurring event such that appropriate actions can be taken. The appraisal of situations occurs before any action is taken. Several theorists thus attempt the formal description of the antecedents to emotion by parsing the functional domains against which the occurring event is appraised.

Appraisal theories of emotion emerged in the historical context of heated discussions about the nature of emotion as opposed to cognition (see Lazarus 1999 for a recap of this debate and Schorr 2001 for a history of appraisal theories). For historical reasons, emotion (passionate and impetuous) has always been opposed to cognition (reasoned and calculated), and this opposition often extends into the concepts used to formulate theories. Most domains ascribed to so-called cognition (calculation or reading being extreme cases, for instance) would see theories spelling out the functional components that give rise to a particular outcome. In contrast, the domain of emotion comprises very disparate theories that often focus more on the outcome (e.g. a labelled emotion, or a category of reactions, expressed in a dimension for instance) than the source (i.e. the functional components that give rise to emotion). Appraisal theories of emotion go beyond this debate (Leventhal and Scherer 1987) by assuming that emotions are *issued from* cognitive processes, in much the same way as any other brain function. These processes take some input, related to the current state of the organism, and produce some output (Roesch *et al.* 2007; Korsten *et al.* in press). Predictions can thus be made about emotional correlates, which can be measured in the brain and the behaviour.

In this chapter, appraisal theories of emotion will help us by providing some context to the necessary low-level descriptions generated through the methods of computational neuroscience. These methods allow for the formal description of the mechanisms of the brain (see Arbib 2003 for an example of such an attempt), with the aim of making predictions that can be tested in neuroimaging experiments. This effort to 'bridge the gap' is, however, bound by the scope of the techniques available to both sides, and the theoretical assumptions that researchers have to make to develop theories further. These limitations have an impact on the biological plausibility of simulations, as well as on the interpretations that can be made of the results.

Simulating brain mechanisms

Artificial neural networks can be used to simulate neural processes, thereby connecting physical structure to psychological or behavioural function; a working model of a neural mechanism produces detailed predictions both on the behaviour of the individual and that of the neuronal hardware. But ANN modelling is not only a valuable tool because it allows for such a connection. As current methodologies for probing the (human) brain cannot produce data that are detailed both temporally and spatially, comparisons of the different data sets to one single computational model can connect different methodologies for gathering neural information, such as EEG and fMRI.

Useful as this tool may be, modelling the brain is not a straightforward task. As the brain contains 10^{11} neurons supporting 10^{14} connections, each containing additional parameters related to morphology of the neuron and different neurotransmitters, it is impossible to catch every detail of one particular function in a single simulation. In response to this problem, different methods of simplification were proposed, with benefits and drawbacks. Inevitably, an increase in quantity of elements being modelled yields a decrease in (biologically plausible) detail.

More than half a century ago, Hodgkin and Huxley (1952) first presented an analysis and a computational model of a biological neuron, including many complex parameters and properties. As this model still included many biological subtleties, it was simplified further in subsequent years. This resulted in a neuronal model in which the essential functional properties of a real model were isolated: the leaky integrate-and-fire neuron. As the name suggests, the input signals of this model neuron are integrated over time, minus a constant 'leak'. When a certain threshold is reached, the neuron produces an output signal—also referred to as a 'spike'—and the integration process restarts from zero. Although this is a large simplification of the complex processes taking place in a real neuron, this mechanism closely resembles their behaviour, which makes it an ideal tool for building large networks of neurons. Therefore, and because it is easily implementable, it became one of the most widely used neuronal models. Recently, a number of somewhat more sophisticated models of spiking neurons have been proposed, that incorporate more subtleties of neuronal behaviour, yet do not require (substantially) more computational resources (most prominently Izhikevitch 2003; see Izhikevitch 2004 for an overview). More detailed simulations of the internal properties of single neurons have also been created, but that is beyond the scope of this chapter.

An alternative to neural networks with spiking neurons is presented by so-called graded nodes, which contain more complex methods of integration, and mimic the behaviour of a group of neurons rather than a single one. When the behaviour of a group of neurons is aggregated, single spikes are no longer prominent. Instead, a signal emerges that changes more gradually and spans a longer period of time. Simulations of larger networks, involving several neural areas, with nodes dedicated to a specific stimulus or concept, would typically be modelled through graded nodes. One notable example of such methodology is the Balloon model for haemodynamic brain response (Buxton *et al.* 1998; Friston *et al.* 2000), which offers a mechanistic account of the process by which evoked changes in blood flow are transformed into a blood oxygenation level dependent signal, as measured by functional magnetic resonance imaging (fMRI).

Discussing the advantages and disavantages of these methodologies is not our intention. Preference is generally dictated by the level under investigation (e.g. single-unit cell recording, functional connectivity between distant brain areas; see Figure 4.2.1), and a compromise between realism and efficiency—neural modelling can be very time-consuming (see Fidjeland *et al.* 2009). The simulations reviewed in this chapter may use one or several of these methodologies, and the extent to which their results can be used to inform theories is of course tied to the choices made by modellers.

Emotional learning

Conditioning is the process whereby the simultaneous or successive presentation of an unconditioned stimulus (US) that has a particular value for the subject and a conditioned stimulus (CS) that does not causes the conditioned stimulus to evoke a conditioned response (CR), which is (a weakened version of) the response originally associated with the unconditioned stimulus. Although the unconditioned stimuli have a particular positive or negative value to the subject that would often evoke an emotion, conditioning is not an exclusively emotional process; it can be automatic and subconscious and can occur without producing an emotional response. Nevertheless, as emotional responses occur frequently and play a prominent role in the conditioning process, it remains a valuable tool in researching the neuroscience of emotion.

Positive and negative emotional stimuli lead to different types of conditioning: reward and fear conditioning, respectively. Largely separate research traditions have evolved to investigate these different types of conditioning, although evidence exists that the underlying neural processes may be similar (see Korsten 2009, for a review). This separation has led to the development of neural models specific to either fear or reward conditioning.

Grossberg (1971) pioneered the modelling of reward conditioning, mathematically describing the neural dynamics involved in the process, particularly the interweaving temporal dynamics of stimulus events and learning dynamics of neurons. Subsequently, a model including a delay or interstimulus interval (ISI) between the onset of the US and the CS was developed (Sutton and

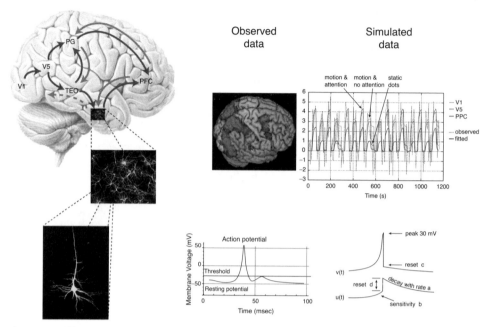

Fig. 4.2.1 Different levels of investigation require different tools. Left: The human brain can be seen as a network of brain areas, each of which can be seen as a network of neurons. The brain contains approximately 10^{11} neurons. Right: Simulating a particular level of investigation requires a particular tool (e.g. fMRI on top, single cell recording at the bottom) and produces different results (e.g. simulated blood oxygenation level dependent signal on top, a single spike at the bottom) (see plate 8).

Barto 1981), as conditioning has been shown to be optimal when the US and CS arrive successively rather than simultaneously. This incorporates the idea that the CS creates an expectation, which is resolved by the arrival of the US. More sophisticated models created in later decades took into account more detailed behavioural and neuroscientific data, culminating in the actor–critic model (Suri and Schultz 1999) and a related model by Brown *et al.* (1999).

The experimental phenomenon that was essential for the development of these models is prediction error. It has long been known that an unexpected, rewarding stimulus causes a dopamine reward signal to emerge from the ventral tegmental area (VTA) and substantia nigra, projecting to the nucleus accumbens, striatum, and many areas in the neocortex including the prefrontal cortex (Schultz 2002). This dopamine reward signal has very specific characteristics for conditioned rewards: throughout the course of conditioning, the reward signal evoked by the US is literally transferred to the CS. In other words, after conditioning, dopamine neurons that were preferentially sensitive to the US stop responding to the US altogether, and become sensitive to the CS. If the expected reward is not presented, dopamine neurons are depressed at the time when the reward would normally be presented.

The resulting simulations reflect this data. In the actor–critic model, Suri and Schultz (1999; see Figure 4.2.2) hypothesized that the learning occurs in an architecture comprised of two interoperating nodes: the 'actor', which is responsible for evaluating the environment and choosing the appropriate behavioural action, and the 'critic', as analogous to dopamine neurons, that produces a prediction error (detected in the ventral tegmental area) based on temporal information, and whose role is to bias the actor. Testing their model against a number of paradigms, they show that

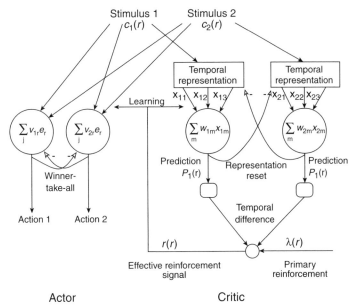

Fig. 4.2.2 Architecture of the Actor–Critic model by Suri and Schultz (1999). Two nodes, the actor (left) and the critic (right), receive inputs from the environment that are coded as functions of time. The critic computes a reinforcement signal that serves to bias the weights of the connections in the system. The actor learns to associate a particular input with a behavioural action, informed by the critic. (Arrowheads are excitatory and circles denote inhibitory pathways.)

reinforcement signals from the critic exhibit many of the characteristics of the midbrain dopamine signals demonstrated in non-human primates in similar conditions.

In a subsequent model of the dopamine data (see Figure 4.2.3), Brown *et al.* (1999) created two different pathways for CS information, where one pathway receives primary reward information and the other contains adaptive timing. This allows for the learning of a range of interstimulus intervals (ISI), rather than one fixed ISI as in the actor–critic. In this model, the US triggers a dopamine signal that strengthens connections in reward-related areas. The temporal latency intrinsic to the dopamine system gradually yields the signal to be transferred from the US to the CS. After conditioning, the distribution of weights in the system is such that presenting the CS alone is sufficient to trigger the conditioned response. A delayed inhibitory response from striosomes (a part of the striatum) suppresses the reward signal initially evoked by the presentation of the US, which is then transferred to the CS.

Of course, reward conditioning only constitutes one aspect of emotional learning, and much effort has been deployed in the investigation of fear conditioning. Interestingly, even though the experimental paradigms are somehow similar, researchers emphasized very different aspects of the underlying brain mechanisms. Modellers especially focused on the amygdala, as large amounts of experimental evidence indicate this area is central in the fear conditioning process. The most important results from rodent research (for a review see Kim and Jung 2006) include the information that amygdala lesions shortly after conditioning abolish the conditioned response while lesions before conditioning prevent acquisition altogether. Additionally, electrical and chemical

Fig. 4.2.3 Architecture of the model proposed by Brown *et al.* (1999). Cortical input enhanced by the CS propagates to both the ventral pathway and time-delay striosomes. The lateral hypothalamus acts as a reinforcement signal to the ventral pathway. Striosomes gradually suppress the dopamine burst response evoked by the reward signal (GABAergic inhibition), accounting for the transfer of activation from the US to the CS. (Arrowheads are excitatory; and circles denote inhibitory pathways.)

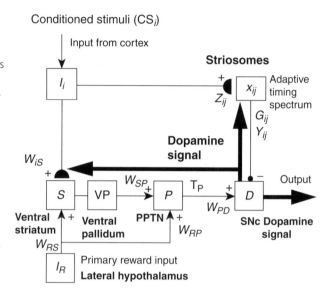

stimulation of the amygdala elicits conditioned fear-like responses, and drug manipulations of the amygdala can impair or enhance aversive memories.

Based mainly on LeDoux's (1992) investigations of the neuroanatomical functionality involved in fear conditioning, Armony *et al.* (1995, 1997) developed a range of models employing cortical and thalamic modulation of the amygdala, reproducing experimental results mentioned above, as well as many others, in great detail. An outline of the main structure of these models is presented in Figure 4.2.4. These results shed some light on the evaluative role of the amygdala, and allowed LeDoux and colleagues to bring forth hypotheses as to the connectivity of the networks at play. In recent years, the functional domain ascribed to the amygdala has elicited a lot of discussion (see Chapter 2.2, this volume), and it is believed to act as a relevance detector that would inform higher-level brain areas (Sander *et al.* 2003; Vuilleumier 2005; Whalen and Phelps 2009).

Refined efforts include the investigation of the inner circuitry of the amygdala as it not only evaluates incoming stimuli, but also informs many—if not most—other brain areas. *In vitro* and *in vivo* results in rodents, for instance, point to the importance of reverberating dynamics within and between the groups of neurons that compose the nuclei of the amygdala (Johnson *et al.* 2009). To ensure consistency, it is thus essential to investigate the other domains for which the role of the amygdala seems to be crucial. Given its (early) position in the perceptual stream, the amygdala is indeed likely to play a major role in all tasks that involve perception, attention, and reaction to emotion-laden stimuli.

Attention

For the last 15 years or so, a growing amount of research has focused on the interaction between attentional and emotional systems, with the hope that addressing one will help to resolve questions about the other. 'Attention is an emergent property of many neural mechanisms working to resolve competition for (visual) processing and control of behavior' (Desimone and Duncan 1995, p. 194, our parentheses). In other words, attention is the ability of the brain to filter the incoming flow of information—from any modality, not just visual—and to focus the

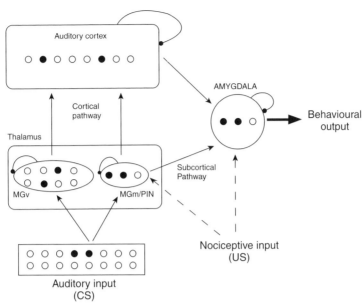

Fig. 4.2.4 Architecture of the model by Armony *et al.* (1995). The model reproduces the connectivity of the main brain areas thought to be involved in fear conditioning of a sound to an aversive shock in rodents. This architecture allows the researchers to test *in vitro* hypotheses about the spreading of node activations when one of several of the connections are disrupted through lesioning.

processing of particular stimuli from the environment, with a view to engage the brain with it (Roesch 2009; Roesch *et al.* 2010). In this context, emotion involves the appraisal of the incoming stimuli, somehow informing the attentional system and biasing perception.

A tentative theory describing the interaction of these two systems, however, yields some controversy about the automaticity of emotional processing, and the extent to which attention is a necessary condition for its occurrence in the first place. Protagonists arguing that emotional processing is automatic and can occur outside of the attentional focus show, for instance, that the amygdala is activated by the perception of emotional facial expressions even if attention is focused on different stimuli in the perceptual space (e.g. Vuilleumier *et al.* 2001), perhaps through crude, low-level perceptual features (e.g. low spatial frequencies) readily transmitted to the cortex. Other results, however, show that attentional load may have an impact on amygdala activation (e.g. Pessoa *et al.* 2002) thus, possibly, degrading perception. However intense this debate may have been, it may simply reflect how difficult it is to frame this particular question. A sensible hypothesis could indeed see reciprocal influences, leaving enough room for both sides of the dispute to be reconciled. For instance, the amygdala may very well preferentially respond to emotion-laden crude information of some kind, while being subject to other contextual control mechanisms that would regulate its influence in the rest of the brain.

Attention is often described as *operating on* cortical sites, either by enhancing the processing of selected stimuli or by diminishing the processing of irrelevant stimuli. This conceptualization led Taylor and colleagues to propose a controller model of attention through which they put to the test a number of hypotheses and experimental paradigms from neuroimaging. Dubbed the COrollary Discharge of Attention Movement (CODAM; see Figure 4.2.5) model, in reference to an engineering control approach, this model simulates the interactions amongst brain

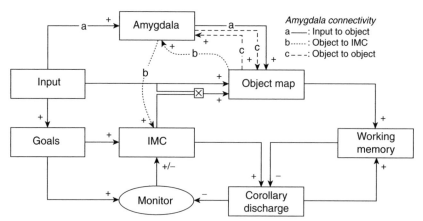

Fig. 4.2.5 Architecture of the COrollary Discharge of Attention Movement (CODAM) model, including subcortical–cortical connections from the amygdala (Fragopanagos *et al.* 2005). See text for details.

areas commonly discussed in the neuroimaging literature (Taylor 2002; Korsten *et al.* 2006). An attentional signal, dispatched by an inverse model controller (IMC, sited in the parietal cortex), modulates working memory through an object map (associative cortices). The IMC also gives rise to a corollary discharge signal (cingulate cortices), facilitating target processing and preventing intrusion after comparison of the input to current goals (areas of the prefrontal cortex). To investigate emotional influences on this attentional system, the authors simulated a modulatory signal ignited from the amygdala to areas of parietal and sensory cortices (Fragopanagos *et al.* 2005). They obtained results that were in agreement with those obtained in the healthy population and amygdala patients, using both EEG and fMRI (Taylor and Fragopanagos 2005). In particular, the recurrent connections between the amygdala and the IMC could explain why the activation of irrelevant emotional information seems to be reduced to such a level that it may hardly interfere with ongoing processing. The authors, however, note that a residual activation still remains in the amygdala, which, in some cases, might still be strong enough to interfere with ongoing processing, but may be too weak to be caught by fMRI analyses.

The interference between different perceptions is best addressed through dual-task paradigms. One such paradigm gives rise to an attentional deficit dubbed the attentional blink (AB), owing to the apparent shutting off of perception for a period of time that can last for up to 400 ms. During this transient period of time, the cognitive system is engaged in processing a first (often visual) target, and is thereby unable to process a subsequent target (Raymond *et al.* 1992). In other words, if a second target appears during that narrow window of time, it fails to reach conscious awareness. Varying the time interval between the two targets makes it possible to assess the availability of the target to the cognitive system over time. Interestingly, emotion-laden information presented as second targets seems to benefit from a processing bias such that, compared to neutral stimuli, they do access central processing yielding conscious awareness and correct identification (see Roesch *et al.* 2009 for a review). Using CODAM, Taylor and colleagues were not only able to show that the AB may occur due to a modulatory signal ignited by the first target, but also that the amygdala plays a crucial role in the attentional influences of emotional stimuli (Fragopanagos *et al.* 2005); this is in accordance with other simulations that focused on the implication of the locus ceruleus–norepinephrine system, a tiny structure in the brainstem—functionally related to the amygdala—that has been implicated in the maintenance of arousal states (Aston-Jones *et al.* 1998; Dayan and Yu 2006). An extension of this work may see the investigation of the time course of the AB curve, which plots the ability to respond correctly to the second target against the time interval between the two targets. Novel methods allow for the decomposition of this curve into different periods of time (Cousineau *et al.* 2006), and each period of time seems differently sensitive to emotion-laden information. In particular, Roesch *et al.* (2009) found evidence for the presence of an attentional control mechanism preventing emotion-laden stimuli from reaching awareness and interfering with the ongoing processing during a period of 0–150 ms after the first target, and a processing bias favouring emotion-laden stimuli, starting 350 ms after the first target, as hypothesized in the framework of appraisal theories.

A competing model of the AB builds on the global workspace theory, according to which the different high-level, specialized areas of the brain involved in the processing of visual stimuli interconnect to each other to form a global workspace, processing targets into a unitary assembly supporting conscious reportability (Baars 1988, 2002; Shanahan 2007). To investigate the hypothesis that at least part of the AB may be due to the exclusive recruitment of this workspace, Dehaene *et al.* (2003) simulated early sensory regions and higher association areas (see Figure 4.2.6). The model exhibited synchronized activity of the simulated thalamo-cortical columns in much the same way as cortical event-related potentials (ERPs) observed in a typical AB experiment comparing seen and unseen/blinked words in healthy participants (Sergent and Dehaene 2004). Describing the cortical activation evoked by unseen words, the authors report a drop in the waveform of components peaking around 300 ms post-stimulus, which correlated with behavioural

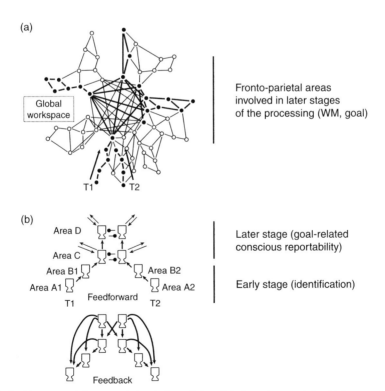

Fig. 4.2.6 Architecture of the neural simulation of the global workspace (after Deheane *et al.* 2003). WM, Working memory. See text for details.

visibility ratings. They report that seen words, when compared to unseen words, yielded an intense spread of activation within left temporal and inferior frontal regions (about 300 ms after stimulus onset), which would then spread to lateral prefrontal and anterior cingulate cortices (about 440 ms), before extending to more posterior regions (about 580 ms). Dehaene and colleagues thus conclude that perceived stimuli may compete to recruit this global workspace that, once activated, only affords exclusive access, leading to the inability to process subsequent stimuli for a transient period of time. Areas in the global workspace theoretically map on to the description of the processing streams involved in visual perception, from perceptual areas to higher associative areas of temporal, parietal, frontal, and cingulate cortex, which is to say that the bottleneck described in AB studies would therefore lie in the top-down influence of higher-level areas, like the PFC or more parietal areas, over the lower-level areas involved in the visual streams.

Subjective feeling and embodiment

So far, we have purposely remained open as to what the concept of emotion entails, because it was being used in a wide variety of contexts. In this section, however, we will address the 'felt' part of emotion, the so-called subjective feeling, and some clarification is thus in order. As pointed out in appraisal theories, emotion is too broad a concept, and it helps to break it down into components (see Chapter 2.1, this volume). One such component is the feeling, which integrates the 'central representation of appraisal-driven response organization in emotion' (Scherer 2004). In other words, the folk representation of the feeling is proposed to be the part of emotion that acts as a monitor to the emotional process, providing the organism with some insight as to what is being experienced—note how close to the debate on consciousness this brings us. It is to be distinguished from the (often unconscious) appraisal component that we described earlier. This idea is tightly related to the Jamesian perspective according to which 'bodily changes follow directly the perception of the exciting fact, and (…) our feeling of the same changes as they occur is the emotion' (James 1884, p. 190). The perceptive reader will have understood that what James refers to as 'emotion' is, in fact, what we called the 'felt' part of emotion, the feeling. Emphasizing the involvement of visceral changes during emotional episodes, James's views set in motion a whole area of investigation (see Chapter 2.4, this volume). Through this research the proposal originated that the feeling is the integrative mechanism through which the dynamic modulations of visceral states, the context in which the eliciting event is occurring, as well as the result of its appraisal are combined to form a tangible affective representation of the occurring situation. In the line of appraisal theories, Grandjean et al. (2008) suggest that the degree of coherence amongst these components may be a determining factor in the differentiation of emotional feelings.

Thagard and Aubie (2008) describe EMOCON (Figure 4.2.7), a neural simulation that contains representations of the environment, of the accompanying bodily state, as well as some crude representation of valence and arousal. This model suggests that dedicated brain areas (amygdala, insula) integrate this information, and then contribute to the elaboration of a neural representation in working memory (dorsolateral prefrontal cortices). The coherent activation of this network of areas constitutes the emotion evoked by the emotion-laden external event, and its representation in working memory is the part of the emotion that can be consciously accessed, the feeling as we defined it earlier. We refer the reader to Chapter 2.2, this volume, for a discussion of the integrative function of the amygdala and the insula and related neuroimaging results.

In a second step, Thagard and Aubie (2008) investigated the coherence between the nodes of the network that gives rise to correlates of emotional awareness through the feeling. Coherence has been proposed as one of the main mechanisms for communication between neural assemblies

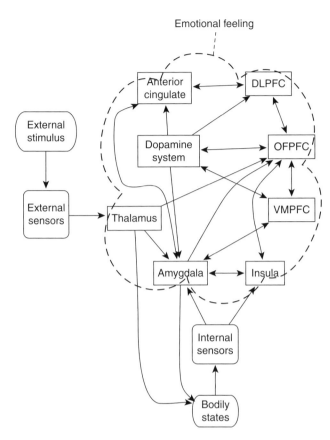

Emotional feeling

Fig. 4.2.7 Architecture of EMOCON by Thagard and Aubie (2008). The model demonstrates the integration of both perceptions of changes in the environment with perceptions of bodily states. Notice that all the brain areas we have discussed so far are represented. The amygdala acts as a integrator of all perception, receiving input from most other areas. The midbrain dopamine system computes some degree of valence. Prefrontal brain areas act as a working memory. The general pattern of activation of the system is proposed to represent the particular emotions that are being 'experienced' by the simulation.

(Singer 1999*a*, *b*; Fries 2005), and one can expect it to be expressed at different levels: within a neural structure, the insula, for instance, which gathers numerous afferent connections from the body (Craig 2009), and between neural structures. Thagard and Aubie (2008) describe NECO (Figure 4.2.8), which they used to investigate the coherence behaviour between the amygdala and different areas of the prefrontal cortex. In NECO, the coherence between brain structures is used to make motivated inferences about the extent to which the network is accomplishing its goal in a particular environment. The inference process is based on the satisfaction of parallel constraints (Thagard 2003), and generates a feeling that can be accessed in memory. In other words, in the explanatory coherence network formed by the prefrontal cortices and the amygdala, the system will select the appropriate action, given a particular context, on the basis of the positive (excitatory) and negative (inhibitory) constraints expressed by each of the node of the network.

Decision making and value system

The respective influences of cognitive and emotional processes on decision making are highly relevant to our day to day functioning. As such, much research has been dedicated to delineating these influences. In psychology as well as in neuroscience, the viewpoint that the emotional counterpart of the decision process has no merit, is irrational, and should be disregarded has been replaced with the idea that an emotional reaction can provide valuable information that has been lost in the complex workings of the cognitive mind. Values play a large role in decision processes,

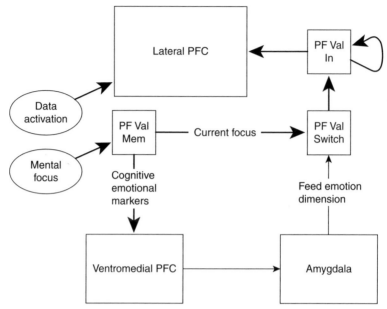

Fig. 4.2.8 Architecture of NECO, by Thagard and Aubie (2008), investigating the coherence between areas of the prefrontal cortex and the amygdala. See text for details.

as decisions tend to be based on the comparison of the value of the expected outcome of one choice to the alternative.

A highly influential research paradigm in the neuroscience of decision making is the IOWA gambling task, in which subjects' choice across four decks of cards determines how much monetary reward or punishment they receive (Bechara *et al.* 1994). Subjects are not informed as to which decks of cards are better or worse than others, or about the proportion of good or bad cards in a good or bad deck. In this task, the skin conductance response (SCR; an indicator of the affective arousal of the participant) can be measured after the choice is made, when the subject anticipates the outcome. On average, this anticipatory SCR is higher when the subject has chosen a bad deck, even when the subject has no conscious knowledge about one deck being better than another (Bechara *et al.* 1994; Wagar and Thagard 2004).

A computational model of this decision process was proposed by Wagar and Thagard (2004), where the nucleus accumbens (NAcc) is a central structure in the integration of cognitive and emotional neural signals for decision making, while the ventromedial prefrontal cortical (VMPFC) activation represents a prediction of the outcome of a given response (see Figure 4.2.9 for an outline of this model). The amygdala module is active only if the response is emotionally laden, and hippocampal activation represents the current context, while VTA activation only serves to continuously deactivate the NAcc so that more than one input is needed to elicit a response from this module. So, when both the hippocampus and VMPFC are active, suggesting the VMPFC prediction applies to the current context, a response is elicited. A response can also be elicited when VMPFC and amygdala are simultaneously active but, because these activations tend to be short as they respond to nonpermanent stimuli (unlike the context), there is a very short time frame in which this coactivation can produce a response. Implementation of this model with spiking neurons performing the IOWA gambling task produces simulated NAcc output data that are similar to behavioural data in normal subjects, and to data in VMPFC lesioned patients: when

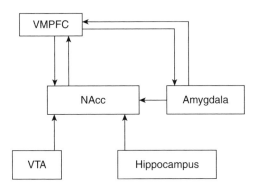

Fig. 4.2.9 Architecture implemented in GAGE (Wagar and Thagard 2004). See text for details.

the VMPFC module is damaged the response is only based on the immediately preceding outcome, rather than a long-term prediction.

This model provides a computational account of somatic marker theory (Damasio 1994), in which emotion influences decision making through somatic markers (a kind of emotional memory) associated with the stimulus. Here, these markers are stored in the VMPFC and expressed through activation of the amygdala. Thus, this model provides a potential, neurally realistic mechanism for partly emotion-based decision making.

A model that more directly relates value to emotional output is that proposed recently by Korsten (2009). The basis of this computational model is the interplay between four different assessments of values created by current events. Three of these assessed values, of currently perceived or predicted valenced stimuli, are compared to a stable norm and to one another. Discrepancies between experience, expectation, and norm of one particular value type (such as reward/punishment or self-esteem) can give rise to emotional responses. This connection between emotion and prediction can be found in other emotion research as well: implication is one of the four main stimulus evaluation checks in the CPM (Sander *et al.* 2005; see also Chapter 2.1, this volume) and predictions are widely accepted to be part of conditioned learning mechanisms in the brain. In this model, different degrees and types of discrepancy give rise to different emotions, which allows for differentiation between a large range of emotions (see Table 4.2.1). Fear, for example, arises when the expected value is lower than the actual (current) value, whereas hope arises when it is higher. Note that two different expected values (exp1 and exp2) are used, where exp1 represents the expectation based on currently perceived stimuli, and exp2 represents a value that was expected previously—analogous to a working memory for expectation.

The neural architecture presented in Figure 4.2.10 provides a basis for all of the comparisons contained in Table 4.2.1. This includes a system of comparator modules, with each node in the output module corresponding to one particular emotion. Learned predictions of future reward or punishment for current and past stimuli are represented in the exp1 and exp2 modules, respectively, and compared to currently experienced values from the act module and a set standard from the norm module. The values in the exp1 and act modules are based on the current context, represented in the ctxt module. A spontaneous inhibition (SI) module ensures that, once a discrepancy has been detected, emotional output continues to be produced until the discrepancy is resolved by a different stimulus.

Many functions and concepts employed in this model—value, comparisons, context—have been subject to neuroscientific research. Thus, neuroanatomical correlates can be assigned to the separate modules. Nevertheless, the model also proposes a clear method for categorizing and delineating a wide range of different emotions. As such, this model provides an excellent starting

Table 4.2.1 Predictions issued from the model by Korsten (2009)

	Reward/punishment	Self-esteem	Outcome of action	Outcome of other's action
exp1 < norm	Fear	Shyness	Guilt	Contempt
exp1 > norm	Hope	Confidence	Hope	Admiration
act < norm & exp1 > act	Anger	Anger	Regret	Empathy
act < norm & exp1 = < act	Sadness	Shame	Regret	Pity
exp2 < norm & exp1 > exp2	Relief	Gratitude	Relief	
exp2 < norm & act < = exp2			Guilt	Schadenfreude
exp2 > norm & exp1 < exp2	Disapp'tm't	Disapp'tm't	Frustration	Pity
act > norm & exp2 < act	Surprise	Surprise	Surprise	
act > norm	Joy	Pride, triumph	Satisfaction	Jealousy

point in bridging the gap between neuroscientific and behavioural knowledge on the subject of emotion.

Furthermore, this model succeeds in categorizing emotions discretely from a limited number of continuously fluctuating evaluations of the situation. This incorporates different, seemingly incompatible aspects of previous emotion theories in a computational model, thus proposing emotion to be a more quantifiable, measurable, and thereby testable phenomenon with a relatively simple process at its core.

Conclusion

What have we learned from computational neuroscience about the neural correlates of emotions?

Methods of computational neuroscience impose the decomposition and the formal description of the functional components that yield correlates of emotion that can be measured in the

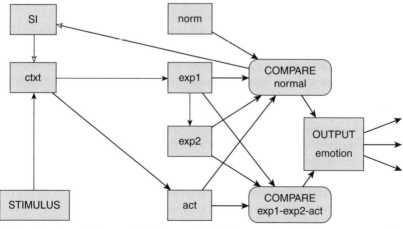

Fig. 4.2.10 Architecture of the model by Korsten (2009). See text for details.

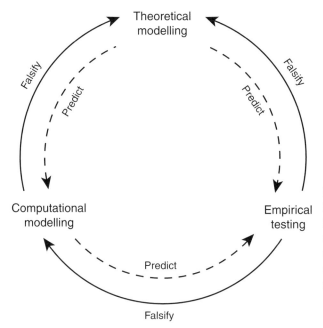

Fig. 4.2.11 Interactions between methods of investigation. The gap between computational modelling and experimental testing could be resolved if both parties used similar inference methods.

brain and the behaviour. Results issued from this paradigm thus point to possible mechanisms, highlight the interactions between neural systems, challenge common theories, and make novel hypotheses that can be tested in experiments (Figure 4.2.11; see Roesch *et al.* 2007). In this chapter, we reviewed some of the models that investigate particular emotional phenomena, allowing us to describe provisions that ought to be taken into account by any theory of emotional processing.

- Any computation in the brain involves some learning, and this is especially true for emotional processes. Learning occurs at multiple levels, and takes multiple forms. At the neural level, several mechanisms are proposed that take into account valenced input. At the network level, dedicated nodes handle more complex information processing, and learning is evident during the integration of multiple perceptual dimensions, including affective dimensions, into one coherent percept.

- The investigation of these dedicated processing nodes imposes the decomposition and the parsing of the functional domains of the systems that underlie the perception and appraisal of emotional stimuli, as well as the interaction of emotion with other functions of the brain, like attention and decision making. This decomposition emphasizes the role and the complexity of subcortical systems. The amygdala, for instance, is shown to play a crucial role in most areas of emotional processing. The scope of its functional domain is, however, heavily debated (see Sander *et al.* 2003), and this debate is likely to result in the need to describe more lower-level subsystems, specialized in their own right (Johnson *et al.* 2009).

- The intricacies of emotional processing with other cognitive phenomena, like attention, consciousness, or decision making, make it difficult to ascribe one brain structure to one function. As can be gathered from our review, most brain areas are shown to be implicated, to some extent, in most of the brain functions we focused on. A successful methodology to investigate emotional processing will thus attempt to relate different phenomena together, in an effort to understand the mechanisms in common. We argue that computational neuroscience constitutes a middle ground that allows theories to be combined to generate new concepts.

What can neural network simulation contribute to the scientific study of emotion?

◆ Neural simulations attempt to describe how brain areas may be involved in several brain functions, such as attention and decision making. The results of these simulations may thus be used to construct novel experimental paradigms tailored to investigate the boundary between brain functions and to propose new concepts that can be used to perfect theories.

◆ This being said, up to now, the gap between simulation and empirical testing is still wide open and very little comes back to experimentalists. This is regrettable because it is not difficult to imagine modellers making predictions for EEG or fMRI. One explanation for this state of affairs may be that modellers often do not use the same inference methods as experimentalists, thus making it difficult for experimentalists to exploit results from simulations.

◆ The reasons for this (unfortunate) state of affairs may lie in the illusion of thick and incommensurable boundaries between scientific disciplines—most likely erected by the very Darwinian need for funding. Researchers are often bred in self-sufficient and self-replicating environments and only seldom are they given the opportunity to experience science through different and often unorthodox perspectives. Therefore, methods that are described in disciplinary publications do not come across as valuable outside the boundaries of the discipline.

Fortunately, in recent years, unifying efforts have been made to formulate truly interdisciplinary dialogues in the form of thematic research foci. The present volume constitutes, of course, a perfect example of this endeavour, and perhaps some of the methods and theories we described will appeal to the reader. The development and rise of affective sciences as a discipline *per se*, encompassing affective psychology, affective neuroscience, and affective computing, amongst others, will hopefully support the healthy curiosity it requires to grow.

Section 5

Approaches to an implementation of affectively competent agents

This section introduces the perspectives of several applied domains in engineering and computer sciences on emotional reactions and their conceptualization in the respective fields. The individual contributions in this section are articulated around specific applications, describing concrete implementations of different agents or networks as linked to specific aspects of emotional mechanisms or competences, in a wide variety of different contexts. In many cases, the authors also address propositions made in Section 2, discuss their feasibility with respect to the state of the art in the respective applied field, and outline the possibilities and limitations of current technologies and methods available in engineering and computer sciences to address and/or incorporate models and paradigms developed by psychologists and neuroscientists for the study of emotional reactions.

In Chapter 5.1, 'Expression of affects in embodied conversational agents', Hyniewska, Niewiadomski, Mancini, and Pelachaud place their work on the conceptual and theoretical framework outlined in Section 1 and specifically address the level of display of expressions of emotions as well as how these displays are perceived. The central aim is to create complex expression in ECAs (described as blends of expressions as in the case of masking one expression by another one or the case of superposition of two expressions). Their model of multimodal sequential expressions of emotions is based on observational studies of emotional behaviours while a model of behaviour expressivity is taken from results of perceptual studies. Specifically, the authors explain how they derived an expressivity model based on the theoretical propositions and empirical data mentioned before and describe the set of parameters used to represent behaviour expressivity and how these parameters have been implemented. This model was tested in a series of studies and the authors report how different types of empirical data can be used to refine a computational model of expressive behaviour.

In Chapter 5.2, 'Synthesis of emotional speech', Schröder, Burkhardt, and Krstulovic address the vocal channel of emotional communication, focusing specifically on the issue of synthesizing emotional speech. They show how the central emotion concepts outlined in the introduction index important aspects of communicative situations, in particular, the emotional state of the (simulated) speaker, the interpersonal stance of the speaker towards a listener, the attitude of the speaker about the topic of the conversation, as well as, in a wider sense, aspects such as underlying mood or personality or even the constraints deriving from the communicative situation. Emotional speech synthesis aims at building models that link such emotion-related concepts to their acoustical or articulatory manifestation in speech. The authors identify the challenges faced by efforts to create speech capabilities for an affectively competent agent, in particular, a technological one arising from the fact that existing synthesis technologies are either natural-sounding or allow for a flexible control of acoustic parameters, but not both. Following a brief historical overview of the area, two approaches—rule-based synthesis based on production models and data-driven statistical models—are discussed in detail. In addition, a methodological challenge is identified. How can generative models of emotional prosody be grounded in theoretically motivated models of emotion, overcoming current practice where emotional prosody rules are often formulated for a limited set of unrelated emotion categories? The authors report on first steps in this direction using a coarse emotion description in terms of emotion dimensions, and end by suggesting a more elaborate approach based on an appraisal model.

In Chapter 5.3, 'Automatic detection of emotion from vocal expression', Devillers, Vidrascu, and Layachi also focus on the vocal communication modality, dealing with analysis rather than synthesis. They postulate that automatic emotion detection by an affectively competent agent must ideally be based on a model of the dynamic emotion process underlying the constantly changing nature of the expression of emotions, contrasting this perspective with many current engineering models of emotion that assume unambiguous responses to fixed conditions corresponding to a static model of emotion. They start from the assumption that 'emotion primitive descriptions' (affective markers) are an important alternative to classical emotion categories for describing a human's affective expressions and propose to detect affective markers such as valence, activation but also control, novelty, and others (as described by dimensional theories and appraisal models) on the basis of suprasegmental features. Specifically, the authors demonstrate how the introduction of some appraisals such as control or novelty into a dimensional structure allows the introduction of some variables that are particularly useful for the real-time detection of emotion from short vocal utterances.

In Chapter 5.4, 'Body gesture and facial expression analysis for automatic affect recognition', Castellano, Caridakis, Camurri, Karpouzis, Volpe, and Kollias centrally consider one of the main requirements of efficient, emotionally competent systems—the recognition of the intended emotions and other affective states by users. Given the multicomponential nature of the emotional processes this requires a multimodal approach. Specifically, the authors describe methods for the analysis of non-verbal multimodal data from users for the understanding of emotional information. In particular, they describe the study of human full-body movement, gesture, and facial expressions as channels (or components) of emotion communication, presenting state of the art of computational models and techniques for the automated analysis of emotional state.

In Chapter 5.5, 'Communicating emotional states with the Greta agent', Niewiadomski, Mancini, Hyniewska, and Pelachaud provide an in-depth case study for the particular embodied conversation agent that they developed, Greta. They provide a detailed review of Greta's competences with respect to the production of emotional expressions in the verbal and non-verbal modalities, specifically, gaze, head and torso movements, facial expressions, and gestures, and discuss functionalities and communication protocols and the animation standards they used. They provide a detailed overview of how the agent's architecture can be used to achieve a number of important conversational aims as identified by the literature on social interaction and communication. Finally, they demonstrate how a number of simple parameter adjustments allow them to provide the agent with a number of individuating dispositional qualities.

Chapter 5.1

Expression of affects in embodied conversational agents[1]

Sylwia Hyniewska, Radosław Niewiadomski, Maurizio Mancini, and Catherine Pelachaud

Summary

Providing virtual agents with expressive faculties is a contemporary challenge. The generated emotional behaviour for embodied conversational agents (ECAs) has to be particularly credible and varied. Cowell and Stanney (2005) showed that well chosen behaviours and emotional expressions improve the credibility of an agent. Behaviour expressivity can be conveyed through the choice of the non-verbal signals and their realization.

Some researchers argue that creating an 'internal state' for an ECA and giving the ECA the possibility to express emotions contributes to a richer human–machine interaction (Walker *et al.* 1994). The internal states can be expressed on the behaviour level through the choice of the non-verbal signals and the modulation of their realization.

In this chapter several algorithms that enrich the behaviour repertoires of ECAs are presented. Although a great number of models use interpolations to create new expressions based on formerly defined basic emotions (e.g. Tsapatsoulis *et al.* 2002; Albrecht *et al.* 2005; Paradiso 2002), a particular attention is paid to the models of emotional expressions going beyond these so-called universal expressions. Some computational models of perceptively verified expressions have been created, mostly using fuzzy methods (Arya and DiPaola 2007; Arya *et al.* 2009). Niewiadomski and Pelachaud have also elaborated a model for the generation of complex facial displays such as superposition or masking of expressions (Niewiadomski and Pelachaud 2007*b*; see Chapter 5.5, this volume).

Other researchers grounded their expression generation systems in a dimensional approach, with a link between points in the space defined mostly by the pleasure, arousal, and dominance (PAD) dimensions and the generated expressions (e.g. Zhang *et al.* 2007; Courgeon *et al.* 2008). Some models also integrate modalities other than the face into the expressions of emotions. A different approach is to focus on the modelling of facial expressions as a sequence of multimodal signals rather than expressions presented at their apex. Such a model of expression animation may increase the agent's communicative capabilities.

Another issue to be treated when modelling agents' displays of internal states is the expressive realization of the behaviours. Different parameters have been defined as having an impact on the

[1] The authors of this chapter have been supported by the EU funded Human–Machine Interaction Network on Emotion Network of Excellence (HUMAINE: http://emotion-research.net/) and by the IP-CALLAS project IST-034800 (http://www.callas-newmedia.eu).

behaviour expressivity. This set of parameters is used in tasks such as animation synthesis, but also in the manual annotation of video corpora or automatic analysis.

Introduction

In this chapter we present several algorithms that model expressive capabilities in embodied conversational agents. An embodied conversational agent (ECA) is a computer-generated character with autonomous capacities in verbal and non-verbal communication that possesses a human-like appearance. Recent progress in the development of ECAs fosters expectations concerning their ability to express emotions in a credible way. Recent research in the field of emotional expressions in humans shows that such expressions go beyond a simple facial expression presented at its apex. In fact, emotions recruit massive resources to cope with a relevant situation, leading to a high activation of the autonomous and somatic nervous system (Sander *et al.* 2005). This activation will have an impact on the behaviour of an individual: emotional cues can be observed in the speech parameters (Banse and Scherer 1996; Schuller *et al.* 2009*a*), in posture (Coulson 2007), and so on (see Chapter 2.3, this volume). In general, expressions should be seen as multimodal (see Chapter 1.1 and 2.3, this volume; de Gelder *et al.* 2010) and composed of many signals (Levenson 2003; Shiota *et al.* 2003). Also the relation of each of these signals may contribute to the emotional interpretation of the overall expression (Scherer and Ellgring 2007*b*; Keltner 1995; Harrigan and O'Connell 1996). One may argue that a human–machine interaction should also include all these non-verbal signals emitted by the user and the embodied virtual interlocutor.

When working with virtual agents, it is important to keep in mind that the interaction of the humans with virtual characters is similar to the human-to-human interaction (Schilbach *et al.* 2006; Brave *et al.* 2005). Therefore, it seems plausible that for the emotional expression synthesis in ECAs it would be appropriate to apply a psychological model of human behaviour. Comprehending the processes implied in the emotional states is still a problem. Researchers involved in the animations of virtual characters rely on different models of emotional behaviour coming from distinct approaches. Classically, animators who seek emotions' definitions in the psychology domain see emotions in one of three major ways: in a discrete approach, i.e. as an automatic reaction to a situation; in a dimensional approach, i.e. as a state characterized by a position in a continuous multidimensional space; or in a componential approach as a dynamic cognitive evaluation of a situation. (For a closer look at the emotional theories mentioned here see Chapter 1.1, this volume.) Different theories on emotions lead to different models of emotional behaviours in ECAs.

During a face-to-face interaction, whether between humans or in a human–machine context, an emotional message can be transmitted verbally or non-verbally. Since the first modelization of a virtual face, work has been realized for the synthesis of emotional expressions (Parke 1972; Platt and Badler 1981). Studies have shown that agents that possess emotional expressivity faculties are engaging users more in the interactions than agents with non-emotional behaviours (Walker *et al.* 1994). In frustrating situations, agents that showed appropriate emotional reactions to users' situations also tended to diminish users' stress level, compared to an interaction with an agent showing no empathy (Mori *et al.* 2003; Prendinger *et al.* 2005). Similarly, when an agent has to interrupt the user in its task, the interruption is perceived as less frustrating when the agent's verbal messages are emotionally coloured (Picard and Liu 2007).

Although the relevance of full-body emotional activity has been stressed (e.g. Lazarus 1991; Argyle 1988; Bull 1987), some ECAs display no emotion expressions or only a limited number, mostly through the face. Usually facial expressions are defined using one of the two standards of facial expression coding: the facial action coding system (FACS; Ekman *et al.* 2002) and

MPEG-4 (Ostermann 2002). FACS is an anatomically based system that makes it possible to describe the muscle movements that are perceived in the face. The minimum change that can be perceived is called an action unit (AU). The MPEG-4 is a graphic standard that defines the point displacements of the face and the joint rotation for the body.

In this chapter different systems that enrich the expressive capabilities of an ECA are presented. First of all, several models of facial expressions have been proposed to extend the agents' facial behaviour. Most of them use some arithmetic operations like averaging facial parameters to generate new expressions. On the other hand, models of complex facial expressions like masking or superposition are usually modelled with fuzzy methods. Sometimes perceptive studies have been used to test the validity of the generated expressions and some models determined in that way have placed expressions in multidimensional spaces. Sequential expressions models have also been proposed by researchers. Some of these models were applied to the face signals, others to several modalities. Several models have also been developed in order to integrate several modalities of expressions into ECA animations. Finally, several agent systems exist that allow one to alter or modulate the way in which non-verbal behaviours are executed. These models are presented in the following sections.

Facial expression models of emotion

Several models of facial expressions have been proposed to enrich the agents' facial behaviour. Most models use interpolations, mainly between predefined basic emotions' expressions. Other models are based on perceptive studies; mainly these have divided the facial area into different parts in order to generate the new expressions by reconstructing differentially from several predefined subexpressions. A few models introduce some physiological changes, such as blushing or sweating, into facial expression.

Whole face interpolation models

The existing solutions usually compute new expressions by 'averaging' the values of the parameters of the expressions of the 'basic' emotions (see Chapter 1.1, this volume). The model called 'emotion disc' (Ruttkay *et al.* 2003) uses a bilinear interpolation between two basic expressions and the neutral one. In the emotion disc six expressions are spread evenly around the disc, while the neutral expression is represented by the centre of the circle. The distance from the centre of the circle represents the intensity of expression. The spatial relations are used to establish the expression corresponding to any point of the emotion disc.

Models of Tsapatsoulis *et al.* (2002) and Albrecht *et al.* (2005) can be used to compute expressions based on a similar approach. Both use the expressions of two 'neighbouring' emotions to compute the facial expressions for non-basic emotions. For this purpose they use different multidimensional spaces, in which emotional labels are placed. In both approaches new expressions are constructed starting from the six Ekman expressions: anger; disgust; fear; happiness; sadness; and surprise. To be more precise, in Tsapatsoulis *et al.* (2002) a new expression is generated by looking for the spatially closest two basic emotions as defined within the dimensional space proposed by Whissell (1989) and Plutchik (1980) and weighting the parameters of these expressions with their coordinates. Albrecht and colleagues (2005) proposed an extended approach. The authors use a three-dimensional space of emotional states defined by activation, evaluation, and power as proposed in (Cowie *et al.* 1999) and an anatomical model of the face is used. As a consequence, they work with a numerical representation of muscle contradictions.

Paradiso (2002) introduced an algebraic structure for facial expression transformations with arbitrary chosen operators. More specifically, he used three operators defined over a set of MPEG-4 facial animation parameters. The sum operator is the weighted mean of two expressions, when the amplifier operator is a product of a real number and an expression. The probable intention of the first parameter was to simulate blends of emotions. Finally, the overlap operator combines two expressions by choosing some facial expression parameters of the first expression and others from the second one. Then by using these arithmetical operations different facial expressions can be generated.

Facial region compositional models

Several authors suggest that the intermediate expressions generated using interpolations may not be (perceptually) valid (e.g. Arya *et al.* 2009; Pelachaud and Poggi 2002). Compositional approaches combine separately different regions of facial expressions (mouth, eyebrows, etc.). Among others, Mäkäräinen and Takala (2009) rely on the blending of existing expressions to synthesize new ones. Their system enables the blending of facial actions defined as partly based on the FACS and the MPEG-4 standard. New expressions can be computed by combining facial actions at the AUs level or at the expressions level. In the latest case, the generated blends can be of two or three basic emotion expressions. Rather than using an additive operator, Bui (2004) uses a set of fuzzy rules to determine the blending expressions of six basic emotions based on Ekman's findings (Ekman and Friesen 1975). A subset of rules is attributed to each pair of emotions. The fuzzy inference determines the degree of muscle contractions of the final expression as a function of the input emotion intensities. Niewiadomski and Pelachaud (2007b) have also used a partitioning approach based on fuzzy inferences, in which each facial expression is defined by a set of eight facial areas. Each part of the face displays an emotion. In complex facial expressions, different emotions can be expressed on different areas of the face (see Chapter 5.5, this volume). The authors use an algorithm (Niewiadomski and Pelachaud 2007b) based on fuzzy similarity to generate superposed, masked, fake, or inhibited expressions.

A different type of facial expression differentiation was considered by Rehm and André (2005). In a study on deceptive agents, they showed that users were able to differentiate between the agent displaying an expression of a felt emotion versus an expression of a fake emotion (Rehm and André 2005). For this purpose they manually defined facial expressions according to Ekman's description of expressions for fake emotions. These expressions are more asymmetric and miss reliable features.

Arya and colleagues (Arya and DiPaola 2007; Arya *et al.* 2009) propose a perceptively valid model for expression blending. That is, the authors aim to create new expressions that can be attached to a meaning (e.g. an emotional state). In a perceptive study human participants had to create facial expressions associated to mixed emotions on a three-dimensional face model. For this purpose they were asked to illustrate short stories with blending expressions. The expressions were evaluated by participants in terms of different dimensions. From the results of this study, a set of fuzzy rules that link specific facial actions with the three-dimensional space of valence, arousal, and agency has been developed. Rules are generated from the statistical analysis of the images created in the experiment by participants. Contrary to Bui whose fuzzy rules were activated depending on the intensity of emotions, in Arya *et al.* the fuzzy values in three emotional dimensions are used to activate the virtual character's face. Interestingly, the blending expression is a combination of the emotion expressions that are provided as input to the model.

Mao and colleagues (Mao *et al.* 2008) propose a layered model of facial behaviour. The authors stress that three processes contribute to any expressive behaviour: emotional; physiological; and social. In Mao *et al.* (2008) the generation of the expression is realized in three layers, the first one being the physiological, the second the emotional, and the third the social layer. At the moment the authors consider: 14 physiological variables on the physiological level (e.g. adrenaline, blood pressure, or sneezing); 36 emotional expressions (e.g. fear, reproach, or satisfaction); and 6 social expressions (e.g. disagree or wink). The final facial behaviour is composed of the output of each layer processed separately, while taking into account the priorities given to each layer. In the case of the second layer (emotional expressions) the output is the result of the processing of the fuzzy relation matrix between expressions and emotions. This matrix contains the mapping from the fuzzy emotion vector to the fuzzy facial vector. Each value (e, f) in this matrix is a degree of membership expressing the probability that an emotion e is mapped to the expression f. Thus the mapping between emotions and expressions is many-to-many. Given an input of a vector of emotional states, the output is the fuzzy facial vector that is defuzzified. Working in parallel, the first layer may influence the way facial behaviour is realized, while the last layer may facilitate or inhibit emotional expressions and/or use some social signals instead of the direct expression of an internal state. The layers define the hierarchical system. The output of each layer may be modified by the output of the layer that has a higher priority.

Modelling physiological changes

Other researchers (de Melo and Gratch 2009; Jung *et al.* 2009) have shifted their focus of attention on to the visible expressions of vegetative functions controlled by the autonomic nervous system, such as the blushing, sweating, or weeping that accompany many emotional states (e.g. Levenson 2003). Thus de Melo and Gratch (2009) concentrated on the integration of blushing, sweating, and wrinkles into the facial animations. The tearing and sweating animation relies on the modelling of water's properties and dynamics. The wrinkles' changes are synchronized with the muscular-based model of the face. An evaluation study shows that wrinkles and blushing add to the expressivity of anger, sweating to the expressivity of fear expressions, wrinkles to the surprised expression, wrinkles and tears to the sadness expression, and blushing to the shame expression when coupled with the appropriate facial muscle expression (de Melo and Gratch 2009).

Multidimensional models based on perceptive studies

Several models of emotional behaviour are placed in the PAD model which is a three-dimensional model defining emotions in terms of pleasure (P), arousal (A), and dominance (D) (Mehrabian and Russell 1974).

Among others, Zhang and colleagues proposed an approach for the synthesis of facial expressions from PAD values (Zhang *et al.* 2007). It allows for the generation of facial expressions of any emotional state that is described in terms of the three PAD variables. First, the authors proposed a new parametrization of facial expressions, namely, partial expression parameters (PEPs). Similarly to MPEG-4, each PEP defines a facial movement in a specific area of the face. The main advantage is that it covers MPEG-4 space with a similar amount of detail, while it relies on a more restricted number of parameters. A perceptive study evaluated how their set of PEPs is linked to participants' attributions of P, A and D values. The validity of the expressions generated from PAD values was confirmed in an evaluation study, where participants had to attribute the PAD and emotional labels to the perceived animations (Zhang *et al.* 2007).

The same dimensional model was also used in a study where participants navigated in a PAD space with corresponding facial animations using a three-dimensional control device (Courgeon *et al.* 2008). Eight expressions (fear, admiration, anger, joy, reproach, relief, distress, satisfaction) were attributed to the extreme points of the three dimensions (valence, activation, and dominance) while an interpolation of FAPS (facial animation parameters of the norm MPEG-4) values allowed for the generation of intermediate expressions. The movement in space was recorded through three-dimensional joystick movements, which included its vertical rotation (Courgeon *et al.* 2008).

Another facial expression model was based on the Russell and Mehrabian three-dimensional model which relies on reverse engineering (Boukricha *et al.* 2009). An empirical study enabled the authors to map a correspondence between randomly generated facial expressions composed of several action units as defined with FACS (Ekman *et al.* 2002) and ratings in term of PAD values. These PAD ratings resulted from naive participants' evaluation of bipolar adjectives using a Likert scale (Semantic Differential Measures of Emotional State or Characteristic (Trait) Emotions, as proposed in Mehrabian and Russell 1974). The evaluated expressions were placed in the dimensional space, where dominance takes one of two discrete values (high or low dominance) while pleasure and activation values are mapped into a continuous space. A facial expression's control space is thus constructed with multivariate regressions, which enabled the authors to associate a facial expression to each point in the space.

A similar method was applied previously by Grammer and Oberzaucher (2006), whose work relies only on the two dimensions of pleasure and arousal. The authors also performed a perceptive study to place randomly generated facial expressions in the dimensional space and apply to the results a multiple multivariate regression, enabling the mapping between AUs and the two dimensions. Moreover, the authors validated this model by checking the position of the six basic emotions in their two-dimensional space. In their approach they partially tried to integrate different theories of facial expressions of emotions. It can be used for the creation of facial expressions relying on the action units defined in the FACS (Ekman *et al.* 2002) and situated in the dimensional space.

Sequenced expression models of emotions

While the previously described models deal with static facial expressions (i.e. expressions described at their apex), few models have been proposed for creating dynamic expressions. Some use the discrete approach but offer means to act on the temporal course of the expressions (Ruttkay 2001; Stoiber *et al.* 2009). Others are based on the appraisal approach (Paleari and Lisetti 2006; Malatesta *et al.* 2009). Some works consider the expressions of emotions as the result of temporal sequences of facial actions. They do not explicitly link these sequences to any appraisal checks.

Ruttkay (2001) proposed a system that allows the human designer to modify a facial expression animation defined by default by a trapezoidal attack–hold–delay. The system permits one, for any single facial parameter, to define manually the course of the animation. The plausibility of the final animation is assured by a set of constraints. The constraints are defined on the key-points of the animation and concern facial animation parameters. One can, for example, force the facial expressions to be symmetric (i.e. all facial parameters have identical values for each key-point). Stoiber and colleagues (2009) propose another interface for the generation of facial expression of a virtual character. Using its two-dimensional custom control space the user might deform both the geometry and the texture of a facial model. The approach is based on the principal component analysis of the images database showing a variety of facial expressions of one subject. It allows the generation of realistic still images as fluent sequences of expressions but deprived of any psychological grounding.

Other researchers were inspired by the component process model (CPM; see Chapter 2.1 for more information on this theory). Paleari and Lisetti (2006) and Malatesta *et al.* (2009) use manually defined sequential expressions inspired by the CPM (Scherer and Ellgring 2007*b*). They consider a limited number of emotions and put the emphasis on the temporal relations between the different dynamic elements of an expression. The authors are also interested in the manner in which the elements are linked to the consecutive stages of cognitive evaluations predicted by the CPM. In Paleari and Lisetti's work (2006), the different facial action parameters are activated at different moments and the expression evolves through time. The final result is an animation consisting of a sequence of several facial movements expressing cognitive evaluations. In the work realized by Malatesta and colleagues (2009), the expressions of anger, disgust, fear, joy, and sadness were generated manually according to Scherer's predictions and the focus was on the intensities and on the temporal constraints of facial signals. This work differs from Paleari and Lisetti's work (2006) where each expression is derived from the addition of a new AU to the former ones. What is more, Malatesta and colleagues compared the additive approach with the sequential one. Results show a recognition rate well above chance level in the case of the additive approach, whereas the sequential approach gives recognition results only marginally above random choice (Malatesta and colleagues 2009).

Several studies show that emotional expressions are composed of signals arranged in a specific sequence (Scherer and Ellgring 2007b; Shiota *et al.* 2003; Keltner 1995; Harrigan and O'Connell 1996). Keltner, for example, showed that it is the temporal unfolding of the non-verbal behaviours that enables one to differentiate the expressions of embarrassment and amusement, which in some studies (e.g. Edelman and Hampson, 1981) tend to be confused by judges as they have a similar set of signals involving smiling and numerous sideways gazes and head shifts (Keltner 1995).

In behaviour animations in ECAs, Pan and colleagues (2007) proposed an approach to display emotions that cannot be expressed by static facial expressions but that are expressed by certain sequences of signals (facial expressions and head movements). First of all, certain sequences of signals were extracted from a video-corpus. From this real data, Pan *et al.* built a directed graph (called a motion graph) in which the arcs are the observed sequences of signals and the nodes are possible transitions between them. Different paths in the graph correspond to different expressions of emotions. Thus, new animations can be generated by reordering the observed displays. Niewiadomski and colleagues have also proposed a system that allows an ECA to display multimodal expressions that respect sequentiality constraints defined in an algorithm. Their system enables the generation of expressions of any duration, while respecting the duration of individual signals composing it and their order of occurrence (Niewiadomski *et al.* 2009b; see Chapter 5.5, this volume).

Multimodal expression models of emotions

An emotion being a *dynamic episode* that produces a sequence of response patterns on the level of gestures, voice, and face (Scherer and Ellgring 2007b), it is interesting to introduce more than one modality of emotional expression into agent animations—especially since not only do body movements tend to influence the interpretation of the facial expression (Meeren *et al.* 2005) but also some of them seem to be specific to particular emotional states (e.g. Wallbott 1998; Pollick *et al.* 2001).

Very few multimodal behaviour models have been created so far. Clavel and colleagues (2009) studied the input of facial and posture in ECAs' emotional expressions. One study showed that the integration of the facial and postural changes into the ECAs' emotional behaviour affects users' overall perception of basic emotions, and has an impact on the attribution of the valence and activation values to the animations. The participants attributed the intended valence to the animations, whether these presented the face only, the posture only, or the face and posture conditions, but not the intended activation. The activation was correctly attributed in the posture only condition, in the majority of the face and posture animations, but not in the face only condition. A second study shows an improvement of the emotion recognition when facial and postural changes are congruent. The authors observed that the judgements were mainly based on the information sent by the face, although adding congruent postures improves the interpretation of the facial expression (Clavel *et al.* 2009).

Michael Kipp proposed a system that automatically generates non-verbal behaviours that are synchronized with the verbal content in four modalities using a set of predefined rules (Kipp 2006). These rules determine the triggering conditions of each behaviour as a function of the text. Thus a non-verbal behaviour can be triggered, for example, by a particular word, sequence of words, type of sentence (e.g. question), or when the agent starts a turn. The system also offers the possibility of discovering new rules. Similarly Hofer and Shimodaira (2007) proposed an approach to generate head movements based on speech. Their system uses hidden Markov models to generate a sequence of behaviours. Data to train the model were manually annotated with four classes of behaviours: postural shifts; shakes and nods; pauses; and movement.

Lance and Marsella (2007) also explored head and body movements occurring in emotional displays and more particularly during gaze shifts. They placed their work in the theoretical context of the PAD dimensional model. Lance and Marsella defined a set of parameters enabling the differentiation of the multimodal emotional displays from the neutral ones based on extractions from the recordings of acted emotional displays. The gaze, head, and body movements data were captured through three motion sensors. Animations that were generated based on the motion captures were evaluated by human coders in terms of arousal and dominance. A set of proposed parameters contains temporal scaling and spatial transformations. Consequently, emotionally neutral displays of gaze, head, and body movements can be transformed using this model into multimodal displays showing, for example, different levels of dominance and arousal.

Behaviour expressivity models

Given that the quality of behaviour execution can be specific to or at least influenced by emotional states (Wallbott and Scherer 1986), several agent systems allow one to alter or modulate the way in which non-verbal behaviours are executed (Nayak 2005; Kipp 2006; Allbeck and Badler 2003; Neff and Fiume 2005). An agent could produce a non-verbal signal with straight and quick arm/hand movements and another signal with smooth, curved, and slow movements. In some systems these movement characteristics are statically assigned to an agent. In other cases they depend on the agent's emotional state or personality. For example, an excited agent could perform quick and rapid movements while a depressed agent could perform slow and heavy ones.

Allbeck and her colleagues created a system to select the most appropriate non-verbal behaviours (gestures and facial expressions) and control the movement quality of the Jack agent (Badler *et al.* 1993) depending on its personality and emotional state (Allbeck and Badler 2003). The user can give commands to the agent to make it conduct some actions. The system analyses the user input and selects the most appropriate behaviours that have to be performed to accomplish the given task. The way in which the agent performs its movements is influenced by a set of high level parameters, embedded in the expressive motion engine (EMOTE). EMOTE is an implementation of the *effort* and *shape* movement components of the Laban movement analysis system (Laban and Lawrence 1947). The effort component defines how a movement is modified in terms of: its *space* (relation with the surrounding space: indirect versus direct); *weight* (impact of movement: light versus strong); *time* (urgency of movement: sustained versus sudden); and *flow* (control of movement: free versus bound). The shape component modifies the movement's coordination (how the mover's body parts change their relative position, e.g. a contracted posture is obtained by bending the shoulders and torso toward the legs), direction (how movements are performed in relation to the environment), and shaping (how movements relate to the horizontal, vertical, and sagittal planes: spreading versus enclosing; rising versus sinking; advancing versus retreating). The EMOTE parameters are applied to the agent's movements depending on the agent's personality and emotional state. Allbeck *et al.* use two parametric models of emotion and personality, in which emotional states and personality traits are expressed as predefined distributions of the EMOTE parameters.

Neff and Fiume (2004, 2005) implemented some key movement properties by reviewing arts and literature, such as theatre and dance. They found that the body and the movement characteristics, such as balance, body silhouette (contour of the body), position of torso and shoulder, influence the way in which people perceive others. They have implemented three motion properties into animated characters: the pose of the character; the timing of movements; and the transition from one pose to another. The shape is the character's body posture, which is expressed by some of its properties, like its tension, balance, and extent. A posture can be relaxed or tensed, depending, for example, on the character's emotional state. By modifying the position of the character's centre of gravity relative to its feet, posture must be varied to keep balance. The extent is the quantity of space used by the character. To perform a movement, the arms, for example, can be fully stretched away from the body or kept near to it. The timing is described as tempo and rhythm. The tempo is simply the speed with which we perform a movement. The rhythm corresponds to the movement pattern. The same rhythm can be performed with different tempos. The tempo is linked to the character's emotional states: for example, sadness is communicated through slow movements, while joy is associated with small and quick ones. Movements' transitions can happen smoothly by keeping the same constant speed, or be interrupted and accelerated/decelerated. These different styles can reveal different character's emotional states and attitudes. For example, interrupted movements can communicate hesitation and doubt, while accelerated movement can be used to give emphasis.

Conclusions

This chapter presents different models of emotional expressions for ECAs. As ECAs are interactive by definition, the social and affective behaviour is crucial for their communication, which should not be limited to the verbal canal.

In the non-verbal domain of ECAs, some researchers use simple interpolations between a limited number of facial expressions, such as the basic emotion expressions, to generate an unlimited number of new ones. Some authors reached beyond the linearity between expressions in their expression generation by partitioning the face and applying mostly fuzzy methods or by grounding the facial generation in a multidimensional model. Work has also been realized on the integration of sequencing in the presentation of expressive behaviour and of its multimodality. Several systems have also been developed to modify the behaviour expressivity characteristics, such as quality of movements or frequency of an expressive feedback of an agent.

Recapitulating, the overall tendency in the research on emotional expressions of ECAs is to enrich a set of multimodal emotional signals. Temporal aspects of behaviours that contribute to emotional expressions should be analysed both in the framework of theoretical advances in the affective sciences and from real data studies, whether from observational or experimental settings. Emotional displays are defined by a set of signals; however, these signals themselves have to be generated in synchrony across modalities, while respecting the constraints imposed by the sequence of appearance and by the modulation of their expressivity parameters in concordance with the specific states.

Chapter 5.2

Synthesis of emotional speech

Marc Schröder, Felix Burkhardt, and Sacha Krstulović

Summary

This chapter describes the state of the technology available for generating synthetic speech with emotions, and proposes a possible methodology for establishing a control structure for speech acoustics in terms of non-trivial models of affect.

We first review the history of speech synthesis, briefly characterizing the various generations of synthesis technologies, from formant synthesis through diphone concatenation and unit selection synthesis to recent statistical model based synthesis technologies. For the two major current technologies, unit selection and statistical synthesis, we describe approaches for generating expressive speech. We also comment on the potential of articulatory speech synthesis, which, despite the limited quality that can be reached with state of the art systems, is scientifically promising, since it makes explicit the relation between physiological changes and resulting acoustic effects.

In the second part, we discuss the problem of predicting voice parameters for a given affective state. Since current technological approaches are data-driven, it is necessary to first record a suitably variable speech corpus from a single speaker. This corpus must be annotated in terms of the affective states that are to be used as control parameters for the voice, and the speech acoustics must be appropriately described. Finally, the two layers must be related to one another, e.g. by machine learning algorithms, to allow for the prediction of speech acoustics based on the affective states.

Introduction

Speech generated by an affectively competent agent would ideally model emotions in a way that is motivated by models from emotion theory. Wherever the human voice expresses or reflects an affective state, the agent's voice should be able to do the same. More than just a small collection of distinct full blown emotion categories, such as anger, fear, happiness, sadness, etc., the agent's voice should be able to express the entire range of affective states, including aspects relevant for communication, such as interpersonal stance, attitude, and mood (Scherer 2003). Whenever humans infer such states from subtle changes in voice intonation, hesitation, voice quality, etc., a truly affectively competent agent should be able to express them. Furthermore, it should be possible to control the agent's voice directly in terms of the affective state that should be expressed, and the agent should have a way of generating appropriate voice features leading to the desired perception by the listeners.

The current state of the art in expressive speech synthesis is very far from this ideal situation. Existing work has mostly been determined by pragmatic considerations and technological limitations and shows only limited grounding in emotion theory. The research community is still concerned with proving that any expressive states can be reliably conveyed at all; it is only beginning to ask which states it would be most important to express in real-world applications.

This chapter is organized as follows. The next section, 'A brief history of speech synthesis', outlines the history and current state of different speech synthesis technologies in general. The application of these technologies to the expression of emotions is described in 'Approaches and technological challenges for expressive speech synthesis', and the technological challenges are pointed out. Abstracting from technological challenges, then, 'A methodological challenge: grounding generative models in emotion theory' outlines a methodology for addressing the problem of developing systematic control models for expressive synthesis, based on emotion theory, in order to link an intended affective state to the synthesis of suitable voice features.

A brief history of speech synthesis

In the early 1980s, the first challenge of automatic speech synthesis was intelligibility. Commercially available systems of those days (e.g. DECTalk in 1983) were based on simple source plus filter models derived from the electronic sciences and from the early techniques of the digital signal processing domain. The vocal tract resonances were modelled as a series of time-varying filters that would apply some formant shaping with a time-varying glottal source. The glottal source would be approximated by a series of pulses for the voiced part, with a fundamental frequency varying according to some prosodic contour, or a white noise in the unvoiced part. Some more elaborate glottal waveform models, such as the Liljencrants–Fant model (Fant *et al.* 1985), could also be used.

A formant synthesizer is driven by inputting explicitly the trajectory of the model parameters, which are roughly the three formants and their bandwidths, the fundamental frequency, and the voiced/unvoiced switch or other parameters of the glottal waveform model. The trajectories can be formed according to a set of linguistically relevant rules. Such systems are very flexible in the sense that they rely on a finite set of easily modifiable parameters that drive some simple mathematical functions or their on-chip equivalents. However, these systems are based entirely on rules and expert knowledge that achieve reasonable intelligibility but poor naturalness. Although attempts at modelling expressive speech (Cahn 1989; Abadjieva *et al.* 1993) were made, naturalness remained the biggest challenge. Nowadays, rule-based formant synthesis is still used in specialized speech synthesizers because of its superiority over data-based approaches with respect to footprint and flexibility. For example, ultrafast speech as needed by blind users can be generated by simply interpolating between the phoneme states in a shorter time duration.

Around 1986, the invention of a new signal processing technique called pitch synchronous overlap–add (PSOLA) marked the birth of diphone synthesis (Moulines and Charpentier 1990). This synthesis technique proceeds by concatenating small units of recorded speech taken from a minimal set that covers a given language. While PSOLA is used to modify pitch and durational features, voice quality is preserved by the natural waveform shaping of the recorded diphone units, thus achieving greater naturalness than rule-based formant synthesizers. In order to control voice quality, some experiments introduced multiple diphone databases from the same speaker (Schröder and Grice 2003). Although diphone synthesis still uses hand-crafted rules to modify the voice acoustics, such systems shifted the speech synthesis paradigm from entirely knowledge-based to some degree of being data-driven. From the 1990s on, diphone concatenation became the primary instrument for a large number of studies in emotional speech synthesis (e.g. Montero *et al.* 1999; Mozziconacci and Hermes 1997; Murray *et al.* 2000). In these works, the modelling of expressions was still rule-based.

The generalization of diphone synthesis to unit selection from large speech corpora, in 1995, achieved greater naturalness at the expense of flexibility (Black and Campbell 1995). Such systems proceed by chopping a large set of naturally spoken sentences into a database of smaller speech units (half-phones, phones, syllables, words, etc.) and indexing the units on the basis of the linguistic context in which they originally happened (type of sentence, position in the sentence, lexical accentuation of the word, etc.). For an incoming sentence, a series of units and their linguistic context are predicted from text. Then, a set of natural speech units that would match the predicted linguistic context as closely as possible is extracted from the database, and subsequently concatenated. Some modification of the prosody can be applied with PSOLA, but it tends to be kept to a minimum in most systems in order to avoid distorting the natural waveform. Unit-selection systems provide more natural synthetic speech, due to reducing as much as possible the degree of tweaking of the natural speech waveform, but the voice quality or the expressiveness of the speech they synthesize is rigidly tied to the contents of the speech unit database.

One of the newest speech synthesis technologies, statistical parametric synthesis (Yoshimura *et al.* 1999), aims at combining the naturalness and data-drivenness of unit selection with the flexibility of signal manipulation. In this technique, the examples contained in a speech database are summarized into a rich parametric model of the speech acoustics, after some semi-supervised training of the model. The model itself is based on a set of Gaussian mixture models, and can be transformed in a mathematically tractable way to reflect a range of voice qualities or a range of speaking styles. A speech parameter generation algorithm is used to re-generate speech from this abstract, parametric, and flexible model.

Approaches and technological challenges for expressive speech synthesis

The human ear is not easily cheated into perceiving a certain expression from synthetic speech. The following sections describe the approaches that were developed to induce such perceptions, based on the different technologies outlined above.

Approaches based on unit selection

The simplest method for generating emotional speech with state-of-the-art speech synthesis technology is also the most natural-sounding one. It is based on the property of the unit selection framework to retain the speaking style of the underlying speech recordings when selecting and re-sequencing speech snippets. Indeed, creating a 'happy' voice is as easy as recording a set of 'happy' utterances portrayed by an actor, and building a synthesis voice from it. In order to create a 'sad' voice, sad recordings are needed, etc. The approach was pioneered by Iida and Campbell (2003), who built a speaking device for amytrophic lateral sclerosis (ALS) patients. The quality of unit selection always depends on the availability of suitable units; therefore, it is possible to attain very high quality in limited domains, by recording domain-specific speech material. This general fact also applies to expressive speech: for example, Johnson *et al.* (2002) built a synthesizer for military shouted speech, Pitrelli *et al.* (2006) recorded voices for conveying 'good news' versus 'bad news', and Gebhard *et al.* (2008) created a poker player's voice for a computer game.

While this approach provides quick and high-quality solutions for individual application domains, it is severely limited by the fact that there is no control over the expressive tone—it is solely determined by the actor's portrayal during recordings. In order to change the expression, even slightly, it would be necessary to record a new voice database with the same speaker.

It is difficult to increase the degree of control over expressivity in the unit selection framework, because modifications of the speech signal tend to introduce substantial distortions. Nevertheless, there are attempts to introduce some control.

One approach is to select suitably expressive units from a voice database containing speech with several different expressions. In the simplest case, all units in the database are tagged with a symbolic label of expressivity, which is included in the selection process. Using a carefully designed speech database containing the annotation of emphasis on individual words, Strom *et al.* (2007) have successfully generated speech with emphasis on individual words. More flexibility is introduced by defining a 'cost matrix' (Fernandez and Ramabhadran 2007) that indicates the perceptual similarity of one expression to another one and thereby allows the system to select a unit from a 'similar' style if necessary.

Potentially more powerful and flexible is a method to select units based on their acoustic properties rather than symbolic annotations. If it were possible to describe the acoustic features that are most relevant for the perception of a certain expression, then these acoustic features could be used as selection criteria. Campbell and Marumoto (2000) used hand-crafted prosody rules as well as automatically trained hidden Markov models (HMMs) to select units for synthesizing happy, angry, and sad speech from a database containing recordings in all three expressive styles. Perception tests showed a partial success, with hand-crafted selection rules performing better than automatically trained ones. Fernandez and Ramabhadran (2007) modelled emphasized versus neutral speech by training an acoustic model of emphasis on a small annotated database, and selecting speech material from a larger, unannotated database using this acoustic model.

A very different approach to more flexible expressivity is to apply voice conversion technology to the speech signal resulting from unit selection. Voice conversion is used for making one speaker's voice sound like another speaker's voice. For example, it is possible to convert a person's voice into the voice of a celebrity, even in a language that the celebrity does not speak (Türk 2007). The more similar the two voices, the smaller the distortions will be that are introduced by the conversion. The technology can also be used with synthetic speech (Kain and Macon 1998). For every conversion between a source and a target speaker, speech data from source and target speaker are required for training a conversion function.

Rather than converting between different speakers, the same technology can also be used to convert between different speaking styles or expressions by the same speaker. Türk and Schröder (2008) have used recordings in neutral, cheerful, aggressive, and depressed speaking styles by the same speaker to train a range of different conversion functions and applied them either to natural neutral speech or to synthesized neutral speech. The converted speech was perceived as intended, but distortions were audible. While this method requires training data for every expressive target style, there are two potential advantages over the simplistic method described above. First, the amount of training data may be considerably smaller than a full synthesis database and, second, if voice conversion is combined with voice interpolation (Türk *et al.* 2005; Schröder 2007), it is possible to synthesize a continuum of intermediate expressions between the styles for which training material is available. It is interesting to note that one of the most successful speech modification techniques involves using Gaussian mixture models (GMM), which are a form of statistical model of the speech acoustics, to derive unit-dependent speech transformation functions (Baudoin and Stylianou 1996; Türk and Schröder 2008).

The challenge for the near future in this area is to improve both selection and conversion technology, and to make the unit selection approach more robust against missing data. In the very long term, however, model-based approaches, which are inherently more flexible, may supersede unit selection technology if their quality approaches that of unit selection. They are described in the following subsection.

Data-driven statistical models

Instead of addressing the explicit modelling of speech production, at one end of the spectrum, or using the speech acoustics as a rigid raw material to assemble new sentences, at the other end of it, data-driven statistical models provide a middle way that combines the flexibility of the parametric models with the 'automatically generated insight' brought by data-driven methods.

Of such data-driven statistical models, speech synthesis based on hidden Markov models (HMMs; Yoshimura *et al.* 1999) is currently the most successful. HMM-based synthesis primarily models the acoustical characteristics of speech. The speech acoustics are observed through a source plus filter model, which can be related to production characteristics via Mel-frequency cepstrum coefficients (MFCC), themselves related to vocal tract shaping, or via line spectrum pairs (LSP), related to the formants' positions. More interestingly, the MFCC or LSP parameters have the property that they define a mathematical vector space where linear distance measures, such as the Euclidean distance or the Mahalanobis distance, correspond to a perceptually meaningful acoustical contrast (Gray and Markel 1976). This means that any acoustical difference between some given speech classes, such as different speakers or different emotional or expressive speech modes, can in theory be modelled by linear translations and rotations across the MFCC or the LSP space.

HMM-based synthesis builds on this property by modelling clusters of speech units, usually phones or phones in context, as a set of multidimensional Gaussian probability density functions (pdfs). A set of such density functions defines a partition of the acoustic space, where each Gaussian cluster in the partition identifies a speech class in a soft way. For example, a speech unit corresponding to a series of MFCC coefficients can be observed in a zone where it has 60% chance of being an /a/ and 40% chance of being an /o/, /a/ and /o/ being each modelled by a Gaussian pdf. Such models are therefore very well suited to modelling the variability of speech. Furthermore, the parameters of the Gaussian probability density functions that underlie the HMMs can be trained in an unsupervised and data-driven way, with the help of large quantities of recorded speech data. After their training, the HMMs can be understood as an efficient summary of the training database: the multiple instances of the speech units contained in the database are described by a small set of parameters that are the means, the variances, and the weights of the Gaussian densities. With the help of an HMM-based speech parameter generation algorithm (Yoshimura *et al.* 1999), synthetic speech can thereafter be recovered from the model.

In this framework, and given the convenient linearization properties of the MFCC or LSP space, the model can be linearly deformed and adapted to account for different speech acoustic modes. Here, linearly means 'in a simple mathematical way'. For example, linear transforms can be applied through simple algebraic operations to shift a speaker-dependent model, trained on one speaker's acoustical observations, towards another speaker's zone in the acoustic space (Leggetter and Woodland 1995). Such model adaptation processes can work with very little data from the target speaker. The speech model can also be explicitly manipulated via multi-linear regression (Nose *et al.* 2007), which means that a finite number of knobs can be manually tuned to adjust the model characteristics across some informed axes such as gender or age.

In practice, the model complements the MFCC or LSP observations of speech, which capture mainly the timbre or voice quality of the speech sounds, with some observations related to the intonation (the fundamental frequency contour) and to the segmental durations (the phone durations) (Yoshimura *et al.* 1999). In addition, some linguistic knowledge is added via decision trees to model the acoustical contrast resulting from the various linguistic situations that arise in speech. For example, indications as to the position of a phone unit in a sentence can help in retrieving a phone model where the prosody is relevant to that specific place in the sentence (e.g. falling or rising prosody contour at sentence endings, or microprosody for phones in context). In text-to-speech synthesis systems, such linguistic factors can be thought of as an intermediate layer that makes the link between the input text and the resulting acoustics, via a selection process able to retrieve the units or Gaussians which are relevant to a particular linguistic context.

Just as linear transformation techniques can be used to transform an HMM-based speech model between various speaker-related classes, they can be used to adapt models across speaking style or emotional classes. For example, Yamagishi *et al.* (2003) have investigated the modelling of four speaking styles for the Japanese language (reading, rough, joyful, and sad) and for a single speaker, by introducing style-dependent questions in the tree-based context modelling process. In a follow-up of this work, Miyanaga *et al.* (2004) have proposed a method to control the speaking style explicitly. Their method is based on the adaptation of the HMM parameters through a multiple linear regression piloted by a style control vector. Alternatively, Tachibana *et al.* (2004) have successfully rendered a continuous range of speaking styles by applying some model interpolation techniques between the three speaker-dependent models of read, joyful, and sad Japanese speech. Such results do not seem to be limited to the Japanese language: in some preliminary experiments, Krstulović *et al.* (2007) have applied HMM-based synthesis to the modelling of football comments in German. These works illustrate the capacity of HMM-based synthesis to produce expressive or emotional synthetic speech in a flexible framework that combines the advantages of a parametric model with the analytic power of data-driven methods.

However, even if the flexibility of the model is now widely acknowledged, some challenges remain regarding the naturalness of the produced synthetic speech. The lack of naturalness of HMM-based synthesis is mainly due to the vocoding stage in the process, which corresponds to observing speech via its decomposition into MFCCs/LSPs plus intonation (fundamental frequency) and duration, and rebuilding it from the parametric model trained in this particular observation space. Indeed, such a decomposition of the speech waveform introduces signal distortions, as opposed to the more direct usage that unit selection makes of the untouched speech waveform. One of the weak points of the vocoding process specifically resides in the modelling of the vocal tract excitation. This topic has become one of the main focuses of research in the area of HMM-based speech synthesis, and solutions to this problem have only recently started to appear (e.g. Maia *et al.* 2007). Such recent works back up the hope that a solution to the naturalness problem should come from the area of speech coding in a near future.

Rule-based synthesis based on production models

In contrast to purely data-based statistical approaches, production models synthesize human speech by modelling aspects of the human production mechanism to a varying degree. These can be summarized by the term 'system modelling' approaches, in contrast to 'signal modelling' ones. Essentially, articulatory models interpolate between target positions of the articulators while kinetic limitations with respect to velocity and degree of freedom are taken into account; the speech signal is then generated based on aerodynamic acoustic models. With the simulation of emotional speech in mind, articulatory synthesis is very attractive because the relation between the influence of emotional arousal on muscles and tissue and the acoustic properties of the body parts that are involved in the speech production process can be directly modelled.

However, it must be noted that articulatory synthesis is still suffering from an insufficiency of data. The correlation between speech and articulator movements is not well researched due to the lack of efficient measurement methods. Also the connection between laryngeal and articulator positions and the sound wave is highly complex; existing tube models are only a rough simplification of the human vocal tract. Nevertheless, experiments with re-synthesis of natural speech and vowel–consonant–vowel logatoms show promising results (Birkholz *et al.* 2006) and clearly constrained phenomena like co-articulation can be studied in a controlled environment (Perrier *et al.* 2005). Furthermore, the database is improving due to advanced technology. For example, using new electromagnetic measurement methodologies, Lee *et al.* (2005) have recently investigated the influence of emotional arousal on articulatory movement.

Articulatory synthesis is a process based on three steps: at first a chain of phoneme descriptions must be transferred into an articulator movement specification that can then be used to retrieve parameters for a physical model describing the lung air flow, the glottal folds, and vocal tract configuration, from which the acoustic signal can then be calculated.

As an approximation of this process, so-called quasi- or pseudo-articulatory synthesis approaches have been proposed based on formant synthesis (Stevens 2002; Iles and Edmondson 1994). With these systems, formant synthesis is used to generate the speech signal from articulatory movement descriptions.

Articulatory models can be used to generate speaking style variations. This has been shown for fast speech by Iles and Edmondson (1994). To indicate exhausted speech, less air pressure, less muscle tension, and softer tissue features can be used by the articulatory models, just as, for increased arousal, stronger muscle tension and rigidity of the tissue might be set. To mimic imprecise or over-articulated speech, the articulatory precision and degree of co-articulation can directly be set in most articulatory models (e.g. Birkholz *et al.* 2006; Stevens 2002; Iles and Edmondson 1994).

It seems strange, therefore, that up to now no direct undertaking to investigate emotional speech with an articulatory synthesizer has been done. Nevertheless, in the long term, articulatory synthesis may become the instrument of choice for research on vocal effects of emotion if not for speech synthesis in general. Reasons are given (e.g. in Shadle and Damper 2001): the ideal speech synthesizer should be able to express certain speaker characteristics, speaking styles, and sound like a specific person. Such flexibility can only be obtained when the parameters of the underlying physical models can be modified.

Besides the articulatory movements, another important aspect of speech production models is the modelling of the glottal flow. Although for intelligible speech, a simple pulse train is sufficient to model the voice source, more complex models are needed to provide for source filter interaction as well as for speaking style variation. On the one hand, the glottal flow can be described using mechanical models such as the two-mass model (de Vries *et al.* 2002). Mechanical models are used, in particular, as parts of articulatory synthesizers. An alternative with more proximity to the speech signal is the Liljencrants–Fant (LF) model (Fant *et al.* 1985), a five-parameter model of the glottal flow.

Klatt and Klatt (1990) introduced their revised KLSYN88 parallel formant synthesizer with a specific glottis model based on the LF model to increase the naturalness of the resulting speech. This synthesizer has been used in numerous studies to investigate voice source variation (e.g. by Gobl and Ni Chasaide 2003; Burkhardt and Sendlmeier 2000).

The connection to emotional speech models is given by the possibility for these models to generate distinct voice quality or phonation types, which play an important role in affect display. Laver (1980) characterized different phonation types and described modal, breathy, whispery, creaky, tense, and lax voices based on physical descriptions of different glottis constellations as well as assigning them to emotion-related states.

Gobl and Ni Chasaide (2003) investigated the relation between voice quality and a range of affective states: emotions, moods, and speaker attitudes. Using the KLSYN88 synthesizer, the authors simulated several phonation types by altering the glottis parameters and related the outcome to emotional impression by means of a perception experiment. It showed that there was not a one-to-one relation between phonation types and emotion-related states, but these qualities were considerably more effective in signalling milder affective states than the strong emotions and tended to be associated with a cluster of affective attributes.

Modelling the voice source is also important with respect to the data driven statistical models mentioned in the previous section as it can be used for speaking style variation. It is a problem though to generate the source signal independently from the filter configuration. The unnatural 'buzziness' inherent in current parametric techniques may in part be due to insufficient models concerning source filter interaction.

In conclusion, the holy grail of speech synthesis—to create a system unlimited by text, language, speaker characteristics, or speaking style—can clearly not be reached by approaches that totally ignore the underlying physical mechanisms. In the long run synthesis based on physical modelling will become more attractive.

A methodological challenge: grounding generative models in emotion theory

Even if the technologies described in the previous section could provide perfectly malleable high-quality synthesis, there would still be a gap towards forming the voice of an affectively competent agent. The missing link is a control structure, providing a relationship between a representation of the agent's affective state and the expressive voice parameters.

If the affective state is conceptualized as a small set of discrete states, as is often the case in research on expressive speech synthesis, the link between the description of affect and its expression is trivial. However, as soon as more plausible models from emotion theory are introduced, possibly involving emotion alongside mood, interpersonal stance, attitude, etc. (Scherer 2003), the task of linking various layers of affect to observable expressions in a coherent, quantitative model becomes a real challenge.

A simplified approach was pursued by Schröder (2006). In a multispeaker database of natural-istic emotional speech, observers' ratings of the emotion dimensions, activation, evaluation, and power, were correlated with acoustic measures. Quantitative generative rules were derived, predicting for any given point in the three-dimensional emotion space the corresponding prosodic settings to be realized in synthetic speech. The appropriateness of the generated prosody was evaluated in a perception test, which showed that activation but not evaluation was conveyed as intended in the synthetic voice.

This approach has illustrated a method for linking emotional descriptions to a generative model of synthetic speech, but it has three shortcomings.

1 It uses speech from many speakers, resulting in large acoustic variations unrelated to the emotional state under study; as a consequence, analysis of this data allows only for the identification of rough trends, not for direct quantitative modelling.

2 The acoustic parameters investigated are the ones that can be measured but with limited consideration for the questions of which parameters can be controlled in synthesis and which are the most relevant perceptually.

3 The research uses a very general description of the emotional state, which does not consider any specific properties of vocal communication.

A more sophisticated approach to creating a generative model of emotional vocal expressiveness could address these shortcomings as outlined in the following section.

Speech material

The predominance of data-driven approaches to speech synthesis suggests that the most promising approach for creating a high-quality quantitative model of vocal expressiveness may be a data-driven approach as well. A data-driven model can only be as good as the data it starts from; therefore, the choice of speech material to use is the most crucial decision in the process.

An essential factor for speech synthesis modelling is that all speech must come from a single speaker, in order to avoid any interspeaker variation that would only introduce noise with respect to the emotional effects to be modelled. Ideally, the speech material should be usable also as a speech database for speech synthesis. Therefore, the audio quality of recordings must be high.

One option is to collect spontaneous speech from a speaker in a longitudinal study, as Campbell (2005) has done; as a result, the data contains the kinds of emotion-related phenomena that play a role in the speaker's life. Alternatively, speech could be recorded from an actor, ideally coached by a director to produce naturalistic examples of the intended types of emotional expressivity (Bänziger and Scherer 2007; Chapter 6.1, this volume); this approach would allow control over the exact types of affective phenomena to be represented in the speech corpus, and ensure the intended coverage. Between these two extreme points, a large range of compromises between naturalness and control exist, as exemplified in the HUMAINE database (Douglas-Cowie *et al.* 2007; see also Chapter 6.2, this volume).

Emotion description

A necessary condition for modelling emotions and related states in the speech material is appropriate annotation. For acted material, the classification of intended states exists from the recording plans, but perceptual verification is needed to ensure that the intended expression is indeed conveyed. For naturalistic material, an assessment is required in terms of listener ratings or expert labelling. A suitable descriptive scheme is required for this purpose.

Indeed, the choice of a descriptive framework is crucial for being able to model the emotion-related variation in the speech material. For example, it would be pointless to attempt using basic emotion categories for describing, for example, a conversational situation in which interpersonal stance towards an interlocutor is mixed with an attitude towards a topic. This may be obvious to emotion researchers, but it seems necessary to make this explicit in the context of research in a technological context such as expressive speech synthesis. The emotion markup language under development at the World Wide Web Consortium (Schröder *et al.* 2008) is being designed in order to make available, in the context of technological applications, a broad range of descriptions from emotion theory. Indeed, one of its aims is to provide a framework and support for annotating emotion-related states in data sets of various kinds.

In the specific context of speech modelling, we should also consider whether all aspects of an emotion description are equally relevant for vocal expression. For example, it seems that the dimension of activation is more easily conveyed through the voice than the evaluation dimension (Schröder 2006).

Acoustic modelling

Unless a speech re-sequencing approach such as unit selection is used, it will be necessary to generate the acoustic parameters that cause the perception of the intended affective state. To generate, it is necessary to describe the data in the first place, and the appropriate descriptions for the vocal correlates of emotions are by no means clear.

One option is to use brute-force methods, computing hundreds of parameters from the speech signal and letting machine learning techniques select the most informative ones (Schuller *et al.* 2006). However, it cannot be guaranteed that the perceptually salient properties of the speech are actually covered in these predefined sets. A different approach is to use expert investigation to identify the kinds of vocal properties that are perceptually relevant (Douglas-Cowie *et al.* 2003*a*). These appear to include local effects that are not necessarily picked up by global, automatic descriptors or that may be treated as statistical noise. Both expert-driven and automatic approaches will need to verify with the speech synthesis technology used whether the parameters considered to be relevant can actually be controlled in the speech generation process.

A promising approach in this context is analysis-by-synthesis: a certain speech utterance from the database is described in terms of the parameters considered to be relevant, and synthesized from these parameters. If the synthesis result is perceptually equivalent to the original, then the parameters are appropriate; otherwise relevant information is lost in the process. Whereas analysis-by-synthesis can be used with any generative model, including statistical-parametric models, it seems particularly useful for production models such as articulatory synthesis or glottal flow models, for which there is no direct way to compute internal model parameters from observations. Where possible, internal configurations can be initially estimated using an inverse generation approach followed by iterative adaptation of model parameters (Revéret *et al.* 2000). An alternative is a brute-force approach, systematically trying out all configurations of the model and selecting the one that comes closest to the observation (Vincent *et al.* 2005).

Linking emotion and acoustics

Once suitable data is annotated in terms of emotions and in terms of relevant speech features, the final step is the creation of the actual generative model: a link from emotion-related descriptions to their acoustical correlates. A broad range of machine learning techniques can be used to establish this link. It remains to be seen whether linear or piecewise linear transforms are sufficient to describe the relation, or whether nonlinear methods such as support-vector machines or neural networks are better suited for the task. Whichever method is used, it will be important to ensure that for continuous predictor variables, such as emotion dimensions, the model will generalize in a stable way to unseen values of the predictor variables. A set of constraints, as inherent in production models, may be able to ensure this stability.

The resulting model predicts the speech features that correspond, for the given speaker, to a given emotion-related state. In combination with an adequate synthesis technology, as outlined in the section 'Approaches and technological challenges for expressive speech synthesis', this system will be able to generate speech that conveys an intended affective state.

Conclusion and outlook

This chapter has outlined the state of the technology at the basis of an affectively competent agent's voice. We have outlined the most relevant speech synthesis technologies and have described how they are used for generating expressive speech. In this description, it has become clear that the main concern of current research in expressive speech synthesis is how to overcome technological obstacles, such as a lack of flexibility in controlling expressiveness-related speech parameters, or the limited naturalness of some approaches.

We have also pointed out that, while technological progress is important, it is also necessary to know how to express the affective states relevant for an agent, which are likely to involve a complexity going beyond a small number of discrete states. We have outlined a method for creating an emotional control model for the voice, which would provide synthesis controllable in terms of the emotional properties that are considered most relevant for the voice.

Research in the area is likely to make some progress in the coming years. Real-world application concerns, e.g. from telephony applications or navigation systems, are pushing towards expressiveness in natural-sounding synthetic voices. At the same time, the area of affective computing is maturing, and is likely to provide descriptions of suitable affective states for a range of real-world human–computer interaction scenarios. The combination of both may pave the way for a sufficiently large-scale effort to create a control model for synthetic expressiveness, yielding a high-quality, controllable voice for an affectively competent agent.

Chapter 5.3

Automatic detection of emotion from vocal expression

Laurence Devillers, Laurence Vidrascu, and
Omar Layachi

Summary

This chapter provides an overview of the state of the art and best practice in the automatic
detection of emotion from vocal expression. We also discuss what needs to be done in this field to
improve emotion detection. The term 'speech emotion detection technology' is used to designate
the use of a system that can detect and identify the emotion of a speaker by extracting affect markers in the voice, focusing on both the non-verbal and verbal content of speech. In emotion detection studies, emotions are considered in the broad sense of emotion-related states, such as
emotions, moods, attitudes, and interpersonal stances.

We first briefly describe the emotional corpora generally used to train statistical models, highlighting the importance of using naturally occurring emotional data rather than acted data. Next,
we give an overview of non-verbal (acoustic or paralinguistic) and verbal (linguistic) features. We
describe the classifiers generally used in the scientific community, and discuss their effectiveness
and how they can be evaluated. Automatic detection of emotion by an affectively competent
agent should ideally be based on a model of the dynamic emotion process incorporating real-time
constraints. This approach is linked to Scherer's theory (see Chapter 2.1, this volume) in that it
tackles the dynamic and constantly changing nature of the expression of emotions. It stands in
sharp contrast to many of the current models of emotion that assume unambiguous responses to
fixed conditions based on a static model of emotion.

We then go on to consider the idea of using 'affective markers' as a hierarchical structure with
different time windows in which low-level markers, such as vocalizations (breathing, laughing),
which require only a short time, inform mid-level markers, such as emotion dimensions and
appraisals, which can need a longer time window, and which are used to recognize high-level
categories of emotion. Descriptions of emotions with affective markers offer a valuable alternative
to conventional emotion categories for detecting human affective expressions. We propose to try
to identify affective markers, such as valence and activation but also control and novelty, and
other supra-features such as pauses, laughter, etc. Our aim is to derive meaningful supra-segmental
(mainly prosodic) and segmental (spectral) events from affective speech in order to construct a
multistage and multi-time window emotion classifier, and to combine this more effectively with
linguistic content.

This chapter ends by pointing out some of the questions that remain to be answered about
what needs to be done if we are to try to improve the automated detection of emotion. In order
to construct a hierarchical emotional classifier based on affective markers, more research is
necessary into extracting features such as vocal quality and rhythmic features. In addition, so far
most studies have focused on just a few basic emotions, but in future research will need to look at

more complex emotions occurring in real-world contexts. If we are to achieve real-time emotion detection, we have to be able to cope with realistic, i.e. vague and mixed, emotional user states/affects without any pre-segmentation. The other problems that remain to be tackled before we can hope to achieve emotion recognition from speech using real-life technology are the independence of the speakers and the robustness of noisy environments (recordings without a nearby microphone). To improve the detection of emotion-related states, we also need to build emotion detection benchmarks based on naturally occurring emotional data collected in real-world situations to evaluate the different technologies.

Introduction

A large body of work on emotion has been reported in the psychological literature, notably theories on perception and production models of emotion, such as the appraisal theory (Scherer 1999*a*, 2009*a*; Chapters 1.1 and 2.1, this volume). There have also been numerous studies in the field of neurobiology of how the human brain recognizes emotional states (e.g. Grandjean and Scherer 2006; Chapter 2.2, this volume). Within the broad area of cognitive science, the dominant paradigm used in computer science over the past decade has been information processing. This paradigm has been successfully applied to cognitive processes at different levels, such as basic vision, spoken language, and higher level thoughts—such as emotion. So far, the facial channel of emotional expression has received more attention than the vocal channel. This situation is changing, because there is now considerable interest in potential applications of emotional speech detection technology, e.g. for call centres, games, robotics, and data mining. There are also a growing number of research papers being published in the field of speech emotion detection (e.g. Batliner *et al.* 2000; Ang *et al.* 2002; Devillers *et al.* 2005; Steidl *et al.* 2005; Vogt and André 2005*a*; Lee and Narayanan 2005; Grimm *et al.* 2007; Ververidis and Kotropoulos 2006; Clavel *et al.* 2007; Vidrascu and Devillers 2007; Kim *et al.* 2007; Schuller *et al.* 2009*b*).

'Speech emotion detection' describes the use of a system that detects and identifies the emotion of a speaker by extracting affect markers in the voice, focusing on both the non-verbal and verbal content of speech. In emotion detection studies, emotions are considered in the broad sense of emotion-related states such as emotions, moods, attitudes, or interpersonal stances. Both the verbal and non-verbal content of speech encode emotion-related states. A set of parameters can be objectively measured via the non-verbal channel, because emotional states involve physiological reactions that modify voice production. Emotion detection is complex, because there are several sources of variability that complicate the search for invariant emotional cues in the voice, such as verbal content, differences between speakers, the expression of spontaneous and strategic emotion. Furthermore, the verbal and non-verbal contents often encode different emotions.

After an overview of the current state of technology, we will try to outline a method for creating a new hierarchical model suitable for real-time emotion detection systems. We introduce the concept of the affective markers as a new classification, including both vocal and emotional features, whose inclusion depends on their relevance and discriminating power regarding affective states. Descriptions of emotions with affective markers offer an important alternative to conventional emotion categories for describing human affective expression. We propose detecting affective markers such as valence and activation, but also control and novelty, and other supra-features such as pauses, laughter, etc. The aim is to derive meaningful supra-segmental (mainly prosodic) and segmental (spectral) events from affective speech, and to use them to construct a multistage and multi-time window emotion classifier and to combine this more effectively with linguistic content.

Commonly used approaches

Most of the existing studies of emotion in computer science have been conducted on induced or recalled data using a small set of archetypal emotions such as anger, joy, fear, sadness (based on a subset of the big-six 'basic' emotions described by Ekman 1999). Everyday emotions in real-world contexts are still rarely studied. There is a significant gap between the emotion-related states observed using artificial data (acted data or contrived data produced in laboratories), and those observed using naturally occurring emotions (Devillers *et al.* 2005; Batliner *et al.* 2000). In the artificial data, the context is 'removed' or 'manipulated', and so we see much simpler 'full-blown' affective states, which are quite remote from genuine emotional states. The emotional state of a person at any given time is a mixture of emotion, attitude, mood, and interpersonal stance, often in response to multi-trigger events (internal or external) occurring at different times. Thus, far from being simple entities like 'basic emotions', emotional state data collected in real-life contexts are a subtle blend of more complex and often seemingly contradictory factors that are very relevant to human communication and that are perceived without any conscious effort by any native speaker of the language being used or member of the same cultural group. Most of the systems intended to detect and identify the 'emotional state' are trained using acted data, which reflect prototypical expressions of emotional states. In contrast, spontaneous data collected in an ecological context are always annotated with external observations given by several labellers using task-dependent emotional states. Thus, the pattern annotated and learned is the subjective experiential component of the emotional reaction (or feeling), rather than the actual emotion of a person, which remains hidden. The feeling is characterized by the expression of controlled or uncontrolled external manifestations, which are due to internal states that are inaccessible to the perception of others. These internal states include the emotional states: emotions, attitudes (interpersonal or preferential), moods, etc. These internal states may be genuine, or may be simulated, as enacted by actors. The contributions of the different voice cues vary greatly, depending on the database used. Feature extraction is a crucial aspect of automated emotion recognition. So far, there has been no comparison of different types of features on a large common database collected in a real-life context. For example, linguistic cues are obviously irrelevant to acted data with fixed speech content but are very relevant for natural data. To summarize, studies using different corpora are difficult to compare, and reviews of the literature identify different sets of best voice cues characterizing specific emotions depending on the corpus used.

After switching from acted to naturally occurring emotion-related states or from fixed text to spontaneous speech, one of the challenges that remains is how to integrate emotion recognition into real-life technology. Systems for the automatic classification of emotional states are based on training methods, because they have the capacity to learn—given enough data— the properties of every class of emotions. Virtually all the existing systems for detecting feelings from vocal characteristics fail to take this constraint into account, and detection actually takes place *post-factum*. The goal of operating in real time implies limiting the length of vocal sequence chosen for analysis, and also knowing only the current sequence and the ones that have preceded it.

New approaches

Recently, databases have been produced that include people in various spontaneous emotional states in response to natural situations. We can hope that these databases will make it possible to develop more sophisticated systems for recognizing the relevant emotional states in such data. Automatic detection systems based on different types of machine-learning architecture, such as localized or distributed connectionist systems, may make it possible to achieve a deeper understanding of the perception of emotion by identifying relevant cues for emotion detection in spontaneously occurring emotional states.

Working in real time involves two main technological challenges: first improving the performances of *post-factum* detectors, which are far from being totally satisfactory for all classes of emotional expression, and, second, using the findings of recent studies of feelings and emotions to help to produce a theoretical model that can be successfully used as an emotion detection system. Automatic emotion detection by an affectively competent agent would ideally be based on a model of the dynamic emotional process with real-time constraints. This idea is linked to Scherer's theory (Chapter 2.1, this volume) in that it tackles the dynamic and constantly changing nature of the expression of emotions. It stands in contrast to many of the current engineering models of emotion that assume unambiguous responses to fixed conditions, and are based on a static model of emotion.

An emotion-related state is not only a very complex phenomenon, but also a very complex process. It is not limited to its static features, but extends to dynamic behaviour without which we cannot hope to understand, interpret, or model, let alone recognize the affective state of a human agent. The purposes now defined for emotional state recognition involve more than simply retrieving one emotional label as being the most characteristic of the vocal sequence or whatever relevant unit we may have chosen. This is why we believe it to be pertinent to introduce the concept of the 'affective marker' as a new classification, including both vocal and emotional features. Increasing the number of relevant markers for automatic affective state recognition will allow us to use a more modular and hierarchical structure. The purpose behind this choice is mainly to gain as much advantage as possible from the dynamic process and from appraisals linked to affective behaviour. It will also make it possible to use a more flexible recognition system that we could modify to suit the target performance level or the model used.

How should we define affective markers? We propose the following definition: variables that are relevant to the expression of affective or emotional behaviour. Some of them are prosodic or vocal features, which are commonly used as input features in emotion recognition, such as the trajectory of the fundamental frequency and mean energy, whereas some of the others are higher level vocal and verbal features, affect bursts such as laughter and sighs, and rhythmic features, such as rate of speech. There are also some other markers that are not directly related to verbal or vocal expression, but involve affective appraisal and dimensional variables, such as emotional dimensions or stimulus evaluation checks (SEC) and appraisals (Scherer 1986).

We propose to divide affective markers into three main classes according to the degree to which each marker discriminates between affective states:

- Low-level affective markers. These markers do indeed influence the appraisal of the affective state, although they do not discriminate sufficiently between different affective states; for instance, an increase in energy could indicate either laughter or crying. They can also be high-level prosodic and vocal features or low-level indicators. At a high vocal level we find jitters, rhythmic features, sighs, laughter, crying, onomatopoeia, and pauses. At a lower level: energy and frequency variations.

- Appraisal and dimensional affective markers. These provide either hierarchical (in terms of successive appraisals) or dimensional discrimination between affective states: this class of marker comprises SECs and appraisals (Scherer 2009*b*), as well as any affective dimension chosen.

- High-level affective markers. These are at the top of the 'food chain' and consist either of discrete emotions, such as happiness or fear, or of more behavioural and stance-related affective states, such as boredom or suspicion.

Multiplying the levels of affective markers, and therefore of inputs into the system, provides a way of designing a hierarchical overall structure. In a nutshell, each level of affective marker will provide a level of decision. The final affective state—which can be a complex of two or more states—will be the result of successive steps, each leading to a more accurate discrimination of the affective state. Discrimination occurs as a result of inputting relevant affective markers into the classifying system.

Challenges in detecting emotion from speech

To summarize, we can say that four main problems have to be solved if an affectively competent agent is to be able to recognize a speaker's affective state.

- The first concerns the choice of the appropriate database used to train the statistical models for the specific application (see Chapter 3.1, this volume). In the next section 'Naturalistic databases and dimensional descriptors of emotion', we focus on the use of dimensional and appraisal descriptors for the purp ose of detection, which we believe offers a way to construct a hierarchical detection system.

- The second problem is how to select the 'right' features for the various emotional-states that we would like to be able to discriminate. This involves both the choice of normalization techniques and the segmentation of emotional units (see the section 'Features used to characterize the different emotional-states' in this chapter).

- The third problem concerns the training phase. This involves the design of the system architecture and the generalization power of the models. We describe the challenge of trying to overcome the limitations of the current technology, and suggest new approaches based on dimension and appraisal models, such as the dynamic unfolding of vocal cues (see the section 'A posteriori and real-time emotion detection systems' in this chapter).

- Finally, the fourth problem is that of real-time detection and the evaluation of the system (see the 'Conclusion').

Naturalistic databases and dimensional descriptors of emotion

If machines are to be made sensitive to emotional information, we need more naturalistic corpora upon which to base research. The expression of affective information by computers will require them to be able to recognize the human affective context, as well as to consider goals and predict outcomes for each interaction. Affective corpora are therefore fundamental both to develop sound conceptual analyses, and to train these 'affective-oriented systems' at all levels.

One of the main challenges when using real-world speech is the categorization and annotation of emotions; this requires the definition of a pertinent and limited set of labels. Most of the previous studies of emotion have been conducted on induced or recalled data with archetypal emotions. A taxonomy commonly used for emotion databases classifies them as acted/non-acted, induced, and naturalistic databases (Douglas-Cowie et al. 2007; Ververidis and Kotropoulos 2006). Some have been produced using artificial controls and acted data (Dellaert et al. 1996), whereas others are naturalistic, such as children (11–12 years old) in a play situation in the AIBO database (Batliner et al. 2004). Everyday emotions in a real-world context (e.g. call centre data; Devillers et al. 2005) are still rarely studied, and most studies focus on a limited number of emotions and on broad classes. For spontaneous data in particular, various different strategies are adopted with regard to the expression of emotions: mixing cues associated with different levels of the acoustic and linguistic channels. Some of the problems arise from the dynamic and constantly changing expression of emotions. Dimensional and appraisal theory could provide a way of coping with these problems.

The dimensional theory was introduced at an early stage (Wundt 1913), but only developed from the late 1970s (Osgood *et al.* 1975; Russell 1997*b*). The communication of emotion is conceptualized using several dimensions such as valence, dominance, and activation. The emotions themselves are then defined using continuous abstract dimensions, rather than being named as discrete categories. The grid study (Fontaine *et al.* 2007) shows a highly consistent structure of four emotional dimensions in three Western languages and Mandarin Chinese: valence, control, activation, and unpredictability.

The emotional state is dynamically assessed by evaluating internal or external stimuli. The emotional response of the agent is classified according to 18 SEC variables, which are grouped to form five broad categories (Chapter 2.1, this volume).

- Novelty.
- Pleasantness: intrinsic and overall pleasantness. This class can be viewed as a subclass of the valence category described in dimensional theory.
- Implications: relationship to expectations; conduciveness to goals. Some of these variables, such as conduciveness to goals, are also linked to the valence dimension.
- Coping potential: the variables in this group are linked to the dominance dimension.
- Compatibility of the situation with external and internal standards; the variables in this group complete the valence dimension.

Scherer has proposed a series of predictions concerning the impact of various types of evaluations on the vocal expression. All the systems used to produce vocalizations (the respiratory system, and the systems responsible for phonation and articulation) are affected by the reactions of the subject. These reactions include changes in the respiratory rate, and in muscular tension or salivation (Scherer 1986). For example, in a novel situation (novelty SEC), the effect on the voice can be an interruption of phonation, silence, a sudden inhalation, an inhalation via the mouth (a fricative sound or gasp), with glottal occlusion (burst or gulp). It would be interesting to include these short vocal cues in a potential real-time detection system, but in fact they are quite difficult to detect in real applications due to ambient noise, inadequate signal capture, the subject's distance from the microphone, etc.

Even a partial correspondence between the two-dimensional theories makes it easier to provide a temporal model of emotions. The dimensional theory introduces a hierarchical organization, which facilitates the detection of emotion (Xiao *et al.* 2007; Grimm *et al.* 2006). The introduction of some appraisals within a dimensional structure would make it possible to introduce some variables based on short vocal sequences, which are more suitable for real-time detection.

Features used to characterize the different emotional states

The speech signal contains many linguistic and paralinguistic features indicating emotional states. Among the features mentioned in the literature as being relevant for characterizing the manifestations of speech emotions, the most widely employed are prosodic features. This is because the earliest studies of emotion detection were carried out using acted speech, where the linguistic content was controlled.

For the accurate detection of emotion in natural, real-world, and prosodic speech, the spectral and voice quality must also be taken into consideration, and not only the prosodic information. Since there is no consensus about the best features, and the choice of features seems to be data-dependent (Devillers *et al.* 2005; Juslin and Laukka 2003), the usual strategy is to use as many features as possible, even if many of them are redundant, and to optimize the choice of features by using attribute selection algorithms. Normalization is a critical step in the recognition of emotional expression. We want to eliminate the variability attributable to the speaker and the recording, while keeping the emotional discrimination.

Acoustic features

We usually distinguish between segmental and supra-segmental features. Segmental features consist mainly of short-term spectra and of features derived from them: Mel-frequency cepstrum coefficients (MFCCs), linear predictive coefficients (LPC), perceptual linear prediction (PLP), etc. Hitherto, these features have been used to recognize speech rather than emotion, but recent research has shown that they can also contain important information for the detection of emotion. Supra-segmental features model the classic prosodic types: pitch, intensity, duration, and also voice quality and long-term spectra. Prosodic features involve two steps: extracting the raw, basic prosodic features and then calculating structured features based on this data. These prosodic features are perceived as stress, accentuation, speech rhythm, and intonation, and are thus relevant to characterizing the speaker's emotional state. Emotional manifestations are not limited to prosodic variations, and the variations in terms of vocal effort also carry relevant information concerning the emotional state of the speaker.

The acoustic content of the emotional state is represented with various levels of temporality. Beyond the choice of relevant acoustic descriptors to characterize the emotional contents, an essential question remains: what time span do we have to envisage for these descriptors? The behaviour of every descriptor is indeed dependent on the time frame within which it is considered.

There are two main approaches: the first approach (e.g. as in Vidrascu and Devillers 2007) uses descriptors of a statistical type, proposing an overall model for all descriptors over various durations, such as the voiced segment, the phone, the syllable, the word, or the phrase. These features are computed every 10 ms. In order to model the change over time of each feature, derivates and statistics (min, max, range, mean, standard deviation, etc.) are often computed over longer intervals, corresponding, for example, to the voiced trajectory for pitch-related features.

The second approach is based on extracting the acoustic descriptors from every window of analysis (Inanoglu and Caneel 2005) or on combining a local and an overall model of the descriptors (Clavel *et al.* 2007). Modelling at the level of the window of analysis and the trajectory has the advantage of not making any assumption about the structure of the word, and does not require any knowledge about the linguistic content associated with the signal of the word. It is essential for a real-time emotion detection system.

Prosodic features

There are three main classes of prosodic features: pitch; intensity; and duration. *Pitch* (F0) and *intensity* contours are often extracted using Praat (Boersma 1993). Some of the features mentioned above vary not only with the emotional content, but also with other factors such as the speaker and the phonetic content. This is typically true of pitch-related features, and the first two formants, which are strongly dependent on the speaker and on the phonetic content, respectively (Clavel *et al.* 2007). However, normalization by speaker is not so simple. One solution would be to use two models—one for males and one for females—or to use clusters of speakers.

Gender detection has achieved a high level of accuracy. Differences between features in male and female speakers are a well-known problem, and it is now established that gender-dependent emotion recognizers perform better than gender-independent ones (Vogt and André 2005*a*).

The normalization by phonemes is also not usually performed, as it relies on the use of a speech recognition tool in order to be able to align the transcription and the speech signal.

Voice quality features

Voice quality is a complicated issue. The best known measures of voice quality are the *jitter* (pitch modulation), the *shimmer* (amplitude modulation), the *unvoiced rate* (corresponding to the proportion of unvoiced frames in a given segment), and the *harmonics to noise ratio* (HNR). The HNR allows us to characterize the contribution of noise to speech during the vocal effort. The perceived noise is due to irregular oscillations of the vocal cords and to additive noise. The algorithm relies on the degree of substitution of harmonics by noise. Some other features, such as the normalized amplitude quotient (Campbell and Mokhtari 2003), which is based on inverse filtering methods that require a microphone located quite close to the speakers' mouth, cannot easily be used for a real-life detection system with less-than-perfect signal capture.

Spectral features

Voice quality is also characterized by spectral features such as *the first two formants and their bandwidths* computed by an LPC (linear prediction coding) analysis. Perception-based spectral and cepstral features, such as *standard Mel frequency cepstral coefficients* (MFCC), classically used in automatic speech recognition (ASR) and more recently used for emotion detection (Shafran *et al.* 2003), *Bark band energy*, and the *spectral centroid* (Ehrette *et al.* 2003), are also considered.

Affect bursts

Affect bursts are defined as short, emotional, non-speech expressions that interrupt speech. (Schröder 2000) shows that affect bursts, presented without their context, can convey a clearly-identifiable emotional meaning. (Vidrascu and Devillers 2007) have also shown that affect bursts such as *inspiration*, *expiration*, *mouth noise laughter*, *crying*, and the number of *truncated words* and *unintelligible voice* noted during a transcription phase can be meaningful for detecting emotion. If we are to be able to add features such as affect bursts to a real-time detection system they must be detected automatically. For example, the success rate of the automatic detection of affect burst laughter is 85% (Devillers and Vidrascu 2007*b*).

Disfluencies

Disfluencies are also interruptions of speech. In (Devillers *et al.* 2004), assuming that negative emotions allow the production of unexpected speech breaks to occur more frequently than neutral behaviour, we calculated the mean of the maximum duration of silences, a measure illustrating the number of silent pauses per utterance, and the emotion class. We also considered the autonomous main French filler pause 'euh' (which is used similarly to 'emm' in English). It occurs as an independent item, and has to be differentiated from vocalic lengthening. In this study, we correlate filler pauses and silent pauses with negative emotions.

Linguistic features

Two methods seem to be used most frequently for dealing with linguistic features: N-Grams (a class-based method; e.g. Ang *et al.* 2002; Lee *et al.* 2002; Devillers *et al.* 2003) and Bag-of-Words (vector space modelling; Schuller *et al.* 2005). As an example, the lexical model used for detecting emotion in (Devillers *et al.* 2003) is a unigram model based on manual transcription, where the similarity between an utterance and an emotion is the normalized log likelihood ratio between a model of emotion and a general task-specific model (eqn 5.3.1). The emotion of an unknown sentence is determined by the model yielding the highest score for the utterance, u, given the emotion model, E.

$$\log P(u/E) = \frac{1}{L_u} \sum_{w \in u} tf(w,u) \log \frac{\lambda P(w/E) + (1-\lambda)P(w)}{P(w)}$$

where $P(w/E)$ is the maximum likelihood estimate of the probability of word, w, given the emotion model, $P(w)$ is the general task-specific probability of w in the training corpus, $tf(w,u)$ are the term frequencies in the incoming utterance u, and L_u is the utterance length in words. Stemming procedures are commonly used in information retrieval tasks for normalizing words in order to increase the likelihood that the resulting terms will be relevant. The integration of linguistic information from the previous sequence (e.g. a few words earlier) is very useful for predicting emotion in a real-time emotional expression detection system.

A *posteriori* and real-time emotion detection systems

One of the crucial problems for all emotion recognition systems is how to select the most appropriate set of relevant features to use with the most efficient machine-learning algorithm. In recent research, a lot of different sets and classifiers have been used, but the best set of features and the most efficient model have yet to be identified and, from the results published, appear to be data-dependent. Virtually all the current systems for detecting emotional states from vocal characteristics fail to integrate the real-time constraint; the detection is carried out *a posteriori*.

Commonly used approaches

The classification of emotional states from the voice has already been the subject of several publications. First step is to choose the appropriate databases and the unit of analysis, e.g. a speaker turn or an 'emotional segment' (manually obtained). Then, a typical approach is to extract paralinguistic features for training a classifier. Different studies have already shown that the same feature vector can yield different performances using different algorithms. Furthermore, feature selection methods often result in higher reliability of the results. The complexity of the recognition task increases the higher the number of classes and the finest and closest these classes are. Finding relevant features of various types becomes essential in order to improve the detection performances.

- *Segmentation*. Segmentation is a determining factor in this issue: to remain consistent with the principles of appraisal theory, the voiced segments used for emotion recognition must be emotionally relevant. We therefore suggest using variable length segments, a segment being defined by the voiced sequence between two slight pauses. Since an emotion has a beginning, a corpus, and an end (according to Scherer's appraisal theory), a sliding window would make it possible to analyse the emotions more accurately across a sequence of segments, each segment corresponding in a way to an affective 'step'. The use of such a window also implicitly permits a feedback loop within the system by taking into account part of the preceding feature vector.

- *Selection of features*. The choice of the features analysed has an important effect not only on the reliability of the model's ability to learn and understand the phenomena involved, but also on the speed and the complexity of the calculations necessary for detection. This becomes of greater importance with the prospect of carrying out real-time tests. One of two approaches is usually used for data mining: selecting the most relevant attributes or applying linear transformations to reduce the volume of data. Feature selection and reduction methods, such as PFS (promising first selection), FS (forward selection), and PCA (principal composant analysis), have been shown to enhance performance (e.g. as shown in Lee *et al.* 2002; Petrushin 1999).

♦ Classification. The best known classifiers for emotion recognition are linear discriminant classifiers (LDC), k-nearest neighbour (k-NN), support vector machines (SVM), feedforward ANNs, also known as multi-layered perceptron, decision tree algorithms, random forests (RF). Dynamic classifiers, such as hidden Markov models (HMMs) or recurrent neural networks (RNNs) or Bayes networks, normalize the feature observed over time. The only dynamic classifiers to have been studied are the HMMs, but the results are not as good as expected. (A comparison of classifiers for detecting emotions from speech is reported in Shafran *et al.* 2003; Devillers *et al.* 2005; Seppi *et al.* 2008.)

♦ Evaluation. Current state of the art *a posteriori* detection based on realistic data yields a correct recognition rate of around 60–70% when used to classify four emotions, and 80–90% for two emotions. However, it is rather difficult to understand what these performance levels really mean and also to what extent performance is impaired in real-time emotion detection. In the next section we will describe new ideas about how to deal with real-time detection systems.

A case study: five emotion classes' detection in real-world call centre data

The case study reported makes use of a corpus of naturally occurring dialogues recorded in a real-world medical call centre. The dialogue corpus contains real agent–client recordings obtained from cooperation between a medical emergency call centre and the LIMSI-CNRS. The use of these data carefully respected ethical conventions and agreements ensuring the anonymity of the callers, the privacy of personal information, and the non-diffusion of the corpus and annotations.

This study focuses on five emotion classes: anger; fear; sadness; relief; and neutral (Vidrascu and Devillers 2007). Anger includes hot and cold anger and different levels of intensity. Fear is the bigger class with, in this experiment, fear, anxiety, stress, and panic segments. Relief is more confined in the corpus with strong lexical markers that are very specific to this emotion ('thanks', 'I agree'). The experiments were made on a subcorpus containing segments (manually obtained) from coarse classes with no emotion mixtures. There are more than 450 speakers in the training set and about 200 different speakers in the test set. Even if in our annotation scheme the same emotion label (e.g. fear or anger) can be assigned to a caller and an agent, the emotions are clearly not the same. Callers' anger and fear are linked to the urgency of the calls while, for the agents, anger and fear are much more linked to the stress of their work and to fatigue (a large part of the calls are also during the night).

Our usual strategy was to use as many features as possible (219 features: MFCCs; prosodic; spectral; disfluency; and non-verbal events cues), even if many of the features are redundant, and to optimize the choice of features with attribute selection algorithms. The same train and test sets have been used for these experiments. An SVM Gaussian classifier was therefore used for all experiments with the software Weka (Witten *et al.* 1999). Because SVMs are two-class classification, the multiclass classification is solved using pairwise classification. Detection results are given using the CL score (class-wise averaged recognition rate, i.e. average of the diagonal of the matrix).

It would be difficult using the raw data to rcompare our detection rates to those from other studies. For example, in Vogt and André (2005*b*), 77% of good detection was obtained on acted speech with 7 classes, 28% with 7 classes with WOZ data, and 39% with 5 classes on the same data. Indeed, very different scores might be obtained depending on the realism of the data, the classes one is interested in, and the certitude with which a label is given. However, we can compare different sets of parameters, especially by keeping the same test and train sets for all experiments. To ensure that the scores obtained on our test set can be reflective of our data and to compare different scores, we need a confidence interval. In order to find one, 80% of all instances of our subcorpus are randomly selected (in such a way as to create the same class distribution as the initial set) to train a SVM model and the 20% left are used as test. This is repeated 250 times so as to obtain a mean and a standard deviation of the CL. The interval [mean-standard deviation, mean + standard deviation] is used as a confidence interval. With only acoustic features (107 features) and without any knowledge about the speech transcription, we obtained a detection rate of 45% for the five emotions of the caller. By adding knowledge derived from the orthographic transcription (disfluences, affect bursts, phonemic alignment) and after the selection of the best 25 features, we achieved 56% of good detection.

New approaches for real-time emotion detection systems

The first study to report the investigation of a real-time emotion detection system was that of (Kim *et al.* 2007). They distinguished between two classes: anger and the neutral state. The system uses two classes of indications—segmental and intrasegmental—which are prosodic and spectral, respectively. Two classification systems are used in parallel and are combined at the end of the process: the first is a classifier GMM (Gaussian mixture model) of MFCCs and the second uses k-NN (k nearest neighbours), which is used for prosodic features. The real-time constraint appears at the level of the choice of the duration of the vocal sequences: from 1 s to 5 s. The results obtained are mixed; high rates of correct detection were only obtained for the sequences lasting 5 s, which severely limits the possibility of operating in real time.

Recognition systems must be able to provide output information about the affective behaviour of an agent, consisting not only of affective labels, but also of the emotional markers linked to appraisals such as novelty, pleasantness, relevance to the goal, etc., whether on the basis of major prosodic variations such as marked increases in energy or pitch, or higher level affect bursts, such as laughter or sighs. The aim is to derive meaningful supra-segmental (mainly prosodic) and segmental (spectral) events from affective speech in order to construct a multistage emotional classifier. We suggest that these emotional markers could be used as expert information for a classifier. This could be done in several ways, for instance, by inferring rules within a fuzzy classifier, thus improving the system introduced by Narayanan (Lee and Narayanan 2003). Or using a hierarchical tree as a model involving several classifying nodes, allowing the step-by-step construction of an emotional image of the agent's state, each classifier providing new information by discriminating between two or more classes of supra-features and appraisals.

The affective markers we propose in this chapter are linked to Scherer's appraisals, and also to emotional dimension theory. We have already used these appraisal dimensions in investigating emotion perception in order to describe the complex blended emotional behaviour of video-taped subjects (Devillers *et al.* 2006). This study also highlighted some of the difficulties involved in the manual labelling of appraisal dimensions. Several dimensions can be annotated reliably, such as conduciveness to goals, pleasantness, relation to expectations, and controllability of the consequences of events. The overall scheme will consist of several major classifiers. The output from each consists of a value or a label for one of the emotional markers linked to existing theories such as valence, novelty, control, and activation, not forgetting other supra-features such as pauses, laughter, and rhythm. The overall structural design will include several successive stages. In a nutshell, we will first process a vocal features vector to obtain various low level affective markers. These markers will be then added to the features vector, and transferred as an output to a staged classifier, which then will carry out successive discriminations of relevant components of the feature vector. The final decision will be made following a decision tree structure; each node will contain an appraisal or dimensional affective marker classifier, and will decide the value for each of the subsequent decision branches. This value can be either Boolean or numerical, depending on whether we want to obtain a single class or wish to model more complex affective behaviour by recognizing mixed affective states.

As an example, we can choose the appraisal and dimensional affective markers—valence, novelty, control, and activation—to discriminate between the following high level affective markers—anger, sadness, satisfaction, fear, and joy. Rhythm, pitch variation, intensity variation, and pauses are low level affective markers that could be used as the input. In the overall decision tree structure adopted (it is an *ad hoc* assumption), valence can be assessed and a value assigned to each of its positive and negative outcomes. Activation can be used to discriminate between the two positive valence states or high level affective markers: joy and satisfaction. Novelty can be used to discriminate between sadness on the one hand, and anger and fear on the other, control being used to discriminate between the last two high level affective markers.

Through a decision process we assign values to each branch. These values (either Boolean or numerical) are then pooled to give an overall score for each high level affective marker. This yields confidence values for each of the affective states, as well as values for the lower level affective markers if these are needed for subsequent processing or applications. This is a decision frame in which any classifier can be used, and which can be modified in order to include or exclude different affective markers from different levels, according to the interpretations and explanations of 'affective theories'.

In this framework, temporality and time variability can be provided by a loop execution: this is enhanced by our definition of affective markers of any level as potential inputs. This means that the output from one time sequence can be used as the input for the next one. The design of each module of the multistage emotion detection system will depend on the desired output, and on the segmental feature sets used. Any models, such as support vector regression (SVR) and fuzzy rules (FR), can be used to infer affective markers.

Conclusion

We have described the current state of emotion detection technology and outlined a method for creating a new hierarchical model for a real-time emotion detection system. Descriptions of emotions, i.e. 'affective markers', are an important alternative to the conventional emotional categories for describing a person's affective expressions. We propose detecting affective markers such as valence and activation, but also control, novelty, and other supra-features such as pauses, laughter, etc. The aim is to derive meaningful supra-segmental (mainly prosodic) and segmental (spectral) events from affective speech in order to construct a multistage emotional classifier.

We conclude by considering the prospects for future research, and the questions that remain to be answered about trying to use emotion theory to overcome the limitations of the current technology. First, *what* exactly should we be trying to detect (emotion, mood, etc.)? At present, this question is often ignored or oversimplified. Second, databases and annotation both have essential contributions to make in constructing and testing systems. Previous studies have highlighted some of the difficulties involved in the manual labelling of appraisals (and also of dimensions). Annotation validation is clearly very important if we are to ensure the quality of a database. The way to evaluate different systems is to test them against the same standard databases. The CEICES ('combining efforts for improving automatic classification of emotional user states'; Batliner *et al.* 2006), a forced cooperation initiative, was the first attempt to do this followed by 'the first emotion challenge in Interspeech 2009' (Schuller *et al.* 2009*b*). Both attempts used the AIBO database developed by Batliner (Batliner *et al.* 2004) with a realistic emotional corpus obtained in a context of a play between of children of 10–12 years old, and using Wizard-of-OZ (WoZ) to drive the AIBO robot. This will provide the benchmarks, without which it is really difficult to know how to assess the progress of research. Third, more complex normalization techniques, such as those used for speaker recognition (e.g. feature warping), could indeed improve the robustness of real-time detection of emotional expression. Finally, in order to construct a hierarchical emotional classifier based on affective markers, more research is necessary into how to extract vocal quality features: for example, we still do not know which features should be extracted for the control or novelty dimensions in real-life applications.

In addition, most studies have focused on just a few 'basic emotions'. Future pertinent work must concern more complex emotions occurring in a real-world context. Real-time emotion detection implies the ability to cope with realistic, i.e. vague and mixed, emotional user states/affects without any pre-segmentation. The other problems that remain to be tackled before we can hope to achieve emotion recognition from speech using real-life technology are the independence of the speakers and the robustness of the system in noisy environments (recordings without a nearby microphone). To improve performance in the detection of emotion, we also need to devise emotion-detection benchmarks for emotional data collected in real-world contexts in order to evaluate the different technologies.

Body gesture and facial expression analysis for automatic affect recognition

Ginevra Castellano, George Caridakis, Antonio Camurri, Kostas Karpouzis, Gualtiero Volpe, and Stefanos Kollias

Summary

Affect recognition plays an important role in everyday life. This explains why researchers in the human–computer and human–robot interaction community have increasingly been addressing the issue of endowing machines with affect sensitivity. Affect sensitivity refers to the ability to analyse verbal and non-verbal behavioural cues displayed by the user in order to infer the underlying communicated affect.

This chapter describes affect sensitivity as an important requirement for an affectively competent agent. An affectively competent agent should be able to exploit affect sensitivity abilities to successfully interact with human users. The perception and interpretation of affective states and expressions are important to enable such an agent to act more socially and engage with users in a truly natural interaction.

In this chapter, affective facial and bodily expressions are addressed as channels for the communication of affect that must be taken into account in the design of an affect recognition system. A survey of state of the art computational approaches for affect recognition, based on the automatic analysis of facial and bodily expressions and their combined information, is presented. Relevant contributions in the field are reviewed and affect sensitivity is discussed with respect to key issues that arise in the design of an automatic system for affect recognition. This chapter draws particular attention to a number of challenges in face and body affect recognition research that have to be addressed in a more comprehensive manner in order to successfully design an affectively competent agent. First of all, an affectively competent agent should be capable of perceiving naturalistic expressions conveying states different from prototypical emotions. Second, such an agent should be able to analyse multiple modalities of expressions: new fusion methods that take into consideration the relationships and synchronization of different modalities are required. Another important issue is the dynamic account of affect and affect-related expressions: automatic analysis of temporal dynamics is required for an affective competent agent to be able to monitor the evolution of the affective states displayed by the user over time. Robustness in the real-world environment is an issue not to be neglected as, to date, many automatic systems for the analysis of affective facial and bodily expressions only work well in controlled environments. Finally, context sensitivity is currently an underexplored topic that has to be taken into consideration in the design of an affectively competent agent, as the detection of the most subtle affective states can be achieved only through a comprehensive analysis of their causes and effects.

The main contribution of this chapter is a review of studies on affect recognition from face and body and the role played by a subset of these in addressing the challenges described above. The above issues should be more extensively investigated by the affect recognition community in order to successfully carry out the design of an affectively competent agent.

Introduction

The ability to communicate with humans intelligently and in a sensitive manner is an important requirement for an affectively competent agent. Research in the area of human–computer and human–robot interaction has increasingly been addressing the problem of modelling intelligent agents by exploiting communication channels that are typical of humans. Affect plays a key role in human–human communication: recognition and expression of affective states are vital for people to understand and be understood, to ensure that the communication has succeeded. This explains why there is an increasing interest in the development of paradigms of interaction endowing artificial agents with affect sensitivity (Picard 1997; Zeng *et al.* 2009).

Affect sensitivity refers to the ability to analyse verbal and non-verbal social affective cues displayed by humans in order to infer their affective states. These range from prototypical emotions (e.g. basic emotions such as joy, anger, sadness, etc.) to more complex affective and mental states such as interest, boredom, frustration, engagement, etc. An affectively competent agent should be able to exploit affect sensitivity abilities to successfully establish an affective interaction with human users: the perception and interpretation of affective states and expressions is important in order for such an agent to be able to provide an appropriate response to the user's behaviour, i.e. to act more socially and engage in a truly natural interaction with users.

Given the key role of affect and emotion in our daily lives, technology for the design of affectively competent agents is attracting increasing interest. It is expected that many applications will benefit from the efforts made by the affect recognition community to build affect-sensitive machines. Applications cover a large range of domains, from security to therapy of people with disabilities, from entertainment to assistive technology.

Several examples of affect sensitive systems are reported in the human–computer and human–robot interaction literature. The affective wearable system by el Kaliouby and colleagues, for example, can help people affected by autism improve their social communication abilities and learn to express emotions (el Kaliouby *et al.* 2006; Madsen *et al.* 2008). Kapoor *et al.* (2007) designed a system for the detection of frustration in students using a learning companion based on automatic analysis of multimodal non-verbal cues including facial expressions, head movement, posture, skin conductance, and mouse pressure data. In the robotics domain, one of the most famous examples of an affect-sensitive robot is Kismet, which is endowed with an attention system based on low-level processing of perceptual stimuli (Breazeal *et al.* 2001; Breazeal 2003). There are several other examples of affectively competent agents. All of them require several types of abilities, but the understanding of the nature of human affect is a basic requirement for scientists to be able to design affect sensitive machines.

There is no doubt that the design of an affect recognition system should be addressed from a multidisciplinary perspective. The development of new technologies must be accompanied by critical studies of the psychological issues that arise from these developments. In this respect, the inclusion of affect representation into a framework for affect recognition is of primary importance. Incorporating models and paradigms developed by psychologists for the classification of affective states (Scherer 2000*a*; Chapter 1.1, this volume) is a pressing need and still a challenging issue.

According to the *Component Process Model* of emotion proposed by Scherer (1984; Chapter 2.1, this volume), a necessary condition for an emotional episode to occur is the synchronization of different processes, as a consequence of a situation/event appraised as highly relevant for an individual's well-being. These processes include appraisal, physiological arousal, action tendency, subjective feeling, and motor expression.

People communicate emotions consciously or unconsciously and can use some channels of expression more than others. Some expressions can be directly perceived, such as facial expressions and voice intonation, while others, such as changes in physiological parameters, can be detected only by using specific sensors. Another channel of affective information is the body: people can express emotions through gestures, postures, and head and full-body movements. The human sensory system performs multimodal integration of all this information, allowing people to recognize emotions by exploiting different channels (Meeren *et al.* 2005; Stein and Meredith 1993). Similarly, an affectively competent agent should be endowed with the ability to analyse different types of affective expressions and fuse them together to infer emotions. At the same time, such an agent must be able to evaluate how different affective expressions influence each other, as well as the amount of information each of them provides about emotion.

This chapter focuses on facial and bodily expressions and their combined information as channels of affect expression. The ability for a system to recognize affective states requires successful association with their patterns of expression (Picard 1997). Nevertheless, a lot of work still has to be conducted in order to establish which affective expressions are the best indicators of an affective state. Several researchers, mainly from psychology, have investigated the relationship between emotion, facial expressions, and body gestures (e.g. Boone and Cunningham 1998; De Meijer 1989; Ekman 1994*b*; Ekman and Friesen 1975; Wallbott 1998). Face and body appear to be the most important channels for communicating behavioural information, including affective states (Ambady and Rosenthal 1992).

While research on affect recognition based on face and body gesture has been extensively addressed in the literature (Zeng *et al.* 2009), several challenges still have to be properly investigated.

- *Spontaneous and non-prototypical affective expressions and states.* Research on automatic affect recognition needs to move towards systems sensitive to spontaneous, non-prototypical affective expressions and states. The design of many existing affect recognition systems was based on databases of acted affective expressions displaying basic emotions (Zeng *et al.* 2009). Although acted affective expressions present several advantages that recordings in a controlled environment can provide (e.g. precise definition, many expressions recorded from the same individual, very high quality of recordings, etc.), they are often exaggerated and decontextualized (Bänziger and Scherer 2007) and mainly reflect stereotypes rather than genuine affective states.

- *Multimodal affective expressions.* Humans can rely on different channels of information to understand the affective messages communicated by others. Similarly, it is expected that an automatic affect recognition system should be able to analyse different types of affective expressions. In this respect, an important issue to be addressed is the fusion of different modalities of expression, which must be designed by taking into account the relationship and correlation across different modalities.

- *Dynamic account of affective expressions.* The dynamics of affective expressions is an important factor in the understanding of human behaviour. Affect and its expressions vary over time: analysis of static affective expressions cannot account for the dynamic changes in the behavioural responses characterizing an affective state and in the affective state itself.

- *Robustness to real world scenarios.* Real-world applications require affect recognition systems built upon face and body detectors and facial and body features tracking systems able to efficiently function in uncontrolled environments: this requires, for example, robustness to noisy backgrounds, occlusions, rigid head motions, etc.

◆ *Context sensitivity.* As suggested by the *Component Process Model* of emotion (Scherer 1984; Chapter 2.1, this volume), appraisal is as important as behavioural responses to characterize affect. This highlights the need for an automatic affect recognition system to take into account the conditions that elicited an emotional response. A context-sensitive affect recognition system must be sensitive to several types of contextual information, such as individual differences in expressing affect, the personality of the person expressing affect, preferences, goals, underlying mood, task, environment, etc.

This chapter presents an overview of computational models and techniques for the analysis of facial and bodily expressions and the automatic recognition of affective states that have been reported in the literature. Relevant contributions in the field are discussed and examples of studies addressing the challenges highlighted above are reported.

The chapter is organized as follows. The next two sections present an overview of affect recognition methods based on the analysis of facial and bodily expressions. Subsequently, a survey of studies and techniques for achieving a fusion of face and body information is provided. Different fusion strategies are discussed. The chapter ends with an overview of the limitations and challenges in the field of automatic affect recognition from face and body.

Affect recognition from the face

Most of the work on affect recognition reported in the literature focuses on the automatic analysis of facial expressions (Zeng *et al.* 2009).

Two main streams of research in affect recognition from the face can be identified: facial affect recognition and facial muscle action recognition (for an extensive survey see Pantic and Bartlett 2007; Zeng *et al.* 2009). While the first aims to map facial expressions directly onto affective categories, the second attempts to recognize facial signals. These two streams are associated with two major approaches for behaviour measurement adopted in psychology: message judgement, which tries to infer what is behind a displayed facial behaviour, and sign judgement, which merely provides an objective description of facial signals (Cohn 2006).

As far as the latter is concerned, the Facial Action Coding System (FACS) introduced by Ekman and colleagues (Ekman and Friesen 1978) allows for an objective and comprehensive description of facial expressions and is the most frequently used method to describe facial behaviour. FACS describes expressions in terms of action units (AUs), which relate to the contractions of specific facial muscles. Once AUs are detected, they can be mapped onto affective categories using high-level rules such as FACSAID (FACS Affect Interpretation Database; Ekman *et al.* 2002). An alternative method to model facial expressions is that based on MPEG-4 metrics (Tekalp and Ostermann 2000). MPEG-4, which mainly focuses on facial expression synthesis and animation, defines the facial animation parameters (FAPs), which are strongly related to the AUs.

Most of the systems for automatic analysis of facial expressions are based on two-dimensional spatio-temporal features. These include *geometric features*, such as the positions of salient facial points (e.g. mouth corners, etc.) or the shape of face components (e.g. eyes, mouth, etc.), and *appearance features*, which represent the texture of the facial skin. Systems based on methods using geometric features include, for example, those of Pantic and colleagues (e.g. Pantic and Patras 2006; Valstar *et al.* 2007), Gunes and Piccardi (2009), Chang and colleagues (Chang *et al.* 2006). Examples of methods using appearance features are those of Bartlett and colleagues (e.g. Bartlett *et al.* 2003) and Anderson and McOwan (2006).

The majority of the affect recognition systems based on automatic analysis of facial expressions have focused on the recognition of basic emotions (Zeng *et al.* 2009). A few attempts to detect non-basic affective states have been reported in the literature. el Kaliouby and Robinson (2004), for example, developed a computational model that detects, in real time, complex mental states such as agreeing, concentrating, disagreeing, being interested, being unsure, and thinking from facial expressions and head movement in video. Littlewort *et al.* (2007) used an automatic system for facial expression recognition to detect expressions of pain. Yeasin *et al.* (2006) developed a system that recognizes six universal facial expressions and uses them to compute levels of interest.

Furthermore, most of the approaches are based on databases of acted affective expressions. Naturalistic data goes beyond extreme emotions and concentrates on more natural affective episodes that happen more frequently in everyday life. To date, a few efforts to develop systems for the automatic detection of spontaneous affective expressions have been reported. Examples include the neurofuzzy system for emotion recognition by Ioannou *et al.* (2005), which allows for the learning and adaptation to specific users' naturalistic facial expressions, and the works by Valstar *et al.* (2007) and Littlewort *et al.* (2007), who reported results on the automatic discrimination between posed and spontaneous facial expressions.

Another key challenge in facial affect recognition is the dynamics of affective expressions. Littlewort *et al.* (2006) suggest that natural and posed expressions are inherently different in terms of temporal dynamics, providing arguments from psychological research (Ekman and Friesen 1982; Frank and Ekman 1993). Other studies show that the dynamics of expressions is a key factor in the discrimination between posed and spontaneous facial behaviour (Cohn and Schmidt 2004; Littlewort *et al.* 2007; Valstar *et al.* 2007). Valstar *et al.* (2007), for example, showed the important role of the temporal dynamics of face, head and shoulder expressions in discriminating posed from spontaneous smiles. Other efforts towards a dynamic account of affective expressions include the work by Pantic and Patras (2006), which deals with facial actions dynamics recognition, and the work by Cowie *et al.* (2008), who proposed a dynamic approach for affect recognition based on a recurrent neural network whose short-term memory and approximation capabilities allow for a dynamic modelling of events and classification of input patterns into affective states.

Context sensitivity in facial affect recognition is still an underexplored challenge. Systems for facial affect recognition need to take into account and adapt their knowledge to the specific user or context of interaction. Adaptation in terms of environment variables or personalized expressivity has to be considered. Neural networks are well suited to fulfilling the adaptation requirement. Caridakis and colleagues (2008), for example, proposed an approach that uses neural network architectures to detect the need for adaptation of their knowledge.

Another example in which context is taken into account in facial affect recognition is the work by Pantic and Rothkrantz (2004), who proposed a case-based reasoning system capable of classifying facial expressions into the emotion categories learned from the user.

Finally, robustness in real-world scenarios is an important factor in facial affect recognition. Most existing approaches in facial feature extraction only work well in controlled environments and are either designed to cope with a limited diversity of video characteristics or require manual initialization or intervention. Examples of exceptions are the system by Pantic and Patras (2006), which is robust to illumination changes, and the system by Anderson and McOwan (2006), characterized by its robustness to rigid head motions.

Affect recognition from the body

Although most of the studies on affect recognition reported in the literature have focused on the automatic analysis of facial expressions, some attempts have also been made towards the design of systems capable of analysing expressive body movement to infer human affect. Different streams of research in affect recognition from body movement can be identified depending on the type of information analysed to recognize affect. Some systems, for example, base the prediction of the conveyed affective content on the type of gesture performed, others on the way a gesture is performed, while others analyse body postures.

As far as systems based on analysis of the type of gesture performed are concerned, examples include: the system by Balomenos and colleagues (2005), which uses the position of the centroid of the head and hands to recognize gesture classes and map them onto emotions; the work by Gunes and Piccardi (2009), who presented a method for the recognition of acted affective states based on analysis of affective body displays and automatic detection of their temporal segments; and the work by Shan *et al.* (2007), who used spatio-temporal features for modelling affective body gestures.

Other studies addressed automatic affect recognition from the perspective of movement expressivity, attempting to predict affect based on the way gestures are performed (Bernhardt and Robinson 2007; Camurri *et al.* 2003, 2004; Castellano *et al.* 2007, 2008*b*). Camurri and colleagues (2005) developed a multilayered conceptual model for multimodal analysis of affective, emotional content in human full-body movement and gesture based on movement qualities. The model (see Figure 5.4.1) is based on four different layers, following a bottom-up approach (Camurri *et al.* 2004). Layer 1 includes techniques for pre-processing of data from different kinds of sensors such as video cameras and on-body (e.g. accelerometers) and environmental sensors. Layer 2 extracts from sensor data a collection of expressive motion features describing the movement being performed (Volpe 2003). Features are derived from research in psychology (e.g. Wallbott 1998; Boone and Cunningham 1998) and human sciences. For example, an important set of features are those relating to the *Theory of effort* by choreographer Rudolf Laban (Laban and Lawrence 1947; Laban 1963). EyesWeb XMI, a platform for synchronized analysis of

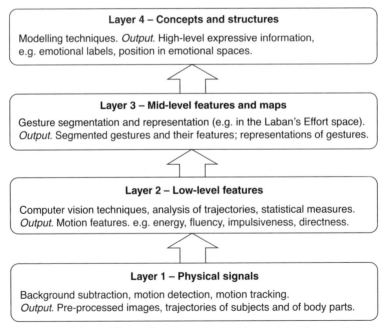

Layer 4 – Concepts and structures
Modelling techniques. *Output.* High-level expressive information, e.g. emotional labels, position in emotional spaces.

Layer 3 – Mid-level features and maps
Gesture segmentation and representation (e.g. in the Laban's Effort space). *Output.* Segmented gestures and their features; representations of gestures.

Layer 2 – Low-level features
Computer vision techniques, analysis of trajectories, statistical measures. *Output.* Motion features. e.g. energy, fluency, impulsiveness, directness.

Layer 1 – Physical signals
Background subtraction, motion detection, motion tracking. *Output.* Pre-processed images, trajectories of subjects and of body parts.

Fig. 5.4.1 A snapshot of the multilayered conceptual model for analysis of expressive gesture worked out in Camurri *et al.* (2005).

multimodal data streams developed by Camurri and colleagues (2007; www.eyesweb.org), allows for the extraction of a wide collection of motion features from video and sensor data streams. Layer 3 deals with two major issues: segmentation of movement in its composing gestures and representation of such gestures in suitable spaces. Layer 4 is conceived as a conceptual network mapping the extracted features and gestures into conceptual structures. The model was tested in a study aiming to automatically discriminate between four emotions (anger, fear, grief, and joy) in dance performances (Camurri *et al.* 2003, 2004).

Work on affect recognition from movement expressivity includes the study by Bernhardt and Robinson (2007), who proposed a framework for affect recognition in knocking motions using motion-captured data. They computed motion cues (e.g. velocity and acceleration of the hand, etc.) over motion primitives obtained using a method based on segmentation by motion energy and clustering of motion segments. Support vector machines were then trained for each motion primitive using statistical measures of the extracted motion cues.

The literature provides some examples of work on affect recognition from postures. Bianchi-Berthouze and Kleinsmith (2003) proposed an approach to self-organize postural features into affective categories to provide robots with the ability to incrementally learn to recognize affective human postures through interaction with human partners. Mota and Picard (2003) explored how sequences of postures can be used to predict affective states related to a child's interest level during a learning task performed with the computer. Based on posture data collected through pressure sensors mounted on a chair, hidden Markov models were used to predict the affective state related to sequences of postural behaviour. D'Mello and Graesser (2009) investigated the effectiveness of detecting affective states (boredom, confusion, delight, flow, and frustration) of learners interacting with an intelligent tutoring system using automatically extracted body pressure data carrying information about body position and arousal.

Despite the fact that studies on affect recognition from body movement are less numerous than those based on facial expressions, the literature includes a few studies that address some of the challenges in affect recognition research. Castellano *et al.* (2008b), for example, proposed an approach based on movement expressivity analysis to classify non-prototypical expressions in music performance into different emotionally expressive intentions (i.e. sad, allegro, serene, personal, and overexpressive). Varni and colleagues (Varni 2008; Varni *et al.* 2008) reported initial results in the attempt to measure emotional synchronization and identify leadership relationships in musicians using analysis of head motion expressivity.

As far as attempts to take into consideration the dynamics of affective expressions are concerned, Castellano (2008) proposed an approach for affect recognition based on the dynamics of movement expressivity, arguing that human affect can be recognized not only from the type of gestures performed, but also from the way they are performed. The approach was inspired by recent theories from psychology (Scherer 2001) claiming that emotional expression is reflected to a greater extent in the timing of the expression than in absolute or average measures. By focusing on the dynamics of expressive motion cues, the proposed approach addresses how motion qualities vary at different temporal levels. A mathematical model that allows for the extraction of information about the dynamics of movement expressivity was proposed. The idea behind this model is to use information about temporal series of expressive motion cues in a format that is suitable for feature vector-based classifiers. The model provides features conveying information about the dynamics of movement expressivity, i.e. information about fluctuations and changes in the temporal profiles of cues (Castellano 2008; Castellano *et al.* 2008b).

Based on this model, Castellano *et al.* (2008b) analysed upper-body and head gestures in musicians expressing emotions and reported that features related to the timing of expressive motion cues, such as the quantity of motion and the velocity of the head, are more effective for

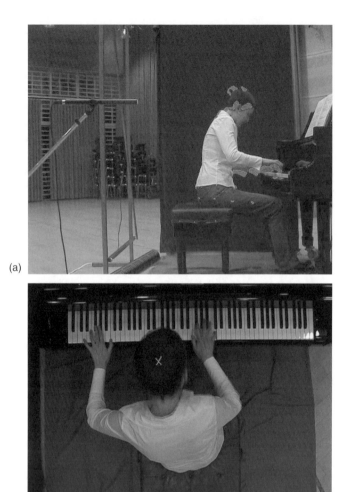

Fig. 5.4.2 (a) A measure of quantity of motion using silhouette motion images (the shadow along the pianist's body) and (b) the tracking of the head. (From Castellano *et al.* 2008*b*) (see plate 9).

the discrimination of affective states than traditional statistical features, such as the mean or the maximum. Figure 5.4.2 shows a measure of the quantity of motion of a pianist's upper body and the tracking of the head.

Finally, a noteworthy effort is that of Gunes and Piccardi (2009), who explored how the modelling and detection of temporal phases of body displays can improve the accuracy of affect recognition.

Affect recognition through multiple modalities: face and body

An affectively competent agent should be endowed with the ability to analyse different types of affective expressions: fusing different affective cues can allow for a better understanding to be achieved of the affective message communicated by the user. Hence the need for a multimodal affect recognition system.

While unimodal systems have received a thorough investigation, studies taking into account the multimodal nature of the affective communication process are still not numerous (Zeng *et al.* 2009). Some efforts combining the face and body modalities of expressions for the purpose of affect recognition have been reported in the literature. el Kaliouby and Robinson (2004), for example, proposed a vision-based computational model to infer mental states from head movements and facial expressions. Their approach uses hidden Markov models for real-time head and facial actions recognition and dynamic Bayesian networks to model mental states over time. Other examples include: the work by Balomenos *et al.* (2005), who used gestures, recognized with hidden Markov models, to support the output of the facial expression analysis in a bimodal emotion recognition system; the system of Gunes and Piccardi (2009), which allows for the recognition of affective states via synchronization of temporal phases of face and body displays; the work by Shan *et al.* (2007), who combined face and body features for bimodal affect recognition using canonical correlation analysis to establish the relation between the two modalities; and the work by Valstar *et al.* (2007), who combined multimodal information conveyed by facial expressions and head and shoulders movement to discriminate between posed and spontaneous smiles.

Other studies have considered the use of multiple channels of information in addition to face and gesture. Kapoor *et al.* (2007), for example, designed a system capable of detecting frustration using multimodal non-verbal cues such as facial expressions, blink, head movement, posture, skin conductance, and mouse pressure. Castellano *et al.* (2008*a*) proposed an approach in which facial expressions, body gesture, and speech data are fused at the feature and decision level to predict eight affective states in a speech-based interaction scenario.

A few of the proposed multimodal systems integrate contextual information for the purpose of affect recognition. The system by Kapoor and Picard (2005) allows for the detection of interest in a learning environment by combining non-verbal cues and information about the learner's task (e.g. the level of difficulty and the state of the game). Castellano *et al.* (2009) proposed an approach to predict the level of engagement of children playing chess with an iCat robot in a naturalistic scenario. Their approach is based on the fusion of non-verbal behaviour (i.e. eye gaze and smiles) and contextual features such as the state of the game and the display of facial expressions by the robot.

An important issue in multimodal affect recognition is the fusion of different modalities. Features from different modalities of expressions can be fused at different levels (Wu *et al.* 1999).

◆ *Feature-level fusion* can be performed by merging features from different modalities and inputting them into a single classifier. In this framework, correlation between modalities can be taken into account during the learning phase. In general, feature-level fusion is more appropriate in the case of closely coupled and synchronized modalities such as speech and lip movements, but tends not to generalize very well if the temporal characteristics of features from different modalities differ substantially, as is the case for speech and facial expression or gesture. Moreover, due to the high dimensionality of input features, large amounts of data are required for training purposes.

◆ *Decision-level fusion* is preferred when the integration of asynchronous, but temporally correlated modalities, is needed. With this approach each modality is classified independently and the outputs of different modalities are combined to obtain the final classification. Although several approaches have been proposed (Kittler *et al.* 1998), designing suitable strategies for decision-level fusion is still a challenge. The knowledge of the characteristics of each modality could inform the choice of different classification schemes for different modalities and the dynamic interconnection among them.

A major issue for both decision-level and feature-level fusion is the synchronization of the different modalities. As far as the feature extraction process is concerned, raw data can be collected at a different sampling rate and different modalities can be processed at different timescales. On the other hand, in the case of decision-level fusion, different classifiers may provide classification results at a different frequency. Multimodal synchronization remains a challenging issue that requires further investigation.

Results from studies in neurology (Stein and Meredith 1993) suggest that the integration of different perceptual signals occurs at an early stage of human processing of stimuli. This seems to suggest that different modalities should be processed in a joint feature space rather than combined with the results of a late fusion. Features from different modalities are often complementary and redundant, and their relationship is often unknown. The development of novel methods for multimodal fusion should take into consideration the underlying relationships and correlations between the feature sets in different modalities (Shan *et al.* 2007; Zeng *et al.* 2006), how different affective expressions influence each other, and how much information each of them provides about the communicated affect.

Conclusion

This chapter investigated affect sensitivity as an important requirement for an affectively competent agent. Specifically, face and body gestures were addressed as channels for the communication of affect. A survey of the state of the art in computational approaches for affect recognition based on the automatic analysis of facial and bodily expressions and their combined information was presented. Affect sensitivity was discussed with respect to key issues that arise in the design of an automatic system for affect recognition.

Although affect recognition from face and body movement has been increasingly investigated as of late (Zeng *et al.* 2009), several challenges still have to be addressed in a more comprehensive manner by the affect recognition community.

- First of all, despite a few attempts (el Kaliouby and Robinson 2004; Kapoor *et al.* 2007; Littlewort *et al.* 2007), many proposed approaches have focused on the detection of prototypical emotions, while it is expected that an affectively competent agent will be sensitive to affective signals conveying more subtle states. Moreover, the majority of the existing systems have been trained using acted and exaggerated expressions rather than with spontaneous samples of human behaviour. The design of real-world applications will require affectively competent agents that are sensitive to spontaneous, real-life affective expressions and states. This will necessitate advances in the definition of new methodologies for labelling naturalistic affective data, currently a non-trivial issue in affect recognition research.

- A second important issue is the need for new systems and methods that analyse multiple modalities for the purpose of affect recognition. New challenges to be addressed by the affect recognition community include the development of new methods for fusing different modalities that take into consideration their intrinsic relationships and synchronization.

- Third, the temporal dynamic of affective expressions has been shown to play an important role in the interpretation of affective displays (Cohn and Schmidt 2004; Castellano *et al.* 2008*b*; Gunes and Piccardi 2009; Valstar *et al.* 2007). The segmentation and analysis of the temporal phases of facial and bodily expressions are still challenging issues, as well as their relationships with the dynamics of the underlying affect.

- Fourth, the design of an affectively competent agent requires further advances in the development of methods robust in uncontrolled environments. Expression detectors must be robust to noisy backgrounds, changes in the illumination conditions, rigid head motions, occlusions, etc.

◆ Fifth, despite a few efforts (e.g. Kapoor and Picard 2007; Castellano *et al.* 2009), context sensitivity is still an underexplored topic. In the design of an affectively competent agent, it is recommended that information about the context in which an affective state or expression is displayed is taken into consideration, as the interpretation of behavioural signals and the underlying affective states is context-dependent.

◆ The current state of the art in affect recognition represents a valuable resource for the design of an affectively competent agent. One of the drawbacks of the richness of studies in the field is that results are often not comparable due to the different experimental conditions, the different databases of affective expressions used to train the affect detectors, the different data used, and so on. Research on an affect-sensitive agent should aim to establish common guidelines for the design of affect recognition frameworks suitable for real world applications.

◆ Finally, we believe that the inclusion of affect representation into a framework for affect recognition is an important issue for the design of an affectively competent agent. Strengthening the connection with psychological models, although still challenging, would allow the first steps towards the detection of more complex affective states and their components (e.g. appraisals, blends of emotions, preferences, mood, etc.) to be undertaken.

Communicating emotional states with the Greta agent[1]

Radosław Niewiadomski, Maurizio Mancini, Sylwia Hyniewska, and Catherine Pelachaud

Summary

Recent technological progress has made the creation of a humanoid interface to computer systems possible. An embodied conversational agent (ECA) is a computer-generated animated character that is able to carry on natural, human-like communication with users. For this purpose agent systems have been developed to simulate verbal and non-verbal communicative behaviours. ECAs can carry on dialogue with users using synthesized speech, gestures, gaze, and facial expressions.

In this chapter we present our ECA called Greta and focus on its capabilities of generating emotional expressive behaviours. Our three-dimensional agent is able to communicate using verbal and non-verbal channels such as gaze, head and torso movements, facial expressions, and gestures. It follows the SAIBA framework that defines functionalities and communication protocols for ECA systems. The system generates the output animation in the MPEG-4 standard. Our system is optimized to be used in interactive applications. It has a rich repertoire of expressive emotional behaviours.

Several studies demonstrate that the application of facial expressions in embodied agents is justified. The agents that use emotional displays are perceived as more engaging (Walker *et al.* 1994), increase the user's interest level, and influence the perception of the agent, as the same ECA with different facial expressions is perceived as more credible and trustworthy (Rehm and André 2005). No wonder many models of emotional expressive behaviours for an ECA were proposed (see Chapter 5.1, this volume). In this chapter we present the algorithms that enrich the emotional expressive behaviours of the Greta agent. First we describe an algorithm that extends a set of facial expressions in the repertoire of the ECA, introducing complex facial expressions like superposition or masking. Complex expressions are composed of the facial areas of its constituent expressions but they can be distinguished from them and they can signal different meanings. They were used in our agent to show socially acceptable behaviours (Niewiadomski and Pelachaud 2007b) or to display empathy (Niewiadomski *et al.* 2008). Then we show how our agent may display emotional states using different modalities. These expressions are composed of different

---

[1] We are very thankful to Björn Hartmann for defining Greta's set of expressivity parameters, and for implementing them in Greta's gesture generation engine. We are very grateful to Ginevra Castellano for her help. The works presented in this chapter have been supported by the EU-funded Human–Machine Interaction Network on Emotion Network of Excellence (HUMAINE: http://emotion-research.net/) and by the IP-CALLAS project IST-034800 (http://www.callas-newmedia.eu).

signals partially ordered in time and belonging to different non-verbal communicative channels. Multimodal expressions are particularly useful for an ECA to communicate subtle emotions such as pride or relief (Niewiadomski *et al.* 2009*a*) that are difficult to signal using only the facial channel.

In the second part of this chapter we describe how full-body expressive behaviours are modulated in our agent using a small set of parameters. These parameters may express certain constant characteristics of the agent as well as modulate its single behaviours in particular emotional states. In the latter case they may modify any non-verbal behaviour such as multimodal or complex expressions of emotion. We also show how to extract the values of these parameters automatically from visual data.

Introduction

In recent years there has been a growing interest in developing embodied agents with expressive capabilities. This is motivated by the effort to enhance human–machine interaction. To be able to express internal states, intentions, or motivations our agent needs to be endowed with non-verbal communication skills and to access data on how to communicate in a human-like manner.

The non-verbal emotional behaviours of our agent can be conveyed through the choice of the non-verbal signals and their realization. Although humans communicate through several modalities at the same time, it is the face that is a privileged place for the expression and the decoding of emotions, as suggested by interdisciplinary theorists (e.g. Kaiser and Wehrle 2001; Ekman 1972). Facial expressions do not always correspond to felt emotions: they can be fake (showing an expression of an unfelt emotion); masked (masking a felt emotion by an unfelt emotion); superposed (showing a mixed of felt emotions); inhibited (masking the expression of emotion with the neutral expression); suppressed (de-intensifying the expression of an emotion); or exaggerated (intensifying the expression of an emotion). We call *complex facial expressions* the expressions that are different from the spontaneous facial displays of simple emotional states (e.g. display of anger or sadness). They can be displays of some combinations of emotions as well as expressions of emotions that are modified according to some social rules. In this chapter we describe a model of complex facial expressions that is based on the partitioning approach proposed by Ekman (Ekman and Friesen 1975; Ekman 2003*a*, *b*). With this algorithm our agent is able to display superposed, masked, fake, and inhibited expressions of emotions. The novelty of our system, compared to the solutions presented in Chapter 5.1, this volume, is that our agent is able to express different types of facial expressions such as inhibited, masked, or fake expressions. Complex facial expressions are computed by composing facial areas of facial expressions, i.e. the final expression is a combination of facial areas of input expressions.

Nevertheless, some studies show that emotions are also expressed through several other modalities such as, for example, body movements (Wallbott 1998; Pollick *et al.* 2001). Some observational studies have explored the complexity of emotional expressions in terms of their dynamics (Keltner 1995; Shiota *et al.* 2003; Harrigan and O'Connell 1996). Among others, Keltner (1995) studied the sequence of facial and body movement in embarrassment. The typical expression of embarrassment starts from gaze downing or gaze shifts, which are followed by 'controlled' smiles. These smiles are often accompanied by a pressure of the lips. At the end of the expression the movement of the head to the left was often observed as well as some face touching gestures (Keltner 1995). We called these expressions *multimodal sequential expressions* of emotions. They might be composed of non-verbal behaviours displayed over different modalities that change dynamically over time. Our agent is able to display *multimodal sequential expressions*. For this purpose we developed a language for the formal description of such expressions from real data and an algorithm that uses this description to automatically generate emotional displays. In comparison to the exisitng solutions (see Chapter 5.1, this volume), this algorithm system generates automatically a variety of multimodal emotional expressions. It is based on a high-level symbolic description of non-verbal behaviours. In contrast to many other approaches that use captured data for behaviour reproduction, in this approach the observed behaviours are interpreted by a human who creates constraints. The sequences of non-verbal displays are independent behaviours that are not driven by the spoken text. The system allows for the synthesis of any number of emotional states and is not restricted by the number of modalities. While it uses a discrete approach in its use of labels to refer to emotions, it is also linked to the componential approach by the underlined importance of the sequence of elements in the perception of emotions. Its advantage is to generate a variety of animations for one emotional label avoiding repetitiveness in the behaviour of a virtual character.

What is more, any expression can be performed slowly or quickly, jerkily or fluently, etc. With the term *expressivity* we identify the ways in which the single non-verbal behaviours are synthesized. They are the external, visible qualities of a movement, like its speed, amplitude, fluidity, and so on. The *expressivity of behaviour* is an important aspect of the non-verbal behaviour. Expressivity is an integral part of the communication process as it can provide information on the emotional state, mood, and personality of a person (Wallbott 1998). The non-verbal behaviour in Greta may be modulated by the use of six expressivity parameters. Moreover, the expressivity parameters in Greta are related to the current emotional state as well as to the characteristics of an overall individuality of the agent.

The remainder of this chapter is organized as follows. In the next section we present a general overview of the architecture of our agent. Then in the third section we describe our model of complex facial expressions, while in the following section the algorithm that generates multimodal sequential expressions in Greta is presented. In the next section we explain how we model the expressivity of non-verbal behaviours. We conclude this chapter in the final section.

Greta the interactive embodied conversational agent

This section presents an overview of the architecture of our ECA. Our agent's architecture follows the design methodology proposed by Thórisson *et al.* (2005) and is compatible with the SAIBA framework (Vilhjálmsson *et al.* 2007). The architecture is modular and distributed. Each module exchanges information and data through a central message system. We use the concept of a whiteboard (Thórisson *et al.* 2005), which allows internal modules and an external software to be integrated easily. The system is designed to be used in interactive applications working in real-time.

Generic architecture for embodied conversational agent

SAIBA (Vilhjálmsson *et al.* 2007) is an international research initiative whose main aim is to define a standard framework for the generation of virtual agent behaviour. It defines a number of levels of abstraction, from the computation of the agent's communicative intention to behaviour planning and realization. The *Intent Planner* module decides on the agent's current goals, emotional state, and beliefs, and encodes them into the Function Markup Language (FML) (Heylen *et al.* 2008). To convey the agent's communicative intentions, the *Behaviour Planner* module schedules a number of communicative signals (e.g. speech, facial expressions, gestures), which are encoded with the Behaviour Markup Language (BML). It specifies the verbal and non-verbal behaviours of ECAs (Vilhjálmsson *et al.* 2007). Finally, the task of the third element of the SAIBA framework, *Behaviour Realizer*, is to realize the behaviours scheduled by the Behaviour Planner.

It receives input in the BML format and generates the animation. There exist several implementations of the SAIBA standard, among others SmartBody (Thiebaux *et al.* 2008; Lee and Marsella 2006), BMLRealizer (Árnason and Porsteinsson 2008), RealActor (Cerekovic *et al.* 2009), and EMBR (Heloir and Kipp 2009).

Our general purpose ECA system is almost a full implementation of the SAIBA framework offering a solution for the *Behaviour Planner* and the *Behaviour Realizer* layers and a partial implementation of the *Intent Planner* for the listener. In our implementation of the SAIBA standard we focus on the *Behaviour Planner* rather than on the *Behaviour Realizer* as the other implementations do. Our *Behaviour Planner* generates a large set of non-verbal behaviours from a single communicative intention. We also provide an advanced *Intent Planner* for the listener that includes reactive, cognitive as well as mimicry backchannels.

Architecture

Figure 5.5.1 illustrates the architecture of our agent. It follows the SAIBA framework and is composed of three main modules. In SAIBA the Intent Planner is dedicated to the speaker. To be able to control a listener agent, we have introduced the *Listener Intent Planner*. This module generates automatically the communicative intentions of the listener. On the other hand, in the current state of our system, the intentions of the speaker are defined manually in an FML-APML input file. In the future they will be generated by the *speaker intent planner*. The *Behaviour Planner* module receives as input the agent's communicative intentions, be it a speaker or a listener, written in FML-APML and generates as output a list of signals in the BML language. These signals are sent to the *Behaviour Realizer*, which generates the MPEG-4 FAP and BAP frames. Finally, the animation is played in the *FAP–BAP player*. All modules are synchronized by the Central Clock and communicate with each other through the Psyclone whiteboard (Thórisson *et al.* 2005).

- *Listener Intent Planner.* The listener Intent Planner module is in charge of the computation of the agent's behaviours while being a listener when conversing with a user (or another

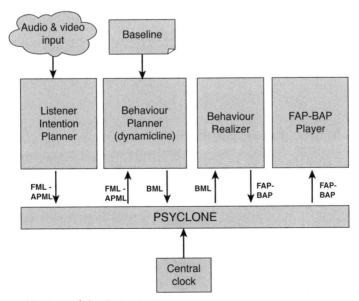

Fig. 5.5.1 The architecture of the Greta agent.

virtual agent). This component encompasses three modules called reactive backchannel, cognitive backchannel, and mimicry.

- The *reactive backchannel module* prompts a backchannel signal when our system recognizes certain speaker's behaviours; for example, a head nod or a variation in the pitch of the user's voice will trigger a backchannel with a certain probability.

- On the other hand, the *cognitive backchannel module* computes when and which backchannel should be displayed using information about the agent's beliefs concerning the speaker's speech. The cognitive module selects which signals to display from the lexicon depending on the agent's reaction towards the speaker's speech.

- The third module is the *mimicry module*. This module determines when and which signals the agent is to mimic.

- *Behaviour Planner.* The Behaviour Planner takes as input both the agent's communicative intentions specified by the FML-APML language and some agent's characteristics (i.e. *baseline*). The main task of this component is to select, for each communicative intention, the adequate set of behaviours to display. The output of the Behaviour Planner is described in the BML language. It contains the sequence of behaviours with their timing information to be displayed by our virtual agent.

- *Behaviour Realizer.* This module generates the animation of our agent following the MPEG-4 format (Ostermann 2002). The input of the module is specified by the BML language. It contains the text to be spoken and/or a set of non-verbal signals to be displayed. Facial expressions, gaze, gestures, torso movements are described symbolically in the repository files. Each BML tag is instantiated as a set of key-frames that are then smoothly interpolated. The Behaviour Realizer synchronizes the behaviours across modalities. It solves also eventual conflicts between the signals that use the same modality. The speech is generated by an external TTS and the lips movements are added to the animation. When the Behaviour Realizer receives no input, the agent does not remain still. It generates some idle movements. Periodically a piece of animation is computed and is sent to the FAP-BAP Player. This avoids unnatural 'freezing' of the agent.

- *FAP–BAP player.* The FAP–BAP player receives the animation generated by the behaviour eealizer and plays it in a graphic window. The player is MPEG-4 compliant. Facial and body configurations are respectively described through FAP and BAP frames.

- *Synchronization.* The synchronization of all modules in the distributed environment is ensured by the Central Clock that regularly broadcasts timestamps through the whiteboard. All other components are registered in the whiteboard to receive timestamps.

Model of complex facial expressions

We base our model of complex facial expressions on Paul Ekman's studies (Ekman and Friesen 1975; Ekman 2003a, b). We define complex facial expressions using a face partitioning approach. Each facial expression is defined by a set of eight facial areas F_k (i.e., F_1 brows, F_2 upper eyelids, F_3 eyes direction, F_4 lower eyelids, F_5 cheeks, F_6 nose, F_7 lips, F_8 lips tension). An expression is a composition of these facial areas, each of which can display signs of emotion. For complex facial expressions, different emotions can be expressed on different areas of the face; e.g. when sadness is masked by happiness, sadness is shown on the eyebrows area while happiness is displayed on the mouth area.

The main task of our algorithm is to assign expressions of emotion to different areas of the face. For this purpose we define for each type of complex facial expression a set of rules that describe

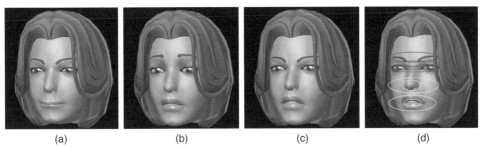

Fig. 5.5.2 Superposition of anger and sadness. From left to right: (a) anger; (b) sadness; (c) superposition of anger and sadness; (d) superposition of anger and sadness with significant areas marked.

the composition of the facial areas. These rules, based on the description proposed by Ekman, refer to six emotions, namely, anger, disgust, fear, joy, sadness, and surprise. For an input emotion for which the facial expression is not defined explicitly by our rules (e.g. expression of contempt or disappointment) our algorithm chooses the most appropriate solution. For this purpose we use an algorithm (Niewiadomski and Pelachaud 2007a) based on fuzzy similarity. In this approach each facial expression is described by fuzzy sets. Fuzzy similarity is used to compute the degree of visual similarity between them. Our algorithm compares any two facial expressions and produces an index of similarity in the interval $[0\ldots1]$, where 0 means 'not similar at all' while 1 means identical expressions. Once the most similar expression, chosen among the six is known the algorithm applies the corresponding rules to the input expression. The rules determine which elements of the input expression are used in the complex facial expression. (More details about the algorithm and its evaluation can be found in Niewiadomski and Pelachaud (2007a, b) and Buisine et $al.$ (2006).)

For different types of complex facial expressions: superposition, masking, fake, or inhibited expressions can be generated with our algorithm. For example, the expression of superposition happens when two emotions are felt at the same time. Figure 5.5.2 shows an example of the superposition expression computed by our model. Figures 5.5.2(a) and (b) show the expressions of anger and sadness respectively. Figures 5.5.2(c) and (d) show the superposition as a composition of face areas of both input expressions. In Figure 5.5.2(d) we see which parts of the face correspond to sadness and which ones to anger. In that image the areas F_5, F_6, F_7, and F_8 (expressing sadness) are marked out with by the light grey circles while areas F_1, F_2, F_3, and F_4 (expressing anger) by a dark grey colour.

Figure 5.5.3 shows the agent displaying the expression of disappointment masked by a fake happiness. We applied our similarity algorithm and found that disappointment has a facial expression very similar to that of sadness. In our model the features of felt sadness that leak over the masking expression are: forehead, brows, and upper eyelids. These elements are represented by the facial areas F_1 (forehead and brows) and F_2 (upper eyelids). According to the inhibition hypothesis, they can be observed in masked sadness. On the other hand, the mouth area displays a smile (sign of happiness).

Sequential expressions of emotions

From the analysis of expressions of emotions like embarrassment (Keltner 1995), awe, amusement, pride (Shiota et $al.$ 2003), or anxiety (Harrigan and O'Connell 1996; see also Chapter 5.1, this volume) it was shown that certain emotions are expressed by a set of signals that are arranged

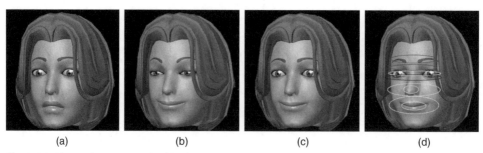

(a)	(b)	(c)	(d)

Fig. 5.5.3 Disappointment masked by happiness. From left to right: (a) disappointment; (b) happiness; (c) disappointment masked by happiness; (d) disappointment masked by happiness with significant areas marked (see plate 10).

in a certain interval of time rather than by a static facial expression (i.e. an expression at its apex). The expressions of emotional states are dynamical and they can be displayed over different modalities like face, gaze and head movement, gestures, or even posture. Interestingly, these signals do not have to occur simultaneously (Keltner 1995).

To go beyond agents showing simply static facial expressions of emotions, we have defined a representation scheme that encompasses the dynamics of the facial expressions of an emotion. The main task of our algorithm is to generate multimodal sequential expressions of emotions, i.e. expressions that are composed of different signals partially ordered in time and with the use of different non-verbal communicative channels. These multimodal expressions can be of any duration, while the duration of constitutive signals is limited, e.g. facial expressions of emotions usually last no longer than 4 seconds (Ekman and Friesen 1975) and gestures often have at least a minimum duration. We define for each emotional state a *behaviour set,* a set of signals through which the emotion is displayed, and a *constraint set* that defines logical and temporal relations between the signals in the behaviour set. These two sets are defined from literature and from manual annotation conducted on a video-corpus (Niewiadomski *et al.* 2009b).

The single signals like a *frown, head nod,* or *self-touch gesture* are described in the repositories of the agent's non-verbal behaviours and are grouped in the behaviour sets. Each behaviour set associates one emotional state with a set of plausible signals that might be displayed by the agent. For each signal in a behaviour set one may define the probability of occurrence, the minimum and maximum duration, and the number of repetitions. All the signals that belong to one behaviour set may occur in the displays of the emotion associated with it, but their occurrence is not random. We developed an XML-like language to describe a set of relations, that is, the constraint set, between the signals of one behaviour set. Two types of constraints are possible.

- *Temporal constraints*, which define arithmetic relations on the start time and end time of a signal, e.g. 'signal s_i cannot start at the beginning of animation' or 'signal s_i starts immediately after the signal s_j finishes'. The temporal constraints are defined using arithmetical relations: $<, >, =$.

- *Appearance constraints*, which describe more general relations between signals like inclusion or exclusion, e.g. 'signals s_i and s_j cannot co-occur' or 'signal s_j cannot occur without signal s_i'.

The constraints of both types can be composed using the logical operators: *and, or, not.*

From the single label of an emotional state e (e.g. anger or embarrassment) our system generates a sequence of multimodal expressions, i.e. the animation A of a given duration t composed of a sequence of signals $\{s_{i(j)}\}$ on different modalities. It chooses a coherent subset of signals from the behaviour set BS_e, computes their durations, and their display order. Thus, at time-step

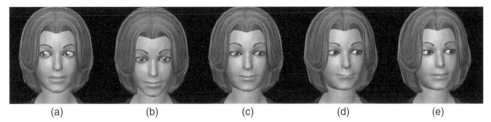

Fig. 5.5.4 An example of an expression of embarrassment.

t_i (1...n-1, $t_n = t$) it chooses one signal s_j from the behaviour set BS_e; it decides its duration and checks if the constraints CS_e are satisfied against the partial animation A (0...t_{i-1}). Consequently, either it adds s_j to A, or it repeats the procedure with the different signal.

Our algorithm is a part of the *Behaviour Planner* module of the Greta agent. It can generate several sequences of signals, each of them satisfying the constraint sets. (More details about the algorithm and its evaluation can be found in Niewiadomski *et al.* (2009*a*, *b*).

In Figure 5.5.4 an example of the animation for the expression of embarrassment is shown. The images present the frames of the animation of Greta displaying respectively the signals: (a) *look_right*; (b) *head_down* and *gaze_down*; (c) *gaze_left*; (d) *gaze_left* and *non-Duchenne_smile*; (e) *gaze_left*. Figure 5.5.5 shows another example of animation of the same emotion. In Figure 5.5.5 the following signals are displayed: (a) *neutral expression*; (b) *smile*; (c) *smile* and *gaze_right*; (d) *gaze_left*; (e) *gaze_down* and *head_down*; (f) *face touching gesture*.

Behaviour expressivity model

In this section we describe a set of parameters that we use to represent the behaviour expressivity. We will show how these parameters may be used to define some global characteristics of the agent as well as how they modulate the synthesis of any emotional signal. Finally, we explain the process of capturing the expressivity values automatically from video corpora.

Expressivity parameters

In order to increase the life-likeness of the Greta ECA, Hartmann *et al.* (2005) have defined and implemented a set of parameters that allow one to alter the way in which the agent expresses its actual communicative intention.

♦ Overall activity (OAC): amount of activity (e.g. passive/static versus animated/engaged). As this parameter increases (or, respectively, decreases), the number of head movements, facial expressions, gestures, and so on increases (or, respectively, decreases).

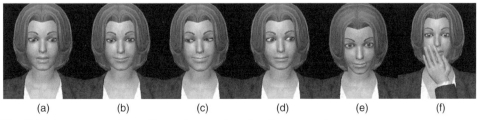

Fig. 5.5.5 An example of a multimodal expression of embarrassment.

- Spatial extent (SPC): amplitude of movements (e.g. expanded versus contracted). It determines the amplitude of, for example, head rotations and hand positions.

- Temporal extent (TMP): duration of movements (e.g. quick versus sustained actions). This parameter modifies the speed of execution of movements. They are slow if the value of the parameter is negative, or fast when the parameter is positive.

- Fluidity (FLD): smoothness and continuity of movement (e.g. smooth, graceful versus sudden, jerky). Higher values allow smooth and continuous execution of movements while lower values create discontinuity in the movements.

- Power (PWR): dynamic properties of the movement (e.g. weak/relaxed versus strong/tense). Higher (or, respectively, lower) values increase (or, respectively, decrease) the acceleration of the head or limbs rotation, making the overall movement look more (or, respectively, less) powerful.

- Repetitivity (REP): this parameter permits the generation of rhythmic repetitions of the same rotation/expression/gesture. For example, a head nod with a high repetitivity becomes a sequence consisting of very fast and small nods.

Baseline and dynamic line

People vary in their behaviours, depending on their personality, the environmental situation, social rules, and so on. Argyle (1988) and Gallaher (1992) state that there is an *underlying tendency* that is constantly present in each person's behaviour. People that tend to look more and perform wide gestures will continue to do so in most situations.

This is the idea we are capturing with the concept of a *baseline* for ECAs. The baseline represents the agent's general, underlying expressive behaviour tendencies. We define the baseline as a set of expressivity parameters *Expr* that represent the agent's general behaviour expressivity, as explained in the previous section: for example, an agent could tend to perform slow and smooth gestures (low temporal and high fluidity), while another agent could tend to move in a fast and jerky manner (high temporal and low fluidity).

When communicating an emotional state or an intention, one may vary one's general tendencies, e.g. one can gesture in a very different way. For example, a person who is always slow in performing hand gestures while talking may change her behaviour quality when being very angry at someone. One of the contributions of our work is the creation of a system in which the agent's general expressive behaviour tendencies can be modulated depending on the agent's emotional state and communicative intention. We aim to model such influences as 'an agent A with general expressive tendencies T, with an emotional state E tends to behave as T_E', where T_E is a particular 'version' of T obtained by a modulation induced by E. In this way the agent's general behaviour tendencies T become *local* to the agent's actual emotional state. We embody the agent's local behaviour tendencies with the concept of a *dynamic line*. The dynamic line structure is the same as that of the baseline; they differ in their meaning and in the way they are computed. The dynamic line is a set of expressivity parameters *Modulated-Expr* that represent the agent local behaviour expressivity, that is, the dynamic line is a set of parameters that derive both from the agent's baseline and its current communicative intention (e.g. its emotional state). It is the dynamic line that represents the agent's current expressivity, the one that influences the execution of the agent behaviour. Figure 5.5.6 outlines how the dynamic line is computed from the baseline at runtime.

This process is executed by the *behaviour quality computation* (BQC) module, which is a part of the *Behaviour Planner* module. The input to the BQC module is the agent's baseline, which is a constant, and the emotional state the agent aims to communicate. Each time the emotional state varies the module computes a new dynamic line for the agent. During the BQC process, the

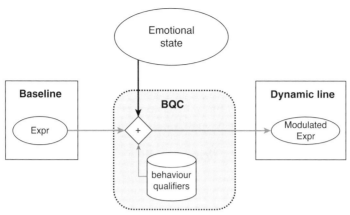

Fig. 5.5.6 Behaviour quality computation (BQC): the agent's baseline and communicative intention are used in the computation of the agent's dynamic line.

expressivity parameters contained in the baseline are modulated depending on the agent's actual emotional state and the resulting expressivity values are stored in the dynamic line.

This means that different emotional states have different impacts on the dynamic lines of two agents that have different baselines. For example, if an agent has a general tendency (baseline) to perform many movements with an average speed/amplitude then in a sad state it could simply stop moving, as the sad state reduces its activation parameter. On the other hand, an agent with a general tendency to move a lot with fast and large movements continues to make movements even when sad, although with a lower frequency and with a lower expressivity (average speed and amplitude).

As shown in Figure 5.5.6, the way in which the agent baseline is modulated into its dynamic line is determined by the agent *behaviour qualifiers*, which are described in detail in the next section.

Behaviour qualifiers

We call a *behaviour qualifier* a set of *modulations* that, given an emotional state, act on the behaviour tendencies of a conversational agent. By *modulation* we mean a variation over one of the expressive parameters contained in the agent's baseline.

As an example, the following description can be modelled by a behaviour qualifier: '*a hot anger state (i) increases the degree of bodily activation and at the same time (ii) the speed, amplitude, and energy of movements are very high*'. We can notice that the behaviour qualifier described in this sentence has two kinds of influences: a *relative* and an *absolute*. In this example, part (i) of the sentence indicates that we may increase the degree of the bodily activation. This is a relative variation because we give an indication of the current behaviour tendency (dynamic line) in terms of the general tendencies (baseline). Instead, part (ii) of the sentence indicates that speed, amplitude, and energy of movement should be very high: in this case we talk about absolute values, that is, the current behaviour tendencies (dynamic line) are explicitly defined, and we do not refer to a general tendency (baseline).

Thus the behaviour qualifier in the example will act on the *overall activation* (OAC) expressivity parameter of the agent's *torso*, *face*, and *gesture* modalities by increasing them by a relative value as described in part (i) of the example sentence. It will also act on the *temporal*, *spatial*, and *power* expressivity parameters of the agent's gesture modality by assigning high absolute values to them, as described by part (ii) of the example sentence.

The task of defining behaviour qualifiers to allow us to perform BQC in ECAs is neither obvious nor simple. There are no certain data about the expressivity modulations induced by emotional states in humans. Only some experimental data is available, and we used the results reported in Argyle (1988), Gallaher (1992), and Wallbott and Scherer (1986) to define the behaviour qualifier of the Greta ECA. For example several researchers observed that in a sad emotional state people tend to move slowly, perform few gestures, and exhibit a contracted posture. Anger and joy induce wide and powerful movements with differences in fluidity: angry movements exhibit low fluidity while happy movements are smoother.

Determining dynamic line automatically

In order to compute the agent's dynamic line, behaviour qualifiers need to be specified. This specification can be done manually following data from the literature (Argyle 1988; Gallaher 1992; Wallbott and Scherer 1986) or can be extracted automatically from visual data. In this section we present a system that takes video data as input, extracts movement expressivity, and finally determines a dynamic line for the Greta agent.

The EyesWeb system (www.eyesweb.org; Camurri *et al.* 2004) is used for the analysis of human movement. A mapping between the extracted expressive parameters and the corresponding expressive parameters of the agent's dynamic line is then established.

Figure 5.5.7 shows an overview of the system architecture and its different modules.

◆ *Human movement analysis*: we perform the automatic extraction of motion expressivity from a video source by using the EyesWeb platform and the EyesWeb Expressive Gesture Processing Library. More specifically, we extract the following motion expressive cues.
  • *Contraction index* (CI): this is a measure, ranging from 0 to 1, of how contracted a movement or gesture is (i.e. performed near to the body) or expanded (i.e. performed with a use of the space surrounding the body). It is calculated by extracting the body *silhouette* from the background.
  • *Velocity*: we find the two-dimensional coordinates of the actor's right or left hand in the image and from them we compute its velocity, taking into account its horizontal and vertical components.

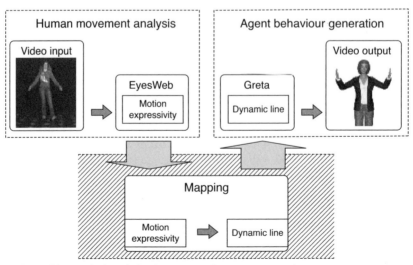

Fig. 5.5.7 From video analysis to behaviour generation: system overview.

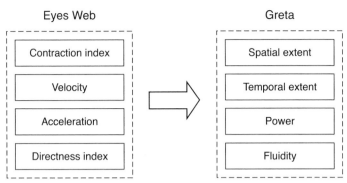

Fig. 5.5.8 Mapping between video parameters extracted with EyesWeb and the Greta expressivity parameters.

- *Acceleration*: by computing the derivative function of the velocity of the actor's hand we obtain its acceleration.
- *Directness index* (DI): this is a measure of how direct or flexible a trajectory between two points in space is. We obtain it by comparing the length of the minimal distance between two points with the length of the trajectory of the actor's right or left hand. We apply the DI to the coordinates of the hand to obtain an indicator of the fluidity of the movement.
- ◆ *Mapping*: the extracted motion expressive cues are mapped on to the agent's dynamic line expressivity parameters and rescaled. We define the following (see Figure 5.5.8).
  - Contraction index is mapped on to spatial extent, since they provide a measure of the amplitude of movements.
  - Velocity is mapped on to temporal extent, as they refer to the velocity of movements.
  - Acceleration is mapped on to power, as both are indicators of the acceleration of movements.
  - Directness index is mapped on to fluidity, as they refer to the degree of the smoothness of movements.
- ◆ *Agent behaviour generation*: this module is part of the Greta agent animation system. It receives as input the agent dynamic line and computes the animation of Greta.

This method allows us to extract qualitative information on behaviour execution in real-time. From these data we are able to elaborate behaviour qualifiers for different emotional states. When these qualifiers are integrated in the agent system, a dynamic line can be computed. The system can model behaviour distinctiveness on the one hand and behaviour quality modulation on the other hand to convey specific messages.

Conclusion

In this chapter we have presented models of the emotional expressive behaviours of our ECA. Each model captures an aspect of the complexity of emotion expressions. The algorithms described in this chapter aim at enriching the expressive capabilities of Greta by considering expressions that go beyond the stereotypical facial expressions in their apex. First of all, we presented the algorithm that generates superposed, masked, inhibited, and fake expressions.

We also introduced to our ECA multimodal sequential expressions. They may be composed of non-verbal behaviours displayed over different modalities, of a sequence of behaviours, or of expressions within one modality that change dynamically.

Finally, we have also presented an algorithm that modulates the behaviour expressivity of agents. Expressivity is an important cue of emotional expressions. It can also be used to define the general characteristics of the agent's behaviours. We have presented a system where the expressivity parameters are captured automatically from real human behaviour.

In the future we will continue the research on multimodal emotional signals. Our work will focus on the synchronization between different modalities (including the verbal channel) as well as on the perception of emotions from different modalities. We also plan to work on full-body emotional expressions, e.g. including the postures. We would like to improve our expressivity model so it will be more related to the emotional state of the agent. This can be achieved through perceptive studies.

Approaches to developing expression corpora and databases

This section consists of two case studies in which the general principles to be heeded in the use of corpora and databases (see Section 3), particularly with respect to plausible and believable samples of emotional expression, are exemplified. While the first example is focused on actor portrayals, the second deals with different ways of inducing emotions to obtain spontaneous emotion expressions.

In Chapter 6.1, 'Introducing the Geneva Multimodal Emotion Portrayal (GEMEP) corpus', Bänziger and Scherer recall the frequent use of emotion portrayals by actors and lay posers in research on emotional expression and point out a number of shortcomings in existing emotional expression corpora. They enumerate a number of requirements for the systematic construction of a corpus that is likely to allow systematic research and to serve as ground truth as well as an evaluation standard for artificial emotional agents. They present the Geneva multimodal emotion portrayals (GEMEP) which was developed according to these criteria. It consists of more than 7000 audio-video emotion portrayals, representing 18 emotions, portrayed by 10 different actors with the help of a professional theatre director. In this contribution, the authors describe the development of the corpus, which is available to other researchers in psychology and affective computing, and report the results of a massive validation study involving observer recognition and believability ratings, demonstrating the utility of the corpus as an instrument to study shared codes of emotional communication

In Chapter 6.2, 'Induction techniques developed to illuminate relationships between signs of emotion and their context, physical and social', Cowie, Douglas-Cowie, Sneddon, McRorie, Hanratty, McMahon, and McKeown suggest that emotion induction is well suited to collecting data that reveal how push and pull effects shape expressive patterns. They describe a variety of data collection techniques designed to address the issue of context, physical and social, that their research teams in Belfast have explored. Four main categories are discussed: (1) a three-stage induction procedure (EM3), which is robust enough to affect performance on demanding activities for a considerable period; (2) emotion induced by passive observation of films and listening to music; (3) observing and recording participants who have been asked to engage in highly emotionally charged activities; and (4) conversational interactions involving multiple, contrasting orientations (especially the SAL paradigm, which provides models of interactions between a human user and an artificial agent with some affective competence). The authors show that these techniques provide models of the way induction can engage with the complexity of 'push' and 'pull' effects that typify everyday environments.

Chapter 6.1

Introducing the Geneva multimodal emotion portrayal (GEMEP) corpus[1]

Tanja Bänziger and Klaus R. Scherer

Summary

In this chapter we outline the requirements for a systematic corpus of actor portrayals and describe the development, recording, editing, and validating of a major new corpus, the Geneva multimodal emotion portrayal (GEMEP). This corpus consists of more than 7000 audio-video emotion portrayals, representing 18 emotions (including rarely studied subtle emotions), portrayed by 10 professional actors who were coached by a professional director. The portrayals are recorded with optimal digital quality in multiple modalities, using both pseudo-linguistic utterances and affect bursts. In addition, the corpus includes stimuli with systematically varied intensity levels, as well as instances of masked expressions. From the total corpus, 1260 portrayals were selected and submitted to a first rating procedure in different modalities to establish validity in terms of inter-judge reliability and recognition accuracy. The results show that the portrayed expressions are recognized by lay judges with an accuracy level that, in the case of all emotions, largely exceeded chance and that compares very favourably with published tests of emotion recognition that use highly selected stimulus sets. The portrayals also reach very satisfactory levels of interrater reliability for category judgements and ratings of believability and intensity of the portrayals.

The validity of the corpus is further confirmed by replicating results in earlier work on the role of expression modality and the corresponding communication channel for cue utilization in emotion recognition. We show that, as expected, the highest accuracy results if both auditory and visual information (voice, face, and gestures) are available, but that sizeable accuracy is achieved even when only one modality is available. The video modality is slightly superior to the audio modality, probably reflecting the fact that facial and gestural cues are more discrete and iconic than vocal cues. However, there are important interactions between emotion and modality, as particular emotions seem to be preferentially communicated by visual or audio cues. The results also raise important issues concerning the relationships between intensity of expression, accuracy, and believability, thereby challenging earlier assumptions.

[1] The research reported here has been supported by the German and the Swiss National Research Foundations, the Swiss Center for Affective Sciences, and the FP6 IST European Network of Excellence Humaine. The authors gratefully acknowledge important contributions by Steve Binggeli in the construction of the corpus and collection of ratings and by Nele Dael, Martijn Goudbeek, Marc Mehu, and Marcello Mortillaro, in the final data-gathering stages and in valuable comments all along.

Introduction: designing the corpus

Research on emotional expression (EE) is in large part based on facial, vocal, or bodily portrayals of particular emotions by professional or trained actors who have been photographed or audio- and/or video-recorded for systematic stimulus presentation purposes (Banse and Scherer 1996; Ekman and Friesen 1976; Lundqvist *et al.* 1998; Goeleven *et al.* 2008; Gosselin *et al.* 1995; Hawk *et al.* 2009; Maurage *et al.* 2007; Johnson *et al.* 1986). The widespread use of emotion portrayals is due to three main factors.

- Intense emotions are relatively rare, of short duration, strongly subject to social control or self-regulation, and generally occur in an unpredictable fashion and outside of public scrutiny (see Chapter 3.2, this volume). As a consequence, systematic recordings of genuine, spontane- ous emotions are difficult to obtain (see Chapter 6.2, this volume).

- Much of emotional expression research is concerned with the communication of emotional meaning, in particular, the perception of expressions by an observer and the inferences drawn from these. In consequence, the emphasis is on fairly prototypical expressions with an estab- lished signal value rather than on idiosyncratic forms of emotion externalization that may vary greatly according to the respective social context.

- Experimental research in psychology, the neurosciences, and affective computing needs to create a sufficient number of conditions, repetitions, and controls, as well as a high degree of standardization, that can only be obtained by using acted portrayals (see also Bänziger and Scherer 2007).

In this chapter we present a new corpus constructed according to a number of theoretical and methodological desiderata and based on our past experience with similar efforts. Because this corpus of actor portrayals was planned to be shared with different research communities for dif- ferent purposes, careful planning of the set of emotions to be included and the type of portrayal instructions was needed.

Selection of emotions portrayed

The affective states selected for portrayal were partly chosen to represent the states that are frequently studied in the literature that deals with facial and/or vocal expressions of affect, in particular the set of basic emotions as defined by basic emotion theorists (Ekman 1999; Izard 1991). Less frequently examined states were also included to address specific research questions. For example, a relatively large number of positive states—such as pride, amusement, elation, interest, pleasure, and relief—were included to challenge the traditional view in which only one undifferentiated positive state (happiness) can be reliably communicated via facial cues. In a similar attempt, some states corresponding to the same family of emotional reactions were included with various arousal levels (e.g. irritated and enraged anger; anxious and panic fear). This inclusion fulfils two aims.

1 Reviews of studies describing acoustic profiles of EEs have repeatedly reported differences in acoustic features of vocal expressions mostly related to arousal level. Variations of arousal within emotion 'families' should allow us to disentangle the influence of arousal level and emotion family on vocal expressions.

2 The inclusion of more than one type of anger (or fear) should result in increased variability of the expressions portrayed and should allow us to include a range of variations that are more likely to occur in daily interactions, under the assumption, for example, that irritation occurs more frequently than rage and anxiety more frequently than panic fear.

Table 6.1.1 Selection of emotions portrayed

Arousal	Valence	
	Positive	Negative
High	Elation (joy) Amusement Pride	Hot anger (rage) Panic fear Despair
Low	Pleasure Relief Interest	Cold anger (irritation) Anxiety (worry) Sadness (depression)

Note. Additional states: shame, surprise, admiration, disgust, contempt, tenderness.

In choosing the set of emotions, an attempt was made to theoretically order them for a valence and an arousal dimension. This is shown in Table 6.1.1, together with a list of additional emotions added for the reasons outlined earlier.

A further attempt to increase the variability of the expressions was undertaken by including portrayals for some of the emotions with less and with more emotional intensity than what corresponds to the usual intensity for a given emotion (baseline intensity). An underlying assumption is that the portrayals produced with less intensity might be closer to expressions that could occur in daily interactions, whereas the portrayals with more intensity might be more exaggerated (or more stereotypical). To this regulation of the intensity of portrayed states, we added a further condition to partially mask some of the expressions (i.e. to portray an unsuccessful deception attempt for some of the affective states).

The role of different expression modalities in the recognition of emotion

Much of the work in using actor portrayals has been interested in cue utilization in the recognition of the intended emotion by observers, an essential aspect of the study of pull effects. Much of this literature has been concerned with the role of different expression modalities and the respective communication channels, for example, vocal expression as carried in the audio modality versus facial and gestural expression as carried in the video modality. Because researchers have traditionally specialized in the domain of the face (the large majority) or the voice (a small minority), most corpora have been recorded in only one modality. In the case of facial expression, much of the work has even been limited to static photographs (which essentially eliminates the important dynamic character of unfolding emotion). As in our earlier actor portrayal studies (Banse and Scherer 1996; Bänziger *et al.* 2009; Scherer and Ellgring 2007*a,b*), we feel that it is essential to work with multimodal corpora in which the portrayed expressions of each actor are recorded in both the video and audio mode. Only such multimodal corpora allow us to study the relative importance of audio and video cues both in isolation and in interaction. The GEMEP corpus described in the following sections is such a multimodal stimulus set, in which high-quality video recordings (including different close-ups of upper body and face, frontal and side view) and digital audio recordings have been obtained.

This chapter, apart from describing the procedures used to produce the corpus and the results of the validation studies, also presents first data on the effects of available modalities on the accuracy of emotion recognition and the perceived intensity and believability of the portrayals. From the patterns of results reported in the literature (Scherer 1999*c*), we hypothesized that the availability of both auditory (voice) and visual (face, gestures, posture) cues should lead to maximal accuracy.

In addition to this predicted main effect for the audio-plus-visual modality, we expected *emotion by modality interactions*, that is, some emotions being better recognized in the audio-only condition and others in the video-only condition. We also examine the role of the type of utterance used (two different nonlinguistic sentences and the sustained vowel 'aaa') on the accuracy of emotion recognition and the perceived intensity and believability of the portrayals.

Methods used to produce and validate the corpus

This section consists of two parts: (1) a detailed description of the production of the corpus (portrayal procedures, recording, and clip selection) and (2) a description of the methods used to gather data on the recognition of the portrayed emotions in the master set. We expect this description (including the supplementary materials)[2] to be used as the reference for all future analyses or tests derived from this corpus.

Production of the corpus

Actors

Ten actors (5 females) were recruited with the help of a professional director (Andrea Novikov), who also supervised the acting during the recordings. The 10 actors are all professional theater actors living and working in the French-speaking part of Switzerland. They were hired for 1 day each at professional rates.

Portrayal procedures

Several weeks before coming to the laboratory, actors received the list of the emotions they were to portray, together with short definitions of the emotion and brief scenarios to illustrate the labels (see Table 6.1.2 for English translations of the original French definitions). Three scenarios were created to instantiate each affective state (see the supplementary materials). A scenario includes the essential features of a situation, which is assumed to elicit a given emotional reaction. Whenever possible, the scenarios included explicit references to one or more interaction partner(s). The actors were requested to improvise interactions with the director, in which they expressed a given affective state. In addition to the written instructions, the actors participated in a preparatory session with the director.

The 12 categories presented in the four cells of Table 6.1.1 were portrayed by all 10 actors. The six additional categories presented below the table were split into two groups and were portrayed by five actors each. The portrayals of the emotions allotted to a particular actor were produced, with frequent pauses, in the order chosen by the director. The portrayals were produced in an interactive setting, with the director serving as the addressee of the expressed emotions. On the basis of the structural descriptions of the emotions that had been agreed upon with the director, he interactively produced an appropriate mood in each actor by eliciting personal life events in which the actor had experienced the emotion. The procedure followed the philosophy of the

---

[2] Supplementary materials. The complexity of the GEMEP corpus, along with the richness of the rating studies, prevents us from including all the available data in one chapter. Nevertheless, we decided to provide the research community with this descriptive data. The data can be downloaded from www.affective-sciences.org/gemep. The supplementary material is intended to be the reference guide that includes detailed information on the corpus and its creation as well as all the available data generated for the GEMEP corpus. In consequence, it will be continually enriched with newer data.

Table 6.1.2 Definitions of emotions portrayed

Emotion	Definition
Admiration	Amazement at the extraordinary qualities of a person, a landscape, or a work of art
Amusement	Roaring with laughter at something that is very funny
Anger	Extreme displeasure caused by someone's stupid or hostile action
Tenderness	Being moved by a touching action, behaviour, or utterance
Disgust	Revulsion when faced with an unpleasant object or environment
Despair	Distress at a life problem with no solution, together with an unwillingness to accept the situation
Pride	Feeling of triumph following a success or a personal achievement (one's own or that of someone close)
Shame	Self-esteem shaken by an error or clumsiness for which one feels responsible
Anxiety (worry)	Fear of the consequences of a situation that could be unfavourable for oneself or someone close
Interest	Being attracted, fascinated, or having one's attention captured by a person or a thing
Irritation	Experiencing displeasure at something or someone while still remaining calm
Joy (elation)	Feeling transported by a fabulous thing that occurred unexpectedly
Contempt	Disapproval of the socially or morally reprehensible conduct of another person
Panic fear	Being faced with an imminent danger that threatens our survival or physical well-being
Pleasure (sensual)	Experiencing an extraordinary feeling of well-being and sensual delight
Relief	Feeling reassured at the end or resolution of an uncomfortable, unpleasant, or even dangerous situation
Surprise	Being abruptly faced with an unexpected and unusual event (without positive or negative connotation)
Sadness	Feeling discouraged by the irrevocable loss of a person, place, or thing

Stanislavski acting method. Portrayals for each emotion were repeated until the director and the actor were satisfied with their performance.

Modulations of intensity and attempts at masking (regulations) were produced only for the states represented in the four cells of Table 6.1.1 (i.e. not for the additional states represented under Table 6.1.1). Each actor produced the three regulations (less intense, more intense, and masked) for six of the categories represented in Table 6.1.1. Different actors produced modulations of intensity and masking for different subsets of emotions. Actors 1, 3, 6, 7, and 8 portrayed regulations for hot anger (hot), despair (des), anxiety (anx), amusement (amu), interest (int), and pleasure (ple). Actors 2, 4, 5, 9, and 10 portrayed regulations for pride (pri), joy (joy), relief (rel), panic fear (pan), irritation (irr), and sadness (sad). The instructions made it clear for the actors that an emotion could have different degrees of intensity as reflected in the expressions 'I felt a little anger' or 'I was very angry'. The instruction to portray an emotion and to mask it simultaneously might appear paradoxical, but it made perfect sense for the actors who frequently meet this kind of request to impersonate a character who is placed in a situation that elicits strong emotions but who tries to conceal them.

Types of utterances

As the basis for their expression portrayals, the actors were asked to utter, at the apex of the relived or simulated emotion, the following two standardized sentences: (a) 'ne kal ibam sud molen!' and (b) 'kun se mina lod belam?' These pseudo-linguistic phoneme sequences were chosen with the help of a phonetician to represent plausible phoneme combinations, with potentially similar pronunciations in a variety of Western languages. The actors were free to imagine different types of semantic meaning while uttering the meaningless sentences. They were further requested to express each affective state while uttering a sustained vowel ('aaa'), which allowed the recording of brief EEs, reminiscent of affect bursts or interjections (Scherer 1994a), in the absence of articulatory movements.

Recording technology and procedures

The portrayals were recorded in one of the interaction laboratories of the Geneva Emotion Research Group at the University of Geneva. Three digital cameras (SONY DSR-PDX10) were used to simultaneously record: (a) the facial expressions and head orientations of the actors; (b) body postures and gestures from the perspective of an interlocutor; and (c) body postures and gestures from the perspective of an observer standing to the right of the actors (see Figure 6.1.1). Sound was recorded by using three separate microphones located at each of the three cameras, plus an additional headset microphone (SENNHEISER) positioned over the left ear of the actor, providing a separate speech recording with a constant distance to the actor's mouth. The audio and video streams were recorded on four separate PCs by using the DV-AVI (PAL, 720×576) format for video and the PCM WAV (41 kHz) for audio. Each recording session lasted around 6 hours.

Editing of individual clips

Video and audio recordings were aligned (with a precision of 1/24 s because the video cameras were not frame synchronized) and segmented on the level of single sentences. Recordings containing the two standard sentences (pseudo-speech) and the sustained vowel, as well as improvised sentences (in French), were extracted and saved into separate digital files. Over 7300 such sequences, among them about 5000 containing the pseudo-linguistic sentences and the sustained

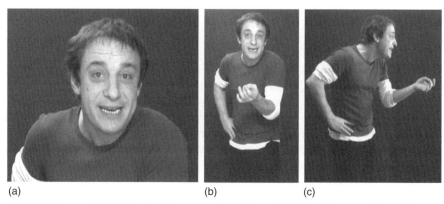

(a)   (b)   (c)

Fig. 6.1.1 Still frames illustrating the three camera angles used in the video recording of the actor portrayals.

vowels, were extracted from the original interactions. This implies that the portrayals are extracted from ongoing interactions and therefore most often start and end with an 'ongoing emotion'. This constitutes a major difference with other corpora of acted emotion portrayals, which often feature brief portrayals that start and end with a 'neutral' expression.

Selection of portrayals for a master set

Expert ratings were carried out to select a reduced number of portrayals with standard speech content for subsequent analyses. Three research assistants (advanced psychology students: 1 male; 2 female) were requested to assess the technical quality of the recordings and the aptitude of the actors to convey the intended emotional impression, in both vocal and facial expressions. Although the three raters showed much disagreement in their judgements, this first assessment of the portrayals allowed us to observe that some actors produced a higher proportion of 'convincing' portrayals than did other actors. Furthermore, there were first indications that some emotions might be more easily conveyed in either facial or vocal displays.

Based on the assessments, a selection of portrayals featuring an equal number of recordings for each actor and each portrayal category was established. Two portrayals for each condition and each actor (i.e. 126 portrayals per actor) were chosen in an iterative selection procedure by three research collaborators. Given the information provided by the expert ratings and their obvious limitations (low agreement, important rater biases, and limited number of raters), the selection had to be based on relatively complex decisions and could not be entirely systematized. In this fashion, a master set of 1260 recordings was established.

Lay ratings of portrayals in the master set

Participants

Ninety participants, mostly undergraduate students from different departments, including psychology, were recruited via announcements in the university buildings and outside the university (e.g. in choirs of amateur singers). The participants were randomly assigned to rating either audio-only (31 participants, 18 female, 29 years old on average), or video-only (31 participants, 25 female, 23 years old on average), or audio-video portrayals (28 participants, 15 female, 29 years old on average). The raters were paid 10 CHF for each rating session and could earn up to 100 CHF if they returned for the total of 10 sessions. However, several raters did not complete all 10 sessions. As a consequence, some portrayals were assessed by a few more raters than others (the count is provided in the supplementary materials).

Procedure

The 1260 selected portrayals were rated in 10 sessions of 126 portrayals produced by separate actors. A rating session always started with a set of written instructions on the rating procedure and the definitions of the emotion categories portrayed by the actors. All sessions took place in a small laboratory equipped with six computers separated by 'open space' walls. Headphones were used to display the sound. One to four raters could take part simultaneously. In each session, a computer interface displayed the portrayals produced by a selected actor in two blocks: the 96 standard sentences produced by the actor were presented first in random order (a new random order for each rater was computed at the start of each session), followed by a short break, and then by the 30 portrayals produced with a sustained 'aaa' by the same actor, also in random order. The intensity of the sound recordings was normalized within each block to accommodate the hearing of the raters (the actors screamed in some recordings and whispered in others; the resulting variability is so large that it would not have been possible to display all recordings at a constant sound level without normalizing the sound level beforehand). The video files were compressed to a DivX format without perceptible quality loss. The video resolution was high, filling most of the screen surface. Several preset orders were defined for the successive sessions to counterbalance the sequence of actors rated. However, perfect counterbalancing was not achievable because we did not request that all raters complete the 10 rating sessions.

Presentation modalities

The ratings were collected with a computer interface that always displayed the portrayal to be rated either in audio-only (A), in video-only (V), or in audio-video (AV) modality, depending on the randomly assigned condition for a given rater.

Instruments and procedures

First, a rating of the 'believability' of each emotional portrayal was requested. Believability was rated on a continuous visual analogue scale, the location of the cursor on screen being transformed to a linear scale ranging from 0 to 10. The scale was defined on screen as the 'capacity of the actor to communicate a natural emotional impression' and ranged from 'very low—one does not get the impression of a real emotion' to 'very high—one gets the impression of a real emotion'.

Upon confirmation of the rater's answer regarding believability, the computer displayed the 15 emotion categories portrayed by the actor on a circle (a variant of the Geneva emotion wheel; Scherer 2005b). The task of the participants was to select one or two categories on this circle and simultaneously rate the level of intensity (on a 4-point scale) for each of the selected categories. The emotional intensity was represented visually by the size of a bubble on screen. A legend specified that the smallest bubble corresponded to a 'very weak emotion', a larger bubble to a 'rather weak emotion', an even larger bubble to a 'rather strong emotion', and the largest bubble to a 'very strong emotion'. The definitions of emotions reproduced in Table 6.1.2 were displayed on screen when the rater was moving the cursor over the respective categories (coloured bubbles). The 15 categories are located on the circle according to their conceptual proximity, with positive emotions to the right side of the screen and negative emotions to the left side of the screen. Raters could select the white bubble in the centre of the circle if they wished to indicate that the recording did not express an emotion. They could also click a button to type another description for the emotion portrayed in any recording (this answer was classified as 'other emotion'). When a rater reported two categories, he or she had to answer a further pop-up question before proceeding to the evaluation of the next portrayal. Raters were asked to indicate if the reason for reporting two answers was either (forced choice) because those two emotions were represented in the portrayal ('mixed emotion') or because the rater was unsure and could not decide which of the two answers was 'correct'. The raters could replay the portrayal as often as they wished, both before rating believability and before selecting one or two categories.

Results of the validation study

In what follows, we present the results on the validity of the GEMEP master set in terms of (1) *reliability* (the greater the degree of agreement between judges the more reliable will be the effects of the use of the portrayals in stimulus presentations) and (2) *accuracy* (the more accurately the portrayals have been recognized the greater the likelihood that the actors produced a valid expression pattern for the respective emotions). As will be shown, the predictions on accuracy score differences between emotions and conditions vary from case to case. In the interest of readability, we do not provide details of all statistical procedures, coefficients, and exact significance levels in the text nor do we discuss peripheral or weak effects. Some of the statistical coefficients are reported in the footnotes to Table 6.1.4; all other detail can be found in the supplementary material (see footnote 2).

Overall accuracy of emotion judgements

We computed accuracy scores for each rater in the form of a percentage of correct answers provided. An answer was defined as correct if a category reported by the participant matched the expressive intention of the actor. In cases in which a second category was reported (the instructions permitted one or two answers for each portrayal to allow for the report of mixed emotions), the answer was still considered correct. Table 6.1.3 shows the mean and range of the accuracy scores for raters in the three groups of raters differing according to presentation modality.

The accuracy score theoretically expected by chance for 17 answer alternatives (15 emotions, no emotion, other emotion) is 5.88%. However, as two responses were allowed and given the problems of differential marginal response tendencies (see Banse and Scherer, 1996), the actual chance level is difficult to estimate. Yet, on the whole there can be no doubt that the overall accuracy levels reported in Table 6.1.3 largely exceed what could be expected by chance, which is unlikely to exceed 10–12%, providing evidence of the validity of the portrayals in terms of the encoding intentions of the actors. This is particularly the case, given the large number of emotion alternatives, greatly exceeding the range used in most earlier studies, and the subtlety of many of the emotions used (as compared to the limited sets of basic emotions used in earlier work).

Interrater reliability of emotion judgements and believability and intensity ratings

For emotion judgements, we computed separate confusion matrices for all raters (including double answers when two answers were provided) and correlated the confusion profiles of each rater with each other rater. An average profile correlation per rater was computed as an agreement index. Mean and range for this index per rater group (after excluding two outliers) are shown in Table 6.1.3. These average profile correlations, ranging from 0.76 to 0.88, are extremely high, given the complex nature of the task, and demonstrate a large extent of agreement between raters in assigning emotion labels. It should be noted that this holds even in cases in which the actor intention was not accurately inferred, suggesting that the portrayals generally provide relatively unequivocal messages even if the actor did not succeed in portraying a specific emotion but rather a close member of the family or a similar emotion (as shown by the lawful patterns of confusion shown in Table 6.1.5).

Table 6.1.3 Accuracy for the three presentation modalities and average interrater profile correlations

	Audio-video	Audio	Video
Number of raters	23	23	25
Average accuracy (%)	57	38	50
Range (%)	35	29	22
Average profile correlation r	0.89	0.76	0.87
Range of r	0.14	0.23	0.09

The reliability of the ratings on the quantitative scale intensity (four levels labelled 1 to 4 from the least intense to the most intense) and believability (continuous visual analogue scale raging from 0 to 10) was estimated with average intraclass correlation coefficients (ICCs) for the raters who provided a complete set of ratings (1260 ratings for the portrayals produced by all 10 actors). For believability, the average ICC varies between 0.63 and 0.69; for intensity, ICC varies between 0.84 and 0.90. Further detail can be found in the supplementary materials. Again, given the complexity and amplitude of the task, as well as the difficulty of defining believability as a dimension, these coefficients compare favourably to what can be expected in most ratings studies (see Rosenthal 1987). The lower level of agreement for believability is accounted for by the high degree of subjectivity in defining and judging this quality.

Accuracy for differences between core emotions, presentation modalities, and verbal content types

First, we will discuss the ratings for the portrayals produced with baseline intensity (i.e. portrayals that are not regulated) and for the 12 core emotions produced by all actors. A four-way repeated measures ANOVA was computed on the accuracy data (defined as the proportion of raters who provided correct answer). Within variables are: Modality (3 levels: audio, video, audio-video) × Emotion (12 levels: pride, joy, amusement, interest, pleasure, relief, hot anger, panic fear, despair, irritation, anxiety, sadness) × Verbal Content (3 levels: sentence 1, sentence 2, 'aaa') and Repetition (2 levels: instance 1 and instance 2). The descriptive results are shown in Table 6.1.4(a).

The ANOVA showed main effects for modality and emotion. The accuracy is lowest (0.42) for portrayals presented in audio-only, somewhat higher (0.55) for video-only modality, and most accurate (0.61) for audio-video modality. For differences among the 12 core emotions—independently of verbal content, presentation modality, and repetition—the average accuracy varies greatly, as shown in the last column of Table 6.1.4, between 0.36 for despair and 0.81 for panic fear. No main effect was found for the two other variables, indicating that neither repetition nor sentence type systematically affected accuracy. It is particularly remarkable that the overall accuracy for portrayals featuring solely a sustained vowel was as high as the accuracy for pseudo-speech portrayals, which were on average much longer and could potentially include more cues.

Significant two-way interaction effects were found for Modality × Emotion and for Emotion × Verbal Content. The former, illustrated in Figure 6.1.2, is due to the fact that some core emotions go against the general trend (audio < video < audio-video. Thus, for hot anger accuracy is slightly higher for video-only than for the other two modalities and, for joy, pride, sadness, and anxiety, accuracy based on video only is at about the same level as in the audio-video modality. The Emotion × Verbal Content effect is due to the fact that for some emotions (e.g. relief, panic fear, and amusement) the portrayals using 'aaa' are better recognized than those for pseudo-speech sentences, independently of the expressive modality considered. The opposite is true for other emotions (e.g. sadness, pride).

The difference between pseudo-speech as used in sentences 1 and 2 and the sustained 'aaa' is theoretically interesting, as it may indicate the differential role of certain phonemic cues. In contrast, the two sentences were construed according to the same principles and only served to examine the effect of different vowel sequences. To test directly the effect of difference between the two pseudo-sentences, a repeated measures ANOVA with the same four factors but including only two levels (sentence 1 and sentence 2) for the variable verbal content was run. No significant effects involving sentence type were found, suggesting that the difference due to the different

Table 6.1.4 Accuracy score means for all emotions by two verbal contents and three display modalities

Accuracy			Audio-Video		Audio		Video		Grand total
Valence	Arousal	Target emotion	Sent 1	aaa	Sent1	aaa	Sent 1	aaa	
(a) Core emotions									
Positive	High	pri	0.64	0.50	0.24	0.10	0.57	0.35	0.40
		joy	0.70	0.55	0.35	0.20	0.67	0.64	0.52
		amu	0.72	0.87	0.57	0.78	0.69	0.74	0.73
	High total		0.69	0.64	0.39	0.36	0.64	0.58	0.55
	Low	int	0.52	0.56	0.26	0.30	0.44	0.52	0.43
		ple	0.61	0.56	0.31	0.40	0.39	0.38	0.44
		rel	0.77	0.90	0.49	0.73	0.64	0.76	0.71
	Low total		0.63	0.67	0.35	0.48	0.49	0.55	0.53
Positive total			0.66	0.65	0.37	0.42	0.57	0.57	0.54
Negative	High	hot	0.69	0.76	0.67	0.72	0.76	0.80	0.73
		pan	0.79	0.97	0.66	0.81	0.66	0.97	0.81
		des	0.43	0.48	0.31	0.33	0.25	0.35	0.36
	High total		0.64	0.74	0.55	0.62	0.55	0.71	0.63
	Low	irr	0.64	0.59	0.51	0.31	0.50	0.48	0.50
		anx	0.57	0.54	0.40	0.29	0.52	0.45	0.46
		sad	0.43	0.26	0.45	0.23	0.43	0.41	0.37
	Low total		0.54	0.46	0.45	0.28	0.49	0.45	0.44
Negative total			0.59	0.60	0.50	0.45	0.52	0.58	0.54
Total			0.63	0.63	0.44	0.43	0.54	0.57	0.54
(b) Additional emotions									
		adm	0.54	0.61	0.39	0.23	0.39	0.51	0.44
		sha	0.22	0.24	0.11	0.03	0.27	0.29	0.19
		con	0.66	0.54	0.25	0.10	0.61	0.57	0.45
		ten	0.45	0.70	0.30	0.22	0.27	0.53	0.41
		dis	0.76	0.98	0.12	0.59	0.50	0.77	0.62
		sur	0.56	0.73	0.33	0.47	0.33	0.59	0.50
Total			0.53	0.63	0.25	0.27	0.40	0.54	0.44
Grand total			0.61	0.63	0.40	0.40	0.51	0.57	0.52

Note. For space efficiency, the table displays only the values for sentence 1 as no significant difference was found between sentence 1 and sentence 2.

Abbreviations. Sent1 = Sentence 1; aaa = sustained vowel "aaa"; pri = pride; joy = joy; amu = amusement; int = interest; ple = pleasure; rel = relief; hot = hot anger; pan = panic fear; des = despair; irr = irritation; anx = anxiety; sad = sadness; adm = admiration; sha = shame; con = contempt; ten = tenderness; dis = disgust; sur = surprise. In this table, accuracy means the average proportion of raters choosing the correct category.

Overall ANOVA main effects for modality, $F(2, 16) = 93.19$, $p < 0.001$, $\eta^2 = 0.92$, and emotion, $F(11, 88) = 19.84$, $p < 0.001$, $\eta^2 = 0.71$. All differences between modality levels are significant in post hoc tests with Bonferroni adjustment. two-way interaction effects for Modality × Emotion, $F(22, 176) = 6.66$, $p < 0.001$, $\eta^2 = 0.45$, and for Emotion × Verbal Content, $F(22, 176) = 5.76$, $p < 0.001$, $\eta^2 = 0.42$. No three-way interaction effects beyond what could be expected by chance.

Valence × Arousal ANOVA: main effect for arousal, $F(1, 9) = 53.90$, $p < 0.001$, $\eta^2 = 0.86$.; two-way interaction between valence and display modality, $F(2, 18) = 19.96$, $p < 0.001$, $\eta^2 = 0.69$; three-way effects, Modality × Valence × Verbal Content, $F(4, 36) = 3.43$, $p = 0.018$, $\eta^2 = 0.28$; Verbal Content × Repetition × Arousal, $F(2, 18) = 4.53$, $p = 0.025$, $\eta^2 = 0.34$; Verbal Content × Valence × Arousal, $F(2, 18) = 37.45$, $p < 0.001$, $\eta^2 = 0.81$; and Repetition × Valence × Arousal. $F(2, 18) = 17.54$, $p < 0.001$, $\eta^2 = 0.66$.

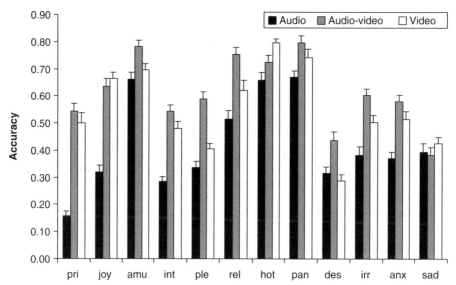

Fig. 6.1.2 Accuracy for modalities and core emotions with baseline intensity. pri, pride; joy, joy; amu, amusement; int, interest; ple, pleasure; rel, relief; hot, hot anger; pan, panic fear; des, despair; irr, irritation; anx, anxiety; sad, sadness.

phonetic material used in the two sentences can be disregarded and that the effects are likely to be similar for phoneme sequences of similar construction. Obviously, we cannot rule out specific effects due to using linguistically meaningful speech material. The absence of an effect for repetition also confirms the high stability of the inferences based on the actor portrayals.

To summarize the results for the different emotions in a systematic fashion according to the underlying Valence × Arousal design of the corpus described in the introduction, a repeated measures ANOVA for the mean accuracy scores computed for the four quadrants of Table 6.1.1 was performed. The results did not show any difference for valence but a main effect for arousal, with high aroused emotions significantly better recognized (average accuracy 0.58) than low aroused emotions (0.48). However, there was also a significant interaction between valence and presentation modality, indicating that the recognition of positive emotions might rely much more on visual cues than that of negative emotions (see Figure 6.1.3). When *only* audio cues are available, accuracy for positive emotions (0.38) is lower than for negative emotions (0.47). But when the portrayals are presented in the *audio-video* modality, accuracy for positive emotions (0.64) increases more than that for negative emotions (0.59), suggesting that the association of audio and visual cues is especially important in order to accurately recognize positive emotions. A three-way interaction between valence, display modality, and arousal (see Figure 6.1.3), shows that the difference between positive and negative emotions is imputable to the negative high aroused emotions (panic fear, hot anger, despair), which are better recognized than other emotions specifically when they are presented in the audio only modality, and to the negative low aroused emotions (anxiety, irritation, sadness), which are less well recognized when presented in audio-video modality. For the sake of economy, we do not describe four additional three-way interactions here because they are of minor interest (see the supplementary materials for further details).

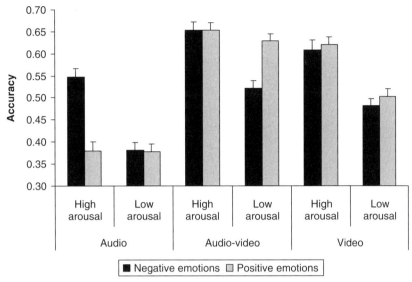

Fig. 6.1.3 Accuracy for modalities, valence, and arousal with baseline intensity.

Accuracy for differences between additional emotions, presentation modalities, and verbal content types

To reduce the total number of portrayals to a manageable size, six additional emotions were portrayed by only half of the actors: actors 2, 4, 5, 9, and 10 portrayed admiration, disgust, and shame, while actors 1, 3, 6, 7, and 8 portrayed tenderness, contempt, and surprise. The mean accuracy scores are listed in Table 6.1.4(b) and plotted in Figure 6.1.4. Two separate repeated measures ANOVAs on those two subsets of data were performed (using the same four factors as before)

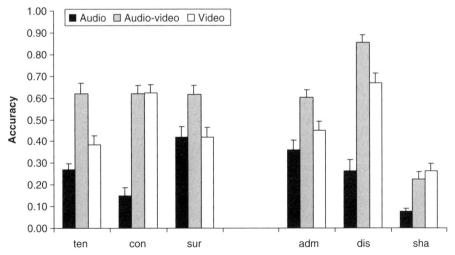

Fig. 6.1.4 Accuracy for additional emotions and different modalities. ten, tenderness; con, contempt; sur, surprise; adm, admiration; dis, disgust; sha, shame.

to analyse the effects on differences in accuracy. In both subsets of data, the ANOVAs showed a significant main effect of modality, again with audio-only less well recognized than those with a video component. A main effect of emotion for group 2 can be attributed to the less accurate recognition of shame portrayals. Significant Emotion × Modality interactions suggest that, for some emotions (especially tenderness, surprise, admiration, disgust), accuracy is relatively higher when the portrayals are presented with sound and picture (audio-video), with the accuracy decreasing when sound is absent (video-only; see Figure 6.1.4). An Emotion × Verbal Content interaction in group 2 indicates that portrayals of disgust using the 'aaa' are more accurately recognized than those for pseudo-speech sentences, an effect that is accentuated when the portrayals are presented in audio-only modality. As for the core emotions, there are no differences between the two types of sentences and for repetition, suggesting a high level of stability of the effects over successive instances when produced by the same actors in the same recording session. The detailed statistics for these effects can be found in the supplementary materials.

Inter-emotion confusions and reports of mixed emotions for core and additional emotions with baseline intensity

Confusion matrices, showing the proportion with which each category is selected for each portrayed emotion, were created separately for the three presentation modalities and for verbal content (sentence 1 versus vowel 'aaa', see note for Table 6.1.4). The detailed tables for these six confusion matrices are available in the supplementary materials. For the sake of economy, only the major confusions (defined as larger than 2 × chance level) are shown in Table 6.1.5, along with the proportion of correct answers. The proportion of correct answers is computed on the basis of the diagonals in the confusion matrices, i.e. including double answers as separate answers, with at least one incorrect answer when a double answer is provided. These proportions are by definition slightly lower than the accuracy figures used to compute the ANOVAs reported earlier (where an answer was considered correct if one of two alternatives was correct).

For some emotions with low recognition accuracy, the answers are spread over several categories, whereas for others the confusions are much more systematic. A particularly striking example is shame produced with a sustained 'aaa' and presented in the audio-only modality. Only 3% of the answers went to the correct category, shame, the remainder being spread over many categories, including the category neutral (i.e. not emotional by our definition). This is not the case for all emotions with low recognition rates; for example, for admiration (in the audio 'aaa' condition), the correct label 'admiration' represents 19% of all answers, whereas the label 'pleasure' represents 31% and the label 'relief' 39% of all answers provided, and other labels are never or rarely used. For some emotions, symmetric confusion patterns are found (for both types of verbal content and for all presentation modalities); thus, sadness is often judged as despair and vice versa. Other confusions are asymmetrical: hot anger is often categorized as irritation, and amusement as joy, but only a few confusions go into the other direction. The fact that the most frequent confusions are not necessarily reciprocal suggests that the categories are not simply equivalent or synonymous.

As shown in Table 6.1.5, there are systematic confusions that are modality-specific (or at least more salient in some modalities), depending on whether audio or video information is available. This suggests that confusions may be partly based on lack of salient cues when only a single channel is available and/or that it takes specific cues in a specific modality to recognize certain emotions.

While the confusion matrix provides very rich information and can be the source of important hypotheses for future research with respect to emotion similarities between and within families

Table 6.1.5 Proportion of answers going to the target category and major confusions (> 0.125)

	AV-sent1		AV-aaa		A-sent1		A-aaa		V-sent1		V-aaa	
	target	maj. conf.	target	maj. conf.	target	maj. conf.	target	maj. conf.	target	maj. conf.	target	maj. conf.
pri	0.56		0.41	joy 0.18	0.20	irr 0.24	0.09	irr 0.16	0.49	joy 0.18	0.31	joy 0.34
joy	0.60		0.47	ple 0.15	0.26		0.16	amu 0.15 and pan 0.14	0.56		0.55	
amu	0.68	joy 0.17	0.81		0.44	joy 0.18	0.63	joy 0.26	0.62	joy 0.19	0.67	joy 0.19
int	0.46		0.47		0.22	neu 0.13	0.24	ple 0.15 & rel 0.18	0.39	irr 0.18	0.48	
ple	0.53	rel 0.17	0.49	rel 0.29	0.26	rel 0.17	0.32	rel 0.36	0.33	rel 0.20	0.33	rel 0.29
rel	0.69		0.82		0.42		0.60	ple 0.22	0.56	ple 0.14	0.70	ple 0.15
hot	0.64	irr 0.31	0.71	irr 0.25	0.51	irr 0.35	0.59	irr 0.27	0.67	irr 0.29	0.75	irr 0.19
pan	0.70	anx 0.18	0.94		0.52	anx 0.20	0.71		0.56	anx 0.20	0.89	
des	0.34	anx 0.17 & sad 0.20	0.41	pan 0.21 & sad 0.21	0.23	anx 0.19 & sad 0.18	0.26	pan 0.26 & sad 0.17	0.20	anx 0.20 & sad .23	0.29	pan 0.15 & sad 0.37
irr	0.58	hot 0.13	0.54	hot 0.13	0.43	hot 0.13	0.26		0.45	hot 0.16	0.43	hot 0.15
anx	0.51	pan 0.13	0.47	pan 0.24	0.34	irr 0.13	0.25	pan 0.15	0.47		0.40	pan 0.15
sad	0.38	irr 0.42	0.24	des 0.26	0.38	des 0.20	0.19	rel 0.17 & des 0.17	0.37	des 0.36	0.37	des 0.32
adm	0.48	ple 0.14	0.52	ple 0.14 & rel 0.15	0.33		0.19	ple 0.31 & rel 0.39	0.35	int 0.18	0.45	rel 0.16
sha	0.19	des 0.29	0.21	des 0.15 & anx 0.18	0.10	sad 0.16	0.03	rel 0.15 & neu 0.14	0.24	des 0.20	0.26	des 0.15 & anx 0.15

(continued)

Table 6.1.5 (continued) Proportion of answers going to the target category and major confusions (> 0.125)

	AV-sent1		AV-aaa		A-sent1		A-aaa		V-sent1		V-aaa	
	target	maj. conf.	target	maj. conf.	target	maj. conf.	target	maj. conf.	target	maj. conf.	target	maj. conf.
con	0.56	irr 0.14	0.48	irr 0.19	0.21		0.08	ple 0.20 & rel 0.23 & irr 0.15	0.54	irr 0.13	0.51	
ten	0.40	ple 0.24	0.65	ple 0.15	0.24	ple 0.15	0.19	ple 0.14 & rel 0.13	0.23	joy 0.15 & amu 0.14 & ple 0.24	0.49	ple 0.13
dis	0.70		0.98		0.10	sad 0.23	0.55		0.43	sad 0.25	0.71	
sur	0.46	anx 0.25	0.60		0.26	anx 0.15	0.40	pan 0.15	0.27	anx 0.29	0.53	sad 0.20

Note. AV, audio-video; A, audio; V, video; sent1, Sentence 1; aaa, sustained vowel 'aaa'; maj. conf., major confusions; pri, pride; joy, joy; amu, amusement; int, interest; ple, pleasure; rel, relief; hot, hot anger; pan, panic fear; des, despair; irr, irritation; anx, anxiety; sad, sadness; adm, admiration; sha, shame; con, contempt; ten, tenderness; dis, disgust; sur, surprise; neu, neutral.

and the nature of the differentiating cues, a more detailed discussion would exceed the confines of this chapter, which is mostly focused on the reliability and validity of the corpus. The latter are confirmed by the fact that the confusions are generally meaningful and give rise to justifiable interpretations.

Accuracy for portrayals produced with regulation attempts (modulations of intensity and masking)

Two separate repeated measures ANOVAs were computed with the accuracy data for the two subsets of emotions portrayed by different actors (see 'Production of the corpus'). The ANOVAs included four within factors: regulation (four levels: masked, less intense, baseline intensity, more intense); emotion (six levels: hot anger, despair, anxiety, amusement, interest, and pleasure in the first analysis; pride, joy, relief, panic fear, irritation, and sadness in the second analysis); modality (three levels: audio, video, audio-video); and repetition (two levels: instance 1 and instance 2). Repeated contrasts were computed to estimate the effect of the four regulations on recognition accuracy. Contrasts were defined on the basis of the hypothesis that the masked portrayals would be the least well recognized (because they are disguised) and that less intense emotion portrayals would be more subtle and therefore less accurately recognized than portrayals produced with baseline intensity or more intense emotion portrayals. Contrasts also tested the assumption that the more intense emotion portrayals would be more accurately recognized than would the portrayals with baseline emotional intensity, provided that more emotional intensity might result in more stereotypical portrayals.

The analysis of those two subsets of data showed differences for emotion and display modality comparable to those described in the previous section. Regarding the influence of the regulations (masking the emotion, baseline intensity, and less and more intense emotions), there was a main effect of regulation in both subsets, shown in Figure 6.1.5. The contrasts showed that the masked portrayals were less accurately recognized than were other portrayals. The differences between the three degrees of intensity go in the expected direction but do not reach significance. Statistical coefficients and further detail are provided in the supplementary materials.

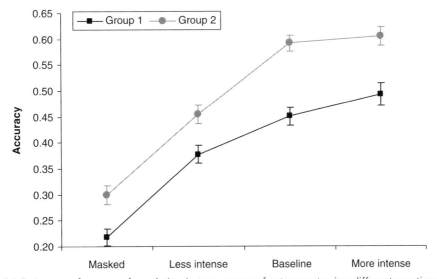

Fig. 6.1.5 Accuracy for types of regulation in two groups of actors portraying different emotions.

Intensity ratings for portrayals produced with regulation attempts (modulations of intensity and masking)

An average intensity rating was computed for each portrayal. When a rater reported two emotion labels with different intensities for one portrayal, the highest intensity reported was retained. When a rater chose to indicate that a portrayal did not express an emotion or that it expressed an emotion not listed among the 15 alternatives proposed for each portrayal, he or she did not explicitly report an intensity level; such answers were therefore not used for the computation of the average intensity score.

We expected that the average intensity ratings would vary in accordance with the instructions provided to the actors regarding intensity regulations (baseline intensity, less intense, and more intense emotion portrayals). To test this assumption, two separate repeated measures ANOVAs were computed on two subsets of data, as described in the preceding section. The masked portrayals were not included in this analysis because we did not expect those portrayals to be as accurately recognized as the other portrayals and made no assumptions regarding their emotional intensity. The ANOVAs included four within factors: regulation (three levels: less intense, baseline intensity, more intense); emotion (six levels: hot anger, despair, anxiety, amusement, interest, and pleasure in the first analysis; pride, joy, relief, panic fear, irritation, and sadness in the second analysis); modality (three levels: audio, video, audio-video); and repetition (two levels: instance 1 and instance 2). Repeated contrasts were computed to estimate the effect of the three intensity regulations on the average intensity rating. Contrasts were defined based on the hypothesis that the less intense emotion portrayals would be rated as less intense than portrayals produced with baseline intensity and that portrayals with more intensity would be rated as more intense than portrayals with baseline intensity.

All main effects except the repetition were significant. Most importantly, the contrasts confirmed the expected differences for regulated portrayals in both groups (see Figure 6.1.6). The less intense emotion portrayals (2.53 in group 1 and 2.46 in group 2) were rated as less intense than were the portrayals produced with baseline intensity (2.73 and 2.71) and the more intense emotion portrayals (3.09 and 3.11) were indeed rated as more intense than were the portrayals

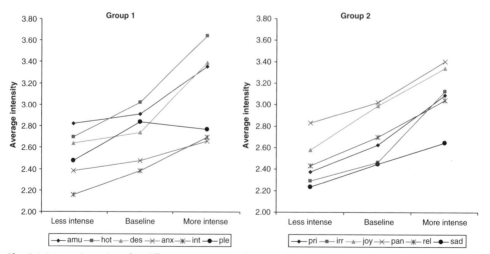

Fig. 6.1.6 Intensity ratings for different emotions and types of regulation in two groups of actors portraying different emotions. amu, amusement; hot, hot anger; des, despair; anx, anxiety; int, interest; ple, pleasure; pri, pride; irr, irritation; joy, joy; pan, panic fear; rel, relief; sad, sadness (see plate 11).

produced with baseline intensity. Further details, statistical coefficients, and a plot of the means can be found in the supplemental materials.

Believability ratings for portrayals produced with regulation attempts (modulations of intensity and masking)

The effects of different regulations (baseline intensity, less intense, more intense, masked), which were previously assessed for accuracy, were tested in the same way for the average ratings of believability computed for each portrayal in each display modality (audio, video, and audio-video). We repeated the statistical analyses described earlier (two independent repeated measures ANOVAs for two data subsets featuring different actors and different emotions), but the assumptions tested by the contrast analyses were different. We predicted that the masked portrayals would be rated as the least believable. This assumption relies on the instructions provided to the actors to disguise their emotional displays; this was thought to introduce conflicting cues that might result in awkward and less believable emotion portrayals. We furthermore speculated that the instruction to produce more intense emotional portrayals might result in overacting and consequently drive raters to perceive the more intense portrayals as less believable than the portrayals with baseline intensity. Finally, we also hypothesized that the instruction to produce less intense portrayals might have the opposite effect (i.e. prime the actors to produce more subtle and perhaps also more realistic emotion portrayals).

The results are shown in Figure 6.1.7. The repeated measures ANOVA computed for the first group yielded significant contrasts showing that the masked portrayals were rated as less believable (average 6.3) than were the other portrayals (average 6.7 for more intense emotion portrayals and for baseline intensity; 6.6 for less intense emotion portrayals). There were no significant differences between degrees of intensity. The low level of believability of masked portrayals was confirmed for the second group, but here significant contrasts showed that the masked portrayals were not rated as significantly less believable (average 6.1) than were the more intense portrayals (average 6.3), whereas the portrayals with baseline intensity (average 6.7) were rated as more believable than were both the less intense emotion portrayals (average 6.4) and the more intense emotion portrayals (average 6.3).

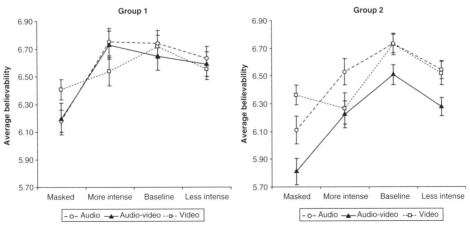

Fig. 6.1.7 Believability ratings for different emotions and types of regulation in two groups of actors portraying different emotions (see plate 12).

Table 6.1.6 Intercorrelations between accuracy proportions, intensity, and believability ratings for three modalities

	Accuracy	Believability
Audio		
Believability	0.483	
Intensity	0.570	0.518
Video		
Believability	0.299	
Intensity	0.573	0.185
Audio-video		
Believability	0.382	
Intensity	0.597	0.472

Note. All correlations are significant at $p < 0.001$ (two-tailed); $N = 1260$.

Relationships between accuracy, believability, and intensity ratings

We computed correlations between accuracy, average believability, and average intensity ratings for all portrayals selected in the corpus ($N = 1260$). Separate correlations were computed for the three presentation modalities (see Table 6.1.6). The relationship between accuracy (proportion of raters who recognize the emotion portrayed in a given audio or video recording) and believability (average ratings for the authenticity of the portrayals) is interesting in several respects. There are explicit speculations about acted emotion portrayals, to the effect that acted emotion portrayals that are highly recognizable are also very stereotypical and would not create an authentic or realistic impression. The significant correlations between accuracy and believability suggest the opposite interpretation. The more readily recognizable a portrayal is, the more believable (authentic or realistic) it was rated in our study. Intensity ratings appear to be correlated with both accuracy and believability, indicating that more extreme portrayals (that are rated as expressing strong emotions) are not only better recognized than less extreme portrayals, but they are also perceived to be more authentic or more realistic.

Discussion and outlook

Validation of the corpus

These results suggest that the GEMEP corpus has been successfully validated, given the satisfactory degree of interrater agreement (reliability) and the high level of accuracy. It is important to note that a complete set of portrayals in all conditions of the corpus design were rated—a total of 1260 portrayals. The degree of accuracy found compares very favourably with established tests of emotion recognition. Table 6.1.7 shows a comparison of the GEMEP results with those of five tests obtained in a recent study (Bänziger *et al.* 2009): the MERT (the multimodal emotion recognition test; Bänziger *et al.* 2009); the PONS (profile of non-verbal sensitivity: Rosenthal *et al.* 1979); the DANVA (diagnostic analysis of non-verbal accuracy; Nowicki and Duke 1994); the ERI (emotion recognition index; Scherer and Scherer in preparation); and the JACFEE (Japanese and Caucasian facial expressions of emotion; Biehl *et al.* 1997). One source of incompatibility between tests stems from differing numbers of response alternatives on the answer sheet. To render the accuracy percentages comparable across tests despite differential answer formats, we computed

Table 6.1.7 Comparison of the proportion index (pi) for accuracy scores in different tests of emotion recognition (for three modalities)

Test	Audio-video	Audio (voice)	Video or picture (face)
GEMEP	0.96	0.90	0.95
MERT	0.95	0.90	0.95
PONS	0.84	0.62	0.81
DANVA		0.88	0.94
ERI		0.88	0.92
JACFEE			0.95

Note. GEMEP, Geneva multimodal emotion portrayal; MERT, multimodal emotion recognition test; PONS, profile of non-verbal sensitivity; DANVA, diagnostic analysis of non-verbal accuracy; ERI, emotion recognition index; JACFEE, Japanese and Caucasian facial expressions of emotion.

the one-sample effect size estimator called the proportion index, or pi (Hall *et al.* 2008; Rosenthal and Rubin 1989) shown in Table 6.1.7. Pi converts any mean accuracy that originates as a proportion, no matter how many response options each item had, to its equivalent proportion were it to have been based on two options.

The pi values for the GEMEP corpus are at least as high and in some cases higher than the pi values for the emotion recognition tests. This is remarkable if one considers that the items used in the tests have generally been carefully selected for accuracy from a larger set of portrayals, whereas the GEMEP values are based on a complete set of portrayals in the corpus that have not been selected earlier for accuracy. It is important to note that this holds not only for the so-called basic emotions, but also for the large number of more subtle, and much less studied, emotions that are included in the corpus.

Another aspect of validation is to establish the believability of the portrayals, which is essential if we are to use the corpus as a valid source for stimulus presentation in studies of the perception of and inference from emotional expression. Actors were instructed to produce expressions that make an authentic impression on the receivers of their performance—as they would attempt to do on the stage. The judges in this study rated the believability of the emotion portrayals defined as the success of the actor in producing an authentic and plausible emotional impression. While the overall level of agreement on this quality is lower than for intensity and category judgements (as is to be expected on the basis of individual difference in the evaluation of this highly subjective construct), there is still substantial agreement suggesting that this dimension can be rated with sufficient reliability. As a consequence, the believability ratings for individual ratings can be used (just as the differential accuracy scores) to select specific items out of the total set for specific subsets of stimulus material.

Another aspect of validity is the assurance that the impressions produced by the portrayals are stable in the sense of not depending too strongly on the nature of the vocal utterances used for the portrayals or on random effects. The results reported above show that the ratings are stable over repetitions and over two different nonlinguistic sentences, suggesting that portrayals can be chosen without having to consider these factors. However, the factor *utterance type*, that is, nonlinguistic sentences versus affect bursts, does make a difference and thus researchers need to determine which utterance type fits best for their respective research purpose. Most likely, the affect burst provides a more primitive and less social instance of EE because it is not influenced by phonological, syntactic, and prosodic factors and may well occur when the sender is alone.

In contrast, the sentence-like utterances can be expected to be determined in part by these linguistic factors and to be closer to a typical utterance in social interaction.

An innovative feature of the GEMEP corpus is the attempt to study masking and variations in the intensity of expression, especially given the frequent critique that actor portrayals are too 'stereotypical'. Importantly, even though recognition accuracy is lower for the masked stimuli as compared to the non-masked ones, they are still recognized at an accuracy level that is higher than chance (Figure 6.1.5), although believability is significantly lower than that for normal portrayals at different intensities (Figure 6.1.7). Apart from this case, the results show that the regulated intensity levels of the portrayals were indeed correctly perceived by the raters, as shown by the intensity ratings in Figure 6.1.6. This means that the corpus can be used to select portrayals at different intensities to systematically study the effect on distal features and emotion inference and attribution.

Modality by emotion effects on accuracy

The empirical results for recognition differences between emotions across modalities provide a first basis for the development of hypotheses about the type of distal and proximal cues that may be involved in the communication of emotion. As one would have expected, the audio-visual condition produces the greatest degree of accuracy, given that it provides all available cues. In comparing single channels, as expected on the basis of an earlier review of channel studies (Scherer 1999), the emotions in the audio modality are less well recognized than they are in the video modality. However, the data show (Figures 6.1.2 and 6.1.4) that this result is mostly due to a few emotions in which audio accuracy is low and video accuracy appreciably higher. These cases seem to be limited to a few emotion families, such as disgust and contempt, which confirms earlier findings. One explanation is that disgust is usually a very brief emotion during which nothing is spoken (Banse and Scherer 1996). Thus, it may not be surprising that actors find it difficult to convey the emotion in a sentence-like utterance. An interesting finding is that the accuracy proportion jumps from 0.12 for the sentence case to 0.59 in the affect burst case (see Table 6.1.4), indicating the existence of specific vocal affect emblems (see Scherer 1994a). Similarly, contempt may be an attitude toward another person that is shown in the face but that rarely colours interactive speech for a longer period. The other emotions in which the audio modality is clearly disadvantaged are the positive emotions of interest, joy, and pride. In the case of interest, little voice change seems to occur from neutral (this being one of the few cases in which the tendency to use the neutral label is strong; see Table 6.1.5). In the case of joy and pride, a number of unambiguous facial signs—including the smile—are apparent, whereas specific cues do not seem to occur in the voice. We find it interesting that pride is systematically confused with irritation in the voice. In the case of sadness and despair, accuracy is low in all modalities, mainly because of the systematic symmetric confusions between the two emotions.

Future development of the GEMEP corpus

As outlined in Chapter 3.2, this volume, one of the essential purposes of actor portrayal studies is to determine the distal and proximal cues and cue utilization in the process of emotion communication. Thus, one important direction of further research is the extraction, coding, or annotation of the behavioural features that distinguish the expression of emotions. The techniques for annotating and analysing these features are extremely costly and time-consuming, and it would thus be unrealistic to analyse all 1260 stimuli. Similarly, for future studies, it would be difficult to have to deal with such a large number of portrayals. In consequence, the selection of a core set is required.

- *Core set.* We decided to identify, on the basis of the ratings reported here, a subset of portrayals, representative of all the emotions and actors, that have received high believability ratings and have a satisfactory level of accuracy, showing that most observers will unambiguously classify them according to portrayal intention. This core set was subjected to another extensive rating study with a much larger number of raters, as well as a categorical response scheme and dimensional ratings (in two separate subgroups of ratings). The results of this study are currently being prepared for publication.

- *Vocal analysis.* In the vocal domain, the state of the art is the extraction of acoustic parameters by using digital signal analysis procedures (see Banse and Scherer 1996; Juslin and Scherer 2005; Scherer *et al.* 2003). Vocal parameter extraction and analysis has been performed for the core set, and an article reporting the results has been submitted for publication (Goudbeek and Scherer, in press). Current work (with J. Sundberg) is focused on a microanalysis of the vocal affect bursts.

- *Facial analysis.* The state-of-the-art instrument to objectively determine the facial movements in expression is the facial action coding system (FACS; Ekman and Friesen 1978). The GEMEP core set is currently FACS coded by certified coders, which constitutes a very time-consuming activity. First results on disambiguating subtly different positive emotions are reported in an article by Mortillaro, Mehu, and Scherer (in preparation). Similar work is under way to study the patterns of action units (AUs) that differentiate families of negative emotions. Because the core set sequences are dynamically coded for onset, apex, and offset of each of approximately 40 AUs, fine-grained analyses of the sequential emergence of AUs and other dynamical aspects of facial expression are currently being performed (Krumhuber and Scherer, submitted for publication). The results will provide a test of Scherer's assumption of sequential unfolding of facial expression as driven by appraisal checks (Aue and Scherer 2008; Delplanque *et al.* 2009; Scherer 1992, 2001, 2009*a*).

- *Gesture and posture annotation.* The study of EE via gesture and posture has been remarkably neglected in the field (but see Wallbott 1998). A new comprehensive gesture and posture coding system has been developed recently in Geneva and the GEMEP core set will be coded by using the same time line as for face and voice. Particular emphasis will also be placed on head movements.

- *Multimodal synchronization.* Because all modalities are coded on the same time line, it will be possible to examine the coherence or synchronization between these systems for the different emotions. As suggested by Scherer (1984, 2005*a*,*b*, 2009*b*), a high degree of subsystem synchronization can be seen as the hallmark for the presence of an emotion. Special attention will be paid to the role of synchronization in perceived emotional authenticity.

- *Regressing behaviour on observer ratings.* As mentioned at the outset, one of the main purposes of this research program is to empirically investigate the Brunswikian lens model in the context of emotion communication. In consequence, much of our work is based on correlating the behavioural data with the subjective ratings to determine the cues used by the observers in their inference and attribution. The crowning piece of this type of analysis is a path analysis or structural modelling to map the data into a Brunswikian lens model.

- *Using the corpus as stimulus material.* An important asset of acted emotion portrayals lies in the absence of contextual cues or variability attached to an emotion-eliciting situation. Unlike 'natural' (spontaneously occurring) EEs, actor portrayals with standard verbal content contain only non-verbal cues to emotions. This allows us to use them to test a variety of hypotheses. Hence, much of the ongoing work uses the GEMEP portrayals as systematic and standardized stimulus material in psychological and neuroscientific studies. Ethofer *et al.* (2009) recently used audio GEMEP portrayals to study the decoding of emotional information in voice-sensitive cortices. The portrayals are currently used in several neuroscience applications. We plan the development of several adaptive tests of emotion recognition for research use, evaluation of emotional competence, and diagnosis of neurological damage. Another area in which the GEMEP corpus is of great utility is in the area of affective computing, for example, the development of dynamic, sequential facial synthesis (Roesch *et al.* 2009). Similarly, the GEMEP portrayals might be used to test the effect of contextual information on the interpretation of the portrayed emotions by providing various explanations alongside the portrayals (e.g. by allocating various meanings to the pseudo-speech sentences pronounced by the actors).

In sum, the GEMEP corpus is a comprehensive, sophisticated, and valid new instrument for research on emotional expression in many different areas such as psychological research on perception and communication of emotion, neuroscience research on the brain structures and circuits underlying emotion expression processing, or work in affective computing (see Chapters 6.2 and 3.2, this volume). The GEMEP corpus is shared with these research communities (see footnote 2 for details) and the complete database with all pertinent annotations will be made available once parameter extraction is finished.

Chapter 6.2

Induction techniques developed to illuminate relationships between signs of emotion and their context, physical and social[1]

Roddy Cowie, Ellen Douglas-Cowie, Ian Sneddon, Margaret McRorie, Jennifer Hanratty, Edelle McMahon, and Gary McKeown

Summary

There are good theoretical reasons to believe that signs of emotion depend on rapid and intricate interplay between inner affective states and their context, reflecting both 'push' and 'pull' effects. Induction is often associated with a more static model, where the aim is simply to induce authentic states on the assumption that authentic signs will then well up. In fact, though, induction is well suited to collecting data that reveal how push and pull effects shape expressive patterns. Teams in Belfast have explored a variety of data collection techniques designed to address the issue of context, physical and social. They fall into four main groups. In the first group, emotion is pre-induced using a three-stage procedure (EM3) that is robust enough to affect performance on demanding activities for a considerable period. The resulting signs depend radically on the nature of the task. When the task is driving, classical signs are very limited, but measures of steering and acceleration show different responses to challenging situations. In contrast, when the task is playing music, the emotion is expressed through the performance. In the second group of techniques, emotion is induced by passive observation, of film and music. The work with film shows that the overt signs depend not only on the presence of others, but also on the familiarity of the other, and these interact with the induced emotion. The responses of musical audiences are marked by synchronies that suggest a distinctive kind of empathy between them and the performer. The third group of techniques considers participants engaging in emotionally charged activities. They show rapid changes of expression associated with changes in the physical context, or the aspects of it being attended, and expression also depends on both the presence of others and awareness of them. Finally, major efforts have gone into studying the signs that mark conversational interactions. These often reflect multiple, contrasting orientations (e.g. negative towards the topic, positive towards the other party). They depend on the goal of the interaction (sociable exchange or negotiating an agreement). Particular effort has been put into the SAL (sensitive artificial listener) paradigm, which provides models of interactions between a human user and

[1] This work was supported by the European Community's Seventh Framework Programme (FP7/2007-2013) under grant agreements no. 211486 (SEMAINE) and 231287 (SSPNet).

an artificial agent with some affective competence. That work has reached a stage where the agent is genuinely automatic, opening the way for systematic variation in agent behaviours so that their emotional significance can be studied with much more rigour than has previously been possible. At least some data from most of these paradigms is available to the research community, and from some the amounts are very substantial. Equally significant, the techniques themselves provide models of the way induction can engage with the complexity of 'push' and 'pull' effects that typify everyday environments.

Introduction

It is natural to think of smiles, laughter, and trembling welling up from an inner pool of feeling. Related images are implicit in the language that we automatically use to describe phenomena of that kind. The most convenient term for them is 'expressions' of emotion, suggesting that their function is giving voice to private experiences. The original use of the word 'expression' (in mediaeval France) is even more telling: it is derived from a Latin word meaning 'what is squeezed or pressed out' (*Oxford English Dictionary* 1971). Six centuries later, Ekman and Friesen (1969) invoked a very similar metaphor when they described the 'leakage' that occurs when people try to conceal emotion. The words reflect what might be called an artesian model, meaning that the internal force of emotion presses various characteristic signs towards the surface.

That kind of image leads naturally to the assumption that the detection task for affectively competent agents is to detect the real upwelling signs, however much they may be attenuated or obscured by forgeries, and, correspondingly, the core task for databases is to provide examples of them. Of course, the image of something welling up from within does sometimes capture what it feels like to reveal emotion. However, there are two kinds of reason why that kind of model needs to be treated with care. They are related to different parts of the theoretical framework outlined by Scherer and his collaborators at different stages in this volume. They acknowledge that, to borrow Gibson's phrase, signs of emotion 'point both ways' (Gibson 1979, p.129). They do reflect the internal state of the agent, but, equally, they reflect the agent's orientation to significant parts of the external world.

The first kind of reason is rooted in the core notion of appraisal, reviewed in Section 2 of this volume, which has been very widely accepted for half a century. Appraisal models trace emotion to the link between an agent and its environment. Fear is not (at least not wholly) an internal feeling: it is (at least partly) an appraisal of an external threat. An interesting consequence of that model is that it suggests signs of emotion may change as rapidly as the focus of perception. My eye can pass in milliseconds from my enemy to the friend a step behind him, and so should my appraisals, and so should the accompanying signs. There are important qualifications. Not all expressive systems can change rapidly: for instance, a flush takes time to fade. It will also be assumed in this chapter that the focus of appraisal need not be physically present: for instance, suddenly remembering an imminent deadline may have effects that are all too like suddenly seeing an enemy.

The second kind of reason is connected to the concept of 'push' and 'pull' effects, which was set out in Chapter 3.2, this volume. It has been less widely assimilated. In terms of the last paragraph, a push effect is one that tends to make expressions an accurate record of the agent's appraisals as they fluctuate with changes in the world and shifts of attention (making due allowance for hysteresis). A pull effect is one that modulates the expressions with the intention that they should be understood. There is a fundamental link in that both concepts consider signs of emotion as a function of the agent's orientation to its world—social or physical, real or imaginary—not as the upwelling of an inner state. That makes it unsurprising that the distinction is not totally clear-cut.

If shifts in expression are social, deliberate, and intended to convey emotion rather than conceal it, then the underlying factors are clearly 'pull'. Letting someone see your feelings about something without consciously choosing to is on the margin. So is smiling in the mirror to dispel a mood of gloom. However, it is better to draw the distinction and tolerate fuzzy boundaries than to lose sight of the important point that orienting to the social world is special.

These ideas have far-reaching implications for research on databases. It is easy to assume that the core challenge for research is to ensure that databases are populated with recordings of people who are feeling authentic instances of particular emotions and therefore showing (to a greater or lesser extent) the true signs that well up from those states. The ideas outlined above suggest that representing authentic inner states is only a small part of the task. In reality, the signs that an affective agent will have to deal with will depend on the interplay between inner affective states and their context—social or physical, real or imaginary—and that interplay is what databases need to capture. To put it crudely, one would expect a person feeling anger to show very different profiles of signs in the following scenarios: with a sympathetic friend; before an unsympathetic judge; in response to a rude gesture; in response to a rude letter; alone in a gym; and alone on a steep ski slope.

The literature on affective computing is not blind to these issues, but they are not often considered explicitly. Attitudes to them tend to divide according to the main source of material considered. The importance of context is stressed in research that concentrates on data collected in the particular practical context where a system is to be applied (e.g. Devillers *et al.* 2005). Research in a second tradition has felt that there must be ways to achieve more generality and more controlled samples, and has focused on induced emotion. It tends to emphasize the authenticity of the underlying state and downplay context. That is reflected in statements like 'we argue for an induced emotion corpus, multiply-labelled by emotional condition and user response to a standard affect scale, obtained in an automated fashion' (Master *et al.* 2006, p. 60) or 'Collection and evaluation of speech corpora reflecting authentic expressions of emotions is necessarily the basis for any research on speech and emotion' (Amir and Ron 2006, p. 25). Others again try to find a middle ground, suggesting that the key is to focus on contexts that seem typical or central. For example, a review of databases by Gunes and Piccardi (2006) proposes that

> ...an ideal multi-modal affect database thus should have the following features:
>
> ◆ The subject is present in his/her natural environment (i.e. office or house).
> ◆ The subject is in a particular affective state due to some real-life event or trigger of events (i.e. stressed at work).
> ◆ The subject does not try to hide what s(he) feels, on the contrary, displays what s(he) feels using multiple communicative channels (i.e. facial expression, head movement, body gestures, voice etc.).
> ◆ The subject is not aware of the recording, hence will not restrain himself/herself unlike the case when s(he) is part of an experiment. [p. 2432]

The proposal seems less attractive in the light of data on the frequency of emotion-related states in everyday environments. Figures given by Cowie (2010) imply that states of emotion as such occupy about 15 minutes of an average day. Other sources (Wilhelm *et al.* 2004) suggest that more than half of those are 'happy', half of the rest are 'angry', and others are rare. On that basis, collecting an informative emotion database along the lines proposed by Gunes and Piccardi would be a very long term project.

This chapter concentrates on a fourth option, which is finding induction techniques that capture some of the key ways that emotional and affective phenomena may appear under diverse combinations of 'pushes' and 'pulls'. Specifically, it describes methods that have been developed and applied in the laboratories at Queen's University in Belfast (QUB for short). They illustrate a range of emotional and affective phenomena as they appear under diverse combinations of 'pushes' and 'pulls'. Examples are used to illustrate the kind of data that the techniques elicit.

The kind of description that is given reflects the motives. The most direct motive is probably the least important. Recordings based on most of the methods that will be described are available to download, and some are suitable for use as training or test material. It is probably more important that the techniques provide models for teams who want to generate data relevant to their own specific needs—theoretical or practical. In that sense, the chapter has a similar function to the various reviews of emotion induction techniques that exist in the psychological literature (Gerrards-Hesse *et al.* 1994; Westermann *et al.* 1996; Coan and Allen 2007), but with an emphasis on the issues that affect computational research on the expression of emotion. The most fundamental aim, though, is to convey that the issues outlined in the introduction are a reality. Concrete examples give a much clearer impression of the issues that research has to address than abstract arguments.

The techniques are grouped under four headings. The grouping may seem eccentric to people who are familiar with different groupings that are used elsewhere (particularly in psychology). The reason for choosing this particular structure is the focus on expression. Techniques that may be considered more or less equivalent in the context of, say, problem solving, may not be at all equivalent in respect of the opportunities that they provide to express emotion. Under each heading we describe the material that has been collected by the teams at QUB.

Separable induction

This section considers paradigms that have a conceptual purity that psychology has found very attractive. They involve two components: procedures that induce an affective state, and indicators that are (or may be) affected by the induced state. The purity of the paradigm comes from the fact that the two components are, as the section heading puts it, separable. In and of itself, the inducing component has no obvious bearing on the indicators. If it affects them (the argument goes), it can only be because an intervening variable, the emotion, came into play. Many of the techniques that are listed in standard psychological summaries of emotion or mood induction are of that type (Gerrards-Hesse *et al.* 1994; Westermann *et al.* 1996; Coan and Allen 2007). Separable induction techniques have also been prominent in some areas that are closely related to affective computing, notably research on speech and emotion (Johnstone and Scherer 1999; Bachorowski 1999).

The research at QUB has explored ways of adapting that general approach to the particular concerns of affective computing. It explores three ideas: that some practically significant activities can be affected by emotion that has been induced by unrelated events; that there are techniques that can induce the relevant kinds of emotion; and that there are signs that can be used to detect the induced emotions. It has considered two sample types of activity: driving (using a high-quality simulator) and musical performance (by accomplished musicians). There are reasons to believe that both of these are open to influence by emotional states (Grimm *et al.* 2007; Mesken 2006; Mesken *et al.* 2008; Juslin 2009). The challenge is to find techniques that allow research to get properly to grips with the effects.

Early work brought the two areas together. Music is routinely used to induce emotion (Kreutz *et al.* 2008), and it was used to induce emotional states in drivers. The strategy was abandoned because separability was clearly a problem. There were effects of playing music while people were driving, and the music affected their emotional state (as measured by the standard SAM (self-assessment mannikin) instrument: Lang 1980). However, there was no obvious way to separate effects due to the emotional impact of music from effects that might be due to its effects on participants' attention and the tempo of their actions.

An alternative that is both conceptually straightforward and well-established is the Velten technique (Velten 1968). It involves inducing participants into a target state by reading a succession of emotionally charged statements about themselves. The state is usually described as a mood rather than an emotion. In early experiments on driving, participants underwent Velten-type induction techniques, and then undertook a simulated drive. Assessments using the SAM self-report scheme were carried out before, during, and after the drive. They confirmed that, in the short term, the Velten technique induced the expected moods. However, the moods dissipated quickly under the influence of a demanding task. That is not unexpected. The underlying principle is nicely captured in an epigram that is attributed to William James, though it is difficult to trace the original source: 'The emotions are not always subject to reason ... but they are always subject to action. When thoughts do not neutralize an undesirable emotion, action will.'[2]

For that reason, a variant technique was developed. It has been called EM3 because it evokes states intermediate between emotion (E) and mood (M) in three steps. The first is to identify issues with a particular kind of affective significance for the participants (the main studies used happiness, anger, sadness, and detached interest). The second step is a Velten-like induction procedure that induces a corresponding mood. The third, which follows immediately, is discussing issues identified in the first step in a way that would be expected to evoke the target emotion. The point of that stage is to change one of the hallmarks of mood, which is that it is usually considered to be 'objectless' (i.e. it is not about anything). The discussion in the third stage ensures that the affect does have an object, in the form of topics that carry an emotional charge for the people involved. Self-reports using SAM and everyday verbal categories showed that the EM3 procedure established states that were robust enough to persist through extended driving. In fact, in some cases, the states persisted long after the experiments were over, in spite of a debriefing that was meant to neutralize them (which raises ethical issues).

The way EM3-induced emotion appears in driving performance reflects the kind of argument that has been made above. In connection with the push–pull distinction, it is striking that participants showed few of the classical signs of emotion when they were driving with no 'pull' to elicit them. What their faces showed was concentration on the task. However, that does not mean that the action of driving had, in James's term, neutralized the emotion. Groups who had experienced different induction procedures showed different responses to various kinds of testing situations embedded in the drives, which appeared in measures of behaviour such as braking, 'weaving', and overtaking. That makes an important point for databases concerned with agents engaged in demanding, non-social tasks. If data collection procedures rely on passive upwelling to provide signs of the agent's emotional state, they will find relatively few. It is the interaction between underlying state and environment that elicits signs, and the signs are specific to the eliciting situations. It is noticeable that other groups who have reported effects of emotion on driving have also associated them with interactions, notably the interaction between the driver and in-car devices (Grimm et al. 2007).

The work on EM3 in musical performance shows contrasting effects that underline the point. The context there provided very powerful and complex pull effects: musicians were invited to express their emotions in their performance, and both the conventions of performance and the presence of an audience reinforced the pull. Correspondingly, the musicians' emotion showed at a wealth of levels (Knapp et al. 2009).

---

[2] http://www.famousquotesandauthors.com/authors/william_james_quotes.html : Uploaded 26/1/10

The work outlined in this section raises some complex issues that cannot be treated at length here, but that should be raised. EM3 induces a kind of state that is neither pure mood nor pure emotion, but has features of both. There is some literature on that kind of composite state (Siemer 2005; Cowie 2010), though not a great deal. It is natural to hypothesize that it is robust because, once ideas with strong and lasting emotional charges have been activated, they tend to go on resurfacing in a way that stops neutrality from re-asserting itself—which would make it somewhat similar to pathological anxiety (Eysenck *et al.* 2007). If its composite structure makes it robust, that kind of state may be more important for affective computing than pure mood. It may also be argued that the gross and obvious differences between musicians and drivers are superficial, and that the true signs of emotion are the same in both cases. It is not obvious that that must be the case. If emotion is thoroughly interactive, then the differences that arise in different contexts are not superficial: they run through and through. And even if it were the case, it would not alter the need for databases that provide examples of the different surface forms: they are a prerequisite for discovering which signs are not context-bound.

Induction during observation

Exposing people to emotive displays is central to psychological research on emotion. It is often part of a separable induction procedure: films are widely used to induce a particular mood before participants carry out an experimental task. However, there is a distinction that is important in the context of databases for affective computing. The signs of emotion that occur while a person is watching a film are likely to be very different from the signs that occur afterwards (at least in surface form). It follows that the signs emitted during the course of observing emotive events are a topic in their own right. An obvious implication is that, if a database uses film to induce emotion, it should not only include the behaviours of people watching a film, but also allow them to be synchronized with the film being watched. It is not a trivial matter if databases deprive research on facial movements (for instance) of the means to consider their relationship to the events that 'pushed' them.

There is also evidence that the signs generated during observation depend on pull effects (Ekman 1972). A study of ours expands that point. 95 individuals were recorded watching a series of three film clips chosen to elicit emotion (amusement, sadness, and anger, respectively) in three conditions: alone; with a friend; or with a stranger. The data collected included both participants' own reports of the extent to which they experienced the target emotion (using both global ratings and continuous self-report ratings) and its apparent intensity as perceived by third parties. The key results involved the agreement between self-rated emotion and the emotion that third parties inferred from the visible signs. For anger, agreement was highest when the person was alone. For amusement, it was similar when the person was alone or with a stranger, but lower in the friend's company. For sadness, there were no significant differences. The implication is that pull effects depend not only on the others who are present, but also on the kind of emotion being expressed.

Here too, music raises particular issues. The audience at a concert responds in a very complex way to the emotional qualities of performance. These effects have been studied at two levels. A longstanding paradigm involves documenting the way indicators of emotionality depend on the music being played (Guhn *et al.* 2007). That provides interesting insights into the features of music that are emotionally significant. Current research at QUB uses indicators of emotion in the audience to influence the performance (Knapp *et al.* 2009). It is worth noting that, because musical performance is significant financially as well as culturally, that kind of work is one of the first areas where affective computing finds large-scale applications. For instance, there is clear commercial interest in the prospect of an agent whose affective competence includes selecting music that suits the listeners' moods (van der Zwaag *et al.* 2009).

Interactions with the inanimate world

The paradigms grouped under this heading set people to interact with inanimate things in ways that are designed to induce emotion. Other people may or may not be present, but interactions with them are assumed to influence the expression of emotion, not to create it. Several demarcation lines in that description are fuzzy; that reflects the real complexity of the situations.

There is a long history of using interactive games to induce emotion (e.g. Kaiser and Wehrle 1996; van Reekum *et al.* 2004). One of the best-known findings in the area comes from a game, albeit not one that is commonly used in laboratories. Kraut and Johnston (1979) showed that bowlers showed emotional expressions after a strike if they were facing other people, but not otherwise. One might expect the presence of other people to be varied routinely in techniques that use games, but that has not generally been the case. It is often difficult to know from descriptions of induction procedures whether expressions might have been influenced by the presence (actual or assumed) of an onlooker.

Computer games are not considered in depth here, partly because they are so well established. Instead the focus is on techniques designed to study emotionally coloured interactions with the physical environment. The most dramatic of these involved 'activity days' where people engaged in challenging tasks, such as balancing on top of a stack of crates, walking a tightrope, or riding a bicycle down a steep bank. The results were recorded using a combination of handheld cameras and cameras mounted on an arm attached to a protective helmet that the participants wore (McRorie and Sneddon 2007*a*).

These situations create intense involvement in complex situations. A striking feature of the data that they yield is the speed with which expressions change. Figure 6.2.1 provides a convenient way to make the point. It shows a trace produced by a rater using a computer interface to record (in real time) the apparent intensity of the emotion shown by an activity day participant. It is easy to

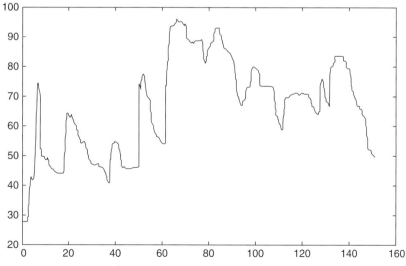

Fig. 6.2.1 Intensity of emotion displayed as a function of time for an activity day participant trying to cross a tightrope (from Hanratty (2010).)

Fig. 6.2.2 Expressions changing in reponse to the 'push' of rapidly changing events (a cyclist speeding past and falling off). (From McRorie and Sneddon (2007a).)

understand why appraisals oscillate when one knows that the participant is trying to cross a tight-rope. Rapid change is not confined to that situation, though. Figure 6.2.2 illustrates how a very different situation elicits change, more in the quality of the expression than in its intensity (the person is watching a cyclist who is racing downhill in the first frame, and has fallen off by the last). The key factors in that example are the 'pushes' exerted by rapidly changing circumstances. 'Pull' effects associated with changes in the participant's focus can also be seen. Figure 6.2.3 shows a striking example. The participant is trying to balance on an unstable stack of crates. When she is concentrating on keeping her balance, her face shows anxiety or mild fear, but, immediately she orients to other people, 'pull' effects come into play, and a smile appears. The intention seems to be reassurance, but it is clearly somewhat mixed. That too is a common feature of the data, and a natural consequence of engaging with situations where there are many things to appraise.

Unobserved – showing fear/ anxiety

Observed - 'putting on a brave face'

Fig. 6.2.3 Contrasting 'push' and 'pull' effects as an activity day participant balances on a stack of crates, initially unaware of onlookers (top row), then registering them and giving a positive signal. (From McRorie and Sneddon (2007a).)

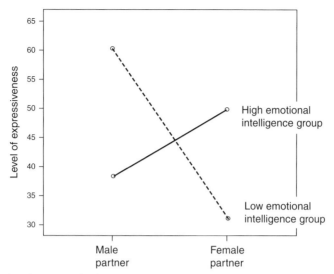

Fig. 6.2.4 Intensity of emotion displayed in a 'spaghetti task' as a function of the participants' emotional intelligence and the gender of the experimenter beside them. (From McRorie and Sneddon (2007b).)

The 'activity day' data is very rich, but its complexity is a problem. That led us to develop emotion-inducing interactions that retained some of the same intensity and spontaneity, but provided more structure. The material has been referred to as 'spaghetti data', for reasons that will become obvious. Participants carried out simple tasks designed to evoke specific emotions. Most involved exploring the contents of a box by feeling inside it with one hand. In one case it contained cold spaghetti (evoking disgust); in another it contained a buzzer that sounded when it was touched (evoking shock); in another the markings suggested that it contained a spider (evoking apprehension); in another it contained a banana with two kiwi fruits placed at one end, one on either side (evoking embarrassment). A final condition involved trying to move a ring from one end of a bent wire to the other without touching the wire, evoking intense concentration and a variety of evaluative appraisals (usually negative). The paradigm produced recordings of strong, spontaneous emotions of very different types.

The paradigm also allows social variables to be examined. An onlooker was always present, and might be the same or different gender. In addition, participants completed a battery of personality-related tests. As might be expected, these factors affected the level of emotional display. The effects were surprisingly complex, though. The level of emotion shown (measured using the same kind of trace as the tightrope example) depended both on the gender of the onlooker and on the emotional intelligence of the participant. Figure 6.2.4 shows the strongest of the interactions. There is a certain logic to the finding that people with low emotional intelligence reveal their feelings to a male. However, the point is not to speculate about the reason for the effect, interesting though that may be. It is to indicate that suitably careful induction techniques can expose very interesting structure within the broad category of pull effects.

Social interactions

Context effects in general, and 'pull' effects in particular, are at their most intricate during social interactions. They take different forms in different kinds of interaction. Social interactions also highlight the issue of multimodality, since speech tends to play a large part in them.

A widely cited source, the Belfast Naturalistic Database (Douglas-Cowie *et al.* 2003*b*), is partly made up of TV material that is not widely available for reasons of copyright and partly of biographical interviews between one of the compilers and people who knew her well. The interviews show a recurring pattern. People talk, in a spontaneous way, about events, some of which were highly traumatic—one being held up at gunpoint during the 'Troubles' in Belfast, and thinking her husband had been shot; one describing the recent and fraught breakup of her marriage. But while the words, and to some extent the voice, suggest genuine distress at these points, the facial expression is usually appropriate to the immediate setting, that is, a conversation with a friend. Cowie *et al.* (2009) provide more information on the discrepancies between face and voice. It may not be wholly accurate, but it is certainly a useful starting point to say that the voice seems to reflect the 'push' of reawakened memories, whereas the face reflects the 'pull' to show positive engagement with the interactant.

Markedly different types of expression are found in a second paradigm that focused on providing and evaluating information on emotive subjects. A resource called the 'green persuasive database' recorded discussions about climate change and the lifestyle adjustments it might call for. The dominant types of expression there involved combinations of affect and cognition, though not quite in the categories proposed by Baron-Cohen *et al.* (2004). Analysis identified six dimensions of expression: emphatic/certain; friendly/amused; attentive/absorbed; argumentative/sceptical; guilty/upset; surprised/curious; and thoughtful/uncertain. Most of these are inherently bound up with the ongoing business of negotiating an understanding acceptable to both parties. It is extremely difficult to disentangle push and pull effects, because the push effects are so intimately bound to the social context. The material reinforces a point made in the context of driving and playing music: engaging in a demanding task transforms the way affect appears.

A third social interaction paradigm will be covered at slightly more length because it has been developed specifically to address a core issue for affectively competent agents—interactions where one party is a machine. It involves a scenario called the 'sensitive artificial listener', SAL for short. SAL agents mimic a style of interaction that was observed in chat shows and at parties, which aroused interest because there seemed to be a real prospect of building a system that could sustain it. When the user speaks, the agent responds with a stock phrase that is keyed to the user's emotional state rather than the content of what he/she says. The stock phrases are calculated to evoke emotion, making it easier for the agent to pick up the kind of information that it relies on. That kind of agent is a realistic prospect because, although it needs some basic emotional and conversational competence, it does not need the kind of competence with fluent speech and language that has proved elusive over decades of effort.

The primary motivation for building SAL type systems is not an immediate application. It is to provide a testbed that allows research to develop emotional and conversational competence in an incremental way. Once an agent exists, it is possible to carry out controlled experiments on the contribution that various components make to affectively satisfying interaction, and to show whether innovations make real improvements. Part of that process is that data generated by interactions with earlier versions can shape the design of their successors. That is the route that the work with SAL has taken.

Early research modelled the scenario by having users interact with a human operator whose responses were restricted to phrases read from a script, with preset rules determining which could be used at any given time. That work developed a structure that allowed sustained interaction. It involved four 'characters', each with a distinct emotional style and a conversational goal of shifting the user towards its own habitual state. They are Prudence, who is even-tempered and sensible, Poppy, who is happy and outgoing, Spike, who is angry and confrontational, and Obadiah, who is depressive. Each 'character' is defined by a script of utterances in keeping with its outlook, and selection rules that choose an utterance that is intended to push the user towards its own habitual state. In spite of its simplicity, that structure turns out to be capable of engaging users in a lively exchange lasting for about half an hour, and involving a rich variety of conversational behaviours.

A substantial body of material has been collected in that scenario. Recordings of the users have been used to develop recognizers, particularly for speech (Eyben *et al.* 2010), that are incorporated in later versions. It was also used to refine the scripts, by identifying points at which the original versions seemed to offer no adequate response. The modified scripts were then used in a 'Wizard of Oz' scenario where an operator navigates a predefined script and decides what the 'agent' should say next. Navigation is based on the operator's assessment of the user's emotional state—clicking to identify it brings up a list of utterances that the 'character' being simulated might make in response to someone in that state. The system then generates the selected utterance. That paradigm produces quite rich emotional interactions. They are noticeably different from the first phase, where it was always clear that the agent was in fact a person. For a substantial proportion of users, the impression that the other party is an artificial system seems to give licence to interact in a strikingly uninhibited way. That is precisely why developing affectively competent agents depends on data from interactions with agents: affective responses to agents are not the same as affective responses to people.

On the other hand, some key conversational elements are very limited in the Wizard of Oz scenario, because the operator spends a good deal of time looking at the script, not the user. A third scenario, 'solid SAL', was developed to overcome that problem. It uses an operator who is thoroughly familiar with the SAL characters, and tries to speak as they would. Several factors help to maintain the impression of machine interaction. The scenario is explained to the user. The interaction takes place at a distance, so that participants hear each other through loudspeakers, and see each other's faces in a teleprompter screen (the teleprompt arrangement allows cameras to point directly at the faces of both parties, which allows full eye contact in a way that offset cameras do not). Probably most important, it quickly becomes clear that the interaction is not following the rules of human–human interaction. Users are not permitted to ask the SAL characters questions. When users do ask questions, they are given a stock reminder that the SAL characters cannot answer questions. The SAL characters also violate normal constraints of politeness and accommodation to the user's emotion. A substantial body of recordings has been collected in that scenario. They show emotional behaviours comparable to previous versions, and also a rich set of conversation-related behaviours, involving eye contact, backchannelling, and turn-taking. Note that the conversational behaviours are not a separate issue from affective competence: they have a very large influence on the emotional climate.

Data from those recordings were used to develop the first fully automatic version of SAL. Recordings of an interaction with it can be seen on the web (at http://www.semaine-project.eu/). The system generates both speech and a visual display for each character: these include both visual and vocal backchannelling informed by the Solid SAL material. Utterance selection is based on detection of user emotion from both visual and acoustic cues: the detectors are trained using recordings from earlier versions. That version in its turn will be used to collect recordings of users interacting with it. Preliminary work indicates that these raise their own new issues. Among the most important are signs of confusion or disengagement, which are likely to be an important feature of human–agent interaction in the foreseeable future, and which need to be recognized in order to initiate repair.

The point of describing the SAL process at length is to convey something that is fundamental to the area. If induction-based methods are to provide the underpinnings for affectively competent agents, their task is not to capture fixed signs that well up whenever a person authentically undergoes a particular affective state. It is to capture the intricate interplay of signs that is involved in both responding to, and shaping, emotionally coloured situations and interactions. The dynamic nature of the interplay puts a premium on paradigms that allow complex dynamics to be studied systematically. Paradigms like SAL, which use artificial interactants, allow a level of control that is very difficult to imagine achieving in experiment where all the interactions are between human beings, and that is one of their great attractions.

Conclusion

Affective computing depends heavily on samples that represent the phenomena adequately, and induction is one of the obvious approaches to obtaining them. It is fair to be wary of approaches that simply try to induce a target state and assume that the rest will follow. This chapter has tried to show that induction does not need to be like that: on the contrary, it offers a particularly promising way of engaging with the way in which signs of emotion are patterned by multiple kinds of push and pull effect in realistically complex situations.

One of the claims that is often made for induction is that it allows investigators to obtain known states. That is not a claim that has been considered here. Some of the techniques do allow states to be identified quite confidently. The 'spaghetti data' in particular provides converging reasons for confidence. The scenario itself makes some options much likelier than others. The format also allowed a follow-up phase, in which participants rated their own experience. The 'spaghetti' material has also been rated by third parties using the trace-type techniques developed in HUMAINE (Douglas-Cowie *et al.* 2007). For ratings of intensity (of the kind illustrated in Figure 6.2.1) coefficients of concordance are usually well above 0.9. That kind of convergence provides samples whose authenticity is difficult to doubt.

The key point, though, is that induction allows investigators to choose their goals. They may make it a priority to generate data where it is possible to say with high confidence what the underlying states were. That was one of the goals behind the spaghetti data. To achieve it, people were put in relatively extreme and artificial situations. That is the price of confidence. The more concerned research is with emotion in complex, ongoing situations, the less it can realistically expect to be sure what the participants' inner state was. So, for instance, the emotional states underpinning the SAL interactions are highly complex—vectors involving multiple pushes and pulls, relating to current and remembered events, real and virtual characters, offences against conversational norms, and so on—all fluctuating over very short timescales. Pinning down that kind of state involves Heisenberg-like uncertainties. Unfortunately, that is what large parts of emotional life are like. To insist that data should have an unambiguous interpretation is to steer investigation away from those parts of emotional life. Induction allows investigators to do that if they choose (and there may be good reasons to). Hopefully, this chapter has shown that it does not force them to.

One of the advantages of induction techniques is that they allow research to create circumstances where emotional states in a certain general area are relatively likely to occur. That is relevant to both the confidence with which material can be interpreted and the likelihood of obtaining it. The other outstanding advantage is epitomized in the SAL recordings: it is possible to ensure recordings that are suitable for automatic analysis. However fascinating they may be, recordings of low technical quality are of little use to affective computing. There are psychological issues to address too, in the sense that the audience, physically present or implicit in cameras, will inevitably affect the signs that participants give. However, these issues can be addressed, provided that the efforts are not derailed by naïve demands for pure signs uncontaminated by the social setting. Reactions to other people, as pushes or pulls, are not contamination: they are an intrinsic part of emotional life and its expression.

For those who want to see and hear samples of the data mentioned here, there are two sources. The HUMAINE database (Douglas-Cowie *et al.* 2007) can be downloaded from the HUMAINE website (http://emotion-research.net/). It includes extracts from the *Belfast Naturalistic Database* (10 clips); SAL with a human script-reader (12 clips in English, 1 in Hebrew); *Activity Data/ Spaghetti Data* (7 clips); and the *Green Persuasive Dataset* (4 clips). These have multilayered trace ratings associated with them.

Much larger quantities of material are available via the MMI database[3]. It includes over 10 hours of solid SAL interactions, with trace-type annotations covering the major dimensions identified by Fontaine *et al.* (2007), intensity (as in Figure 6.2.1), and a range of everyday categories. A proportion of the material is withheld for testing purposes; the rest is available to download. The whole Green Persuasive dataset can also be downloaded, and more of the material described here is gradually being made available.

The fundamental aim of this chapter, though, is not to advertise existing data. It is to alert research groups to the possibilities that open up once induction is seen as a flexible and sophisticated tool. It has been a fundamental theme that everyday emotional expression is driven by multiple pushes and pulls, interacting with individual and profoundly unpredictable shifts of attention and intention. It is inconceivable that such a domain could be understood at all satisfactorily without very large amounts of data. The only way to accumulate material on the appropriate scale is for a large community to engage creatively in the task.

---

[3] http://sspnet.eu/category/sspnet_resource_categories/resource_type_classes/dataset/

Section 7

Conclusions

In Chapter 7.1, we attempt to integrate some of the views presented in the chapters of the earlier sections and to raise tentative propositions regarding the possibilities of enhancing the cross-fertilization across disciplines with respect to the study of emotions in humans and in machines. Based on the contributions in the earlier sections, we also discuss the minimal specifications of an 'affectively competent agent' suitable for application and make some tentative predictions regarding the prospects of such an agent in the near and distant future. Much of the material in Chapter 7.1 has been provided by the contributors to the volume and is summarized or cited here by the editors.

Outlook: Integration and future perspectives for affective computing

Klaus R. Scherer, Tanja Bänziger,
and Etienne B. Roesch

Integration

The contributions in this volume testify to the amount of interdisciplinary integration that has already been achieved in this research domain. We see two major factors that have had a very beneficial impact on this process.

1 The creation of a recognized area of specialization under the name of 'affective computing', based on Picard's (1997) pioneering book and followed by the launch of a major international conference on 'Affective computing and intelligent interaction' (ACII), now complemented by the creation of a journal dedicated to this domain, the *IEEE Transactions on Affective Computing* (http://www.computer.org/portal/web/tac).

2 The funding of a European Network of Excellence by the European Community, the 'Human–Machine Interaction Network on Emotion' (HUMAINE). This network aims to lay the foundations for European development of systems that can register, model, and/or influence human emotional and emotion-related states—'emotion-oriented systems'. It was recognized early on that such systems may be central to future interfaces, but their conceptual underpinnings were not sufficiently advanced to be sure of their real potential or the best way to develop them. As relevant knowledge is dispersed across many disciplines, HUMAINE has attempted to bring together leading experts from key disciplines in a program designed to achieve intellectual integration in six thematic areas cutting across traditional groupings: theory of emotion; signal/sign interfaces; the structure of emotionally coloured interactions; emotion in cognition and action; emotion in communication and persuasion; and usability of emotion-oriented systems. HUMAINE certainly achieved its major purpose, to bring together international experts, and has not only achieved an unprecedented degree of sharing and understanding of the multiple disciplinary approaches available to affective computing but also spawned several multidisciplinary collaborations. Tangible signs of its success are the rapid attraction of interest and participation from outside Europe, the establishing of the interdisciplinary HUMAINE association (http://emotion-research.net/) that is home to a growing number of special interest groups and organizes the yearly ACII conference, and, last but not least, the existence of this book.

Despite this promising start, we are still many decades away from the moment in which an emotional Turing test would fail to identify the artificial alternative. In fact, one might wonder if that is a desirable aim to achieve, as discussed in more detail in the notes on ethical concerns at the end of this chapter. However, there is little doubt that we are slowly getting closer to *believable* emotionally competent agents—that is, robots or virtual characters we are willing and able to interact with in a reasonably efficient, smooth, and agreeable fashion. Similarly, it would be of enormous help for emotion researchers to have access to computer simulation models of emotion processes to test the plausibility of certain assumptions, estimate parameters, or experimentally test alternative hypotheses. Again, the current state of affairs, as reflected in this volume, does not suggest that this will be a commonplace approach tomorrow, although the various types of expressively competent agents described in this volume are a promising first step in this direction.

At the same time, we should be realistic and avoid setting our expectations to an unrealistically high level. The history of artificial intelligence (AI) research should provide a clear warning. After an initial period of grossly exaggerated expectations, assuming that AI would be able to equal if not surpass human intelligence (in the wake of one of the first massive interdisciplinary efforts ever), there was a rude awakening. Yet, there have been unquestionable advances in our understanding of machine intelligence and our ability to use it for a large number of applications benefiting human well-being (as well as some for which this effect is arguable). Most reasonably, the same can be expected for affective computing. In this volume we have argued that we should set our sights on an emotionally competent agent, i.e. a believable personalization of computer routines that converges sufficiently well to our emotional and interpersonal needs to allow automatization of a large number of routine services as well as for entertainment and socializing. We will now explore some of the types of applications, suggested by our contributors, that may go beyond what has been described in the implementation section.

Application

Kreibig, Brosch, and Schaefer (Chapter 2.4) see the following three implications of affective computing based on psychophysiological indicators of emotion.

> 'First, it has the potential to revolutionize safety-relevant work sectors, including pilots, air traffic controllers, and drivers, where such measurements can be used to indicate when one cannot perform one's task properly and have an early warning function to take counteractive measures or to rotate workers. Second, in the medical context, such technology may aid in the diagnosis of emotional disorders and play a role in monitoring the success of treatments for such disorders. Third, it may be appealing to media and entertainment industries by offering a new level of interactiveness.'

Parkinson suggests that the interpersonal approach he sketched in Chapter 2.5 may serve to show that

> 'emotions may be strategically presented in order to influence other people's actions, as happens when anger is used for intimidation or excitement is worked up in order to generate enthusiasm in others. Examples of the application of these principles can be found in the uses of rhetoric, persuasion, or motivational coaching. Correspondingly, awareness of the rhetorical and motivational impact of emotion presentations is a first step towards resisting some of their interpersonal effects.'

Becker-Asano and Wachsmuth (Chapter 4.1) show that the computational simulation of primary and secondary emotion dynamics can be applied to the virtual human Max and they tested its effects in a variety of interaction scenarios.

> 'Some of these applications have been demonstrated to the public for entertainment purposes, whereas others have been used in the laboratory mainly to validate the interplay of the architectural components. The application of the WASABI architecture to robotic agents and androids seems promising and is currently being investigated.'

Hyniewska, Niewiadomski, Mancini, and Pelachaud (Chapter 5.1), who described their attempts to synthesize emotional behaviours in embodied conversational agents (ECAs), said the following

> 'Our work aims to endow virtual agents with a greater spectrum of expressions, to enrich their non-verbal behaviours and their expressivity. Such models may have implications for the display of expressive behaviours for virtual agents. These agents can have different roles such as being an educational tutor, a learning assistant, a conversational mate, or also a virtual companion. Other implications could be for the creation of virtual characters in video games and serious games.'

Schröder, Burkhardt, and Krstulovic (Chapter 5.2), who described issues in the synthesis of emotional speech in the vocal channel of emotional communication, explain:

> 'Emotional speech synthesis comes into play where the automated generation of speech goes beyond pure information presentation. As soon as expressions are needed for a simulated or real communicative situation, the voice must change from a neutral default setting to a speaking style that is appropriate to the emotional or expressive situation. Potential applications can be divided in two broad classes:
>
> ◆ Voice contents authoring: such applications deal with simulated interactions, as they arise from story-telling applications or in computer games, and where human users are in the position of an audience. Here, it is appropriate to generate exaggerated expressions for the purpose of achieving a dramatic effect.
> ◆ Dialogue systems: such applications deal with actual human-machine interactions in task-based scenarios such as telephone-based voice portals. In this context, emotional expressions must be subtler, and situational appropriateness has greater importance because it participates in the emotional dimension of the dialogue with the human user. For example, generating the wrong kind of emotional expression in a dialogue with a customer is likely to result in worse adverse reactions than generating no expression at all.
>
> At present, application prospects involving emotionally expressive synthetic speech in the authoring/ entertainment domain are more advanced than in the dialogue domain.'

Devillers, Vidrascu, and Layachi who authored Chapter 5.3 on the automatic recognition of emotion from specified vocal cues describe three applications that are currently under development.

◆ 'Building a real-time system of emotion detection (four emotional-states) for monitoring an artificial agent by voice. The chosen application is Skype conversations where the speaker is represented by his/her own avatar. When irritation in detected in the speaker's voice, the avatar will display anger-expressive behaviour.

◆ In the domain of robotics real-time emotion detection systems must be able to detect emotional-states in the voices of adults but also the elderly or children to adjust the dialogue strategy to be chosen. Here, challenging problems are posed by signal capture and the large variability of the voices.

◆ In the domain of the call centres the detection of customer satisfaction is of central interest. A combination of paralinguistic and linguistic features extracted from speech are used for emotion detection.'

Castellano, Caridakis, Camurri, Karpouzis, Volpe, and Kollias (Chapter 5.4) remark:

> 'Given the key role of emotion in our daily lives, it is expected that many applications will benefit from the efforts to design affect sensitive machines. Automatic analysis of non-verbal behaviour, such as

facial expressions, gaze, gait, etc., could be exploited for security purposes; for example, it could be used to detect deception or to highlight suspicious behaviour in highly frequented public areas such as airports or train stations. Affect-sensitive machines could also find a use as therapeutic aids for people with disabilities, for example, individuals affected by autism. These tend to have problems in recognizing other people's emotions, as well as expressing their own emotions appropriately and showing empathy: affect-sensitive machines could help them develop emotional skills and take an active role in social interaction. Artificial companions, whether as robots, graphical synthetic characters, or interactive toys, are examples of artefacts that would benefit from the integration of social, affective capabilities into their underlying technology in order to sustain long-term interactions with humans. Affect-sensitive artificial companions could assist in the care for the elderly; they could be used in applications for edutainment and entertainment (e.g. intelligent interactive games, etc.), as personal assistants in smart environments, and be employed as interactive toys for therapy purposes, for example, by encouraging and mediating interactions between people affected by social, cognitive disabilities.'

Obviously, the preceding has only been a sampling of the rich possibilities of applications for emotionally competent agents, as provided by some of our authors, demonstrating the wide range of possibilities but also the need for much more intensive research and development. The editors feel that much of the present research in this area is hampered by a certain short-sightedness of the current granting policies. Many of the research grants and contracts held by the laboratories working on the implementation of some of the ideas concerning the potential of emotionally competent agents are constrained to produce, relatively rapidly, so-called 'exemplars' of applications that seem commercially promising, in one-shot research contracts. Obviously, this puts the emphasis on producing show case examples rather than the solid, cumulative research that is urgently needed in this field. It also tends to augment competitiveness between laboratories working on similar issues and to discourage interdisciplinary approaches as these would be far too costly in the given funding frame. Generally, good applications have been based on strong basic research and good theoretical models are the best basis for both. Unless granting policy in the area of affective computing starts realizing this basic principle of research and development we are likely to continue to see a proliferation of interesting exemplars with little potential for commercial success.

Future

Instead of attempting to predict the development of this new area of research and development on emotionally competent agents—all too likely to be a futile exercise—we offer some utopian futuristic perspectives. Again, we quote our contributors, this time without holding them directly responsible.

'Sensors for taking measurements of bodily functions will be ubiquitous, appearing in form of wireless body area networks in various wearable solutions, such as stand-alone attachable sensors or integrated in garments. Signal processing will be real-time and reliable. Computing applications based on instantaneously measured bodily functioning will be integrated in various everyday applications, including telecommunication (both person-to-person as well as human–computer interaction), entertainment (adaptive program selection for music or television, gaming or virtual reality, interactive music or story line generation), dieting and nutrition, physical and mental fitness programs, as well as the work context (e.g. stress monitoring, motivational engagement).'

'Currently, much of the research into interpersonal causes and effects of emotion as reviewed in this chapter consists of demonstrations that such effects can and do often happen. One can expect to see increasing attention to the specific processes (both individual and interpersonal) that underlie these phenomena. In particular, one can foresee the application of more rigorous distinctions between different kinds of implicit and explicit processes and between strategic operations and more direct adjustments to social pressures and affordances. More generally, one can expect to see diversification of the activities of emotion researchers coupled with acknowledgement that different kinds of emotional phenomena require different kinds of explanation and different kinds of research approaches.'

'Although it is difficult to foresee future trends of technological development, the field of affective computing might hopefully generate a set of technological standards yielding a clearer terminology with respect to its primary topic labelled "emotion". Furthermore, affective computing can be expected to play a significant role in the design of human-centred, sociable technology in general.'

'We foresee that in a few years time there will be a huge increase in the realism of automatically generated animation. Computer graphics models already exist to render human skin and wrinkles with a high degree of realism. High rendering quality can be achieved in near-real time. Animations obtained through motion capture are able to capture subtle and dynamic motion, arriving at a high degree of realism. We believe that hybrid models between computer graphics and autonomous agents will allow for the creation of very realistic and believable three-dimensional human agent. Moreover, agents will have greater autonomy; in particular, behaviour models will be developed taking into account the effect of the context on behaviour appropriateness. Agents will be endowed with emotional and social intelligence. Other aspects we believe will be achieved concern the creation of long-term companions (able to display non-repetitive behaviours as well as having a coherent emotional and behavioural model) and the specification of an individualized agent.'

'In the mid term, it is likely that data-driven technologies will continue to dominate the technologies used in speech synthesis in general and therefore also in expressive speech synthesis, because data-driven methods provide substantially better quality than model-based approaches. In these paradigms, high-quality expressions depend on suitable training data, so that the number and quality of expressions will be limited by the data available. Conceptual advances regarding the types of expressions required for applications can guide the data selection process and thus lead to usable systems with limited but contextually appropriate expressiveness.

In the long term, parametric models such as articulatory speech synthesizers or statistical models of the speech acoustics can be expected to play a role because of their greater flexibility and controllability, and because their parametric nature makes them more suitable to define a low-dimensional linking model between speech acoustics/production and some parametric model of emotion or expression. Such synthesis models may start to play a role if they can be made more natural-sounding. Possible contributions to that advance in quality may come from improved model accuracies or from new ways of including training data in the fine-tuning process of explicit model parameters in automatic ways. Still in the long term, the models linking emotional states to the speech acoustics or speech production are in very early stages, and more complete approaches are yet to be researched. In this domain, the roadmap is likely to follow closely the general advances of affective computing research.'

'Affect in a broad sense—the fact that we feel positive or negative about things, empowered or threatened by them, well or ill treated—is an integral part of natural human communication. Hence, it has to be part of any interaction with computers that allows humans to communicate in ways they find natural. For that reason, increased affective sophistication is bound to be part of the move towards naturalness in interfaces, which has been continuing steadily for decades. That is linked to the increasing part that interfaces with machines play in life. It is acceptable for interfacing to be unnatural if it is occasional, but it becomes wearing if it is continual. The more we interface with automatic systems—as answering machines, automatic tutors, artificial companions, health advisors, and, of course, entertainment—the less acceptable affective incompetence will be; and the more various forms of affective competence will become part of everyday interaction with artificial systems.'

'Effectiveness and complexity of automatic methods for analysis of affective non-verbal behaviour are rapidly increasing. The current interest of affect recognition research is progressively moving towards the design of context-aware systems trained with spontaneous rather than prototypical affective expressions. The need for systems capable of working in real-time in "real world" scenarios will require an increasing attention towards the modelling of the dynamics of affect. To develop systems capable of having a large impact on people's daily lives, the affect recognition community will have to address design issues. What system is more appropriate for a given application or for a given user? How does the system take into consideration individual differences? Personalization of affect recognition abilities is likely to become a crucial aspect in the design of a successful affect recognition system. Further research challenges lie in designing systems that can deal with multiple users, in the direction of social affective interaction.'

A concluding note on ethics

Like most technological developments, emotion-oriented computing raises a large number of ethical issues. In this brief overview, we will address aspects that might arise provided that some goals are attained (e.g. implementing emotionally competent behaviours in embodied agents or robots). We will not discuss the feasibility of those goals, but we nevertheless attempt to focus mostly on current and realistic goals to avoid dwelling on purely fictional scenarios. After a few considerations on the broad-spectrum issues that may arise around the development of 'sentient machines', we will consider a few aspects directly related to: (1) the recognition of emotions in human users and their potential utilizations; (2) attempts to implement or simulate emotional behaviour in machines; and (3) manipulation of emotional processes in order to influence the users' opinions or behaviours.

We will not target any applications specifically but we will mention specific systems, such as robots or (embodied) artificial agents. When an example is cited, the reader is free to consider if the example can be extended also to other systems; examples are not provided to restrict certain issues to certain specific applications only. The reader should also remember that this discussion merely considers the abstract endeavour of allotting emotions or emotional competence to artificial systems. In this respect, the goal only, not the feasibility, of the enterprise matters for the discussion.

Phenomenological consciousness and affective relationships: what would it imply if machines would feel emotions or—more realistically—if humans would develop genuine affective interactions and relationships with machines? We do not know if it will ever be achievable to implement emotional feelings in machines. One might argue that an organic body is a prerequisite in order to feel emotions, but it is nonetheless conceptually unsettling for (many) humans to think that machines might have emotions, especially when this concept includes a phenomenological consciousness of the emotions in the machines. Why is that? Probably because emotions and emotional feelings are thought of being at the core of humanity, i.e. an essential feature that differentiates humans (and also animals) from inanimate objects. Science fiction tells us that expunging this essential distinction might be a problem. In the typical science fiction scenario involving humanoid sentient robots, the robots quickly claim to have the same rights and prerogatives as humans and ultimately want to take over and to rule over humans, just as humans originally create the robots with the idea of ruling over them.

This parallel between the human goals and the potential aspirations of the sentient (and sapient) robots hints to another level of the same problem: what might happen if humans form an attachment (relationship) with a robot that is similar to the relationship formed with a friend, a child, or a pet? This is a quite realistic expectation. One application (goal) for emotion-oriented technology is clearly to create companions (as well as servants) for humans, companions with whom they can engage emotionally and hence develop a form of relationship that they would not tend to develop towards a vacuum cleaner or any other tool or toy devoid of emotional abilities. An ethical issue then is how will humans consider such emotional machines, if they are disposable objects but also have emotions or—more realistically—if humans have feelings for them and form attachments towards them? This would create an obvious dilemma that would not be easy to resolve. Either we would accept that we have human-to-human analogue attachments to machines and then we would not be able to dispose of them so easily any longer, or we would learn that we may actually dispose of 'objects' towards which we have formed attachments that are analogous to the attachments we form towards human beings. In the latter case, the risk exists that this notion could then be transferred also to human–human relationships—that people would learn that they may get rid of (or otherwise abuse) persons with whom they have a relationship that is no longer fully satisfactory (as one would exchange one's computer application for the next upgrade with 'improved features'). Service-robots are the most obvious instantiation of this kind, but such applications could also take the shape of conversational agents. The range of potential customers is wide—from the 'teacher' helping the child with his homework to the 'nurse' helping the elderly (and lonely) widow(er) to remember to take his/her medicine and lock the front door. Outside the issue of the emotional competences of such 'helpers', one can already question the improvements such robots/agents might offer as compared to human nurses, teachers (or secretaries, psychotherapists, social workers, priests, etc.) outside of their full-time exclusive availability for the user. If we add the dimension of emotional behaviour and competences in such agents/robots, it seems clear that the goal is to take an additional step towards interactions that are to be used as substitutes for human–human interactions. This might—ultimately—imply that a robot could replace a human nurse (teacher, psychologist, etc.) in most of her functions and that users might—ultimately—become quite dependent on their artificial helpers. Many individuals are already quite dependent on their computers or mobile phones, but would we really benefit from extending this dependency on technology also towards the fulfilment of our affective needs?

A few further ethical issues become apparent if we consider the range of emotional competences that are developed in affective computing today. We split the following discussion into three sections, taking up first the field of automatic recognition (of human emotions by computers), then of synthesis, simulation, or implementation of emotional behaviour in computers, and, finally, the strategic manipulation of emotions in order to influence computer users' opinions or behaviours.

The first domain—recognition of emotions in human users—is an essential prerequisite in speaking of emotional competence. Without some form of 'knowledge' (information) concerning the emotions experienced by humans in social interactions, any system that operates in interaction with humans will indeed be impaired (at least if one expects the interaction to operate on the same grounds as human interactions). Currently, attempts to uncover emotions in human users are mainly concentrated on analysing facial and/or vocal behaviour in order to identify potential emotions of interest from non-verbal behaviour. Verbal cues, gestures or postures, and physiological signals are also considered, but much effort is directed to extracting information from the face and the voice, probably because vocal and facial cues appear to be the most accessible signs of emotions.

However, one could argue that, in order to get that information (is the user emotional? what emotions are experienced by the user?), no advanced feature detection and decision-making systems need to be implemented. The computer could more simply be programmed to ask the user what emotions he is experiencing (given that we are talking mostly about systems that are interacting with the users, this would be fairly easy). There are at least two reasons that can be invoked against this simple solution. First, we can assume that users are not always aware of their emotions or do not want to disclose them to the computer (if they are unaware of their emotional reactions they obviously cannot disclose them). Second, there are systems that do not interact directly with the user, but that still could use this information, and, even when the system does interact with the human users, explicitly questioning the users about their emotions might be very disruptive for the interaction itself.

There is an inherent ethical issue in this argumentation. If users are sometimes unaware of their emotional reactions or if they do not want to disclose them, there is a potential violation of privacy concern when a computer is gathering and using this kind of information. If one would ask the user about his willingness to confirm the information and to let the system use it, it is likely that the user would refuse (under the assumption that he is either unaware or unwilling to disclose). The second aspect we mentioned earlier aggravates this problem as the system will probably never attempt to confirm its decisions nor ask for permission to use the information, given that this would disrupt the interaction (if there is an interaction; if there is no interaction asking for confirmation or permission to use is impossible anyway).

Let's assume that the system makes an accurate decision about the emotions of the user and uses that decision for the benefit of the user and to the detriment of no one else. There would not be ethical (or legal) unfavourable outcomes (despite the privacy violation, which might be considered an ethical issue in itself). But problems might arise if the system is making a decision that the user would consider mistaken and furthermore if this leads to an expected or unexpected unfavourable outcome for the user. Furthermore, an accurate decision regarding the emotions experienced by the user might also lead to an outcome that is unfavourable for the user and this would also be very problematic if the information leading to this unfavourable outcome were not provided willingly by the user. Hence extreme care ought to be taken with respect to the way this information will be used by the system. One example of a potential application in emergency call centres can be used to illustrate the impending risks. We assume that an automatic recognition system is used in order to prioritize incoming emergency calls and decide which callers will be selected to receive medical attention first. Any caller who would be placed in the queue despite an actual urgent need for medical attention might be quite righteously displeased if this decision were based on an automatic analysis of vocal features, resulting in a decision of low emergency based on a detection of low emotional arousal in the caller's voice. Especially so, if the caller was unaware at the time of the call that his efforts to remain composed when interacting with an 'answering machine' would have led the 'answering machine' to decide that he did not need immediate rescue. On a more general level, the issue is that it will be ethically hazardous in many cases to use information retrieved without the awareness, confirmation, and permission of the users and hence the practical utility of the unobtrusive detection of emotions may be questioned.

A special case in point is the automatic or computer-aided detection of deception. Given the recent increases in crime and terrorism, the good, old 'lie detector' has started a second life in a new cloak and is currently extremely fashionable. The extraordinary computing power of modern computers and the development of extremely sophisticated pattern detection and classification algorithms, as well as the claims of emotion and non-verbal communication researchers concerning the diagnostic value of 'micro-expressions' (small-scale, rapid expressive movements that normally go undetected but that may 'leak' states the sender tries to hide), have made the detection of deception a very fashionable and attractive research and development objective.

Much of this research starts with a fundamentally flawed assumption, namely, that deception can be diagnosed through subtle expressions. But the truth value of statements (or expressed states) does not move muscles; it is emotions, and especially the preparatory action tendencies that they generate, that do. Thus, the 'detection of deception' is always an 'inference of deception' based on conjectures or construals of underlying 'hidden' states and the congruence or incongruence of hidden and advertised states with respect to the situation or context, which requires yet another set of conjectures and interpretations. Clearly, these inference processes are subject to an extraordinary number of factors, including many observer biases, especially given the immense extent of individual differences, and socio-normative constraints, in the evaluation of situations and the production of expressive reactions. What is a dubious exercise even for trained experts in catching liars becomes positively dangerous, and often unethical, if the task is relegated to a machine algorithm.

The second domain—emotional behaviour in machines—currently covers two main approaches. On the one hand, the goal is to give human users the impression that machines react emotionally. For this purpose robots or conversational agents with humanoid appearance or animal appearance will be programmed to display signals (e.g. facial expressions) that are expected to be interpreted as emotional by the users. The final goal of this enterprise is essentially to improve the communication with the users. The idea is that robots or agents that show appropriate emotional expressions are likely to be rated more positively than those that do not and that the involvement of the user in the communication with such systems will be greater. The other domain would include all applications that aim to include emotions as part of programs to generate motivated behaviours. At least some emotions can be considered to contribute to evolutionary functional behaviours (e.g. fear helps to avoid or escape danger). Including something analogous to emotions in models used to program computers is expected to enhance the functional behaviour of computers as well. There is an important conceptual difference between those two approaches. In the first case, the computers are not expected to have emotions but only to display signals that can be interpreted as emotional, in analogy with signals that are usually interpreted to show emotions in humans. In the second case, the goal is to implement something analogous to an emotional reaction in the computer (although usually without the phenomenological 'feeling' component).

Potential ethical issues in the first approach include mostly issues related to the 'make believe' component. The goal is to give the impression of emotionality while there is actually nothing emotional in the system. The users will be 'fooled' into engaging affectively with the robot or the agent, but without reciprocity. One could argue that currently many products are marketed with promises that they in fact do not hold, without leading to major ethical concerns. However, affectively loaded interactions, such as being empathic, enjoying something with you, or feeling sorry for you, or picking a fight, are interactions that many individuals might consider acceptable only if their partner is also affectively engaged in the interaction. If the partner is just playing along a predefined script, showing the appearance of affective engagement but without any actual engagement, one could speak of outright deception. Hence, it is in fact likely that emotionally intelligent adults would not engage in such interactions if they very well knew that there was no reciprocity. However, this might not be the case for children or fragile individuals who might not have the full capacity to understand the difference between the appearance of emotionality and genuine emotionality. In fact, successful imitations in robots or agents might even lead to increased difficulties in making this distinction for some individuals and might favour the notion that many other relationships are similarly unilateral and shallow.

In the second eventuality—aiming at implementing elements of emotional responses into computers in order to orient their behaviours—it might be important to question the validity of the functional view of emotions. While the hypothesis of functionality holds true for many examples, it is equally possible to find other examples of emotional reactions that are detrimental for the well-being or survival of individuals. For example, it is easy to imagine that computers might benefit from mechanisms resembling fear that would alert them to potential threats and tune them to avoid threats or preserve themselves. However, it is already more difficult to imagine how a computer might benefit from mechanisms resembling sadness, grief, or depression. Human emotions, even if they are functional to the ground, can also 'go wrong'. Here we cannot outline a full catalogue of potential affective disorders, but let us only think of the example of fear, which doubtlessly includes evolutionarily functional components. Implementing the capacity to fear in computers might open up the possibility to implement simultaneously the potential for dysfunctional fear responses, such as panic attacks, generalized anxiety, or phobias. Obviously, the ideal scenario would be to implement only 'useful' emotional mechanisms in machines but the model being taken from human emotions might encompass the potential also for associated disorders.

Along the same line of ideas, if we imagine a robot or an agent that would be able to display adequate emotions (i.e. in appearance functional emotional behaviours), a robot or an agent that also would understand the users' emotional reactions and would be able to strategically use both its emotional reactions and the emotional reaction of its users for a number of preset goals, we might speculate that we would have created a fully competent emotional robot/agent. However— if also deprived of emotional feelings and empathy—the previous description could easily be the portrait of a psychopath.

The third and last domain of emotion-oriented computing to be discussed concerns the domain of persuasion and the manipulation of people's opinions and behaviours through emotional mechanisms. Emotions are powerful motivators and as such they are often used and manipulated in marketing or in politics in order to influence the public opinion in one direction or another. For example, political leaders frequently resort to fear (of strangers, of the future, of economical problems) or to pride (national or partisan feelings) in order to influence voting behaviours; marketing campaigns try to associate positive feelings with certain products or businesses because positive emotions will incite people to buy related products. It would therefore be surprising if such mechanisms would not be picked up also in affective computing applications (e.g. in the placement of advertisements in games or on the internet). Manipulating opinions or behaviours obviously involves ethical concerns as it directly deals with issues of freedom of choice and self-determination. However, there are probably no specific concerns to be raised in this respect for emotion-oriented technologies. Ethical issues with respect to opinion or behaviour manipulation lie mostly in the goals of the manipulations (the final result of the manipulation might be more or less 'good'—beneficial for the targeted groups—or more or less 'bad'—detrimental for the targeted groups), and the goals are independent of the media that are used to promote them. Yet it may be advisable for researchers working on the development of the technology to be aware of the fact that it might be used to promote unethical goals and for them to develop means to prevent such uses.

As shown by many examples in the history of science, scientists are powerless to prevent abuse of their discoveries and they often regret the effects of 'the spirits that they have summoned'. Yet, the potential for abuse should not impede scientific progress. Affective computing is clearly here to stay. However, in developing a wide variety of emotion-oriented systems, researchers and practitioners should heed the special nature and function of human emotions and the enormous power these command and show appropriate concern for ethical issues that might arise on the way.

Bibliography

Abadjieva, E., Murray I.R. and Arnott, J.L. (1993). Applying analysis of human emotional speech to enhance synthetic speech. *Proceedings Eurospeech* 1993, Berlin, pp. 909–12.

Adolphs, R. (2003). Cognitive neuroscience of human social behaviour. *Nature Reviews Neuroscience* 4, 165–78.

Adolphs, R., Russell, J.A., and Tranel, D. (1999). A role for the human amygdala in recognizing emotional arousal from unpleasant stimuli. *Psychological Science* 10 (2), 167–71.

Afzal, S. and Robinson, P. (2009). Natural affect data—collection and annotation in a learning context. In *Affective computing and intelligent interaction. International Conference 2009 (ACII 2009)*, pp. 22–8. Amsterdam, The Netherlands. IEEE Computer Society Press, Los Alamitos.

Aggleton, J. (2000). *The amygdala: a functional analysis*. Oxford University Press, Oxford.

Albrecht, I., Schröder, M., Haber, J., and H.-P. Seidel (2005). Mixed feelings: expression of non-basic emotions in a muscle-based talking head. *Journal of Virtual Reality*, Special issue on Language, Speech, and Gesture 8 (4) 201–12.

Allbeck, J. and Badler, N. (2003). Representing and parameterizing agent behaviours. In *Life-like characters: tools, affective functions and applications* (ed. H. Prendinger and M. Ishizuka), pp. 19–38. Springer, Berlin.

Allen, J.J.B., Chambers, A.S., and Towers, D.N. (2007). The many metrics of cardiac chronotropy: a pragmatic primer and a brief comparison of metrics. *Biological Psychology* 74, 243–62.

Ambadar, Z., Schooler, J.W., and Cohn, J.F. (2005). Deciphering the enigmatic face: the importance of facial dynamics in interpreting subtle facial expressions. *Psychological Science* 16, 403–10.

Ambady, N. and Rosenthal, R. (1992). Thin slices of expressive behavior as predictors of interpersonal consequences: a meta-analysis. *Psychological Bulletin* 111 (2), 256–74.

Amir, N. and Ron, S. (2006). Collection and evaluation of an emotional speech corpus using event recollection. In *Proceedings of the LREC Workshop on Corpora for Research on Emotion and Affect*, Genoa, May 2006, pp. 25–8.

Anderson, J.R. (1993). *Rules of the mind*. Lawrence Erlbaum, Hillsdale, New Jersey.

Anderson, J.R. and Lebiere, C. (2003). The Newell test for a theory of cognition. *Behavioral and Brain Sciences* 26, 587–640.

Anderson, K. and McOwan P.W. (2006). A real-time automated system for recognition of human facial expressions. *IEEE Transactions on Systems, Man and Cybernetics, Part B* 36 (1), 96–105.

Anderson, N.H. (1989). Information integration approach to emotions and their measurement. In *Emotion: theory, research, and experience*. Vol. 4. *The measurement of emotion* (ed. R. Plutchik and H. Kellerman), pp. 133–86. Academic Press, New York.

Andreassi, J.L. (2006). *Psychophysiology: human behavior and physiological response*. Routledge, London.

Ang, J., Dhillon, R., Krupski, A., Shriberg, E., and Stolcke, A. (2002). Prosody-based automatic detection of annoyance and frustration in human–computer dialog. *Proceedings of the International Conference on Spoken Language Processing*, Denver, Colorado, pp. 2037–40.

Anliker, U., Ward, J.A., Lukowicz, P., Tröster, G., Dolveck, F., Baer, M., Keita, F., Schenker, E., Catarsi, F., Coluccini, L., Belardinelli, A., Shklarski, D., Alon, M., Hirt, E., Schmid, R., and Vuskovic, M. (2004). Amon: a wearable multiparameter medical monitoring and alert system. *IEEE Transactions on Information Technology in Biomedicine* 8, 415–27.

Arbib, M.A. (ed.) (2003). *The handbook of brain theory and neural networks*, 2nd edn. MIT Press, Cambridge, Massachusetts.

Arbib, M.A. and Fellous, J.-M. (2004). Emotions: from brain to robot. *Trends in Cognitive Sciences* **8** (12), 554–61.

Argyle, M. (1988). *Bodily communication*, 2nd edn. Methuen and Co., London.

Aristotle (1941). *Ethica Nicomachea* [Nicomachean ethics]. In *The basic works of Aristotle* (ed. R. McKeon), pp. 935–1126. Random House, New York.

Ark, W.S., Dryer, D.C., and Lu, D.J. (1999). The emotion mouse. In *Proceedings of HCI International (the 8th International Conference on Human–Computer Interaction) on Human–Computer Interaction: Ergonomics and User Interfaces*, pp. 818–23. Lawrence Erlbaum Associates, Hillsdale, New Jersey.

Armony, J.L., Servan-Schreiber, D., Cohen, J.D., and LeDoux, J.E. (1995). An anatomically constrained neural network model of fear conditioning. *Behavioral Neuroscience* **109** (2), 246–57.

Armony, J.L., Servan-Schreiber, D., Cohen, J.D., and LeDoux, J.E. (1997). Computational modeling of emotion: explorations through the anatomy and physiology of fear conditioning. *Trends in Cognitive Science* **1**, 28–34.

Árnason, B.P. and Þorsteinsson, A. (2008). The CADIA BML Realizer, http://cadia.ru.is/projects/bmlr/.

Arnold, M.B. (1960). *Emotion and personality*, Vol. 1. *Psychological aspects*. Columbia University Press, New York.

Arya, A. and DiPaola, S. (2007). Multi-space behavioural model for face-based affective social agents. *EURASIP Journal on Image and Video Processing*, Special issue on Facial Image Processing, article ID 48757.

Arya, A., DiPaola, S., and Parush, A. (2009). Perceptually valid facial expressions for character-based applications. *International Journal of Computer Game Technology* **2009**, Article ID 462315.

Aston-Jones, G., Rajkowski, J., Ivanova, S., Usher, M., and Cohen, J. (1998). Neuromodulation and cognitive performance: recent studies of noradrenergic locus coeruleus. *Advances in Pharmacology* **42**, 755–9.

Aue, T. and Scherer, K.R. (2008). Appraisal-driven somatovisceral response patterning: effects of intrinsic pleasantness and goal conduciveness. *Biological Psychology* **79**, 158–64.

Aue, T., Flykt, A., and Scherer, K.R. (2007). First evidence for differential and sequential efferent effects of goal relevance and goal conduciveness appraisal. *Biological Psychology* **74**, 347–57.

Austin, J.T. and Vancouver, J.B. (1996). Goal constructs in psychology: structure, process, and content. *Psychological Bulletin* **120** (3), 338–75.

Averill, J.R. (1980). A constructivist view of emotion. In *Emotion*, Vol. 1. *Theory, research, and experience* (ed. R. Plutchik and H. Kellerman), pp. 305–40. Academic Press, New York.

Aviezer, H., Hassin, R.R., Ryan, J., Grady, C., Susskind, J., Anderson, A., Moscovitch, M., and Bentin, S. (2008). Angry, disgusted, or afraid? Studies on the malleability of emotion perception. *Psychological Science* **19**, 724–32.

Baars, B.J. (1988). *A cognitive theory of consciousness*. Cambridge University Press, Cambridge.

Baars, B.J. (2002). The conscious hypothesis: origins and recent evidence. *Trends in Cognitive Sciences* **6** (1), 47–52.

Bach, D.R., Schachinger, H., Neuhoff, J.G., Esposito, F., Salle, F.D., Lehmann, C., Herdener, M., Scheffler, K., and Seifritz, E. (2008). Rising sound intensity: an intrinsic warning cue activating the amygdala. *Cerebral Cortex* **18**, 145–50.

Bachorowski, J-A. (1999). Vocal expression and perception of emotion. *Current Directions in Psychological Science* **8**, 53–7.

Badler, N., Phillips, C., and Webber, B. (1993). *Simulating humans: computer graphics animation and control*. Oxford University Press, Oxford.

Bales, R.F. (1950). *Interaction process analysis: a method for the study of small groups*. Addison-Wesley, Reading, Massachusetts.

Balomenos, T., Raouzaiou, A., Ioannou, S., Drosopoulos, A. I., Karpouzis, K., and Kollias, S. (2005). Emotion analysis in man–machine interaction systems. In *Machine learning for multimodal interaction* (ed. S. Bengio and H. Bourlard), pp. 318–28. Lecture Notes in Computer Science 3361. Springer Verlag, Berlin.

Banse, R. and Scherer, K.R. (1996). Acoustic profiles in vocal emotion expression. *Journal of Personality and Social Psychology* **70** (3), 614–36.

Bänziger, T. (2004). Communication vocale des émotions: perception de l'expression vocale et attributions émotionnelles [Vocal communication of emotion: perception of vocal expression and emotion attribution]. Unpublished PhD dissertation. University of Geneva, Geneva, Switzerland. Retrieved June 7, 2009, from <http://www.unige.ch/fapse/emotion/publications/theses/these325_banziger.pdf>

Bänziger, T. and Scherer, K.R. (2007). Using actor portrayals to systematically study multimodal emotion expression: the GEMEP corpus. In *Affective computing and intelligent interaction, Proceedings of the Second International Conference (ACII 2007), Lisbon* (ed. A. Paiva, R. Prada, and R.W. Picard), pp. 476–87. Lecture Notes in Computer Science 4738. Springer-Verlag, Berlin.

Bänziger, T., Grandjean, D., and Scherer, K.R. (2009). Emotion recognition from expressions in face, voice, and body: the multimodal emotion recognition test (MERT). *Emotion* **9** (5), 691–704.

Bar-Haim, Y., Lamy, D., Pergamin, L., Bakermans-Kranenburg, M.J., and van Ijzendoorn, M.H. (2007). Threat-related attentional bias in anxious and nonanxious individuals: a meta-analytic study. *Psychological Bulletin* **133**, 1–24.

Baron-Cohen, S., Golan, O., Wheelwright S., and Hill, J.J. (2004). *Mind reading: the interactive guide to emotions.* Jessica Kingsley Publishers, London.

Barrett, L.F. (2006). Emotions as natural kinds?. *Perspectives on Psychological Science* **1**, 28–58.

Barrett, L.F. and Russell, J.A. (2009). Circumplex models. In *Oxford companion to emotion and the affective sciences* (ed. D. Sander and K.R. Scherer), pp. 85–8. Oxford University Press, Oxford.

Barrett, L.F., Lindquist, K.A., and Gendron, M. (2007). Language as context for the perception of emotion. *Trends in Cognitive Sciences* **11**, 327–32.

Bartlett, M.S., Littlewort, G., Braathen, P., Sejnowski, T.J., and Movellan, J.R. (2003). A prototype for automatic recognition of spontaneous facial actions. *Advances in Neural Information Processing Systems* **15**, 1271–8.

Bartlett, M.S., Littlewort, G., Frank, M., Lainscsek, C., Fasel, I., and Movellan, J. (2006). Fully automatic facial action recognition in spontaneous behavior. In Proceedings of the 7th IEEE Conference on face and gesture recognition, Southampton, UK.

Bartneck, C. (2002). Integrating the OCC model of emotions in embodied characters. *Proceedings of the Workshop on Virtual Conversational Characters: Applications, Methods, and Research Challenges*, Melbourne.

Barton, R.A., Aggleton, J.P., and Grenyer, R. (2003). Evolutionary coherence of the mammalian amygdala. *Proceedings of the Royal Society of London B: Biological Sciences* **270**, 539–43.

Bates, J., Loyall, B., and Reilly, W.S.N. (1991). Broad agents. *Sigart Bulletin* **2,** 38–40.

Batliner, A., Fisher, K., Huber, R., Spilker, J., and Noth, E. (2000). Desperately seeking emotions or: actors, wizards, and human beings. *Proceedings of the ISCA Workshop on Speech and Emotion*, 195–200.

Batliner, A., Fischer, K., Huber, R., Spilker, J., and Noeth, E. (2003). How to find trouble in communication. *Speech Communication* **40**, 117–43.

Batliner, A., Hacker, Ch., Steidl, S., Nöth, E., D'Arcy, S., Russell, M., and Wong, M. (2004). You stupid ting box—children interacting with the AIBO robot: a cross linguistic emotional speech corpus. *Proceedings of International Conference on Language Resources and Evaluation LREC*, Lisbon, Portugal.

Batliner, A., Steidl, S., Schuller, B., Seppi, D., Laskowski, K., Vogt, T., Devillers, L., Vidrascu, L., Amir, N., Kessous, L., and Aharonson, V. (2006). CEICES: combining dfforts for improving automatic classification of emotional user states: a forced co-operation initiative. *Fifth Slovenian and First International Language Technologies Conference*, Ljubljana, Slovenia.

Baudoin, G. and Stylianou, Y. (1996). On the transformation of the speech spectrum for voice conversion. In *Proceedings of the 4th International Conference on Spoken Language Processing* (Philadelphai, Pennsylvania), pp. 1405–8.

Baumeister, R.F. (2002). Ego depletion and self-control failure: an energy model of the self's executive function. *Self and Identity* 1, 129–36.

Baxter, M.G. and Murray, E.A. (2002). The amygdala and reward. *Nature Reviews Neuroscience* 3, 563–73.

Baylor, A. L. and Kim, S. (2008). The effects of agent nonverbal communication on procedural and attitudinal learning outcomes. In *Intelligent virtual agents, Proceedings of the 8th International Conference (IVA 2008)*, Tokyo, Japan (ed. H. Prendinger, J.C. Lester, and M. Ishizuka), pp. 208–14. Lecture Notes in Computer Science 5208. Springer, Berlin.

Bechara, A., Damásio, A.R., Damásio, H., and Anderson, S.W. (1994). Insensitivity to future consequences following damage to human prefrontal cortex. *Cognition* 50, 7–15.

Bechara, A., Damásio, H., Damásio, A., and Lee, G. (1999). Different contributions of the human amygdala and ventromedial prefrontal cortex to decision-making. *Journal of Neuroscience* 19, 5473–81.

Becker, C., Kopp, S., and Wachsmuth, I. (2004). Simulating the emotion dynamics of a multimodal conversational agent. *International Workshop on Affective Dialogue Systems*, pp. 154–65. Springer, Berlin/Heidelberg.

Becker, C., Prendinger, H., Ishizuka, M., and Wachsmuth, I. (2005). Evaluating affective feedback of the 3D agent Max in a competitive cards game. *Proceedings of 1st International Conference on Affective Computing and Intelligent Interaction* (ed. J. Tao, T. Tan, and R.W. Picard), pp. 466–73. Springer, New York.

Becker, C., Kopp, S., and Wachsmuth, I. (2007). Why emotions should be integrated into conversational agents. In *Conversational Informatics: An Engineering Approach* (ed. T. Nishida), pp. 49–68. John Wiley and Sons Ltd, London.

Becker-Asano, C. (2008). WASABI: Affect Simulation for Agents with Believable Interactivity. PhD thesis for the Faculty of Technology, University of Bielefeld, Bielefeld, Germany.

Becker-Asano, C. and Wachsmuth, I. (2008). Affect simulation with primary and secondary emotions. In *Intelligent virtual agents, Proceedings of the 8th International Conference (IVA 2008)*, Tokyo, Japan (ed. H. Prendinger, J.C. Lester, and M. Ishizuka), pp. 15–28. Lecture Notes in Computer Science 5208. Springer, Berlin.

Becker-Asano, C. and Wachsmuth, I. (2010). Affective computing with primary and secondary emotions in a virtual human. *Autonomous Agents and Multi-Agent Systems* 20 (1), 32–49.

Bennett, D. S., Bendersky, M., and Lewis, M. (2002). Facial expressivity at 4 months: a context by expression analysis. *Infancy* 3, 97–11.

Berger, R.D., Saul, J.P., and Cohen, R.J. (1989). Transfer function analysis of autonomic regulation. I. Canine atrial rate response. *American Journal of Physiology—Heart and Circulatory Physiology* 256 (1), 142–52.

Bernhardt, D. and Robinson, P. (2007). Detecting affect from non-stylised body motions, In *Affective computing and intelligent interaction, Proceedings of the Second International Conference (ACII 2007)*, Lisbon (ed. A. Paiva, R. Prada, and R.W. Picard), pp. 59–70. Lecture Notes in Computer Science 4738. Springer-Verlag, Berlin.

Berntson, G.G., Cacioppo, J.T., and Quigley, K.S. (1991). Autonomic determinism: the modes of autonomic control, the doctrine of autonomic space, and the laws of autonomic constraint. *Psychological Review* 98, 459–87.

Berntson, G.G., Cacioppo, J.T., and Quigley, K.S. (1993). Cardiac psychophysiology and autonomic space in humans: empirical perspectives and conceptual implications. *Psychological Bulletin* 114 (2), 296–322.

Berntson, G.G., Quigley, K.S., and Lozano, D. (2007). Cardiovascular psychophysiology. In *Handbook of psychophysiology* (ed. J.T. Cacioppo, L.G. Tassinary, and G.G. Berntson), Chapter 8, pp. 182–210. Cambridge University Press, Cambridge.

Bevaqua, E. and Pelachaud, C. (2004). Expressive audio-visual speech. *Computer Animation and Virtual Worlds* 15 (3–4), 297–304.

Bianchi-Berthouze, N. and Kleinsmith, A. (2003). A categorical approach to affective gesture recognition. *Connection Science* **15** (4), 259–69.

Biehl, M., Matsumoto, D., Ekman, P., Hearn, V., Heider, K., Kudoh, T., *et al.* (1997). Matsumoto and Ekman's Japanese and Caucasian facial expressions of emotion (JACFEE): reliability data and cross-national differences. *Journal of Nonverbal Behavior* **21**, 3–21.

Birkholz, P. (2007). Control of an articulatory speech synthesizer based on dynamic approximation of spatial articulatory targets. In *INTERSPEECH-2007*, 2865–68.

Birkholz, P., Jackèl, D., and Kröger, B.J. (2006). Construction and control of a three-dimensional vocal tract model. In *Proceedings of the International Conference on Acoustics, Speech, and Signal Processin. (ICASSP 2006)* (Toulouse, France), pp. 561–2.

Biswas, G., Leelawong, K., Schwartz, D., Vye, N., and Tag, V. (2005). Learning by teaching. A new agent paradigm for educational software. *Applied Artificial Intelligence*, Special issue on Educational Agents—Beyond Virtual Tutors **19**, 393–412.

Black, A.W. and Campbell, N. (1995). Optimising selection of units from speech databases for concatenative synthesis. In *Proceedings of Eurospeech 1995 (Madrid)* Vol. 1, pp. 581–4.

Blanchard, A. and Cañamero, L. (2006). Developing affect-modulated behaviors: stability, exploration, exploitation, or imitation? *6th International Workshop on Epigenetic Robotics*, Paris.

Blanck, P.D. (1993). *Interpersonal expectations*. Cambridge University Press, Cambridge.

Blechert, J., Lajtman, M., Michael, T., Margraf, J., and Wilhelm, F.H. (2006). Identifying anxiety states using broad sampling and advanced processing of peripheral physiological information. *Biomedical Sciences Instrumentation* **42**, 136–41.

Boersma P. (1993). Accurate short-term analysis of the fundamental frequency and the harmonics-to-noise ratio of a sampled sound. *Proceedings of the Institute of Phonetic Sciences* **17**, 97–110.

Boone, R.T. and Cunningham, J.G. (1998). Children's decoding of emotion in expressive body movement: the development of cue attunement. *Developmental Psychology* **34** (5), 1007–16.

Borow, K.M. and Newburger, J.W. (1982). Noninvasive estimation of central aortic pressure using the oscillometric method for analysing systemic artery pulsatile blood flow: comparative study of indirect systolic, diastolic and mean brachial artery pressure with simultaneous direct ascending aortic pressure measurements. *American Heart Journal* **103**, 879–86.

Boucsein, W. (1992). *Electrodermal activity*. Plenum Press, New York.

Boukricha, H., Wachsmuth,I., Hofstaetter, A., and Grammer, K. (2009). Pleasure–arousal–dominance driven facial expression simulation. In *Affective computing and intelligent interaction. International Conference 2009 (ACII 2009)*, Amsterdam, The Netherlands, pp. 119–25. IEEE Computer Society Press, Los Alamitos.

Bould, E. and Morris, N. (2008). Role of motion signals in recognizing subtle facial expressions of emotion. *British Journal of Psychology* **99**, 167–89.

Bradley, M.M. and Lang, P.J. (2000). Measuring emotion: behavior, feeling and physiology. In *Cognitive neuroscience of emotion* (ed. R. Lane and L. Nadel), pp. 242–76. Oxford University Press, New York.

Braubach, L., Pokahr, A., Moldt, D., and Lamersdorf, W. (2005). Goal representation for BDI agent systems. In *Programming multi-agent systems*, Lecture Notes in Computer Science 3346, pp. 44–65. Springer, Berlin.

Brave, S., Nass, C., and Hutchinson, K. (2005). Computers that care: investigating the effects of orientation of emotion exhibited by an embodied computer agent. *International Journal of Human–Computer Studies* **62**, 161–78.

Breazeal, C. (2003). Emotion and sociable humanoid robots. *International Journal of Human–Computer Studies* **59** (1–2), 119–55.

Breazeal, C., Edsinger, A., Fitzpatrick, P., and Scassellati, B. (2001). Active vision for sociable robots. *IEEE Transactions on Systems, Man and Cybernetics–Part A* **31** (5), 443–53.

Brosch, T., Sander, D., Pourtois, G., and Scherer, K.R. (2008). Beyond fear: rapid spatial orienting towards emotional positive stimuli. *Psychological Science* **14** (9), 362–70.

Brown, J., Bullock, D., and Grossberg, S. (1999). How the basal ganglia use parallel excitatory and inhibitory learning pathways to selectively respond to unexpected rewarding cues. *Journal of Neuroscience* **19**, 10502–11.

Brownley, K.A., Hurwitz, B.E., and Schneiderman, N. (2000). Cardiovascular psychophysiology. In *Handbook of psychophysiology* (ed. J.T. Cacioppo, L.G. Tassinary, and G.G. Berntson), Chapter 9, pp. 224–64. Cambridge University Press, Cambridge.

Brunswik, E. (1956). *Perception and the representative design of psychological experiments*, 2nd edn. University of California Press, Berkeley.

Buck, R. (1985). Prime theory: an integrated view of motivation and emotion. *Psychological Review* **92** (3), 389–413.

Bui, T.D. (2004). Creating emotions and facial expressions for embodied agents. PhD thesis for Department of Electrical Engineering, Mathematics and Computer Science, University of Twente, Enschede, the Netherlands.

Buisine, S., Abrilian, S., Niewiadomski, R., Martin, J.-C., Devillers, L., and Pelachaud, C. (2006). Perception of blended emotions: from video corpus to expressive agent. In *Intelligent virtual agents, Proceedings of the 6th International Conference (IVA2006), Marina del Rey, USA* (ed. J. Gratch, M. Young, R. Aylett, D. Ballin, and P. Olivier), pp. 93–106. Lecture Notes in Computer Science 4133. Springer, New York.

Bull, P.E. (1987). *Posture and gesture*, Pergamon International Series in Experimental Social Psychology, Vol. 16. Pergamon Books, Oxford.

Bullier, J. (2004). Integrated model of visual processing. *Brain Research: Brain Research Review* **36** (2–3), 96–107.

Bullier, J. and Nowak, L.G. (1995). Parallel versus serial processing: new vistas on the distributed organization of the visual system. *Current Opinion in Neurobiology* **5** (4), 497–503.

Burkhardt, F. (2001). *Simulation emotionaler Sprechweise mit Sprachsystemen*. Shaker Verlag, Aachen.

Burkhardt, F. and Sendlmeier, W.F. (2000). Verification of acoustical correlates of emotional speech using formant-synthesis. In *Proceedings of the ISCA Workshop on Speech and Emotion* (Newcastle, Northern Ireland), pp. 151–6.

Busemeyer, J.R., Dimperio, E., and Jessup, R.K. (2007). Integrating emotional processing into decision-making models. In *Integrated models of cognitive systems* (ed. W.D. Grey), pp. 213–29. Oxford University Press, New York.

Buxton, R.B., Wong, E.C., and Frank, L.R. (1998). Dynamics of blood flow and oxygenation changes during brain activation: the Balloon model. *Magnetic Resonance in Medicine* **39**, 855–64.

Cacioppo, J.T. and Tassinary, L.G. (1990a). Inferring psychological significance from physiological signals. *American Psychologist* **45**, 16–28.

Cacioppo, J.T. and Tassinary, L.G. (1990b). Psychophysiology and psychophysiological inference. In *Principles of psychophysiology: physical, social, and inferential elements* (ed. J.T. Cacioppo and L.G. Tassinary), pp. 3–33. Cambridge University Press, New York.

Cacioppo, J.T., Tassinary, L.G., and Berntson, G.G. (2000a). Psychophysiological science. In *Handbook of psychophysiology* (ed. J.T. Cacioppo, L.G. Tassinary, and G.G. Berntson), Chapter 1, pp. 3–23. Cambridge University Press, Cambridge.

Cacioppo, J.T., Tassinary, L.G., and Berntson, G.G. (Eds.) (2000b). *Handbook of psychophysiology*. Cambridge University Press, Cambridge.

Cacioppo, J.T., Berntson, G.G., Larsen, J.T., Poehlmann, K.M., and Ito, T.A. (2000c). The psychophysiology of emotion. In *The handbook of emotion* (ed. R. Lewis and J.M. Haviland-Jones), pp. 173–91. Guilford Press, New York.

Cacioppo, J. T., Tassinary, L.G., and Berntson, G.G. (2007a). Psychophysiological science: interdisciplinary approaches to classic questions about the mind. In *Handbook of psychophysiology* (ed. J.T. Cacioppo, L.G. Tassinary and G.G. Berntson), pp. 1–18. Cambridge University Press, Cambridge.

Cacioppo, J.T., Tassinary, L.G., and Berntson, G.G. (Eds.) (2007b). *Handbook of psychophysiology*. Cambridge University Press, Cambridge, UK.

Cahn, J.E. (1989). The generation of affect in synthesized speech. *Journal of the American Voice Input/ Output Society* **8**, 1–19.

Calder, A.J., Lawrence, A.D., and Young, A.W. (2001). Neuropsychology of fear and loathing. *Nature Reviews Neuroscience* **2**, 352–63.

Campbell, N. (2000). Databases of emotional speech. In *Proceedings of the ISCA Workshop on Speech and Emotion*, pp. 34–8. <ftp://ftp.cs.pitt.edu/web/projects/nlp/conf/isca2000/speech_emotion/pdfs/ campbell.pdf>

Campbell, N. (2005). Developments in corpus-based speech synthesis: Approaching natural conversational speech. *Institute of Electronics, Information and Communication Engineers Transactions on Information and Systems* **88** (3), 376–83.

Campbell, N. and Marumoto, T. (2000). Automatic labelling of voice-quality in speech databases for synthesis. In *Proceedings of the 6th International Conference on Spoken Language Processing* (Beijing, China), Vol. 4, pp. 468–71.

Campbell, N. and Mokhtari, P. (2003). Voice quality: the 4th prosodic dimension, *Proceedings of the 15th International Congress of Phonetic Sciences* (Barcelona), Vol. 3, pp. 2417–20.

Campos, J. J., Thein, S., and Daniela, O. (2003). A Darwinian legacy to understanding human infancy: emotional expressions as behavior regulators. In *Emotions inside out: 130 years after Darwin's 'The expression of the emotions in man and animals'* (ed. P. Ekman, J.J. Campos, R.J. Davidson, and F.B.M. De Waal), pp. 110–34. New York Academy of Sciences, New York.

Camras, L.A., Lambrecht, L., and Michel, G.F. (1996). Infant 'surprise' expressions as coordinative motor structures. *Journal of Nonverbal Behavior* **20**, 183–95.

Camras, L.A., Meng, Z., Ujiie, T., Dharamsi, S., Miyake, K., Oster, H., Wang, L., Cruz, J., Murdoch, A., and Campos, J. (2002). Observing emotion in infants: facial expression, body behaviour, and rater judgments of responses to an expectancy-violating event. *Emotion* **2**, 179–93.

Camurri, A., Lagerlöf, I., and Volpe, G. (2003). Recognizing emotion from dance movement: comparison of spectator recognition and automated techniques. *International Journal of Human–Computer Studies* **59** (1–2), 213–25.

Camurri, A., Mazzarino, B., Ricchetti, M., Timmers, R., and Volpe, G. (2004). Multimodal analysis of expressive gesture in music and dance performances. In *Gesture-based communication in human– computer interaction* (ed. A. Camurri and G. Volpe), pp. 20–39. Springer Verlag, Heidelberg.

Camurri, A., De Poli, G., Leman, M., and Volpe, G. (2005). Toward communicating expressiveness and affect in multimodal interactive systems for performing art and cultural applications. *IEEE Multimedia* **12** (1), 43–53.

Camurri, A., Coletta, P., Varni, G., and Ghisio, S. (2007). Developing multimodal interactive systems with EyesWeb XMI. In *Proceedings of the 2007 Conference on New Interfaces for Musical Expression*, pp. 305–8.

Cañamero, L. (2009). Autonomous agent. In *Oxford companion to emotion and the affective sciences* (ed. D. Sander and K.R. Scherer). Oxford University Press.

Canli, T., Sivers, H., Whitfield, S.L., Gotlib, I.H., and Gabrieli, J.D. (2002). Amygdala response to happy faces as a function of extraversion. *Science* **21**, 2191.

Cannon, W.B. (1929). *Bodily changes in pain, hunger, fear, and rage*, 2nd edn. D. Appleton and Co., New York and London.

Cannon, W.B. (1939). *The wisdom of the body*. Norton, New York.

Caridakis, G., Karpouzis, K., and Kollias, S. (2008). User and context adaptive neural networks for emotion recognition. *Neurocomputing* **71** (13–15), 2553–62.

Carroll, J.M. and Russell, J.A. (1997). Facial expressions in Hollywood's portrayal of emotion. *Journal of Personality and Social Psychology* **72** (1), 164–76.

Castellano, G. (2008). Movement expressivity analysis in affective computers: from recognition to expression of emotion. Ph.D. Dissertation, Faculty of Engineering, University of Genoa, April 2008.

Castellano, G., Villalba, S.D., and Camurri. A. (2007). Recognising human emotions from body movement and gesture dynamics. In *Affective computing and intelligent interaction, Proceedings of the Second International Conference (ACII 2007)* (ed. A. Paiva, R. Prada, and R.W. Picard), pp. 71–82. Lecture Notes in Computer Science 4738. Springer-Verlag, Berlin.

Castellano, G., Kessous, L., and Caridakis, G. (2008*a*). Emotion recognition through multiple modalities: face, body gesture, speech. In *Affect and emotion in human–computer interaction* (ed. C. Peter and R. Beale), pp. 92–103. Lecture Notes in Computer Science 4868. Springer, Heidelberg.

Castellano, G., Mortillaro, M., Camurri, A., Volpe, G., and Scherer, K. (2008*b*). Automated analysis of body movement in emotionally expressive piano performances. *Music Perception* **26** (2), 103–19.

Castellano, G., Pereira, A., Leite, I., Paiva, A., and McOwan, P.W. (2009). Detecting user engagement with a robot companion using task and social interaction-based features. In *Proceedings of the 2009 ACM International Conference on Multimodal Interfaces (ICMI 2009)*, pp. 119–26. ACM, New York.

Cerekovic, A., Pejsa, T., and Pandzic, I.S. (2009). RealActor: character animation and multimodal behaviour realization system. In *Intelligent virtual agents, Proceedings of 9th International Conference (IVA 2009)*, Amsterdam, The Netherlands (ed. Z. Ruttkay, M. Kipp, A. Nijholt, and H.H. Vilhjálmsson), pp. 486–7. Lecture Notes in Computer Sciences 5773. Springer, Berlin.

Ceschi, G. and Scherer, K.R. (2003). Children's ability to control the facial expression of laughter and smiling: knowledge and behaviour. *Cognition and Emotion* **17**, 385–411.

Chang, Y., Hu, C., Feris, R., and Turk, M. (2006). Manifold based analysis of facial expression. *Journal of Image and Vision Computing* **24** (6), 605–14.

Cheng, A., Eysel, U.T., and Vidyasagar, T.R. (2004). The role of the magnocellular pathway in serial deployment of visual attention. *European Journal of Neuroscience* **20** (8), 2188–92.

Childress, A.R., Ehrman, R.N., Wang, Z., Li, Y., and Sciortino, N. (2008). Prelude to passion: limbic activation by 'unseen' drug and sexual cues. *PLoSone* **3** (1), e1506. Published online: doi: 10.1371/journal.pone.0001506.

Christie, M.J. (1981). Electrodermal activity in the 1980s: a review. *Journal of the Royal Society of Medicine* **74**, 616–22.

Clavel, C., Vasilescu, I., Richard, G., and Devillers, L. (2007). Voiced and unvoiced content of fear-type emotions in the SAFE corpus. *Proceedings of Speech Prosody*, 2007.

Clavel, C. Plessier, J., Martin, J.-C. Ach, L., and Morel, B. (2009). Combining facial and postural expressions of emotions in a virtual character. In *Intelligent virtual agents, Proceedings of 9th International Conference IVA 2009*, Amsterdam, The Netherlands (ed. Z. Ruttkay, M. Kipp, A. Nijholt, and H.H. Vilhjálmsson), pp. 287–300, Lecture Notes in Computer Sciences 5773. Springer, Berlin.

Cleeremans, A. (2008). Consciousness: the radical plasticity thesis. *Progress in Brain Research* **168**, 19–33.

Clore, G. and Palmer, J. (2009). Affective guidance of intelligent agents: how emotion controls cognition. *Cognitive Systems Research* **10,** 21–30.

Clore, G., Schwarz, N., and Conway, M. (1994). Affect as information. In *Handbook of affect and social cognition* (ed. J.P. Forgas). Lawrence Erlbaum, Mahwah, New Jersey.

Coan, J.A. and Allen, J.B. (Eds.) (2007). *Handbook of emotion elicitation and assessment.* Oxford University Press, New York.

Cohen, S. (2004). Social relationships and health. *American Psychologist* **59**, 676–84.

Cohen, S. and Wills, T.A. (1985). Stress, social support and the buffering hypothesis. *Psychological Bulletin* **98**, 310–57.

Cohn, J.F. (2006). Foundations of human computing: facial expression and emotion. In *Proceedings of the 8th International Conference on Multimodal Interfaces (ICMI 2006)* (ed. F.K.H. Quek, J. Yang, D.W. Massaro, A.A. Alwan, and T.J. Hazen), pp. 233–8. ACM, New York.

Cohn, J.F. and Schmidt, K.L. (2004). The timing of facial motion in posed and spontaneous smiles. *International Journal of Wavelets, Multiresolution and Information Processing* **2**, 1–12.

Cohn, J.F., Ambadar, Z., and Ekman, P. (2007). Observer-based measurement of facial expression with the facial action coding system. In *Handbook of emotion elicitation and assessment* (ed. J.A. Coan and J.J.B. Allen), pp. 203–21. Oxford University Press, New York.

Cohn, M.A., Rao, A.S., Broudy, M., Birch, S., Watson, H., Atkins, N., Davis, B., Stott, F.D., and Sackner, M.A. (1982). The respiratory inductive plethysmograph: a new non-invasive monitor of respiration. *Bulletin Européenne de Physiopathologie Respiratoire* **18**, 643–58.

Conati, C. (2002). Probabilistic assessment of user's emotions in educational games. *Journal of Applied Artificial Intelligence, Special issue on 'Merging cognition and affect in HCI'* **16**, 555–75.

Conati, C. and Maclaren, H. (2004). Evaluating a probabilistic model of student affect. *Proceedings of 7th International Conference on Intelligent Tutoring Systems,* Maceio, Brazil. Lecture Notes in Computer Science, Volume 3220, pp. 55–66. Springer, Berlin.

Coulson, M. (2007). Attributing emotion to static body postures: recognition accuracy, confusions, and viewpoint dependence. *Journal of Nonverbal Behavior* **28** (2), 114–39.

Courgeon, M., Martin, J.C., and Jacquemin, C. (2008). User's gestural exploration of different virtual agents' expressive profiles. In *Proceedings of the International Conference on Autonomous Agents and Multi Agent Systems, AAMAS 2008* (ed. L. Padgham, D. Parkes, and J.P. Muller), Vol. 3, pp. 1237–40. Inesc-Id.

Cousineau, D., Charbonneau, D., and Jolicoeur, P. (2006). Parameterizing the attentional blink effect. *Canadian Journal of Experimental Psychology* **60** (3), 175–89.

Cowan, N. (1988). Evolving conceptions of memory storage, selective attention, and their mutual constraints within the human information-processing system. *Psychological Bulletin* **104** (2), 163–91.

Cowell, A. and Stanney, K.M. (2003). Embodiement and interaction guidelines for designing credible, trustworthy embodied conversational agents. In *Intelligent Virtual Agents, Proceedings of the 4th International Workshop (IVA 2003)*, Kloster Irsee, Germany (ed. T. Rist, R. Aylett, D. Ballin, and J. Rickel), pp. 301–9. Lecture Notes in Computer Science 3661. Springer-Verlag, New York.

Cowell, A.J. and Stanney, K.M. (2005). Manipulation of non-verbal interaction style and demographic embodiment to increase anthropomorphic computer character credibility. *International Journal of Human–Computer Studies* **62**, 2, 281–306.

Cowie, R. (2009). Perceiving emotion: towards a realistic understanding of the task. *Philosophical Transactions of the Royal Society B* **364**, 3515–25.

Cowie, R. (2010). Describing the forms of emotional colouring that pervade everyday life. In *The Oxford handbook of the philosophy of emotion* (ed. P. Goldie), pp. 63–94. Oxford University Press, Oxford.

Cowie, R. Douglas-Cowie, E., Apolloni, B., Taylor, J., Romano, A., and Fellenz, W. (1999). What a neural net needs to know about emotion words. In *Computational intelligence and applications* (ed. N. Mastorakis), pp. 109–14. Word Scientific Engineering Society, Singapore.

Cowie, R., Douglas-Cowie, E., Savvidou, S., McMahon, E., Sawey, M., and Schröder, M. (2000). 'Feeltrace': an instrument for recording perceived emotion in real time. *Proceedings of the ISCA Workshop on Speech and Emotion*, Newcastle, Co. Down, UK, pp. 19–24.

Cowie, R., Douglas-Cowie, E., Karpouzis, K., Caridakis, G., Wallace, M., and Kollias, S. (2008). Recognition of emotional states in natural human–computer interaction. In *Multimodal user interfaces* (ed. D. Tzovaras), pp. 119–53. Springer, Berlin and Heidelberg.

Cowie, R., McKeown, G., and Gibney, C. (2009). The challenges of dealing with distributed signs of emotion: theory and empirical evidence. In *Affective Computing and Intelligent Interaction, Proceedings of the International Conference (ACII 2009)*, Amsterdam, Vol. 1, pp. 351–6. IEEE.

Craig, A.D. (2002). How do you feel? Interoception: the sense of the physiological condition of the body. *Nature Reviews Neuroscience* **3**, 655–66.

Craig, A.D. (2009). How do you feel—now? The anterior insula and human awareness. *Nature Reviews Neuroscience* **10**, 59–70.

Critchley, H.D. (2002). Electrodermal responses: what happens in the brain. *The Neuroscientist* **8**, 132–42.

Damásio, A.R. (1994). *Descartes's error: emotion, reason, and the human brain*. Putnam, New York.

Damasio, A.R. (1998). Investigating the biology of consciousness. *Philosophical Transactions of the Royal Society of London B, Biological Sciences* **353** (1377), 1879–82.

Damasio, A. (2003). *Looking for Spinoza: joy, sorrow, and the feeling brain.* Harcourt, Orlando, Florida.

Dan Glauser, E.S. and Scherer, K.R. (2008). Neuronal processes involved in subjective feeling emergence: oscillatory activity during an emotional monitoring task. *Brain Topography* **20**, 224–31.

Darwin, C. (1872/1998). *The expression of emotions in man and animals*, 3rd edn (ed. P. Ekman). Oxford University Press, New York. [Original work published 1872.]

Davidson, R.J. (1995). Cerebral asymmetry, emotion, and affective style. In *Brain asymmetry* (ed. R.J. Davidson, and K. Hugdahl), pp. 361–87. MIT Press, Cambridge, Massachusetts.

Davidson, R.J. and Irwin, W. (1999). The functional neuroanatomy of emotion and affective styles. *Trends in Cognitive Sciences* **3**, 11–21.

Davidson, R.J. and Sutton, S.K. (1995). Affective neuroscience: the emergence of a discipline. *Current Opinion in Neurobiology* **5** (2), 217–24.

Davidson, R.J, Jackson, D.C, and Larson C.L. (2000). Human electroencephalography. In *Handbook of psychophysiology*, 2nd edn (ed. J.T. Cacioppo, L.G. Tassinary, and G.G. Berntson), Chapter 2. Cambridge University Press, Cambridge.

Davidson, R.J., Scherer, K.R., and Goldsmith, H.H. (2003). *Handbook of affective sciences.* Oxford University Press, New York.

Davis, M. and Whalen, P.J. (2001). The amygdala: vigilance and emotion. *Molecular Psychiatry* **6**, 13–34.

Davitz, J.R. (1969). *The language of emotion.* Academic Press, New York.

Dawson, M.E., Schell, A.M., and Filion, D.L. (1990). The electrodermal system. In *Principles of psychophysiology. Physical, social, and inferential elements* (ed. J.T. Cacioppo and L.G. Tassinary), pp. 295–324. Cambridge University Press, New York.

Dawson, M.E., Schell, A.M., and Filion, D.L. (2007). The electrodermal system. In *Handbook of psychophysiology* (ed. J.T. Cacioppo, L.G. Tassinary, and G.G. Berntson), pp. 159–81. Cambridge University Press, Cambridge.

Dayan, P. and Yu, A.J. (2006). Phasic norepinephrine: a neural interrupt signal for unexpected events. *Network* **17** (4), 335–50.

De Gelder, B., Van den Stock, J., Meeren, H.K.M., Sinke, C.B.A., Kret, M.E., and Tamietto, M. (2010). Standing up for the body. Recent progress in uncovering the networks involved in processing bodies and bodily expressions. *Neuroscience and Biobehavioral Reviews* **34**, 513–27.

Dehaene, S., Sergent, C., and Changeux, J.-P. (2003). A neuronal network model linking subjective reports and objective physiological data during conscious perception. *Proceedings of the National Academy of Sciences USA* **100** (14), 8520–5.

Dellaert, F., Polzin, T., and Waibel, A. (1996). Recognizing emotion in speech. *Proceedings of 4th International Conference on Spoken Language Processing*, Vol. 3, pp. 1970–3.

Delplanque, S., Grandjean, D., Chrea, C., Aymard, L., Cayeux, I., Margot, C., Velazco, M. I., Sander, D., and Scherer, K.R. (2009). Sequential unfolding of novelty and pleasantness appraisals of odors: Evidence from facial electromyography and autonomic reactions. *Emotion* **9**, 316–28.

De Melo, C. and Gratch, J. (2009). Expression of emotions using wrinkles, blushing, sweating and tears. In *Intelligent virtual agents, Proceedings of 9th International Conference IVA 2009*, Amsterdam, The Netherlands (ed. Z. Ruttkay, M. Kipp, A. Nijholt, and H.H. Vilhjálmsson), pp. 188–200. Lecture Notes in Computer Sciences 5773. Springer, Berlin.

De Melo, C., Zheng, L., and Gratch, J. (2009). Expression of moral emotions in cooperating agents. In *Intelligent virtual agents, Proceedings of 9th International Conference IVA 2009*, Amsterdam, The Netherlands (ed. Z. Ruttkay, M. Kipp, A. Nijholt, and H.H. Vilhjálmsson), pp. 301–7. Lecture Notes in Computer Sciences 5773. Springer, Berlin.

De Meijer, M. (1989). The contribution of general features of body movement to the attribution of emotions. *Journal of Nonverbal Behavior* **13** (4), 247–68.

D'Entremont, B. and Muir, D. (1999). Infant responses to adult happy and sad vocal and facial expressions during face-to-face interaction. *Infant Behavior and Development* 22, 527–39.

Deonna, J. and Scherer, K.R. (2009). The case of the disappearing intentional object: Constraints on a definition of emotion. *Emotion Review* 2 (1), 44–52.

Derryberry, D. and Reed, M.A. (2002). Anxiety-related attentional biases and their regulation by attentional control. *Journal of Abnormal Psychology* 111, 225–36.

Descartes, R. (1649). *Les passions de l'âme*. Paris.

Desimone, R. and Duncan, J. (1995). Neural mechanisms of selective visual attention. *Annual Reviews of Neuroscience* 18 (0147–006X), 193–222.

Devillers, L. and Vidrascu, L. (2007*a*). Real-life emotion recognition in speech. In *Speaker classification 2* (ed. C. Müller), pp. 34–42. Springer, Berlin.

Devillers, L. and Vidrascu, L. (2007*b*). Positive and negative emotional states behind the laugh in spontaneous spoken dialogs. *Proceedings of the Interdisciplinary Workshop on the Phonetics of Laughter* (Saarbrucken), pp. 37–40.

Devillers, L., Vasilescu, I., and Lamel L. (2003). Emotion detection in a task-oriented dialog corpus. In *Proceedings of IEEE International Conference on Multimedia, (ICME 2003)*.

Devillers, L., Vasilescu, I., and Vidrascu, L. (2004). F0 and pause features analysis for anger and fear detection in real-life spoken dialogs. *Proceedings of Speech Prosody* (Nara, Japan), pp. 205–8.

Devillers, L., Vidrascu, L., and Lamel, L. (2005). Challenges in real-life emotion annotation and machine learning based detection. *Neural Networks* 18, 407–22.

Devillers, L., Cowie, R., Martin, J-C., Douglas-Cowie, E., Abrilian, A., and McRorie, M. (2006). Real-life emotions in French and English TV video corpus clips: an integrated annotation protocol combining continuous and discrete approaches. *Proceedings of the 5th International Conference on Language Resources and Evaluation (LREC 2006)*, pp. 1105–10.

De Vries, M.P., Schutte, H.K., Veldman, A.E.P., and Verkerke, G.J. (2002). Glottal flow through a two-mass model: comparison of Navier–Stokes solutions with simplified models. *Journal of the Acoustic Society of America* 111, 1847–53.

De Waal, F.B.M. (2003). Darwin's legacy and the study of primate visual communication. In *Emotions inside out: 130 years after Darwin's The expression of the emotions in man and animals* (ed. P. Ekman, J.J. Campos, R.J. Davidson, and F.B.M. De Waal), pp. 79–87. New York Academy of Sciences, New York.

Dias, J. and Paiva, A. (2005). Feeling and reasoning: a computational model for emotional agents. *Proceedings of 12th Portuguese Conference on Artificial Intelligence, EPIA 2005*. Springer.

Dignum, F. (1999). Autonomous agents with norms. *Artificial Intelligence and Law* 7, 69–79.

Dimberg, U. (1990). Facial electromyography and emotional reactions. *Psychophysiology* 27, 481–94.

Dimberg, U., Thunberg, M., and Elmehed, K. (2000). Unconscious facial reactions to emotional facial expressions. *Psychological Science* 11, 86–9.

Dindo, L. and Fowles, D.C. (2008). The skin conductance orienting response to semantic stimuli: significance can be independent of arousal. *Psychophysiology* 45, 111–18.

Ding, L. and Martinez, A.M. (2006). A three-dimensional shape and motion reconstruction for the analysis of American sign language. *Proceedings of the 2nd IEEE Workshop on Vision for Human–Computer Interaction*. IEEE Computer Society, Washington DC.

Dittrich, W.H., Troscianko, T., Lea, S.E.G., and Morgan, D. (1996). Perception of emotion from dynamic point-light displays represented in dance. *Perception* 25 (6), 727–38.

D'Mello, S.K. and Graesser, A.C. (2009). Automatic detection of learners' emotions from gross body language. *Applied Artificial Intelligence* 23 (2), 123–50.

Dobson, K.S. (1989). A meta-analysis of the efficacy of cognitive therapy for depression. *Journal of Consulting and Clinical Psychology* 57, 414–19.

Dokhan, B., Setz, C., Arnrich, B., and Tröster, G. (2007). Monitoring passengers' breathing—a feasibility study. In Swiss Society of Biomedical Engineering Annual Meeting, Neuchâtel, Switzerland.

Donato, G., Bartlett, M., Hager, J., Ekman, P., and Sejnowski, T. (1999). Classifying facial actions. *IEEE Transactions on Pattern Analysis and Machine Intelligence* **21** (10), 974–89.

Douglas-Cowie, E., Cowie, R., and Schröder, M. (2003a). The description of naturally occurring emotional speech. In *Proceedings of the 15th International Congress of Phonetic Sciences*, Barcelona, pp. 2877–80.

Douglas-Cowie, E., Campbell, N., Cowie, R., and Roach, P. (2003b). Emotional speech: towards a new generation of databases. *Speech and Emotion* **40**, 33–60.

Douglas-Cowie, E., Cowie, R., Sneddon, I., Cox, C., Lowry, O., McRorie, M., Martin, JC., Devillers, L., Abrilian, S., Batliner, A., Amir, N., and Karpousis, K. (2007). The HUMAINE database: addressing the collection and annotation of naturalistic and induced emotional data. In *Affective computing and intelligent interaction* (ed. A. Paiva, R. Prada, and R.W. Picard), pp. 488–500. Springer, Berlin.

Doyle, J. (2006). *Extending mechanics to minds: the mechanical foundations of psychology and economics.* Cambridge University Press, London.

Draghi-Lorenz, R., Reddy, V., and Costall, A. (2001). Rethinking the development of 'nonbasic' emotions: a critical review of existing theories. *Developmental Review* **21**, 263–304.

Draghi-Lorenz, R., Reddy, V., and Morris, P. (2005). Young infants can be perceived as shy, coy, bashful, embarrassed. *Infant and Child Development* **14**, 63–83.

Edelmann, R.E. and Hampson, S.E. (1981). The recognition of embarrassment. *Personality and Social Psychology Bulletin* **7**, 109–16.

Edwards, P. (1998) Etude empirique de déterminants de la différenciation des émotions et de leur intensité. [An empirical study of the determinants of the differentiation and the intensity of the emotions.] Ph.D. Thesis. University of Geneva. (Download available from http://www.unige.ch/fapse/emotion/theses.html)

Ehrette, T., Chateau, N., d'Allessandro, C., and Maffiolo, V. (2003). Predicting the perceptive judgment of voices in a telecom context: selection of acoustic parameters. In *Eurospeech-2003* (Geneva), pp. 117–20.

Ekman, P. (1972). Universals and cultural differences in facial expression of emotion. In *Nebraska symposium on motivation* (ed. J.R. Cole), pp. 207–83. University of Nebraska Press, Lincoln.

Ekman, P. (1973). Cross-cultural studies of facial expression. In *Darwin and facial expression: a century of research in review* (ed. P. Ekman), pp. 169–222. Academic Press, New York.

Ekman, P. (1982). Methods for measuring facial action. In *Handbook of methods in nonverbal behavior research* (ed. K.R. Scherer and P. Ekman), pp. 45–90. Cambridge University Press, Cambridge.

Ekman, P. (1984). Expression and the nature of emotion. In *Approaches to emotion* (ed. K.R. Scherer and P. Ekman), pp. 319–43. Erlbaum, Hillsdale, New Jersey.

Ekman, P. (1992). An argument for basic emotions. *Cognition and Emotion* **6**, 169–200.

Ekman, P. (1994a). All emotions are basic. In *The nature of emotion: fundamental questions* (ed. P. Ekman and R.J. Davidson), pp. 15–19. Oxford University Press, New York and Oxford.

Ekman, P. (1994b). Strong evidence for universals in facial expressions: a reply to Russell's mistaken critique. *Psychological Bulletin* **115**, 268–87.

Ekman, P. (1999). Basic emotions. In *The handbook of cognition and emotion* (ed. T. Dalgleish and T. Power), pp. 45–60. John Wiley and Sons, Ltd, Chichester.

Ekman, P. (2003a). Darwin, masking, and facial expression. *Annals of the New York Academy of Sciences* **1000**, 205–21.

Ekman, P. (2003b). *The face revealed*. Weidenfeld and Nicolson, London.

Ekman, P. (2003c). *Emotions revealed*. Times Books, New York.

Ekman, P. (2007). The directed facial action task; emotional responses without appraisal. In *Handbook of emotion elicitation and assessment* (ed. J.A. Coan and J.B. Allen), pp. 47–53. Oxford University Press, New York.

Ekman, P. (2009). Lie catching and micro expressions. In *The philosophy of deception* (ed. C. Martin). Oxford University Press, Oxford.

Ekman, P. and Friesen, W.V. (1969). Nonverbal leakage and clues to deception. *Psychiatry* **32**, 88–105.

Ekman, P. and Friesen, W. V. (1971). Constants across cultures in the face and emotion. *Journal of Personality and Social Psychology* **17**, 124–9.

Ekman, P. and Friesen, W.V. (1975). *Unmasking the face: a guide to recognizing emotions from facial clues.* Prentice-Hall, Englewood Cliffs, New Jersey.

Ekman, P. and Friesen, W.V. (1976). *Pictures of facial affect.* Consulting Psychologists Press, Palo Alto, California.

Ekman, P. and Friesen, W.V. (1978). *The facial action coding system: a technique for the measurement of facial movement.* Consulting Psychologists Press, Palo Alto, California.

Ekman, P. and Friesen, W.V. (1982). Felt, false and miserable smiles. *Journal of Nonverbal Behavior* **6**, 238–52.

Ekman, P. and Friesen, W.V. (1986). A new pan-cultural facial expression of emotion. *Motivation and Emotion* **10**, 159–68.

Ekman, P. and Heider, K.G. (1988). The universality of a contempt expression: a replication. *Motivation and Emotion* **12**, 303–8.

Ekman, P. and Rosenberg, E.L. (2005). What the face reveals: basic and applied studies of spontaneous expression using the Facial Action Coding System (FACS), 2nd edn. Oxford University Press, New York.

Ekman, P., Sorenson, E.R., and Friesen, W.V. (1969). Pan-cultural elements in facial displays of emotion. *Science* **164**, 86–8.

Ekman, P., Friesen, W.V., O'Sullivan, M., Chan, A., Diacoyanni-Tarlatzis, I., Heider, K., *et al.* (1987). Universals and cultural differences in the judgments of facial expressions of emotion. *Journal of Personality and Social Psychology* **53**, 712–17.

Ekman, P., Friesen, W.V., and O'Sullivan, M. (1988). Smiles when lying. *Journal of Personality and Social Psychology* **54**, 414–20.

Ekman, P., Irwin W., and Rosenberg, E. (1994). EMFACS-8. Unpublished manual.

Ekman, P., Friesen, W.V., and Hager, J.C. (2002). Salt Lake City, Utah. (Retrieved from: http://www.face-and-emotion.com/dataface/facs/new_version.jsp)

Elfenbein, H.A. and Ambady, N. (2002). On the universality and cultural specificity of emotion recognition: a meta-analysis. *Psychological Bulletin* **128**, 203–35.

Elliott, C. (1992). The affective reasoner: a process model of emotions in a multi-agent system. PhD dissertation, Northwestern University, Institute for the Learning Sciences, Technical Report no. 32.

Elliott, C. and Siegle, G. (1993). Variables influencing the intensity of simulated affective states. In *AAAI technical report for the Spring Symposium on Reasoning about Mental States: Formal Theories and Applications*, pp. 58–67. AAAI, Stanford University, Palo Alto, California.

Ellsworth, P.C. (1991). Some implications of cognitive appraisal theories of emotion. In *International review of studies on emotion* (ed. K. Strongman), pp. 143–61. Wiley, New York.

Ellsworth, P.C. (1994). William James and emotion: is a century of fame worth a century of misunderstanding? *Psychological Review* **101**, 222–9.

Ellsworth, P.C. and Scherer, K.R. (2003). Appraisal processes in emotion. In *Handbook of the affective sciences* (ed. R.J. Davidson, H. Goldsmith, and K.R. Scherer), pp. 572–95. Oxford University Press, New York and Oxford.

El Nasr, M.S., Yen, J., and Ioerger, T. (2000). FLAME: Fuzzy Logic Adaptive Model of Emotions. *Autonomous Agents and Multi-Agent Systems* **3**, 219–57.

Engel, B.T. and Chism, R.A. (1967). Effect of increases and decreases in breathing rate on heart rate and finger pulse volume. *Psychophysiology* **4**, 83–9.

Erickson, R.P. (2008). A study of the science of taste: on the origins and influence of the core ideas. *Behavioral and Brain Sciences* **31** (1), 59–75.

Ernst, J.M., Litvack, D.A., Lozano, D.L., Cacioppo, J.T., and Berntson, G.G. (1999). Impedance pneumography: noise as signal in impedance cardiography. *Psychophysiology* **36**, 333–8.

Esteves, F., Dimberg, U., *and* Öhman, A. (1994). Automatically elicited fear: conditioned skin conductance responses to masked facial expressions. *Cognition and Emotion* **8**, 393–413.

Ethofer, T., Van De Ville, D., Scherer, K., and Vuilleumier, P. (2009). Decoding of emotional information in voice-sensitive cortices. *Current Biology* **19** (12), 1028–33.

Ewbank, M.P., Lawrence, A.D., Passamonti, L., Keane, J., Peers, P.V., and Calder, A.J. (2009). Anxiety predicts a differential neural response to attended and unattended facial signals of anger and fear. *NeuroImage* **44**, 1144–51.

Eyben, F., Wöllmer, M., Graves, A., Schuller, B., Douglas-Cowie, E., and Cowie, R. (2010). On-line emotion recognition in a 3-D activation-valence-time continuum using acoustic and linguistic cues. *Journal on Multimodal User Interfaces*, special issue on Real-Time Affect Analysis and Interpretation: Closing the Affective Loop in Virtual Agents and Robots **3** (1–2), 7–19.

Eysenck, M.W., Derekshan, N., Santos, R., and Calvo, M.G. (2007). Anxiety and cognitive performance: attentional control theory. *Emotion* **7** (2), 336–53.

Fahrenberg, J., Schneider, H.-J., and Safian, P. (1987). Psychophysiological assessments in a repeated-measurement design extending over a one-year interval: trends and stability. *Biological Psychology* **24**, 49–66.

Fant, G. (1960). *Acoustic theory of speech production*. Mouton's-Gravenhage.

Fant, G., Liljencrants, J., and Lin, Q. (1985). A four-parameter model of glottal flow. *Speech Transmission Laboratory, Quarterly Progress and Status Report* **4**, 1–13.

Fasel, I., Stewart-Bartlett, M., Littelwort-Ford, G., and Movellan, J.R. (2002). Real time fully automatic coding of facial expressions from video. In *9th Symposium on Neural Computation*. California Institute of Technology.

Fecteau, S., Belin, P., Joanette, Y., and Armony, J.L. (2007). Amygdala responses to nonlinguistic emotional vocalizations. *NeuroImage* **36** (2), 480–7.

Feeney, B.C. and Collins, N.L. (2003). Motivations for caregiving in adult intimate relationships: influences on caregiving behavior and relationship functioning. *Personality and Social Psychology Bulletin* **29**, 950–68.

Feldman-Barrett, L. (2006). Are emotions natural kinds? *Perspectives on Psychological Science* **1**, 28–58.

Fellbaum, C. (ed.) (1999). *WordNet: an electronic lexical database*. MIT Press, Cambridge, Massachusetts.

Felleman, D.J. and Van Essen, D.C. (1991). Distributed hierarchical processing in the primate cerebral cortex. *Cerebral Cortex* **1**, 1–47.

Fellous, J.M. and Arbib, M.A. (2005). *Who needs emotions? The brain meets the robot*. Oxford University Press, Oxford.

Fellous, J.M., Armony, J.L., and LeDoux, J.E. (2003). Emotional circuits and computational neuroscience. In *The handbook of brain theory and neural networks*, 2nd edn (ed. M.A. Arbib), pp. 398–401. MIT Press, Cambridge, Massachusetts.

Fernandez, R. and Ramabhadran, B. (2007). Automatic exploration of corpus-specific properties for expressive text-to-speech: a case study in emphasis. In *Proceedings of the 6th ISCA Workshop on Speech Synthesis* (Bonn, Germany), pp. 34–9.

Fidjeland, A., Roesch, E.B., Shanahan, M.P., and Luk, W. (2009). NeMo: A platform for neural modelling of spiking neurons using GPUs. In *Proceedings of the 20th IEEE International Conference on Application-specific Systems, Architectures and Processors*, Boston, Massachusetts, pp. 137–44. IEEE.

Fine, C. and Blair, R.J.R. (2000). The cognitive and emotional effects of amygdala damage. *Neuroreport* **6**, 435–50.

Fischer, A.H., Manstead, A.S.R., and Zaalberg, R. (2003). Social influences on the emotion process. *European Review of Social Psychology* **14**, 171–201.

Flykt, A., Dan, E.S., and Scherer, K.R. (2009). Using a probe detection task to assess the timing of intrinsic pleasantness appraisals. *Swiss Journal of Psychology* **68** (3), 161–71.

Fontaine, J.R.J., Scherer, K.R., Roesch, E.B., and Ellsworth, P.E. (2007). The world of emotions is not two-dimensional. *Psychological Science* **18** (12), 1050–7.

Fowles, D.C., Christie, M.J., Edelberg, R., Grings, W.W., Lykken, D.T., and Venables, P.H. (1981). Publication recommendations for electrodermal measurements. *Psychophysiology* **18**, 232–9.

Fragopanagos, N., Kockelkoren, S., and Taylor, J.G. (2005). A neurodynamic model of the attentional blink. *Brain Research Cognitive Brain Research* **24** (3), p. 568–86.

Frank, M. and Ekman, P. (1993). Not all smiles are created equal: the differences between enjoyment and non enjoyment smiles. *Humor: International Journal of Humor Research* **6** (1), 9–26.

Frank, R. (1988). *Passions with reason: the strategic role of the emotions.* W.W. Norton, New York.

French, J.R.P., Jr. and Raven, B.H. (1959). The bases of social power. In *Studies in social power* (ed. D. Cartwright), pp. 150–67. University of Michigan Press, Ann Arbor.

Frick, R.W. (1986). The prosodic expression of anger: differentiating threat and frustration. *Aggressive Behavior* **12** (2), 121–8.

Fridlund, A.J. (1991). Sociality of solitary smiling: potentiation by an implicit audience. *Journal of Personality and Social Psychology* **60**, 229–40.

Fridlund, A.J. (1994). *Human facial expression: an evolutionary view.* Academic Press, San Diego.

Fridlund, A.J. (1997). The new ethology of human facial expressions. In *The psychology of facial expression* (ed. J.A. Russell and J.M. Fernándezo-Dols), pp. 103–29. Cambridge University Press, Cambridge.

Fridlund, A.J., Kenworthy, K., and Jaffey, A.K. (1992). Audience effects in affective imagery: replication and extension to dysphoric imagery. *Journal of Nonverbal Behavior* **16**, 191–212.

Friedman, B.H. and Thayer, J.F. (1998). Anxiety and autonomic flexibility: a cardiovascular approach. *Biological Psychology* **47**, 243–63.

Fries, P. (2005). A mechanism for cognitive dynamics: neuronal communication through neuronal coherence. *Trends in Cognitive Sciences* **9**, 474–80.

Friesen, C.K. and Kingstone, A. (1998). The eyes have it! Reflexive orienting is triggered by nonpredictive gaze. *Psychonomic Bulletin and Review* **5**, 490–5.

Frijda, N.H. (1986). *The emotions.* Cambridge University Press, Cambridge.

Frijda, N.H. (1987). Emotion, cognitive structure, and action tendency. *Cognition and Emotion* **1**, 115–43.

Frijda, N.H. (1993). The place of appraisal in emotion. *Cognition and Emotion* **7**, 357–87.

Frijda, N.H. (2007). *The laws of emotion.* Lawrence Erlbaum Associates, Mahwah, New Jersey.

Frijda, N.H. and Scherer, K.R. (2009). Emotion definition (psychological perspectives). In *Oxford companion to emotion and the affective sciences* (ed. D. Sander and K.R. Scherer), pp. 142–3. Oxford University Press, Oxford.

Frijda, N.H. and Swagerman, J. (1987). Can computers feel? Theory and design of an emotional system. *Cognition and Emotion* **1** (3), 235–57.

Frijda, N.H. and Tcherkassof, A. (1997). Facial expressions as modes of action readiness. In *The psychology of facial expression* (ed. J.A. Russell and J.M. Fernandez-Dols), pp. 57–77. Cambridge University Press, Cambridge.

Frijda, N.H., Mesquita, B., Sonnemans, J., and van Goozen, S. (1991). The duration of affective phenomena, or emotions, sentiments and passions. In *International review of emotion and motivation* (ed. K. Strongman), pp. 187–225. Wiley, New York.

Frischen, A., Bayliss, A.P., and Tipper, S.P. (2007). Gaze cuing of attention: visual attention, social cognition and individual differences. *Psychological Bulletin* **133**, 694–724.

Friston, K.J., Mechelli, A., Turner, R., and Price, C.J. (2000). Nonlinear responses in fMRI: the Balloon model, Volterra kernels, and other hemodynamics. *Neuroimage* **12**, 466–477.

Gallaher, P.E. (1992). Individual differences in nonverbal behaviour: dimensions of style. *Journal of Personality and Social Psychology* **63** (1), 133–45.

Gardner, W.N. (1996). The pathophysiology of hyperventilation disorders. *Chest* **109**, 516–34.

Gebhard, P. (2005). ALMA—a layered model of affect. Paper presented at *Fourth International Joint Conference on Autonomous Agents and Multiagent Systems*, Utrecht, pp. 29–36.

Gebhard, P. and Kipp, K.H. (2006). Are computer-generated emotions and moods plausible to humans? In *Intelligent virtual agents, Proceedings of the 6th International Conference (IVA 2006)*, Marina del Rey, California (ed. J. Gratch, M. Young, R. Aylett, D. Ballin, and P. Olivier), pp. 343–56. Lecture Notes in Computer Science 4133. Springer, New York.

Gebhard, P., Schröder, M., Charfuelan, M., *et al.* (2008). IDEAS4Games: building expressive virtual characters for computer games. In *Intelligent virtual agents, Proceedings of the 8th International Conference (IVA 2008)*, Tokyo, Japan (ed. H. Prendinger, J.C. Lester, and M. Ishizuka), pp. 426–40. Lecture Notes in Computer Science 5208. Springer, Berlin.

Gerrards-Hesse, A., Spies, K., and Hesse, F.W. (1994). Experimental inductions of emotional states and their effectiveness: a review. *British Journal of Psychology* **85**, 55–78.

Ghashghaei, H.T., Hilgetag, C.C., and Barbas, H. (2007). Sequence of information processing for emotions based on the anatomic dialogue between prefrontal cortex and amygdale. *NeuroImage* **34** (3), 905–23.

Gibson, J.J. (1979). *The ecological theory of visual perception*. Houghton Mifflin, Boston.

Gleason, M.E.J., Iida, M., Shrout, P.E., and Bolger, N. (2008). Receiving support as a mixed blessing: evidence for dual effects of support on psychological outcomes. *Journal of Personality and Social Psychology* **94**, 824–38.

Gmytrasiewicz, P. and Lisetti, C. (2000). Using decision theory to formalize emotions for multi-agent systems. *Second ICMAS-2000 Workshop on Game Theoretic and Decision Theoretic Agents*, pp. 391–2. Boston.

Gobl, C. and Ni Chasaide, A. (2003). The role of voice quality in communicating emotion, mood and attitude. *Speech Communication* **40**, 189–212.

Goeleven, E., De Raedt, R., Leyman, L., and Verschuere, B. (2008). The Karolinska directed emotional faces: a validation studies. *Cognition and Emotion* **22** (6), 1094–118.

Goffman, E. (1959). *The presentation of self in everyday life*. Doubleday Anchor, Garden City, New York.

Gosselin, P., Kirouac, G., and Doré, F.Y. (1995). Components and recognition of facial expression in the communication of emotion by actors. *Journal of Personality and Social Psychology* **68**, 1–14.

Goudbeek, M. and Scherer, K.R. (in press). Beyond arousal: valence and potency/control in the vocal expression of emotion. *Journal of the Acoustic Society of America*.

Grammer, K. and Oberzaucher, E. (2006). The reconstruction of facial expressions in embodied systems: new approaches to an old problem. *ZIF Mitteilungen* **2**, 14–31.

Grandjean, D. and Scherer, K. (2006). Examining the neural mechanisms involved in the affective and pragmatic coding of prosody. In *Proceedings of Speech Prosody 2006*, paper 268.

Grandjean, D. and Scherer, K.R. (2008). Unpacking the cognitive architecture of emotion processes. *Emotion* **8**, 341–51.

Grandjean, D., Sander, D., Pourtois, G., Schwartz, S., Seghier, M., Scherer, K.R., and Vuilleumier, P. (2005). The voices of wrath: brain responses to angry prosody in meaningless speech. *Nature Neuroscience* **8**, 145–6.

Grandjean, D., Sander, D., and Scherer, K.R. (2008). Conscious emotional experience emerges as a function of multilevel, appraisal-driven response synchronization. *Consciousness and Cognition* **17** (2), 484–95.

Gratch, J. (2000). Émile: marshalling passions in training and education. *Fourth International Conference on Intelligent Agents*. Barcelona, Spain.

Gratch, J. (2008). True emotion vs. social intentions in nonverbal communication: towards a synthesis for embodied conversational agents. In *Modeling communication with robots and virtual humans* (ed. I. Wachsmuth and G. Knoblich), pp. 181–98. Springer, Berlin.

Gratch, J. and Marsella, S.A. (2004a). A domain-independent framework for modelling emotion. *Journal of Cognitive Systems Research* **5** (4), 269–306.

Gratch, J. and Marsella, S. (2004*b*). Evaluating the modeling and use of emotion in virtual humans. *3rd International Joint Conference on Autonomous Agents and Multiagent Systems*, pp.320–27, New York.

Gratch, J. and Marsella, S. (2005). Evaluating a computational model of emotion. *Autonomous Agents and Multi-Agent Systems* **11** (1), 23–43.

Gratch, J., Wang, N., Gerten, J., and Fast, E. (2007). Creating rapport with virtual agents. In *Intelligent virtual agents, 7th International Conference (IVA 2007)*, Paris, France (ed. C. Pelachaud, J.-C. Martin, E. André, G. Chollet, K.Karpouzis, and D. Pelé), pp. 125–38. Lecture Notes in Computer Science 4722. Springer, Berlin.

Gratch, J., Marsella, S., and Petta, P. (2009*a*). Modeling the antecedents and consequences of emotion. *Journal of Cognitive Systems Research* **10**, 1–5.

Gratch, J., Marsella, S., Wang, N., and Stankovic, B. (2009*b*). Assessing the validity of appraisal-based models of emotion. In *Affective computing and intelligent interaction. Third International Conference (ACII 2009)*, Amsterdam. IEEE, Los Alamitos.

Gray, A. and Markel, J. (1976). Distance measures for speech processing. *IEEE Transactions on Acoustics, Speech and Signal Processing* **24** (5), 380–91.

Gray, J.A. (1990). Brain systems that mediate both emotion and cognition. *Cognition and Emotion* **4** (3), 269–88.

Gray, J.A. (1994). Framework for a taxonomy of psychiatric disorder. In *Emotions: essays on emotion theory* (ed. S.H.M. van Goozen and N.E. Nanne), pp. 29–59. Lawrence Erlbaum Associates, Mahwah, New Jersey.

Gray, J.A. and McNaughton, N. (2000). Anxiolytic action on the behavioural inhibition system implies multiple types of arousal contribute to anxiety. *Journal of Affective Disorders* **61** (3), 161–76.

Green, R.S. and Cliff, N. (1975). Multidimensional comparisons of structures of vocally and facially expressed emotion. *Perception and Psychophysics* **17** (5), 429–38.

Grimm, M., Kroschel, K., and Narayanan, S. (2006). Modeling emotion expression and perception behavior in auditive emotion evaluation. In *Proceedings of ISCA 3rd International Conference on Speech Prosody*, Dresden, Germany, pp. 9–12.

Grimm, M., Kroschel, K., Mower, E., and Narayanan, S. (2007). Primitives-based evaluation and estimation of emotions in speech. *Speech Communication* **49**, 787–800.

Gross, J.J. (1998). Antecedent- and response-focused emotion regulation: divergent consequences for experience, expression, and physiology. *Journal of Personality and Social Psychology* **74**, 224–37.

Gross, J.J. (ed.) (2007). *Handbook of emotion regulation*. Guilford Press, New York.

Gross, J.J. and John, O.P. (2003). Individual differences in two emotion regulation processes: implications for affect, relationships, and well-being. *Journal of Personality and Social Psychology* **85**, 348–62.

Gross, J.J. and Levenson, R.W. (1993). Emotional suppression: physiology, self-report, and expressive behavior. *Journal of Personality and Social Psychology* **64**, 970–86.

Gross, J.J. and Levenson, R.W. (1997). Hiding feelings: the acute effects of inhibiting positive and negative emotions. *Journal of Abnormal Psychology* **106**, 95–103.

Gross, J.J. and Thompson, R.A. (2007). Emotion regulation: conceptual foundations. In *Handbook of emotion regulation* (ed. J.J. Gross), pp. 3–24. Guilford Press, New York.

Grossberg, S. (1971). On the dynamics of operant conditioning. *Journal of Theoretical Biology* **33** (2), 225–55.

Grossman, P. (1983). Respiration, stress, and cardiovascular function. *Psychophysiology* **20**, 284–300.

Grossman, P. and Kollai, M. (1993). Respiratory sinus arrhythmia, cardiac vagal tone, and respiration: within-and between-individual relations. *Psychophysiology* **30**, 486–95.

Guhn, M., Hamm, A. and Zentner, M. (2007). Physiological and musico-acoustic correlates of the chill response. *Music Perception* **24** (5), 473–84.

Gunes, H. and Piccardi, M. (2006). Creating and annotating affect databases from face and body display: a contemporary survey. In *Proceedings of the IEEE International Conference On Systems, Man and Cybernetics*, pp. 2426–33.

Gunes, H. and Piccardi, M. (2009). Automatic temporal segment detection and affect recognition from face and body display. *IEEE Transactions on Systems, Man, and Cybernetics, Part B* **39** (1), 64–84.

Gunes, H., Piccardi, M., and Pantic M. (2008). From the lab to the real world: affect recognition using multiple cues and modalities. In *Affective computing: focus on emotion expression, synthesis, and recognition* (ed. J. Or), pp. 185–218. I-Tech Edu. Publishing, Vienna.

Gunnar, M.R. and Stone, C. (1984). The effects of positive maternal affect on infant responses to pleasant, ambiguous and fear-provoking toys. *Child Development* **55**, 1231–6.

Haag, A., Goronzy, S., Schaich, P., and Williams, J. (2004). Emotion recognition using bio-sensors: first steps towards an automatic system. In *Tutorial and research workshop on affective dialogue systems* (ed. E. André, L. Dybkjaer, W. Minker, and P. Heisterkamp), pp. 36–48. Springer, Kloster Irsee, Germany.

Hall, J.A. and Bernieri, F.J. (Eds.) (2001). *Interpersonal sensitivity: theory and measurement.* Erlbaum, Mahwah, New Jersey.

Hall, J.A. and Matsumoto, D. (2004). Gender differences in judgments of multiple emotions from facial expressions. *Emotion* **4** (2), 201–6.

Hall, J.A., Andrzejewski, S.A., Murphy, N.A., Schmid Mast, M., and Feinstein, B. A. (2008). Accuracy of judging others' traits and states: comparing mean levels across tests. *Journal of Research in Personality* **42**, 1476–89.

Hamann, S. (2003). Nosing in on the emotional brain. *Nature Neuroscience* **6** (2), 106–8.

Hamm, A., Schupp, H.T., and Weike, A.I. (2003). Motivational organization of emotions: autonomic changes, cortical responses, and reflex modulation. In *Handbook of affective sciences* (ed. R.J. Davidson, K.R. Scherer, and H.H. Goldsmith), pp. 187–211. Oxford University Press, New York.

Hanratty, J. (2010). Individual and situational differences in emotional expression. Submitted for the degree of PhD in the School of Psychology, Queen's University, Belfast.

Hansen, C.H. and Hansen, R.D. (1988). Finding the face in the crowd: an anger superiority effect. *Journal of Personality and Social Psychology* **54**, 917–24.

Hareli, S. and Parkinson, B. (2008). What's social about social emotions? *Journal for the Theory of Social Behavior* **38**, 131–56.

Hareli, S. and Rafaeli, A. (2008). Emotion cycles: on the social influence of emotion in organizations. *Research in Organizational Behavior* **28**, 35–59.

Harrigan, J.A. and O'Connell, D.M. (1996). How do you look when feeling anxious? Facial displays of anxiety. *Personality and Individual Differences* **21** (2), 205–12.

Harrigan, J., Rosenthal, R., and Scherer, K.R. (Eds.) (2005). *The new handbook of methods in nonverbal behavior research.* Oxford University Press, Oxford.

Hartmann, B., Mancini, M., Buisine, S., and Pelachaud, C. (2005). Design and evaluation of expressive gesture synthesis for embodied conversational agents. In *Proceedings of International Joint Conference on Autonomous Agents and Multi-Agent Systems (AAMAS)*, Utrecht, The Netherlands (ed. F. Dignum, V. Dignum, S. Koenig, S. Kraus, M.P. Singh, and M. Wooldridge), pp. 1095–6. ACM, New York.

Harver, A. and Lorig, T.S. (2000). Respiration. In *Handbook of psychophysiology* (ed. J.T. Cacioppo, L.G. Tassinary, and G.G. Berntson), Chapter 10, pp. 265–93. Cambridge University Press, Cambridge.

Hatfield, E., Cacioppo, J.T., and Rapson, R.L. (1994). *Emotional contagion.* Cambridge University Press, New York.

Hawk, S.T., Van Kleef, G.A., Fischer, A.H., and Van der Schalk, J. (2009). 'Worth a thousand words': absolute and relative decoding of nonlinguistic affect vocalizations. *Emotion* **9**, 293–305.

Heloir, A. and Kipp, M. (2009). EMBR—a realtime animation engine for interactive embodied agents. In *Intelligent virtual agents, Proceedings of 9th International Conference IVA 2009*, Amsterdam, The Netherlands (ed. Z. Ruttkay, M. Kipp, A. Nijholt, and H.H. Vilhjálmsson), pp. 393–404. Lecture Notes in Computer Sciences 5773. Springer, Berlin.

Hess, U., Banse, R., and Kappas, A. (1995). The intensity of facial expression is determined by underlying affective state and social situation. *Journal of Personality and Social Psychology* **69**, 280–8.

Hess, U., Adams, R., and Kleck, R. (2007). Looking at you or looking elsewhere: the influence of head orientation on the signal value of emotional facial expressions. *Motivation and Emotion* **31**, 137–44.

Hess, W.R. (1948). *Die Organisation des vegetativen Nervensystems*. Benno Schwabe, Basel.

Heylen, D., Reidsma D., and Ordelman R. (2006). Annotating state of mind in meeting data. *Proceedings of the Language Resources and Evaluation (LREC 2006) Workshop on Corpora for Research on Emotion and Affect*, Genoa, pp. 84–7.

Heylen, D., Kopp, S., Marsella, S., Pelachaud, C., and Vilhjálmsson, H. (2008). Why conversational agents do what they do. Functional representations for generating conversational agent behaviour. In *Proceedings of the Workshop on Functional Markup Language at the 7th International Conference on Autonnomous Agents and Multiagent Systems (AAMAS 2008)*, Estoril Portugal.

Hinz, A., Seibt, R., Hueber, B., and Schreinicke, G. (2000). Response specificity in psychophysiology: a comparison of different approaches. *Journal of Psychophysiology* **14**, 115–22.

Hirsch, J.A. and Bishop, B. (1981). Respiratory sinus arrhythmia in humans: how breathing pattern modulates heart rate. *American Journal of Physiology* **241**, 620–9.

Hobson, P. (2002). *The cradle of thought: exploring the origins of thinking*. Macmillan, London.

Hochschild, A.R. (1979). Emotion work, feeling rules, and social structure. *American Journal of Sociology* **85**, 551–75.

Hodgkin, A.L. and Huxley, A.F. (1952). A quantitative description of membrane current and its application to conduction and excitation in nerve. *Journal of Physiology* **117** (4), 500–44.

Hoetink, A.E., Faes, T.J.C., Visser, K.R., and Heethaar, R.M. (2004). On the flow dependency of the electrical conductivity of blood. *IEEE Transactions on Biomedical Engineering* **51**, 1251–61.

Hofer, G. and Shimodaira, H. (2007). Automatic head motion prediction from speech data. In *Interspeech 2007, 8th Annual Conference of the International Speech Communication Association*, Antwerp, Belgium, pp. 722–5.

Hood, B.M., Willen, J.D., and Driver, J. (1998). Adult's eyes trigger shifts of visual attention in human infants. *Psychological Science* **9**, 131–4.

House, J.S. and Kahn, R.L. (1985). Measures and concepts of social support. In *Social support and health* (ed. S. Cohen and S.L. Syme), pp. 83–108. Academic Press, New York.

Hsee, C.K., Hatfield, E., and Chemtob, C. (1992). Assessments of the emotional states of others: conscious judgments versus emotional contagion. *Journal of Social and Clinical Psychology* **11**, 119–28.

Hume, D. (2000). *A treatise of human nature*. Oxford University Press, Oxford.

Hurley, H.H. (2001). The eccrine sweat glands: structure and function. In *The biology of the skin* (ed. R.K. Freinkel and D. Woodley), pp. 47–76. Parthenon Publishing Group, New York.

Iida, A., and Campbell, N. (2003). Speech database design for a concatenative text-to-speech synthesis system for individuals with communication disorders. *International Journal of Speech Technology* **6**, 379–92.

Iida, A., Campbell N., Higuchi, F., and Yasumura, M. (2003). A corpus-based speech synthesis system with emotion. *Speech Communication* **40**, 161–87.

Iles, J. and Edmondson, W. (1994). Quasi-articulatory formant synthesis. In *Proceedings of the International Conference on Spoken Language Processing, ICSLP 1994*, Vol. 3, pp. 1663–6.

Ilies, R, Wagner, D.T., and Morgeson, F.P. (2007). Explaining affective linkages in teams: individual differences in susceptibility to contagion and individualism–collectivism. *Journal of Applied Psychology* **92**, 1140–8.

Inanoglu, Z. and Caneel, R. (2005). Emotive alert: hmm-based emotion detection in voicemail messages. In *Proceedings of Intelligent User Interfaces*. San Diego, pp. 251–3.

Ioannou, S., Raouzaiou, A., Tzouvaras, V., Mailis, T., Karpouzis, K., and Kollias, S. (2005). Emotion recognition through facial expression analysis based on a neurofuzzy method. *Neural Networks* **18**, 423–35.

Ito, J., Pynadath, D., and Marsella, S. (2008). Modeling self-deception within a decision-theoretic framework. In *Intelligent virtual agents, Proceedings of the 8th International Conference (IVA 2008)*, Tokyo, Japan (ed. H. Prendinger, J.C. Lester, and M. Ishizuka), pp. 322–33. Lecture Notes in Computer Science 5208. Springer, Berlin.

Izard, C.E. (1971). *The face of emotion*. Appleton-Century-Crofts, East Norwalk, Connecticut.

Izard, C.E. (1977). *Human emotions*. Plenum, New York.

Izard, C.E. (1991). *The psychology of emotions*. Plenum Press, New York.

Izard, C.E. (1992). Basic emotions, relations amongst emotions and emotion–cognition relations. *Psychological Review* **99** (3), 561–5.

Izard, C.E. (2007). Basic emotions, natural kinds, emotion schemas, and a new paradigm. *Perspectives on Psychological Science* **2**, 260–80.

Izhikevich, E.M. (2003). Simple model of spiking neurons. *IEEE Transactions on Neural Networks* **14**, 1569–72.

Izhikevich, E.M. (2004). Which model to use for cortical spiking neurons? *IEEE Transactions on Neural Networks*, Special issue on Temporal Coding **15**, 1063–70.

Jakobs, E., Manstead, A.S.R., and Fischer, A.H. (2001). Social context effects on facial activity in a negative emotional setting. *Emotion* **1**, 51–69.

James, W. (1884). What is an emotion? *Mind* **9**, 188–205.

James, W. (1890/1898). *The principles of psychology*. Holt, New York.

Jänig, W. (2003). The autonomic nervous system and its coordination by the brain. In *Handbook of affective sciences* (ed. R. Davidson, K.R. Scherer, and H. Goldsmith), Chapter 9, pp. 135–86. Oxford University Press, New York.

Jänig, W. and Häbler, H.-J. (1999). Organization of the autonomic nervous system: structure and function. In *Handbook of clinical neurology*. Vol. 74. *The autonomic nervous system*. Part 1. *Normal functions* (ed. P.J. Vinken, G.W. Bruyn, and O. Appenzeller), pp. 1–52. Elsevier, Amsterdam.

Jänig, W. and Häbler, H.-J. (2000). Specificity in the organization of the autonomic nervous system: a basis for precise neural regulation of homeostatic and protective body functions. *Progress in Brain Research* **122**, 351–67.

Jänig, W. and McLachlan, E.M. (1992*a*). Characteristics of function-specific pathways in the sympathetic nervous system. *Trends in Neurosciences*, **15**, 475–481.

Jänig, W. and McLachlan, E.M. (1992*b*). Specialized functional pathways are the building blocks of the autonomic nervous system. *Journal of the Autonomic Nervous System* **41**, 3–13.

Jarlier, S., Grandjean, D., N'Diaye, K., Delplanque, S., Sander, D., Vuilleumier, P., and Scherer, K.R. (2008). Thermal imaging of facial expressions: investigating thermal correlates of facial action units activities. In *Proceedings of the10th International Conference on Cognitive Neuroscience*, Bodrum, Turkey.

Jennings, J.R., Berg, W., Hutcheson, J., Obrist, P., Porges, S., and Turpin, G. (1981). Committee report. Publication guidelines for heart rate studies in man. *Psychophysiology* **18**, 226–31.

Jennings, J.R., Kamarck, T.W., Stewart, C., Eddy, M., and Johnson, P. (1992). Alternate cardiovascular baseline assessment techniques: vanilla or resting baseline. *Psychophysiology* **29**, 742–50.

John, O.P. and Gross, J.J. (2004). Healthy and unhealthy emotion regulation: personality processes, individual differences, and lifespan development. *Journal of Personality* **72**, 1301–34.

Johnson, L.R., LeDoux, J.E., and Doyère, E. (2009). Hebbian reverberations in emotional memory micro circuits. *Frontiers in Neuroscience* **3** (2), 198–205.

Johnson, W.F., Emde, R.N., Scherer, K.R., and Klinnert, M.D. (1986). Recognition of emotion from vocal cues. *Archives of General Psychiatry* **43**, 280–3.

Johnson, W.L., Narayanan, S.S., Whitney, R., Das, R., Bulut, M., and LaBore, C. (2002). Limited domain synthesis of expressive military speech for animated characters. In *Proceedings of IEEE Workshop on Speech Synthesis* (Santa Monica), pp. 163–6.

Johnston, L., Miles, L., and Macrae, C.N. (2010). Why are you smiling at me? Social functions of enjoyment and non-enjoyment smiles. *British Journal of Social Psychology* **49**, 107–27.

Johnstone, T. and Scherer, K.R. (1999). The effects of emotions on voice quality. In *Proceedings of the XIVth International Congress of Phonetic Sciences,* San Francisco, pp. 2029–32.

Johnstone, T. and Scherer, K.R. (2000). Vocal communciation of emotion. In *Handbook of emotions*, 2nd edn (ed. M. Lewis and J.M. Haviland-Jones), pp. 220–35. Guilford Press, New York.

Johnstone, T., van Reekum, C.M., and Scherer, K.R. (2001). Vocal correlates of appraisal processes. In *Appraisal processes in emotion: Theory, methods, research* (ed. K.R. Scherer, A. Schorr, and T. Johnstone) , pp. 271–84). Oxford University Press, New York.

Johnstone, T., van Reekum, C.M., Hird, K., Kirsner, K., and Scherer, K.R. (2005). The effect of manipulated appraisals on voice acoustics. *Emotion* **5** (4), 513–18.

Johnstone, T., van Reekum, C. M., Bänziger, T., Hird, K., Kirsner, K., and Scherer, K.R. (2007). The effects of gain versus loss and difficulty on vocal physiology and acoustics. *Psychophysiology* **44**, 827–37.

Jones, B.C., DeBruine, L.M., Little, A.C., Conway, C.A., and Feinberg, D.R. (2006). Integrating gaze direction and expression in preferences for attractive faces. *Psychological Science* **17**, 588–91.

Jung, Y., Weber, C., Keil, J., and Franke T. (2009). Real-time rendering of skin changes caused by emotions. In *Intelligent virtual agents, Proceedings of 9th International Conference IVA 2009*, Amsterdam, The Netherlands (ed. Z. Ruttkay, M. Kipp, A. Nijholt, and H.H. Vilhjálmsson), pp. 504–5, Lecture Notes in Computer Sciences 5773. Springer, Berlin.

Juslin, P.N. (1998). A functionalist perspective on emotional communication in music performance. *Comprehensive Summaries of Uppsala Dissertations from the Faculty of Social Sciences 78*. Uppsala University Library, Uppsala.

Juslin, P.N. (2001). A Brunswikian approach to emotional communication in music performance. In *The essential Brunswik: beginnings, explications, applications* (ed. K.R. Hammond and T.R. Stewart), pp. 426–30. Oxford University Press, New York.

Juslin, P.N. (2009). Emotion in music performance. In *Oxford handbook of music psychology* (ed. S. Hallam, I. Cross, and M. Thaut), pp. 377–89. Oxford University Press, New York.

Juslin, P.N. and Bänziger, T. (2009). Brunswikian lens model. In *Oxford companion to the affective sciences* (ed. K.R. Scherer and D. Sander), pp. 80–1. Oxford University Press, New York.

Juslin, P.N. and Laukka, P. (2001). Impact of intended emotion intensity on cue utilization and decoding accuracy in vocal expression of emotion. *Emotion* **1** (4), 381–412.

Juslin, P.N. and Laukka, P. (2003). Communication of emotions in vocal expression and music performance: Different channels, same code? *Psychological Bulletin* **129** (5), 770–814.

Juslin, P.N. and Scherer, K.R. (2005). Vocal expression of affect. In, (Eds.), *The new handbook of methods in nonverbal behavior research* (ed. J.A. Harrigan, R. Rosenthal, and K. Scherer), pp. 65–135. Oxford University Press, Oxford.

Kahneman, D. (2000). Experienced utility and objective happiness: a moment-based approach. In *Choices, values, and frames* (ed. D. Kahneman and A. Tversky), pp. 673–92. Cambridge University Press, New York.

Kain, A. and Macon, M. (1998). Spectral voice conversion for text-to-speech synthesis. In *Proceedings of the 1998 IEEE International Conference on Acoustics, Speech and Signal Processing* (Seattle, Washington), Vol. 1, pp. 285–8.

Kaiser, S. and Wehrle, T. (1996). Situated emotion al problem solving in interactive computer games. In *Proceedings of the VIIIth Conference of the International Society for Research on Emotions (ISRE 1996)* (ed. N.H. Frijda), pp. 276–80. ISRE Publications.

Kaiser, S. and Wehrle, T. (2001). Facial expressions as indicators of appraisal processes. In *Appraisal processes in emotions: theory, methods, research* (ed. K.R. Scherer, A. Schorr, and T. Johnstone), 285–300. Oxford University Press, New York.

Kaiser, S. and Wehrle, T. (2008). Facial expressions in social interactions: beyond basic emotions. In *Advances in consciousness research.* Vol.74. *Animating expressive characters for social interactions* (ed. D. Cañamero and R. Aylett), pp. 53–69. John Benjamins Publishing Company, Amsterdam.

el Kaliouby, R. and Robinson, P. (2004). Real-time inference of complex mental states from facial expressions and head gestures. In *IEEE International Conference on Computer Vision and*

Pattern Recognition, Workshop on Real Time Computer Vision for Human Computer Interaction, Vol. 10, p. 154.

el Kaliouby, R., Teeters, A., and Picard, R.W. (2006). An exploratory social–emotional prosthetic for autism spectrum disorders. In *International Workshop on Wearable and Implantable Body Sensor Networks*, pp. 3–4. MIT Media Lab, Cambridge, Massachusetts.

Kanade, T., Cohn, J.F., and Tian, Y. (2000). Comprehensive database for facial expression analysis. In *Proceedings of the 4th IEEE International Conference on Automatic Face and Gesture Recognition*, Grenoble, France, pp. 46–53.

Kapoor, A. and Picard R.W. (2005). Multimodal affect recognition in learning environments. In *Proceedings of the 13th Annual ACM International Conference on Multimedia*, pp. 677–82. ACM, New York.

Kapoor, A., Burleson, W., and Picard, R.W. (2007). Automatic prediction of frustration. *International Journal of Human–Computer Studies* **65** (8), 724–36.

Kappas, A. (2001). A metaphor is a metaphor is a metaphor: exorcising the homunculus from appraisal theory. In *Appraisal processes in emotion: theory, methods, research* (ed. K.R. Scherer, A. Schorr, and T. Johnstone), pp. 157–72. Oxford University Press, New York.

Kappas, A., Hess, U., and Scherer, K.R. (1991). Voice and emotion. In *Fundamentals of nonverbal behavior* (ed. R. Feldman and B. Rime), pp. 200–38. Cambridge University Press, New York.

Katz, G.S. (1998). Emotional speech: a quantitative study of vocal acoustics in emotional expression. PhD thesis, University of Pittsburgh, Pittsburgh.

Kelley, H.H. (1972). Causal schemata and the attribution process. In *Attribution: perceiving the causes of behaviour* (ed. E.E. Jones, D.E. Kanouse, H.H. Kelley, R.E. Nisbett, S. Valins, and B. Weiner), pp. 151–74. General Learning Press, Morristown, New Jersey.

Keltner, D. (1995). Signs of appeasement: evidence for the distinct displays of embarrassment, amusement and shame. *Journal of Personality and Social Psychology* **68**, 441–54.

Keltner, D. and Buswell, B.N. (1996). Evidence for the distinctness of embarrassment, shame, and guilt: a study of recalled antecedents and facial expressions of emotion. *Cognition and Emotion* **10** (2), 155–72.

Keltner, D. and Buswell, B.N. (1997). Embarrassment: its distinct form and appeasement functions. *Psychological Bulletin* **122**, 250–70.

Keltner, D. and Haidt, J. (1999). Social functions of emotions at four levels of analysis. *Cognition and Emotion* **13**, 505–21.

Keltner, D., Ekman, P., Gonzaga, G.C., and Beer, J. (2003). Facial expression of emotion. In *Handbook of affective sciences* (ed. R. Davidson, K.R. Scherer, and H. Goldsmith), pp. 415–31. Oxford University Press, New York.

Kim, J. and André, E. (2008). Emotion recognition based on physiological changes in music listening. *IEEE Transactions on Pattern Analysis and Machine Intelligence* **30**, 2067–83.

Kim, J. and Jung, M. (2006). Neural circuits and mechanisms involved in pavlovian fear conditioning: a critical review. *Neuroscience and Biobehavioural Reviews* **30**, 188–202.

Kim, S., Georgiou, P.G., Lee, S., and Narayanan, S. (2007). Real-time emotion detection system using speech: multi-modal fusion of different timescale features. In *Proceedings of IEEE 9th International Workshop on Multimedia Signal Processing*, pp. 48–51.

Kipp, M. (2006). Creativity meets automation: combining nonverbal action authoring with rules and machine learning. In *Intelligent virtual agents, 6th International Conference, IVA 2006*; Marina del Rey, California (ed. J. Gratch, M. Young, R. Aylett, D. Ballin, and P. Olivier), pp. 230–42. Lecture Notes in Computer Science 4133. Springer, New York.

Kittler, J., Hatef, M., Duin, R.P.W., and Matas, J. (1998). On combining classifiers. *IEEE Transactions on Pattern Analysis and Machine Intelligence* **20** (3), 226–39.

Klatt, D.H. and Klatt, L.C. (1990). Analysis, synthesis and perception of voice quality variations among female and male talkers. *Journal of the Acoustical Society of America* **87** (2), 820–56.

Kleinsmith, A., De Silva, R., and Bianchi-Berthouze, N. (2006). Cross-cultural differences in recognizing affect from body posture. *Interacting with Computers* **18** (6), 1371–89.

Klesen, M. (2005). Using theatrical concepts for role-plays with educational agents. *Applied Artificial Intelligence special issue 'Educational agents—beyond virtual tutors'* **19**, 413–31.

Kline, R.B. (2005). *Principles and practice of structural equation modeling.* Guilford Press, New York.

Knapp, R.B., Jaimovich, J., and Coghlan, N.L. (2009). Measurement of motion and emotion during musical performance. In *Affective computing and intelligent interaction. Third International Conference (ACII 2009)*, Vol. 1, pp. 735–40. IEEE, Los Alamitos.

Knutson, B. (1996). Facial expressions of emotion influence interpersonal trait inferences. *Journal of Nonverbal Behavior* **20**, 165–92.

Koenigs, M., Young, L., Adolphs, R., Tranel, D., Cushman, F., Hauser, M., and Damásio, A. (2007). Damage to the prefrontal cortex increases utilitarian moral judgements. *Nature* **446**, 908–11.

Koizumi, K., Terui, N., and Kollai, M. (1983). Neural control of the heart: significance of double innervation re-examined. *Journal of the Autonomic Nervous System* **7**, 279–94.

Konno, K. and Mead, J. (1967). Measurement of the separate volume changes of rib cage and abdomen during breathing. *Journal of Applied Physiology* **22**, 407–22.

Korsten, N. (2009). Neural architectures for an appraisal basis of emotion. PhD thesis, King's College London.

Korsten, N.J.H., Fragopanagos, N., Hartley, M., Taylor, N., and Taylor, J.G. (2006). Attention as a controller. *Neural Networks* **19** (9), 1408–21.

Korsten, N., Roesch, E.B., Fragopanagos, N., Taylor, J.G., Grandjean, D., and Sander, S. (in press). Biological and computational constraints to psychological modelling of emotion. In *Handbook for research on emotions and human–machine interactions* (ed. P. Petta, E.B. Roesch, K. Karpouzis, E. Douglas-Cowie, L. Cañamero, M. Zancanaro, and J. Laaksolahti). Springer.

Kosslyn, S.M. and Koenig, O. (1995). *Wet mind, the new cognitive neuroscience.* Free Press, New York.

Krämer, N.C. and Bente, G. (2003). Brauchen Interface–Agenten Emotionen? [Do interface agents need emotions?] In *Mensch UND Computer: Interaktion in Bewegung* (ed. G. Szwillus and J. Ziegler), pp. 287–96. Teubner, Stuttgart.

Krämer, N.C., Tietz, B., and Bente, G. (2003). Effects of embodied interface agents and their gestural activity. In *Intelligent Virtual Agents, Proceedings of the 4th International Workshop (IVA 2003)*, Kloster Irsee, Germany (ed. T. Rist, R. Aylett, D. Ballin, and J. Rickel), pp. 292–300. Lecture Notes in Computer Science 3661. Springer-Verlag, New York.

Kraut, R.E. and Johnston, R.E. (1979). Social and emotional messages of smiling: an ethological approach. *Journal of Personality and Social Psychology* **37** (9), 1539–53.

Kreibig, S.D. (2010). Autonomic nervous system activity in emotion: a review. *Biological Psychology* **84**, 394–421. doi:10.1016/j.biopsycho.2010.03.010.

Kreibig, S.D., Wilhelm, F.H., Gross, J.J., and Roth, W.T. (2005). Specific emotional responses as deviations from the experimental context. *Psychophysiology* **42**, S77.

Kreibig, S.D., Gendolla, G.H.E., and Scherer, K.R. (2007). Sitting, listening, viewing, or performing? Effects of baseline task on quantification of autonomic reactivity in emotion. *Psychophysiology* **44**, S38. Poster presented at the Society for Psychophysiological Research, 47th Annual Meeting, Savannah, Georgia.

Kreibig, S.D., Gendolla, G.H.E. and Scherer, K.R. (2010). Psychophysiological effects of emotional responding to goal attainment. *Biological Psychology* **84**, 474–87. doi:10.1016/j.biopsycho.2009.11.004.

Kreutz, G., Ott, U., Teichmann, D., Osawa, P., and Vaitl, D. (2008). Using music to induce emotions: influences of musical preference and absorption. *Psychology of Music* **36**, 101–26.

Krstulović, S., Hunecke, A., and Schröder, M. (2007). An HMM-based speech synthesis system applied to German and its adaptation to a limited set of expressive football comments. In *Proceedings Interspeech 2007*, Antwerp, Belgium, pp. 1897–900.

Krumhuber, E. and Kappas, A. (2005). Moving smiles: the role of dynamic components for the perception of the genuineness of smiles. *Journal of Nonverbal Behaviour* **29**, 13–24.

Krumhuber, E., Manstead, A.S.R., and Kappas, A. (2007*a*). Temporal aspects of facial displays in person and expression perception: the effects of smile dynamics, head-tilt, and gender. *Journal of Nonverbal Behaviour* **31**, 39–56.

Krumhuber, E., Manstead, A. S. R., Cosker, D., Marshall, D., Rosin, P. L., and Kappas, A. (2007*b*). Facial dynamics as indicators of trustworthiness and cooperative behavior. *Emotion* **7**, 730–5.

Krumhuber, E., Manstead, A.S.R., Cosker, D., Marshall, D., and Rosin, P.L. (2009). Effects of dynamic aspects of smiles in human and synthetic faces: a simulated job interview setting. *Journal of Nonverbal Behavior* **33**, 1–15.

Kubicek, W.G., Krnegis, J.N., Patterson, R.P., Witsoe, D.A., and Mattson, R.H. (1966). Development and evaluation of an impedance cardiac output system. *Aerospace Medicine* **37**, 1208–12.

Kuppens, P. and Van Mechelen, I. (2007). Interactional appraisal models for the anger appraisals of threatened self-esteem, other-blame, and frustration. *Cognition and Emotion* **21**, 56–77.

Laban, R. (1963). *Modern educational dance.* Macdonald and Evans Ltd, London.

Laban, R. and Lawrence, F.C. (1947). *Effort.* Macdonald and Evans Ltd, London.

LaBar, K.S., Gitelman, D.R., Parrish, T.B., Kim, Y.-H., Nobre, A., and Mesulam, M.-M. (2001). Hunger selectively modulates corticolimbic activation to food stimuli in humans. *Behavioral Neuroscience* **115** (2), 493–500.

Lacey, J.I. (1967). Somatic response patterning and stress: some revisions of activation theory. In *Psychological stress* (ed. M.H. Appley and R. Trumbell), pp. 14–37. Appleton-Century-Crofts, New York.

Lacey, J.I. and Lacey, B.C. (1958). Verification and extension of the principle of autonomic response-stereotypy. *American Jouranal of Psychology* **71**, 50–73.

Lagasse, L.L., Neal, A.R., and Lester, B.M. (2005). Assessment of infant cry: acoustic cry analysis and parental perception. *Mental Retardation and Developmental Disabilities Research Reviews* **11**, 83–93.

Laird, J.E., Newell, A., and Rosenbloom, P.S. (1987). SOAR: an architecture for general intelligence. *Artificial Intelligence* **33**, 1–64.

Lance, B. and Marsella, S. (2007). Emotionally expressive head and body movements during gaze shifts. In *Intelligent virtual agents, 7th International Conference (IVA 2007)*, Paris, France (ed. C. Pelachaud, J.-C. Martin, E. André, G. Chollet, K.Karpouzis, and D. Pelé), pp. 72–85. Lecture Notes in Computer Science 4722. Springer, Berlin.

Lanctôt, N. and Hess, U. (2007). The timing of appraisals. *Emotion* **7**, 207–12.

Lang, P. (1980). Behavioural treatment and bio-behavioral assessment: computer applications. In *Technology in mental health care delivery systems* (ed. J.B. Sidowski, J.H. Johnson, and T.A. Williams), pp. 119–37. Ablex, Norwood, New Jersey.

Lang, P.J., Öhman, A., and Vaitl, D. (1988). *The international affective picture system* [photographic slides]. The Center for Research in Psychophysiology, University of Florida, Gainesville.

Lang, P.J., Bradley, M.M., and Cuthbert, B.N. (2005). *International affective picture system (IAPS): Instruction manual and affective ratings.* The Center for Research in Psychophysiology, University of Florida.

Langley, J.N. (1903). Das sympathische und verwandte nervöse Systeme der Wirbeltiere (autonomes nervöses System), *Ergebnisse der Physiologie* **27/II**, 818–27.

Langley, J.N. (1921). *The autonomic nervous system (Pt. 1).* Heffer, Cambridge.

Laukka, P. (2004). Vocal expression of emotion: discrete-emotions and dimensional accounts. Ph.D. dissertation, Uppsala University.

Laukka, P., Juslin, P., and Bresin, R. (2005). A dimensional approach to vocal expression of emotion. *Cognition and Emotion* **19** (5), 633–53.

Laukkanen, A.-M., Vilkman, E., Alku, P., and Oksanen, H. (1996). Physical variations related to stress and emotional state: a preliminary study. *Journal of Phonetics* **24**, 313–35.

Laver, J. (1980). *The phonetic description of voice quality.* Cambridge University Press, Cambridge.

Lazarus, R.S. (1968). Emotions and adaptation: conceptual and empirical relations. In *Nebraska symposium on motivation* (ed. W.J. Arnold), pp. 175–270. University of Nebraska Press, Lincoln.

Lazarus, R.S. (1991). *Emotion and adaptation.* Oxford University Press, New York.

Lazarus, R.S. (1999). The cognition–emotion debate: a bit of history. In *Handbook of cognition and emotion* (ed. T. Dalgleish and M.J. Power), pp. 3–19. John Wiley and Sons Ltd., New York.

Lazarus, R.S., Coyne, J.C., and Folkman, S. (1982). Cognition, emotion, and motivation: the doctoring of Humpty-Dumpty. In *Psychological stress and psychopathology* (ed. R.W.J. Neufeld), pp. 218–39. McGraw-Hill, New York.

Leary, M.R, Landel, J.L., and Patton, K.M. (1996). The motivated expression of embarrassment following a self-presentational predicament. *Journal of Personality* **64**, 619–36.

LeDoux, J.E. (1992). Brain mechanisms of emotion and emotional learning. *Current Opinion in Neurobiology* **2**, 191–7.

LeDoux, J.E. (1996). *The emotional brain.* Simon and Schuster, New York.

LeDoux, J.E. (2008). The amygdala. *Scholarpedia* **3** (4), 2698.

LeDoux, J.E. and Schiller, D. (2009). The human amygdala: insights from other animals. In *The human amygdala* (ed. P.J. Whalen and E.A. Phelps), pp. 43–60. Guilford, New York.

Lee, C.M. and Narayanan, S. (2003). Emotion recognition using a data-driven fuzzy interference system. In *Eurospeech-2003*, pp. 157–60.

Lee, C.M. and Narayanan, S. (2005). Toward detecting emotions in spoken dialogs. *IEEE Transactions on Speech and Audio Processing* **13** (2), 293–303.

Lee, C.M., Narayanan, S., and Pieraccini, R. (2002). Combining acoustic and language information for emotion recognition. *Proceedings of International Conference on Spoken Language Processing,* pp. 873–6.

Lee, J. and Marsella, S. (2006). Nonverbal behaviour generator for embodied conversational agents. In *Intelligent virtual agents, Proceedings of the 6th International Conference (IVA 2006),* Marina del Rey, California (ed. J. Gratch, M. Young, R. Aylett, D. Ballin, and P. Olivier), pp. 243–55. Lecture Notes in Computer Science 4133. Springer, New York. 243–255.

Lee, S., Yildirim, S., Kazemzadeh, A., and Narayanan, S. (2005). An articulatory study of emotional speech production. In *Proceedings of Interspeech 2005,* 497–500.

Leggetter, C. and Woodland, P. (1995). Maximum likelihood linear regression for speaker adaptation of continuous density hidden Markov models. *Computer Speech and Language* **9**, 171–85.

Lepper, M.R. (1988). Motivational considerations in the study of instruction. *Cognition and Instruction* **5** (4), 289–309.

Lerner, J.S., Gonzalez, R.M., Dahl, R.E., Hariri, A.R. and Taylor, S.E. (2005). Facial expressions of emotion reveal neuroendocrine and cardiovascular stress responses. *Biological Psychiatry* **58**, 743–50.

Leßmann, N., Kopp, S., and Wachsmuth, I. (2006). Situated interaction with a virtual human—perception, action, and cognition. In *Situated communication* (ed. G. Rickheit and I. Wachsmuth), pp. 287–323. Mouton de Gruyter, Berlin.

Lester, J.C., Towns, S.G., Callaway, C.B., Voerman, J.L., and Fitzgerald, P.J. (2000). Deictic and emotive communication in animated pedagogical agents. In *Embodied conversational agents* (ed. J. Cassell, J. Sullivan, S. Prevost, and E. Churchill), pp. 123–54. MIT Press, Cambridge, Massachusetts.

Levenson, R.W. (1988). Emotion and the autonomic nervous system: a prospectus for research on autonomic specificity. In *Social psychophysiology and emotion: theory and clinical applications* (ed. H.L. Wagner), pp. 17–42. Wiley, Chichester.

Levenson, R.W. (2003). *Autonomic specificity and emotion*. In *Handbook of affective sciences* (ed. R.J. Davidson, K.R. Scherer, and H.H. Goldsmith), pp. 212–24. Oxford University Press, New York.

Levenson, R.W., Ekman, P., and Friesen, W.V. (1990). Voluntary facial action generates emotion-specific autonomic nervous system activity. *Psychophysiology* 27, 363–84.

Levenson, R.W., Ekman, P., Heider, K., and Friesen, W.V. (1992). Emotion and autonomic nervous system activity in the Minangkabau of West Sumatra. *Journal of Personality and Social Psychology* 62 (6), 972–88.

Leventhal, H. and Scherer, K.R. (1987). The relationship of emotion to cognition: A functional approach to a semantic controversy. *Cognition and Emotion* 1, 3–28.

Levine, D. S. (2007a). Neural network modeling of emotion. *Physics of Life Reviews* 4, 37–63.

Levine, D.S. (2007b). How does the brain create, change, and selectively override its rules of conduct? In *Neurodynamics of higher-level cognition and consiousness* (ed. R. Kozma and L. Perlovsky). Springer-Verlag, Heidelberg.

Levine, D.S. (2009). Brain pathways for cognitive-emotional decision making in the human animal. *Neural Networks* 22 (3), 286–93.

Levine, D.S. and Leven, S.J. (1992). *Motivation, emotion, and goal direction in neural networks*. L. Erlbaum Associates, Hillsdale, New Jersey.

Lewis, M. (2000). The emergence of human emotions. In *Handbook of emotions* 2nd edn (ed. M. Lewis and J.M. Haviland-Jones), pp. 265–80. Guilford Press, New York.

Lewis, M. and Saarni, C. (1997). *Lying and deception in everyday life*. Guilford Press, New York.

Lewis, M., Haviland-Jones J. M., and Feldman Barrett, L. (2008). *Handbook of emotions*. Guilford Press, New York.

Liang, J., Krause, N.M., and Bennett, J.M. (2001). Social exchange and well-being: is giving better than receiving? *Psychology and Aging* 16, 511–23.

Lim, C.L., Rennie, C., Barry, R.J., Bahramali, H., Lazzaro, I., Manor, B., and Gordon, E. (1997). Decomposing skin conductance into tonic and phasic components. *International Journal of Psychophysiology* 25, 97–109.

Lindquist, K.A., Barrett, L.F., Bliss-Moreau, E., and Russell, J.A. (2006). Language and the perception of emotion. *Emotion,* 6, 125–138.

Lisetti, C. and Gmytrasiewicz, P. (2002). Can a rational agent afford to be affectless? A formal approach. *Applied Artificial Intelligence* 16, 577–609.

Lisetti, C.L. and Nasoz, F. (2004). Using non-invasive wearable computers to recognize human emotions from physiological signals. *EURASIP Journal on Applied Signal Processing* 2004, 1672–87.

Lisetti, C.L. and Schiano, D. (2000). Facial expression recognition: where human–computer interaction, artificial intelligence, and cognitive science intersect. *Pragmatics and Cognition* 8, 185–235.

Littlewort, G., Bartlett, M., Fasel, I., Susskind, J., and Movellan, J. (2006). Dynamics of facial expression extracted automatically from video. *Image and Vision Computing* 24 (6), 615–25.

Littlewort, G.C., Bartlett, M.S., and Lee, K. (2007). Faces of pain: automated measurement of spontaneous facial expressions of genuine and posed pain. In *Proceedings of the 9th International Conference on Multimodal Interfaces*, pp. 15–21. ACM, New York.

Llabre, R.W., Spitzer, S.B., Saab, P.G., Ironson, G.H., and Schneiderman, N. (1991). The reliability and specificity of delta versus residualized change as measure of cardiovascular reactivity to behavioral challenges. *Psychophysiology* 28, 701–11.

LoBue, V. (2009). More than just another face in the crowd: superior detection of threatening facial expressions in children and adults. *Developmental Science* 12, 305–13.

Locher, I., Kirstein, T., and Tröster, G. (2005). Temperature profile estimation with smart textiles. In *Proceedings of the 1st International Scientific Conference Ambience 05*, Tampere, Finland.

Lockhart, R.A. and Lieberman, W. (1979). Information content of the electrodermal orienting response. In *The orienting reflex in humans* (ed. H.D. Kimmel, E.H. van Olst, and J.F. Orlebeke), pp. 685–700. Erlbaum, Hillsdale, New Jersey.

Lorig, T.S. (2007). The respiratory system. In *Handbook of psychophysiology* (ed. J.T. Cacioppo, L.G. Tassinary, and G.G. Berntson), Chapter 10, pp. 231–44. Cambridge University Press, Cambridge.

Lorini, E. and Castelfranchi, C. (2007). The cognitive structure of surprise: looking for basic principles. *Topoi: An International Review of Philosophy* **26,** 133–49.

Lozano, D.L., Norman, G., Knox, D., Wood, B.L., Miller, B.D., Emery, C.F., and Berntson, G.G. (2007). Where to B in dZ/dt. *Psychophysiology* **44,** 113–19.

Lundqvist, D., Flykt, A., and Öhman, A. (1998). The Karolinska directed emotional faces—KDEF. CD ROM from the Department of Clinical Neuroscience, Psychology section, Karolinska Institutet, Stockholm, Sweden.

Luo, Q., Holroyd, T., Jones, M., Hendler, T., and Blair, J. (2007). Neural dynamics for facial threat processing as revealed by gamma band synchronization using MEG. *NeuroImage* **34** (2), 839–47.

Lutz, C. and White, G.M. (1986). The anthropology of emotions. *Annual Review of Anthropology* **15,** 405–36.

Madsen, M., el Kaliouby, R., Goodwin, M., and Picard, R.W. (2008). Technology for just-in-time in-situ learning of facial affect for persons diagnosed with an autism spectrum disorder. In *Proceedings of the 10th ACM Conference on Computers and Accessibility (ASSETS)*, pp. 19–26. ACM, New York.

Maes, P. (1991). Situated agents can have goals. In *Designing autonomous agents: theory and practice from biology to engineering and back* (ed. P. Maes), pp. 49–70. MIT Press, Cambridge, Massachusetts.

Maia, R., Toda, T., Zen, H., Nankaku, Y., and Tokuda, K. (2007). An excitation model for HMM-based speech synthesis based on residual modeling. In *Proceedings of the 6th ISCA Workshop on Speech Synthesis*, Bonn, Germany, pp. 131–6.

Mäkäräinen, M. and Takala, T. (2009). An approach for creating and blending synthetic facial expressions of emotion. In *Intelligent virtual agents, Proceedings of 9th International Conference IVA 2009*, Amsterdam, The Netherlands (ed. Z. Ruttkay, M. Kipp, A. Nijholt, and H.H. Vilhjálmsson), pp. 243–9, Lecture Notes in Computer Sciences 5773. Springer, Berlin.

Malatesta, L., Raouzaiou, A., Karpouzis, K., and Kollias, S. (2009). MPEG-4 facial expression synthesis. *Personal and Ubiquitous Computing* (Special issue on Emerging Multimodal Interfaces) **13** (1), 77–93.

Mampe, B., Friederici, A.D., Christophe, A., and Wermke, K. (2009). Newborns' cry melody is shaped by their native language. *Current Biology*, Epub ahead of print **19,** 1994–7.

Mancini, M. and Pelachaud, C. (2008). Distinctiveness in multimodal behaviors. In *Proceedings of the 7th Conference on Autonomous Agents and Multi-Agent Systems* (AAMAS 2008), Estoril, Portugal.

Mandler, G. (1975). *Mind and emotion*. Wiley, New York.

Manstead, A.S.R. and Fischer, A.H. (2001). Social appraisal: the social world as object of and influence on appraisal processes. In *Appraisal processes in emotion: theory, methods, research* (ed. K.R. Scherer, A. Schorr, and T. Johnstone), pp. 221–32. Oxford University Press, New York.

Manstead, A., Fischer, A.H., and Jakobs, E.B. (1999). The social and emotional functions of facial displays. In *The social Context of Nonverbal Behavior* (ed. P. Philippot, R.S. Feldman, and E.J. Coats), pp. 287–313. Cambridge University Press, New York.

Mao, W. and Gratch, J. (2006). Evaluating a computational model of social causality and responsibility. Paper presented at *5th International Joint Conference on Autonomous Agents and Multiagent Systems*. Hakodate, Japan, pp. 985–92.

Mao, X., Xue, Y., Li, Z., and Bao, H. (2008). Layered fuzzy facial expression generation: social, emotional and physiological. In *Affective computing, focus on emotion expression, synthesis and recognition* (ed. J. Or), pp. 185–218. I-Tech Education and Publishing, Vienna.

Marinier, R.P. (2008). A computational unification of cognitive control, emotion, and learning. PhD dissertation, University of Michigan, Ann Arbor, Michigan.

Marinier, R.P. and Laird, J. (2007). Computational modeling of mood and feeling from emotion. In *Proceedings of 29th Meeting of the Cognitive Science Society*, pp. 461–6. Cognitive Science Society, Nashville.

Marinier, R.P., Laird, J.E., and Lewis, R.L. (2009). A computational unification of cognitive behavior and emotion. *Cognitive Systems Research* **10,** 48–69.

Marsella, S. and Gratch, J. (2001). *Modeling the interplay of plans and emotions in multi-agent simulations.* Cognitive Science Societ, Edinburgh.

Marsella, S. and Gratch, J. (2006). EMA: a computational model of appraisal dynamics. In *Agent construction and emotions*, Vienna Austria.

Marsella, S. and Gratch, J. (2009). EMA: a model of emotional dynamics. *Journal of Cognitive Systems Research* **10**, 70–90.

Marsella, S., Gratch, J., and Rickel, J. (2003). Expressive behaviors for virtual worlds. In *Life-like characters tools, affective functions and applications* (ed. H. Prendinger and M. Ishizuka), pp. 317–61. Springer-Verlag, Berlin.

Marsella, S., Gratch, J., Wang, N., and Stankovic, B. (2009) Assessing the validity of a computational model of emotional coping. In *Affective computing and intelligent interaction. Third International Conference (ACII 2009).* IEEE, Los Alamitos.

Martin, J.-C., Niewiadomski, R., Devillers, L., Buisine, S., and Pelachaud, C. (2006). Multimodal complex emotions: gesture expressivity and blended facial expressions. *Journal of Humanoid Robotics* **3** (3), 269–91.

Martin, J.C., Paggio, P., Kuhnlein, P., Pianesi, F., and Stiefelhagen, R. (2007). Special issue on 'Mulitmodal Corpora for Modeling Human Multimodal Behaviour'. *Journal on Language Resources and Evaluation* **41** (3–4), 253–64.

Marwitz, M. and Stemmler, G. (1998). On the status of individual response specificity. *Psychophysiology* **35**, 1–15.

Master, A.S., Jonsson, I-M., Nass, C., Deng, P.X., and Richards, K.L. (2006). A framework for generating and indexing induced emotional voice data. In *Proceedings of the LREC Workshop on Corpora for Research on Emotion and Affect*, Genoa, May 2006 pp. 60–3.

Matias, R. and Cohn, J.F. (1993). Are MAX-specified infant facial expressions during face-to-face interaction consistent with differential emotions theory? *Developmental Psychology* **29**, 524–31.

Matsumoto, D. (1990). Cultural similarities and differences in display rules. *Motivation and Emotion* **14**, 195–214.

Matsumoto, D. (1992). American–Japanese cultural differences in the recognition of universal facial expressions. *Journal of Cross-Cultural Psychology* **23**, 72–84.

Matsumoto D. (2001). Culture and emotion. In *The handbook of culture and psychology* (ed. D. Masumoto), pp. 171–94. Oxford University Press, New York.

Matsumoto, D., Consolacion, T., Yamada, H., Suzuki, R., Franklin, B., Paul, S., Ray, R., and Uchida, H. (2002). American–Japanese cultural differences in judgments of emotional expressions of different intensities. *Cognition and Emotion* **16** (6), 721–47.

Matsumoto, D., Willingham, B., and Olide, A. (2009). Sequential dynamics of culturally moderated facial expressions of emotion. *Psychological Science* **20** (10), 1269–75.

Maurage, P., Joassin, F., Philippot, P., and Campanella, S. (2007). A validated battery of vocal emotional expressions. *Neuropsychological Trends* **2**, 63–74.

Mauss, I.B. and Robinson, M.D. (2009). Measures of emotion: a review. *Cognition and Emotion* **23**, 209–37.

Mauss, I.B., Levenson, R.W., McCater, L., Wilhelm, F.H., and Gross, J.J. (2005). The tie that binds? Coherence among emotion experience, behavior, and physiology. *Emotion* **5**, 175–90.

Mayer, J.D. and Salovey, P. (1993). The intelligence of emotional intelligence. *Intelligence* **17**, 433–42.

Mayer, J.D., DiPaolo, M., and Salovey, P. (1990). Perceiving affective content in ambiguous visual stimuli: a component of emotional intelligence. *Journal of Personality Assessment* **54** (3), 772–81.

McCall, C., Blascovich, J., Young, A., and Persky, S. (2009). Proxemic behaviors as predictors of aggression towards Black (but not White) males in an immersive virtual environment. *Social Influence* **4**, 138–54.

McCool, F.D., Wang, J., and Ebi, K.L. (2002). Tidal volume and respiratory timing derived from a portable ventilation monitor. *Chest* **122**, 684–691.

McDougall, W. (1923). *Outline of psychology*. Charles Scribner's Sons, New York.

McMahon, E., Cowie, R., Wagner, J., and André, E. (2008). Multimodal records of driving influenced by induced emotion. In *Proceedings of the Language Resources and Evaluation Conference (LREC 2008) Workshop on Corpora for Research on Emotion*, Marrakech, Morocco, pp. 48–52.

McRorie, M. and Sneddon, I . (2007*a*). Real emotion is dynamic and interactive. In *Affective computing and intelligent interaction, Proceedings of the Second International Conference (ACII 2007)*, Lisbon, Portugal (ed. A. Paiva, R. Prada, and R.W. Picard), pp. 759–60. Lecture Notes in Computer Science 4738. Springer, Berlin.

McRorie, M. and Sneddon, I. (2007*b*). Contextual and individual differences in expression of induced emotion. Paper presented to the HUMAINE plenary, Paris 2007.

Meeren, H., Heijnsbergen, C., and Gelder, B. (2005). Rapid perceptual integration of facial expression and emotional body language. *Proceedings of the National Academy of Sciences, USA* **102** (45), 16518–23.

Mehrabian, A. (1980). *Basic dimensions for a general psychological theory: implications for personality, social, environmental, and developmental studies*. Oelgeschlager, Gunn and Hain, Cambridge, Massachusetts.

Mehrabian, A. (1995). Framework for a comprehensive description and measurement of emotional states. *Genetic, Social, and General Psychology Monographs* **121** (3), 339–61.

Mehrabian, A. (1996). Analysis of the big-five personality factors in terms of the pad temperament model. *Australian Journal of Psychology* **48**, 86–92.

Mehrabian, A. and Russell, J.A. (1974). *An approach to environmental psychology*. MIT Press, Cambridge, Massachusetts.

Mele, A.R. (2001). *Self-deception unmasked*. Princeton University Press, Princeton, New Jersey.

Melfsen, S. and Florin, I. (2002). Do socially anxious children show deficits in classifying facial expressions of emotions? *Journal of Nonverbal Behavior* **26**, 109–26.

Mellers, B. A., Schwartz, A., Hu, K., and Ritov, I. (1997). Decision affect theory: emotional reactions to the outcomes of risky options. *Psychological Science* **8,** 423–9.

Merriam–Webster Online Dictionary (2009). *Merriam–Webster Online Dictionary*. Merriam-Webster Inc., Springfield, Massachusetts. Retrieved May 16, 2009, from http://www.merriam-webster.com/dictionary.

Mesken, J. (2006). Determinants and consequences of drivers' emotions. PhD thesis, University of Groeningen.

Mesken, J., Hagenzieker, M., and Rothengatter, T. (2008). A review of studies on emotions and road user behaviour. In *Driver behaviour and training*. Vol. 3: *Human factors in road and rail transport* (ed. L. Dorn), pp. 91–106). Ashgate, Aldershot.

Meyer, J.-J.C. (2006). Reasoning about emotional agents. *International Journal of Intelligent Systems* **21,** 601–19.

Miles, L.K. (2009). Who is approachable? *Journal of Experimental Social Psychology* **45**, 262–6.

Mineka, S. and Öhman, A. (2002). Phobias and preparedness: the selective, automatic, and encapsulated nature of fear. *Biological Psychiatry* **52** (10), 927–37.

Minsky, M. (1986). *The society of mind*. Simon and Schuster, New York.

Miyanaga, K., Masuko, T., and Kobayashi, T. (2004). A style control technique for HMM based speech synthesis. In *Proceedings of the 8th International Conference on Spoken Language Processing, Interspeech 2004* (Jeju, Korea), Vol. 2, pp. 1437–40.

Moffat, D. and Frijda, N.H. (1995). Where there's a will there's an agent. In *Proceedings of the Workshop on Agent Theories, Architectures and Languages* (ed. M.J. Wooldridge and N.R. Jennings), pp. 245–60. Springer-Verlag.

Montero, J.M., Gutiérrez-Arriola, J., Colás, J., Enríquez, E., and Pardo, J.M. (1999). Analysis and modelling of emotional speech in Spanish. In *Proceedings of the 14th International Conference of Phonetic Sciences* (San Francisco), pp. 957–60.

Moos, A. and Trouvain, J. (2007). Comprehension of ultra-fast speech—blind vs. 'normally hearing' persons. In *Proceedings of the 16th International Congress of Phonetic Sciences (ICPhS 2007)* (ed. J. Trouvain and W.J. Barry), pp. 677–80. Pirrot, Saarbrücken, Germany.

Moore, R.K. (2007). Spoken language processing: piecing together the puzzle. *Speech Communication* **49** (5), 418–35.

Moors, A. (2009). Theories of emotion causation: a review. *Cognition and Emotion* **23**, 625–62.

Moors, A. (2010). Automatic constructive appraisal as a candidate cause of emotion. *Emotion Review*.

Moors, A. and De Houwer, J. (2005). Automatic processing of dominance and submissiveness. *Experimental Psychology* **52** (4), 296–302.

Moors, A. and De Houwer, J. (2006). Automaticity: a theoretical and conceptual analysis. *Psychological Bulletin* **132**, 297–326.

Moors, A., De Houwer, J., Hermans, D., and Eelen, P. (2005). Unintentional processing of motivational valence. *The Quarterly Journal of Experimental Psychology* **58A**, 1043–63.

Mori, J., Prendinger, H., and Ishizuka, M. (2003). Evaluation of an embodied conversational agent with affective behavior. In *Proceedings of International Joint Conference on Autonomous Agents and Multi-Agent Systems (AAMAS 2003), Workshop on Embodied Conversational Characters as Individuals* (ed. J. Rosenschein and M. Wooldridge), pp. 58–61, Melbourne, Australia, Association for Computing Machinery.

Moskowitz, G.B. and Grant, H. (2009). *The psychology of goals*. Guilford, New York.

Mota S. and Picard R.W. (2003). Automated posture analysis for detecting learner's interest level. In *Proceedings of the Workshop on Computer Vision and Pattern Recognition for Human–Computer Interaction, CVPR HCI*.

Motley, M.T. (1993). Facial affect and verbal context in conversations. Facial expression as interjection. *Human Communication Research* **20**, 3–40.

Motley, M. and Camden, C. (1988). Facial expression of emotion: a comparison of posed expressions versus spontaneous expressions in an interpersonal communication setting. *Western Journal of Speech Communication* **52**, 1–22.

Moulines, E. and Charpentier, F. (1990). Pitch-synchronous waveform processing techniques for text-to-speech synthesis using diphones. *Speech Communication* **9** (5), 453–67.

Mozziconacci, S.J.L. and Hermes, D.J. (1997). A study of intonation patterns in speech expressing emotion or attitude: production and perception. *IPO Annual Progress Report* **32**, 154–60.

Mumme, D. L., Fernald, A., and Herrera, C. (1996). Infants' responses to facial and vocal emotional signals in a social referencing paradigm. *Child Development* **67**, 3219–37.

Murray, I.R., Edgington, M.D., Campion, D., and Lynn, J. (2000). Rule-based emotion synthesis using concatenated speech. In *Speech and Emotion*, ISCA Tutorial and Research Workshop, Newcastle Northern Ireland, pp. 173–7.

Myrtek, M. and Brügner, G. (1996). Perception of emotions in everyday life: studies with patients and normals. *Biological Psychology* **42**, 147–64.

Myrtek, M., Bruegner, G., Fichtler, A., König, K., Müller, W., Foerster, F., and Höppner, V. (1988). Detection of emotionally induced ECG changes and their behavioural correlates: a new method for ambulatory monitoring. *European Heart Journal* **9** (Suppl. N), 55–60.

Myrtek, M., Aschenbrenner, E., and Brügner, G. (2005). Emotions in everyday life: an ambulatory monitoring study with female students. *Biological Psychology* **68** (3), 237–55.

Nadel, J. and Muir, D. (Eds.) (1995). *Emotional development*. Oxford University Press, New York.

Nakanishi, H., Shimizu, S., and Isbister, K. (2005). Sensitizing social agents for virtual training. *Applied Artificial Intelligence*, Special issue, 'Educational agents—beyond virtual tutors' **19**, 341–62.

Narayanan, R.T., Seidenbecher, T., Kluge, C., Bergado, J., Stork, O., and Pape, H.C. (2007). Dissociated theta phase synchronization in amygdalo-hippocampal circuits during various stages of fear memory. *European Journal of Neuroscience* **25** (6), 1823–31.

Nayak, V. (2005). Emotional expressiveness through the body language of characters in interactive game environments. PhD thesis, Media Arts and Technology University of California, Santa Barbara.

Neal Reilly, W.S. (1996). Believable social and emotional agents. PhD thesis, Carnegie Mellon University, Pittsburgh, Pennsylvania.

Neal Reilly, W.S. (2006). Modeling what happens between emotional antecedents and emotional consequents. Paper presented at *Eighteenth European Meeting on Cybernetics and Systems Research*. Austrian Society for Cybernetic Studies, Vienna.

Neff, M. and Fiume, E. (2004). Artistically based computer generation of expressive motion. In *Proceedings of the AISB-2004 Symposium on Language, Speech and Gesture for Expressive Characters*, pp. 29–39.

Neff, M. and Fiume, E. (2005). AER: Aesthetic exploration and refinement for expressive character animation. In *Proceedings of the 2005 ACM SIGGRAPH/Eurographics symposium on Computer animation*, pp. 161–70. ACM Press, New York.

Nesse, R. (2009). Evolution of emotion. In *Oxford companion to emotion and the affective sciences* (ed. D. Sander and K.R. Scherer), pp. 159–64. Oxford University Press, Oxford.

Neumann, R. and Strack, F. (2000). Mood contagion: the automatic transfer of mood between persons. *Journal of Personality and Social Psychology* **79**, 211–23.

Ni Chasaide, A. and Gobl, C. (1997). Voice source variation. In *The handbook of phonetic sciences* (ed. W.J. Hardcastle and J. Laver), Blackwell, Oxford.

Niedenthal, P.M., Halberstadt, J.B., Margolin, J., and Innes-Ker, A. (2000). Emotional state and the detection of change in facial expression of emotion. *European Journal of Social Psychology* **30** (2), 211–22.

Niewiadomski, R. and Pelachaud, C. (2007*a*). Fuzzy similarity of facial expressions of embodied agents. In *Intelligent virtual agents, 7th International Conference (IVA 2007)*, Paris, France (ed. C. Pelachaud, J.-C. Martin, E. André, G. Chollet, K.Karpouzis, and D. Pelé), pp. 86–98. Lecture Notes in Computer Science 4722. Springer, Berlin.

Niewiadomski, R. and Pelachaud, C. (2007*b*). Model of facial expressions management for an embodied conversational agent. In *Affective computing and intelligent interaction, Proceedings of the Second International Conference (ACII 2007)*, Lisbon, Portugal (ed. A. Paiva, R. Prada, and R.W. Picard), pp. 12–23. Lecture Notes in Computer Science 4738. Springer, Heidelberg.

Niewiadomski, R., Ochs, S., and Pelachaud, C. (2008). Expressions of empathy in ECAs. In *Intelligent virtual agents, Proceedings of the 8th International Conference (IVA 2008)*, Tokyo, Japan (ed. H. Prendinger, J.C. Lester, and M. Ishizuka), pp. 37–44. Lecture Notes in Computer Science 5208. Springer, Berlin.

Niewiadomski, R., Hyniewska, S., and Pelachaud, C. (2009*a*). Evaluation of multimodal sequential expressions of emotions in ECA. In *Affective computing and intelligent interaction. Third International Conference (ACII 2009)*, pp. 635–41. IEEE, Los Alamitos.

Niewiadomski, R., Hyniewska, S., and Pelachaud, C. (2009*b*). Modeling emotional expressions as sequences of behaviours. In *Intelligent virtual agents, Proceedings of 9th International Conference (IVA 2009)*, Amsterdam, The Netherlands (ed. Z. Ruttkay, M. Kipp, A. Nijholt, and H.H. Vilhjálmsson), pp. 316–22. Lecture Notes in Computer Sciences 5773. Springer, Berlin.

Nolen-Hoeksema, S., Wisco, B.E., and Lyubomirsky, S. (2008). Rethinking rumination. *Perspectives on Psychological Science* **3**, 400–24.

Nose, T., Kato, Y., and Kobayashi, T. (2007). A speaker adaptation technique for MRHSMM-based style control of synthetic speech. *Proceedings of the 2007 IEEE International Conference on Acoustics, Speech and Signal processing, ICASSP 2007* (Honoluly), Vol. 4, pp. 833–6.

Nowicki, S. and Duke, M.P. (1994). Individual differences in the nonverbal communication of affect: The diagnostic analysis of nonverbal accuracy. *Journal of Nonverbal Behavior* **18**, 9–35.

Oatley, K. (1992). *Best laid schemes: the psychology of emotions*. Cambridge University Press, Cambridge.

Oatley, K. and Johnson-Laird, P.N. (1987). Towards a cognitive theory of emotions. *Cognition and Emotion* **1**, 29–50.

Oatley, K. and Johnson-Laird, P.N. (1996). The communicative theory of emotions: empirical tests, mental models, and implications for social interaction. In *Striving and feeling: interactions among goals, affect, and self-regulation* (ed. L.L. Martin and A. Tesser), pp. 363–93. Erlbaum, Mahwah, New Jersey.

Obrist, P.A. (1981). *Cardiovascular psychophysiology*. Plenum, New York.

Ochs, M., Devooght, K., Sadek, D., and Pelachaud, C. (2006). A computational model of capability-based emotion elicitation for rational agent. *International Workshop on Emotion and Computing*. Bremen.

Öhman, A. (1987). The psychophysiology of emotion: an evolutionary–cognitive perspective. In *Advances in psychophysiology* (ed. P.K. Adeles, J.R. Jennings, and M.G.H. Coles), Vol. 2. The JAI Press, Greenwich, Connecticut.

Öhman, A. and Mineka, S. (2001). Fears, phobias, and preparedness: toward an evolved module of fear and fear learning. *Psychological Review* **108**, 483–522.

Öhman, A. and Wiens, S. (2004). The concept of an evolved fear module and cognitive theories of anxiety. In *Feelings and emotions* (ed. A. Manstead, N. Frijda, and A.H. Fischer), pp. 58–80. Cambridge University Press, Cambridge.

Öhman, A., Flykt, A., and Esteves, F. (2001*a*). Emotion drives attention: detecting the snake in the grass. *Journal of Experimental Psychology: General* **130**, 466–78.

Öhman, A. Lundqvist, D., and Esteves, F. (2001*b*). The face in the crowd revisited: a threat advantage with schematic stimuli. *Journal of Personality and Social Psychology* **80**, 381–96.

Ortony, A. and Turner, T.J. (1990). What's basic about basic emotions? *Psychological Review* **97**, 315–31.

Ortony, A., Clore, G.L., and Collins, A. (1988). *The cognitive structure of emotions*. Cambridge University Press, New York.

Osgood, C.E., Suci, G.J., and Tannenbaum, P.H. (1957). *The measurement of meaning*. University of Illinois Press, Urbana.

Osgood, C., May, W.H., and Miron, M.S. (1975). *Cross-cultural universals of affective meaning*. University of Illinois Press, Urbana.

Oster, H. (2005). The repertoire of infant facial expressions: an ontogenetic perspective. In *Emotional development* (J. Nadel and D. Muir), pp. 261–92. Oxford University Press, Oxford.

Ostermann, J. (2002). Face animation in MPEG-4. In *MPEG-4 facial animation—the standard implementation and applications* (ed. I.S. Pandzic and R. Forchheimer), pp. 17–55. Wiley, Chicester.

O'Sullivan, M. and Guilford, J.P. (1975). Six factors of behavioural cognition: understanding other people. *Journal of Educational Measurement* **12** (4), 255–71.

Oudeyer, P-Y. (2002). The production and recognition of emotions in speech: features and algorithms. *International Journal of Human-Computer Studies* **59** (1–2), 157–8.

Paiva, A., Aylett, R., and Marsella, S. (Eds.) (2004). *Proceedings of International Joint Conference on Autonomous Agents and Multi-Agent Systems (AAMAS)*, Workshop on Empathic Agents, New York.

Paiva, A., Dias, J., and Aylett, R. (2005). Learning by feeling: evoking empathy with synthetic characters. *Applied Artificial Intelligence*, Special issue on 'Educational agents—beyond virtual tutors' **19**, 235–66.

Paleari, M. and Lisetti, C.L. (2006). Psychologically grounded avatars' expressions. In *Proceedings of 1st Workshop on Emotion And Computing* at KI 2006, 29th Annual German Conference on Artificial Intelligence, Bremen, Germany.

Palmer, S.E. (1999). *Vision science: photons to phenomenology*. MIT Press, Cambridge, Massachusetts.

Pan, X. Gillies, M. Sezgin, T.M., and Loscos, C. (2007). Expressing complex mental states through facial expressions. In *Affective computing and intelligent interaction, Proceedings of the Second International Conference (ACII 2007)*, Lisbon (ed. A. Paiva, R. Prada, and R.W. Picard), pp. 745–6. Lecture Notes in Computer Science 4738. Springer, Berlin.

Panksepp, J. (1991). Affective neuroscience: a conceptual framework for the neurobiological study of emotions. In *International reviews of emotion research* (ed. K. Strongman), pp. 59–99. Wiley, Chichester.

Panksepp, J. (1998*a*). *Affective neuroscience: the foundations of human and animal emotions*. Oxford University Press, Oxford and New York.

Panksepp, J. (1998*b*). The periconscious substrates of consciousness : affective states and the evolutionary origins of the self. *Journal of Consciousness Studies* **5** (17), 566–82.

Pantic, M. and Bartlett, M.S. (2007). Machine analysis of facial expressions. In *Face recognition* (ed. K. Delac and M. Grgic), pp. 377–416. I-Tech Education and Publishing, Vienna.

Pantic, M. and Patras, I. (2006). Dynamics of facial expression: recognition of facial actions and their temporal segments from face profile image sequences. *IEEE Transactions on Systems, Man and Cybernetics, Part B* **36** (2), 433–49.

Pantic, M. and Rothkrantz, L.J.M. (2004). Case-based reasoning for user-profiled recognition of emotions from face images. In *IEEE International Conference on Multimedia and Expo (ICME 2004)*, pp. 391–4.

Paradiso, A. (2002). An algebra for combining MPEG-4 compliant facial animations. In *Proceedings of International Workshop on Lifelike Animated Agents:P Tools, Affective Functions, and Applications* in conjunction with the Seventh Pacific Rim International Conference on Artificial Intelligence, Tokyo, Japan.

Parke, F. (1972). Computer generated animation of faces. In *Proceedings of ACM National Conference*, Salt Lake City, Vol. 1, pp. 451–7. ACM, New York.

Parkinson, B. (1996). Emotions are social. *British Journal of Psychology* **87**, 663–83.

Parkinson, B. (2001*a*). Putting appraisal in context. In *Appraisal processes in emotion: theory, research, application* (ed. K.R. Scherer, A. Schorr, and T. Johnstone), pp. 173–86. Oxford University Press, Oxford.

Parkinson, B. (2001*b*). Anger on and off the road. *British Journal of Psychology* **92**, 507–26.

Parkinson, B. (2005). Do facial movements express emotions or communicate motives? *Personality and Social Psychology Review* **9**, 278–311.

Parkinson, B. (2007). Getting from situations to emotions: appraisal and alternative routes. *Emotion* **7**, 21–5.

Parkinson, B. (2008). Emotions in direct and remote social interaction: getting through the spaces between us. *Computers in Human Behavior* **24**, 1510–29.

Parkinson, B. (2009). What holds emotions together? Meaning and response coordination. *Cognitive Systems Research* **10**, 31–47.

Parkinson, B. and Simons, G. (2009). Affecting others: social appraisal and emotion contagion in everyday decision-making. *Personality and Social Psychology Bulletin* **35**, 1071–84.

Parkinson, B., Fischer, A., and Manstead, A.S.R. (2005). *Emotion in social relations: cultural, group and interpersonal processes*. Psychology Press, Philadelphia.

Patel, G.A. and Sathian, K. (2000). Visual search: bottom-up or top-down? *Frontiers in Bioscience* **5**, 169–93.

Pecchinenda, A. (2001). The psychophysiology of appraisals. In *Appraisal processes in emotion: theory, methods, research* (ed. K.R. Scherer, A. Schorr, and T. Johnstone), pp. 301–15. Oxford University Press, New York and Oxford.

Pelachaud, C. (2009). Embodied conversational agent E.C.A. In *Oxford companion to emotion and the affective sciences* (ed. D. Sander and K.R. Scherer). Oxford University Press, Oxford.

Pelachaud, C. and Bilvi, M. (2003). Computational model of believable conversational agents. In *Communications in multiagent systems* (ed. M.-P. Huget), pp. 300–17. Springer-Verlag, New York.

Pelachaud, C. and Poggi, I. (2002). Subtleties of facial expressions in embodied agents. *Journal of Visualization and Computer Animation* **13**, 301–12.

Perrez, M. and Reicherts, M. (1995). *Stress, coping, and health: a situation–behavior approach: theory, methods, applications*. Hogrefe and Huber Publishers, Seattle, Washington.

Perrier P., Ma, L., and Payan, Y. (2005). Modeling the production of VCV sequences via the inversion of a biomechanical model of the tongue: *Proceedings Interspeech 2005* (Lisbon), pp. 1041–4.

Pessoa, L. (2008). On the relationship between emotion and cognition. *Nature Reviews Neuroscience* **9**, 148–58.

Pessoa, L., McKenna, M., Gutierrez, E., and Ungerleider, L. (2002). Neural processing of emotional faces requires attention. *Proceedings of the National Academy of Sciences of the United States of America* **99** (17), 11458–63.

Petrushin, V. (1999). Emotion in speech: recognition and application to call centers. In *Conference on Artificial Neural Network Intelligence Engineering (St Louis, Missouri)*, pp. 7–10.

Petta, P. and Gratch, J. (2009). Computational models of emotion. In *Oxford companion to emotion and the affective sciences* (ed. D. Sander and K.R. Scherer). Oxford University Press, Oxford.

Phan, K.L., Taylor, S.F., Welsh, R.C., Decker, L.R., Noll, D.C., Nichols, T.E., Britton, J.C., and Liberzon, I. (2003). Activation of the medial prefrontal cortex and extended amygdala by individual ratings of emotional arousal: a fMRI study. *Biological Psychiatry* 53 (3), 211–15.

Phelps, E.A. and LeDoux, J.E. (2005). Contributions of the amygdala to emotion processing: from animal models to human behavior. *Neuron* 48, 175–87.

Philippot, P. and Feldman, R.S. (2004). *The regulation of emotion*. Erlbaum, Mahwah, New Jersey.

Picard, R.W. (1997). *Affective computing*. MIT Press, Cambridge, Massachusetts.

Picard, R.W. (2009). Affective computing. In *Oxford companion to emotion and the affective sciences* (ed. D. Sander and K.R. Scherer). Oxford University Press.

Picard, R. and Liu, K. (2007). Relative subjective count and assessment of interruptive technologies applied to mobile monitoring of stress. *International Journal of Human–Computer Studies* 65, 396–75.

Picard, R.W., Vyzas, E., and Healey, J. (2001). Toward machine emotional intelligence: analysis of affective physiological state. *IEEE Transactions on Pattern Analysis and Machine Intelligence* 23 (10), 1175–91.

Piferi, R.L., Kline, K.A., Younger, J., and Lawler, K.A. (2000). An alternative approach for achieving cardiovascular baseline: viewing an aquatic video. *International Journal of Psychophysiology* 37, 207–17.

Pitrelli, J.F., Bakis, R., Eide, E.M., Fernandez, R., Hamza, W., and Picheny, M.A. (2006). The IBM expressive text-to-speech synthesis system for American English. *IEEE Transactions on Audio, Speech and Language Processing* 14 (4), 1099–108.

Platt, S.M. and Badler, N.I. (1981). Animating facial expressions In *Proceedings of Conference on Computer Graphics and Interactive Techniques (SIGGRAPH '81)*, Vol. 15, pp. 245–52. ACM Press, New York.

Plutchik, R. (1980). *Emotion: a psychobioevolutionary synthesis*. Harper and Row, New York.

Poggi, I. and C. Pelachaud, C. (2000). Emotional meaning and expression in performative faces. In *Affective interactions: towards a new generation of computer interfaces* (ed. A. Paiva), pp. 182–95. Springer-Verlag, Berlin.

Pollick, F., Paterson, H.M., Bruderlin, A., and Sanford, A.J. (2001). Perceiving affect from arm movement. *Cognition* 82, 51–61.

Popescu, A.T., Popa, D., and Paré, D. (2009). Coherent gamma oscillations couple the amygdala and striatum during learning. *Nature Neuroscience* 12 (6), 801–7.

Posner, M.I. and DiGirolamo, G.J. (2000). Cognitive neuroscience: origins and promise. *Psychological Bulletin* 126 (6), 873–89.

Power, M. and Dalgleish, T. (1997). *Cognition and emotion: from order to disorder*. Psychology Press, Hove.

Prendinger, H., Mori, J., and Ishizuka, M. (2005). Using human physiology to evaluate subtle expressivity of a virtual quizmaster in a mathematical game. *International Journal of Human–Computer Studies* 62, 231–45.

Price, D.D., Barrell, J.E., and Barrell, J.J. (1985). A quantitative–experiential analysis of human emotions. *Motivation and Emotion* 9, 19–38.

Putnam, L.E., Johnson, Jr., R., and Roth, W.T. (1992). Guidelines for reducing the risk of disease transmission in the psychophysiology laboratory—SPR ad hoc committee on the prevention of disease transmission. *Psychophysiology* 29 (2), 127–41.

Que, C.L., Kolmaga, C., Durand, L.G., Kelly, S.M., and Macklem, P.T. (2002). Phonospirometry for noninvasive measurement of ventilation: methodology and preliminary results. *Journal of Applied Physiology* 93, 1515–26.

Rachman, S.J. (1978). *Fear and courage*. W.H. Freeman and Company, San Francisco.

Rank, S. (2009). Behaviour coordination for models of affective behavior. Ph.D. thesis, Vienna University of Technology, Vienna.

Rank, S. and Petta, P. (2005). Appraisal for a character-based story-world. In *Intelligent virtual agents, Proceedings of the 5th International Conference (IVA 2005), Kos, Greece* (ed. T. Panayiotopoulos,

J. Gratch, R. Aylett, D. Ballin, P. Olivier, and T. Rist), pp. 495–6. Lecture Notes in Computer Science 3661. Springer, Berlin.

Rao, A. and Georgeff, M. (1991). Modeling rational agents within a BDI-architecture. *Proceedings of the International Conference on Principles of Knowledge Representation and Planning*, pp. 473–84. Morgan Kaufmann publishers Inc, San Mateo, California.

Raymond, J.E., Shapiro, K.L., and Arnell, K.M. (1992). Temporary suppression of visual processing in an RSVP task: an attentional blink? *Journal of Experimental Psychology: Human Perception and Performance* **18** (3), 849–60.

Reddy, V. (2000). Coyness in early infancy. *Developmental Science* **3**, 186–92.

Reginald B., J.A. and Kleck, R.E. (2005). Effects of direct and averted gaze on the perception of facially communicated emotion. *Emotion* **5** (1), 3–11.

Rehm, M. and André, E. (2005). Catch me if you can—exploring lying agents in social settings. In *Proceedings of International Joint Conference on Autonomous Agents and Multi-Agent Systems (AAMAS)*, Utrecht, The Netherlands (ed. F. Dignum, V. Dignum, S. Koenig, S. Kraus, M.P. Singh, and M. Wooldridge), 937–44. ACM, New York.

Reisenzein, R. (2009). Emotions as metarepresentational states of mind: naturalizing the belief–desire theory of emotion. *Journal of Cognitive Systems Research* **10**, 6–20.

Revéret, L., Bailly, G., and Badin, P. (2000). MOTHER: a new generation of talking heads providing a flexible articulatory control for video-realistic speech animation. In *Proceedings of the Sixth International Conference on Spoken Language Processing* (ICSLP 2000) (Beijing, China), Vol. 2, pp. 755–8.

Reynolds, D.A.J. and Gifford, R. (2001). The sounds and the sights of intelligence: a lens model channel analysis. *Personality and Social Psychology Bulletin* **27** (2), 187–200.

Rickel, J., Marsella, S., Gratch, J., Hill, R., Traum, D., and Swartout, W. (2002). Toward a new generation of virtual humans for interactive experiences. *IEEE Intelligent Systems* **17** (4), 32–8.

Rimé, B. (2009). Emotion elicits the social sharing of emotion: theory and empirical review. *Emotion Review* **1**, 60–85.

Rimm-Kaufman, S.E. and Kagan, J. (1996). The psychological significance of changes in skin temperature. *Motivation and Emotion* **20**, 63–78.

Riskin, J. (ed.) (2007). *Genesis redux: essays on the history and philosophy of artificial life.* Chicago University Press, Chicago.

Rittweger, J., Lambertz, M., and Langhorst, P. (1997). Influences of mandatory breathing on rhythmical components of electrodermal activity. *Clinical Physiology* **17**, 609–18.

Ritz, T. and Dahme, B. (2006). Implementation and interpretation of respiratory sinus arrhythmia measures in psychosomatic medicine: practice against better evidence? *Psychosomatic Medicine* **68**, 617–27.

Ritz, T., Dahme, B., Dubois, A.B., Folgering, H., Fritz, G.K., Harver, A., Kotses, H., Lehrer, P.M., Ring, C., Steptoe, A., and Woestijne, K.P.V.D. (2002). Guidelines for mechanical lung function measurements in psychophysiology. *Psychophysiology* **39**, 546–67.

Roach, J.R. (1993). *The player's passion: studies in the science of acting.* University of Michigan Press, Ann Arbor.

Robin, O., Rousmans, S., Dittmar, A., and Vernet-Maury, E. (2003). Gender influence on emotional responses to primary tastes. *Physiology and Behavior* **78** (3), 385–93.

Robinson, M. (2009). Levels of processing. In *The Oxford companion to emotion and the affective sciences* (ed. D. Sander and K.R Scherer). Oxford University Press, Oxford and New York.

Roesch, E.B. (2009). Attention meets emotion: temporal unfolding of attentional processes to emotionally relevant information. Ph.D. thesis, Swiss Centre for Affective Sciences, University of Geneva, Geneva, Switzerland.

Roesch, E.B., Sander, D., and Scherer, K.R. (2007) The link between temporal attention and emotion: a playground for psychology, neuroscience, and plausible artificial neural networks. In *Artificial neural networks—ICANN 2007* (ed. J. Marques de Sá, L.A. Alexandre, W. Duch, and D. Mandic), Vol. 2, pp. 859–68. Springer, Berlin.

Roesch, E.B., Sander, D., and Scherer, K.R. (2009). Emotion and motion in facial expressions modulate the attentional blink. *Perception* **38**, 466.

Roesch, E.B., Sander, D., Mumenthaler, C., Kerzel, D., and Scherer, K.R. (2010). Psychophysics of emotion: the QUEST for emotional attention. *Journal of Vision* **10** (3), 1–9.

Roesch, E.B, Tamarit, L., Reveret, L., Grandjean, D., Sander, D., and Scherer, K.R. (in press). FACSGen: a tool to synthesize emotional facial expressions through systematic manipulation of facial action units. *Journal of Nonverbal Behaviour.*

Roggen, D., Bharatula, N. B., Stäger, M., Lukowics, P., and Tröster, G. (2006). From sensors to miniature networked SensorButtons. In *Proceedings of the 3rd International Conference on Networked Sensing Systems*, Chicago. pp. 119–22.

Rolls, E.T. (1999). The functions of the orbitofrontal cortex. *Neurocase* **5**, 301–12.

Rose, A.J. (2002). Co-rumination in the friendships of girls and boys. *Child Development* **73**, 1830–43.

Rose, A.J., Carlson, W., and Waller, E.M. (2007). Prospective associations of co-rumination with friendship and emotional adjustment: considering the socioemotional trade-offs of co-rumination. *Developmental Psychology* **43**, 1019–31.

Roseman, I.J. (1984). Cognitive determinants of emotion: a structural theory. *Review of Personality and Social Psychology* **5**, 11–36.

Roseman, I.J. and Smith, C.A. (2001). Appraisal theory: overview, assumptions, varieties, controversies. In *Appraisal processes in emotion* (ed. K.R. Scherer, A. Schorr, and T. Johnstone), pp. 3–34. Oxford University Press, New York.

Roseman, I.J., Wiest, C., and Swartz, T.S. (1994). Phenomenology, behaviors, and goals differentiate discrete emotions. *Journal of Personality and Social Psychology* **67** (2), 206–21.

Rosenthal, R. (1987). *Judgment studies: design, analysis, and meta-analysis.* Cambridge University Press, Cambridge.

Rosenthal, R. and Rubin, D.B. (1989). Effect size estimation for one-sample multiple-choice-type data: design, analysis, and meta-analysis. *Psychological Bulletin* **106**, 332–7.

Rosenthal, R., Hall, J.A., DiMatteo, M.R., Rogers, P.L., and Archer, D. (1979). *Sensitivity to nonverbal communication: the PONS test.* John Hopkins University Press, Baltimore.

Rosis, F.D., Pelachaud, C., Poggi, I., Carofiglio, V., and Carolis, B.D. (2003). From Greta's mind to her face: modelling the dynamics of affective states in a conversational embodied agent. *International Journal of Human–Computer Studies* **59**, 81–118.

Ruisel, I. (1992). Social intelligence: conception and methodological problems. *Studia Psychologica* **34** (4–5), 281–96.

Russell, J.A. (1980). A circumplex model of affect. *Journal of Personality and Social Psychology* **39**, 1161–78.

Russell, J.A. (1983). Pancultural aspects of the human conceptual organization of emotions. *Journal of Personality and Social Psychology* **45**, 1281–8.

Russell J.A. (1997*a*). How shall an emotion be called? In *Circumplex models of personality and emotions* (ed. R. Plutchik and H. Conte), pp. 205–20. American Psychological Association, Washington, DC.

Russell, J.A. (1997*b*). Reading emotions from and into faces: resurrecting a dimensional-contextual perspective. In *The psychology of facial expression* (ed. J.A. Russell and J.-M. Fernández-Dols), pp. 295–320. Cambridge University Press, Cambridge.

Russell, J.A. (2003). Core affect and the psychological construction of emotion. *Psychological Review* **110**, 145–72.

Russell, J.A. and Bullock, M. (1986). On the dimensions preschoolers use to interpret facial expressions of emotion. *Developmental Psychology* **22**, 97–102.

Russell, J.A., Bachorowski. J.A., and Fernandez-Dols, J.M. (2003). Facial and vocal expressions of emotion. *Annual Review of Psychology* **54**, 329–49.

Ruttkay, Z. (2001). Constraint-based facial animation. *International Journal of Constraints* **6**, 85–113.

Ruttkay, Z., Noot, H., and ten Hagen, P. (2003). Emotion disc and emotion squares: tools to explore the facial expression face. *Computer Graphics Forum* **22** (1), 49–53.

Ruys, K.I. and Stapel, D.A. (2009). Emotion elicitor or emotion messenger? Subliminal priming reveals two faces of facial expressions. *Psychological Science* **19**, 583–600.

Ruzanski, E., Hansen, J.H.L., Finan, D., Meyerhoff, J., Norris, W., and Wollert, T. (2005). Improved 'TEO' feature-based automatic stress detection using physiological and acoustic speech sensors. In *Interspeech-2005*, pp. 2653–6.

Saab, P.G., Llabre, M.M., Hurwitz, B.E., Frame, C.A., Reineke, L.J., Fins, A.I., McCalla, J., Cieply, L.K., and Schneiderman, N. (1992). Myocardial and peripheral vascular responses to behavioral challenges and their stability in Black and White Americans. *Psychophysiology* **29**, 384–97.

Saarni, C. (1979). Children's understanding of display rules for expressive behaviour. *Developmental Psychology* **15** (4), 424–9.

Sackur, J. and Dehaene, S. (2009). The cognitive architecture for chaining of two mental operations. *Cognition* **11**, 187–211.

Saltzman, K.M. and Holahan, C.J. (2002). Social support, self-efficacy and depressive symptoms: an integrative model. *Journal of Social and Clinical Psychology* **21**, 309–22.

Sander, D. and Koenig, O. (2002). No inferiority complex in the study of emotion complexity: a cognitive neuroscience computational architecture of emotion. *Cognitive Science Quarterly* **2**, 249–72.

Sander, D. and Scherer, K.R. (Eds.) (2009). *Oxford companion to emotion and the affective sciences*. Oxford University Press, Oxford.

Sander, D., Grafman, J., and Zalla, T. (2003). The human amygdala: an evolved system for relevance detection. *Reviews in the Neurosciences* **14** (4), 303–16.

Sander, D., Grandjean, D., and Scherer, K.R. (2005). A systems approach to appraisal mechanisms in emotion. *Neural Networks* **18**, 317–52.

Saul, J.P., Berger, R.D., Albrecht, P., Stein, S.P., Chen, M.H., and Cohen, R.J. (1991). Transfer function analysis of the circulation: unique insights into cardiovascular regulation. *American Journal of Physiology* **261** (4.2), 1231–45.

Schachter, S. and Singer, J.E. (1962). Cognitive, social, and physiological determinants of emotional state. *Psychological Review* **69**, 379–99.

Schaefer, A., Braver, T.S., Reynolds, J.R., Burgess, G.C., Yarkoni, T., and Gray, J.R. (2006). Individual differences in amygdala activity predict response speed during working memory. *The Journal of Neuroscience* **26** (40), 10120–8.

Schell, A.M., Dawson, M.E., and Filion, D.L. (1988). Psychophysiological correlates of electrodermal lability. *Psychophysiology* **25**, 619–32.

Scherer, K.R. (1978). Personality inference from voice quality: the loud voice of extroversion. *European Journal of Social Psychology* **8**, 467–87.

Scherer, K.R. (1982). Methods of research on vocal communication: paradigms and parameters. In *Handbook of methods in nonverbal behavior research* (ed. K.R. Scherer and P. Ekman), pp. 136–98. Cambridge University Press, Cambridge.

Scherer, K.R. (1984). On the nature and function of emotion: a component process approach. In *Approaches to emotion* (ed. K.R. Scherer and P. Ekman), pp. 293–317. Erlbaum, Hillsdale, New Jersey.

Scherer, K.R. (1985). Vocal affect signaling: a comparative approach. In *Advances in the study of behavior* (ed. J. Rosenblatt, C. Beer, M. Busnel, and P.J.B. Slater), pp. 189–244. Academic Press, New York.

Scherer, K.R. (1986). Vocal affect expression: a review and a model for future research. *Psychological Bulletin* **99**, 143–65.

Scherer, K.R. (1987). Toward a dynamic theory of emotion: the component process model of affective states. *Geneva Studies in Emotion and Communication* **1**, 1–98 [online version]. Retrieved June 5, 2009, from http://www.unige.ch/fapse/emotion/publications/geneva_studies.html

Scherer, K.R. (1988). On the symbolic functions of vocal affect expression. *Journal of Language and Social Psychology* 7, 79–100.

Scherer, K.R. (1992). What do facial expressions express? In *International review of studies on emotion* (ed. K. Strongman), Vol. 2. pp. 293–318. Lawrence Erlbaum, Hillsdale, New Jersey.

Scherer, K.R. (1993). Studying the emotion-antecedent appraisal process: an expert system approach. *Cognition and Emotion* 7, 325–55.

Scherer, K.R. (1994*a*). Affect bursts. In *Emotions: Essays on emotion theory* (ed. S. van Goozen, N.E. van de Poll, and J.A. Sergeant), pp. 161–96. Erlbaum, Hillsdale, New Jersey.

Scherer, K.R. (1994*b*). Toward a concept of 'modal emotions'. In *The nature of emotion: Fundamental questions* (ed. P. Ekman and R.J. Davidson), pp. 25–31. Oxford University Press, New York.

Scherer, K.R. (1995). A simple demonstration of neural network modeling of appraisal predictions. Unpublished manuscript. University of Geneva.

Scherer, K.R. (1997). Profiles of emotion-antecedent appraisal: testing theoretical predictions across cultures. *Cognition and Emotion* 11, 113–50.

Scherer, K.R. (1999*a*). Appraisal theories. In *Handbook of cognition and emotion* (ed. T. Dalgleish and M. Power), pp. 637–63. Wiley, Chichester.

Scherer, K.R. (1999*b*). On the sequential nature of appraisal processes: indirect evidence from a recognition task. *Cognition and Emotion* 13 (6), 763–93.

Scherer, K.R. (1999*c*). Universality of emotional expression. In *Encyclopedia of human emotions* (ed. D. Levinson, J. Ponzetti, and P. Jorgenson), Vol. 2, pp. 669–74. Macmillan, New York.

Scherer, K.R. (2000*a*). Psychological models of emotion. In *The neuropsychology of emotion* (ed. J. Borod), pp. 137–62. Oxford University Press, New York.

Scherer, K.R. (2000*b*). Emotions as episodes of subsystem synchronization driven by nonlinear appraisal processes. In *Emotion, development, and self-organization: dynamic systems approaches to emotional development* (ed. M.D. Lewis and I. Granic), pp. 70–99. Cambridge University Press, New York/Cambridge.

Scherer, K.R. (2001). Appraisal considered as a process of multi-level sequential checking. In *Appraisal processes in emotion: theory, methods, research* (ed. K.R. Scherer, A. Schorr, and T. Johnstone), pp. 92–120. Oxford University Press, New York.

Scherer, K.R. (2002). Emotion, the psychological structure of. In *International encyclopedia of the social and behavioural sciences* (ed. N.J. Smelser and P.B. Baltes), pp. 4472–7. Pergamon, Oxford.

Scherer, K.R. (2003). Vocal communication of emotion: a review of research paradigms. *Speech Communication* 40, 227–56.

Scherer, K.R. (2004). Feelings integrate the central representation of appraisal-driven response organization in emotion. In *Feelings and emotions: The Amsterdam Symposium* (ed. A.S.R. Manstead, N.H. Frijda, and A.H. Fischer), pp. 136–57. Cambridge University Press, Cambridge.

Scherer, K.R. (2005*a*). Unconscious processes in emotion: the bulk of the iceberg. In *The unconscious in emotion* (ed. P. Niedenthal, L. Feldman-Barrett, and P. Winkielman), pp. 312–34. Guilford, New York.

Scherer, K.R. (2005*b*). What are emotions? And how can they be measured? *Social Science Information* 44, 693–727.

Scherer, K.R. (2007). Component models of emotion can inform the quest for emotional competence. In *The science of emotional intelligence: knowns and unknowns* (ed. G. Matthews, M. Zeidner, and R. D. Roberts), pp. 101–26. Oxford University Press, New York.

Scherer, K. R. (2009*a*). The dynamic architecture of emotion: evidence for the component process model. *Cognition and Emotion* 23 (7), 1307–51.

Scherer, K.R. (2009*b*). Emotions are emergent processes. They require a dynamic computational architecture. *Philosophical Transactions of the Royal Society, Series B* 364, 3459–74.

Scherer, K.R. (2009*c*). Emotion theories and concepts (psychological perspectives). In *Oxford companion to emotion and the affective dciences* (ed. D. Sander and K.R. Scherer), pp. 145–9. Oxford University Press, Oxford.

Scherer, K.R. and Brosch, T. (2009). Culture-specific appraisal biases contribute to emotion dispositions. *European Journal of Personality* **23**, 265–88.

Scherer, K.R. and Ellring, H. (2007*a*). Are facial expressions of emotion produced by categorical affect programs or dynamically driven by appraisal? *Emotion* **7**, 113–30.

Scherer, K.R. and Ellring, H. (2007*b*). Multimodal expression of emotion: affect programs or componential appraisal patterns? *Emotion* **7** (1), 158–71.

Scherer, K.R. and Grandjean, D. (2008). Facial expressions allow inference of both emotions and their components. *Cognition and Emotion* **22**, 789–801.

Scherer, K.R. and Kappas, A. (1988). Primate vocal expression of affective states. In *Primate vocal communication* (ed. D. Todt, P. Goedeking, and E. Newman), pp. 171–94. Springer, Heidelberg.

Scherer, K.R. and Peper, M. (2001). Psychological theories of emotion and neuropsychological research. In *Handbook of neuropsychology* (ed. F. Boller and J. Grafman), Vol. 5, *Emotional behaviour and its disorders* (ed. G. Gainotti), pp. 17–48. Elsevier, Amsterdam.

Scherer, K.R and Wallbott, H.G. (1985). Analysis of nonverbal behaviour. *Handbook of discourse analysis* **2**, 199–230.

Scherer, K.R. and Wallbott, H.G. (1994). Evidence for universality and cultural variation of differential emotion response patterning. *Journal of Personality and Social Psychology* **66**, 310–28.

Scherer, K.R., Walbott, H.G., and Summerfield, A.B. (1986). *Experiencing emotion: a cross-cultural study*. Cambridge University Press, Cambridge.

Scherer, K.R., Schorr, A., and Johnstone, T. (ed.). (2001). *Appraisal processes in emotion: theory, methods, research*. Oxford University Press, New York.

Scherer, K.R., Johnstone, T., and Klasmeyer, G. (2003). Vocal expression of emotion. In *Handbook of the affective sciences* (ed. R.J. Davidson, K.R. Scherer, and H. Goldsmith), pp. 433–56. Oxford University Press, New York and Oxford.

Scherer, K.R., Wranik, T., Sangsue, J., Tran, V., and Scherer, U. (2004*a*). Emotions in everyday life: probability of occurrence, risk factors, appraisal and reaction pattern. *Social Science Information* **43** (4), 499–570.

Scherer, K.R., Zentner, M. R., and Stern, D. (2004*b*). Beyond surprise: the puzzle of infants' expressive reactions to expectancy violation. *Emotion* **4**, 389–402.

Scherer, U., Helfrich, H., and Scherer, K.R. (1980). Internal push or external pull? Determinants of paralinguistic behaviour. In *Language: social psychological perspectives* (ed. H. Giles, P. Robinson, and P. Smith), pp. 279–82. Pergamon, Oxford.

Scheutz, M. and Schermerhorn, P. (2009). Affective goal and task selection for social robots. In *The handbook of research on synthetic emotions and sociable robotics* (ed. J. Vallverdú and D. Casacuberta), pp. 74–88. Information Science Reference, London.

Scheutz, M. and Sloman, A. (2001). Affect and agent control: experiments with simple affective states. *Proceedings of IAT-01*, pp. 200–9. World Scientific Publisher.

Schilbach, L., Wohlschläger, A., Krämer, N., Newen, N., Shah, A., Fink, G., and Vogeley, K. (2006). Being with virtual others: neural correlates of social interaction. *Neuropsycholgia* **44**, 718–30.

Schmidt, K.L., Ambadar, Z., Cohn, J.F., and Reed, L.I. (2006). Movement differences between deliberate and spontaneous facial expressions: zygomaticus major action in smiling. *Journal of Nonverbal Behavior* **30**, 37–52.

Schorr, A. (2001). Appraisal—the evolution of an idea. In *Appraisal processes in emotion: theory, methods, research* (ed. K.R. Scherer, A. Schorr, and T. Johnstone), pp. 20-34. Oxford University Press, New York.

Schröder, M. (2000). Experimental study of affect bursts. In *Proceedings of ISCA workshop Speech and Emotion*, pp. 132–7.

Schröder, M. (2003). Experimental study of affect bursts. *Speech Communication* **40**, 99–116.

Schröder, M. (2004). Dimensional emotion representation as a basis for speech synthesis with non-extreme emotions. In *International Workshop on Affective Dialogue Systems* (ed. E. André, L. Dybkjaer, W. Minker, and P. Heisterkamp), pp. 209–20. Springer, Berlin/Heidelberg.

Schröder, M. (2006). Expressing degree of activation in synthetic speech. *IEEE Transactions on Audio, Speech and Language Processing* **14** (4), 1128–36.

Schröder, M. (2007). Interpolating expressions in unit selection. In *Affective Computing and Intelligent Interaction, Second International Conference (ACII 2007)* (ed. A. Paiva, R. Prada, and R.W. Picard), pp. 718–20. Lecture Notes in Computer Science 4738. Springer, Berlin.

Schröder, M. (2009). Expressive speech synthesis: past, present, and possible futures. Affective information processing. In *Affective information processing* (J. Tao and T. Tan), pp. 111–26. Springer, London.

Schröder, M. and Grice, M. (2003). Expressing vocal effort in concatenative synthesis. In *Proceedings of the 15th International Conference of Phonetic Sciences*, Barcelona, pp. 2589–92.

Schröder, M., Wilson, I., Jarrold, W., *et al.* (2008). What is most important for an emotion markup language? In *Proceedings of the Third Workshop on Emotion and Computing, KI 2008*, Kaiserslautern, Germany (ed. D. Reichardt).

Schuller, B., Müller, R., Lang, M., and Rigoll, G. (2005). Speaker independent emotion recognition by early fusion of acoustic and linguistic features within ensembles. *Interspeech-2005*, pp. 805–8.

Schuller, B., Arsic, D., Wallhoff, F., and Rigoll, G. (2006). Emotion recognition in the noise applying large acoustic feature sets. In *Proceedings of the 3rd International Conference on Speech Prosody* (Dresden, Germany), paper 128.

Schuller, B., Batliner, A., Steidl, S., and Seppi, D. (2009*a*). Emotion recognition from speech: putting ASR in the loop. In *Proceedings of the International Conference on Acoustics, Speech, and Signal Processing (ICASSP 2009)*, Taipei, Taiwan, pp. 4585–8. IEEE.

Schuller, B., Steidl, S., and Batliner A. (2009*b*). The INTERSPEECH 2009 emotion challenge. In *Proceedings Interspeech 2009*, pp. 312–15.

Schultz, W. (2002). Getting formal with dopamine and reward. *Neuron* **36**, 241–63.

Schwartz, S.H. and Bilsky, W. (1987). Toward a universal psychological structure of human values. *Journal of Personality and Social Psychology* **53**, 550–62.

Seppi, D., Batliner, A., Schuller, B., Steidl, S., Vogt, T., Wagner, J., Devillers, L., Vidrascu, L., Amir, N., and Aharonson, V. (2008). Patterns, prototypes, performance: classifying emotional user states. *Interspeech-2008*, pp. 601–4.

Sergent, C. and Dehaene, S. (2004). Is consciousness a gradual phenomenon? Evidence for an all-or-none bifurcation during the attentional blink. *Psychological Science*, 15(11), p. 720–728.

Sergerie, K., Chochol, C., and Armony, J.L. (2008). The role of the amygdala in emotional processing: a quantitative meta-analysis of functional neuroimaging studies. *Neuroscience and Biobehavioral Reviews* **32** (4), 811–30.

Seth, A.K., Dienes, Z., Cleeremans, A., Overgaard, M., and Pessoa, L. (2008). Measuring consciousness: relating behavioural and neurophysiological approaches. *Trends in Cognitive Sciences* **12** (8), 314–21.

Seyfarth, R.M., Cheney, D.L., and Marler, P. (1980). Monkey responses to three different alarm calls: evidence for predator classification and semantic communication. *Science* **210**, 801–3.

Shadle, C.H. and Damper, R.I. (2001). Prospects for articulatory synthesis: a position paper. In *Proceedings of the 4th ISCA Tutorial and Research Workshop on Speech Synthesis (SSW4-2001)*, paper 116.

Shafran, I., Riley, M., and Mohri, M. (2003). Voice signatures. In *IEEE Automatic Speech Recognition and Understanding Workshop*, pp. 31–36.

Shaikh, M.A.M., Prendinger, H., and Ishizuka, M. (2007*a*). SenseNet: a linguistic tool to visualize numerical-valance based dentiment of textual data. In *Proceedings of the 5th International Conference on Natural Language Processing (ICON-2007)*, Hyderabad, India, pp. 147–52.

Shaikh, MA., Prendinger, H., and Mitsuru, I. (2007*b*). Assessing sentiment of text by semantic dependency and contextual valence analysis. In *Affective computing and intelligent interaction* (ed. A. Pavia, P. Prada, and R.W. Picard), pp. 191–202. Springer, Berlin.

Shan, C., Gong, S., and McOwan, P.W. (2007). Beyond facial expressions: learning human emotion from body gestures. *Proceedings of the British Machine Vision Conference (BMVC'07)*, Warwick, UK.

Shanahan, M. (2007). A spiking neuron model of cortical broadcast and competition. *Consciousness and Cognition* 17 (1), 288–303.

Shaver, K.G. (1985). The attribution of blame: causality, responsibility, and blameworthiness. Springer-Verlag, New York.

Shaver, P., Schwartz, J., Kirson, D., and O'Connor, C. (1987). Emotion knowledge: further exploration of a prototype approach. *Journal of Personality and Social Psychology* 52, 1061–86.

Sherwood, A., Allen, M.T., Fahrenberg, J., Kelsey, R.M., Lovallo, W.R., and van Doornen, L.J. (1990). Methodological guidelines for impedance cardiography. *Psychophysiology* 27, 1–23.

Shields, S.A., MacDowell, K.A., Fairchild, S.B., and Campbell, M.L. (1987). Is mediation of sweating cholinergic, adrenergic, or both? A comment on the literature. *Psychophysiology* 24, 312–19.

Shiota, M. N., Campos, B., and Keltner, D. (2003). The faces of positive emotion: prototype displays of awe, amusement, and pride. *Annals of the New York Academy of Sciences* 1000, 296–9.

Shweder, R.A. (1993). The cultural psychology of the emotions. In *Handbook of emotions* (ed. M. Lewis and J.M. Haviland), pp. 417–34. Guilford Press, New York.

Si, M., Marsella, S.C., and Pynadath, D.V. (2008). Modeling appraisal in theory of mind reasoning. In *Intelligent virtual agents, Proceedings of the 8th International Conference (IVA 2008)*, Tokyo, Japan (ed. H. Prendinger, J.C. Lester, and M. Ishizuka), pp. 334–47. Lecture Notes in Computer Science 5208. Springer, Berlin.

Siddle, D.A.T. (1991). Orienting, habituation, and resource allocation: an associative analysis. *Psychophysiology* 28, 245–59.

Siemer, M. (2005). Moods as multiple-object directed and as objectless affective states: an examination of the dispositional theory of moods. *Cognition and Emotion* 19 (6), 815–45.

Simon, H.A. (1967). Motivational and emotional controls of cognition. *Psychological Review* 74, 29–39.

Sinaceur, M. and Tiedens, L.Z. (2006). Get mad and get more than even: when and why anger expression is effective in negotiations. *Journal of Experimental Social Psychology* 42, 314–22.

Singer, W. (1999*a*). Neurobiology. Striving for coherence. *Nature* 397 (6718), 391–3.

Singer, W. (1999*b*). Neuronal synchrony: a versatile code for the definition of relations? *Neuron* 24 (1), p. 49–65.

Sinha, R. and Parsons, O.A. (1996). Multivariate response patterning of fear and anger. *Cognition and Emotion* 10, 173–98.

Sloman, A. (2002). How many separately evolved emotional beasties live within us? In *Emotions in humans and artifacts* (ed. R. Trappl, P. Petta, and S. Payr), pp. 35–114. MIT Press, Cambridge, Massachusetts.

Sloman, A. and Croucher, M. (1981). Why robots will have emotions. *International Joint Conference on Artificial Intelligence*. Vancouver, Canada.

Smith, C.A. (1989). Dimensions of appraisal and physiological response in emotion. *Journal of Personality and Social Psychology* 56, 339–53.

Smith, C.A. and Ellsworth, P.C. (1985). Patterns of cognitive appraisal in emotion. *Journal of Personality and Social Psychology* 48, 813–38.

Smith, C.A. and Kirby, L. (2000). Consequences require antecedents: toward a process model of emotion elicitation. In *Feeling and thinking: the role of affect in social cognition* (ed. J.P. Forgas), pp. 83–106. Cambridge University Press, New York.

Smith, C.A. and Kirby, L.D. (2001). Toward delivering on the promise of appraisal theory. In *Appraisal processes in emotion: theory, methods, research* (ed. K.R. Scherer, A. Schorr, and T. Johnstone), pp. 121–40. Oxford University Press, New York.

Smith, C.A. and Kirby, L.D. (2009). Putting appraisal in context: toward a relational model of appraisal and emotion. *Cognition and Emotion* 23, 481–503.

Smith, C.A. and Lazarus, R.S. (1990). Emotion and adaptation. In *Handbook of personality: theory and research* (ed. L.A. Pervin), pp. 609–37. Guilford, New York.

Smith, C.A. and Scott, H.S. (1997). A componential approach to the meaning of facial expressions. In *The psychology of facial expression* (ed. J.A. Russell and J.M. Fernández-Dols), pp. 229–54. Cambridge University Press, New York.

Smith, M.C., Bentin, S., and Spalek, T.M. (2001). Attention constraints of semantic activation during visual word recognition. *Journal of Experimental Psychology: Learning, Memory, and Cognition* 27 (5), 1289–98.

Soltis, J. (2004). The signal functions of early infant crying. *Behavioral and Brain Sciences* 27, 443–90.

Sonnemans, J. and Frijda, N.H. (1994). The structure of subjective emotional intensity. *Cognition and Emotion* 8 (4), 329–50.

Sorce, J.F., Emde, R.N., Campos, J., and Klinnert, M.D. (1985). Maternal emotional signaling: its effect on the visual cliff behavior of 1 year olds. *Developmental Psychology* 21, 195–200.

Soussignan, R. (2002). Duchenne smile, emotional experience, and autonomic reactivity: a test of the facial feedback hypothesis. *Emotion* 2, 52–74.

Staller, A. and Petta, P. (2001). Introducing emotions into the computational study of social norms: a first evaluation. *Journal of Artificial Societies and Social Simulation* 4 (1).

Stanislavski, C. (1980). *An actor prepares*. Methuen, London.

Steidl, S., Levit, M., Batliner, A., Nöth, E., and Niemann, H. (2005). 'Of all things the measure is man'—classification of emotions and inter-labeler consistency In *IEEE Proceedings of ICASSP 2005—International Conference on Acoustics, Speech, and Signal Processing*, Philadelphia, Pennsylvania, Vol. 1, pp. 317–20.

Stein, B. and Meredith, M.A. (1993). The merging of senses. MIT Press, Cambridge, Massachusetts.

Stein, M. and Luparello, T.J. (1967). Measurement of respiration. In *Methods in psychophysiology* (ed. C.C. Brown), pp. 75–94. Williams and Wilkins, Baltimore.

Steinel, W., Van Kleef, G.A., and Harinck, F. (2008). Are you talking to *me*?! Separating the people from the problem when expressing emotions in negotiation. *Journal of Experimental Social Psychology* 44, 362–9.

Stekelenburg, J. J. and van Boxtel, A. (2002). Pericranial muscular, respiratory, and heart rate components of the orienting response. *Psychophysiology* 39, 707–22.

Stemmler, G. (1984). Psychophysiologische Emotionsmuster. Dissertation im Fachbereich Psychologie, University of Hamburg.

Stemmler, G. (1988). Effects of profile elevation, scatter and shape on discriminant analysis results. *Educational and Psychological Measurement* 48, 853–71.

Stemmler, G. (1989). The autonomic differentiation of emotions revisited: convergent and discriminant validation. *Psychophysiology* 26, 617–32.

Stemmler, G. (1992a). *Differential psychophysiology: persons in situations*. Springer, New York.

Stemmler, G. (1992b). The vagueness of specificity: models of peripheral physiological emotion specificity in emotion theories and their experimental discriminability. *Journal of Psychophysiology* 6, 17–28.

Stemmler, G. (2003). Methodological considerations in the psychophysiological study of emotion. In *Handbook of affective sciences* (ed. R.J. Davidson, K.R. Scherer, and H. Goldsmith), pp. 225–55. Oxford University Press, New York.

Stemmler, G. (2004). Physiological processes during emotion. In *The regulation of emotion* (ed. P. Philippot and R.S. Feldman), pp. 33–70. Erlbaum, Mahwah, New Jersey.

Stemmler, G., Heldmann, M., Pauls, C.A., and Scherer, T. (2001). Constraints for emotion specificity in fear and anger: the context counts. *Psychophysiology* 38, 275–91.

Stemmler, G., Aue, T., and Wacker, J. (2007). Anger and fear: separable effects of emotion and motivational direction on somatovisceral responses. *International Journal of Psychophysiology* 66, 141–53.

Stevens, K.N. (2002). Toward formant synthesis with articulatory controls. In *Proceedings of 2002 IEEE Workshop on Speech Synthesis*, pp. 67–72.

Stoiber, N., Séguier, R., and Breton, G. (2009). Automatic design of a control interface for a synthetic face. In *Proceedings of the 2009 International Conference on Intelligent User Interfaces*, pp. 207–16.

Strack, F., Martin, L., and Stepper, S. (1988). Inhibiting and facilitating conditions of the human smile: a nonobtrusive test of the facial feedback hypothesis. *Journal of Personality and Social Psychology* **54**, 768–77.

Strom, V., Nenkova, A., Clark, R., *et al.* (2007). Modelling prominence and emphasis improves unit-selection synthesis. In *Proceedings Interspeech 2007* (Antwerp, Belgium), pp. 1282–5.

Stroufe, L.A. (1996). *Emotional development.* Cambridge University Press, New York.

Suri, R. and Schultz, W. (1999). A neural network model with dopamine-like reinforcement signal that learns a spatial delayed response task. *Neuroscience* **91**, 871–90.

Sutton, R. and Barto, A. (1981). Toward a modern theory of adaptive networks: expectation and prediction. *Psychological Review* **88**, 135–70.

Swanson, L.W. and Petrovich, G.D. (1998). What is the amygdala? *Trends in Neurosciences* **21**, 323–31.

Swartout, W., Gratch, J., Hill, R., Hovy, E., Marsella, S., Rickel, J., and Traum, D. (2006). Toward virtual humans. *AI Magazine* **27**, 96–108.

Tachibana, M., Yamagishi, J., Onishi, K., Masuko, T., and Kobayashi, T. (2004). HMM-based speech synthesis with various speaking styles using model interpolation. In *Proceedings of Speech Prosody 2004*, Nara, Japan, pp. 413–16.

Tallon-Baudry, C. and Bertrand, O. (1999). Oscillatory gamma activity in humans and its role in object representation. *Trends in Cognitive Sciences* **3**, 151–62.

Tallon-Baudry, C., Bertrand, O., Delpuech, C., and Pernier, J. (1996). Stimulus specificity of phase-locked and non-phase-locked 40 Hz visual responses in human. *Society for Neuroscience* **16** (3), 4240–9.

Task Force of the European Society of Cardiology and the North American Society of Pacing Electrophysiology (1996). Heart rate variability: standards of measurement, physiological interpretation, and clinical use. *Circulation* **93**, 1043–65.

Taylor, J.G. (2002). A control model of the movement of attention. *Neural Networks* **115**, 309–26.

Taylor, J.G. and Fragopanagos, N.F. (2004). Modelling human attention and emotion. In *Proceedings of the International Joint Conference on Neural Networks (IJCNN)*.

Taylor, J.G. and Fragopanagos, N.F. (2005). The interaction of attention and emotion. *Neural Networks* **18** (4), 353–69.

Taylor, J. and Fragopanagos, N. (2007). Resolving some confusions over attention and consciousness. *Neural Networks* **20** (9), p. 993–1003.

Taylor, J.G. and Korsten, N. (2009). Connectionist models of emotion. In *Oxford companion to emotion and the affective sciences* (ed. D. Sander and K.R. Scherer). Oxford University Press, Oxford.

Tcherkassof, A., Bollon, T., Dubois, M., Pansu, P., and Adam, J-M. (2007). Facial expressions of emotions: a methodological contribution to the study of spontaneous and dynamic emotional faces. *European Journal of Social Psychology* **37**, 1325–45.

Tekalp, A.M. and Ostermann, J. (2000). Face and 2-D mesh animation in MPEG-4. *Signal Processing: Image Communication* **15**, 387–421.

Thagard, P. (2003). Why wasn't O. J. convicted: emotional coherence in legal inference. *Cognition and Emotion* **17**, 361–83.

Thagard, P. and Aubie, B. (2008). Emotional consciousness: a neural model of how cognitive appraisal and somatic perception interact to produce qualitative experience. *Consciousness and Cognition* **17** (3), 811–34.

Thiébaux, M., Marsella, S., Marshall, A.N., and Kallmann, M. (2008). SmartBody: behaviour realization for embodied conversational agents. In *Proceedings of 7th Conference on Autonomous Agents and Multi-Agent Systems* (ed. L. Padgham, D. Parkes, J. Müller, and S. Parsons), pp. 151–8. INESC-ID.

Thomas, F. and Johnston, O. (1995). *The illusion of life: Disney animation.* Hyperion, New York.

Thórisson, K.R., List, T., Pennock, C., and Dipirro, J. (2005). Whiteboards: scheduling blackboards for semantic routing of messages and streams. In *AAAI-05 Workshop on Modular Construction of Human-Like Intelligence*, pp. 8–15.

Tiedens, L.Z. (2001). Anger and advancement versus sadness and subjugation: the effect of negative emotion expression on social status conferral. *Journal of Personality and Social Psychology* **80**, 86–94.

Tobin, M.J., Jenouri, G., Lind, B., Watson, H., Schneider, A., and Sackner, M.A. (1983). Validation of respiratory inductive plethysmography in pulmonary disesase. *Chest* **83**, 615–20.

Tomai, E. and Forbus, K. (2007). Plenty of blame to go around: a qualitative approach to attribution of moral responsibility. *Proceedings of QR-07: the 21st International Workshop on Qualitative Reasoning*. Aberystwyth, U.K.

Tomkins, S.S. (1962). *Affect, imagery, consciousness*. Vol. 1. *The positive affects*. Springer, New York.

Tomkins, S.S. (1963). *Affect, imagery, consciousness*. Vol. 2. *The negative affects*. Springer, New York.

Tomkins, S.S. (1984). Affect theory. In *Approaches to emotion* (ed. K.R. Scherer and P. Ekman), pp. 163–96. Erlbaum, Hillsdale, New Jersey.

Tomkins, S.S. and Messick, S. (1963). Computer simulation of personality: frontier of psychological theory. Wiley, New York.

Tononi, G. (2004). An information integration theory of consciousness. *BMC Neuroscience* **5** (42), 1–22.

Totterdell, P. (2000). Catching moods and hitting runs: mood linkage and subjective performance in professional sports teams. *Journal of Applied Psychology* **85**, 848–59.

Totterdell, P., Kellett, S., Teuchmann, K., and Briner, R.B. (1998). Mood linkage in work groups. *Journal of Personality and Social Psychology* **74**, 1504–15.

Traum, D., Rickel, J., Gratch, J., and Marsella, S. (2003). Negotiation over tasks in hybrid human-agent teams for simulation-based training. In *Proceedings of the International Conference on Autonomous Agents and Multiagent Systems*, Melbourne, Australia, pp. 441–8.

Trevarthen, C. (1984). Emotions in infancy. In *Approaches to emotions* (ed. K.R. Scherer and P. Ekman), pp. 129–57. Erlbaum, London.

Tsapatsoulis, N., Raouzaiou, A., Kollias, S., Cowie, R., and Douglas-Cowie, E. (2002). Emotion recognition and synthesis based on MPEG-4 FAPs. In *MPEG-4 facial animation—the standard, implementations, applications* (ed. I. Pandzic and R. Forchheimer), pp. 141–68. John Wiley and Sons, Chichester.

Türk, O. (2007). Cross-lingual voice conversion. PhD Thesis, Bogaziçi University, Istanbul, Turkey.

Türk, O. and Schröder, M. (2008). A comparison of voice conversion methods for transforming voice quality in emotional speech synthesis. In *Proceedings Interspeech 2008* (Brisbane, Australia).

Türk, O., Schröder, M., Bozkurt, B., and Arslan, L. (2005). Voice quality interpolation for emotional text-to-speech synthesis. In *Proceedings Interspeech 2005* (Lisbon, Portugal), pp. 797–800.

Ullman, S. (1995). Sequence-seeking and counter-streams: a model for information flow in the cortex. *Cerebral Cortex* **5**, 1–11.

Valstar, M.F., Gunes, H., and Pantic, M. (2007). How to distinguish posed from spontaneous smiles using geometric features. In *Proceedings of the 9th International Conference on Multimodal Interfaces (ICMI 2007)*, pp. 38–45. ACM, New York.

Van den Hoogen, W., IJsselsteijn, W., and de Kort, Y.A.W. (2008). Exploring behavioral expressions of player experience in digital games. In *Proceedings of the Workshop on Facial and Bodily Expression for Control and Adaptation of Games, ECAG 2008* (ed. R.P.A. Nijholt and R. Poppe), pp. 11–19. Amsterdam.

Van der Linden, M. (2004). Fonctions exécutives et régulation émotionnelle. [Executive functions and emotional regulation]. In *Neuropsychologie des fonctions exécutives [Neuropsychology of executive functions]* (ed. T. Meulemans, F. Collette, and M. Van der Linden), pp. 137–53. Solal, Marseille.

van der Zwaag, M., Westerink, J., and van den Broek, E. (2009). Deploying music characteristics for an affective music player. In *Affective computing and intelligent interaction. International Conference 2009 (ACII 2009)*, Amsterdam, The Netherlands, p. 459. IEEE Computer Society Press, Los Alamitos.

Van Diest, I., Thayer, J. F., Vandeputte, B., Van de Woestijne, K.P., and Van den Bergh, O. (2006). Anxiety and respiratory variability. *Physiology and Behavior,* **89**, 189–95.

Van Kleef, G.A. (2009). How emotions regulate social life: the emotions as social information (EASI) model. *Current Directions in Psychological Science* **18**, 184–8.

Van Kleef, G.A. and Côté, S. (2007). Expressing anger in conflict: when it helps and when it hurts. *Journal of Applied Psychology* **92**, 1557–69.

Van Kleef, G.A., De Dreu, C.K.W., and Manstead, A.S.R. (2004). The interpersonal effects of anger and happiness in negotiations. *Journal of Personality and Social Psychology* **86**, 57–76.

Van Kleef, G.A., De Dreu, C.K.W., and Manstead, A.S.R. (2006*a*). Supplication and appeasement in conflict and negotiation: the interpersonal effects of disappointment, worry, guilt and regret. *Journal of Personality and Social Psychology* **91**, 124–42.

Van Kleef, G.A., De Dreu, C.K.W., Pietroni, D., and Manstead, A.S.R. (2006*b*). Power and emotion in negotion: power moderates the interpersonal effects of anger and happiness on concession making. *European Journal of Social Psychology* **36**, 557–81.

Van Reekum, C.M. and Scherer, K.R. (1997). Levels of processing for emotion–antecedent appraisal. In *Cognitive science perspectives on personality and emotion* (ed. G. Matthews), pp. 259–300. Elsevier Science, Amsterdam.

Van Reekum, C., Banse, R., Johnstone, T., Etter, A., Wehrle, T., and Scherer, K.R. (2004). Psychophysiological responses to appraisal responses in a computer game. *Cognition and Emotion* **18** (5), 663–88.

Varni, G. (2008). Multimodal non-verbal interaction based on sound and music. Toward enactive and social interfaces. Ph.D. dissertation, University of Genoa, 2009.

Varni, G., Camurri, A., Coletta, P., and Volpe, G. (2008). Emotional entrainment in music performance. In *Proceedings of the 8th IEEE International Conference on Automatic Face and Gesture Recognition (FG 2008)*, pp. 1–5.

Velásquez, J. (1998). When robots weep: emotional memories and decision-making. In *Proceedings of the Fifteenth National Conference on Artificial Intelligence*. AAAI Press, Madison, Wisconsin.

Velten, E. (1968). A laboratory task for inductions of mood states. *Behaviour Therapy and Research* **6**, 473–82.

Venables, P.H. and Christie, M.J. (1980). Electrodermal activity. In *Techniques in psychophysiology* (ed. I. Martin and P.H. Venables), pp. 3–67. Wiley, Chichester.

Verduyn, P., Delvaux, E., Van Coillie, H., Tuerlinckx, F., and Van Mechelen, I. (2009). Predicting the duration of emotional experience: two experience sampling studies. *Emotion* **9**, 83–91.

Ververidis, D. and Kotropoulos, C. (2006). Emotional speech recognition: resources, features and methods. *Speech Communication* **48** (9), 1162–81.

Vidrascu, L. and Devillers, L. (2007). Five emotion classes detection in real-world call center data: the use of various types of paralinguistic features, *Proceedings of Workshop Paraling07*.

Vilhjálmsson, H.H., Cantelmo, N., Cassell, J., *et al.* (2007). The behaviour markup language: recent developments and challenges. In *Intelligent virtual agents, 7th International Conference (IVA 2007)*, Paris, France (ed. C. Pelachaud, J.-C. Martin, E. André, G. Chollet, K.Karpouzis, and D. Pelé), pp. 99–111. Lecture Notes in Computer Science 4722. Springer, Berlin.

Vincent, D., Rosec, O., and Chonavel, T. (2005). Estimation of LF glottal source parameters based on an ARX model. In *Proceedings Interspeech 2005* (Lisbon, Portugal), pp. 333–6.

Vingerhoets, A.J. (1985). The role of the parasympathetic division of the autonomic nervous system in stress and the emotions. *International Journal of Psychosomatics* **32**, 28–34.

Vlemincx, E., Van Diest, I., De Peuter, S., Bresseleers, J., Bogaerts, K., Fannes, S., Li, W., and Van den Bergh, O. (2009). Why do you sigh: sigh frequency during induced stress and relief. *Psychophysiology* **46**, 1005–13.

Vogt, T. and André, E. (2005*a*). Improving automatic emotion recognition from speech via gender differentiation. *Proceedings of IEEE International Conference on Multimedia, ICME 2005*.

Vogt, T. and André, E. (2005*b*). Comparing feature sets for acted and spontaneous speech in view of automatic emotion recognition. *Proceedings of IEEE International Conference on Multimedia, ICME-2005*, pp. 474–7.

Volpe, G. (2003). Computational models of expressive gesture in multimedia systems. Ph.D. Dissertation, Faculty of Engineering, University of Genoa, April 2003.

Voskuhl, A. (2007). Motions and passions: music-playing women automata and cultural commentary in late 18th-century Germany. In *Genesis redux: essays on the history and philosophy of artificial life* (ed. J. Riskin), pp. 293–320. Chicago University Press, Chicago.

Vuilleumier, P. (2005). How brains beware: neural mechanisms of emotional attention. *Trends in Cognitive Sciences* **9**, 585–94.

Vuilleumier, P. (2009). The role of the amygdala in perception and attention. In *The human amygdala* (ed. P.J. Whalen and E.A. Phelps), pp. 220–49. Guilford Press, New York.

Vuilleumier, P., Armony, J. L., Driver, J., and Dolan, R.J. (2001). Effects of attention and emotion on face processing in the human brain: an event-related fMRI study. *Neuron* **30**, 829–41.

Vuilleumier, P., Armony, J., Driver, J., and Dolan, R.J. (2003). Distinct spatial frequency sensitivities for processing faces and emotional expressions. *Nature Neuroscience* **6**, 624–31.

Wagar, B.M. and Thagard, P. (2004). Spiking phineas gage: a neurocomputational theory of cognitive–aæctive integration in decision making. *Psychological Review* **111** (1), p. 67–79.

Wagner, H.L. and Smith, J. (1991). Facial expression in the presence of friends and strangers. *Journal of Nonverbal Behavior* **15**, 201–14.

Walker, J.H., Sproull, L., and Subramani, R. (1994). Using a human face in an interface. *Proceedings of the SIGCHI Conference on Human factors in Computing Systems: Celebrating Interdependence*, Boston, Massachusetts (ed. B. Adelson, S. Dumais, and J. Olson), pp. 85–91. Association for Computing Machinery.

Wallace, R.K., Benson, H., and Wilson, A.F. (1971). A wakeful hypometabolic physiologic state. *American Journal of Physiology* **221**, 795–9.

Wallbott, H.G. (1988). Big girls don't frown, big boys don't cry—gender differences of professional actors in communicating emotion via facial expression. *Journal of Nonverbal Behavior* **12**, 98–106.

Wallbott, H.G. (1998). Bodily expression of emotion. *European Journal of Social Psychology* **28**, 879–96.

Wallbott, H.G. and Scherer, K. R. (1986). Cues and channels in emotion recognition. *Journal of Personality and Social Psychology* **51** (4), 690–9.

Wallin, B.G. (1981). Sympathetic nerve activity underlying electrodermal and cardiovascular reactions in man. *Psychophysiology* **18**, 470–6.

Watson, D. and Tellegen, A. (1985). Toward a consensual structure of mood. *Psychological Bulletin* **98**, 219–35.

Wehrle, T. and Kaiser, S. (2000). Emotion and facial expression. In *Affect in interactions: towards a new generation of interfaces* (ed. A. Paiva), pp. 49–64. Springer, Heidelberg.

Wehrle, T. and Scherer, K.R. (2001). Towards computational modelling of appraisal theories. In *Appraisal processes in emotion: theory, methods, research* (ed. K.R. Scherer, A. Schorr, and T. Johnstone), pp. 350–65. Oxford University Press, New York.

Wehrle, T., Kaiser, S., Schmidt, S., and Scherer, K.R. (2000). Studying dynamic models of facial expression of emotion using synthetic animated faces. *Journal of Personality and Social Psychology* **78** (1), 105–19.

Weiner, B. (1985). An attributional theory of achievement motivation and emotion. *Psychological Review* **92**, 548–73.

Weiner, B. (1995). *The judgment of responsibility*. Guilford Press, New York.

Westermann, R., Spies, K., Stahl, G., and Hesse, F.W. (1996). Relative effectiveness and validity of mood induction procedures: a meta-analysis. *European Journal of Social Psychology* **26**, 557–80.

Whalen, P.J. and Phelps, E. (Eds.) (2009). *The human amygdala*. The Guilford Press, New York.

Whalen, P.J., Shin, L.M., McInerney, S.C., Fischer, H., Wright, C.I., and Rauch, S.L. (2001). A functional MRI study of human amygdala responses to facial expressions of fear versus anger. *Emotion* **1**, 70–83.

Whalen, P.J., Kagan, J., Cook, R.G., Davis, F.C., Kim, H., Polis, S., McLaren, D.G., Somerville, L.H., McLean, A.A., Maxwell, J.S., and Johnstone, T. (2004). Human amygdala responsivity to masked fearful eye whites. *Science* **306** (5704), 2061.

Whissell, C. (1989). The dictionary of affect in language. In *Emotion: theory, research, and experience*, Vol. 4. *The measurement of emotions* (ed. R. Plutchik and H. Kellerman), pp. 113–31. Academic Press, San Diego.

Widen, S.C. and Russell, J.A. (2002). Gender and preschoolers' perception of emotion. *Merrill-Palmer Quarterly* **48**, 248–62.

Wiens, S. (2005). Interoception in emotional experience. *Current Opinion in Neurology* **18**, 442–7.

Wilhelm, F.H., Kolodyazhniy, V., Kreibig, S.D., Roth, W.T., and Gross, J.J. (2007). Affective computing: Using computational intelligence techniques to classify the psychophysiological signatures of emotions. *Psychophysiology* **44** (S1), S110.

Wilhelm, F.H., Roth, W.T., and Sackner, M.A. (2003). The LifeShirt: an advanced system for ambulatory measurement of respiratory and cardiac function. *Behavior Modification* **27**, 671–91.

Wilhelm, F.H., Pfaltz, M.C., Grossman, P., and Roth, W.T. (2006). Distinguishing emotional from physical activation in ambulatory psychophysiological monitoring. *Biomedical Sciences Instrumentation* **42**, 458–63.

Wilhelm, P., Schoebi, D., and Perrez, M. (2004). Frequency estimates of emotions in everyday life from a diary method's perspective: a comment on Scherer et al.'s survey-study 'Emotions in everyday life'. *Social Science Information* **43** (4), 647–65.

Wilkowski, B.M., Robinson, M.D., and Friesen, C.K. (2009). Gaze-triggered orienting as a tool of the belongingness self-regulation system. *Psychological Science* **20** (4), 495–501.

Winkielman, P., and Berridge, K.C. (2003). What is an unconscious emotion? The case for unconscious 'liking'. *Cognition and Emotion* **17**, 181–211.

Winston, J.S., Gottfried, J.A., Kilner, J.M., and Dolan, R.J. (2005). Integrated neural representations of odor intensity and affective valence in human amygdala. *Journal of Neuroscience* **25**, 8903–7.

With, S. and Kaiser, S. (2009). Multimodal annotation of emotion signals in social interactions. In *Current and future perspectives in facial expression research: topics and methodological questions* (ed. E. Bänninger-Huber and D. Peham). Innsbruck University Press, Innsbruck.

Witten, I.H., Frank, E., Trigg, L., Hall, M., Holmes, G., and Cunningham, S.J. (1999). Weka: practical machine learning tools and techniques with Java implementations. *Proceedings of the ICONIP/ANZIIS/ANNES'99 International Workshop on Emerging Knowledge Engineering and Connectionist-Based Information Systems*, pp. 192–6.

Wollermann C. and Lasarcyk E. (2006). Modeling and perceiving of (un)certainty in articulatory speech synthesis. In *Proceedings of the ISCA Workshop on Speech Synthesis SSW06*.

Wollmer, M., Eyben, F., Reiter, S., Schuller, B., Cox, C., Douglas-Cowie, E., and Cowie R. (2008). Abandoning emotion classes—towards continuous emotion recognition with modelling of long-range dependencies. *Interspeech-2008*, pp. 597–600.

Wright, P. and Liu, Y. (2006). Neutral faces activate the amygdala during identity matching. *Neuroimage* **29**, 628–36.

Wu, L., Oviatt, S., and Cohen, P. (1999). Multimodal integration—a statistical view. *IEEE Transactions on Multimedia* **1** (4), 334–41.

Wundt, W. (1900). *Völkerpsychologie. Eine Untersuchung der Entwicklungsgesetze von Sprache, Mythos und Sitte. Band I. Die Sprache* [Cultural psychology: a study of the developmental mechanisms of language, myths, and customs. Vol. 1. Language]. Kröner, Leipzig.

Wundt, W.M. (1905). *Grundriss der Psychologie* [Fundamentals of psychology], 7th revised edn. Engelman, Leipzig.

Wundt, W.M (1913). Lectures on human and animal psychology. *Grundriss der Psychologie*. Alfred Kröner, Leipzig.

Wundt, W. (1922/1863). *Vorlesung über die Menschen- und Tierseele*. Voss Verlag.

Xiao Z., Dellandrea, E., Dou, W., and Chen, L. (2007). A dimensional emotion model driven multi-stage classification of emotional speech. Research report RR-LIRIS-2007-033. LIRIS, CNRS.

Xu, X., Li, Y., Hu, L., and Tao, J. (2009). Categorizing terms' subjectivity and polarity manually for opinion mining in Chinese. In *Affective Computing and Intelligent Interaction, Proceedings of the International Conference (ACII 2009)*, Amsterdam. IEEE.

Yamagishi, J., Onishi, K., Masuko, T., and Kobayashi, T. (2003). Modeling of various speaking styles and emotions for HMM-based speech synthesis. In *Proceedings Eurospeech 2003*, Geneva, Switzerland, pp. 2461–4.

Yeasin, M., Bullot B., and Sharma, R. (2006). Recognition of facial expressions and measurement of levels of interest from video. *IEEE Transactions on Multimedia* 8 (3), 500–7.

Yik, M., Meng, Z., and Russell, J.A. (1998). Adults' freely produced emotion labels for babies' spontaneous facial expressions. *Cognition and Emotion* 12, 723–30.

Yoshimura, T., Tokuda, K., Masuko, T., Kobayashi, T., and Kitamura, T. (1999). Simultaneous modeling of spectrum, pitch and duration in HMM-based speech synthesis. In *Proceedings of Eurospeech 1999* (Budapest), pp. 2347–50.

Zajonc, R.B. (1980). Feeling and thinking: preferences need no inferences. *American Psychologist* 35, 151–75.

Zara, A., Maffiolo, V., Martin, J.C., and Devillers, L. (2007). Collection and annotation of a corpus of human–human multimodal interactions. In *Affective Computing and Intelligent Interaction, Second International Conference (ACII 2007)* (ed. A. Paiva, R. Prada, and R.W. Picard), pp. 464–75. Lecture Notes in Computer Science 4738. Springer, Berlin.

Zeman, J., Penza, S., Shipman, K., and Young, G. (1997). Preschoolers as functionalists: the impact of social context on emotion regulation. *Child Study Journal* 27, 41–67.

Zeman, J., Cassano, M., Perry-Parrish, C., and Stegall, S. (2006). Emotion regulation in children and adolescents. *Journal of Developmental and Behavioral Pediatrics* 27, 155–68.

Zeng, Z., Hu, Y., Liu, M., Fu, Y., and Huang, T.S. (2006). Training combination strategy of multi-stream fused hidden Markov model for audio-visual affect recognition. In *Proceedings of the 14th Annual ACM International Conference on Multimedia*, pp. 65–8. ACM, New York.

Zeng, Z., Pantic, M., Roisman, G.I., and Huang, T.S. (2009). A survey of affect recognition methods: audio, visual, and spontaneous expressions. *IEEE Transactions on Pattern Analysis and Machine Intelligence* 31 (1), 39–58.

Zhang, S., Wu, Z., Meng, H.M., and Cai, L. (2007). Facial expression synthesis using PAD emotional parameters for a Chinese expressive avatar. In *Affective Computing and Intelligent Interaction, Second International Conference (ACII 2007)* (ed. A. Paiva, R. Prada, and R.W. Picard), pp. 24–35. Lecture Notes in Computer Science 4738. Springer, Berlin.

Ziemke, T. (1998). Adaptive behavior in autonomous agents. *Presence* 7, 564–87.

Zillmann, D., Weaver, J.B., Mundorf, N., and Aust, C.F. (1986). Effects of an opposite gender companion's affect to horror on distress, delight and attraction. *Journal of Personality and Social Psychology* 51, 586–94.

Appendix

A non-exhaustive list of online resources

The reader will find below a non-exhaustive list of websites of general interest to affective computing, of some research projects, labs and individuals. Compared to other fields, affective computing is still in its infancy. The broad nature of its goals and the scope of interest it generates, contribute to blurring boundaries between very different disciplines. Entering the field might thus feel disconcerting. We hope this appendix will provide useful points of entry to start a fascinating journey.

We compiled this non-exhaustive list of websites at the time of publication of this book. Future editions will contain updates.

General

http://www.scholarpedia.org Peer-reviewed encyclopedia written by academic leading experts in their fields. It includes a number of relevant areas for affective computing in general, and adjacent fields.

http://www.scholarpedia.org/article/Affective_computing

http://www.scholarpedia.org/article/Encyclopedia_of_computational_neuroscience

http://www.scholarpedia.org/article/Encyclopedia_of_computational_intelligence

http://www.scholarpedia.org/article/Encyclopedia_of_dynamical_systems

http://home.earthlink.net/~perlewitz/ Annotated index for computational neurobiology. It includes a who's who, where, as well as list of modelling software, databases, community resources (frequently asked questions, mailing lists), books, journals, conferences and graduate programmes.

http://emotion.nsma.arizona.edu/emotion.html The Emotion Home Page by Fellous & Hudlicka references emotion-related events, journals, and research labs around the world.

Research centres and projects

http://www.emotion-research.net/ European Network of Excellence "Human-Machine Interaction Network on Emotion" (HUMAINE, IST-507422), the EU research project that prompted the realization of this volume. The project ended in 2004, and is now replaced by the HUMAINE Association, which centralises academic efforts in affective computing. The HUMAINE Association is open to all researchers related to emotion-oriented computing throughout the world. It supports the IEEE Transactions on Affective Computing, as well as the International Conference on Affective Computing and Intelligent Interaction (ACII).

http://www.affective-sciences.com The Swiss Centre for Affective Sciences is one of 20 National Centres of Competence in Research established by the Swiss federal government.

http://www.media.mit.edu/ The Media Lab at the Massachusetts Institute for Technology, Cambridge, USA.

http://www.peopleandrobots.org/ People & Robots, at Carnegie Mellon University, Pittsburgh, USA.

http://www.reading.ac.uk/cinn Centre for Integrative Neuroscience and Neurodynamics, Reading, UK.

http://www.eucognition.org/ Second edition of the European Network for the Advancement of Artificial Cognitive Systems, Interaction and Robotics. EUCognition is a network of researchers in artificial cognitive systems and related areas who want to connect to other researchers and reflect on the challenges and aims of the discipline. It funds and organises regular events.

http://isre.org International Society for Research on Emotion

http://sspnet.eu/ European Network of Excellence in Social Signal Processing, fostering and supporting research activities in Social Signal Processing with the aim of bringing Social Intelligence in computers. It started in 2009 for a duration of 4 years.

http://www.cyberemotions.eu/ EU consortium started in 2009 for a duration of 4 years, which aims at investigating different aspects of collective emotions in cyberspace.

http://musart.dist.unige.it/ InfoMus Lab, Genova, Italy; emotion in performing art.

http://www.image.ntua.gr/ Image, Video and Multimedia Systems Lab (IVML) in the National Technological University of Athens, Greece.

http://www.limsi.fr/ The Computer Sciences Laboratory for Mechanics and Engineering Sciences (LIMSI) is a CNRS laboratory (UPR 3251) associated with UPMC and Paris-Sud 11 Universities, France.

http://emotions.usc.edu/ Computational Emotion Group at the University of Southern California, USA.

http://www.ofai.at/ The Austrian Research Institute for Artificial Intelligence, Vienna, Austria.

http://specs.upf.edu/ Synthetic, Perceptive, Emotive and Cognitive Systems Group, Barcelona, Spain

Mailing lists

Artificial Emotions http://groups.google.com/group/artificial-emotion

ISRE Mailing List http://isre.org/membership.php

HUMAINE http://emotion-research.net/publicnews/new-announcement-mailing-list-humaine-news/

Connectionists http://www.cnbc.cmu.edu/connectionists

Comp-Neuro http://www.neuroinf.org/mailman/listinfo/comp-neuro

Journals and conferences

Emotion Review (http://emr.sagepub.com/)

IEEE Transactions in Affective Computing (http://www.computer.org/portal/web/tac)

International Conference on Affective Computing & Intelligent Interaction (http://emotion-research.net/acii)

ACII'09 (http://www.acii2009.nl/)

ACII'07 (http://gaips.inesc-id.pt/acii2007/)

ACII'05 (http://www.affectivecomputing.org/2005/)

Individuals and labs

Elisabeth Andre (http://mm-werkstatt.informatik.uni-augsburg.de) – Virtual Character

Christian Becker-Asano (http://www.becker-asano.de/) – Modelling

Cynthia Braezeal (http://web.media.mit.edu/~cynthiab/) – Robotics

Joanna Bryson (http://www.cs.bath.ac.uk/~jjb/) – Modelling

Lola Cañamero (http://homepages.feis.herts.ac.uk/~comqlc/) – Robotics

Elliot Clark (http://condor.depaul.edu/~elliott/) – Modelling

Jeffrey Cohn (http://www.pitt.edu/~jeffcohn/) – Automatic analysis of facial expressions

Garrison Cottrell (http://www-cse.ucsd.edu/~gary/) – Classifiers, Emotion, Facial expression

Roddy Cowie (http://www.psych.qub.ac.uk/Staff/Profiles/cowie) – Emotion Psychology

Antonio Damasio (http://www.usc.edu/schools/college/bci/) – Affective Neuroscience

Richard Davidson (http://psyphz.psych.wisc.edu/) – Affective neuroscience

Jean-Marc Fellous (http://www.u.arizona.edu/~fellous/) – Modelling, Affective Neuroscience

Didier Grandjean (http://cms.unige.ch/fapse/neuroemo/) – Affective Neuroscience

Paul Ekman (http://www.paulekman.com/) – Facial expressions

Dylan Evans (http://www.dylan.org.uk/)

Jean-Marc Fellous and Eva Hudlicka (http://emotion.nsma.arizona.edu/Emotion/EmoRes/CompAI/CompAI.html) – Review emotion theories

John Gratch (http://people.ict.usc.edu/~gratch/) – Modelling

Kristina Höök (http://www.sics.se/~kia/) – Human-Computer Interaction

Stacy Marsella (http://ict.usc.edu/~marsella) – Modelling

Marvin Minsky (http://web.media.mit.edu/%7Eminsky/) – Philosophy, Modelling

Shrikanth Narayanan (http://sail.usc.edu/) – Speech Analysis

Andrew Ortony (http://www.cs.northwestern.edu/~ortony/) – Modelling

Ana Paiva (http://gaips.inesc-id.pt/gaips/people/anapaiva.html) – Virtual Character

Maja Pantic (http://www.doc.ic.ac.uk/~maja/) – Multimodal analysis of human nonverbal behaviour

Brian Parkinson (http://www.chch.ox.ac.uk/college/profile/academics/brian-parkinson) –

Catherine Pelachaud (http://perso.telecom-paristech.fr/~pelachau/) – Embodied Conversational Agents

Paolo Petta (http://www.ofai.at/~paolo.petta/)

Diego Pizzagalli (http://www.wjh.harvard.edu/~daplab/) – Affective Neuroscience

Rozalind Picard (http://affect.media.mit.edu/)

Etienne B. Roesch (http://etienneroes.ch) – Modelling, Affective Neuroscience

Gerd Ruebenstrunk (http://www.ruebenstrunk.de/) – Review emotion theories

David Sander (http://cms.unige.ch/fapse/EmotionLab/) – Affective Neuroscience

Matthias Scheutz (http://hri.cogs.indiana.edu) – Human-Robot Interaction

Marc Schröder (http://www.dfki.de/~schroed/) – Emotion in Synthesized Speech

Aaron Sloman (http://www.cs.bham.ac.uk/~axs/#contentslist) – Modelling

John G. Taylor (http://www.mth.kcl.ac.uk/~jgtaylor/) – Modelling, Affective Neuroscience

Patrik Vuilleumier (http://labnic.unige.ch/) – Affective Neuroscience

Author Index

Index